"This book about people's power mo[...]
years makes the case, convincingly, tha[...]
worldwide new left. Reading it will broaden the perspective of activists
and analysts in North America and Europe, a very important task."
—Immanuel Wallerstein, Senior Research Scholar, Yale University

"Visionary historian George Katsiaficas writes like a novelist with
the eye for detail of a poet and the moral weight of a philosopher.
He has circled the globe applying his seminal theory of the Eros
Effect. *Asia's Unknown Uprisings* is the latest chapter of his grand
epic. Like Pablo Neruda's *Canto General*, Katsiaficas's works are a
blueprint for hope for 'all the peoples struggling for freedom.'"
—Richard Cambridge, author of *One Shot News—Poetry of Conscience*

"In *Asia's Unknown Uprisings*, George Katsiaficas inspires readers with
an exciting yet scholarly examination of the rise and interlinking
of mass revolutionary waves of struggle. In no way Pollyannaish,
Katsiaficas presents readers with an analysis of the successes and
failures of these late twentieth-century movements. In view of the
phenomenal Arab democratic uprisings begun in late 2010 and
early 2011, Katsiaficas's analysis is profoundly relevant in helping us
understand how the metaphorical flight of a butterfly in one part of
the planet can contribute to a hurricane thousands of miles away."
—Bill Fletcher, Jr., coauthor of *Solidarity Divided*, and
BlackCommentator.com editorial board member

"George Katsiaficas is America's leading practitioner of the method of
'participant-observation,' acting with and observing the movements
that he is studying. This study of People Power is a brilliant narrative
of the present as history from below. It is a detailed account of the
struggle for freedom and social justice, encompassing the different
currents, both reformist and revolutionary, in a balanced study that
combines objectivity and commitment. Above all, he presents the
beauty of popular movements in the process of self-emancipation."
—James Petras, author of *The Arab Revolt and the Imperialist Counterattack*

"George Katsiaficas has written a majestic account of political
uprisings and social movements in Asia—an important contribution
to the literature on both Asian studies and social change that is highly
recommended reading for anyone concerned with these fields of
interest. The work is well-researched, clearly argued, and beautifully
written, accessible to both academic and general readers."
—Carl Boggs, author of *The Crimes of Empire* and *Imperial Delusions*,
and professor of social sciences, National University, Los Angeles

Asia's Unknown Uprisings

Volume 2: People Power in the Philippines, Burma, Tibet, China, Taiwan, Bangladesh, Nepal, Thailand, and Indonesia, 1947–2009

George Katsiaficas

Asia's Unknown Uprisings Volume 2: People Power in the Philippines, Burma, Tibet, China, Taiwan, Bangladesh, Nepal, Thailand, and Indonesia, 1947–2009
George Katsiaficas
© George Katsiaficas
This edition © 2013 PM Press

ISBN: 978-1-60486-488-5
Library of Congress Control Number: 2011917551

Cover: John Yates / www.stealworks.com
Interior design by briandesign

10 9 8 7 6 5 4 3 2 1

PM Press
PO Box 23912
Oakland, CA 94623
www.pmpress.org

Printed in the USA on recycled paper, by the Employee Owners of Thomson-Shore
in Dexter, Michigan.
www.thomsonshore.com

For Shin Eun-jung, 1972–2012
Activist, filmmaker, and author
My partner and inspiration

The anonymous people

WE
Are the anonymous people
No photos
No paintings
To record our pasts
Our forefathers
Collected no stamps
No public wall
Bears our names
No awards for us
In public games

WE
Are the anonymous people
Our forefathers were the same
Age's suffering
Connects us to the past
No memories of us
But our world is vast

WE
Are the anonymous people
Silence is our mask

—Basil Fernando (1970)

Contents

List of Tables   xiii

List of Charts and Graphs   xiv

List of Photographs   xiv

List of Abbreviations   xvi

PREFACE   xix

CHAPTER 1   **A World of Uprisings**   1
Asia's People Power Insurgencies
Civil Insurgencies from 1968 to 1998
Global People Power
From 1968 to 1989: The Fall of Soviet Communism
Rethinking Huntington's Third Wave
What Is Democracy?
Ideology and Science
Evaluating Uprisings
The Continuing Wave

CHAPTER 2   **The Philippines**   37
The Marcos Regime
The Assassination of Benigno Aquino
The Snap Election
The Mutiny inside the Military
People Power Emerges
The Final Battle
International Effects of People Power 1
The Aquino Government

From Ramos to Estrada
People Power 2: From Estrada to Arroyo
EDSA 3: Poor People Power

CHAPTER 3   **Burma**   80
8–8–88
Councils Come to Power
Thermidor: The Iron Fist Comes Down
Long Road Since 1988
The Economics of Military Rule
The 2007 "Saffron Revolution"

CHAPTER 4   **Tibet**   104
The 1959 Uprising
Exile and Occupation
The Late 1980s
Continuing Resistance

CHAPTER 5   **China**   125
The Cultural Revolution's Contribution to the Movement of 1989
Economic Reform
The 1989 Crisis
Students Take the Initiative
Students Under Attack
The Hunger Strikers' Coup d'État
"Commander-in-Chief of the Headquarters of Tiananmen Square"
From Martial Law to the Bloodshed of June 4
The Aftermath of the Uprising
China's Prosperity amid Repression
Continuing Resistance and State Incorporation

CHAPTER 6   **Taiwan**   173
The 1947 Uprising and Massacre
From the "Silent Generation" to the Kaohsiung Incident
Grassroots Protests and the End of Martial Law
Democratization Upsurge
The Wild Lily Student Movement
Toward a Democratic Transition

CHAPTER 7   **Nepal**   211
Nepali Civil Society
Preparing the *Jana Andolan*
Political Parties and People's Movement
Liberated Patan
The Uprising's Climax
Negotiations and Compromise
Unfinished Character of *Jana Andolan* 1

The Uprising's Renewal of Civil Society
The Interim Government
The Maoist Impetus
October 4, 2002, Royal Coup d'État
Jana Andolan 2—The 2006 *Loktantra Andolan*
A Difficult Harvest
Who's in Power?

CHAPTER 8   **Bangladesh**   265
Bangladesh's Bloody Birth
Students to the Fore
Bangladeshi Student Power
The Democratic Breakthrough
Women's Movement
Class Struggles of Garment Workers

CHAPTER 9   **Thailand**   287
Nation, Religion, King
The 1973 Student Revolution
The Postuprising Surge
The 1976 Massacre of Students
Neoliberalism's Thai Face
1992 "Black May"
Showdown on May 17
The Outcome of Black May
"Cell Phone Mob"
The 1997 People's Constitution
The 1997 IMF Crisis
Red Shirts and Yellow Shirts

CHAPTER 10   **Indonesia**   344
The IMF Crisis
The 1998 Student Uprising
The *Reformasi* Era

CHAPTER 11   **People Power and Its Limits**   359
The Global Imperative
From 1968 to Uprisings 2.0
The Arab Spring
Revisiting the Eros Effect
Activating the Eros Effect

CHAPTER 12   **The Commune: Freedom's Phenomenological Form**   380
From the Paris Commune to the Gwangju People's Uprising
Differences Between the Two Uprisings
The Role of the Military
The Paris Commune's Role in the Gwangju Uprising

Peter Kropotkin and People's Uprisings

CHAPTER 13 **Organizations and Movements**   400
Aesthetic Avant-Gardes
Political Avant-Gardes
Uprisings 2.0: Building the Virtual Commune
The Role of NGOs
NGOs and the Changing Character of U.S. Intervention

CHAPTER 14 **The Changing Face of the Proletariat**   422
Enlarged Base of Revolution: Middle Strata and
Lumpenproletariat
Gender and Uprisings
Female Archetypes and Democratization
Antigone and Chunhyang

CHAPTER 15 **Uprisings in Comparative Perspective**   438
Economic Factors
Protest Peaks and Depth of Democratization
Counting the Deaths
Role of Military and Regime Insiders
Civil Society
Autonomy and Centralization

CHAPTER 16 **The System Is the Problem**   455
The Best and the Brightest
In the Name of Freedom and Democracy
Structural Imperatives of the World System
First Structural Imperative: Wars and Weapons
Second Structural Imperative: Crisis of Bubbles and Busts
Third Structural Imperative: Billionaires and Beggars
Fourth Structural Imperative: Profits and Pollution
Toward a Reasonable System
The Ongoing Global Uprising

Interviews   479

Credits   482

About the Author   483

Index   484

LIST OF TABLES

TABLE 1.1	Dictators Deposed by People Power Uprisings	2
TABLE 1.2	Asian People Power Uprisings, 1986–1998	8
TABLE 2.1	Foreign Direct Investments in the Philippines (in million U.S.$)	43
TABLE 2.2	Number of Strikes and Workers by Year (Philippines)	45
TABLE 2.3	Strikes in the Philippines, 1983–1987	60
TABLE 2.4	Comparison of People Power 1 and 2	68
TABLE 2.5	Number of Filipino NGOs and Unions, 1984–1997	69
TABLE 2.6	Average Number of Strikes, 1986–2003 (Philippines)	71
TABLE 2.7	Mean Per Capita Daily Food Consumption, in Grams	71
TABLE 2.8	Estimated Percentage of Underweight and Underheight Children	72
TABLE 4.1	Chinese Government Estimate of Tibetan Monasteries and Monks	113
TABLE 5.1	Rates of Real Growth and Inflation, 1983–1991	135
TABLE 5.2	Comparison of the Present Power Structure and Feudal China's Power Structure	143
TABLE 5.3	Number of Protests, May–June 1989	154
TABLE 5.4	Rates of Real Growth and Inflation, 1997–2006	163
TABLE 5.5	Incidents of Social Unrest, 1993–2005	165
TABLE 6.1	Distribution of Gross Domestic Product	190
TABLE 6.2	Labor Disputes in Taiwan, 1965–1986	191
TABLE 6.3	Growth of Civil Society Groups in Taiwan, 1980–2001	202
TABLE 6.4	Taiwan NGOs	202
TABLE 7.1	Enrollment in Secondary and Higher Institutions	216
TABLE 7.2	National Election Results, May 1991	240
TABLE 7.3	Comparison of *Jana Andolan* 1 and 2	246
TABLE 7.4	2008 Election Results for Constituent Assembly (Top 12 of 55 Parties)	255
TABLE 8.1	Officially Registered NGOs in Bangladesh, 1990–2006	277
TABLE 9.1	Strikes in Thailand, 1972–1980	311
TABLE 9.2	Foreign Direct Investments (in million U.S.$)	312
TABLE 9.3	Rural Protests, May 20, 1992	324
TABLE 10.1	Violence in Aceh, 1999–2002	356
TABLE 13.1	Number of Transnational Social Movement Organizations, 1973–2003	413
TABLE 14.1	Contemporary Asian Antigones	430
TABLE 15.1	Inflation and GDP Growth Rate Before Uprisings	440
TABLE 15.2	GNP Per Capita at the Time of Uprising	441
TABLE 15.3	Peaks of Urban Protests	443

TABLE 15.4	Deaths During Uprisings	444
TABLE 16.1	Banking Crises and Decontrol of Financial Sectors	465
TABLE 16.2	World Social Forum Attendance	472

LIST OF CHARTS AND GRAPHS

FIGURE 1.1	Orange Tree, 1968–2006.	18
FIGURE 9.1	Thailand's Coups, 1932–2006	291
FIGURE 9.2	Organization of the National Student Center of Thailand	297
FIGURE 9.3	Structure of Thailand's Assembly of the Poor	331

LIST OF PHOTOGRAPHS

Popular intuition in the Philippines dictated Marcos's departure.	12
Rebel military leader Juan Ponce Enrile called the U.S. and Japanese ambassadors.	49
Nuns with rosaries faced down Marcos's army.	51
Massive occupation of public space made it impossible for Marcos to use tanks.	53
To seize control of television stations, rebel soldiers killed troops loyal to Marcos.	57
On the third day of EDSA 2, people flooded the streets.	67
On 8-8-88, millions of Burmese joined protests.	87
In a vain attempt to persuade soldiers to join protests, some people kissed their feet.	88
Monks played key roles in the Burmese uprising.	91
Wherever Aung San Suu Kyi spoke, throngs of people gathered.	95
Tibetan dob-dob monks.	108
Thousands of women rallied the population to protect the Dalai Lama.	111
Champa Tenzin's heroism was greeted enthusiastically in the streets of Lhasa.	115
Monks initiated protests on March 5, 1988.	116
Massive media presence in Beijing stimulated activists to compete for fame.	144
After preventing soldiers from reaching Tiananmen Square on June 3, Beijing citizens offered them food.	153
Burning military vehicles reveal the intensity of the fighting in Beijing.	160
Mutilated corpse of soldier Liu Guogeng.	161
Thousands of native Taiwanese were massacred in 1947.	182
Beginning in 1986, protests against Taiwan's martial law led to government promises to lift the decades-old state of emergency.	192
Thousands of students occupied Chiang Kai-shek Memorial Hall plaza.	199
The people of Patan took down the sign in front of the district court and held their liberated turf for days.	222
In liberated Patan, citizens spoke freely about strategy and tactics.	224
Women armed with farm tools took to the streets.	228
Women brought flowers to help persuade security forces to be gentle.	247
Madhav Kumar Nepal addressed people in Kalanki.	249
Maoist victory rally in Kathmandu, June 2, 2006.	251
Student Jahad's corpse was carried back to Dhaka University.	273
Students played a major role in uniting and leading the Bangladeshi movement in 1990.	274
Women television stars led a celebration after Ershad was overthrown.	275
The gathering at Thammasat University grew beyond anyone's expectations.	296

Smiling young people with portraits of the king and queen led the "Day of Joy."   298
Many people were shot dead in the streets.   299
Tanks were ordered to disperse crowds in Bangkok.   300
As army attacks continued, small groups set fire to symbolically significant targets.   301
Mobs of police, soldiers, and civilians attacked Thammasat University students in 1976.   309
An "army of motorcycles" swept through the streets.   322
Soldiers stripped and tied up thousands of people.   323
On July 27, 1996, thousands of Indonesians rose against the dictatorship.   347
IMF Director Michel Camdessus watched as Suharto was compelled to sign an agreement.   349
The army cooperated with students as they took over parliament.   351
After the overthrow of Suharto, teachers massively called for improved working conditions and higher pay.   354

LIST OF ABBREVIATIONS

AHRC	Asia Human Rights Commission
AID	Agency for International Development
BB	Black Bloc
FDI	Foreign Direct Investment
IMF	International Monetary Fund
NED	National Endowment for Democracy
NGOs	Non-Governmental Organizations
PGA	People's Global Action
POs	People's Organizations
WB	World Bank
WSF	World Social Forum
WTO	World Trade Organization
YMCA	Young Men's Christian Organization
YWCA	Young Women's Christian Organization

Philippines

CPP	Communist Party of the Philippines
EDSA	Epifanio de los Santos Avenue; the acronym also enumerates a series of uprisings that began there
GABRIELA	General Assembly Binding Women for Reform, Integrity, Leadership, and Action
KOMPIL	Congress of the Filipino People (Kongreso ng Mamamayang Pilipino)
LABAN	Philippine Democratic Party
MNLF	Moro National Liberation Front
NAMFREL	Citizens' Movement for Free Elections
NDF	National Democratic Front
NPA	New People's Army
RAM	Reform the Armed Forces Movement (Rebolusyonaryong Alyansang Makabansa)
TUPAS	Trade Union Congress of the Philippines

| UNIDO | United National Democratic Organization |
| WAND | Women's Action Network for Development |

Burma

CPB	Communist Party of Burma
GUB	Government of the Union of Burma
NCUB	National Council of the Union of Burma
NLD	National League for Democracy
RIT	Rangoon Institute of Technology
RU	Rangoon University

Tibet

| CCP | Communist Party of China |
| PLA | People's Liberation Army |

China

ACFTU	All China Federation of Trade Unions
ASU	Autonomous Student Union
BASU	Beijing Autonomous Student Union
BAWF	Beijing Autonomous Workers' Federation

Taiwan

DPP	Democratic Progressive Party
KMT	Kuomintang
SC	Settlement Committee
TNU	Taiwan National University

Nepal

COCAP	Collective Campaign for Peace
CPN-M	Communist Party of Nepal–Maoist
CPN-ML	Communist Party of Nepal–Marxist-Leninist
CPN-UML	Communist Party of Nepal–Unified Marxist-Leninist
FDO	Feminist Dalit Organization
INSEC	Informal Sector Service Center
MRD	Movement for the Restoration of Democracy
NC	Nepali Congress Party
NUTA	Nepal University Teachers' Association
PLA	People's Liberation Army
RNA	Royal Nepalese Army
SPA	Seven Party Alliance
ULF	United Left Front
UNPM	United National People's Movement
UPF	United People's Front

Bangladesh

AL	Awami League
APSU	All Party Students' Unity
BNP	Bangladesh Nationalist Party
JSD	Socialist National Organization
RAB	Rapid Action Battalion

Thailand

AOP	Assembly of the Poor
CFD	Confederation for Democracy
CPB	Crown Property Bureau
CPD	Campaign for Popular Democracy
CPT	Communist Party of Thailand
FCT	Farmers' Confederation of Thailand
FIST	Federation of Independent Students of Thailand
FLUT	Federation of Labor Unions of Thailand
GLBT	Gay, Lesbian, Bisexual, and Transgender Movement
ISOC	Internal Security Operation Command
NARC	National Administrative Reform Council
NSCT	National Student Center of Thailand
PAD	People's Alliance for Democracy
PDP	Power of Virtue Party (Palang Dharma Party)
PPP	People Power Party
SFT	Student Federation of Thailand
UDD	United Front for Democracy against Dictatorship

PREFACE

THIS BOOK HAS its origins in a suggestion made over dinner in Gwangju, South Korea, in May 2000. That evening, as I sat across the table from East Timor's Bishop Carlos Belo, he looked at me, peering deeply into my eyes. With a modesty that underlies his great intelligence, Bishop Belo very politely asked, "Professor, you've written books about European and American social movements. Why don't you write about Asia?" With his simple question, the next decade of my life took an unexpected turn.

In 2001 and 2008, I returned to live in Gwangju, where translations of my previous books opened doors through which few foreigners had walked. In the course of my research, dozens of people graciously took time to explain nuances of their experiences and to guide me as I tread on unfamiliar ground. With Korea as my base, I traveled extensively in East Asia, often to meet activists I had first encountered in Gwangju. They, in turn, introduced me to key insiders in their home countries. In addition to opening my eyes to struggles that were far more advanced than those in the United States, where there is only peripheral support from the population, these activists shared memories of years of sacrifice and hardship that sustained me in my decade-long quest to finish this book.

South Korea's movement is situated at the center of Asian People Power because of the role of Gwangju in shaping the entire region's insurgency. As I observed in *Asia's Unknown Uprisings Volume 1*, the Gwangju People's Uprising propelled the country out of the orbit of an American-backed military dictatorship. Along with the nineteen-day June Uprising in 1987, Gwangju is the reason for the existence today of Korean democracy. While Korea's rich history of twentieth-century uprisings is of no small significance to the nine other places analyzed in this book, it is not essential to have read the first volume in order to understand this one. Readers will be able to start afresh here.

While many of the uprisings I discuss were successful in ousting dictators, none has been able to realize participants' highest aspirations. In many cases, global corporations rode on the backs of insurgencies in order to open markets previously closed to them and to exploit the labor-power of people formerly employed by local capitalists. In my view, this is no reason to discount the significance of grassroots movements as vehicles for social transformation. From the American Revolution to the French and the Russian, no past insurgency has successfully won its makers' fondest dreams—nor should we expect any single episode to be able to do so. While past revolutions "perfected the machine instead of smashing it," popular uprisings also qualitatively enhanced millions of people's lives and increased individual and collective freedoms. For that, we should all be eternally grateful—especially given the enormous costs often paid by participants.

In my previous study of the global movement of 1968, I uncovered the simultaneous international emergence of congruent actions and aspirations—a phenomenon I named the "eros effect." Much to my surprise, I also found it to be a significant dimension of Asian democratization movements from 1986 to 1998. Using the case studies in this book, I extend my empirical understanding of the eros effect and deepen my analysis of it.

My hope is that future scholars and activists will build upon this work, correcting its flaws, and revealing new connections among a seemingly divergent array of movements. I would be very pleased if these two volumes were to contribute, however modestly, to the self-conscious synchronization of future global uprisings, to help empower them to break the stranglehold of militarized nation-states and global capitalism.

I owe a great debt to many who do not wish to be named. Many others, including prominent political leaders like Nepal's former president Ram Baran Yadav, former prime minister Madhav Kumar Nepal, and Philippine Senator Gregorio Honasan kindly took time to answer my sometimes very difficult inquiries. A list of interviewees is contained in an appendix. I wish to acknowledge financial assistance from the Korea Research Foundation as well as a Bistline Grant and sabbatical leave from Wentworth Institute of Technology, whose library staff, especially Dan O'Connell and Pia Romano, have been an unending source of help. A Fulbright Senior Research Grant made it possible for me to live in Korea from 2007 to 2008. For years, the Sociology Department and May 18 Institute at Chonnam National University in Gwangju warmly hosted me as a visiting professor and provided me with intellectual space of no small importance.

To complete this book, many colleagues provided intellectual sustenance, often in the form of critical interventions. I wish particularly to thank Victor Wallis, James Petras, and Basil Fernando, whose careful readings and gentle suggestions often pointed me in directions I had not considered. Eddie Yuen, Jack Hipp, Ngo Vinh Long, Teodros Kiros, Loren Goldner, and David Martinez provided valuable encouragement and advice. Jordi Gomez offered helpful editorial comments. In many countries I visited, I was fortunate to be guided by activists and scholars: Pete Rahon and Mary Racelis in the Philippines; Sann Aung, Aung Kyaw So, and Thura for Burma; Kim Jin-ho and Kim Jae Kwan for China; Michael Hsiao and Frank Chen in Taiwan; Samantha and Jon Christiansen, Parvin Akhi, and Ataur Rahman in Bangladesh; Suresh Pokharel, Ram Chandra Pokharel, Bimal Sharma, Bhawana Bhatta, and Lok Raj Baral in Nepal; and Sor Rattana and Jiranan Hanthamrongwit in Thailand. Korean colleagues Park Hae-kwang, Kim Chanho, Na Il-sung, and Na Kahn-chae played significant roles in my capacity to complete this study. I am particularly grateful to my daughter, Cassandra, whose help on the book kept me going in the final months. She and Dalal provided great support and enlivening conversations. Shin Eun-jung is a model of hard work whose companionship nurtures my own endeavors.

Cambridge, Massachusetts
September 21, 2011

CHAPTER 1

A World of Uprisings

The likelihood of democratic development in Eastern Europe is
virtually nil. . . . With a few exceptions, the limits of democratic
development in the world may well have been reached.
—Samuel Huntington, 1984

We, the old ones, may never see the decisive battles of the coming
revolution.
—V.I. Lenin, January 1917

UPRISINGS ARE TERRIBLE, beautiful events. They break out so unexpectedly that
they surprise their partisans as much as they bewilder their opponents. Far more
than we realize, the world we live in has been created by revolutionary insurgencies. From the American Revolution to the Russian, from the Gwangju Uprising
to the Arab Spring, uprisings occur with astonishing regularity.

Leading up to the 1980s, East Asian dictatorships had been in power for
decades and seemed unshakable, yet a wave of revolts soon transformed the
region. These insurgencies threw to the wind the common bias that Asians are
happier with authoritarian governments than democracy. They ushered in greater
liberties and new opportunities for citizen participation—as well as for international capital. One of the purposes of this book is to assess the contradictory
character of these changes and the forces that produced them.

Asia's Unknown Uprisings focuses on people's forms of interaction with each
other during moments of confrontations with the forces of order. I seek to let the
actions of hundreds of thousands of people speak for themselves as a means to
portray freedom's concrete history. The oft-repeated phrase "the people make
history" cannot be comprehended without a central focus on popular uprisings. In the first volume, I provided a view of Korean history through the prism

of social movements. In a country whose unique character meant three consecutive dynasties each lasted nearly half a millennium, Korea's long twentieth century produced an unmatched richness of uprisings and upheavals. From the 1894 Farmers' Movement against Japanese colonialism to the 2008 candlelight protests against U.S. "mad cow" beef, insurgencies continually built upon each other. Popular movements assimilated lessons from previous protest episodes, and people improvised tactics and targets from their own assessments of past accomplishments and failures.

This volume is international in scope and deals with uprisings in nine places, yet connections can be found in popular insurgencies' capacities to learn from each other, to expand upon preceding examples, and to borrow each other's vocabulary, actions, and aspirations. Almost overnight, "People Power" simultaneously became activists' common global identity—cutting across religious, national, and economic divides. Through empirical analysis of specific uprisings, this book's focus is the unfolding development of Asian uprisings in the Philippines (1986), Burma (1988), Tibet (1989), China (1989), Taiwan (1990), Nepal (1990), Bangladesh (1990), Thailand (1992), and Indonesia (1998).

The 1989 revolutions in Eastern Europe against Soviet regimes are well known, yet Eurocentric (and anticommunist) bias often diminishes the significance of their Asian counterparts, rendering them largely invisible. Although the accomplishments of Asian uprisings are noteworthy and their character significantly more grassroots than contemporaneous turmoil in Eastern Europe (where Gorbachev's willingness to abandon the Russian empire triggered the movements), they remain unknown, even within the region where they transpired. East Asia's string of uprisings from 1980 to 1998 had a huge political impact, overthrowing eight entrenched regimes: Philippine dictator Ferdinand Marcos was forced into exile; South Korea's Chun Doo-hwan was disgraced and compelled to grant direct presidential elections before being imprisoned; Taiwan's forty-year martial law regime was overturned; Burma's mobilized citizenry overthrew two dictators only to see their successors massacre thousands; Nepal's monarchy was made constitutional; military ruler Muhammad Ershad in Bangladesh was forced to step down and eventually sent to prison; Army Chief Suchinda Kraprayoon in Thailand was forced to vacate the office of prime minister; and Indonesia's longtime dictator Suharto was ousted after three decades in power.

Despite more than a century of research, modern social science is utterly incapable of predicting political upheavals. Democratization theorists have identified

TABLE 1.1 **Dictators Deposed by People Power Uprisings**

Dictator	Country	Year of Ouster
Ferdinand Marcos	Philippines	1986
Chun Doo-hwan	South Korea	1987
Ne Win, Sein Lwin	Burma	1988
Ershad	Bangladesh	1990
Suchinda	Thailand	1992
Suharto	Indonesia	1998

an array of major variables posited to be significant indicators of the possibility for lasting democracy. Half a century ago, Seymour Martin Lipset hypothesized a correlation between economic development and democracy, asserting that once societies reach a wealth threshold, their chances of being democratic are significantly higher than those of poorer societies. Various theorists have subsequently operationalized Lipset's "modernization theory" with specific quantitative predictions correlating wealth and survival rate of democratic systems of governance.[1] Samuel Huntington's observation that urbanization is a prerequisite for democratization led him to recommend "forced-draft urbanization," a notorious policy that resulted in free-fire zones and rural saturation bombing of Vietnam as a means of forcing peasants into cities. The United States dropped more bombs on Vietnam to "create the preconditions for democracy" than had been used everywhere during World War II, yet Vietnamese nationalism prevailed. Max Weber's notion of a correlation between capitalism and the Protestant ethic was adapted to Asia through analysis asserting an inverse relationship between Confucian values and democratization. Although East Asia's economic rise has given such theorists pause, communal Confucian values remain seen as the "kernel of traditional culture that is unfavorable to democracy."[2] For Huntington, Confucian democracy was an oxymoron, a "contradiction in terms."[3] Following his lead, Euro-American theorists have understood a dearth of American-style "civil society" as a reason for an absence of democracy.

To the above list of explanatory variables for democratic governance should be added the precise character of uprisings. Protesters' mutual relationships (their capacity to bond and organize themselves in moments of extreme crisis, their hierarchical or horizontal patterns of authority, and their behavior toward those within their own ranks who violate group norms and values) are significant predictors of future political relationships. Similarly, insurgents' interaction with opposing forces (their treatment of prisoners, tactics of mobilization and confrontation, and forms of justice meted out to traitors and enemy combatants) give insight into the quality of democratic norms that likely would become operative if the movement were successful. Comparing the intensity of peaks of protest may also be a means of gauging democratization's subsequent depth. Noting with care specific social strata that mobilize during crises may be a better means of comprehending political opinions than one hundred telephone opinion polls conducted in quieter moments. Individuals who seem to be agreeing with the course of politics-as-usual often have other streams of thought in the back of their minds. The tremendous power of the mass media notwithstanding, uncontrolled intuitions and insights remain operative even when they are not overtly expressed.

Seeking to better understand social movements is one reason for my admittedly belabored reconstruction of civil insurgencies in this book, but it is not my only one: I hope to glean useful lessons and insights for future generations' freedom struggles. In my view, without a fundamental break with a few hundred billionaires' control of humanity's vast social wealth and the allocation of that wealth through the profit motive, our planet will continue to be ravaged by reckless industrialization and unending wars. Without systematic transformation of corporate capitalism, hundreds of millions of people will remain condemned to live in hell on earth because of poverty, starvation, and disease. As I see it, it is entirely unlikely that the kind of social reorganization required for lasting peace, environmental salvation, and shared prosperity can be achieved through continuing evolution of inherited economic and political structures. Rather, global revolutionary change is a prescriptive remedy needed in large doses to cure the diseases of militarized nation-states, power-hungry politicians, and wealth-grabbing billionaires.

Like art, revolution is an important dimension of uniquely human activity, a form of species-constitutive behavior that contains its own grammar and logic. While it is true that humans are creatures of habit and routine, we are also capable of enormous changes. We grow accustomed to our daily lives, and fantasize—or fear—that our current conditions will last forever. Nation-states today are everywhere hegemonic, yet uprisings can transform overnight even the most apparently entrenched social relationships.

One of the problems with a nationalist construction of history is that it refutes in advance the idea that human beings in various places might actually be more closely tied to each other than they are to their own "countrymen," that ordinary people's aspirations and dreams, their conscious and unconscious desires and needs, might be more similar to each other's than to those of their nations' elites. Even addition of one country's history to another can lead to assertions that are both untrue and unimportant, while obscuring transnational simultaneity, commonalities, and parallel grassroots developments. It matters little whether or not the first nationalist revolution in Asia took place in the Philippines with the uprising against the Spanish in 1896.[4] Korea's Great Farmers' War, or Tonghak movement, came two years earlier. What is important is they both fought for freedom from foreign conquest. The great international synthesis achieved by Tonghak, China's Taiping Rebellion, and Vietnam's Cao Dai have much more in common than many scholars realize precisely because of nationalist constraints on research.

Today, as planetary integration accelerates, human beings are rapidly becoming self-conscious as a species—one of the very best dimensions of globalization. World history opens new possibilities, and it is also a necessary means to assimilate properly the recent past. If citizens in country A were motivated to overthrow their ruler because they witnessed people in country B do so, then a history of either country alone would not do justice to its freedom movement. Even more significant is the *simultaneous* emergence of freedom struggles in many places. When conceptualized across national boundaries, a more accurate representation of uprisings becomes possible, and a more promising future comes into focus. This endeavor lies at the center of all my books on urban insurgencies in the late twentieth century.

The inability of analysts to comprehend the global nature of social movements is due in part to a lack of empirical studies of uprisings, even in national contexts. With respect to Korea, the best English-language historians have often neglected (and sometimes misstated) basic facts related to insurgencies and paid scant attention to their significance, emphasizing instead "Great Men" and "Great Women." In the case of Thailand, as Somchai Phatharathananunth wrote in 2006, "There are still few major works on Thai civil society organizations in the form of social movements."[5] Much as I tried, I could find no comprehensive German or English-language history of many of the uprisings discussed in this book, so I wrote them myself.

Moving from periphery to center of the world system (a phenomenon commonly understood in economic terms), East Asia is positioned today to take the lead in the unfolding of world politics. The huge losses of indigenous people's lives in U.S. wars—more than three million killed in the Korean War and at least two million more in Indochina—served as crucibles of fire, precipitated refugees by the tens of millions, and conditioned unprecedented social movements that sought to transform their societies. In three devastating years, Korea's *yangban* aristocracy was decimated and the country completely destroyed, compelling its citizens arduously to rebuild.

Koreans' spirit and energy through destruction and reconstruction positioned them in the center of the groundswell of Asian popular uprisings, and their subsequent cultural wave (*hallyu*) swept the continent at the end of the twentieth century. In 1960, South Korean students led the country against U.S.-imposed dictator Syngman Rhee. After police slaughtered 186 young people in the streets of Seoul, Rhee was forced into exile, and democracy won. In 1973, Thai students mobilized hundreds of thousands of citizens against their military dictator, and after seventy-three were gunned down, they also won a short-lived democracy. In 1980, citizens in Gwangju courageously rose up against the brutality of the South Korean army. After driving the military out of the city, they governed themselves through citizens' general assemblies. Although overwhelmed by the army (abetted by U.S. President Carter) at the cost of hundreds of lives, they continued their struggle to overthrow the junta in 1987 and to imprison former dictators Chun Doo-hwan and Roh Tae-woo a decade later.

Asia's People Power Insurgencies
Even in defeat, popular insurgencies transform people and subsequently reappear in unexpected forms. The sudden emergence of eight People Power uprisings within six short years from 1986 to 1992 is a case in point. The term "People Power" was born in the actions of hundreds of thousands of Filipinos in February 1986, when citizens overthrew the Marcos dictatorship in an eighteen-day uprising. Set off by electoral fraud and a mutiny by key elements of the military, people stubbornly took to the streets to block loyalist tanks and troops. Despite being continually threatened with great harm, people's courageous flooding of public space provided critical support to the mutineers. While mythologized today, people's nonviolent resistance should not obscure the critical roles played by armed soldiers, whose guns and helicopters were vital to the ouster of Marcos. Nor should the grassroots rebellion obscure the importance of the Catholic Church hierarchy, which called for citizens to go into the streets of Manila.[6] After the uprising began, U.S. President Ronald Reagan continued to support his longtime friend Marcos,

but once the bulk of the military defected to the side of the opposition, the United States insisted the time had come for Marcos to go. Soon thereafter he went reluctantly into exile, but not before the phrase "People Power" became well known enough to frighten entrenched dictators no matter where in the world they ruled.

The overthrow of Marcos helped to animate the 1987 June Uprising in South Korea, a marathon endeavor of nineteen consecutive days of illegal protests in which more than one million people mobilized on three separate days. Hundreds of thousands of Koreans evidently were inspired and instructed by their Filipina fellows. Alongside Korea's legendary student movement, Christian groups also played a leading role in winning direct presidential elections and other political reforms. Civil society played a crucial role in the popular uprising through formation of a "grand coalition with the opposition political party, ultimately pressuring the authoritarian regime to yield to the 'popular upsurge' from below."[7]

As South Koreans won democracy, people's movements sprang up in many neighboring countries. An end to thirty-eight years of martial law was won in Taiwan in 1987, less than a month after the Korean military capitulated to opposition demands. Anecdotal evidence tells of people singing Korean democracy movement songs in the streets of Taipei.[8] Three more years of struggles culminated in students taking over Chiang Kai-shek Square in March 1990 to insist upon—and gain—democratic elections for president and parliament (the Legislative Yuan).

In Burma, popular aspirations for loosening central controls bloodily collided with the forces of order beginning in March 1988.[9] As in 1980 in Gwangju, students in Rangoon led the population into the streets, and the military went on a killing spree ordered by ruthless generals at the highest levels of power. Despite horrific repression, popular resistance continued, compelling President Ne Win to step down after twenty-six years of rule. When he named the police commander responsible for the butchery of so many innocent lives as his replacement, five days of new student-led protests forced yet another resignation. In the resulting vacuum of power, popular councils of workers, writers, monks, ethnic minorities, and students emerged as the leadership of a nationwide movement for multiparty democracy. Undeterred by people's clear desire for more freedom, the military decided to preserve its rule by massacring even more protesters—killing at least three thousand people before order was restored. Arresting thousands in 1990, including over a hundred newly elected parliamentarians, the Burmese military government ignored the huge electoral mandate won by Aung San Suu Kyi's National League for Democracy (NLD) and kept her under house arrest for most of the next twenty years.

In March 1989, three decades after their failed uprising against Chinese invasion, Tibetans rose again. When Chinese police attacked small protests against Han settler-colonialism, demonstrators counterattacked, turning their wrath on Chinese businesses. Party leaders sent in the army and declared martial law in Lhasa on March 8, a precursor of what would come to Beijing less than two months later. In May 1989—months before Eastern European communism faced its stiffest challenges—student activists in Tiananmen Square activated a broad public outcry for democracy. Hundreds of thousands of workers and citizens soon joined the movement as it spread to nearly all cities and grew beyond any-one's expectations. Following the tactics of Filipinos who had mobilized to stop Marcos's army in Manila, citizens of Beijing held off the People's Liberation Army for days and prevented it from implementing the government's declaration of martial law. Despite splits in the armed forces and inside the Communist Party, order was ultimately imposed after hundreds were killed around Tiananmen Square. For years afterward, activists were hunted and imprisoned.

The revolt in China originated from outside the ranks of the party, but it had significant allies even in the party's highest echelons. Within the halls of com-munism in neighboring Vietnam, as the *Zeitgeist* of revolt against dictatorship was at work, a member of the Politburo, General Tran Do, publicly called for multiparty democracy in 1989, an unprecedented event. Inspired by Asian revolts, Europeans began to take more decisive actions to overthrow Soviet-backed dic-tatorships. There, too, dissidents within ruling communist parties significantly affected activists. A flood of change inundated Eastern Europe, and new govern-ments were won in Hungary, Poland, Czechoslovakia, and Romania. In November 1989, the Berlin Wall came down, and Germany quickly reunified. The Baltic countries seceded from the Soviet Union, which toppled under its own top-heavy weight and soon dissolved into more than a dozen new republics.

In 1990, people in Bangladesh and Nepal massively mobilized to overthrow their rulers. Only after students in Bangladesh compelled warring opposition parties to unite against military dictator Muhammad Ershad was the movement able to compel his resignation. In Nepal, fifty-three days of illegal protests begin-ning in April 1990 forced the king to accept opposition leaders' generous offer of a constitutional monarchy. (In 2006, after a new king seized control, a nineteen-day popular uprising abolished the monarchy.)

As country after country was affected, Thailand underwent a bloody upris-ing in 1992 that strengthened democratic forces. The mobilization there began humbly enough when an opposition politician went on a hunger strike against coup leader General Suchinda Kraprayoon's ascension to the office of prime min-ister. As a movement for civilian control of government and democracy spread, hundreds of thousands of people went into the streets. On May 18, 1992, more than fifty people were killed when the military used bullets to suppress street demonstrations. As a result of his army's brutality, Suchinda was forced to step down.[10] Years of grassroots involvement in writing a new constitution produced one of the best in Asia, which went into effect in 1997.

In 1998 in Indonesia, students called for a "People Power Revolution." After days of campus protests, tens of thousands of them surged into the parliament building and ended three decades of Suharto's presidency. Protesters used new Internet technology—chat rooms, web pages, and e-mail—to organize and mobi-lize. Given the country's unreliable progovernment media, they adapted the web to publicize their movement and used encrypted messages to send intelligence reports to each other about the positions and size of military and police. Since student organizations were heavily infiltrated, one of their main organizations, Forum Kota, insisted on a rotation of leadership and office location every week.[11]

The variety of movements examined in this book is summarized in TABLE 1.2. Despite libraries of books written about them, these uprisings' synchronous appearance and relationships to each other have yet to be explored. As the

TABLE 1.2 **Asian People Power Uprisings, 1986–1998**

Country	Year	Type of Movement	Short-Term Result	Long-Term Outcome
Philippines	1986	Military mutiny supported by Catholic hierarchy and People Power	Elite-led democracy; neoliberal reforms	"People Power II" in 2001 overthrows President Estrada; death squads still active as late as 2008
South Korea	1987	People's Uprising; 19 days of illegal protests	Direct presidential elections; increased liberties; strike wave	End to military dictatorship; increased liberties and prosperity; Korean wave
Taiwan	1987–1990	Extraparliamentary opposition (*tangwai*); student protests	End of four decades of martial law; wave of protests; elections	Illiberal democracy; increased prosperity
Burma	1988	Student-led popular uprising; councils	Two dictators overthrown; movement suppressed violently—thousands killed	Continuing military dictatorship
Tibet	1989	Monk-led protests turn into riots	Martial law; heavy repression	Continuing military dictatorship
China	1989	Student protests leading to popular contestation of power	Repression; increased prosperity	Continuing one-party rule but with greater prosperity
Nepal	1990	53-day popular uprising and general strike	Constitutional monarchy; strikes; reforms	Second Uprising in 2006 overthrew monarchy
Bangladesh	1990	Student-led popular uprising	Overthrew Ershad; new elections; strikes	Continuing dictatorship/ illiberal democracy
Thailand	1992	Citizen coalition led protests; intense fighting after military attacks	Violent suppression leading to new constitution (1997)	2006 military coup d'état; continuing struggles; polarization of Red and Yellow Shirts
Indonesia	1998	Student-led uprising; occupation of parliament	Ouster of Suharto; neoliberal reforms	Illiberal democracy

relationship of these revolts to each other is an understudied dimension of their history, so is their place in an even larger intercontinental wave of insurgencies beginning with the global 1968 New Left.

Belief that the 1960s belong to the distant past ignores their continuation at the end of the twentieth century. While New Left insurgencies were characterized by the rapid spread of revolutionary aspirations and actions in 1968, they had significant long-term effects. The shift in values they created meant that it was only a matter of time before the apartheid regime in South Africa collapsed, only a question of when—not if—dictatorships everywhere would be swept away. Forms of direct democracy and collective action developed by the New Left of the 1960s continue to define insurgencies' aspirations and structures, precisely why the New Left was a world-historical movement.[12]

Civil Insurgencies from 1968 to 1998

In almost every country in the world, insurgent social movements synchronously emerged in 1968. From France to Senegal, China to the United States, and Poland to Mexico—as in dozens of other countries—militant students were at the cutting edge, and they sometimes detonated wider social explosions. In France, after a student rebellion, a general strike in May 1968 of at least nine million workers demanded an end to lives of drudgery in factories and offices. When the communist-dominated trade unions negotiated a settlement calling for higher wages, thousands of workers threw bottles and lunches at their union leaders, and booed them off the stage. Around the country, workers rejected the communists' proposed settlement. They wanted new kinds of lives—not better pay for enduring stultifying assembly lines and boring offices for the better part of their lives. They rejected the entire system and called for self-management and an end to capital's domination.

Opposing capitalism and communism because neither kind of society was free, 1960s movements became known as "New Left" to distinguish them from their communist—or "Old Left"—predecessors (or, as some insisted, nemeses). When the Prague Spring, the Czechoslovakian experiment of "socialism with a human face," was brought to an end by half a million invading Russian troops, people in Prague took down street signs and buildings' identification markers. It took the Soviet Union's army a week to find the post office. Borrowing a page from the U.S. peace movement, young protesters put flowers in the gun barrels of tanks. In Poland and Yugoslavia, student movements emerged along the global fault lines of protest.

The international revolt in 1968 was touched off by one of the greatest armed uprisings of the twentieth century—the Tet Offensive in Vietnam. On the night of January 31, 1968, nearly every city in the Southern part of the country and all U.S. bases came under surprise attack. More than half a million U.S. troops and a vast intelligence apparatus failed to anticipate the nationally synchronized uprising during which seventy thousand South Vietnamese guerrillas attacked in a single night. Vietnam's second-largest city, Hue, was liberated and held out for three weeks, and the U.S. embassy grounds in Saigon were overrun.[13] Planned to coincide with presidential elections in the United States, the Tet Offensive resulted in President Lyndon Johnson's decision not to run for reelection and led to upheavals in Germany, France, Spain, Senegal, and Mexico—even in the heartland of the United States. A few months later, on April 4, Martin Luther King Jr. was assassinated, and riots took place in over 150 cities. More damage was done to Washington, D.C., than when the British captured it during the war of 1812. All these movements converged in a process of mutual amplification.[14]

The spontaneous chain reaction of uprisings and the massive occupation of public space in 1968 signaled the sudden entry into history of millions of ordinary people who acted in solidarity with each other. People intuitively believed that they could change the direction of the world from war to peace, from racism to solidarity, and from patriotism to humanism. In my book on the global imagination of 1968, I developed the concept of the eros effect to explain the rapid spread of revolutionary aspirations and actions.[15] During moments of the eros effect, universal interests become generalized at the same time as dominant values of society (national chauvinism, hierarchy, and domination) are negated. As Marcuse so clearly formulated it, humans have an instinctual need for freedom—something that we grasp intuitively, and it is this instinctual need that is sublimated into a collective phenomenon during moments of the eros effect.[16] Dimensions of the eros effect include: the sudden and synchronous emergence of hundreds of thousands of people occupying public space; the simultaneous appearance of revolts in many places; the intuitive identification of hundreds of thousands of people with each other; their common belief in new values; and suspension of normal daily routines like competitive business practices, criminal behavior, and acquisitiveness. In the course of this book, I discuss many such moments. People's intuition and self-organization—not the dictates of any party— are key to the emergence of such protests. Actualized in the actions of millions of people in 1968, the eros effect is a tool of enormous future potential. In relation to the 1980 Gwangju Uprising, this phenomenon was named the "absolute community."[17] With the Arab Spring in 2011, transnational eruptions of protests have become widely visible.

Although often thought to have climaxed in 1968, the global movement intensified afterward. In 1969, the Italian Hot Autumn saw hundreds of thousands of workers challenge factory authority and institute autonomous forms of shop floor governance. In 1970, the U.S. movement reached its high point at the Black Panthers Revolutionary People's Constitutional Convention, the culmination of the "American 1968," a remarkable five-month upsurge from May to September 1970, during which the movement simultaneously climaxed among a wide range of constituencies: a political strike of four million students and half a million faculty on the campuses after the killings at Kent State and Jackson State Universities; the National Organization for Women's general strike of women (and the design of the modern symbol for feminism); the massive entry of Vietnam veterans into the peace movement; the first Gay Pride week; and the Chicano Moratorium on August 29 in Los Angeles. As the whole society was disquieted, Puerto Ricans, Native Americans, and a rainbow of constituencies flocked to

Philadelphia in answer to the Black Panther Party's call to write a new constitution for the United States. A visionary draft was produced through a participatory process involving more than ten thousand people. The consensus included replacement of the nation's standing army with popular self-defense and equitable redistribution of the world's wealth.[18]

Also in 1970, the Polish workers' movement revived. Chanting "We apologize for 1968!"—when workers had failed to rally to students' support—thousands went into the streets of Gdansk. Fighting with police escalated, and at least 45 people were killed, hundreds wounded, and 19 buildings set on fire—including the ruling United Polish Workers' Party headquarters. The movement spread to Gdynia and Szczecin. Only after Party Chief Edward Gierek resigned could the insurgency be contained.[19] Fighting in the streets subsided, but the trade union movement slowly rebuilt itself into *Solidarność*—the organization that went on to overturn Poland's government in 1989.[20]

At the end of 1972, when the U.S. government bombed the dikes of Northern Vietnam and mined Haiphong harbor, campus protests again involved millions of students. In October 1973, Thai students mobilized, led by some who had studied in the United States and returned with New Left ideas. After dozens of people were shot down in the streets of Bangkok, students overthrew the Thanom military dictatorship and created one of the most open periods in the country's history.

A month later, students in Greece took over Athens Polytechnic to oppose the U.S.-imposed Papadopoulos dictatorship. They chanted slogans that praised the courage of their counterparts in Thailand. The 1973 Greek student movement's mammoth "OXI!" ("NO!") poster drew inspiration from what Herbert Marcuse had characterized as the New Left's "Great Refusal." On November 17, soldiers using a tank, bazooka, and automatic weapons gunned down thirty-four people and retook the Polytechnic. Eight days after the slaughter, Papadopoulos was overthrown from within his own army's ranks, but the military's days in power were numbered, and it fell within a year.

From 1974 to 1991, after the floodgates of change had been knocked open by this global revolt, some forty countries democratized. Beginning with the overthrow of the Portuguese dictatorship on April 25, 1974, the "Carnation Revolution" was quickly followed by the demise of the junta in Spain (1977). In Peru, strikes and popular insurgencies toppled the government in 1977. In dozens of countries, people fought the structural adjustment demands of the International Monetary Fund (IMF). From 1978 to 1979, widespread strikes against the IMF broke out in Bolivia. Popular movements in Nicaragua and Iran overthrew U.S. imposed dictators. History's *Zeitgeist* suddenly appeared everywhere, if not in the form of popular uprisings and movements in the streets, then in the backrooms of power. Everyone rushed to catch the wave: Senegal (1978), Ghana (1979), Nigeria (1979), Bolivia and Honduras (1982), and Turkey (1983). In 1982, a general strike in Argentina mobilized people against the military dictatorship for the first challenge to it in years. In Uruguay, monthly rallies beginning in May 1983 culminated in a mammoth protest of four hundred thousand people (in a country of only three

Popular intuition in the Philippines dictated Marcos's departure.
Photo by Joe Galvez Jr. Source: Monina Allarey Mercado, editor, *People Power: An Eyewitness History* (Manila: The James B. Reuter, S.J. Foundation, 1986), 145.

million) demanding release of political prisoners and an end to dictatorship. In 1984, millions of Brazilians mobilized for direct presidential elections.

As a popular uprising developed step by step, Haiti's dictator, Duvalier, in power for decades, was forced to flee early in February 1986. In the Philippines, people took hope from Duvalier's ouster and mobilized massively against Marcos later that same month. In the photo above, one group sat on their sandbagged barricade with a homemade sign reading: "Marcos—Duvalier Waits for You!!!" Such global relationships are often ignored or deemed anecdotal, yet people's intuitive connections are powerful resources in challenging existing powers.

Global People Power

As People Power swept through Asia after 1986, citizens rose up all over the world—from Eastern Europe to Latin America, back again to Asia and into Africa. Civilian governments replaced military rulers in Colombia, Brazil, and Chile; multiparty democracy appeared in the Ivory Coast, Zaire, Gabon, and Algeria. In December 1987, Palestinians under Israeli occupation launched their first Intifada. Even in Pakistan, democratic elections were held after Zia-ul-Haq was killed in an air crash on August 17, 1988. In January 1989, Benin's Marxist-Leninist government faced a paralyzing general strike and was subsequently forced to conduct free elections. At the end of February 1989, Venezuelans rose in a tremendous popular rebellion against an IMF-imposed austerity package. At least 276 people were killed (some counted the slaughter in the thousands) before the massive mobilization could be halted. Over the next decade, the country realigned its political priorities, and Hugo Chávez was swept into power. As South Africa's movement continued to build momentum, millions of people worldwide galvanized an antiapartheid boycott, and Nelson Mandela walked out of prison on February 11, 1990, after thirty-seven years in captivity.

This wave of insurgencies was not characterized by armed insurrections led by centralized parties or ideologically united groups. Neither pacifist nor communist, these movements were generated from the grassroots. Generally not armed, they were neither called into being nor led by trained cadre (such as the Proletarian Hundreds or Red Guards); nor were they mainly productions of traditionally defined sectors of the working class. In contrast to political insurgencies led by centralized parties, these were social insurgencies produced by global civil society, a diverse and autonomous manifestation of popular wisdom that has continually grown since 1968. The movements' popularity and festive character often befuddled those in power. During the June Uprising in South Korea, even the military's loyalties were so thrown into confusion that top generals thought military intervention would not be helpful and might provoke another Gwangju Uprising.[21]

Within the veritable tidal waves of protests that swept the planet, people intuitively awakened to their power and took control of cities. In the Philippines, Romania, and East Germany, crowds of people overran presidential palaces. The 1986 "People Power" uprising in the Philippines clearly encouraged South Koreans (whose 1980 Gwangju Uprising had also inspired Philippine resistance), and "People Power" became the name adopted for mobilizations in Burma, Taiwan, and China. The overthrow of Romanian dictator Ceausescu had profound effects in Nepal, since Ceausescu had visited Kathmandu in 1987. In 1998, Indonesians took the name "People Power" from the Philippines, and Jakarta's reform movement bequeathed its name ("*reformasi*") to the Malaysian movement soon thereafter.[22] In victory as well as defeat, people intuitively identified with one another: after Chinese protesters were brutalized in the streets of Beijing on June 4, 1989, East German activists worried they would soon face a "Chinese solution."

In 1968, connections among protests were, for the most part, immediate and unreflective, but in 1989, citizens became self-consciously tied together. As a result of mass communications, people are increasingly capable of interpreting world events and drawing appropriate lessons within days of events in distant parts of the planet. From my earlier study of the actions of millions of people in 1968, I gleaned five defining principles of the global New Left:

1. Opposition to racial, political, and patriarchal domination as well as to economic exploitation
2. Concept of freedom as not only freedom from material deprivation but also freedom to become new kinds of human beings
3. Expansion of democracy and the rights of the individual, not their constraint
4. Enlarged base of revolution, including the "proletarianized" middle strata
5. Emphasis on direct action.[23]

These principles existed in the actions of millions of people and embodied their capacity for self-management and international solidarity.

Uprisings at the end of the twentieth century demonstrate patterns astonishingly similar to these defining features of New Left movements. Unlike hostility toward the church in classical Left movements from the French Revolution and 1871 Paris Commune to the Russian and Chinese Revolutions, New Left movements emerged from within the church and used it as a base of support, whether in African-American civil rights struggles or East Germany's Protestant church refuges. Movements of the 1960s involved thousands of pastors like Martin Luther King Jr. and a changed Catholic Church after the promulgation of liberation theology in Medellín. During Gwangju's 1980 uprising, the YMCA and YWCA were key organizing centers, and in 1986, Cardinal Jaime Sin of Manila played a huge role in the 1986 Philippine People Power victory, as did Korean Protestants and Cardinal Stephen Kim in the following year's June Uprising.

A key New Left characteristic was an enlarged constituency of revolution—a factor discerned in the significant participation of the lumpenproletariat among Gwangju's armed resistance fighters; mobilization of the new working class (offline office and clerical employees) as Seoul's "necktie brigade" in 1987; in committed protests of Nepalese medical professionals, lawyers, and journalists in 1990; and in what is erroneously referred to as the "mobile phone mob" in Thailand in 1992.[24] While more recent movements assimilated completely new technologies like fax machines, cell phones, the Internet, and social media, they also reactivated New Left playfulness, humor, irony, and autonomous artistic expression as opposition tactics.

New Left forms of participatory democracy were central to the movement's identity in the 1955 struggle to desegregate buses in Montgomery, Alabama; student movements in dozens of countries; the international counterculture embracing Christiania's communards in Copenhagen, San Francisco's Diggers, Amsterdam's Provos, and Berkeley's People's Park; as well as the Black Panther Party's Revolutionary People's Constitutional Convention. Continuing in the 1960s tradition of participatory democracy, the autonomous movement (or Autonomen) in Germany used consensus in general assemblies to make key decisions and has sustained itself over several generations of activists. Allied with farmers and ecologists, the Autonomen successfully stopped the German nuclear power industry's attempt to produce bomb-grade uranium. As they developed through militant actions, the Autonomen transformed themselves from civil Luddism into a force resisting the corporate system as a whole.

Asian uprisings contained parallel forms of "deliberative democracy" during the 1980 Gwangju Uprising in South Korea, the Lily student movement in Taipei's Chiang Kai-shek Square in 1990, and Kathmandu's liberated Patan in 1990. In this same tradition, Seattle protests against the WTO in 1999 were largely prepared by networks for direct action based upon strict principles of participatory democracy. In the anti–corporate globalization movement that grew by leaps and bounds after Seattle, forms of consensual decision-making emerged among many groups, and decentralization of communication made possible by projects like Indymedia allowed for the participatory ethic to proliferate. Even the armed Zapatista uprising in Mexico shares many New Left characteristics. Not a traditional working-class constituency, they bring questions of participatory democracy and everyday life to the center of the movement. They did not try to seize state power directly but sought to change their lives through counterinstitutions. They even talked about the idea of creating a "new person." All of these developments are extraordinarily important and help to highlight and intensify a globally interconnected movement.

Asian activists were greatly influenced by—and should be seen as part of—the New Left. Thailand's 1973 uprising was to a large extent organized by students whose studies in the United States had exposed them to 1960s ideas and actions. The 1973 generation not only led that uprising but also went on to participate significantly in the 1992 democratic insurgency. The Philippines movement was also a product of energy from the 1960s. During years of preparation for their historic task, members of the Reform the Armed Forces Movement (RAM)—the central organization of the 1986 military mutiny—studied Egyptian officers who overthrew King Farouk in 1952, reviewed the history of social movements in many countries, "in particular Gandhi's work and people's experiences in Czechoslovakia and Hungary," and contacted civil activists to organize "flower brigades" designed to block roads into Manila and thereby prevent troops loyal to Marcos from coming to his rescue.[25] They modeled these flower brigades on "those the American youth movement of 1968 had used to disarm troops breaking up demonstrations against the Vietnam War."[26] In 2009, I interviewed Philippine Senator Gregorio Honasan, a key leader of the mutiny in 1986. He described RAM as "children of First Quarter Storm," the Philippine movement of 1970.[27]

In her 1986 presidential campaign against Marcos, Cory Aquino ran under the banner of LABAN (*Lakas ng Bayan*) or "Power of the People"—an amazingly similar phrase to the chief slogan of the Black Panther Party, "All Power to the People." Today that exact phrase is used in many contexts, for example in Venezuela where it has been painted on police cars. While the phrase's exact origin lies in the flux of popular creativity that congeals in social movements, its common usage speaks volumes about these movements' similarities to each other.[28] One analyst reported that East German participants in their democratic revolution of 1989 were familiar with "People Power" but did not trace it to the Philippines. Similarly, activists in Nepal used the term without reference to the Philippines.[29]

Tracing the empirical history of Eastern European insurgencies, it is apparent that Asia's predated and inspired them. Asian uprisings were understood by participants in Europe's 1989 revolutions as vital, even "central to the global movement."[30] One participant in East Europe's democratization noted that television news reports of the Chinese movement played a significant role: "Everywhere in East Europe people were talking about it. Everybody told me: 'without the Chinese, we could not have done anything.'"[31] Televised reports of Chinese repression of protesters in Tiananmen Square also apparently played an important part in persuading Eastern Europe's Soviet leaders to go peacefully into the sunset (with the sole exception of Ceausescu in Romania). The Chinese movement followed forerunners in the Philippines and Korea—both of which were within the U.S. sphere of power and therefore heavily reported in China. When Czech President Havel visited Manila in 1995, he spoke out about the inspirational role played by Filipina People Power for the Czech movement.[32]

Beginning with the global insurgency of the 1960s, people collectively recognized that they neither needed nor desired a single vanguard party. The history of the Russian Revolution and the dearth of liberty in Eastern Europe became commonsense proof of that strategy's limitations—as did the similarity between mammoth states in the United States and the USSR, a common realization reflected even in Beatles songs. Disenchantment with the corporate/communist behemoth grew as people came to understand that liberty without racial and economic equality (as in the United States) was not genuine freedom any more than equality without liberty (as in the USSR). All over the world, more and more people knew that war should be made obsolete, nuclear weapons abolished, and police repression ended. The New Left emphasis on spontaneity grew precisely from the wisdom and intelligence of ordinary people.

The global movement of 1968 profoundly changed people's expectations of their political leaders and economic structures. More than anything else, however, what changed were people's conceptions of themselves and their own power. Unlike the Euro-American New Left, activists in Asia did not need to invent a new counterculture in order to sustain their struggle. Rather, Asian movements rejuvenated traditional music, art, philosophy, and theater, and strengthened their communal ties as they mobilized against decrepit political relationships and postcolonial structures of capital accumulation.

From 1968 to 1989: The Fall of Soviet Communism

After 1968, grassroots movements continue to be structured according to a grammar of increasing democracy, autonomy, and solidarity. These now seemingly universal desires stand in stark opposition to the entrenched system of capitalist patriarchy. With these unifying aspirations, social movements remain globally connected, and internationally synchronized actions are increasingly common. From this perspective, late twentieth-century democratization movements were delayed results of 1968's high points. They were the 1960s' gift to the future. Without anyone predicting their downfall, Eastern Europe's communist regimes in Hungary, Poland, East Germany, Czechoslovakia, Bulgaria, Yugoslavia, and Romania were all transformed in 1989. The Soviet Union could not remain aloof and it soon dissolved. Looking back at the string of uprisings that swept away East Asian dictatorships and East European Soviet regimes, Immanuel Wallerstein, Terrence Hopkins, and Giovanni Arrighi called the movements of 1989 "the continuation of 1968."[33]

Among many historical connections and robust similarities between insurgencies in 1968 and 1989, New Left insurgencies that opposed communist Old Left governments in Czechoslovakia, Poland, and Yugoslavia in 1968 were direct links. In Czechoslovakia, when the new government first convened on December

28, 1989, delegates chose Alexander Dubček, leader of the 1968 Prague Spring, as their first speaker of parliament. Within the Soviet Union, many prominent Party intellectuals, especially those grouped around the journal *Problems of Peace and Socialism*, were greatly affected by the Czech movement. Soviet leader Mikhail Gorbachev himself acknowledged his debt to the Prague Spring as he rose in the ranks of the Communist Party: "The Czechoslovakia of 1968 was for me a major impulse toward critical thinking. I understood that there was something in our country that was not right. But this impulse came from the outside world."[34] Gorbachev's college friend from Moscow State University, Zdeněk Mlynář, was a future Czech dissident and one of the architects of the 1968 reform program. After the Prague Spring was crushed, Gorbachev was part of the Soviet delegation sent to reconstruct the two countries' relationship. He noted how workers refused to meet with the Soviet representatives, an "eye-opening" experience for him. Nineteen years later, when he was asked what the differences were between 1968 in Czechoslovakia and his own program, he quipped, "Nineteen years."[35]

Not only was Gorbachev directly changed and inspired by the Prague Spring, Czech activists remained committed to the process of social transformation and carried it through as best they could. We can trace a direct line of key activists who kept alive the dream of the Prague Spring and helped spread it to many other countries, including Hungary, the USSR, Bulgaria, Romania, and Poland, as illustrated in Figure 1.1.[36]

An additional dimension of the impact of 1968 is located in Western European peace movements, which grew out of the New Left and helped transform frozen Cold War power relations, that is, to navigate their societies out of the dead end to which political elites had so ineptly steered them. Without the European peace movement in the streets protesting U.S. Pershing missiles (and Soviet SS-20s), Gorbachev and other members of the Soviet establishment would never have been prepared to loosen their grip on Eastern European buffer states— their insurance against a new German invasion. After massive protests against the possibility of nuclear war erupted on both sides of what was then called the Iron Curtain, neither buffer states nor short-range missiles were required to provide Soviet leaders with the assurances they needed. Millions of people who took to the streets in Europe in the fall of 1981 against U.S. policies helped to convince Gorbachev that Western military intervention in Russia was out of the question. These mobilizations are historically responsible for breaking up the stalemated military confrontation produced by the world's political elites.

Grassroots movements against Russian domination, of course, have a long history. By the 1980s, they had grown into forces nagging Gorbachev and Soviet leaders, but after Asian uprisings brought People Power onto the stage of history, movements in Eastern Europe gained encouragement and inspiration. For example, on August 23, 1987, less than two months after Korean dictator Chun Doo-hwan was forced to agree to presidential elections, the Lithuanian Freedom League brought out several hundred people to protest the anniversary of the 1939 Molotov-Ribbentrop Pact—the first time public opposition to it had ever been mounted. The pact had sealed the Baltic countries' fate as Moscow's

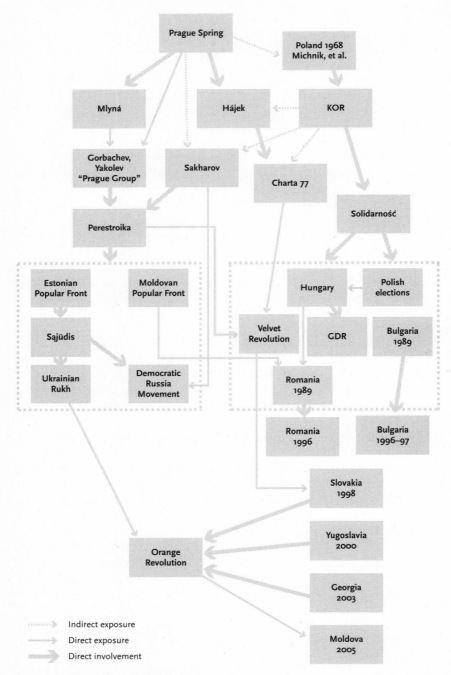

FIGURE 1.1 **Orange Tree, 1968–2006.**
Source: Fredo Arias-King, "Orange People: A Brief History of Transnational Liberation Networks in East Central Europe," *Demokratizatsia* 15, no. 1 (January 2007): 35.

satellites. On June 10, 1988, thousands of Lithuanians publicly sang forbidden nationalist songs, sparking a movement later dubbed the "Singing Revolution." Within two weeks, on June 24, intellectuals organized *sajudis* ("co-movements" in Lithuanian) to publicly lead an independence struggle against Soviet domination. *Sajudis* were comprised of artists, scholars, journalists, musicians, philosophers, and writers, and these intellectuals were as surprised as anyone when within a few months, they found tens of thousands of supporters.[37] On August 23, more than a hundred thousand people demonstrated for national independence. Merging with the Green Movement, the movement brought tens of thousands of citizens to join hands and form human chains along the Baltic shoreline, protesting the Ignalina nuclear plant and the possibility of catastrophic pollution. Activists revived folk songs and festivals, and by using their traditional culture, they activated massive resistance. On September 11, neighboring Estonians' "Song of Estonia" attracted about three hundred thousand people, more than one-fourth of the country's population.

Following these protests, on December 7, 1988, Mikhail Gorbachev told the UN General Assembly that "force and the threat of force can no longer be, and should not be instruments of foreign policy." Once Gorbachev renounced Soviet use of force to maintain its defense line against another German invasion, a wave of change engulfed Eastern Europe. Soon thereafter, tens of thousands of Soviet troops began pulling out of Eastern Europe. One of the most visible protest venues was in Leipzig, where beginning in the spring of 1989, people chanted, "*Wir wollen raus!*" (We want out!). Few people expected that before the end of the year, the Berlin Wall would be pulled down.

In June 1989, Imre Nagy—executed hero of the 1956 Hungarian Uprising in which as many as twenty thousand people died—was reburied in a symbolic act indicating the regime's desire to move toward independence from the Soviet Union.[38] In late August, on the fiftieth anniversary of the Molotov-Ribbentrop Pact, some two million people from Estonia, Latvia, and Lithuania joined hands in a six-hundred-kilometer human chain from Tallinn through to Vilnius and called for freedom from Russian domination. When Hungary opened its borders to the West on September 11, 1989, East Germans flooded through, and their leaders did not repress growing Monday marches in Leipzig. On October 16, one hundred thousand people marched, the next week three hundred thousand, until finally on Monday, November 4, half a million people gathered in Berlin with live television coverage. On November 9, the wall was breached.

History changed at breathtaking speed in this moment. One day after the Berlin Wall was broken through, Bulgarian dictator Tudor Zhivkov was forced from power. One month and a day later, the Velvet Revolution won power in Czechoslovakia. The demise of East Germany had helped stiffen resistance since the East German secret police had long been one of the most powerful forces propping up the Czech regime. The Velvet Revolution involved six weeks of spontaneous protests. On November 17, after it was rumored Prague police killed a student, about fifteen thousand people rallied near the university at Strahov.[39] As people came down the hill to the main part of the city, soldiers in red berets broke up their peaceful candlelight vigil. In support of the ensuing student strike, actors turned over their theater for public meetings. With Havel as leader, Civic Forum—the name given to the political movement—called for liberal democracy and a market economy. Three days later, a crowd of more than a hundred thousand jammed Wenceslas Square. Jingling keys and calling for the return to power of Dubček, hero of the 1968 Prague Spring, they insisted it was time for the communists to vacate the house of government. The next day, even more people congregated, this time with a sound system. On November 27, the student strike turned into a two-hour national strike, convincing communist president Gustav Husak to step down, and the next month, the Federal Assembly unanimously acclaimed Havel as new president.

The same day that Czech President Husak resigned, December 10, the student-based Mongolian Democratic Union formed after sparking protests in Ulan Bator.[40] In a large public square, the rock band *Khonkh* ("bell") played outdoors as people paraded with banners protesting "bureaucratic oppression." A week later, a second rally drew two thousand people, and students returned with banners calling for freedom of the press, a multiparty system, and human rights. On January 21, with temperatures sliding to about −30°C, they sang traditional folk songs praising long-banned national hero Genghis Khan and resolved to hold weekly demonstrations. Beginning a hunger strike on March 7, traditionally dressed activists in Ulan Bator (inspired by Chinese students in Tiananmen) drew tens of thousands of supporters and set off strikes in the capital. As protests mushroomed, the government quickly granted a multiparty system. In mid-April, a postreform surge among coal miners and truck drivers demanded greater economic rights.

Despite the tectonic shift in Eastern Europe elites, ruthless dictator Nicolae Ceausescu had no intention of stepping aside. A week after Czech President Husak resigned, Romania's city of Timisoara convulsed in violence when soldiers opened fire and killed nearly one hundred people. During a general strike in Timisoara in response to the killings, soldiers began conversations with citizens. Within a week, the army withdrew, and a revolutionary committee became the town's de facto government.[41] On December 22, after the army suddenly changed sides, its tanks led a crowd in Bucharest that overran Ceausescu's headquarters and captured him. On Christmas Day, he and his wife were executed, and a new communist government quickly replaced them.

As the process of change continued, on March 11, 1990, Lithuania declared independence. That same day in Estonia, a democratically elected alternative parliament convened in the capital and also moved toward a declaration of independence. Despite Lithuania's resolution to depart from the Soviet Union, Russian troops retained control of much of the country's infrastructure. On January 13, 1991, they clamped down so hard that the day remains etched in people's minds as "Bloody Sunday." At least 14 people were killed (including a KGB officer) and 702 wounded when tanks and armor-piercing bullets were used to secure Soviet control of the main television tower in Vilnius.[42] People massively revolted, taking down street signs to confuse Russian troops (as had been done in Prague in 1968), and offered active resistance to defend the parliament building and television tower.

Less than a week later in neighboring Latvia, six protesters were killed, and half a million people converged in downtown Riga. They built barricades to defend their parliament and broadcast centers, reinforced them with heavy trucks and tractors, strung barbed wire and flammable materials into the blockades, and organized round-the-clock patrols. Citizens provided meals, firewood, medicines, and prepared for a Soviet siege.[43] When the dust settled on the scurry of grassroots activity, no invasion by Russia materialized.

Within a few short months, Eastern Europe's Soviet regimes had been overthrown. In Hungary and Poland, governments adopted reform-oriented measures and integrated their oppositions into power through a process of institutional compromise. In Czechoslovakia and East Germany, regimes that refused to bend in the wind were swept from power by popular insurgencies. In Albania, Bulgaria, and Romania, after the top rung of communist leaders had been deposed, entrenched communist cadre retained control of capital and political power.

With its empire collapsing, hardline Soviet leaders sought to retake their power. Gorbachev's ambitious reform program so angered Party conservatives that they mounted a coup against him beginning on August 19, 1991. Elements of the Communist Party, the KGB, and the army mobilized in synchronized actions. Gorbachev and his family were placed under house arrest, but popular resistance to the hardline communist counteroffensive was widespread. In Moscow, people poured into the streets to protect the Russian parliament. Women and students called on soldiers to join them. Religious people knelt in the streets in prayer, pacifists passed out writings on the methods of nonviolent struggle, and newspapers and radio stations that had been closed by the state quickly set up alternative media. In Palace Square in Leningrad, more than a hundred thousand people assembled. The mayor appealed to the military not to support the coup, and the head of the Russian Orthodox Church threatened excommunication to anyone who followed coup leaders' directives. Russian President Boris Yeltsin dramatically called for resistance from the top of a friendly tank, and even some members of the KGB refused to follow orders, risking death for their defiance. Eventually the coup collapsed, opening the way for the dissolution of the Soviet Union. One by one, each of its fifteen republics declared independence. In early December, Yeltsin and leaders of other republics dissolved the USSR—a move later described as an "unconstitutional coup" by Gorbachev. Weakened by the August coup, Gorbachev was powerless to stop the USSR's collapse after seven decades of Communist Party rule.

In this time of accelerated change, former U.S. ambassador to NATO, Harlan Cleveland, observed that, "Across the world, the general public is now the driving force for political and social change, with their 'leaders' struggling to keep up with them. It is hard to think of a time in world history when the political leaders of powerful nations have seemed so irrelevant to important outcomes. Well-known names—presidents and prime ministers of the world's military powers and economic powerhouses—have been staring at the nightly news with ill-concealed astonishment."[44] While acknowledging grassroots movements' power, top leaders in Eastern Europe also played significant roles. In many cities of Eastern Europe, including Leipzig, Berlin, Budapest, and Prague, crowds chanted "Gorby! Gorby!" They wanted a leader to liberate them, a new Peter the Great who would institute progress from the highest level of government. Despite elite attempts to manage the reform process, when the breakthrough came, its results were different than anyone expected. West Germany swallowed the East in one big gulp, producing enormous budgetary nightmares and cultural dislocations like the emergence of neo-Nazi pogroms. The demise of the USSR was beyond Soviet reformers' expectations or desires. No one could impede the rapid penetration of the former Soviet Union by corporate capitalism, and Russia was ravaged by a neoliberal offensive led by Harvard economists. Long-term movements, intense uprisings, grassroots insurgencies, and activist groups are key to producing robust, lasting democratic change. Yet, because key catalysts behind changes in the communist world emanated from above, democratization was neither lasting nor deep, and a new elite seized control and aligned itself with global capital.

With the collapse of the Soviet Union, American triumphalists proclaimed victory in the Cold War and prepared for another century of U.S. world hegemony. According to the misguided views of Francis Fukuyama, we had arrived at the "end of history." Although he subsequently recanted, many people believed that the entire world would welcome U.S.-style representative democracy as the best possible form of government. Paul Wolfowitz and Dick Cheney sent U.S. troops into Iraq, fully expecting them to be greeted with flowers in the streets of Baghdad. With mounting U.S. casualties, a continuing economic crisis that began in 2008, and the rising fortune of China, the illusion of U.S. global hegemony vanished as quickly as a desert mirage. In 2009, President Obama's bow to the emperor of Japan and his quiescence in Beijing were only surface indications of a much deeper American decline yet to come. Nonetheless, an ideological interpretation of the late twentieth century that maintains the United States is at the center remains operative in Samuel Huntington's concept of the third wave.

Rethinking Huntington's Third Wave

Few theorists besides Samuel Huntington have enjoyed the widespread application of their ideas through national policies. With the ears of Pentagon insiders and their worldwide academic network listening carefully to his every word, the power of his ideas should not be underestimated. A lifelong "Cold Warrior," Huntington praised the military as a "motor of development" even in repressive, Third World dictatorships supported by the United States. After the collapse of the Soviet Union, "Mad Dog" (as his students called him) warned of a "clash of civilizations," thereby laying the groundwork for U.S. global military intervention to focus on the Islamic world. Under President Richard Nixon, the United States implemented "forced-draft urbanization" in Vietnam through massive bombings of "free-fire zones" in which U.S. troops were permitted to kill anything that moved. For every minute Nixon was president, the United States dispensed more than a ton of explosives on Vietnam—a total of 3.2 million tons, more than during the Eisenhower, Kennedy, and Johnson regimes combined.[45] As Carl Boggs recounted, "By the end of this warfare the United States had destroyed 9,000 out of 15,000 hamlets, 25 million acres of farmland, 12 million acres of forest, and 1.5 million farm animals. Towns and villages were bombed, torched, and bulldozed, their inhabitants often rounded up and slaughtered. Nearly one million orphans were left along with 181,000 disabled people and one million widows. More than 19 million gallons of toxic herbicides were dumped in the South alone, by far the greatest use of chemical weaponry ever."[46]

Despite the sacrifice of more than fifty-eight thousand American lives and slaughter of two million people, Huntington's attempt to "democratize" Southern Vietnam was shattered by the heroic resistance of Vietnamese freedom fighters and a global peace movement. Shaken by U.S. defeat in Vietnam, Huntington wrote a report to the Trilateral Commission in which he named the "democratic distemper" as a cause of 1960s protests. He concluded that less democracy was called for in the United States.[47] At that time, many people worried about the health of liberty, of its capacity to survive assaults by jaundiced paragons of virtue from Harvard, such as Samuel Huntington and Henry Kissinger.[48]

In 1984, Huntington incorrectly surmised that, "The likelihood of democratic development in Eastern Europe is virtually nil. . . . With a few exceptions, the limits of democratic development in the world may well have been reached."[49] He was not alone in his mistaken assessment. In a multivolume study of democratization published in 1989—just before the wave of collapse of Soviet regimes—Juan Linz, Seymour Martin Lipset, and Larry Diamond (leading lights of mainstream democratization theory) did not include a single communist country because "there is little prospect among them of a transition to democracy."[50] These predictive failures cannot be blamed on a lack of information. U.S. media continually gave wide coverage to communism's internal problems while scarcely covering events within the U.S. sphere of influence. By comparison to the U.S. media frenzy during Tiananmen Square protests in China, the tiny space afforded the 1980 Gwangju Uprising helps explain why it is today called "Korea's Tiananmen" even though it preceded the Chinese movement by nine years.

As dictatorships fell one after another in East Asia and Eastern Europe, Huntington quickly abandoned his pessimism and promulgated the idea of a "third wave" of democratization. Previously, his ideological presuppositions caused him to disregard the profound transvaluation of values ushered in by the movements of the 1960s. In the aftermath of the civil rights movement and New Left, South Africa's apartheid regime's days were numbered, as were the reigns of other dictatorships supported by the United States (and Huntington) in places like Greece, Portugal, Spain, the Philippines, and many other countries. Whether behind the communist "Iron Curtain" or in the capitalist "Free World," tyrannical governments could not last after the global wave of 1968 had changed the world. When unpopular regimes were subsequently swept aside, Huntington crafted the "third wave" as a tool to sever democratization movements from their origins in the New Left—and to aggrandize the U.S. role in the "democratic wave."

What Is Democracy?

Few political questions confronting humanity today are of greater importance than that of the meaning of democracy. Universally valued, democracy remains an elusive concept. Minimally defined as elections, democracy worthy of the name involves the existence of justice as well as citizens' input into significant decisions affecting their everyday lives. Despite such considerations, Huntington maintained that "elections, open, free, and fair, are the essence of democracy, the inescapable *sine qua non.*"[51] In so doing, he ascribes a universal truthfulness to Western-style representative governments, to "formal democracy," in which members of the economic elite vie for positions of political power in elections, and only a fraction of the population bothers to vote.

In U.S. national elections, candidates not loyal to the Pentagon and transnational corporate power routinely cannot even be included in televised debates—let alone be able to mount major fund-raising efforts. As a result, the vast majority of U.S. elections carry less choice than between Coke and Pepsi. Voting seldom, if ever, offers meaningful choices to citizens, such as the possibility to abstain from wars. Whether Democrats or Republicans are in office, corporate looting of the public treasury and massive Pentagon budgets feed the war machine's unending appetite. Voting every few years may help people feel like they have a say in government, but it does little to ensure real democracy.

Even if we accept Huntington's perspective for the moment, major problems arise. His notion of democracy simply as voting makes for ease of measurement. Whether or not there are elections becomes his method to determine whether or not "democracy" exists—which, for him, means simply that 50 percent of adult males are eligible to vote and a "responsible executive" is supported by an elected legislature or chosen in direct elections.[52] Contemporary thinkers might wonder why 50 percent of men alone were sufficient for Huntington, why he excluded women. With rates of voter participation hovering around 60 percent, elections by men only would mean only about 30 percent of citizens would vote. A candidate could then be elected with a "majority" of 16 percent of citizens—hardly a number worthy of being considered democratic. Even if the franchise is extended to everyone, a majority of the 60 percent who vote is still only 30 percent of the electorate.

In contrast to Huntington's minimalist definition of democracy, a different understanding has repeatedly been formulated within popular movements since the 1960s: ordinary citizens should have real power through direct participation in decision-making. Popular input could help bring an end to wars and a phasing out of the military's weapons of mass destruction. Precious resources could be democratically allocated rather than controlled by a handful of billionaires. (Instead of a Murdoch-controlled global media, for example, we could have citizen-reporters providing news from around the world.) Self-managed institutions could determine society's goals and means of operation based upon human needs, not corporate greed. Democratization could be "measured on the basis of the decentralization of power and wealth and creation of an independent 'public sphere' in which rational discussion among people can take place and decision-making [can be] pursued."[53] A democracy worthy of the name would empower all individuals to participate in deliberating upon political matters and to decide what policies to undertake. This kind of deliberative democracy is prefigured within the practice of popular insurgencies, but it is out of the realm of possibilities offered to us by the prevailing system of representative governments.

Existing forms of representative democracy are ideally suited to the corporate market economy. Candidates can compete like products through advertisements, and voting on personalities rather than on substantive issues involves the same kind of choice that consumers make in supermarkets. Parliamentary democracy is a suitable vehicle for legitimization of rule by economic elites, for expansion of corporate and consumer markets, for coordination of the global capitalist economy, and for providing banks with a safe and reliable financial infrastructure, but it is not the alpha and omega of democracy. The more Huntington's notion of "democratization" is accepted, the more real the risk becomes to freedom. He considered "democracy" good only when it did not interfere with U.S. strategic needs or business interests. In Allende's Chile, Chávez's Venezuela, or when Americans protest wars, he believed democracy should be limited, even overthrown if necessary. Huntington's notion of the "third wave" was a tool designed to open markets and bring deeper penetration by U.S. transnational corporations.

Following Huntington, a veritable parade of political scientists proclaimed that the essence of democracy is voting. In so doing, they prepared the groundwork for illiberal democracies like Pervaz Musharraf in Pakistan and Hamid Karzai in Afghanistan, petty dictators maintained in power only through wasting thousands of American lives, hundreds of thousands of indigenous people's lives, and hundreds of billions of U.S. taxpayer dollars—all legitimated by elaborate ideological obfuscation and media campaigns that portray them as necessary for "democracy." The type of "democratization" that Huntington's theories sought to impose on the world includes Abu Ghraib and the CIA's rendition program, unending wars in which the vast majority of those killed are civilians, environmental devastation, and trade liberalization that spells death to millions at the periphery of the world system—policies implemented without any substantive popular discussions or choice between real alternatives.

In order to provide ideological justification for U.S. wars, Huntington went to great lengths to rewrite history. In *The Third Wave* (1991), he argued that democracies have been created in three great waves: the first wave, 1828 to 1926; the second wave, 1943 to 1962 (post–World War II); and the third wave, 1974 to the time of the book's publication in 1991. Consistent with his bias against grassroots power, his periodization of the "first wave" severed democracy from the American and French Revolutions—social movements that created modern representative democracy—just as his "third wave" cut democracy from its roots in 1960s insurgencies. While he excluded 1960s social movement insurgencies, he did not exclude economic developments prior to 1974: "In considerable measure, the wave of democratizations that began in 1974 was the product of the economic growth of the previous two decades."[54] Huntington's three waves correspond to victories of capitalist elites and as such relate more to expansion of market economies than to genuine democracy. He did not ignore political developments—only those of which he did not approve—and when he did acknowledge the contribution of activism, it was elite action. He was convinced that "the third wave of the 1970s and 1980s was overwhelmingly a Catholic wave."[55] He located the origin of this Catholic wave in the change in the Catholic Church during the 1960s due to Pope John XXIII—but he did not link it to 1960s movements that were the point of origin of the "Christian Left" at the base of the church. His bias against 1960s movements prevented him from understanding that tens of thousands of people in the Christian Left, advocates of the Theology of Liberation, were not simply subjects of the Pope but active creators of changes in the church and themselves autonomous participants in the global grassroots movement.[56]

Huntington framed his third wave as a tribute to U.S. imperial power and democratic prestige: "Movements for democracy throughout the world were inspired and borrowed from the American example. In Rangoon supporters of democracy carried the American flag; in Johannesburg they reprinted *The Federalist*; in Prague they sang 'We Shall Overcome'; in Warsaw they read Lincoln and quoted Jefferson; in Beijing they erected the Goddess of Democracy."[57] Here Huntington made a critical error that led him to misconstrue events. He claimed the "Goddess of Democracy" in Tiananmen Square was a copy of the U.S. Statue of Liberty. In fact, Chinese art students explicitly rejected the idea of copying the U.S. statue as too "pro-American" and instead modeled theirs on Russian communist Vera Mukhina's monumental sculpture, "A Worker and a Collective Farm Woman," which held aloft a torch with two hands on the top of the USSR's pavilion at the 1937 Paris World Fair.[58]

Similarly, the Athens Polytechnic students who sacrificed their lives in the movement to overthrow the Greek dictatorship were profoundly anti-American. As was well known to Greeks, the United States and Israel had overthrown their democracy in 1967 and imposed the Papadopoulos junta in its place.[59] With an accurate understanding of the actual character of the global insurgency unleashed in this period, we can better comprehend Athens Polytechnic students, whose actions were a key event in the process of overturning dictatorships in the Southern Mediterranean. The global student movement of 1968, which mightily opposed the U.S. war in Vietnam, animated Greek students.[60] Athenian protesters in 1973 identified with Thai students, who also opposed the U.S. war and had overthrown their military rulers only a few months earlier. Huntington ignored Greek and Thai students and instead placed Portugal's military coup against the Salazar dictatorship at the beginning of the third wave. Even in that case, he failed to link the Portuguese colonels to insurgent African guerrillas in Mozambique, Angola, and Guinea-Bissau, key grassroots movements that greatly influenced Portugal's colonial officers before they successfully overthrew Salazar in 1974.

To be sure, the democratic luster of the United States remained bright in the 1980s. During the Gwangju Uprising, the most militant fighters nicknamed themselves the "SWAT" team after a popular U.S. television show, and many citizens believed that the entry of U.S. aircraft carrier Coral Sea into Korean waters during the uprising meant it had come to save them—when in fact the opposite was true. After the United States abetted Korea's military dictatorship in crushing the uprising, anti-Americanism emerged with a vengeance in South Korea. The dialectical character of the United States, one of the freest societies in world history and simultaneously one of its most warlike, evidently still allowed for a variety of enthusiastic support in the 1980s. For Huntington, the United States "conveyed an image of strength and success."[61] For others, the image was of a free society, where ordinary citizens could live prosperously and enjoy liberties like nowhere else.

Huntington's exogamous model of political development understood democracy as a system that could be imposed upon people from the outside, as in his post–World War II "second wave," when "Allied occupation promoted inauguration of democratic institutions in West Germany, Italy, Austria, Japan, Korea."[62] Leaving aside the slaughter of a hundred thousand South Koreans prior to the beginning of the Korean War, the question remains: was Korea then a democracy? When we ask which "open, free, and fair" elections (according to his own definition) in Korea he could have meant, there is none to which anyone can point. Admiring more recent democracies imposed from the outside, Huntington welcomed U.S. invasions of Grenada and Panama as bringing them democracy.[63] It quite eluded him that any system of government imposed from the outside hardly qualifies as democracy—unless of course, something other than "rule by the people" is meant. In a world where Henry Kissinger, who bombed Hanoi on Christmas 1972, and Barack Obama, who expanded the war in Afghanistan, both received a Nobel Peace Prize, it should be no wonder that mainstream scholarly research is also flawed—yet I cannot help but make note of it.

Ideology and Science

In the late 1980s, the U.S. National Academy of Sciences twice refused to admit Huntington on the grounds that his work was "ideology," not "science." In his campaign against Huntington's application for membership, Yale mathematics professor Serge Lang pointed to the book *Political Order in Changing Societies* (1968), in which Huntington called South Africa under apartheid a "satisfied society." Huntington's ideological posturing is far from unique. Much of mainstream political science in the United States routinely accepts value-laden research as "science." Huntington's Cambridge colleague, MIT professor Ithiel de Sola Pool, kept interrogation records of tortured Viet Cong suspects in file cabinets in his office as "data" to analyze enemy motivation, implicitly becoming part of the entire torture apparatus. Despite his complicity in war crimes in Vietnam— or should I say because of them?—Pool's name today is attached to an annual award of the American Political Science Association. Like Pool, Huntington did not see himself merely as an academic but infused his books with advice for and praise of the military as a "motor of development."

For "dispassionate" and "value-free" political scientists like Huntington, elite dynamics are primary variables. Since they assume an elite will always govern, the only questions become: "Which elite?" and "Can democratic transitions be managed for the maintenance of elements of an old elite?" Huntington's administrative social research categorized the character of transitional regimes, classifying them as transplacement in which key leaders maintain themselves within a new arrangement of power, unlike a wholesale *replacement* of an old elite, or a *transformation* of an old elite into a new elite. *Abolition* of elite rule altogether and creation of substantive democracy remained out of his realm of possibilities. As a self-described "aspiring democratic Machiavelli," Huntington offered "tips" to leaders on how to isolate radical opposition.[64]

Emphasizing elite actions, Huntington downplayed the role of civil society in the democratization groundswell at the end of the twentieth century. He claimed "demonstrations, protests and strikes played central roles in only six transitions completed or underway at the end of the 1980s [in the Philippines, South Korea, East Germany, Poland, Czechoslovakia, and Romania]."[65] Only reluctantly did he acknowledge that, "It seems probable, although little evidence is available, that events in the Philippines and Korea helped stimulate the demonstrations for democracy in Burma in 1988 and those in China in the fall of 1986 and the spring of 1989, as well as having some impact on the liberalization that occurred in Taiwan."[66] Like Huntington, Guillermo O'Donnell and Philippe Schmitter believe that it is preferable for elites to transfer power to some fraction of their supporters or to negotiate a transition with reform-minded members of the opposition than to be outright overthrown by opposition movements.[67] That is one reason why elites embrace and propagate widely nonviolence: it permits negotiations between old and new rulers and facilitates the peaceful accommodation of the old within the new. It is also why reformist parties can be so useful. Stephen Haggard and Robert Kaufman realized that "as we have seen in several of our cases, reforms have sometimes been more effective when they are implemented by 'Left' parties that can provide some possibility of political influence and compensation to those negatively affected by the reform process."[68] According to their view, popular movements cannot lead to more democracy; they may prove to be "uncontrollable" and lead either to revolutionary overthrow of the existing system in its entirety or increased repression.[69]

Whatever their different purviews, mainstream sociologists, economists, and political scientists subscribe to the notion of the "rational" individual actor at the core of society. As with Adam Smith's "invisible hand," they believe that "rational choice," or personal advancement of compartmentalized self-interests will lead to maximization of the social good. In the first place, individualized instrumental rationality is but one form of rational action—and often an unreasonable form at that. Collective instrumental rationality and value-rationality are other forms, which play central roles in animating social movements. With important exceptions like E.P. Thompson and George Rudé, social scientists have traditionally viewed crowds as less rational than individuals. In extreme interpretations, crowds were understood to embody a form of "contagion," of authoritarian domination and unintelligent action, such as lynch mobs. According to this conventional wisdom, crowds lead individuals to suspend their individual rationality and act according to "base" instinctual passions.

In contrast to this view, millions of ordinary people who unite in social movements can be regarded as proof of another dynamic: ordinary people, acting together in the best interests of society, embody a reasonability and intelligence far greater than that of elites which rule nation-states and giant corporations. One does not need to be a radical to subscribe to the idea of group intelligence. Recent observers of technology have penned simple insights that speak volumes: the Internet and the World Wide Web have facilitated "the wisdom of crowds" and "smart mobs."[70]

In the case of South Korea, political scientists' bias in favor of elite-led transitions compelled the Carnegie Commission to ignore the contribution of the insurgent movement in the country's democratic transition. Instead they credited Roh Tae-woo (who was subsequently imprisoned for his crimes against the people of Gwangju).[71] Juan Linz and A. Stepan studied East Germany and came to the conclusion that "regime collapse" had occurred despite substantial evidence that popular mobilizations transformed the political landscape.[72] When fractions of previous dictatorships are permitted to play some role in new democratic regimes (as in South Korea, East Germany, Romania, and Indonesia), the reasonability, and even gullibility, of insurgent movements is a key reason, not their lack of influence. People's generosity even allowed many deposed dictators to keep much of their ill-begotten fortunes—as Duvalier, Marcos, Chun, Ershad, and Suharto all did.

Evaluating Uprisings

Uprisings are the best of times; they are the worst of times. Tremendous changes occur, but great setbacks are possible. People make new lifelong friends, others watch in horror as their loved ones are murdered and blood flows in the streets. Are the sacrifices worth the benefits?

For Huntington, as for most political scientists, the impacts of uprisings are mainly understood in terms of changes in elite power. That is certainly one analytical approach, yet there are far more significant outcomes. One is to assess broad indications of people's well-being and happiness, new rights won by subaltern groups, and expanded liberties. To what extent have onerous burdens and dictatorships been brought to an end? A second evaluative dimension was enunciated more than two hundred years ago, when Immanuel Kant searched for indications of the degree to which reason becomes an important determinant of morality and culture. If we extrapolate his insight into a framework of gauging freedom in people's lives, we can ask: Have people been able to become deliberative subjects of their social and political affairs? To what extent have liberties won by ordinary citizens resulted in free public conversations, increased ordinary citizens' involvement in policymaking, changed patterns of authority, and activated civic organizations? What kinds of resources for future freedom movements have been produced?

Bound as they are to maintaining the political control center, Huntington and mainstream political science fail to recognize such outcomes. As is often said, victors write history in large script. Yet at the margins, a more accurate understanding, one not tied to predominant ideology, is possible. Every revolutionary upheaval prepares the ground for future insurgencies. Although apparent failures since they did not seize power, previous waves of social movements in 1848, 1905, and 1968 profoundly changed values and ushered in new political epochs.[73] After 1848, workers won greater employment rights, and citizens' voting rights expanded; after 1905, struggles for national liberation became increasingly legitimate; and since 1968, women's rights, justice for subaltern groups, and the environment have become central concerns. Similarly, subsequent Asian uprisings expanded freedom without seizing power. The transvaluation of values produced by robust insurgent movements may be longer-lasting and of greater significance than transitory fluctuations in elite composition or implementation of new voting systems. After successful insurgencies, Taiwan's forty-year martial law regime finally was brought to an end, and Thais, Nepalis, Filipinos, and South Koreans all won new, more progressive constitutions. In South Korea, workers won annual double-digit pay raises for years after 1987, and workers in Thailand, Nepal, South Korea, and China won greater union rights.

Yet uprisings can also lead to regression in people's standards of living, civil demobilization, and less political engagement in state matters. In the aftermath of successful overthrows of dictatorships in Thailand, South Korea, Indonesia, and the Philippines, elite corporations, aided by the World Bank, IMF, and WTO, used the openings provided by popular movements to batter down barriers to U.S. and Japanese goods and investors. The resultant situation led to increased poverty in the Philippines and to the 1997 IMF crisis in Thailand and South Korea. In Burma, dire poverty reigns supreme—along with a ruthless predatory state whose commanding generals enrich themselves while the vast majority suffers in marginalized states of existence. In the former Soviet Union, hunger rose and life expectancy fell. In 1989, only 2 percent of Russians lived below the poverty line. Within ten years of the coming of "democracy," half of all children lived in poverty, and more than 23 percent of Russians were impoverished—living on two dollars per day or less.[74] Fully 40 percent of Russians survived on four dollars per day, as tuberculosis and infant mortality rates rose to an all-time high. Within twenty years, average life expectancy for men fell by five years to sixty.

One common result of the nine case studies in this book is that in country after country, an afterglow surge occurred after uprisings. Insurgencies energized civil societies, outcomes evident in workers' strikes and farmers' movements, motion among minorities and subaltern strata, and a mushrooming of independent newspapers, cooperatives, and political activism. Clearly uprisings gave rise to expanding circles of actions. Insurgent confrontations transformed clients into citizens, compelled elites to reevaluate goals and adjust policies, and empowered grassroots organizations. After individuals and groups engaged in illegal regime-altering actions, they found ways to engage in new forms of political participation to remake established procedures and create new space for others to become involved. The world's greatest natural resources are human imagination and will—the forces animating, and empowered by, upheavals at the end of the twentieth century.

At the same time, some uprisings' afterglow outcomes, such as NGOs proliferation, lead to the emergence of a new stratum of professional activists who presented fertile grounds for recruitment by U.S. agencies seeking supplicants concerned with the promotion of democracy—but not with challenging the global elite's power and wealth. As specialized activism came to dominate the movement, insurgencies simultaneously disintegrated, as even well-intentioned activists were co-opted into vehicles that served the very system they formerly opposed. In the 1980s, as People Power revolts transformed political dynamics, U.S. global strategy changed from sole reliance on repressive military interventions and covert CIA actions to include a public component called "democracy promotion," the attempt to penetrate and control emergent civil societies in targeted countries (those with regimes deemed unfriendly or unstable by American policymakers). Tens of millions of U.S. dollars were poured into programs formerly managed by the CIA, such as creating "friendly" trade unions, political parties, feminist alliances, activist clusters, and media that would support U.S. transnational interests.[75] In combination with the National Endowment for Democracy, the AFL-CIO, the international committees of the Democratic and Republican parties, and the U.S. Chamber of Commerce, NGOs chosen by U.S. officials were funded with the aim of building friendly voices within emergent civil societies in order to channel them into transnational alliances with global elites.[76]

Often this effort required undermining indigenous radical formations that organically developed through struggles against U.S.-backed dictatorships—as in the Philippines under Marcos or more recently in Egypt before the overthrow of Mubarak. The goal in both these cases was to suppress popular demands that arose from below. American policymakers are well aware that the radical impetus in the streets, if left to develop according to its own logic, could well continue to expand and become a threat to both U.S. strategic military interests and corporate domination. U.S. infiltration of indigenous civil society groups is often a preventative measure meant precisely to undermine movements' radical potential. As James Petras observed during the Arab Spring, "The risk of waiting too long, of sticking with the dictator, is that the uprising radicalizes: the ensuing change sweeps away both the regime *and* the state apparatus, turning a political uprising into a social revolution."[77] (In cases where entrenched regimes unfriendly to the United States cannot be overthrown through military intervention, such as Milošević in Yugoslavia, strategic nonviolent opposition led by NGOs was used as an alternative tactic.)[78]

As the global economy developed, authoritarian dictatorships became fetters to economic expansion or were unable to defeat local insurgencies. Previously friendly regimes were sacrificed one after another to make room for new subelites better equipped to facilitate new phases of capitalist expansion. Under the guise of overthrowing "cronyism," indigenous capitalists who operated according to the logic of local accumulation were replaced with transnational banks and corporations, eager to penetrate previously closed labor markets and consumers.

One after another, insurgencies at the end of the twentieth century illustrate that ordinary people's collective wisdom is far greater than that of entrenched elites, whether democratically elected or self-appointed. Without highly paid trainers, insurgent activists adapted new technologies and brought them into use faster than the corporate elite. The throngs of ordinary citizens who went into the streets and faced violence and arrest, endangering their own lives and their families' futures, had visions of freedom writ large. It is these visions that I seek to portray in the following chapters, to uncover goals expressed during actions involving thousands of people. I aim to probe into people's deepest aspirations—ones that remain in their hearts even when the events in which they are involved are short-lived or produce unintended results. Empirical analysis of the actions of hundreds of thousands of ordinary people—millions if we sum the total number of participants—reveals that ordinary people want peace, greater democratic rights, equality, and simple forms of progress, while elites are more concerned with cutting taxes on the rich, extending national sovereignty, and protecting corporate profits. In the transformed reality constructed by People Power, mobilized throngs have newfound capacities to enact change. Inspired by previous movements of common people to overturn elites at the apex of power, popular movements continue to enlarge the scope of human liberty. By reconstructing the actions of hundreds of thousands of people in insurgencies, I hope to construct a philosophical history not simply from my own mind but from the actions of masses of people. As Susan Buck-Morss put it, what is needed is to "construct not a philosophy of history, but a philosophy out of history, or (this amounts to the same thing) to reconstruct historical material as philosophy."[79]

The Continuing Wave

The late twentieth-century wave of uprisings is inseparable from the ongoing contestation of elite rule that continues today in global insurgencies against the neoliberal economic system. The global movement that yesterday won formal democracy today demands an end to world poverty. By challenging the concentration of humanity's collective wealth in the hands of a few billionaires and a few hundred corporations, the global justice movement is a continuing democratic wave. Without anyone telling them to do so, millions of people all over the world have selected the world capitalist regime as the target of their protests. Most publicly visible in world media after the battle of Seattle in 1999, popular confrontations of elite power seek democratic deliberation of the global economic system's goals and rules. All over the world, thousands of protesters have challenged summit meetings of the IMF, G-8, WTO ministerials, and World Bank. A new pluralist and decentralized global economy is envisioned by thousands of participants in the World Social Forum in Porto Alegre and in regional alliances autonomous of the WTO/World Bank/IMF axis. How much longer will humanity tolerate the current abomination of waste and warfare that condemns millions of human beings to living hell on earth?

Despite apparent setbacks, social movements' energies resonate from the grassroots across national boundaries, stimulating each other with greater velocity and more force than ever before in history. Groups form and disband, crowds gather and scatter—but they leave behind a residue of collective capacity for thought and action that builds upon previous incarnations. As people are transformed through insurgencies, they refuse to tolerate previously accepted forms of domination. Popular wisdom grows in each iteration of the movement's emergence; ever-new aspirations animate action. In the never-ending struggle for freedom, we continually advance part of the way to our goal but never arrive at the end of history.

NOTES

1   Two prominent examples are Adam Przeworski and Fernando Limongi, "Modernization: Theory and Facts," *World Politics* 49, no. 2 (January 1997), 155–83; and Fareed Zakaria, *The Future of Freedom: Illiberal Democracy at Home and Abroad* (New York: W.W. Norton and Co., 2003).

2   Liu Jianfei, "Chinese Democracy and Sino-U.S. Relations," Institute of International Strategic Studies, The Central Party School of the Chinese Communist Party, September 2007, 8.

3   Samuel Huntington, *The Third Wave: Democratization in the Late Twentieth Century* (Norman: University of Oklahoma Press, 1991), 307.

4   See Mark R. Thompson, *Democratic Revolutions: Asia and Eastern Europe* (London: Routledge, 2004), 131.

5   Somchai Phatharathananunth, *Civil Society and Democratization: Social Movements in Northeast Thailand* (Copenhagen: NIAS Press, 2006), ix.

6   See Monina Allarey Mercado, ed., *People Power: An Eyewitness History* (Manila: The James B. Reuter, S.J. Foundation, 1986), 226, 258, 308.

7   Sunhyuk Kim, "Civic Mobilization for Democratic Reform," in *Institutional Reform and Democratic Consolidation in Korea*, eds. Larry Diamond and Doh Chull Shin (Stanford: Hoover Institution Press, 1999), 281. For details on the June Uprising, see *Asia's Unknown Uprisings Volume 1*, chap. 9.

8   As explained to me by Seung Hee Jeon in Cambridge, Massachusetts, in 2006.

9   The military government changed the country's name to Myanmar and its largest city to Yangon, but the democracy movement insists on retaining the old names, and I follow them in that regard.

10   Human rights activists maintain that hundreds were killed or disappeared.

11   Jørgen Johansen, "Waves of Nonviolence and the New Revolutionary Movements," unpublished paper, 37; revised and published with the same title in *Seeds of New Hope: Pan-African Peace Studies for the Twenty-First Century* (2 vols.), eds. Elavie Ndura-Ouedraogo, Judith Atiri, and Matt Meyer (Trenton, NJ: Africa World Press, 2008).

12   For more on the world-historical character of the movements of 1968, see chapter 1 of my book *The Imagination of the New Left: A Global Analysis of 1968* (Boston: South End Press, 1987), hereafter *Imagination*.

13   The preeminent role of Vietnam was preconditioned by an earlier insurgency there during World War II. In 1945, after millions of Vietnamese had starved to death under Japanese rule, a nationwide uprising had captured the country's rice stocks and food supplies. In 1968, master planning by Ho Chi Minh, who had studied European and Chinese armed urban insurrections of the 1920s and 1930s for the Comintern, was a critical component of the synchronized Tet offensive. See A. Neuberg, *Armed Insurrection* (London: New Left Books, 1970). The authors were actually Mikhail Tukhachevsky, Ho Chi Minh, Osip Piatnitsky, and Erich Wollenberg.

14   See *Imagination*, chap. 2.

15   See *Imagination* and *The Subversion of Politics: European Autonomous Social Movements and the Decolonization of Everyday Life* (Oakland: AK Press, 2006) for discussion of what I call the "eros effect."

16   For Marcuse's formulation of instinct and revolution, see *Essay on Liberation* (Boston: Beacon Press, 1969).

17   Choi Jungwoon, *The Gwangju Uprising: The Pivotal Democratic Movement that Changed the History of Modern Korea* (Paramus: Homa and Sekey Books, 2006), 85, 131.

18   These documents and analysis are contained in *Liberation, Imagination, and the Black Panther Party*, eds. Kathleen Cleaver and George Katsiaficas (New York: Routledge, 1997).

19   For a brief overview of events in Poland as well as New Left insurgencies in Yugoslavia and Czechoslovakia, see *Imagination*, 58–70.

20   See "Poland," *Imagination*, 66–70. For continuity with even earlier development of the Polish movement, see Jane Leftwich Curry on "Poland's permanent revolution" in Jane Curry and L. Fajfer, *Poland's Permanent Revolution: People vs. Elites 1956 to the Present* (Washington, D.C.: American University Press, 1996).

21   Jung-Kwang Cho interviewed General Chun Doo-hwan in his private residence years later as a friendly interlocutor. He also met with other top members of the South Korean military elite and reported that the majority had opposed the use of force. See Jung-kwan Cho, "The Kwangju Uprising as a Vehicle of Democratization" in *Contentious Kwangju: The May 18 Uprising in Korea's Past and Present*, eds. Gi-Wook Shin and Kyung Moon Hwang (Lanham, Maryland: Rowman & Littlefield, 2003), 76–77.

22   Thompson, *Democratic Revolutions*, 3.

23   *Imagination*, 23–27.

24   For more on the Korean uprisings of 1987, see *Asia's Unknown Uprisings Volume 1*, chap. 9.

25   Almonte quoted in Angela Stuart Santiago, *1986: Chronicle of a Revolution* (Manila: Raintree Publishing, 1996), 49.

26   Jose T. Almonte, *My Part in the People Power Revolution* (Manila: n.p., 2006), 14.

27   See chap. 2 below.

28   Poder Popular is also the name of Cuban institutions of government established in the 1975 Constitution. Earlier, a slogan was widely chanted in Chile: "Crear, crear; Poder Popular!" In 2007, I was astonished to see "Todo el Poder al Pueblo!" on the sides of police cars in Caracas, Venezuela.

29   Thompson, *Democratic Revolutions*, 131.

30   Edward Friedman, ed., *The Politics of Democratization: Generalizing East Asian Experiences* (Boulder: Westview Press, 1994), 24.

31   Christopher Neck, *Actual* (April 1990); *World Journal* (April 6, 1990): 33. Quoted in Friedman, *Politics*, 54.

32   V.G. Kulkarni and R. Tasker, "Promises to Keep," *Far Eastern Economic Review* 159 (February 29, 1996): 22.

33   Giovanni Arrighi, Terence K. Hopkins, and Immanuel Wallerstein, "1989: The Continuation of 1968," *After the Fall: 1989 and the Future of Freedom*, ed. George Katsiaficas (New York: Routledge, 2001), 35.

34   Mikhail Gorbachev and Zdeněk Mlynář, *Conversations with Gorbachev: On Perestroika, the Prague Spring, and the Crossroads of Socialism* (New York: Columbia University Press, 2002), 47, as quoted in Fredo Arias-King, "Orange People: A Brief History of Transnational Liberation Networks in East Central Europe," *Demokratizatsia* 15, no. 1 (January 2007): 38.

35   Mark Almond, *Uprising! Political Upheavals that Have Shaped the World* (New York: Barnes and Noble Books, 2002), 98.

36   Arias-King, "Orange People," 31.

37   Grazina Miniotaite, *Nonviolent Resistance in Lithuania: A Story of Peaceful Liberation* (Boston: The Albert Einstein Institution, 2002), 26.

38   Johansen, "Waves of Nonviolence," 24.

39   For years, the rumor passed as truth, but it was recently determined that it was

purposely spread to help build the opposition. See Dan Bilefsky, "Velvet Revolution's Roots Still Obscure 20 Years Later," *New York Times*, November 17, 2009.

40 Peter Ackerman and Jack Duvall, *A Force More Powerful: A Century of Nonviolent Conflict* (Palgrave: New York, 2000), 439.

41 Ibid., 436.

42 Miniotaite, *Nonviolent Resistance*, 49; Johansen, "Waves of Nonviolence," 29; Richard Deats, "The Global Spread of Active Nonviolence," Fellowship of Reconciliation, http://www.forusa.org/nonviolence/0900_73deats.html.

43 Olgerts Eglitis, *Nonviolent Action in the Liberation of Latvia* (Boston: The Albert Einstein Institution, 1993), 32–33.

44 Harlan Cleveland, "The Age of People Power," *The Futurist* (January–February 1992): 15.

45 George Katsiaficas, ed. *Vietnam Documents: American and Vietnamese Views of the War* (Armonk, NY: M.E. Sharpe, 1992), 143.

46 Carl Boggs, *The Crimes of Empire* (London: Pluto Press, 2010), 55.

47 Michael Crozier, Samuel Huntington, and Joji Watanabe, *The Crisis of Democracy: Report on the Governability of Democracies to the Trilateral Commission* (New York University Press, 1975), 106, 113–15.

48 For an overview of Harvard's involvement in eugenics as well as other dimensions of its impact on foreign policy, see the award-winning film by Shin Eun-jung, *Verita$: Everybody Loves Harvard* (2011).

49 Samuel P. Huntington, "Will More Countries Become Democratic?" *Political Science Quarterly* 99, no. 2 (Summer 1984): 217–18.

50 Friedman, *Politics*, 33.

51 Huntington, *Third Wave*, 9.

52 Ibid., 16.

53 Peter Hering in *The Role of Civil Society and Democratization in Nepal*, ed. Ananda P. Srestha (Kathmandu: Nepal Foundation for Advanced Studies, 1998), i.

54 Huntington, *Third Wave*, 61.

55 Ibid., 76.

56 See *Imagination*, 71–73.

57 Huntington, *Third Wave*, 286.

58 Han Minzhu, ed., *Cries for Democracy: Writings and Speeches from the 1989 Chinese Democracy Movement* (Princeton: Princeton University Press, 1990), 343–44.

59 Stephen Rousseas, *The Death of a Democracy: Greece and the American Conscience* (New York: Grove Press, 1967).

60 Eraklis Anastasiadis, "The Athens Polytechnic Uprising: The Uprising that Brought Down a Dictatorship," Wentworth Institute of Technology, Summer 2007.

61 Huntington, *Third Wave*, 287.

62 Ibid., 18.

63 Ibid., 40, 164.

64 Ibid., xv.

65 Ibid., 146.

66 Ibid., 103–4.

67 See Guillermo O'Donnell and Philippe Schmitter, eds. *Transitions from Authoritarian Rule: Tentative Conclusions about Uncertain Democracies* (Baltimore: Johns Hopkins University Press, 1986).

68 Stephen Haggard and Robert Kaufman, *The Political Economy of Democratic Transitions* (Princeton: Princeton University Press, 1995), 377.

69 Guillermo O'Donnell and Philippe Schmitter, eds., *Transitions from Authoritarianism: Comparative Perspectives* (Baltimore: Johns Hopkins University Press, 1986).

70   See the recent books by non-academic and non-movement observers James Silewecki, *The Wisdom of Crowds* (New York: Random House, 2005) and Howard Rheingold, *Smart Mobs: The Next Social Revolution* (Cambridge, MA: Perseus Publishers, 2003).

71   See *Asia's Unknown Uprisings Volume 1*.

72   Juan J. Linz and Alfred Stepan, *Democratic Transitions and Consolidation: Southern Europe, South America, and Post-Communist Europe* (Baltimore: Johns Hopkins University Press, 1996), 316–28.

73   *Imagination*, 13–18.

74   Joseph E. Stiglitz, *Globalization and Its Discontents* (New York: Norton, 2002), 153.

75   One of the first analyses of this phenomenon is in William I. Robinson, *Promoting Polyarchy: Globalization, U.S. Intervention, and Hegemony* (Cambridge, UK: Cambridge University Press, 1996).

76   Ibid., 95.

77   James Petras, *The Arab Revolt and the Imperialist Counterattack* (Atlanta: Clear Day Books, 2011), 16.

78   Compared with the enormous sacrifices required to bring communism to power, comparatively little effort was needed to overthrow it—a tribute to its capacity for peaceful evolution.

79   Susan Buck-Morss, *The Dialectics of Seeing: Walter Benjamin and the Arcades Project* (Cambridge: MIT Press, 1989), 77, 55.

CHAPTER 2

The Philippines

The Dialectic of Power and Resistance is one of the great motor forces of history. Power produces conflict, and conflict between antagonistic forces gives rise to ever new solutions.

—Benigno Aquino

Out of this confrontation, ordinary street Filipinos, Tondo people and faceless, joined with the middle class, and both discovered a kind of spontaneous collective will that they had never exerted before, and a common bond they had never nurtured. It electrified them. Tears streamed down their faces. Some began to sing. "People Power" was born.

—Sterling Seagrave

CHRONOLOGY	
January 30, 1970	"Black Friday": six people killed by police attack on protest
September 21, 1972	President Ferdinand Marcos declares martial law
August 21, 1983	Benigno Aquino assassinated
November 1984	Secret U.S. National Security Council memo: Marcos must go
February 7, 1986	Snap presidential election between Marcos and Corazon Aquino
February 9, 1986	Thirty election tabulators walk out in protest of Marcos's people rigging results
February 16, 1986	More than one million people rally in Rizal Park against Marcos
February 19, 1986	U.S. Senate votes that Philippine election was characterized by "widespread fraud"

February 22, 1986	Four-day People Power Revolution (EDSA 1) begins with mutiny in the military
February 22, 1986	Cardinal Jaime Sin calls for people to protect the rebels in the military
February 23, 1986	Crowd at EDSA swells from fifty thousand in morning to one million by evening
February 24, 1986	Marcos loyalists mount assault but air force goes over to the rebel side
February 24, 1986	As Marcos announces emergency, television station captured by rebels after gun battle
February 24, 1986	Rebel helicopters attack Malacañang presidential palace
February 25, 1986	In separate ceremonies, Marcos and Aquino each sworn in as country's president
February 25, 1986	Rebel attack captures last television station; Marcos inauguration taken off air
February 26, 1986	Marcos is sedated aboard U.S. flight to Hawaii
July 6, 1986	First anti-Aquino coup attempt
September 26, 1986	Nationwide campaign to occupy land by farmers launched
November 20, 1986	Labor leader Rolando Olalia killed; funeral march attended by tens of thousands
December 10, 1986	Ceasefire with leftist National Democratic Front
January 22, 1987	"Mendiola Massacre": 21 peasants marching for land shot to death in Manila
August 26, 1987	Nearly two million workers and supporters march against Aquino's policies
August 28, 1987	Fifth and bloodiest coup attempt against Aquino (Honasan Coup)
September 16, 1991	Philippine Senate rejects plan to extend lease on U.S. bases
December 7, 2000	President Joseph Estrada's impeachment trial begins in Senate
January 16, 2001	People Power 2 begins after Senate effectively acquits Estrada
January 18, 2001	Crowd at EDSA swells to over five hundred thousand
January 19, 2001	Armed Forces leaders defect to opposition
January 20, 2001	President Estrada overthrown by EDSA 2
April 25, 2001	Insisting he is still president, Estrada is arrested on charges of plunder
April 25, 2001	People Power 3 ("Poor People Power") begins in support of Estrada
April 26, 2001	Crowd at EDSA surpasses one million
May 1, 2001	EDSA 3 marches on Malacañang to support Estrada; three people killed by police

"HISTORY REPEATS ITSELF, first as tragedy, then as farce." So often repeated, this tired formula has been accorded the status of absolute truth. The cunning of history finds ways to disprove every attempt to generalize laws of its development—even "iron" ones.

The experience of three People Power uprisings in the Philippines reveals a different pattern. In February 1986, hundreds of thousands of Filipinos courageously and illegally occupied the streets of Manila until entrenched president Ferdinand Marcos left office and went into exile. Far from tragic, their victory has become mythologized as the first nonviolent "People Power" uprising. Fifteen years later, many of the same participants gathered again on January 20, 2001, for People Power 2 in the same place, Epifanio de los Santos Avenue (EDSA)—one of Manila's main thoroughfares. Continuing protests forced President Joseph Estrada out of Malacañang presidential palace, and Vice President Gloria Macapagal-Arroyo was sworn in as the new chief executive on EDSA's holy ground. Arroyo's ascension to the presidency proved to be catastrophic. A little more than three months later, Estrada's supporters regrouped at EDSA to support his claim to be the legitimately elected president. Flooding the streets with more than a million people, People Power 3 (or "Poor People Power") culminated in a march on Malacañang presidential palace by tens of thousands of Estrada supporters, slum dwellers, and working-class denizens of Manila. Police had been restrained when faced with middle-class protesters, but this time they opened fire, killing three and wounding more than a hundred people.

The international "eros effects" of People Power have been enormous, yet detailed examinations of the reasons for the 1986 uprising's success—and the limitations of the changes it brought—have been far less robust. Pacifists have mythologized People Power 1, enshrining the omnipotence of nonviolent protest by more than a million people in the streets, but the actual unfolding of the 1986 uprising reveals a different story. Top military leaders supported by the Catholic Church and the United States led an armed mutiny that overthrew Marcos, and firepower was an essential ingredient in victory. At two critical moments, armed mutineers shot their way into the main television stations of Manila, and rebel helicopters attacked the presidential palace and loyalist air base.[1] All in all, at least a dozen people were killed in the 1986 transfer of power. The CIA provided rebel military leaders with real-time intelligence on Marcos's troop movements.[2]

If they are to be accurate, accounts of People Power 1 must begin with the military mutiny, and they should not fail to record the role of the United States in easing Marcos out of the country. While the oft-neglected rebels within the Philippine military were the instigators of the uprising, it is doubtful they could have succeeded without the support of Catholic Cardinal Jamie Sin and hundreds of thousands of ordinary Filipinos who flooded into the streets despite the threat of military force being used against them.

The 1986 uprising ushered Marcos out of the country and replaced him with Corazon Aquino, daughter of one of the country's wealthiest families. No matter how inspirational People Power 1 may have been, the "revolution" it accomplished was little more than a transfer of power between sections of the pro-American elite. The insurgency's top-down character meant that while the presidency changed hands, the underlying economic and social system remained intact, even strengthened because ordinary people considered the new regime less oppressive. Although a new constitution empowered NGOs and led to a popular referendum that forced U.S. bases to close, Filipino society remains mired in many of the same problems that plagued it under the Marcos dictatorship. Seemingly intractable poverty affects nearly half of all citizens. Malnutrition and stunted growth afflict millions of children. Development is stymied, and one-fourth of the country's workforce finds jobs abroad to support their families at home.

Three hundred years of Spanish colonialism eviscerated indigenous Filipino cultures, forging what novelist F. Sionil José calls "a modern country but not yet a nation."[3] Living on three thousand islands, Filipinos speak eighty languages. With the collapse of the Spanish Empire at the end of the nineteenth century, the United States claimed the Philippines. For refusing to submit to the "manifest destiny" of Americans, some two hundred thousand natives were massacred by the United States before the independence movement was crushed. Although Mark Twain and other luminaries formed an Anti-Imperialist League that sought to restrain U.S. imperial ambitions, massacres went on for years as the United States "liberated" its "little brown brothers." Largely forgotten in U.S. history texts, continuing tensions in Filipina-American relations originate in the brutal conquest of islanders guilty of nothing more than wanting to live as free people.[4]

Conquered and humiliated by Japan during World War II, many Filipinos fought alongside the United States in a fierce guerrilla war—although the country's elite, accustomed to accommodating occupiers, generally worked alongside Hirohito's servants. After the war, U.S. commanding general Douglas MacArthur personally exonerated Manuel Roxas, one of the chief collaborators with Japan, and positioned him to become the elected president of the Republic of the Philippines.[5] Members of the landed gentry were transformed into captains of industry, while those who preferred to remain tied to their rural estates received U.S. backing for the decimation of the Huk rebels fighting for land reform.

At the end of World War II, the Philippines was the most modern country in all of Southeast Asia. As Sionil José recalled, "Students from the region came to our schools. When I traveled, the backwardness everywhere amazed me. Jakarta and Kuala Lumpur were villages. The tallest structure in Bangkok was Wat Arun. Seoul and Taipei were quiet, with horse drawn carts, bicycles, and those low brick buildings left by the Japanese. . . . Manila has skyscrapers now but everywhere are the slums that show how we have decayed."[6] The country was "the second richest country in the region, next only to Japan; our universities attracted students from all over Asia, and we had the best professionals, the most modern stores and hospitals."[7] By the 1980s, the Philippines were one of the region's basket cases, and the island republic continues to slide downhill as most of the region makes "miraculous" progress. In 1940, the Philippines had the highest literacy rate in all of Southeast Asia—no doubt a result of the government's generous expenditures on education in previous decades (some 50 percent of its total budget). Today, half the population has had only elementary schooling, and only 43 percent of incoming elementary school children are expected to finish high school.[8]

The Marcos Regime

Much of the blame for the decline of the Philippines has been laid at the feet of the Marcos regime. From humble beginnings, provincial politician Ferdinand Marcos climbed to the country's top position in 1965, where he soon usurped total power and amassed a huge fortune, conservatively estimated at between $5 billion and $20 billion in 1986.[9] For more than two decades, he ruled with the blessing of U.S. corporate and political leaders. Applauded by the American Chamber of Commerce for overturning Supreme Court decisions that threatened foreign businesses' property holdings, Marcos was able to parlay support from the United States into lavish wealth. Locals spoke of "guns, goons, and gold" rather than "law and order" to characterize his regime.

Heeding the advice of U.S. mentors, on May 1, 1972, Marcos announced a shift in economic policy from import substitution (production for the domestic market to keep the country's balance of payments favorable) to export-oriented and labor-intensive industry. A few months later, on September 21, 1972, using a contrived "assassination attempt" on his defense secretary, Juan Ponce Enrile, Marcos declared martial law—thereby avoiding term limits on his presidency. Other provisions prohibited strikes, intensively controlled the media, and led to thousands of arrests. Even Jesuit monasteries were not immune: the military mounted a surprise helicopter raid in August 1974—raising the ire of Cardinal Sin—a deed for which Marcos would subsequently pay dearly.

For decades, the Marcos family and their close associates plundered the treasury, reducing the Philippines to bankruptcy while relegating its citizens to hardships. Alongside dictators like South Korea's Park Chung-hee, the Shah of Iran, and Taiwan's Chiang Kai-shek, Marcos ingratiated himself with U.S. presidents through generous campaign contributions.[10] He rented out an army construction battalion to the United States for use in Vietnam. In exchange for his largesse, he was compensated handsomely, garnering $80 million from Westinghouse Corporation for one contract alone—a nuclear power plant with financing arranged via the U.S. Export-Import Bank.[11] In the eyes of one prominent American journalist at the time of the Tet Offensive, "Marcos was riding high, new in office, young, dynamic, saying the right things to foreigners as well as to Filipinos, impressing us all with plans and promises."[12]

Unconcerned that as many as three-fourths of the country's forty-five million human beings were impoverished, that Manila's street children seemed to congregate everywhere, Marcos married a former beauty queen and lived large. The Marcoses commissioned a monumental mural in Malacañang that portrayed themselves as Adam and Eve. They named highways after each other and threw lavish parties. Their eventual ouster is not surprising. What I find difficult to comprehend is people's magnanimous capacity to forgive them, to allow them to keep billions of dollars of the impoverished nation's wealth. For years, Marcos's body has remained embalmed in public view, like Communist idols Lenin, Mao, Kim, and Ho—a public display of reverence for a man whose people unceremoniously sent him into exile.

As president, Marcos permitted little dissent—even when it was peaceful. In nearly every country in the world in 1968, student protests rocked governments. In the Philippines, the unrest became known as the First Quarter Storm. On January 30, 1970, six people were killed in cold blood as they rushed to escape a police onslaught on a demonstration at the Mendiola Bridge approaching Malacañang palace.[13] Named "Black Friday" by then-senator Benigno Aquino, that incident was one of many that illustrated the regime's brutality. From torture and disappearances to long prison terms, dissidents had little choice but to go underground. Scion of one of the country's leading families, firebrand orator, and teenage Korean War photographer for the *Manila Times*, Senator Aquino soon became Marcos's chief nemesis. Instead of running for president, Aquino found himself serving hard prison time. When his health deteriorated, he was released to the United States, where he and South Korean dissident Kim Dae Jung became colleagues at Harvard University's Center for International Affairs.

As in many other countries, the more the regime repressed university students, the more radical they became. All over the world, communists split from mainstream Soviet-aligned parties and founded Maoist ones—such as the Communist Party of the Philippines (CPP). Inspired by the Maoist victory in China, the CPP's New People's Army (NPA) grew rapidly into the only opposition. While their revolt was unsuccessful in seizing power, one of its consequences was to help spark a reform movement within the armed forces—much as insurgent African guerrillas in Mozambique, Angola, and Guinea-Bissau had accomplished within Portugal's colonial army before the military's successful overthrow of the Salazar dictatorship in 1974.

Officers fighting the NPA were dissatisfied with the regime's siphoning off millions of dollars of U.S. financial support meant for the military, nor were they pleased by Marcos's penchant for appointing officers loyal to him—rather than those most qualified to fight a war. While Marcos ordered his command-ers to ruthlessly suppress rural communities, rank-and-file soldiers were being cheated on food and clothing allocations. Guerrilla fighters of the emergent Moro National Liberation Front (MNLF) were sometimes better armed.[14] A small coterie of officers grew increasingly unhappy with the government's failure to provide them with reliable air transport, medical support, and adequate logistics for their counterinsurgency wars. Gregorio "Gringo" Honasan explained to me that after army pacification campaigns in rural areas, he promised local leaders that roads and medical facilities would soon be built. Called back into the same areas years later, "nothing had changed."[15] To do something about these problems, Honasan organized fellow officers into Reform the Armed Forces Movement (RAM, or Rebolusyonaryong Alyansang Makabansa)—the group that would go on to initiate the 1986 People Power revolt.

The global U.S. war against communism, in the 1980s still a very powerful impetus for American policy despite its defeat in Vietnam, was faltering in the

TABLE 2.1 **Foreign Direct Investments in the Philippines (in million U.S.$)**

	1980	1985	1990	1995	1997
Indonesia	180	310	1,092	4,346	4,677
Thailand	189	164	2,562	2,068	3,626
Philippines	-106	12	550	1,459	1,249

Source: UNCTAD as quoted in Dae-oup Chang, "Neoliberal Restructuring of Capital Relations in East and South-East Asia," in *Neoliberalism: A Critical Reader*, eds. Alfredo Saad-Filho and Deborah Johnston (London: Pluto Press, 2005), 254.

hands of Marcos's authoritarian regime. In 1983, while the Philippine army fought without proper medical care and boots, U.S. intelligence estimated that the NPA and the Philippine army had reached a "strategic parity."[16] From a few hundred rebels in 1972, the NPA had grown to as many as thirty thousand combatants by 1985 according to a U.S. Senate estimate.[17] The NPA was present in sixty-eight of the seventy-three provinces, and exerted some degree of control over 20 percent of the country's villages—a sea of support of at least half a million people.[18] In the estimation of the Pentagon's high command, a more democratic parliamentary regime—if controlled by members of the elite favorable to the United States like Aquino—was far preferable to Marcos as a means to prevent a communist victory. Ultimately, Marcos's biggest mistake in Washington's eyes was to increasingly cut himself off from members of the traditional elite.

To finance his lavish spending, Marcos borrowed heavily—no doubt encouraged by the easy terms afforded him by global financial institutions. By the early 1980s, the Philippine debt crisis contributed mightily to the economy's freefall. In October 1983, the country stopped servicing its debt, making international investors nervous and the U.S. government less than pleased. To compensate for the decline in foreign investments, the national bank expanded the money supply. In the first seven years of martial law, the economy had grown by an average of 6 percent per year, but growth fell to 3 percent in 1982 and 2.6 percent a year later. Real wages slowly rose until 1980, when serious annual declines began to be felt in both urban and rural settings. In 1984, as the country reeled from its worst recession since 1945, the economy's output fell by 6 percent.[19] At the same time as inflation weighed heavily—averaging 47 percent in 1983 and 23.5 percent in 1984—shortages and hoarding appeared.[20] The currency was devalued by more than 100 percent from 1982 to 1985. By 1986, the recession was yet to be resolved; that year, output fell by nearly 8 percent, and international investors moved to the Thailand and Indonesia. The regime's habitual doling out of favors to cronies and family did little to endear it among the nation's businesspeople. As indicated in TABLE 2.1, investors began a capital flight as early as 1980, an indication of how little faith they had in Marcos.

The Assassination of Benigno Aquino

As a geopolitical construct, East Asia hardly existed before Western domination of the region. At the end of the twentieth century, the latter was so powerful that even opposition leaders discovered in the United States a waiting room for future heads of state. In the early 1980s, Kim Dae Jung and Benigno Aquino, popular, pro-American leaders of vast democratic strata, sat together in exile in Newton, Massachusetts, each having escaped death sentences from their countries' systems of justice. Getting acquainted and exchanging views on how best to overcome dictatorships, on at least one occasion, they shared breakfast at Aquino's home as they discussed their situations.[21] Both men's fates were tied to political changes in their homelands. No one would have guessed that their cook that morning, Aquino's wife, Corazon, would herself be pressed into service as head of state within a few short years.

In the midst of economic turmoil in his homeland, Benigno Aquino decided it was time to return home from his safe refuge in the United States to rescue the nation. On August 21, 1983, as soon as his flight landed, he was killed. Within hours of his assassination, demonstrations against Marcos broke out. In the ensuing expression of grief, more than one million people (some say twice that number) attended his funeral procession, undeterred by torrential rain. For the first time, office workers, business executives, housewives, and teachers joined protests normally confined to students, unions, and leftists. At the forefront of opposition to Marcos stood the Makati Business Club, leaving little doubt that the nation's economic elite perceived the murder of Aquino as the last straw in Marcos's total mismanagement of the nation. At an appointed hour every Wednesday and Friday, prominent businessmen ordered work stopped as tons of yellow confetti rained down from Makati's high rise buildings, a regular ritual that spread to other parts of Manila and as far South as Davao in Mindanao.

After the assassination of Benigno Aquino, Washington became increasingly aloof. It did not take much intelligence to come to the conclusion that Marcos was bad for the country. As early as June 1984, a secret study by the U.S. embassy blamed Marcos for the Communists' growing influence, and that November, a secret NSC Directive (National Security Council) called for a "transition" in the Philippines, "dismantling 'crony' monopoly capitalism and allowing the economy to respond to free market forces."[22] Using its embassy staff as point men and women, Washington quietly began to undermine Marcos's rule.[23] Marcos's incompetence was also noted in 1985 by U.S. admiral William Crowe, chair of the joint chiefs, who recommended that Marcos be retired in order for the military to better fight the guerrillas. Although then-president Ronald Reagan was a friend of Marcos, his advisors listened when the Pentagon spoke.

By the 1984 congressional elections, two opposition parties fielded candidates—the Philippine Democratic Party (LABAN or People Power) and the United National Democratic Organization (UNIDO). With widespread allegations of fraud, the opposition won 56 of 183 seats. Marcos ordered his police not to permit the opposition to mobilize in the streets. In September 1984, at least thirty-four protesters were hospitalized when police used guns and clubs to disperse thousands of antigovernment protesters. Refusing to be intimidated, the next month, ten times as many protesters took to the streets—and under leadership of Cardinal Sin, they were allowed to rally peacefully.[24] Alongside antigovernment demonstrations and rallies, strikes spread, as TABLE 2.2 illustrates.

TABLE 2.2 **Number of Strikes and Workers by Year (Philippines)**

Year	Number of Strikes	Workers Involved
1972	69	33,396
1973	0	0
1974	0	0
1975	5	1,760
1976	86	70,929
1977	33	30,183
1978	53	33,731
1979	48	16,728
1980	62	20,902
1981	260	98,585
1982	158	53,824
1983	155	33,638
1984	282	65,306
1985	371	111,265
1986	581	168,779
1987	436	89,600

Sources: Bureau of National Labor Relations; Bach M. Macaraya, *Workers' Participation in the Philippine People Power Revolution* (Manila: Friedrich Ebert Stiftung, 1988), 1, 27; ILO, *Year Book of Labor Statistics*; Haggard and Kaufman, *Political Economy*, 62.

Although the labor movement was internally divided between pro-Marcos and left-wing tendencies, strikes escalated in 1984 and 1985, from a little more than half a million days lost in 1983 to nearly five times that many two years later.

From the grassroots, people emerged to organize the Congress of the Filipino People, Kongreso ng Mamamayang Pilipino (KOMPIL)—a wide coalition of NGOs, issue-oriented protest groups, labor and faith-based organizations, left-wing groups, and prominent individuals—all dedicated to ending the Marcos dictatorship. Theater groups formed by the dozens, and traversed the archipelago spreading the word of Marcos's corruption, his subservience to the United States, and his importation of dangerous nuclear power technology.[25] Ordinary Filipinas knew the country was in a terrible downward spiral, while for his part, Marcos threw huge parties for his family and relied on U.S. support for his continued rule.

Anti-Marcos forces inside the Church, academia, and middle class quickly drew in workers and poor people. As yellow confetti protests gathered momentum, a cross-class alliance developed with the Trade Union Congress of the Philippines (TUPAS), which urged its members to join the weekly rallies in Makati. These regular protests were significant preparation for the 1986 explosion. TUPAS helped form a broad front, the United Filipino Workers, aimed at carrying out a general strike against the regime. In the early 1980s, a strike in the Bataan Export Processing Zone helped convince TUPAS leaders that Marcos could be overthrown only by united action with other sectors of the opposition.[26]

In the process of the opposition enlarging its base, the early anti-imperialism and far-reaching vision of the movement became subsumed under a new consensus that Aquino was the person to replace Marcos. Randolf David described the change: "By the time the February events began to unfold, democratization and social justice had already become faint notes on EDSA's agenda. Anti-imperialism completely disappeared almost overnight, together with the campaign against militarization. What took their place were the hegemonic symbols of the flower and the rosary."[27]

The Snap Election

Senior American officials like Secretary of State George Schulz fretted that the regime was crumbling. They challenged Marcos in private to improve his government's policies and to reconcile with opposition forces. Marcos's health was deteriorating rapidly, and the man who appeared to be next in line, General Fabian Ver, had been found (along with others) to be indictable for the murder of Aquino. Marcos came under pressure to justify U.S. support for his continuing rule. To prove his popularity and placate his U.S. protectors, he proposed a special "snap election" on U.S. television. (It was subsequently revealed that CIA director William Casey had originally proposed the election.[28]) At the time, little did anyone guess that this seemingly arbitrary decision would cost Marcos his presidency.

The Catholic Church was no latecomer to the movement to unseat Marcos. With the snap election approaching, Cardinal Sin encouraged Corazon Aquino to run for president. Cory told him her husband was talking to her from the grave, inspiring her to run for president. Sin advised her to pray more, since "It is not a joke to go against Marcos." Cory retreated to the Pink Sisters Convent, where she made up her mind. In her words: "All right, I will run. I have decided . . . to run. It is God's will." Sin responded: "All right, kneel down. You are going to be president. You are the Joan of Arc."[29] Cory adopted yellow for her campaign (the same color as the confetti that rained down at anti-Marcos protests), wearing it so often she was dubbed "the canary."

The church mobilized to ensure the election's fairness. Tens of thousands of volunteers for the National Citizens' Movement for Free Elections (NAMFREL) were officially accredited as election observers. Created by the CIA in 1953, NAMFREL, a nonpartisan volunteer organization with over two hundred thousand members from nongovernmental groups, was formally reorganized in 1983 in preparation for congressional elections.[30] Some seven thousand members of the Trade Union Congress of the Philippines (a small, conservative federation affiliated with U.S. interests) were financed by the U.S. National Endowment for Democracy to participate in NAMFREL's observation of elections.[31] Central to the group's mission were the "NAMFREL Marines," Cardinal Sin's elite "strike force" of 600 nuns who could be sent into the field at a moment's notice. Vincente Paterno, NAMFREL chairman for Metro Manila, recalled: "I thought 300 people in twenty-five strike forces would be enough. And we fielded 600 nuns—the NAMFREL Marines . . . we had the strike forces; we probably had about 30,000 volunteers. We had an army."[32]

True to form, Marcos tried to rig the election. Fraudulent vote tallies compelled thirty computer technicians (led by a RAM leader's wife) to walk out of the official tabulation center on the night of February 9, 1986. At that moment of high drama, no one—not even high ranking Americans paying attention to every detail of daily developments—guessed that the next week would be so tumultuous. Despite the church's warnings to Marcos, to say nothing of threats to the eternal souls of anyone tampering with the votes, the clergy's insistence on fair elections was ignored. In this delicate moment when the nation's attention was riveted on the election's result, U.S. President Reagan declared on February 11 that "hard evidence" of fraud was lacking. Shocking the opposition, he suggested that cheating might have happened "on both sides."

While many people attributed Reagan's remarks to his friendship with Marcos, Washington's main concern were U.S. bases at Clark and Subic Bay. "I don't know of anything more important than those bases," he uttered at a press conference. Larry Speakes, Reagan's press secretary, opined Aquino had lost. He encouraged her to help Marcos form a government.[33] To Filipinos who witnessed ballot boxes disappear, who saw voters paid to favor Marcos, who were intimidated or harassed, who read about murders of anti-Marcos leaders, it was everywhere evident that Reagan was wrong. Two days after Reagan's statement, the Catholic Bishop's Conference publicly declared the election was "unparalleled in the fraudulence of its conduct" and called upon people to engage in a "nonviolent struggle for justice." The next day, it declared that a government that "retains power through fraud" has "no moral basis."

Aquino called for her supporters to rally on February 16 at the Luneta in Rizal Park. When her forces had assembled, she called them "the biggest crowd of our lives"—a throng ranging from one to two million people.[34] Aquino announced a broad plan to boycott specific banks and companies known to be close to Marcos, to delay payment of utility bills, and for a one-day strike scheduled for the day after Marcos's inauguration. In an outpouring of popular support, nuns and religious workers lined up to withdraw money from the targeted banks, and all four labor formations supported the Aquino plan by endorsing a general strike for Wednesday, February 26, 1986. (Little did they know that Marcos would be driven into exile then.) Even Nestle Corporation ceased advertising on government television's Channel 4 as well as in one of the newspapers on Aquino's boycott list. On February 19, the U.S. Senate voted 85–9 to declare the election in the Philippines to have been marked by "widespread fraud." Testifying before the House of Representatives the next day, Reagan administration official Paul Wolfowitz announced that new U.S. aid was being suspended as long as Marcos remained in office.

In this ripe moment, all that was needed was for forces inside the country to act. While church leaders and opposition politicians did their utmost to unseat Marcos, communists decided to sit out the revolt because there was "little difference between Aquino and Marcos." Since both represented the wealthy, the NDF sat out the elections and attended to internal problems. Throughout Mindanao in 1985, the NPA had engaged in a brutal purge of its members after reports that secret military agents had infiltrated it. In six months, some 950 cadres were executed, decimating the fastest growing regional branch of the party and leading to claims that the CPP was the "new Khmer Rouge." As thousands of people left its ranks, the party's membership fell from nine thousand to three thousand.[35] When party leaders decided to sit out the snap election, members and front organizations followed their commands closely—lest they arouse the ire of the party's security forces.[36] The extent of communist misunderstanding of the popular mood was revealed in the fact that voter turnout was over 90 percent.

The Mutiny inside the Military

Just after midnight on Saturday, February 22, 1986, a small group huddled in the home of Defense Minister Juan Ponce Enrile to put the finishing touches on a bold plan to overthrow Marcos. At 2:00 a.m. on February 23, Colonel Gregorio Honasan was to lead a commando assault on Malacañang and arrest the presidential family. His former classmates at the Philippine Military Academy, Colonels Eduardo Kapunan and Victor Batac, would simultaneously stage diversionary actions. By showing their resolve to better the country at the risk of their own lives, they believed dissident officers in RAM's secret network (conservatively estimated to include five thousand of all fifteen thousand officers in the military) would rally behind them. Honasan and his coconspirators vowed to accept no personal rewards for their efforts. Instead they decided on a transitional government that included Cory Aquino, Cardinal Sin, Juan Ponce Enrile, and army chief of staff Fidel Ramos. From humble beginnings as a beer-drinking discussion group, RAM spawned a steering committee that met regularly in the headquarters of the national police.[37] Colonel Jose Almonte contacted Cardinal Sin and informed him of RAM's plan. When he asked for the church's support, Cardinal Sin told him, "Colonel, you do your duty, and I'll do mine!"

As the small group of conspirators gathered together on February 22 in Enrile's home, little did they know that one of their members had turned informant, and at that very moment, was spilling the beans to General Ver inside the presidential palace. Ver rapidly reinforced presidential security with thousands of his best troops, and arrested 19 Marines, all key members of RAM, at 2:00 a.m. on Feb 22.[38] In the middle of the night, when Honasan and Kapunan secretly reconnoitered the key point they planned to attack, they observed a full Marine battalion waiting in ambush. After studying Ver's troops, Honasan rushed to Enrile's house, informing him that all of them were about to be arrested. Then and there, they decided to act as soon as possible.

Agreeing on an alternate plan, Honasan gave the signal for all their forces to regroup at Camp Aguinaldo on EDSA at about 3:00 p.m. Reached by telephone, Fidel Ramos agreed to join them there. As soon as Enrile arrived by helicopter at the camp, he called U.S. Ambassador Stephen Bosworth and Japanese Ambassador Kioshi Somiya. Perhaps his most important call for support went to Manila Cardinal Sin. Speaking on Catholic Radio Veritas, Sin exhorted the people of Manila not to be alarmed and to stay home.[39] When the rebels finished counting their forces, they totaled 320 armed officers and men, plus about 300 civilians organized into twelve teams.[40] The officers worked the telephones calling colleagues and asking for their support. As the RAM telephone tree grew, one key pledge of support came from Air Force Colonel Antonio Sotelo—commander of

Rebel military leader Juan Ponce Enrile called the U.S. and Japanese ambassadors.
Photo by Franz Lopez in *People Power: An Eyewitness History*, 114.

the Fifteenth Strike Wing. Assembling his squadron commanders, they armed and fueled five attack helicopters.

When the media flooded into the camp for a press conference, Enrile and Ramos openly declared their revolt and asked the public to join them. They declared they had no food. Popular support was immediate—thousands of people brought so much food that RAM asked people to stop bringing uncooked rice. Some of the first meals were served on silver trays.[41] Colgate-Palmolive sent in boxes of toothpaste, toothbrushes, and soap.[42] "Piles and piles" of cigarettes were suddenly available.

Around 9:00 p.m., Cardinal Sin again went on Radio Veritas and asked people to support "our two good friends."[43] From then on, Radio Veritas worked closely with the rebels, even helping them communicate with each other—"the first time in military history, anywhere in the world, that private broadcast media, run by concerned citizens, were used to transmit military orders or directives to military units in the field."[44] Jesuit priest James Reuter was a key link in the entire operation. He was in continual direct contact with Ramos in Camp Crame, with Radio Veritas, and by telephone, with the U.S. embassy.[45] In a back office of the defense ministry, CIA agents informed Enrile and Ramos of "everything Ver did, and passed on all communications coming out of Malacañang. Enrile stayed in frequent contact with Ambassador Bosworth through this backroom CIA link."[46] Ramos subsequently acknowledged he "was constantly in touch with U.S. defense and air force attaché, Colonel Tom Halley, who was assigned as my counterpart by the U.S. ambassador."[47] The U.S. Seventh Fleet stood by in Philippine waters—further boosting rebel morale.

At this critical moment, Aquino was hundreds of miles away in Cebu. Unwilling to trust Enrile (Marcos's defense minister), she was considering her own declaration of a provisional government in Davao.[48] The next day, she conferred by telephone with Cardinal Sin, telling him the "third force" (RAM) was a problem. "No," he replied, "I am sure they are staging this because they want you to be the president. Go there and thank them. Without this, you could be demonstrating every day and would still not be president. But now you will be. You can see the hand of God. This is the answer to our prayers."[49] While many people subsequently questioned whether it was the hand of God or of the CIA, the cardinal's remark was on target insofar as the military's revolt was central to the movement's success. Neither a miracle nor a CIA conspiracy, the grassroots insurgency—of which RAM was one expression—was the moving historical force that drove Marcos out of the country.

Shortly after midnight on Day 2, Sunday, February 23, Ramos strengthened his forces inside Camp Crame with seventeen tanks and two helicopters. During the night, the number of supporters outside the camp fell from twenty thousand to about two thousand. At 4:00 a.m., an attack appeared imminent, but it never materialized, largely because still undiscovered RAM members refused to carry out orders. As the city awoke, people began streaming to EDSA in ever-greater numbers. By 8:00 a.m., the crowd had swelled to some fifty thousand. Hours later, when loyalist forces commanded by Ver finally mounted an attack, all seven of their tanks were stopped by throngs of people at the intersection of EDSA and Ortigas. By that time, Ramos and Enrile had enlisted the support of a majority of Constabulary commanders and military commanders of forty provinces.

Early Sunday morning, armed loyalists destroyed Radio Veritas, but within hours, it continued broadcasting using a short-lived emergency transmitter. By the time that gave out, Cardinal Sin had already called James Reuter and asked him to find another transmitter. Soon a new station, calling itself Radio Bandido, secretly resumed broadcasts so essential to morale and coordination of those in the streets. Hundreds of nuns arrived, flooding the stairways leading to the new station to prevent loyalist troops from entering the building.

By lunchtime, hundreds of thousands of people were crowded around the rebel troops—some counted more than one million people at EDSA. To help defend themselves, people cut down trees and lampposts. City buses were commandeered to form barricades alongside Mercedes and private cars. Sandbags were quickly thrown onto the piles, adorned by dozens of religious icons. When a large Marine force led by tanks and APC's attempted to attack Camp Crame, nuns with rosaries faced them down. As the tanks edged forward, people refused to budge. So many people jammed the highways and streets around the rebel camps that military units loyal to Marcos could not advance.

Now more confident, rebel commanders decided to combine their positions. Enrile and Honasan led their forces from Camp Aguinaldo and crossed EDSA to join Ramos inside Crame. Once there, Enrile informed the U.S. ambassador of his move, and then called General Ver. He gave both men the same message: if Ver's tanks continued any farther, a bloody battle would result. Marcos offered all rebels complete amnesty—but RAM leaders quickly refused even to consider it. Simultaneously, rebel soldiers decided not to distribute arms to the thousands of supporters encircling them.

Nuns with rosaries faced down Marcos's army.
Photo by Pete Reyes in *People Power: An Eyewitness History*, 178.

People Power Emerges

Staying in the streets day and night, the people of Manila changed not only the course of Filipino history—they transformed themselves. The struggle against Marcos brought them together in exhilarating new ways. A new identity of the nation was forged. Three centuries of Spanish colonization and one of U.S. domination had brought Catholicism and profound cultural influences—but islanders' indigenous identities had been destroyed, leaving Filipino identity a work in progress. Foreign influence penetrated consciousness so deeply felt that that even

the guerrillas of the MNLF use the Spanish designation "Moro" to name themselves, and guerrilla fighters of the NPA play basketball, originally an American
game, in their spare time at base camps.

As F. Sionil José told me, the Philippines is "A country but not yet a nation,
outside the influence of major East Asian streams of culture (Confucianism,
Hinduism, and Buddhism). The Philippines has no Angkor Wat or Borobudur."
In conversation with Thai activist Sulak Sivaraksa, José expressed the same sentiment another way: "We have a great inferior[ity] complex when it comes to
Thailand, Indonesia and to much of continental Southeast Asia because the
remnants of your ancient civilizations are there for you to see and to learn from,
and your history is a continuum from the past."[50]

People Power provided a new unity and sense of purpose to the Philippines.
As the EDSA Revolution website remembers, "It's about the people. It's about the
rich and the poor, the old and the young, the geek and the jock, losing their status,
interlocking their arms, standing together in the long stretch of the highway, and
for one moment, they were just Filipinos. All of them, one."[51] In itself, the movement forged a unified Filipino identity as strong as any since the U.S. conquest. As
one writer expressed it: "Out of this confrontation, ordinary street Filipinos, Tondo
people and faceless, joined with the middle class, and both discovered a kind of
spontaneous collective will that they had never exerted before, and a common
bond they had never nurtured. It electrified them. Tears streamed down their faces.
Some began to sing. 'People Power' was born."[52] What I've called the eros effect
is here evident in the emotions and actions of hundreds of thousands of Filipinos.

People's normal values changed overnight. One mother recalled, "I used to
hate the military and the police, but on Sunday I found myself preparing sand-
wiches for them. I heard over the radio that they needed food. I had to squeeze
through a crowd just to bring food to the soldiers. I remembered all the times I had
cursed them during rallies and was amazed that now I walked so far and worked
so hard for them."[53] For Enrile the change was palpable: "I heard the people
shouting, 'We love our soldiers!' I never heard that before in my life. In all my
years with the military, I never heard that. We have to be worthy of that. Our allegiance is to the people."[54] Cory Aquino recalled, "Everything was so spontaneous.
There was no director. It was really the people wanting to make changes happen,
and they did make them happen. It was the people themselves coming together
and becoming one and finally identifying with each other. . . . Finally Filipino
people were identifying with all that's good about the Filipino—the sharing of
food, the praying together, the kindness and support shown for everybody, the
total giving of oneself . . . "[55] For Rene Cruz, "It really felt like a miracle was happening. Soldiers not firing when ordered to, my own children and wife out in
EDSA and actually enjoying it, and the weather so nice and cool throughout the
four days . . . there was no report of pick-pocketing, no mugging, no untoward
incident."[56] NGO leader Corazon Juliano-Soliman told me "Everyone witnessed
ordinary people doing heroic acts, guarding polling places and chaining themselves to ballots. The whole movement was built on each other's courage, and
felt like one big family."[57]

Massive occupation of public space made it impossible for Marcos to use tanks.
Photo by Joey D. Vera in *People Power: An Eyewitness History*, 155.

Workers' participation was so widespread that some observers considered the uprising a "workers' revolution against the abuses of the Marcos regime."[58] Refusing to charge anything, cab drivers brought carloads of people to the camps for free. While many workers joined the protests, they did so as individuals—that is, outside the structures of their trade unions.[59] Disagreements within TUCOP prevented it from directly supporting the opposition; the Federation of Free Workers steadfastly maintained its principle to remain "free from politics"; and the leftist Kilusang Mayo Uno remained faithful to a boycott of the elections and refused formally to endorse the uprising.

Although mainly centered in Manila, actions occurred in other parts of the country. In Cebu City, people thronged in front of a Philippine Constabulary camp known to be friendly to the mutiny and succeeded in preventing it from being attacked by pro-Marcos forces. In Iloilo City, bonfires and dancing in the streets celebrated Aquino. In Marawi, prayer rallies targeted politicians who supported Marcos.[60]

People's courageous intransigence persuaded whole units of the military, arms in hand, to cross over to the side of the rebels. What had begun on February 22 with two hundred soldiers turned into a majority of the two hundred thousand armed forces within forty-eight hours. Marcos was horrified as key military commanders turned against him while the whole world was watching. At 7:00 p.m. on February 23, the Pope delivered a letter to Marcos via the Papal Nuncio appealing for a peaceful settlement. Soon thereafter, for the first time, the U.S. government publicly questioned the "credibility and legitimacy" of his government. Privately, the United States offered Marcos refuge, but he refused, insisting he would stay on as president. Late that evening, Ramos and Enrile traveled separately to the house of Cory Aquino's sister in Greenhills to meet with Aquino, who had arrived by private plane without arousing public attention. Aquino was still hesitant about working with Enrile, since she had been compelled to deal with him as her husband's captor during his lengthy imprisonment.[61]

As dusk fell on EDSA, a Jesuit priest convinced a pro-Marcos tank commander to withdraw his forces for the night. As the tanks rumbled off, people shouted, "Good night! See you tomorrow!" Unbeknownst to the commander, some of his troops had quietly passed word to people to "please stay so we don't have to attack each other."[62] Throughout the night, people at EDSA heard repeated ringing of the church bells—a signal that Marcos's forces were going to attack. As rumors spread of troop movements, droves of people set off to block streets. Spirits were kept high through prayers and songs. At the front gate of Camp Crane, nuns sang while soldiers briefed citizens on the proper use of Molotov cocktails.[63] A loyalist truck approached the crowd and insisted on passing through to bring food to troops supporting Marcos. Ramos was called and told people, "Let them through. Hungry soldiers are dangerous." The food got through.[64] At 2:00 a.m. Ramos announced to the crowd that a Huey helicopter had defected to the side of the rebels, and popular singer Freddie Aguilar sang "Bayan Ko" ("My Country"—a popular song long banned by Marcos). After conferring with President Reagan in Washington, Secretary of State George Shultz called U.S. Ambassador Bosworth at 4:00 a.m. Manila time and told him to inform Marcos that his "time was up."[65] Marcos was assured that his departure to the United States would be facilitated as long as he controlled the violence. Yet Marcos still refused to leave.

The Final Battle

As dawn broke on February 24, rebel soldiers inside Camp Crame expected an all-out assault in which they would sacrifice their lives. They embraced each other and said their final goodbyes. As the radio played the Philippine Military Academy song, all stood—many with tears in their eyes. A few minutes later, Marcos could be heard over the radio ordering General Ver to "wipe them out." Behind a volley of tear gas, riot troops with clubs scattered people in their path. Simultaneously, hundreds of loyalist troops attacked the east side of Camp Aguinaldo, breaking through the wall facing Camp Crame.

With the destiny of the country hanging in the balance, a miracle decided the outcome of the battle. A strong gust of wind blew the tear gas back in the direction of the loyalist forces that had fired it. Everyone paused—including the attacking soldiers. Having witnessed the "hand of God," they suddenly crossed over to the side of insurgents amid hugs and cheers from the assembled throng. Almost at the same time, five helicopter gunships took to the air with orders to attack the mutineers, but all the pilots and crews—led by Colonel Antonio Sotelo—defected to the side of the rebels and landed their machines at Camp Crame. As the sixteen aviators walked smartly to Ramos's war room, they were wildly applauded. Nuns offered them flowers. All along EDSA cheering broke out. Commodore Tagumpay

Jardiniano, commander of the Naval Defense Force, announced to cheers of fifty officers that he had gone over to the rebel side for a "cause worth fighting for."[66] Soon thereafter in the Pasig River, a frigate moved into position and trained its guns on Malacañang. Two fighter jets were sent to attack rebels inside Camp Crame. After circling overhead, they broke off and landed at Clark Airbase, where they remained grounded for the remainder of the revolt.

At the same moment that the tide of battle at EDSA was shifting to the insurgents, Cory Aquino was told that Enrile was no longer mentioning her name. In effect, her advisers believed Enrile was seizing power for himself. She "called in the lawyers" and made preparations to take an immediate oath of office.[67] As a rumor spread that Marcos had left the country, crowds swelled to what some insisted were millions of people.[68] Only a few miles away inside Malacañang, Marcos ordered Channel 4 to broadcast him live so people would know he had not left the country. At 9:15 a.m., Marcos appeared on Channel 4, surrounded by his wife, Imelda, and his grandchildren. He declared a state of emergency and insisted he had no plans to resign. In the middle of his press conference, General Ver asked permission to attack Camp Crame. Marcos restrained his general, telling him "not to attack" and authorizing him only to use small arms fire.

Inside Camp Crame, Enrile sent troops to take over Channel 4. He also ordered a helicopter group armed with rockets to hit the area around the palace— but not the building itself. A few minutes passed before two truckloads of rebel soldiers surrounded Channel 4. Shots rang out as a sniper on the transmission tower defended the building. The rebels returned fire, killing the sniper. At 9:56 a.m. Marcos's image on Channel 4 blacked out. His forty-one minutes of airtime failed to rally sufficient support for him to remain president.

A half hour later, rebel helicopters attacked Malacañang and Villamor Air Base to destroy loyalist helicopters.[69] Six rockets were fired at the palace, and two soldiers guarding it were wounded. Enraged, General Ver ordered his air force to bomb Camp Crame, but the reply that came back indicated how far his situation had deteriorated: "Yes, Sir! Proceeding to bomb Malacañang Palace now!" So unanimous did the air force defect to the rebel side that, "The helicopters were busy all day Monday, February 24, firing warnings into the Malacañang Palace grounds, destroying three presidential helicopters at Villamor air base, and providing air cover to rebel troops who captured the government-controlled television station, Channel 4."[70] Inside liberated Channel 4, five ad hoc committees quickly formed to resume production, including ones for radio, TV, production, accreditation, and news. Outside the lobby, people cheered as a portrait of Marcos was carried out and burned. At 11:45 a.m., Radio Veritas resumed broadcasting, and at 1:25 p.m., Channel 4 went back on the air, this time promising "Now you will get the truth from this channel." Camera operators and technicians came back to work voluntarily, not knowing how the situation might turn out.

Late that afternoon, Ver sent a Marine battalion and army units on a "suicide assault" on Camp Crame. Learning of Ver's move, the U.S. embassy immediately notified Washington, and President Reagan was awoken. For the first time, he agreed to call publicly for the resignation of his old friend.[71] That night, the

Marcos family madly packed their vast wealth into crates—gold bullion, bonds, freshly printed currency, jewels, works of art, and cultural artifacts were all sent by boat to a staging area adjacent to the U.S. embassy. At 2:45 a.m. in Manila, Marcos put a call through to Senator Paul Laxalt of Nevada, who was meeting with Secretary Shultz and key members of Congress. Marcos wanted to know if Reagan had really called for him to leave. On another line, Imelda called Nancy Reagan to ask the same question. At about 5:00 a.m. their answers arrived. Laxalt counseled Marcos that "The time has come." Nancy told Imelda that they would be welcome to live in the United States if violence was avoided.[72]

Marcos adhered to his final instructions from Washington, but not all confrontations ended peacefully. A little past midnight, several people were wounded by loyalist soldiers who fired through barbed wire at citizens who blocked tanks trying to retake Channel 4. The next day, February 25, sporadic gun battles echoed through various parts of the city. Around 7:00 a.m., loyalist snipers reportedly wounded at least four people near Channel 9's transmission tower in Quezon City (far from the hundreds of thousands of people at EDSA and Malacañang).[73] Later that morning, both Aquino and Marcos were sworn in as the country's next president. In a battle to control the airwaves, about sixty insurgents shot it out with some thirty loyalist soldiers for control of Channel 9's transmitter—the only remaining channel broadcasting Marcos. When three Marcos loyalists climbed the transmitter tower to take the high ground, a helicopter gunship quickly killed them.[74] The attack incapacitated the transmitter, shutting down Channels 2, 9, and 13—and effectively blacking out Marcos's inauguration ceremony. Deprived of his last media outlet, Marcos's position was futile, but he still refused to surrender. At the junction of Tomas Morato and Timog around 3:46 p.m., a truck and jeep full of loyalists shot their way through crowds, wounding several people, to get through their barricades.[75]

That morning, Cory Aquino's inauguration ceremony at luxurious Club Filipino was sparsely attended. The wealthy group that assembled could not be certain they would prevail, yet like the signers of the Declaration of Independence in 1776, they were willing to stake their lives and fortunes on winning. According to an account in the *Manila Times*, "One is disappointed that none of the people of the lower orders of Philippine society is represented at the head table. Most of the people inside are still members of the old political families whose social and economic backgrounds put them in key positions to influence policy decisions. New forces in society crying out for recognition are invisible within the Club Filipino power elite."[76] Aquino quickly signed Executive Order Number 1 naming Enrile her defense minister (just as Marcos had done) and Ramos chief of staff of the armed forces.

In the streets around Mendiola, loyalist troops and citizens fought a running battle with thousands of citizens. A contingent of thirty priests and seminarians, including at least four foreign priests, stood between loyalist marines and protesters. A dozen people lay seriously wounded, but the quick action of the priests prevented more injuries.[77] Thousands of people remained in place, encircling the palace. Finally, all the troops were ordered away from Malacañang—but remained in the streets approaching it.

To seize control of television stations, rebel soldiers killed troops loyal to Marcos.
Photo by Pete Reyes in *People Power: An Eyewitness History*, 259.

About 9:00 p.m., five U.S. helicopters arrived to take Marcos away. At this, the very last moment, Enrile crossed the lines to say goodbye to his boss of thirty years. As Marcos departed, witnesses reported their meeting ended with a long embrace.[78] Another account told of Marcos refusing to get aboard and being compelled to leave.[79] As soon as the helicopters spirited the Marcos family away, people's cheers resounded across EDSA, including those from a contingent of gays and transvestites who happily screamed, "Marcos is gone! We will finally get to see Malacañang."[80] With marine guards gone, hundreds of people swept into the building, destroying documents, and looting—but leaving for posterity Imelda's discarded collection of three thousand pairs of designer shoes.

Still the contest was not complete. Once Marcos landed at Clark Air Base, he asked Ambassador Bosworth if he could spend time in his home province before going into exile. Bosworth called Aquino, but she insisted Marcos must leave straight away. Nonetheless, Marcos called his aides and ordered them to organize an "Ilocano Army" to take back Manila in a countercoup. The United States would hear nothing of it. The next morning, after a bitter exchange with U.S. officials, Marcos insisted on going home one last time. Finally he boarded his plane. Ordered to transport him out of the country, American pilots insisted they would not comply with his demands to go home. The former president had to be sedated to stop him from arguing.[81]

International Effects of People Power 1

Despite the many limitations of the regime that emerged to replace Marcos and the failure of the movement to develop into a social revolution, the 1986 People Power Uprising was clearly a great victory. By demonstrating the possibility of removing an entrenched dictatorship in a relatively bloodless manner, it nourished the dream of ordinary people's capacity to overthrow governments, no matter how powerful they may appear to be. Global repercussions of People Power reverberated immediately, generating a wave of insurgencies, as illegal occupation of public space by hundreds of thousands of citizens became a new tactic in the arsenal of popular movements. The appropriation of public space is an enduring tactic that continues to reappear all over the world—most recently in Cairo's Tahrir Square. Intense concentration of capital in contemporary societies has necessitated urban webs at the heart of the system. Without any party or central committee ordering them to do so, citizens have learned to take over such essential spaces, creating a demilitarized form of protest in which popular aspirations can be aired and movements nourished and sustained.

The Philippine People Power revolution helped animate the June Uprising of 1987 in South Korea, a nineteen-day marathon endeavor in which Christian groups also played a leading role.[82] In Taiwan, the overthrow of Marcos "was an inspiration to the middle class and made them realize it was time for democracy. It gave them hope that perhaps their own protest movement would succeed."[83] In 1998, students in Indonesia called themselves a "People Power movement" and helped overthrow longtime dictator Suharto (see chapter 10 below). During the Arab Spring, many insurgents labeled their movement "People Power." The 1986 uprising was itself a creation of global dynamics unleashed from the world-historical movements of 1968, in whose aftermath cross-border movement surges have grown in importance as international connections among movements emanate from the grassroots—and not only in Asia. The Philippine revolt against Marcos broke out only months after Haitian dictator Jean-Claude Duvalier was forced to flee; on page 12 is a photo taken in the streets of Manila during the uprising that depicts a protester with a handmade sign: "Marcos: Duvalier Waits for You!!!"

A decade after 1986, Manila's *Sunday Times* reported, "The entire world watched. Hundreds of correspondents had been sent from all over the world to cover the election. What they got was a ringside seat for a revolution—a bloodless revolution that observers worldwide are now studying so that they may apply the same system in some African and South American countries whose people have yet to rid themselves of their own versions of Marcos and Imelda."[84]

Cory Aquino passed away in 2009. Eulogizing her, Ramos remembered that, "For her, revolution was the first of the wave of 'velvet revolutions' that liberated countless millions from Manila to Seoul to Johannesburg to Prague, Warsaw and Moscow. President Aquino's 'People Power' revolution, indeed, is among the proudest moments in my country's history, and the distinctive contribution of our people to the saga of mankind's long struggle for freedom and dignity."[85] During a visit to Manila in 1995, Czech President Vaclav Havel noted, "Your peaceful People Power Revolution was an inspiration to us for our own revolution."

The Aquino Government

Limited to a political revolution in which power was transferred from one pro-American section of the Filipino elite to another, the overthrow of Marcos restored democracy in name only. Within a few weeks of coming to power, President Aquino freed political prisoners, including Jose Maria Sison, founder of the CPP then languishing in prison at Fort Bonifacio. Despite the best of intentions, she could not neglect her own people, the landowning wealthy who opposed land reform. Her government's lackadaisical approach to land reform drew criticisms even from her bastion of support in the World Bank—an institution she needed to help renegotiate the debt left by Marcos, at least $26 billion, a sum requiring 39 percent of the 1988 national budget to service.[86] She partially fulfilled her promise to make land available to the poor and enacted redistribution programs covering six million hectares, but she did not include more than two million hectares controlled by the country's superrich landowners—including her own holdings at Hacienda Luisita. A few weeks after she came into office, a U.S. State Department official reported, "Our objective was to capture . . . to encourage the democratic forces of the center, then consolidate control by the middle and also win away the soft support of the NPA. So far, so good."[87] U.S. financing assured her administration of economic success.

Human rights abuses were even a more glaring problem during Aquino's administration than under Marcos. Amnesty International reported that the overall number actually increased under Aquino.[88] During her first seven months in office, at least 239 cases of torture were reported. In that same period of time, her troops routinely destroyed villages in remote parts of the country as they conducted counterinsurgency operations. Dozens of mass evacuations of rural areas were ordered.[89] On November 13, 1986, labor leader Rolando Olalia was brutally assassinated. As head of the trade union confederation, Kilusang Mayo Uno (May First Movement), Olalia represented over eight hundred thousand workers. At the time, as many as three-fourths of all Filipinos lived in poverty, and many workers made little more than sixty cents an hour (half that for female sweatshop employees in Export Processing Zones, where global corporations were largely unregulated). Olalia was also secretary-general of Partido ng Bayan (People's Party), a broadly based coalition of many constituencies. At the intersection of so many grassroots forces, Olalia publicly spoke for peace between the government and the leftist NDF. His murder was rumored to be the work of people who favored stepping up the war against the insurgency, especially those close to Defense Minister Juan Ponce Enrile, but such allegations were never proven. His funeral march on November 20, 1986, was attended by tens of thousands.

In the days and weeks following the democratic upsurge, workers mobilized in strike actions that far exceed previous strike numbers, a dynamic also observed in South Korea.[90] A slowly building number of strikes in the late Marcos era gave way to a torrent of workers' demands for equitable compensation after the dictator was forced to flee. In 1986, there were 581 reported strikes—more than double the number of strikes in any year since 1972 with the exception of 1985, when there were 371. Aggregate days lost to strikes rose from a little more than half a million in 1983 to five times that many in 1986, as shown in TABLE 2.3.

Sadly, people's unity and optimism after their ouster of Ferdinand Marcos lasted only a few months: on January 22, 1987, at least twenty-one people were shot dead on Mendiola Bridge and nearly a hundred wounded when police opened fire on a peaceful demonstration of landless people piously requesting that the Aquino government make good on its campaign promises of land. With her own Mendiola massacre—killing more than three times the number of people in what her husband had called Marcos's "Black Friday" in 1970—Aquino's government lost much support—and Cory lost the Nobel Peace Prize she seemed certain to win.[91] The next month Aquino declared total war on communism, telling graduates of the Philippine Military Academy on February 11 that the time had come to "unsheathe the sword of war."

By February 1987, the ceasefire proclaimed on December 10, 1986, with the insurgent NPA collapsed. Artists like Renato Habulan, Orlando Castillo, and Pablo Baen Santos were some of the first to criticize publicly Aquino's drift away from her promises. Calling themselves "socialist realists," they helped to spark opposition against Aquino's conservative policies. On August 26, 1987, nearly two million workers and supporters marched against her policies, and two days later, the fifth and bloodiest coup attempt against her was mounted (the Honasan coup).

TABLE 2.3 **Strikes in the Philippines, 1983–1987**

Year	Number	Workers Involved	Aggregate Days Lost
1983	155	33,600	581,300
1984	282	65,300	1,907,800
1985	371	111,300	2,457,700
1986	581	169,500	3,637,900
1987	436	89,600	1,907,700

Source: ILO, *Year Book of Labor Statistics*; Stephen Haggard and Robert Kaufman, *The Political Economy of Democratic Transitions* (Princeton: Princeton University Press, 1995), 62.

Aquino quickly changed many of her positions. She permitted vigilante groups to carry arms and even praised one of them, NAKASAKA, as a manifestation of "people power." Before the end of 1987, she publicly endorsed the notoriously violent anticommunist vigilante group, Alsa Masa.[92] Aquino had helped legalize previously underground groups, like the People's Party, which found its members being killed since making itself public. Evidence points to the continuity in CIA involvement in death squads from Operation Phoenix in Vietnam to anticommunist death squads in the Philippines like Alsa Masa. Specifically Colonel James Rowe of the Joint U.S. Military Advisory Group and U.S. General John Singlaub are believed to have participated in the government's "total war" on insurgents.[93] Arrest warrants were issued once again for previously imprisoned political activists like Sison. (Unlike many others, he was able to find refuge in the Netherlands.)

The fact that the military and Catholic Church led the uprising, steering it in the direction of changing elite rulers, helped deprive the popular movement of its central role in the process of social transformation. Unlike South Korea, where the marginalized forces of the democracy movement were able to weed out many of the military dictatorship's elite and spread prosperity to a large middle class, in the Philippines the everyday lives of most people remain enchained in a web of poverty and domination. The fact that the possibility of systematic change was lost can be attributed to the character of the democracy movement—its leadership by the church hierarchy and military rather than by ordinary citizens. The possibility of real change was no illusion: As one observer explained, "Had Filipinos decided to go on and struggle for a more equitable distribution of wealth, the abolition of the military, or a decentralized government that was more responsive to their needs, who knows what more amazing things they might have achieved."[94] After her consolidation of power, Aquino eased RAM out of power. Some officers felt betrayed, and others believed they could do a far better job for the country than Aquino—and that they would be supported by a majority of people. Despite her elite support and apparent success, Aquino faced six attempted coups in her first year and a half in office.

Although Aquino liked to portray herself as a political neophyte who reluctantly agreed to run for president in order to get rid of Marcos, she was also heir to one of the nation's wealthiest family fortunes, and personally helped balance the books on her family's vast plantation enterprises. Ruling by decree (in much the same manner as Marcos) during her first eighteen months in office, her neoliberal policies—including market-based reforms like trade liberalization, exchange rate flexibility, privatization, and tax reform—restored short-term growth to the country's ailing economy.

A new constitution was drafted and elections held in 1987, but no organized pro-Marcos force even bothered to contest the elections. The new constitution limited the president's capacity to exercise emergency powers, and it also recognized health as a basic right—a huge victory for health workers.[95] Significantly it enshrined the role of NGOs and POs (People's Organizations) in the country's decision-making processes, asserting government shall encourage NGOs, "respect the role of POs," and facilitate "participation at all levels of decision-making." One of the lasting transformations Aquino helped accomplish was to encourage and stimulate NGOs among women (then estimated to earn only 39 percent of what men made).[96] In the 1980s, two different networks congealed, Lakas ng Kababaihan (Group of 10 or G-10), and the Women's Action Network for Development (WAND). In the mid-1990s these two groups contained some two hundred organizations. In 1989, a Philippine-U.S. women's solidarity organization formed; when it was five years old, GABRIELA (General Assembly Binding Women for Reform, Integrity, Leadership and Action) had more than a hundred organizations working with it; and KABAPA, a national women's group had about thirty thousand members.[97] The first public lesbian march took place in 1993.[98]

Aquino retired from the presidency as a heroic person in her nation's history, yet her record as president left much to be desired. Despite her many moralistic appeals and promises, Philippine politics remain corrupt and violence-prone. To no one's surprise but to many people's disappointment, the old elite remained firmly in control. In congressional and Senate elections on May 11, 1987, out of two hundred congressional seats, families traditionally in control of districts won 169. Some local officials were dismissed, but the new constitution's promises of agrarian reform and indigenous rights remained a dream. Along with six attempted coups d'état, Aquino faced two attempts to impeach her.

In August 1987, one of the bloodiest coups lasted for three days until it was finally brought to an end. Part of the support for Aquino arrived in the form of a motorcade of cars—in a society where a sizeable proportion of people barely have enough to eat and only a small proportion owned cars.[99] Although a 1991 decentralization law passed, power remained centralized in Manila. Once a legislature had been elected and a new constitution approved, GDP grew nearly 5 percent from 1987 to 1991, not numbers on a par with Asian tigers, but certainly robust when compared to less than 1 percent growth from 1981 to 1985 and a decline of nearly 8 percent in 1986.

As economic problems caused by the regime's consistent adoption of neoliberal policies emerged in 1989, Aquino raised the domestic price of oil, a move that immediately led to widespread protests and a military coup deemed a failure only after the United States let it be known that it would use airpower to keep the neoliberal Aquino regime in power.[100] Of the six coups launched against Aquino, the one in December 1989 attempted by RAM and the Young Officers Movement nearly succeeded. It was defeated only after defense secretary Fidel Ramos asked U.S. Ambassador Nicholas Plat for U.S. aircraft support to prevent rebel forces from attacking.[101] Once the U.S. aircraft had flown, the coup collapsed. In the words of one of its leaders, General Edgardo Abenina, "We were about to take over the government. Then the U.S. warplanes appeared. We simply cannot hope to win against the strong power of the U.S. air force."[102] In gratitude, Aquino did all she could to save the U.S. bases, even calling a mobilization at the Luneta. Few people attended, and on September 16, 1991, the Senate rejected a plan to extend the lease on U.S. bases.

Despite the pessimist appraisal of Filipina People Power sketched above, the impetus for change continued, notably in the successful mobilization against U.S. bases. Clark Airfield and the mammoth Subic Bay facility were finally closed by popular referendum—despite more than $1 billion annual aid provided by the United States to maintain them. While anti-Americanism played a central role in the Senate's failure to renew the leases, another factor was the declining financial contributions being made by the United States. Between the EDSA Uprising of 1986 and the 1991 decision to close the bases, U.S. aid totaled $750.19 million; in the same period, Japan sent $4.19 billion into the country.[103] By 1996, Japanese aid totaled more than $1 billion per year; U.S. aid was less than 5 percent of that figure—some $50 million annually—an apparent reversal of roles delineated in the secret Taft-Katsura Agreement of 1905 under which the Japan's colonization of Korea and U.S. rule of the Philippines were mutually agreed.[104] After Marcos was overthrown, Japanese corporations used the Asian Development Bank to lend money to themselves in order to build ports, roads, power plants, and other mammoth projects. Foreign corporate interests—not the needs of local people—defined the character and location of huge investments.

The IMF and World Bank substantially subsidized Aquino's government, and she was able to negotiate an "extraordinary" refinancing of the country's debt. By 1991, the regime was able to begin substantially paying down the principal after Aquino imposed a structural adjustment program that included import liberalization, lifting restrictions on financial markets, and privatization of public enterprises.[105] In 1992 obstacles to the flow of foreign currency were lifted. Soon huge trade deficits were felt, but their effect was offset by a debt-restructuring plan that substantially reduced payments. Monies sent home by Filipina workers abroad played a vital role in the country's economic growth. As the currency was devalued and exports as a portion of GDP rose, an anti-Aquino coalition formed, but the legislators were kept in IMF lockstep. The president of the Senate, a long-time opponent of structural adjustment programs, was replaced by an Aquino ally.

From Ramos to Estrada

A key leader of the 1986 uprising, Fidel Ramos ascended to the presidency in 1992. A graduate of West Point who had served in both Korea and Vietnam under American commanders, Ramos opened the country to foreign investments as never before. Under his neoliberal policies, the economy continued to grow, but not rapidly: GDP growth averaged 3.2 percent annually compared with 3.8 percent under Cory Aquino.[106] Foreign sources of money sent into the Philippines—especially by migrant workers—soared under Ramos, increasing from $24.65 billion during Aquino's tenure in office to $40.9 billion in the first three years of Ramos's administration.[107] So many Filipinas were finding employment in Japanese brothels masquerading as "entertainers" that the U.S. State Department eventually placed Japan on its watch list for trafficking.[108] Although government statistics indicated declining poverty, the number of homeless children begging in the major cities mushroomed, as did the presence of families living under bridges or out of pushcarts. One estimate told of 30 percent of Manila's population (about 2.5 million people) living as squatters in 1993.[109]

Ramos appointed some 150 retired officers to government posts and positions in state-owned enterprises, and he did his best to invite U.S. troops back to the Philippines. By the end of his term in office, he mounted an effort to change the constitution to permit him to continue as president. Only after NGOs and civil society successfully mobilized more than half a million people to flood the streets of Manila in 1997 did Fidel Ramos abandon his scheme to remain in power.[110]

In 1998—despite public opposition from Cardinal Sin, Cory Aquino, and the country's elite—Vice President Joseph Estrada, running on a platform openly opposing U.S. bases, won 40 percent of the vote in an eleven-candidate race for the presidency. President Estrada appointed distinguished economists to continue Ramos's free-market policies at the same time as he sought to transfer lands owned by absentee landlords to farmers who toiled on them. Like Ramos, Estrada had risen in the ranks under Marcos—and much of his campaign financing originated among former Marcos supporters. Once in power, he offered Imelda Marcos a favorable settlement of the government's claims against her wealth, and floated a proposal to allow foreigners to own land. Called into the streets by Sin, Aquino, and civil society leaders, in August 1999, thousands of protesters compelled him to back down.[111]

Unlike Ramos, Estrada's roots and base of support were among the country's poor, whose overwhelming support had propelled him into the presidency—and the president never shied away from showing his gratitude. "My only dream is to help the poor. . . . I would like to be known as the president who championed the cause of the masses," he told *Asiaweek* in early 2000. Although Estrada grew up in the upper-middle class, he dropped out of college to become an action movie star, a role in which he struck nationalist themes and championed the poor. Former mayor of a suburban city, he was elected vice president in 1992. Estrada's record was not entirely without merit. When he came into office, more than half the country lived in poverty, but with him in Malacañang, the poor felt they had a friend as president. More importantly, from January to November 2000, only eight extrajudicial killings were reported, as were only an equal number of disappearances—although two of the disappeared were later found alive.[112] Moreover, from 1999 to 2000 the number of reported rapes in the country declined substantially: from 903 to 650.[113]

The economy, however, was in disarray. GDP growth rate increased to around 4 percent, but the Philippines still had not recovered from the 1997 IMF crisis. By the end of 2000, when the rest of the region had returned to growth, the country stagnated: unemployment was still in double digits, the value of the peso remained low, and investments were few and far between.[114] Three administrations' neoliberal policies, especially lifting of restrictions on financial markets, led to increased vulnerability to global dynamics. Decades of compliance with neoliberal imperatives of international institutions devastated the economy. Within three years of honoring WTO commitments, four million jobs were lost, 710,000 in agriculture alone from 1996 to 1998.[115] As the country's reliance on imports grew, consumption of basic food decreased.[116] In the first decade since its WTO membership in 1995, rice imports increased by over a million metric tons—a 587 percent jump.[117] In the decade after Marcos's ouster, economic growth in the Philippines was a paltry 2.9 percent per year—compared to 7.8 percent per year in China and 6.3 percent annually in Indonesia during the same period of time.[118] When the IMF crisis of 1997 hit, the country weathered the crisis better than other more globally integrated economies, but like the entire region, many people suffered catastrophe. The stock exchange fell below 50 percent of its value in January 1998 compared to the year before. The exchange rate fell from 26.3 peso/dollar in July 1997 to 35 peso/dollar in 1998.[119] Unfinished buildings started to haunt the Manila skyline and property values plummeted.

People Power 2: From Estrada to Arroyo

While the economy's dim performance unsettled people, Estrada's lifestyle made him unacceptable to key forces that had overthrown Marcos: the church, the urban middle class, and the military. Publicly enjoying his many children from a bevy of "wives"—each living in a luxury residence—Estrada's ostentatious philandering meant he could never gain the approval of the Catholic hierarchy, so he courted fundamentalist Protestants and non-Vatican El Shaddai. He flaunted his "midnight cabinet"—a coterie of card-playing close friends with whom million dollar bets alternated with important decisions about the country's future. As much as he enraged the moralistic Catholic majority, Estrada's sexual conquests and public displays of wealth vicariously satisfied many of his poor constituents.

Estrada enriched himself and his cronies through sweetheart contracts. Although he promoted human rights in Asia—speaking on behalf of Anwar Ibrahim when the Malaysian prime minister was imprisoned and honoring the husband of Aung San Suu Kyi—he was less than generous with the Philippine press. After the *Manila Times* alleged his involvement in selling off public lands at reduced prices to benefit cronies, he compelled the paper's owners to sell it. He later tried to silence criticisms by the *Philippine Daily Inquirer*, but the paper refused to back down. After a falling out, one of his closest collaborators revealed illegal gambling profits, and the press was only too eager to carry the allegations prominently. Once the Pandora's box of presidential corruption had been opened, a slew of shell companies—perhaps six hundred in all—became visible, and Estrada's fortune, allegedly garnered through presidential privileges, became a hot topic for public discussions.

Beginning in October 2000, key players of EDSA 1—among them Cardinal Sin and Cory Aquino—began to rally people at the EDSA shrine the church had built to commemorate the 1986 uprising. More than two thousand activists launched KOMPIL 2, a coalition modeled on the one that helped overthrow Marcos.[120] Countermobilizations by Estrada supporters drew even larger crowds—as many as one million on November 11.[121] Nonetheless, in mid-November, the House of Representatives voted to impeach the president, and his trial in the Senate (a process almost the mirror image of U.S. constitutional procedures) began on December 7, 2000. This first trial of a Philippine president became a national sensation. The entire country was glued to their televisions every day starting when the proceedings began at 2:00 p.m. to their conclusion six or more hours later. Polls indicated that an astonishing 90 percent of people followed the trial closely or occasionally during its twenty-four-day duration. Experts testified the president had used a false name to open a bank account with tens of millions of dollars in it. He and his friends were shown to profit from artificially inflating stock prices and laundering illegal gambling proceeds using government banks and pension funds.

Well-attended rallies against Estrada were organized from distant Mindanao in the South (where he had stepped up the army's war against rebel fighters, displacing nearly a million people) to the Northern city of Baguio, where a sizeable contingent of gays and lesbians was part of mobilizations against the president.[122] Even fraternity boys at the University of Philippines found a way to join the festivities by jogging around campus wearing nothing but black ski masks.

Estrada's trial reached its decisive moment at 10:00 p.m. on January 16, 2001, when senators voted by a slim 11–10 margin not to open an envelope containing key evidence, thereby acquitting the president. Within hours, without anyone asking them to do so, thousands of protesters gathered at the EDSA shrine. KOMPIL had discussed the possibility of a massive mobilization and had agreed to wear black clothes, black ribbons, and black armbands—but not to gather at EDSA.[123] The experiences of hundreds of thousands of people in 1986 helped facilitate this spontaneous outburst. Once people began to assemble, text messaging spread the word so rapidly that circuits overloaded. Estimates told of as many as seventy million text messages a day during the uprising, so many that Globe wireless company brought in special equipment to make sure they got through.[124] NGO leaders involved in KOMPIL first went to Vice President Gloria Macapagal-Arroyo's house, where she insisted they all go to EDSA. They quickly formed into three shifts to coordinate the protests and brought in computers, printers, and cables to hook up a coordination center.

By midnight, Aquino and Sin had arrived, joining about twenty thousand others.[125] In the middle of the night, the crowd thinned considerably and the number of youthful rockers rose, but by the next afternoon, many people returned from a good night's sleep. The next evening, Sin told the gathering of about a hundred thousand to "Stay here until evil is conquered by good. Stay here until corruption is overcome by integrity." People listened and remained in the streets. While Cardinal Sin played an active role, only thirty out of a hundred bishops actively involved themselves in the protests.[126] When the peso fell to a record low against the dollar, traders walked out of the Manila stock exchange to demand Estrada's resignation.

On the third day, January 18, protests continued with no end in sight. The crowd grew to at least five hundred thousand; some estimated one million people.[127] Polls subsequently determined that 65 percent—perhaps even more—of the participants who gathered in Manila were from the upper 10 percent of the class structure.[128] Seeking compromise, President Estrada offered to allow the now infamous envelope to be opened in public—but it was already too late. At that same moment, the chief of the armed forces, General Angelo Reyes, was canvassing his top officers to determine in what direction they were leaning. Horrified to discover that a civil war among dissident factions within the military was possible, he decided on the morning of January 19 to preempt any such possibility. After calling Gloria Macapagal-Arroyo, Reyes telephoned the president and informed him of his decision to defect to the opposition. He beseeched Estrada to resign for the sake of the country. Then the entire military top brass went to EDSA amid cheers, as hundreds of thousands of people tasted victory. Applause and adulation soon gave way to a massive street party—more a carnival than protest—with confetti and firecrackers, not tear gas and bullets.

On the morning of January 20, leftist forces—veterans of innumerable street battles—led the throng from EDSA to Malacañang, where presidential security forces, police officers, and angry Estrada supporters were waiting. As the crowd was underway, Supreme Court Justice Davide quietly arrived at the near-empty EDSA shrine, where he swore in Arroyo as the country's new president, thereby averting what surely would have been a bloody confrontation at Malacañang—but sidestepping the constitutional procedure for removal of the president. Estrada also wished to avoid bloodshed, and he left the presidential palace to defuse the looming confrontation. Without any of the high drama of 1986, Arroyo became the new president. So smooth was the transition that on Monday, January 22, when financial markets opened, the peso returned to precrisis levels, and the stock market surged as foreign investors poured funds back into the country.[129]

People Power 2 built on the legacy of the 1986 uprising but was quite different than People Power 1, as detailed in TABLE 2.4.

People Power 2 further consolidated the military's prominence in the country's politics.[130] For Jose Abueva, "People Power 2 was a massive exercise in direct

On the third day of EDSA 2, people flooded the streets.
Source: *EDSA 2: A Nation in Revolt* (Manila: AsiaPix/Anvil, 2001), 147.

TABLE 2.4 **Comparison of People Power 1 and 2**

People Power 1: 1986	People Power 2: 2001
Marcos out, Aquino in	Estrada out, Arroyo in
New constitution	No new constitution
Limited role of NGOs	Major role of NGOs
Local government officials dismissed	Few local government officials dismissed
Cross-class alliance	Professionals and upper-middle class
Last four days of long movement	Three days to push out a corrupt president
Twelve people killed	No one killed
Military mutiny initiated the uprising	People spontaneously gathered at EDSA

democracy after the institution of impeachment had failed because of the inability of the senator-judges, and the senate as an institution, to act with the integrity, impartiality, and wisdom that the people had expected of them."[131] Such a view justifies Estrada's nonconstitutional ouster by referring to "direct democracy" to characterize the uprising. In fact, the defection of the military elite to Arroyo was what swung the outcome to her. Neither "mob rule"—as some in the foreign press believed—nor "direct democracy," EDSA 2 was a military coup brought on by mobilization of influential segments of society. As such, it demonstrated how NGOs might skillfully construct the correct constellation of forces to overthrow governments—including democratically elected ones. The kind of "direct democracy" that involves devolving power to neighborhoods and individual institutional settings like workplaces and universities, where people can directly manage their own affairs and determine their destinies through reasonable deliberation (as we saw in Gwangju in 1980), had little to do with Estrada's overthrow.

While People Power 2 took three days to push out a corrupt president, it was "the fruit of years of organizing."[132] People's accumulation of experiences since 1986 included activists who worked diligently to get Estrada out of the presidency. NGO activists organized by Dinky Juliano-Soliman took on the name Task Force Transition. Funded by the Ayala Foundation and the Metrobank Foundation, a core group of twenty-five to thirty people began meeting in November 2000.[133] Besides NGO activists, they included businesspeople, civil society people, and other leaders who worked to develop a specific plan for the first hundred days of a post-Estrada administration. Subgroups intensively discussed economic policy, social development, politics, and security (including some members of the military). One of their concerns was how quickly landowners had consolidated themselves after People Power 1. At one point, someone proposed the idea of a transitional revolutionary government, but the group's consensus was to follow constitutional procedure—meaning Arroyo would become president.

The preeminent role of NGOs in the uprising is a significant new dimension of People Power 2. Returning from fourteen years abroad in the early 1990s, sociologist Mary Racelis observed profound changes after People Power 1, that "Filipinos of all classes have been vigilant—fighting for, guarding, and nurturing their right to have a say in their country's development." In Racelis's view, thousands of NGOs and POs tell us "A vibrant civil society is being formed with parallels in no other country I know."[134] As I discuss in a subsequent chapter, NGOs are a powerful tool for mobilizations, and their effects are not entirely beneficial.

People Power 1 developed soon after the UN had legitimated NGOs as a forum for civic action, and Aquino's 1986 constitution, drafted by forty-eight commissioners she chose, specifically referred to NGOs and POs as part of the process of democratic governance. In Racelis's view, "proto-NGOs" could even be found in nineteenth-century Spanish colonial and Catholic organizations.[135] The heritage of grassroots organizing additionally includes 1960s Saul Alinsky–style community groups like the Urban Industrial Mission (a church-based organizing group also active in Korea, India, Indonesia, Sri Lanka, Kenya, and South Africa).[136] These earlier forms of grassroots activism may be seen as a basis for subsequent developments, but after People Power 1, the number and influence of NGOs mushroomed. The steady growth is remarkable, as TABLE 2.5 summarizes. Racelis reckoned that there were as many as ninety-five thousand NGOs in 2000, along with thirty-five thousand co-ops.[137]

EDSA 3: Poor People Power

Eleven days after Estrada vacated Malacañang, he insisted publicly that he was still president. In response, criminal charges of plunder were almost immediately filed against him, leading thousands of his supporters to gather at his home to protect him. On April 25, police arrived to arrest Estrada. After a four-hour stand-off, he agreed to be taken into custody peacefully. His supporters then marched to EDSA and kept vigil for five days, in what has become known as EDSA 3 or "Poor People Power." The number of people at the shrine exceeded those who had gathered for People Power 2.[138] Unlike the middle and upper-class constituents who

TABLE 2.5 **Number of Filipino NGOs and Unions, 1984–1997**

Year	NGOs	Trade Unions
1984	23,800	1,680
1985	26,100	1,868
1986	27,100	2,217
1987	28,700	2,694
1988	31,300	3,242
1989	34,000	3,793
1990	41,100	4,293
1991	44,400	4,843
1992	53,000	5,258
1993	57,200	5,836
1994	61,200	6,725
1995	70,200	7,283
1996	n/a	7,610
1997	n/a	8,576

Source: Aurel Croissant, *Von der Transition zur Defekten Demokratie* (Wiesbaden: Westdeutscher Verlag, 2002), 125, 160–61.

had compelled Estrada's removal, People Power 3 involved mostly slum dwellers from Manila's squatter colonies. At 2:00 a.m. on the morning of May 1, at least fifty thousand people formed a determined column and set off in the direction of the presidential palace where Arroyo had taken up residence. Massive police forces stopped them with water cannons, tear gas, and live ammunition. Pitched battles erupted, and when they were finally over, three citizens lay dead and more than a hundred had been wounded. Arroyo declared a state of national emergency and ordered arrests of opposition leaders—including three officers in her military. Although Poor People Power mobilized more people than People Power 2, the revolt lacked major support among the Church hierarchy, business community, trade unions, political parties, NGOs, and—most importantly—the military.

In the following years, Arroyo's regime plundered the treasury to the tune of billions of dollars, murdered hundreds of human rights workers, and reversed the popular mandate against the presence of U.S. troops in the Philippines. While Arroyo enriched herself, Estrada, accused of stealing less than $45 million (4 billion pesos) from public funds, was found guilty of two counts of plunder for receiving bribes from illegal gambling operations and stock manipulation. (He was acquitted of perjury.) The court ordered him to return less than $10 million (a little over 700 million pesos) in bank accounts and real estate—a pittance in comparison to what his successor stole. Arroyo's corruption became so terrible that activists who had helped overthrow Estrada and place her in the presidency became convinced they had not so much participated in a restoration of democracy as they had abetted an avaricious family's designs on wealth and power. The Arroyo family's stolen fortune is routinely estimated to be in the billions—not the millions of Estrada. With the tacit approval of the church and civil groups who brought her to power, her administration removed nearly all government regulation of foreign investment—opening the country to more intensified degradation, decapitalization, and debt.

Under President Arroyo, death squads emerged once again at the same time as U.S. troops were involved in suppressing the Muslim insurgency in Mindanao and other islands. After the Arroyo administration took office, more than ten judges and fifteen lawyers were killed—as were fifty media workers.[139] Since 2001, at least twenty-three church leaders—including pastors, priests, and a bishop— were murdered. In addition to the killings, thousands more people experienced torture, assault, illegal arrest, unlawful detention and displacement.[140] Between 2001 and July 2007, a minimum of 886 extrajudicial killings of social activists and 179 forced disappearances were reported. Almost none resulted in court investigations, let alone trials or convictions. In the first eight months of 2008, the AHRC reported forty-two killings by vigilantes in the country's South.[141] UN Special Reporter Philip Alston found the military to be responsible for the majority, especially private militias supported by the military. Bishop Alberto Ramento of the Iglesia Filipina Independiente was found dead in his parish on October 3, 2006. Police claim it was a burglary with homicide, but they neglected to report that the bishop had been threatened on at least three previous occasions for his work on behalf of the poor. Less than a month before his murder, he had openly

TABLE 2.6 **Average Number of Strikes, 1986–2003 (Philippines)**

Years	President	Average Number of Strikes
1986–1991	Aquino	308
1992–1997	Ramos	104
1998–2000	Estrada	70
2001–2003	Arroyo	39

Source: http://www.dole.gov.ph/news/details.asp?id=N000000242, accessed June 10, 2009.

called for President Arroyo to step down because of the government's failure to stop the wave of killings.[142]

The Arroyo administration's record of repression terrified many people, including workers who lost their willingness to strike when death squads patrolled at night. Arroyo presided over a country in which there were only thirty-six strikes in 2002, the lowest in twenty-one years.

As she finished serving the remainder of Estrada's electoral mandate, Arroyo clung desperately to power, telling an election official after the 2004 votes had already been placed that she desired a winning margin of at least one million. To no one's surprise, she got the numbers she was looking for. Whatever the level of voters' performance, however, democracy remains a precarious venture. President Gloria Arroyo survived a 2003 military rebellion, but was unable to push through constitutional amendments to permit her to serve beyond 2010.

Between 2001 and 2005, the country's top thousand corporations increased their net income by 325 percent, while seven of ten farmers were landless, and the prices fetched for their products declined because of cheap imports.[143] A handful of billionaires sits atop the economy—and as in a typical neoliberal pyramid—a 2006 IBON national survey found more than 70 percent of people considered themselves poor.[144] So badly are ordinary Filipinos doing that per capita food consumption is declining, as TABLE 2.7 portrays.

Foreign investment has poured back into the region in the past decade, but the Philippines continues to lose huge investments to Thailand and faces growing competition in electronics from China (which accounts for more than half of Philippine exports). Government borrowing has left little money for banks to lend to businesses to create new jobs, leaving the country in a stagnant, or even deteriorating, economic dilemma. While GNP increased, family income from 2003 to 2006 declined slightly to $3,200 per year.[145] Per capita food supply decreased

TABLE 2.7 **Mean Per Capita Daily Food Consumption, in Grams**

Food Group	1978	1982	1987	1993
Cereals	367	356	345	340
Fish, Meat, Poultry	133	154	157	147
Vegetables	145	130	111	106
Fruits	104	102	107	77
Miscellaneous	104	102	107	77

Source: Bureau of Fisheries and Aquatic Resources, Alice Raymundo, "Trade Liberalization and the Struggle for Food Sovereignty in the Philippines," in *Putting People at the Centre: Human Security Issues in Asia*, ed. Anuradha M. Chenoy, (New Delhi: ARENA, 2006), 138.

TABLE 2.8 **Estimated Percentage of Underweight and Underheight Children**

	1989–90	1992	1993	1996	1998	2001
0–5 Years Old Underweight	34.5	34.0	29.9	30.8	32.0	30.6 (3.670 million)
0–5 Years Old Underheight	39.9	36.8	34.3	34.5	34.0	31.4 (3.766 million)
6–10 Years Old Underweight	34.2	32.5	30.5	28.3	30.2	32.9 (3.065 million)
6–10 Years Old Underheight	44.8	42.8	42.2	39.1	40.8	41.1 (3.828 million)

Sources: Food and Nutrition Research Institute, "2001 Updating of Nutritional Status of Filipino Children of the Regional Level"; Raymundo, "Trade Liberalization," 139

in 2000–2001 from the previous year.[146] The hardest hit are the young, who are still underweight and underheight, as shown in TABLE 2.8.

The anti-neoliberal movement congealed around Stop the New Round Coalition and joined international efforts to stop the 2003 Cancun WTO negotiations. A Confederation of Farmers, Fishers, and Rural Women's Organizations was formed from twenty-eight provincial federations, and the group sponsored Sumilao farmers' continuing struggle for lands. Linked to Via Campesina and the Cancun anti-WTO protests, the group was inspired by Korean farmers and began a 1,700 km march to Manila in 2008.[147] Besides the reformist opposition, communists are estimated to have between 6,000 and 10,000 armed members in more than a hundred guerrilla fronts—down from a high of more than 25,000 in the late 1980s.[148] In their liberated areas, they have established cooperatives, reduced land rent, liberated women, and created the basis for grassroots empowerment. While the NPA's power base has been weakened, the Moro Islamic Liberation Front and Moro National Liberation Front were estimated to have anywhere from 10,000 to 160,000 well-trained troops complete with anti-aircraft defenses as early as 1995.[149]

In February 2008, claiming there was a plot to assassinate president Arroyo by Islamic groups (or by the communist NPA—which ever suited its purposes), the armed forces put the Philippine military on full alert one day before demonstrations were scheduled by a broad coalition accusing the president of corruption and calling for her resignation.[150] NGOs and other civil society groups planned the protests in response to Senate testimony confirming suspicions that the president's husband, Jose Miguel Arroyo and another crony were going to receive $130 million in kickbacks from a $329 million broadband project between the government and a Chinese company. While the contract was subsequently cancelled, the Arroyo family's wealth continued to soar—as did repression needed to safeguard it. Even the government's crack investigator was assassinated as he left home.[151] In June 2009, the opposition successfully defeated a proposal by Arroyo and her allies to change the constitution away from a presidential system—a transparent move to permit Arroyo to remain the country's leader as prime minister. Many people were reminded of Marcos's imposition of martial law in 1972 to perpetuate his own presidency.

According to World Bank figures in 2007, one quarter of the workforce—some eight million Filipinos—work overseas. As the country's leading export, they send home about $17 billion a year, accounting for 13 percent of gross domestic product. At home, as Arroyo and the elite enriched themselves, the poor have little choice but to gaze abroad—leaving their homeland increasingly impoverished. Remittances by workers abroad totaled at least $7.56 billion in 1996—not counting money hand carried back into the country.[152] A recent report showed there were an average of thirty-five thousand annual reports by workers abroad of abuse ranging from failure to receive wages to rape and murder.

Despite the success of two uprisings in forcing corrupt presidents from office, the Filipino people have failed to change significantly their social system. The 1986 uprising has become loved internationally yet its empirical history reveals that it accomplished a transfer of power from one section of the pro-U.S. elite to another. The central role of armed units of the military and the conservative Catholic hierarchy (supported by the U.S. government and CIA) leaves people discussing even today whether it was the hand of God or those of the CIA, the power of the people or of the military's guns, that overthrew Marcos. Of course, it was the combination of all those forces. The Left's boycott of elections permitted pro-U.S. forces to seize the historic opening and manage the uprising.

Both successful uprisings—People Power 1 and 2—combined vast popular mobilizations of hundreds of thousands of people with support from the military. In 1986, the rebels in the armed forces took the initiative, but by themselves they would in all likelihood not have had sufficient forces to defeat an all-out counterattack by Marcos's forces. The protection afforded by people in the streets was vital to the uprising's success.

During People Power 2, the popular mobilization came first from the spontaneous initiative of thousands of people, many of whom had experiences in People Power 1. People knew where to gather and what to bring. Many veterans of People Power 1 arrived with their children. At that time, NGO activists were far better organized than in 1986, and the defection of the chiefs of all armed services, so critical to the movement's ouster of Estrada, came as the final act—not the opening scene. People Power 2 demonstrated how activist leadership—through advance planning and careful preparation—can seize the initiative. The NGO leaders who prepared an agenda for the first hundred days of the new administration provide a great model for people involved in future uprisings. While they were disappointed by their betrayal at the hands of Arroyo, a member of their group who became president, even that betrayal carries a valuable lesson: the shortcomings of relying upon individual leaders, especially when not subject to immediate recall.

The failure of Poor People Power was a result of the armed forces and police remaining loyal to the Arroyo presidency—a faithfulness they enforced through guns and clubs. Without the military's defense of her presidency, Arroyo would probably have been forced from office.

While popular insurgencies seem doomed to fail without support from within the military, the failure of coup after coup reveals the impotence of the military without popular movements. To their credit, the Philippine military—unlike those in Burma and Thailand—refrained from using overwhelming force against citizens as a means to enforce their views on the people.

The changeover from Marcos's "cronies" to transnational capital suited international investors, like the Carlyle Group. The hero of People Power 1 and subsequently Philippine president Fidel Ramos was Carlyle Asia Advisory Board member until 2004. (Carlyle has had connections to both U.S. presidents Bush as well as members of the Bin Laden family.) Here is graphic illustration of the ways in which People Power uprisings serve the interests of transnational capital. The country's economic and social structures remain fundamentally unchanged. In 2010, Aquino's son (Benigno S. Aquino III) was elected president, and Marcos's widow, son, and daughter all won seats in Congress, testament to a handful of families' continuing domination of Filipina politics.

While People Power failed to transform the underlying economic Philippines society, it inspired movements around the world. That may well be its most lasting contribution.

NOTES

1 Mercado, *People Power*, 226, 258, 308.
2 Interview with Senator Gregorio Honasan, Manila, June 2, 2009.
3 Interview with F. Sionil José, Manila, June 1, 2009.
4 Leon Wolff, *Little Brown Brother* (Baltimore: Johns Hopkins University Press, 2006). Two hundred thousand is a very conservative figure of Filipinos killed by the U.S. military. John Tirman estimated a *minimum* of that number and as many as four hundred thousand people. See *The Deaths of Others* (New York: Oxford University Press, 2011), 18.
5 See John J. Carroll, *Forgiving or Forgetting: Churches and the Transition to Democracy in the Philippines* (Manila: Institute on the Church and Social Issues, 1999), 10; Benedict Anderson, "Cacique Democracy in the Philippines," *New Left Review* 169 (May–June 1988): 13, 14, 19.
6 F. Sionil José, "Literature as History," speech at Stanford University, May 5, 2005. Copy given to me by the author.
7 F. Sionil José, "Why Are We a 'Nation of Servants'?" *Philippine Star*, April 5, 2009.
8 Lorna Kalaw-Tirol, ed., *1996: Looking Back, Looking Forward* (Manila: Foundation for Worldwide People Power, 1995), 166; Joseph Yu, "Elections and Poverty," *Education for Development* 6, no. 2 (March–April 2007): 23. As government expenditures on education decline, the number of secondary school teachers fell from 1996 to 2004 (from over 145,000 to 120,000). Edna E.A. Co et al., *Philippine Democracy Assessment: Economic and Social Rights*, 122.
9 Immediately after Marcos's ouster, Jose Almonte was officially empowered to seek return of these monies. He documented U.S. $3.8 billion "ready for release" in late 1986 and identified another $4 billion. His Swiss contacts led him to believe the government should be able to recover between $10 and $20 billion (Almonte, *My Part*, 2006, 20). Donald Kirk estimated the Marcos fortune at $8.5 billion and reported that some $48 billion "disappeared" from government holdings since 1983. Donald Kirk, *Philippines in Crisis: U.S. Power versus Local Revolt* (Manila: Anvil Publishing, 2005), xiii, 179. Ackerman and Duvall, *A Force More Powerful*, 373. Although some believe only about $400 million of Marcos's loot has been recovered, in 1998, the *New York Times* estimated the Marcos holdings at somewhere between $5 and $10 billion, and reported that about $1 billion of the hidden money had been returned (Seth Mydans, "Suharto and Co.," *New York Times*, May 25, 1998, A6).
10 Anderson, "Cacique Democracy," 21–22.
11 Raymond Bonner, *Waltzing with a Dictator* (New York: Times Books, 1987), 307–9; Anderson, "Cacique Democracy," 23.

12 Kirk, *Philippines in Crisis*, vi.
13 See Benigno Aquino Jr., *A Garrison State in the Making* (Manila: Benigno S. Aquino Jr. Foundation, 1985), 243.
14 Almonte, *My Part*, 7–8.
15 Interview with Senator Gregorio Honasan, Manila, June 2009.
16 Manuel L. Quezon III, "The Long View: Left and Right Sides of People Power," *Philippine Daily Inquirer*, January 5, 2009.
17 Daniel Schirmer and Stephen Shalom, eds., *The Philippines Reader* (Boston: South End Press, 1987), 315–16. This estimate may be a bit high. Other sources place the number of mainstream fighters at twenty-four thousand, about half of whom were armed.
18 Lawyers Committee for Human Rights, *Vigilantes in the Philippines: A Threat to Democratic Rule* (New York: 1988), 3.
19 Haggard and Kaufman, *Political Economy*, 48.
20 Joseph Y. Lim, "The Philippines and East Asian Economic Turmoil," in *Tigers in Trouble: Financial Governance, Liberalisation and Crises in East Asia*, ed. Jomo K.S. (London: Zed Books, 1998), 199–200.
21 Conversation with Ed Baker, Cambridge, Massachusetts, 2007. On the day I visited the Tarlac museum dedicated to Aquino, his address book from his days in Massachusetts happened to be open to the page beginning with letter K. Beneath entries for Ted Kennedy and Stanley Karnow were two phone numbers for Kim Dae Jung.
22 Schirmer and Shalom, *Philippines Reader*, 322–23.
23 Lee Jae-eui, "Operation Fascinating Vacation," in *The Kwangju Uprising: Eyewitness Press Accounts of Korea's Tiananmen*, eds., Henry Scott-Stokes and Lee Jae-eui (Armonk: M.E. Sharpe, 2000), 40.
24 Huntington, *Third Wave*, 199.
25 One estimate put the number of theater groups at four hundred by 1987. Eugène Van Erven, *The Playful Revolution: Theater and Liberation in Asia* (Bloomington: Indiana University Press, 1992), 92.
26 Bach M. Macaraya, *Workers' Participation in the Philippine People Power Revolution* (Manila: Friedrich Ebert Stiftung, 1988), 42–43.
27 Randolf David, "A Movement Dies, a Regime Is Born," *Kasarinlan* 3 (1988), 3.
28 Santiago, *1986*, 12.
29 Mercado, *People Power*, 48.
30 Huntington, *Third Wave*, 82.
31 Robinson, *Promoting Polyarchy*, 130.
32 Mercado, *People Power*, 71.
33 Stanley Karnow, *In Our Image: America's Empire in the Philippines* (New York: Random House, 1989), 414.
34 "The Philippine Revolution and the Involvement of the Church," (Manila: Social Research Center of University of Santo Tomas, 1986), 12; Macaraya, *Workers' Participation*, 49.
35 Patricio N. Abinales, "When a Revolution Devours Its Children," in *The Revolution Falters: The Left in Philippine Politics After 1986*, ed. Patricio N. Abinales (Ithaca: Cornell Southeast Asia Program, 1996), 156–57.
36 Patricio Abinales estimated that NPA/CPP had 16,018 regular fighters under arms in 1986. See ibid., 169. Of course, the People Power uprising precipitated a crisis among the CPP, especially since the boycott was a monumental error that marginalized the party in the time of unparalleled motion among the Filipina people. After the uprising's success in expelling Marcos, dissent was openly voiced within the party, and the ensuing divergence of opinions led to several splits—all of which rendered the group increasing irrelevant. See Kathleen Weekley, "From Vanguard to Rearguard," in *The*

Revolution Falters: The Left in Philippine Politics After 1986, ed. Patricio N. Abinales (Ithaca: Cornell Southeast Asia Program, 1996), 30, 53.

37 Interview with Senator Gregorio Honasan, Manila, June 2, 2009.
38 Patricio Mamot, *Profile of Filipino Heroism* (Quezon City: New Day Publishers, 1986), 52.
39 Santiago, *1986*, 38.
40 Ibid., 25, 32.
41 Ibid., 54.
42 Ibid., 53.
43 Ibid., 38.
44 Fidel Ramos quoted in ibid., 52.
45 Ibid., 53. There was another first as well here. James Carroll told me that this was "the first time the church had approved revolution in advance" (interview with the author, Manila, June 4, 2009).
46 Sterling Seagrave, *The Marcos Dynasty* (New York: Harper and Row, 1988), 414, as quoted in Santiago, *1968*, 55.
47 Ibid., 172.
48 Ibid., 41.
49 Ibid., 60.
50 M. Bernad, ed., *Conversations with F. Sionil Jose* (Quezon City: Vera Reyes, 1991), 215, as quoted in Joseph Scalise, "Articulating Revolution: Rizal in F. Sionil Jose's *Rosales Saga*." (Essay in author's possession.)
51 The EDSA Revolution website, http://library.thinkquest.org/15816/therevolution.article5.html
52 Seagrave, *The Marcos Dynasty*, 415, as quoted in Santiago, *1968*, 79.
53 Yolanda Lacuesta, quoted in ibid., 65.
54 Ibid., 169.
55 Ibid., 194.
56 Ibid., 135, 141.
57 Interview with Dinky Corazon Juliano-Soliman, Manila, June 2, 2009.
58 Bonifacio Tupaz, president of the Trade Unions of the Philippines and Allied Services, was interviewed on July 9, 1987. See Macaraya, *Workers' Participation*, 12–13.
59 Ibid., 36.
60 Benedict Kerkvliet and Resil Mojares, *From Marcos to Aquino: Local Perspectives* (Honolulu: University of Hawaii Press, 1992), 4.
61 Santiago, *1968*, 87.
62 Interview with James Carroll, Manila, June 4, 2009.
63 Santiago, *1968*, 95.
64 Interview with James Carroll, Manila, June 4, 2009.
65 Santiago, *1968*, 99.
66 Ibid., 108.
67 Ibid., 112.
68 *Sunday Inquirer Magazine*, June 1, 1986; *Bulletin Today*, February 25, 1986 as cited in Santiago, *1968*, 130. Using space and density of people as a guide, an interesting calculation of the number of people at EDSA, Luneta, Liwansang Bonifacio, and Ugarte Field placed the number between 1,986,376 and 2,494,028. This figure, however, included space occupied by cars, monuments, trees, buildings, and posts. It therefore seems to safe to say there were over one million people in the streets supporting the insurgents. See Renato Constantino, *Malaya*, April 30, 1986, reprinted in Santiago, *1968*, 131–32.
69 Mercado, *People Power*, 308.
70 Ackerman and Duvall, *Force More Powerful*, 390.
71 Santiago, *1968*, 137.

72 Ibid., 151.

73 Mercado, *People Power*, 232.

74 Mercado, *People Power*, 258.

75 Santiago, *1968*, 170.

76 Amando Doronila in *Manila Times*, February 26, 1986, cited in Santiago, *1968*, 161.

77 Mercado, *People Power*, 241.

78 Santiago, *1968*, 180.

79 Arturo Aruiza, *Ferdinand E. Marcos: Malacañang to Makiki* (Quezon City: ACA, 1991), 159–60. Col. Aruiza was Marcos's aide for over two decades.

80 Santiago, *1968*, 182.

81 Santiago, *1968*, 197.

82 Lee Jae-eui, "The Seventeen Years of Struggle to Bring the Truth of the Gwangju Massacre to Light," in *Gwangju in the Eyes of the World*, 143.

83 V.G. Kulkarni and Rodney Tasker, "Promises to Keep," *Far Eastern Economic Review* 159 (February 29, 1996): 22–23.

84 Joaquin R. Roces in *Sunday Times Magazine*, reprinted in Santiago, *1986*, 173. This insight is borne out by my interviews. In exile after being released from long-term imprisonment, Filipino activist Edicio de la Torre was asked by South African ANC leaders to interpret events in the Philippines in order to optimize their own democratic transition. Interview with de la Torre in Manila, June 5, 2009.

85 Fidel Ramos, "Vale Cory Aquino: a lifetime of service and a precious legacy," *Taipei Times*, August 12, 2009.

86 Walden Bello, *The Anti-Development State: The Political Economy of Permanent Crisis in the Philippines* (Manila: Anvil Publishers, 2009), 13. Other estimates of the debt left by Marcos were as high as $56 billion, much of it in loans floated to the dictatorship by the IMF and World Bank. By 2005, the nation's debt had soared to around $70 billion.

87 Robinson, *Promoting Polyarchy*, 139.

88 Kathleen Weekley, "From Vanguard to Rearguard," 54. Also see the data in Kalaw-Tirol, *1996*, 79.

89 Van Erven, *Playful Revolution*, 56–57.

90 See *Asia's Unknown Uprisings Volume 1*, chapter 10.

91 Interview with F. Sionil Jose, Manila, June 1, 2009.

92 David, "A Movement Dies," 5; Lawyers Committee for Human Rights, *Vigilantes*, 139–43.

93 Roland Simbulan, "The CIA's Hidden History in the Philippines," Lecture at the University of the Philippines, August 18, 2000.

94 "People Power in the Philippines," http://fragmentsweb.org/TXT2/philiptx.html.

95 Maria Ela L. Atienza, "Health Devolution and Central-Local Relations in the Philippines: The Tripartite Partnership of the Department of Public Health, Local Government Units and Civil Society Organizations," *Journal of Democracy and Human Rights* 9, no. 1 (April 2009): 241; Interview with Mary Racelis, Manila, May 29, 2009.

96 GABRIELA, *The Situation of Women under the Estrada Administration*, 1999 as cited in Philippine Alliance of Human Rights Advocates (PAHRA), *Human Rights Report, 2000: A Prelude to Estrada's Curtain Call* (Quezon City: 2001), 73. Female labor force participation comprised only 49 percent of women in 1995, while the male rate was 82 percent. Miriam Coronel Ferrer, "Human Rights and Democracy in the Philippines," in *Democracy and Human Rights in the New Millennium*, International Symposium on the 20th Anniversary of the Kwangju Uprising Program (Gwangju: May 18 Institute, 2000), 141.

97 Carolyn I. Sobritchea, "Engendering Democracy and Nation-Building," in *Democratization Movements and Women*, Conference Proceedings of the Third 5.18

Memorial International Conference for Democratization and Human Rights (Gwangju: Chonnam National University May 18 Institute, 2002), 94. At the same time, the United States financed KABATID, a network of elite women designed to compete with existing feminist organizations and to advocate U.S. interests, such as maintaining U.S. bases and keeping the ban on the Communist Party and Left forces. See Robinson, *Promoting Polyarchy*, 132–33.

98 Amrita Basu, "The Many Faces of Asian Feminism," *Asian Women* 5 (Fall 1997): 11.

99 Vincent Boudreau, "Of Motorcades and Masses: Mobilization and Innovation in Philippine Protest," in *The Revolution Falters: The Left in Philippine Politics After 1986*, ed. Patricio N. Abinales (Ithaca: Cornell Southeast Asia Program, 1996), 60.

100 Haggard and Kaufman, *Political Economy*, 225.

101 Eva-Lotta E. Hedman, "Beyond Boycott: The Philippine Left and Electoral Politics After 1986," in *The Revolution Falters: The Left in Philippine Politics After 1986*, ed. Patricio N. Abinales (Ithaca: Cornell Southeast Asia Program, 1996), 90.

102 Kalaw-Tirol, *1996*, 57.

103 Kirk, *Philippines in Crisis*, 174.

104 See *Asia's Unknown Uprisings Volume 1*, chap. 2.

105 Haggard and Kaufman, *Political Economy*, 219.

106 Kalaw-Tirol, *1996*, 110–11.

107 Ibid., 138.

108 Kirk, *Philippines in Crisis*, 226.

109 Kalaw-Tirol, *1996*, 150.

110 Muthiah Alagappa, ed., *Civil Society and Political Change in Asia: Expanding and Contracting Democratic Space* (Stanford: Stanford University Press, 2004), 4.

111 Mary Racelis, "New Visions and Strong Actions: Civil Society in the Philippines," in *Funding Virtue: Civil Society Aid and Democratic Promotion*, eds. Marina Ottaway and Thomas Carothers (Washington: Carnegie Endowment, 2000), 179.

112 See PAHRA, *Human Rights Report*, 39–42.

113 Ibid., 74.

114 Carl H. Lande, "The Return of 'People Power' in the Philippines," *Journal of Democracy* 12, no. 2 (April 1991): 92.

115 Alice Raymundo, "Trade Liberalization and the Struggle for Food Sovereignty in the Philippines, in Anuradha M. Chenoy, *Putting People at the Centre: Human Security Issues in Asia* (New Delhi: ARENA, 2006), 132.

116 See IBON Database and Research Center, *WTO: Supreme Instrument for Neoliberal Globalization* (Manila: IBON Books, 2005).

117 IBON Foundation, "RP is Asia's Top Rice Importer," *Education for Development* 6, no. 2 (March–April 2007): 10.

118 Amando Doronila, ed., *Between Fires: Fifteen Perspectives on the Estrada Crisis* (Makati and Pasig: Inquirer Books and Anvil Publishing, 2001), 101.

119 Jomo, *Tigers in Trouble*, 213.

120 Jennifer C. Franco, "The Philippines: Fractious Civil Society and Competing Visions of Democracy," in *Civil Society and Political Change in Asia: Expanding and Contracting Democratic Space*, ed. Muthiah Alagappa (Stanford: Stanford University Press, 2004), 123; Doronila, *Between Fires*, 239.

121 Doronila, *Between Fires*, 15, 240.

122 Sheila S. Coronel, *EDSA 2: A Nation in Revolt* (Pasig City: Anvil, 2001), 17; Lande, "The Return," 94, cites sources giving the figure at between five hundred thousand and one million on January 18. For Mindanao displacements, see PAHRA, *Human Rights Report*, 27.

123 Interview with Dinky Corazon Juliano-Soliman, Manila, June 4, 2009.

124 Coronel, *EDSA 2*, 127; Interview with Dinky Corazon Juliano-Soliman, Manila, June 4, 2009.

125 Doronila, *Between Fires*, 171.

126 John J. Carroll, "Civil Society, the Churches, and the Ouster of Erap," in Doronila, *Between Fires*, 246.

127 PAHRA, *Human Rights Report*, 9.

128 Doronila, *Between Fires*, 8.

129 Lande, "The Return," 96.

130 Teresa S. Encarnacion Tadem, "Philippine Social Movements and the Continuing Struggle to Confront the Challenges of the Martial Law Period," *Journal of Democracy and Human Rights* 9, no. 1 (April 2009): 281.

131 Doronila, *Between Fires*, 83.

132 Interview with Dinky Corazon Juliano-Soliman, Manila, June 2, 2009.

133 Ibid.

134 Mary Racelis, "From the Fringes to the Mainstream," *Intersect* 8, no. 4 (April–May 1994): 7–8, as cited in Kalaw-Tirol, *1996*, 30.

135 Racelis, "New Visions, Strong Actions," in *Funding Virtue*, 164.

136 Interview with Edicio de la Torre, Manila, June 5, 2009.

137 Racelis, "New Visions, Strong Actions" 160–61, 181. As Racelis notes, from 1980 to 1997 U.S. AID contributed $54.5 million to Philippine NGOs and U.S. private voluntary agencies in the country; and in 1991, foreign donors gave $102 million to NGOs. Thus, there is some question whether or not these agencies are actually nongovernmental.

138 Coronel, *EDSA 2*, 226.

139 Asia Human Rights Commission, *The State of Human Rights in Eleven Asian Nations— 2006* (Hong Kong, 2006), 222.

140 IBON Foundation, *A New Wave of State Terror in the Philippines* (Manila: IBON Books, 2005), 59.

141 Asian Human Rights Commission, "Arbitrary Deprivation of Life in the Philippines," (Hong Kong, September 2008), 3.

142 Asian Human Rights Commission, "Rotten to the Core: Unaddressed Killings, Disappearances and Torture in the Philippines," *Article 2 of the International Covenant on Civil and Political Rights* 6, no. 1 (February 2007): 43.

143 Antonio Tujan Jr., "Political Killings Stem from Opposition to Arroyo's Economic Policies," *Education for Development* 6, no. 2 (March-April 2007): 7.

144 Ibid., 74.

145 Tadem, "Philippine Social Movements," 286.

146 Edna E.A. Co et al., *Philippine Democracy Assessment: Economic and Social Rights* (Pasig City: Anvil Publishing, 2007), 19.

147 Interview with Raul Socrates Banzuela, Manila, May 30, 2009.

148 Kirk, *Philippines in Crisis*, 151; Information Bureau, CPP, *Images of the New People's Army* (2004), xi.

149 Kalaw-Tirol, *1996*, 140; PAHRA, *Human Rights Report* estimated the strength of MILF at eight thousand to forty thousand; the group claimed 120,000 armed and unarmed fighters and many more supporters (20).

150 Carlos H. Conde, "Philippines on Alert After Plot," *New York Times*, February 15, 2008.

151 Keith Bradsher, "The Philippines Struggles to Cope with Deficits and Insurgents," *New York Times*, October 26, 2003.

152 Kirk, *Philippines in Crisis*, 182.

CHAPTER 3

Burma

It is not power that corrupts, but fear.

—Aung San Suu Kyi

Any high-ranking army officer who had taken an armed infantry unit into the capital and declared his support for the uprising would have become a national hero immediately, and the tables would have been turned.

—Bertil Lintner

CHRONOLOGY

March 12, 1988	Tea shop incident; Rangoon Institute of Technology students attacked
March 15, 1988	Dozens of students killed while marching in Rangoon
March 18, 1988	Major protests in downtown Rangoon set fire to government buildings
March 21, 1988	Dozens of police and protesters killed in heavy fighting in Rangoon
July 23, 1988	Ne Win resigns and names Sein Lwin ("the Butcher") as his successor
August 3, 1988	Amid peaceful protests, people use "People Power" to describe themselves
August 8, 1988	8:08 a.m., dockworkers go on strike; marches all over the country
August 8, 1988	11:30 p.m., army opens fire, killing hundreds of people
August 19, 1988	Sein Lwin resigns
August 19, 1988	Maung Maung forms government; strike councils control most cities and towns

August 26, 1988	Aung San Suu Kyi makes first public speech to half a million people
September 8, 1988	More than a million people march in both Rangoon and Mandalay
September 18, 1988	Hundreds killed as Saw Maung seizes power and represses councils
September 19, 1988	Killings continue
September 24, 1988	National League for Democracy (NLD) forms
October 3, 1988	General strike collapses
July 20, 1989	Aung San Suu Kyi is placed under house arrest for most of next twenty-one years
May 27, 1990	NLD wins more than 58 percent of the vote and 392 of 492 seats in elections
May 28, 1990	Military ignores election results, arrests winners, and rules with iron fist
December 19, 1990	Escaped parliamentary representatives form government in exile
October 14, 1991	Aung San Suu Kyi wins Nobel Prize
August 15, 2007	Regime raises fuel prices more than 100 percent
August 18, 2007	"Generation 88" mobilizes hundreds of protesters; massive arrests ensue
September 5, 2007	"Saffron Revolution" erupts as hundreds of monks march
September 18, 2007	Daily protests by thousands of monks begin
September 26, 2007	Army attacks monks in Rangoon; many people killed
September 27, 2007	Monasteries raided; thousands of people arrested
May 2, 2008	Cyclone Nargis strikes Burma; more than 138,000 people perish
November 7, 2010	New elections under a constitution created by the military; boycott by NLD
November 13, 2010	Aung San Suu Kyi released from detention

THE WINDS OF change emanating from the Philippines and Korea lifted the spirits of people in Burma, who chafed under the yoke of a decades-old military dictatorship. In March 1988, a popular movement mushroomed when students took to the streets of Rangoon. Within a few months, protests spread throughout the country, and even brutal repression could not contain them. On July 23, President Ne Win was compelled to step down after twenty-six years in power. Beginning on 8-8-88, five days of new student-led protests forced his replacement also to resign after hundreds more people had been gunned down in the streets. Councils and "general strike committees" representing workers, writers, monks, and students exercised de facto power in cities and towns for weeks. Grassroots councils coordinated a nationwide movement for multiparty democracy.[1] On September 18, a new military regime seized power and used overwhelming firepower to take back control of the country. Thousands more people were shot dead—bringing the number killed that year to at least three thousand (some estimate as many as ten thousand were killed). Arresting thousands more, including over one hundred elected parliamentary representatives, the Burmese military government has continued to use an iron fist to remain in power.

Students have long been in the popular movement's forefront in Burma, and the country has a long history of government violence against protesters. In 1920, they went on strike against British colonial rule, when at least one student succumbed to British clubs and sticks wielded by police on horseback. Nearly all of the five hundred students at Rangoon University went on strike against a new education law, and the strike wave spread to high schools and other parts of the country. Townspeople supported the students with food and money, and the strike won some of its demands. Although the movement was suppressed, schools using Burmese as their language were established and helped provide centers for subsequent struggles.

In 1936, students waged another strike, and two years later, year 1300 in the Burmese calendar, a nationalist uprising broke out. As peasants and workers joined students in the streets, the colonial authorities gunned down seventeen people on February 15, 1939. The bloody suppression convinced many people of the need for more strategic organization. Activists surged into the new Communist Party of Burma (CPB) and fought decades of rurally based armed struggle. A student activist in 1936, Aung San led the country against both Japanese and British attempts to dominate it, leading to independence in 1948. A rival "comrade" assassinated Aung San in 1947, turning the country's fallen leader into a preeminent national hero.[2]

After independence, many ethnic groups joined the CPB's continuing armed struggle against the new government—which also had its hands full dealing with Chinese Kuomintang (KMT) troops loyal to Chiang Kai-shek who ensconced themselves along the Burmese-China border after the communist victory in China in 1949. In November 1953, when Vice President Nixon visited Rangoon, hostile throngs greeted him, helping alert policymakers in Washington that ending support for Chinese counterrevolutionaries inside Burma might be in the best interests of the United States. On January 26, 1961, more than twenty thousand Chinese troops finally crossed over the border to end KMT raids. When Burmese Army units subsequently found stockpiles of U.S. arms and supplies in the abandoned KMT camps, riots erupted outside the U.S. embassy.

Despite the KMT's defeat, for more than half a century, U.S. policy has remained oriented to surrounding China with American bases, one reason why Burma's regime has been supported by communist authorities in Beijing. Similar to the notorious Khmer Rouge regime that ravaged Cambodia from 1975 to 1979, Burma's military rulers have brought misery and poverty to the country, and used weapons of utmost brutality against their own population. Revolts by Shan and Kachin minorities remained sources of self-government opposed to the regime's centralized power. (One-third of Burma's people are ethnic minorities, and the regime has long fought to control them.) As ethnic leaders and Burmese politicians discussed the possibility of a new federal structure, a Revolutionary Council under the control of General Ne Win seized power early on the morning of March

1, 1962. Many prominent political leaders were arrested or simply disappeared as Ne Win led the country on the road to a "Burmese Way to Socialism." With Burma's army firmly in control of the country, becoming in Samuel Huntington's ill-advised phrase, the "motor of development," the country went from one of the wealthiest in the region to the poorest.

With the advent of dictatorship, the country needed only an excuse to rise. Only weeks after Ne Win seized power, final examinations were improperly leaked to the children of government officials at Rangoon University. Students immediately mobilized, barred the police from the university by shutting the main gate, and proclaimed Rangoon University a "fortress of democracy." Inside campus, the consensus at meetings favored restoration of democracy. The rector rebuffed the students who approached him for help, after which he left the campus. Later that day, July 7, 1962, more than one hundred students were gunned down by automatic weapons.[3] The next day, the Student Union Building, center of the movement and longtime symbol of the students' struggle against the British, was dynamited and completely destroyed.

Continuing popular resistance to the military regime could not surmount intense repression. In 1970, armed insurgencies united to overthrow Ne Win, and although initially successful, their campaign soon dissipated. In May and June 1974, wildcat strikes spread outward from the oil fields to Rangoon, but the regime killed dozens of strikers. Any form of autonomous political activity was attacked. In November 1974, Rangoon University students performed a public funeral for U Thant, former Burmese secretary-general of the United Nations. They buried him on the site of their dynamited student union building, but troops arrived, brutally killed dozens, and snatched U Thant's corpse. When students continued to protest, troops again opened fire, causing hundreds of casualties.

With the military firmly in control for twenty-six years, Burma's predatory state impoverished the country, while Ne Win amassed a huge personal fortune. In 1987, the United Nations declared Burma a Least Developed Country. The economic stress—particularly massive foreign debt and practically nonexistent foreign exchange reserves—was compounded when Ne Win demonetized 25, 35, and 75 kyat bank notes, making more than half of the currency in circulation worthless and lowering prices farmers received for their produce. His motivation was partly a result of his faith in numerology: he believed the number nine was lucky. Protests in the country's two largest cities, Rangoon and Mandalay, were immediate. Everywhere, student activists were greeted as heroes. The government closed universities and conducted a wave of arrests. In this volatile atmosphere, any incident could have ignited a major confrontation. As chance would have it, that spark was set off in a teashop. No one could have guessed it at the time, but in the spring of 1988, a tempest in a teashop would develop into a nationwide general strike.

8–8–88

On March 12, 1988, students from Rangoon Institute of Technology (RIT) were drinking tea in a café near campus, when a fight broke out with other customers who objected to students' playing a new tape by popular singer Sai Hti Hseng that they had brought with them. A few drunken rowdies attacked and severely beat one student. The police arrested the attackers, but when they discovered that one of them was the son of a prominent member of the local People's Council, they released them. Upset with this latest incident of favoritism for the elite, a few dozen students protested at the offices of the People's Council, and riot police (Lon Htein) were called in. One student was shot to death.[4]

Spontaneously called meetings on campus lasted until midnight, and despite their peaceful character, Lon Htein invaded the RIT campus on March 15 and arrested hundreds of students. The next day, students from nearby Rangoon University rallied on their campus to show solidarity with the technology students. As their ranks swelled, someone suggested marching to RIT. Thousands of people, fists pumping the air amid chants for democracy and an end to one-party rule, soon set off for RIT. High schoolers and citizens joined the procession before barbed wire and hundreds of armed riot police near Inya Lake halted them. The crowd sang the national anthem and even the army song, but soon riot police charged, inflicting a level of violence on peaceful protesters few thought possible. When the attack stopped, dozens lay mortally wounded—some placed the number of casualties at more than two hundred.

Despite the carnage, workers, slum residents, and students had stood up to the regime—a threat that could not be ignored. The next day, police invaded RU campus and arrested more than a thousand people. On this sweltering day, students were packed so tightly into police vans parked in the sun that dozens died of suffocation. Such inhuman repression bred resistance; in this case, youthful intelligence led the new generation of activists to reach out to their predecessors from the 1970s, and with their elders' advice, a new student union was established. Its information department produced and distributed leaflets, and a social welfare department collected money and provided food and water to rallies. An intelligence unit, sometimes called the protection department, was formed to identify infiltrators. A prison was set up in a dorm, and three students who were found guilty of informing were summarily executed.[5] This early act of violence was an ominous sign.

As the movement debated its next steps, no one could predict what would happen. Suddenly, on March 18, some three hundred students converged around Sule pagoda in the heart of Rangoon. Within an hour, their ranks swelled to more than ten thousand people. Slum residents, workers, and students joined to rise against the military. All over the city, people blocked fire engines and even set one on fire, while others selectively picked out government targets for destruction. Carefully chosen buildings in downtown Rangoon were set afire. In the words of a West German tourist: "The people were very selective. They smashed traffic lights, burned government cars and targeted other state property. I did not see any destruction of private property or widespread looting." As people braved the military's guns with rocks and Molotovs, dozens of protesters were killed. Across the country, campuses were closed down. Rangoon's crematoria billowed black smoke as the military destroyed the bodies of those they had killed, but a first wave of movement leaders was born, their organizations steeled in the crucible of murderous violence. If the military thought they could erase the memory of its brutality and weather the storm, they were sadly mistaken.

One van full of arrested students had waited outside Insein Jail for hours, and forty-two arrested people inside suffocated to death. When the campuses reopened on May 30, former arrestees came forward and disclosed the torture and gang rapes to which they had been subjected. Such revelations shocked the nation. The military curtailed plans for new protests, but on June 14, a masked student stepped up in front of a hastily assembled group near the RU campus recreation center and announced a demonstration for the next day. Warily assembling around a makeshift stage near the library on June 15, a daring handful of masked people demanded release of those still in prison. Only a few people gathered, but the number of protesters quickly grew. When a critical mass of thousands had formed, the group marched off campus to the empty site of the dynamited student union building, stopping at an adjacent memorial for a student killed in the 1938 anti-British movement.

In the next days, monks and textile workers joined campus meetings, and high school students massively rallied to the movement. All universities in Rangoon responded, as did students in outlying regions—notably Pegu and Moulmein. Flash demonstrations seemed to appear out of nowhere, scattering leaflets denouncing the regime and calling for action against it, before disappearing as quietly as they had assembled. When students again sought to march to downtown Rangoon on June 21, the military attacked, running over two thirteen-year-olds. People from the neighborhood then counterattacked. For the first time, *jinglees* (sharpened bicycle spokes fashioned into poisonous darts) were fired from catapults at soldiers. Protesters scattered throughout the city and were joined by throngs of people. Street vendors, workers, and even gangs fought bloody battles against the military in many parts of the city. When a female student who had been holding the students' Fighting Peacock flag was forced inside a police station, people stormed the building and got her released. At least ten Lon Htein were killed, and perhaps ten times as many people. On June 23, some seventy people were killed in Pegu before order was restored.

Although a dusk-to-dawn curfew was in force, activists defied it and announced the creation of a strike center in Shwe Dagon pagoda—headquarters of strikes in 1920 and 1936. After being dispersed by the army, they regrouped into secret organizations. The dictatorship's curfew wreaked havoc on outdoor markets, and prices of essential foodstuffs doubled or tripled. The government tried to blame Burma's problems on its Muslim minority, and a wave of sectarian violence swept the country, even reaching Ne Win's hometown.

Worried that the popular uprising would overwhelm the forces of order, the government made concessions. Imprisoned students were released, and officials in charge of the police resigned. Most startling was Ne Win's sudden announcement that he would resign and that the country would get a multiparty democracy. Hopes for change soared, but soon disbelief and anger set in when Ne Win announced that he would be succeeded by Sein Lwin, Lon Htein chief and commander of the troops who had so bloodily suppressed student demonstrations in 1962 and 1988. Quietly optimistic, people compared Ne Win to Marcos, hoping he, too, would be forced into exile so that a multiparty democracy could be established. Ne Win was also compared to Marcos because both had amassed personal fortunes of billions of dollars.

The brutalities to which they had been subjected and the regime's apparent capitulation made citizens more determined than ever to overthrow the entire system. Ne Win may have left office, but behind the scenes, he controlled his handpicked successor. With overwhelming grassroots support, the movement prepared for massive protests on August 8, 1988, the fiftieth anniversary of the 1300 movement that had marked the anti-British struggle. The first venue in which the protests were announced was in a popular monthly magazine, *Cherry*, where a cartoonist drew the Statue of Liberty breaking chains in the shape of four eights. The BBC picked up the story of the date and helped spread news of it throughout the country.[6] On August 1, the underground All-Burma Students' Union sent out small groups of students to distribute leaflets calling for a general strike on 8–8–88. The teams would suddenly appear at bus stops and teashops, pass out their handbills, and vanish into the city. By "strike" much more was meant than bringing a particular workplace or even an entire industry to a halt; rather it is a general closure of businesses and everyday activities in an area—allowing everyone to go in the streets, like the Nepalese or Indian *bandh* (countrywide general strike). On August 2, monks joined students outside the Shwe Dagon Pagoda and appealed for national actions against the regime. The next day, after a spirited demonstration in Rangoon, the military declared martial law in Rangoon—but the public largely ignored it.

Amid demonstrations that continued to be peaceful and spirited, people borrowed the term "People Power" to describe themselves. In Maung Maung's words: "The crowds were big in Rangoon and grew bigger and bolder, defying military administration, curfew and orders to disperse. Restraint on the part of troops who patrolled the affected areas only encouraged the crowds, who called upon the soldiers to join them and establish 'people power,' a popular term borrowed and applied with strained analogy. Young girls garlanded soldiers and coaxed them to throw in their lot with them. Often the surging sea of people threatened to swallow the troops."[7]

At 8:08 a.m. on August 8, 1988, Rangoon dockworkers walked off their jobs, a signal for a general strike that would cause the entire country to halt and bring about democratic elections for the first time in decades. Sadly, the nationwide movement was met by a barbarous military, which would kill thousands of people and rule the country with an iron grip for decades to come. Like the Jeju Uprising of April 3, 1948, the uprising was organized in advance, but the Burmese uprising did not have a strong organization like the South Korean Labor Party. In the words of one of the people involved in meetings the night before, "There was actually no central organization for the demonstrations. We had only agreed on some basic principles, the main one being that every march should converge outside City Hall."[8] From all over Rangoon, marches streamed downtown. It seemed as if

On 8–8–88, millions of Burmese joined protests.
Photo by Tom Lubin in *Burma's Revolution of the Spirit* (New York: Aperture Foundation, 1994), 37.

every group in the diverse country was involved—Indians, Chinese, Tibetan, Thai, and a dozen more ethnic minorities marched with colorful banners, as did young and old, workers and even government employees. In a carnival-like atmosphere, the country put itself on display. Fists in the air, immigration, customs, and railroad police marched, as did sailors and air force members. Notable was a disciplined column of monks who carried their bowls upside down as a sign of the general strike. Everywhere the Fighting Peacock flag of the All-Burma Students' Union fluttered overhead. The festive mood of people was reflected in their calling

In a vain attempt to persuade soldiers to join protests, some people kissed their feet.
Photo by Ryo Takeda.

members of the armed forces confronting them on the streets—protected from attacks by students—"elder brothers." Many people called upon them to join the uprising. Nearly every city in the country experienced their most massive protests in memory.

At 5:30 p.m. in Rangoon, the Rangoon army commander addressed the crowd, telling them they must disperse or his troops would open fire. No one left. Instead the crowds grew bigger. People exhorted the soldiers not to fire and chanted, "This is a peaceful demonstration!" Thousands of people knelt before the soldiers, imploring them, "We love you; you are our brothers. All we want is freedom. You are the People's Army. Come to our side."[9] Some people kissed the feet of soldiers, hoping to persuade them to side with the movement.

For hours, as the stalemate continued, many people believed they had won. But shortly before midnight, when people in the streets were singing the national anthem, troops started shooting. For at least three long hours, they continued to fire. Armored cars opened up on crowds with automatic weapons, and trucks full of soldiers stopped suddenly and shot anyone in the streets. Soldiers invaded emergency rooms and killed many people as they lay in beds. All over the country, no less than 360 people were killed that day.[10] Thousands were arrested.

Despite the state's violence, people refused to stay home. Monks led a march near the Japanese embassy, but the army opened fire and killed more than thirty people. In the working-class suburb of North Okkalapa, troops fired on markets, teashops, and homes, but people fought back with whatever they could find: *jinglees*, swords, clubs, rocks and Molotovs. They overturned a vehicle with a machine gun mounted on it and burned it. Monks joined in the attacks and were dubbed the "yellow army." As one monk stood in a meditative pose in the midst of the turmoil, a sniper shot him in the head. Some protesters bravely drove a fire engine into the local riot police headquarters and burned it down. The next day, another police station was torched, and four captured policemen were executed in the street—beheaded by a young man with a rusty sword. Barricades to prevent the police from entering neighborhoods were everywhere constructed. In one neighborhood, troops barricaded themselves inside a local party office. They called in air support, but people refused to let them escape. Finally, when night descended, they were able to withdraw.

By the afternoon of Tuesday, August 9, Rangoon General Hospital was running out of supplies to treat the wounded. A group of nurses marched outside, carrying the national flag and a sign imploring the army to stop shooting. Incredibly, they too became victims of the army's shoot-to-kill orders. *Newsweek* reported that in North Okkalapa on August 10, "Witnesses at the cemetery said they heard cries of shooting victims who had been brought to Kyandaw [crematorium] while they were still alive—and were cremated along with the corpses." Although exact numbers will never be known, thousands were killed, as the armed forces routinely turned automatic weapons on any public gathering.

On August 12, after three days of bloody massacres and people's stubborn refusal to give up, Sein Lwin announced his resignation. People joyfully rushed into the streets. Dancing happily, they banged pots and pans, laughed, cried, and celebrated their victory in a "carnival of democracy." The previously spontaneous movement began to organize itself more systematically. Lawyers signed a declaration calling the shootings unconstitutional. Former government leaders and newly repatriated Aung San Suu Kyi signed a public letter suggesting the formation of a "People's Consultative Committee." On August 19, the ruling party appointed Maung Maung, a graduate of Oxford, as the next leader of the country, but people's desire for an end to the one-party state was too strong to accept a new ruler appointed by the same government that had murdered so many. Tens of thousands of people went back into the streets, demanding an end to the one-party state. Although the army refrained from shooting in many cities, in Moulmein, dozens of people were killed. In response, citizens attacked the homes of two ruling party functionaries who ordered the army to fire. The bureaucrats escaped, but the crowd emptied their homes of a substantial hoard of consumer goods and sold them on the streets to raise money for the strike council, the town's new de facto government.

Councils Come to Power

All over Burma, government officials abandoned their offices, and strike councils moved in. It seemed that every group of citizens, from transvestites to gravediggers and blind people,[11] organized strike committees. Victory parades were hastily assembled, newspapers published, and representatives sent to make contact with other cities and regions. In more than 200 of the country's 314 towns, strike centers emerged. In areas where Muslims and Buddhists had only recently been fighting, unity prevailed. "Communal frictions and old grudges were forgotten, and maybe for the first time ever, all national and political groups across the country joined together for a common cause. . . . The yellow banner of Buddhism fluttered beside Islam's green flag with the crescent moon."[12] Priests paraded with signs reading, "Jesus Loves Democracy." According to Maung Maung, "banks and telecommunication departments, railways, petrol dumps, were under the control of the dissidents."[13] Once martial law was lifted from Rangoon on August 24, 1988, the army withdrew, and monks and street gangs took over the task of providing security for people. In Mandalay, a committee of monks and lawyers organized daily rallies.

Despite the opportunity for a national strike council to form, activists instead chose a few prominent personalities to direct the movement. A meeting of national figures was convened, including Aung San Suu Kyi, General Tin Oo, former prime minister U Nu, and Aung Gyi. They came together briefly, but unity among these leaders proved to be elusive. Like no one else, Aung San Suu Kyi galvanized the opposition into a unified force. On the afternoon of August 26, she gave her first public speech to a gathering of at least half a million people. Visiting Burma from England to attend to her sick mother, she had remained politically marginal until the massacres convinced her to get involved. As other prominent opposition voices joined hers, the ruling party lost its membership base. Thousands of officials resigned. Defections from the government were so massive that even journalists who worked for the government's press went on strike, saying they would "no longer broadcast propaganda."

Monks played key roles in the Burmese uprising.
Photo by Alain Evrard in *Burma's Revolution of the Spirit*, 41.

With everyone on strike, people's lives were transformed. Local citizens' committees took over the normal functions of the police. Citizens patrolled the streets, and monks often were the judges when a criminal was brought to justice. In many places, monks also supervised garbage collection, made sure clean water was available, and directed traffic. For some time, it appeared that Buddhist harmony was a "technology of resistance" directed against authoritarian state power.[14] Voluntary community spirit emerged simultaneously in many disparate neighborhoods. Rock groups serenaded demonstrations. Workers in factories and offices formed independent trade unions. Railroad workers announced they would not provide any more special trains for "dictators of the one-party system." In North Okkalapa, where the fighting had been especially intense, people erected a concrete monument in memory of those killed that was exactly 8 feet 8.8 inches high. In neighborhoods near Rangoon General Hospital, hundreds of people donated blankets and pillows for wounded people, and black market vendors of medicines handed over their wares for free.

Despite the eros effect of People Power, not all actions were joyful. In some cases, rising crime rates caused citizens to erect bamboo fences around neighborhoods, and guard forces consisting of monks were organized.[15] When police agents were caught red-handed as they tried to poison a hospital's water supply, two confessed and were released, but three who refused to confess were beheaded publicly. Bertil Lintner saw that, "What had started as a carnival-like, Philippine-style 'people's power uprising' was beginning to turn nasty and coming more and more to resemble the hunt for the *tonton macoutes* in Haiti after the fall of 'Baby Doc' Duvalier in 1986."[16] In South Okkalapa, as many as twenty agents of the army were beheaded after they looted a warehouse and took hostage monks and students who had tried to stop them. In another case, a boy who confessed to having been sent by the military to shoot *jinglees* at demonstrators in South Okkalapa was set free. Although there was little space for hearings by truth commissions, the judgment of the crowd was certainly less severe and more discriminating than that of the army, whose guns sprayed death for thousands of people in the crowds.

On August 25, despite vocal protests by bank workers, the military suddenly withdrew a huge amount of money from the Foreign Trade Bank. All soldiers were then paid six months salary in advance. The next day at notorious Insein Jail where many political prisoners were incarcerated, a fire started. When prisoners tried to flee the inferno, hundreds—perhaps as many as a thousand—were shot dead. Mysteriously, thousands of other convicts were able to "escape" from prisons around the country. As they looted and raped, panic ensued. Rumors spread that water jars enjoyed by demonstrators were being poisoned. Secret police began looting warehouses and offering rewards for delivery of members of the citizens' councils to the authorities. In the midst of such turmoil, is it any wonder that suspected government agents were executed in the streets?

The general strike committee of Rangoon issued an ultimatum calling on the government to install an interim government or face an indefinite strike. On September 6, nine of the eleven living members of the "30 Comrades," the national heroes who had led the independence movement during World War II, called on members of the armed forces to support the uprising. Many soldiers and police officers did join the protests. On September 9, some 150 Air Force members went on strike, and two other units soon joined them. Uniformed columns of police, complete with their marching bands, also attended the demonstrations. In the opinion of Bertil Lintner, "Any high-ranking army officer who had taken an armed infantry unit into the capital and declared his support for the uprising would have become a national hero immediately, and the tables would have been turned." Unfortunately, no such hero, no Burmese version of

Fidel Ramos or Gregorio Honasan, stepped forward. Rumors circulated wildly, one even placing a U.S. aircraft carrier in Burmese waters on a mission to "liberate Rangoon."[17] People thought the United States would help them, and the U.S. embassy was often the rallying point for demonstrations. As in 1980 Gwangju, where the rumor spread of a U.S. aircraft carrier arriving to support democracy, the fantasy revealed more about people's dreams than about the real world of political expediency. No U.S. ships arrived to help Burmese insurgents in 1988, and although a U.S. aircraft carrier was dispatched to Korea during the Gwangju Uprising, it was sent to support the Chun Doo-hwan dictatorship, not the movement for democracy.

On September 8, more than a million people marched in both Rangoon and Mandalay, and three days later, the parliament voted to end one-party rule. Rather than install a caretaker regime, however, Maung Maung insisted on first holding a party congress. On September 10, even though the ruling party's convention affirmed that "free, fair multiparty elections" should be held, they refused to first step down, meaning the elections would be held under their control. Their actions indicated that they would still make decisions, even though public confidence in them was at an all-time low. Demonstrators insisted that the ruling party relinquish control of the government. Protests grew in size, reaching half a million people for the third consecutive day on September 16. The next day, soldiers shot at a peaceful student procession on Merchant Street. Enraged students, monks, and workers armed themselves with knives, slingshots and *jinglees*, surrounded the Trade Ministry where the attacking soldiers had taken refuge, and captured twenty-four of them (including their arms and ammunition).[18] As the situation deteriorated that night, army units shot hunger strikers in front of the U.S. embassy.

Thermidor: The Iron Fist Comes Down

On September 18, 1988, many people believed that Burma was on the verge of a democratic breakthrough, although others remained skeptical. As weeks of protests took their toll, students began to suffer from "demonstration fatigue." Nonetheless, hundreds of thousands of people again took to the streets of Rangoon. The promised elections did not deter protesters from demanding that the ruling party step down immediately.

Unwilling to permit the liberalization process to proceed any further, the military intervened. Around 4:00 p.m., General Saw Maung announced an end to Maung Maung's rule. Seizing power, he sent the army out in force to enforce a nighttime curfew and banned public assemblies. As in August, people's response was swift. Neighborhoods autonomously barricaded themselves for self-defense, especially in North and South Okkalapa and Tingangyun. Unwilling to be compliant victims of the military's wanton violence, many people armed themselves with crossbows, slingshots, Molotovs, swords and *jinglees*, but the army's cranes, bulldozers, and machine guns were far superior. Barricades were systematically removed, and any resistance obliterated. Estimates of the number of people massacred that day range from hundreds to thousands. Miraculously, when several hundred students were surrounded at Rangoon University, a monk somehow led them out a back door to safety.

The next day, September 19, when protests resumed near the City Hall, carefully placed machine guns opened fire, and troops in formation appeared out of nowhere and fired volley after volley into the crowd. Nearly every strike center was attacked, schoolgirls shot dead, and funerals attacked. Two young boys were killed in front of their parents in South Okkalapa. People fought back, but the overwhelming force of the military was deployed without mercy. One small group of protesters was able to destroy a microwave antenna in Rangoon, temporarily knocking out key lines of communication, but the military refused to submit, instead killing between five hundred and a thousand people to defend the coup d'état. Years later, Maung Maung would write: "The government was 'defunct' and wanted to remain so, leaving the dirty job of breaking up the mobs to the *Tatmadaw* [the army] . . . the mobs had gone berserk and started looting homes and factories and, armed with lethal weapons, were ready to kill and chop off heads,"[19]

All through September and October, homes and monasteries were raided. Police with photographs sought out activists, arresting the lucky ones and summarily executing the less fortunate—although some insisted the reverse was the case. Hundreds of government workers were detained, thousands fired. On October 3, when the new military regime issued an ultimatum for people to return to work or face severe consequences, the strike collapsed. Autonomous media were shut down; the monument in North Okkalapa razed; and residents in the big cities ordered to paint their houses to cleanse any signs of the fighting. Only when the official media broadcast the list of strike centers that had been shut down, did movement activists realize how far the ripples from their actions had spread. Small towns and villages all over the country had autonomously organized themselves into participants in the national uprising, but it was too late to reconstitute the grassroots impetus.

Thousands of people began a long trek to the Thai border, where at least eight thousand students organized the All-Burma Students' Democratic Front and began an armed struggle to liberate the country. Waiting for foreign countries to arm them to fight for democracy, the students were not prepared for the jungle. Trainers in nonviolence from the United States were suddenly active among all opposition groups, armed or not.[20] Arriving at the Thai border around the same time as Burmese student activists did, Gene Sharp helped "disarm and make the Burmese movement less powerful."[21]

Although armed ethnic groups gave them hospitality and training, the armed struggle in Burma was never developed fully. Students had accumulated experience and insight from decades of urban struggle, and they were quick to acknowledge the debt they owed to previous generations. "The uprising of 8–8–88 did not only happen because of our efforts," one activist told me, "but from the efforts of activists in 1962, 1967, 1969, 1973, 1975, and 1976. All these small uprisings are still working."[22] At the same moment, urban activists had enormous difficulties in adapting to jungle life.

Wherever Aung San Suu Kyi spoke, throngs of people gathered.
Photo by Dominic Faulder in *Burma's Revolution of the Spirit*, 55.

On September 24, the National League for Democracy (NLD) was formed, and the group went on to win the overwhelming majority in elections. Although back in command, the military was compelled by the 1988 parliamentary decision to hold multiparty elections, and it did so in 1990. In the preelection campaigning, massive crowds appeared wherever Aung San Suu Kyi spoke, and she crisscrossed the country tirelessly.

In July 1989, troops arrested hundreds of people (mainly students) who had camped out at her house since the 1988 uprising. The NLD won a landslide victory in May 1990, garnering 392 of the 485 seats in the National Assembly and over 80 percent of the votes, but the government did not honor people's votes. The military imposed house arrest on Aung San Suu Kyi, arrested over a hundred elected representatives, and severely repressed any public protests.

Long Road Since 1988

The tragic defeat suffered in 1988 scarred Burma's public life. For decades, even peaceful assemblies were severely repressed. Rangoon's neighborhoods near the city center were cleared of residents, and as many as five hundred thousand people were forcibly relocated. As thousands of people were arrested, military tribunals replaced civilian courts, and summary execution became a common sentence for political offenses. It became a crime to send e-mail, invite foreigners into your home, and own a modem.[23] Filming anyone in uniform became punishable by up to twenty years in prison. To sap the strength of the democracy movement, the police made heroin widely available, cooperating in its distribution. Dubbed "freedom from fear," the same title as Aung San Suu Kyi's most famous essay, heroin and AIDS epidemics ravaged Burma's youth.[24]

While thousands of students and more than a dozen armed ethnic minority groups waged an armed struggle in the countryside, the NLD organized secret groups in the cities. On April 17, 1989, ethnic Wa fighters—the core of the army of the Burmese Communist Party—mutinied and took over their headquarters near the Chinese border. Soon thereafter, other ethnic blocs within the People's Army left the organization and pursued their own negotiations with the regime. While her father had united the various groups to fight as one against the colonial government, Aung San Suu Kyi discouraged them, abdicating the role of unifier to become the champion of nonviolence. In effect, she doomed the national movement to impotency and division.

Only too happy to see armed resistance to it crumble, the dictatorship negotiated deals one by one over the next few years. In exchange for localized ceasefires, leaders of some ethnic groups were allowed to smuggle gold, drugs, timber, and gems, while rank-and-file foot soldiers were named "Special Police" with salaries, rations, and rank among the "Border Troops." Still other groups held out for limited autonomy. Ultimately, at least seventeen ceasefires were counted among the ethnic minorities, while two formerly armed groups surrendered outright. All were forbidden to make contact with illegal organizations like the NLD.

On August 8, 1990, the second anniversary of the 1988 uprising, thousands of monks marched in Mandalay, holding their alms bowls upright. People turned out to offer them food and money, but after someone hoisted the Fighting Peacock flag (adopted by the NLD in their election campaign), the army opened fire to disperse the crowd. The state-run media subsequently denied the army had used firearms and instead reported attacks by monks and students. At the end of August, monks again mobilized, this time promising not to accept donations from (or provide services for) members of the armed forces—endangering the souls of impressionable young men. This Buddhist revolt, although nonviolent, threatened the government's hold on its young soldiers, and they responded viciously by raiding more than 130 monasteries and arresting hundreds of monks.

On December 19, 1990, elected members of parliament who were able to escape the country formed a government in exile, the National Coalition Government of the Union of Burma. Representing all ethnic minorities and the NLD, they called for the restoration of democracy within a federal system. Aung San Suu Kyi won the Nobel Peace Prize in 1991, but for more than fifteen of the next twenty-three years, she was subjected to house arrest. The junta's treatment of ordinary people has been less restrained. More than two thousand political prisoners endure lives of anguish and brutality.

The armed struggle in Burma was never supported by outside forces—a lack of international aid that stands in stark contrast to the massive aid funneled by the governments of Norway, Sweden, Switzerland, the United States, and Canada to nonviolent groups, to say nothing of Aung San Suu Kyi's 1991 Nobel Peace Prize. Without the arms they needed, insurgent groups in the jungles were unable to make advances. Over time they became isolated from urban struggles, while the NLD's public refusal to cooperate with the military led to a continuing stalemate. Aung San Suu Kyi was briefly released from house arrest from 1995 to 1997, but the movement, although massively supported by people, was largely quieted. In May 1996, the NLD attempted to convene a party convention, but the military arrested hundreds of people—including 238 who had been legally elected in 1990. The next year, a possible prison term of twenty years was declared for anyone listening to Aung San Suu Kyi at her weekly meetings outside her home.

Briefly released again from house arrest, Aung San Suu Kyi was not permitted to travel freely. On May 30, 2003, less than a month after being permitted to leave her home, crowds of government supporters near the northern village of Depayin set upon her convoy. In what many consider a premeditated assassination attempt, dozens—possibly as many as 282 of her supporters—were massacred. Along with Tin Oo, NLD cofounder and vice chairperson, she was one of many people who were then sentenced (again) to detention, part of a general crackdown on the NLD. She remained a prisoner until 2010.

The military has changed the name of the country to Myanmar, but the democracy movement insists that the current government is completely illegitimate and continues to use Burma to name their country. With all citizens required to contribute labor to the country, the military has continued the country's long history of building magnificent Buddhist temples. It also spent a fortune building a new capital city in Naypyidaw, far from any concentration of people. When the capital was inaugurated in 2005, Burmese numerology defined the timing of its celebration: at 11:00 a.m. on November 11, 11 government ministries and 11 battalions of troops left Rangoon in 1,100 trucks.

For two decades, the NLD was not allowed to publish, copy, make international phone calls, hold meetings in its offices; it had no freedom of speech or assembly. According to a 2006 report on public television in the United States, at least 128 activists died in custody, and more than another 1,100 remain locked away. One in three children are malnourished and one in ten die before the age of five. Although the military ratified a new constitution and held elections in 2010, the NLD refused to participate.

The Economics of Military Rule

Just after the 1988 uprising, global oil companies paid more than $5 million each for drilling rights in Burma. Among the takers were Amoco and Unocal of the United States, Dutch Shell, BHP of Australia, Yukong from South Korea, Idemitsu from Japan, Petro-Canada, and the UK's Croft and Kirkland. In 1990, Texaco and Total Oil from France signed a $300 million agreement to build a natural gas pipeline into Thailand. Deforestation was so extreme that an area the size of El Salvador was cleared every year during the 1990s. Thailand and China both sent delegations to improve trade. More than three-fourths of all oil imported to China passes through the Straits of Malacca, and control of the region around that narrow passageway is of enormous strategic importance. With U.S. wars in the Middle East, China's growing insecurity concerning oil supplies made the country redouble its efforts to ensure friendly relations with regimes in Burma, Cambodia, and Thailand.

Using the sale of oil, timber, fishing, and mining rights, the military expanded the size of its army (doubling its size to more than four hundred thousand) and upgraded its weapons. One estimate placed the military's budget at 60 percent of the government's expenditures.[25] Arms dealers and timber buyers from China, Israel, Singapore, and Thailand were willing business partners. After purchasing more than $1 billion of weapons from China, the dictatorship used a scorched earth policy and ruthless raids to defeat most of the ethnic groups, whose peoples were subjected to arbitrary domination of the Burmese military. Murder of ethnic peoples became commonplace, and rapes were widespread, especially of Shan women. A 2002 report told of 625 rapes of women and girls—some as young as eight years old. In the following three years, 188 more females were raped in Shan state, with more than half the crimes committed by military officers. Some 65 percent were gang rapes.[26] In 2004, women of the Karen ethnic minority reported 126 cases of rape by soldiers.[27]

While the Western media often singles China out as the main supporter of the Burmese military, the king of Thailand plays a huge role. In 2004, Thailand accounted for nearly 40 percent of all Burmese exports (compared to only 6 percent for China). Thailand also benefits from the low-cost labor provided by Burmese refugees. More than 334,123 Burmese migrant workers were counted by Thai immigration in 1994.[28] Labor experts estimated the number of people pushed across the border at 1.5 million. At least 150,000 more languish in nine camps in Thailand, but many more wander outside the camps, often without passports and subjected to detention, deportation, and degradation. On April 9, 2008, some fifty-four illegal immigrants from Burma suffocated in the back of a container truck that was smuggling them to the tourist resort island of Phuket.

An economic basket case, Burma remains one of the world's poorest countries. Hundreds of thousands of displaced people inside the country live from hand to mouth. Top military leaders amass huge fortunes while 90 percent of Burmese live on less than one dollar per day. Estimates tell of 270 to 400 children who die everyday from preventable diseases.[29] In 2007, economists estimated an average family of five needed more than 80,000 kyat (about $110) a month to live, including food, medicine, and transport but excluding luxury goods. The average monthly income of a professional worker—teacher, university professor, or government official—was less than 10,000 kyat ($13). Human rights groups say forced labor is still used in Burma. Unlike South Korea's "developmental state" (the military dictatorship's policies aimed at expanding the nation's economy), Burma is a "predatory state" (where the military forces millions of people to provide free labor to state projects). Human rights groups estimate three thousand villages have been destroyed and one million people made refugees in a program of systematic expropriation of ancestral lands of ethnic minorities.

The 2007 "Saffron Revolution"

The Saffron Revolution was sparked by a government decision in mid-August to significantly increase the price of fuel and other commodities over which it held a strict monopoly. Only released from prison a few short years before, "Generation 88" (survivors of the 1988 uprising) pulled together an alternative leadership to the NLD and organized protests in Rangoon. Soon similar peaceful marches took place throughout the country. Hundreds of people took to the streets. Paramilitary forces roughed up their marches, and thirteen government-identified "leaders"—many only recently released from prison—were arrested. By August 21, some one hundred people were in police custody. Once protests began, activists creatively utilized SMS text-messages, e-mail, blogs, Facebook, Wikipedia, and video-equipped cell phones to spread knowledge of the movement outside the country. Within hours, foreign radio like BBC broadcast reports back into Burma. On August 22, in a major police success, seven key members of the 88 Generation were located and arrested. Despite international opposition to its continuing repression, the military rounded up hundreds of people.

It appeared that protests had ended, but about a month later, monks mobilized by the tens of thousands, and throngs of people joined the new wave of actions. On September 5, hundreds of saffron-robed monks took to the streets of Pakokku, north of Mandalay. Unwilling to tolerate even a peaceful march, police fired warning shots to disperse the crowd. A contingent of monks is a major challenge in a society where there are about as many monks as soldiers—more than three hundred thousand of each.[30] At the beginning of their protests, monks did their best to keep citizens from joining them. They wanted it clear they were taking significant steps against the regime and its supporters, and they did not want to cause injury to anyone beside themselves.[31]

By September 18, daily protests broke out all over the country. In Mogok, monks gathered and deliberated long and hard before deciding to turn bowls over and bring a strike into the streets. Still the center of Rangoon, gold-domed Shwedagon Pagoda became a gathering place for the daily protests that lasted until the September 27, the day after monasteries were raided.[32] Twenty-four-year-old Ashin Kovida was elected by fourteen fellow monks to lead the protests. Inspired by videos of the popular uprising in Yugoslavia against Slobodan Milosevic, his group drafted and distributed thousands of leaflets to other monasteries. On September 19, as about two thousand protesting monks sat together in Sule Pagoda, Kovida called for others to step forward and provide leadership. Fifteen people who did so formed the Monks Representative Group and helped coordinate protests until September 26.

Protests grew in size until they culminated in a march of twenty thousand in Rangoon on September 23. The next morning two famous entertainers offered alms to the monks, and thousands of citizens joined them, chanting slogans for democracy, and demanding freedom for Aung San Suu Kyi. The Burmese Bar Association joined Generation 88 and monks in publicly calling for a peaceful solution to the country's political deadlock. On the evening of September 24, state television warned of severe action against protesters, and trucks with loudspeakers circled Rangoon with warnings of arrests and worse. Nonetheless, the feeling on the streets the next day resembled a "carnival atmosphere" in the eyes of at least one Western reporter.[33] With residents applauding buoyant marchers from balconies, monks turned over their alms bowls, students unfurled forbidden Fighting Peacock flags, and Buddhist nuns led chants against the dictatorship. That night a sixty-day nighttime curfew was declared.

The next day, people were made to pay for their joyous celebration and refusal to stay home. As protesters gathered, police charged them behind a barrage of smoke bombs and tear gas. Police attacked with sticks, soldiers began shooting, and many people were killed. Nonetheless some fought their way out and marched downtown. As they reached Sule Pagoda, trucks full of soldiers tailed them. Despite the danger, the crowd jeered the troops and threw rocks to keep them away. Monks admonished soldiers they would suffer in their next lives for their sins. While some soldiers cried—the vast majority carried out their orders and attacked again. As night fell and the streets emptied, the army began raiding monasteries. That night in the Ngwe Kyar Yan monastery, which had taken a leading role in 1988, blood ran onto the floors, forming puddles alongside the pockmarked walls.

In the early morning hours of September 26, heavily armed riot police and soldiers surrounded protesters who sought to march out of Shwedagon Pagoda. Soon, police attacked and brutalized passive monks and citizens. At least one monk was bloodily beaten to death. Soldiers shot into the crowd and ran over people with vehicles, killing many.[34] After the protest was broken up, thousands of monks were rounded up all over Burma with the help of progovernment paramilitary groups.

On Thursday, September 27, the army killed Japanese photographer Kenji Nagai as he covered a demonstration. Backed by the military, hundreds of riot police with shields and clubs cleared the streets. Gunfire rang out and then settled into a steady staccato. The next day, the regime claimed a total of only ten dead, while a UN official guessed forty dead and three thousand arrested—about a third of whom were monks. Even these estimates seemed low to many observers. On October 4, the U.S. Campaign for Burma reported that about two hundred protesters had been killed since September 26, and that figure did not include a bloody raid at a high school on September 29. The army reportedly cremated many bodies (possibly including many still alive) at the crematorium in Yay Way Cemetery.

Arrests ran into the thousands. The military claims 2,100 people were rounded up. *Der Spiegel* reported that 800 arrested monks were brought to Rangoon Institute of Technology.[35] While Kovida escaped to Thailand, eight of the fifteen other leading monks were missing after the roundups. Because of the brutal repression, citizens began switching off lights and televisions during the nightly news broadcasts as a form of protest.

On June 27, 2007, human rights groups counted 1,192 political prisoners, including sixteen elected MPs. A year after the Saffron Revolution, the number of political prisoners stood at 2,123. The military has released over 9,000 common criminals, but political prisoners languish in intolerable conditions. On July 18, 2008, Khin Maung Tint died after ten years in Mandalay prison, bringing the number of political prisoners to die in custody to 137. Nonetheless, Burmese activists have persisted, working together across generations. Most recently, Zeyar Thaw (a hip hop artist) and Kyaw Ko Ko, president in 2007 of the All-Burma Students' Union, have emerged in the forefront of grassroots resistance. In 2008, poet Saw Wai was arrested for his eight-line Valentine's Day verse, "February 14." The first word of each line read, "Power crazy senior general Than Shwe."

CIA involvement in the Saffron Revolution may be a factor of some importance. William Engdahl indicates the U.S. intelligence services learned from the 1986 Philippine revolt and implemented prepackaged destabilization programs—including color-coded T-shirts, musicians, and the tactic of massive nonviolent occupation of public space aimed at unfriendly governments:

> Burma's "Saffron Revolution," like the Ukraine "Orange Revolution" or the Georgia "Rose Revolution" and the various Color Revolutions instigated in recent years against strategic states surrounding Russia, is a well-orchestrated exercise in Washington-run regime change, down to the details of "hit-and-run" protests with "swarming" mobs of Buddhists in saffron, Internet blogs, mobile SMS links between protest groups, well-organized protest cells which disperse and reform. CNN made the blunder during a September broadcast of mentioning the active presence of the NED [U.S. government funded National Endowment for Democracy] behind the protests in Myanmar. [36]

On top of the misery caused by the country's military, in May 2008 Hurricane Nargis struck, killing some 138,000 people and displacing hundreds of thousands more. Later that year, military leaders again promised a general election in 2010, but they refused to permit Aung San Suu Kyi to be a candidate. Although the National Council of the Union of Burma (NCUB) has been active for years as an umbrella group comprising the broad spectrum of democratic opposition (the NLD, the Democratic Alliance of Burma, the National League for Democracy-Liberated Area, the Ethnic and Nationalities Council, and the Members of Parliament Union), Aung San Suu Kyi remains the movement's supreme authority.[37]

With the movement divided by questions of tactics and ethnicity, many have little alternative but to fight on in isolation from potential allies. For the Karen, who have been waging an armed struggle continuously since 1947, Burmese chauvinism remains an issue, while for Aung San Suu Kyi, nonviolence is an absolute. The question of tactics is worth close examination. How do we explain why Nelson Mandela no longer languishes in Robbin Island prison and became president of South Africa, while Suu Kyi has spent most of her adult life under house arrest? As one analyst observed, "Arguably the uprising failed not because some of its participants turned to violence, but because, as a whole, it was not forceful enough."[38]

Despite suffering a crushing defeat in 1988, the Burmese People Power movement inspired others, especially in neighboring Tibet. Tenzin Gyatso, the Dalai Lama, eloquently spoke of how "humanity's innate desire is for freedom, truth, and democracy. The nonviolent 'people power' movements that have arisen in various parts of the world in recent years have indisputably shown that human beings can neither tolerate nor function properly under tyrannical conditions. In their demonstrations for democracy, the Burmese people, too, spoke from their hearts, asserting their natural desire for freedom."

NOTES

1. Interviews with Aung So and Aung Moe Zaw, Maesot, Thailand, November 4 and 5, 2008.
2. Aung San is today known as the father of modern Burma. So great is the esteem in which people hold him that when his daughter, Aung San Suu Kyi, returned from years of exile to care for her ailing mother in 1988, she quickly became the leader of the Burmese movement for democracy.
3. In an interview in Maesot, Thailand, on November 5, 2008, Karen National Union vice president and longtime activist David Tharekabaw remembered that 104 students were killed.
4. Bertil Lintner's *Outrage: Burma's Struggle for Democracy* (London and Bangkok: White Lotus, 1990) provides a compelling and detailed report on these events. Lintner's work on Burma is without peer, and I have relied heavily on his books.
5. Ibid., 9.
6. See the discussion in ibid., 90–92.
7. Maung Maung, *The 1988 Uprising in Burma* (New Haven: Yale Southeast Asia Studies, 1999), 93.
8. Lintner, *Outrage*, 95.
9. Alan Clements and Leslie Kean, *Burma's Revolution of the Spirit* (New York: Aperture Foundation, 1994), 36.
10. *Voices from the Jungle* (Tokyo: Center for Christian Response to Asian Issues, 1989), 1. Hereafter *Voices*.
11. Vincent Boudreau, "State Repression and Democracy Protest in Three Southeast Asian Countries," in *Social Movements: Identity, Culture and the State* (Oxford: Oxford University Press, 2002), 35.
12. Lintner, *Outrage*, 114.
13. Maung Maung, *1988 Uprising*, 226.
14. William A. Callahan, *Cultural Governance and Resistance in Pacific Asia* (Abingdon: Routledge, 2006), 94.
15. Confirmed to me in e-mails with Bertil Lintner, April 9, 2006. Lintner also saw this

development as an indication that "law and order" did not break down as many post–September 18 accounts claimed.

16   Lintner, *Outrage*, 121–22.
17   Lintner, *Outrage*, 127; Maung Maung, *1988 Uprising*, 226.
18   *Voices*, 5.
19   Maung Maung, *1988 Uprising*, 267.
20   See Gamanii, "Putting Out Fires—The Burmese Way," unpublished pamphlet, Mae Sot Thailand, 2008.
21   Interview with Aung Kyaw So, Maesot, Thailand, November 2008.
22   Interview with Aung Moe Zaw, Maesot, Thailand, November 5, 2008.
23   *New York Times*, November 14, 2000, 11.
24   Clements and Kean, *Burma's Revolution*, 89.
25   *Burma: Anatomy of Terror*, a film by John Pilger.
26   Shan Women's Action Network, http://www.shanwomen.org.
27   Alternative ASEAN Network on Burma, *Burma Briefing: Issues and Concerns* (Bangkok: 2004), 85.
28   Walden Bello, Shea Cunningham, and Li Kheng Poh, *A Siamese Tragedy: Development and Disintegration in Modern Thailand* (Oakland, CA: Food First Books, 1998), 88.
29   Teddy Buri, "International Community and Democratic Change in Burma," in *Gwangju International Peace Forum*, May 16, 2009, 31.
30   Andrew Marshall, "Blood, Robes, and Tears: A Rangoon Diary," *Time*, October 22, 2007, 24.
31   Awzar Thi, "Burma's Saffron Revolution," *Human Rights Solidarity* 17, no. 5 (Hong Kong: Asian Human Rights Commission, September 2007): 3.
32   Thomas Fuller, "A Monk's Tale of Protest and Escape from Myanmar," *New York Times*, October 26, 2007.
33   Marshall, "Blood, Robes, and Tears," 27.
34   Pankaj Mishra, "The Revolt of the Monks," *New York Review*, February 14, 2008, 36.
35   Jürgen Kremb, "Die Stadt der leeren Klöster," *Der Spiegel* 41 (2007): 157.
36   F. William Engdahl, "Chokepoint! The Geopolitical Stakes of the Saffron Revolution," October 15, 2007, http://www.engdahl.oilgeopolitics.net/Geopolitics___Eurasia/Myanmar/myanmar.html.
37   Interview with Sann Aung, Bangkok, Thailand, November 4 and 5, 2008.
38   Justin Wintle, *Perfect Hostage: A Life of Aung San Suu Kyi* (London: Hutchinson, 2007).

CHAPTER 4

Tibet

When iron birds fly and horses are on wheels, Tibetans will be scattered over the world.
—Eighth-century Tibetan prophecy

A people which enslaves others forges its own chains.
—Karl Marx

CHRONOLOGY

March 10, 1959	Uprising in Lhasa begins; more than twenty thousand people protect the Dalai Lama
March 10, 1959	Popularly elected leaders declare Tibet independent; fighting units organized
March 11, 1959	Lhasa engulfed in a sea of black flags as thousands acclaim independence
March 12, 1959	Five thousand women march; huge meeting at Shol (under the Potala)
March 17, 1959	Dalai Lama flees to India; Kashag formally declares independence
March 19, 1959	Chinese forces fire artillery to inflict enormous casualties; days of heavy fighting
March 19, 1959	Beijing declares twenty-one-year-old Panchen Lama the new leader of Tibet
March 28, 1959	Chinese premier Chou En-lai orders government of Tibet dissolved
September 27, 1987	Police arrest twenty-one monks and three others for protesting

October 1, 1987	About forty monks walk in a circle of protest; police arrest many people
October 1, 1987	Several thousand people demand prisoners' release, set police station on fire
October 1, 1987	At least six people killed; more than five hundred Tibetans arrested
October 6, 1987	More protests, and arrests and killings of Tibetans
March 5, 1988	More than twelve people killed after monks demand freedom for prisoners
March 5, 1988	Barricades protect sections of the Barkhor; slingshots and stones used
December 10, 1988	At least eighteen people killed and seventy wounded
January 28, 1989	Panchen Lama dies of a heart attack
March 5, 1989	Monks and nuns lead demonstration
March 6, 1989	Citizens join the protests
March 7, 1989	Heavy fighting in Lhasa
March 8, 1989	Martial law declared in Tibet for 387 days; as many as 250 people killed
May 2, 1989	Martial law declared in Beijing
June 4, 1989	Dozens of protesters killed in Beijing
March 10, 2008	Uprising begins and lasts until June; in 125 incidents, 220 Tibetans are killed, 1,300 wounded, and nearly 7,000 detained or imprisoned

FOR CENTURIES, TIBETANS carved out their own unique civilization on their remote high plateau sheltered by the Himalayas. The emergence of the Tibetan nation has been traced to 127 BCE, when Nya-Tri-Tsenpo inaugurated forty generations of royal rule.[1] Nearly a millennium later, war between China and Tibet broke out during the reign of Tr-Dhi-Tsuk-Ten (thirty-sixth of these kings) in the eighth century, and Tibet conquered several Chinese provinces. A stone pillar commemorating the Tibetan victory remained standing in front of the Potala to the end of the twentieth century.

Despite Tibet's close proximity to Nepal and India, Buddhism arrived relatively late, and when it did, unique mountainous beliefs were infused into the subcontinent's more standard versions. In a nation of warriors, Buddha's *ahimsa*, or nonviolence, took root as strongly as anywhere, and nearly everyone laid down their arms. More than the forces of the world's many armies, Tibetans' gentle religion and esoteric beliefs—intuition, fortune-telling through oracles, past lives, and trance—finally subdued the Mongolian conquerors who ruled much of Eurasia. The Mongols adopted Tibetan Lamaism as their religion, and during both the Yuan dynasty (1271–1368) and Manchu-led Qing dynasty (1644–1911), Tibetan Buddhism was the official religion of China.

By the time the twentieth century arrived, perhaps 10 percent of all Tibetans were monks or nuns. While their social system was feudal, the monasteries were egalitarian in the sense that anyone could enter and rise according to their ability—and monks were free to leave. Buddhism's leveling effect is profoundly liberating, and Tibetan people—while impoverished in the eyes of the materialistic many—were immeasurably wealthy in spiritual terms.

As the religious center of China, Tibet enjoyed autonomy and peace. Beginning in 1896, however, Qing military forces began to attack. Although initially repulsed, in 1903, Chinese General "Butcher" Feng and his armies slaughtered their way into Tibet's heartland. When the democratic revolution of 1911 overthrew China's Manchu rulers, Tibet enjoyed a temporary respite from Chinese influence. The Chinese mission in Lhasa was evicted and the Dalai Lama returned from India—where he had taken refuge. The current Dalai Lama tells us, "from 1912 until the Chinese invasion of 1950, neither the Chinese nor any other state had any power whatever in Tibet."[2] Those parts of Eastern Tibet that remained subject to the new Kuomintang (KMT) administration in Beijing during the first half of the twentieth century continually sought to expel the Han Chinese.

In 1931, monks in Dhargay monastery north of Nyarong in Eastern Tibet (Kham) in alliance with local leader Sonam Wangdu led a rebellion that liberated the city.[3] Chinese counterattacks recaptured it about a year later, and continuing incursions constituted Tibetans' main problem. Indigenous Tibetans did not distinguish between communists and nationalists, so even Red Army units on the Long March were ambushed as they passed through Kham lands.[4]

In 1939, a decade before Chinese "liberation" of Tibet from feudalism, there were some six thousand monasteries in the country, and one in four boys was a monk. Official communist policy specified that "Mongolia, Tibet and Xinjiang exercise autonomy as democratic, autonomous states." As early as the party's second congress in 1922, the Chinese Communist Party (CCP) promised "to unite the Chinese territory proper as a real democratic republic." Soon after their 1949 victory over Chiang Kai-shek and the KMT, one of the CCP's main priorities was to consolidate its territory and "to liberate 3,000,000 Tibetans from imperialist aggression."

During more than half a century of Chinese occupation policies, estimates of the number of Tibetans killed because of revolt, imprisonment, and starvation are well over one million out of a population of only about five million.[5] Hundreds of thousands of others have been forced to seek refuge abroad. Population transfer of ethnic Han Chinese appears to have been so successful that today more than half of the people in Tibet are Chinese settlers, who are subsidized, protected, and encouraged by the Chinese state.

Tibet is one-quarter of China's landmass and contains some 40 percent of China's mineral wealth (including gold, zinc, lead, copper, and borax), significant uranium deposits, and key missile sites. Besides millions of acres of virgin forests, it also may hold oil.

During that same half-century, U.S. world strategy has been to encircle and isolate China, an endeavor in which millions of Koreans and Vietnamese were sacrificed. Tibet, too, could not escape the dynamic conflict between the world great powers. In April 1950, after thirty thousand troops—the advance unit of China's Eighteenth Army—marched through Tibet, the Dalai Lama appealed to the United Nations, but that august body had only recently approved an invasion force in Korea, and it refused to act—a "grievous blow" to Tibet in the estimation of the Dalai Lama. According to Chinese sources, the People's Liberation Army (PLA)—the army of the communist government—killed more than 5,700 Tibetan fighters in Eastern Tibet in October 1950.[6] China and Tibet reached a Seventeen-Point Agreement in 1951, which the Dalai Lama later insisted had been imposed at bayonet point and that the Tibetan seal stamped on it had been fabricated in Beijing. Thousands of Chinese troops arrived in Lhasa and demanded food, disrupting the delicate balance between population and barley so heartily maintained for centuries. Inflation caused by shortages in Lhasa meant food prices increased tenfold, and many people starved. Mao had promised in 1952 that Tibetan lands, when they were eventually redistributed, would be done so "by Tibetan people themselves."[7]

Although the UN refused to assist Tibet, the United States willingly stepped in. In the mid-1950s, the CIA flew dozens of anti-Chinese Tibetan fighters to the Pacific island of Saipan for training in armaments and communications, and then helped them infiltrate back into Tibet.[8] Others were flown to the U.S. state of Colorado and to Cornell University to prepare them to overthrow Chinese rule. As fighting continued for the next decade in Amdo, some ten thousand Tibetan independence fighters were killed in action. In Sichuan as well, a revolt by the Tibetan (Khampa) minority was said by the New China News Agency to have been staged by "inhuman slave owners and feudal lords."

In 1955, conflicts broke out in Kham province as peasants resisted collectivization of agriculture, and they quickly escalated into war. In Sichuan in May and June 1956, major revolts against party policies occurred among the region's predominantly Tibetan population, and the PLA was called out and forcibly restored order. One report told of two thousand Chinese troops having their noses cut off by Golok fighters supplied by the KMT.[9] Communist sympathizer Anna Louise Strong reported that rebels in Eastern Tibet mounted about ten thousand armed troops. On July 18, 1956, The *Times of India* reported that all routes into Lhasa that pass through Eastern Tibet were closed by guerrillas, and only a single route through the northeast was open. Again in 1957, Tibetans defied party reforms. Internal reports described crowds that "besieged government buildings, burned government stores and warehouses, disrupted communications, robbed the masses, killed cadres, attacked the PLA . . . The party and government were compelled to wage an armed struggle to put down the rebellion."[10] On the Chinese side, the "struggle against superstition, demons and gods" had only begun.

The PLA used overwhelming force, including bombing runs, to suppress indigenous Tibetan resistance. In October 1958, Khampa fighters shot down a Chinese plane that had bombed and strafed their camp, killing many family members.[11] As PLA forces streamed to the area, they ambushed the families, and by the time remnants had regrouped, only about four thousand of the original fifteen thousand had survived.[12] During the 1950s, a thousand or more of the Tibetan army's total force of ten thousand lightly equipped fighters were killed, while on the Chinese side, casualties appear to have been even higher. On

Tibetan dob-dob monks.
Photo by Joseph F. Rock. Collection of National Geographic Society.

September 29, 1956, Reuters reported fifty thousand Chinese killed along with fifteen thousand Tibetans in a two-year period.[13]

While CIA disinformation campaigns make such reports suspect, it is fair to say that resistance in the country's East was most intense, and as a result its people suffered terribly. Under communist rule, a secret association, the Mimang, or People's Party, drew wide support. It encouraged people to refrain from fraternizing with Han people and to refuse to send their children to Chinese schools.[14] Many dob-dob, a special detachment of fighting monks from the great monasteries of Drepung (7,700 monks), Sera (5,500 monks), and Ganden (3,300 monks) were members of the Mimang. One Indian report told of the underground People's Party's main force of 26,000 monks "each of whom has a rifle wrapped somewhere among his prayer flags." [15]

Even though he did not support their militant resistance, Tibetans were overwhelmingly loyal to the Dalai Lama, many of whom believe he is the reincarnation of the Bodhisattva of Compassion. When a joint Tibetan-Chinese constitutional committee to create a new administration was announced in Lhasa at the beginning of 1956, people spontaneously rose against it. As the Dalai Lama described the situation, "The resentment of ordinary people against the Chinese had created something totally new in Tibet: political leaders spontaneously chosen by the people. These men were not government officials. They had no official standing at all, but came from all ordinary walks of life. And when I describe them as political leaders, I do not mean they were political in any Western sense."[16] As leaflets were prepared and posted all over Lhasa denouncing the committee, the Dalai Lama and his cabinet acceded to a Chinese demand and had three of the leaders arrested—one of whom died in prison.

The 1959 Uprising

Tibetan New Year (Losar) calls for three weeks of feasting and prayers followed by a great prayer festival (Monlam). In early 1959, with thousands of refugees camped outside Lhasa and about seventeen thousand monks arriving for Monlam, the city's population doubled to about a hundred thousand. Outside the city, war against the Chinese invaders raged. With the help of Chinese deserters, dob-dob warrior-monks and insurgents led by Chuzhi Gangdruk killed around six hundred PLA soldiers who had dug tunnels under a heavily fortified camp in Tsetang (less than fifty miles from Lhasa near the Bhutan border). Using chili peppers to smoke the PLA troops out, the Tibetan fighters killed many Chinese who were gunned down as they attempted to surrender.[17]

On March 9, 1959, the Dalai Lama, then twenty-four years old and only recently having completed his religious examinations, contemplated an invitation he received from Chinese commander Tan Kuan-san. The note specifically called for him to attend a theater performance without his armed bodyguards or other ministers the next evening in the Chinese camp. In the past two years, many high lamas had disappeared after being similarly invited to visit Chinese authorities, and as word spread of the "invitation," people immediately became fearful for the Dalai Lama's life.[18] As word spread that the Dalai Lama was to go to the Chinese camp without bodyguards, *ragyabas*—men who specialize in cutting up corpses for sky burials—went door to door to mobilize protection for him. The abbots of Sera monastery sent word to monks in outlying areas—especially for dob-dob—to come to Lhasa. Old rifles were dusted off, but even they were few in number, and ammunition was scarce. One report claimed volunteers from Amdo and Golok acquired five thousand rifles.[19] Yet, a dob-dob monk involved in the movement claimed only about four hundred rifles were available at Sera.[20]

On March 10, in response to the perceived threat on the Dalai Lama's life, more than twenty thousand people responded to a call to form a living wall to protect him by surrounding his summer palace, the Norbulingka. As people gathered, spokespeople from a Freedom Committee read a Declaration of Tibetan Independence and burned copies of the contested Seventeen-Point Agreement signed by the traitor Ngabo in Beijing on May 23, 1951 (under which Beijing assumed control of Tibet's military and foreign affairs but recognized the Dalai Lama's position). Dozens of public meetings and government officials soon endorsed similar statements.[21] At 6:00 p.m., the Dalai Lama's bodyguards, government figures, and popularly elected leaders again declared an end to the Seventeen-Point Agreement and declared Tibet independent. Fighting units were organized from trades and monasteries.[22]

In this volatile moment, a Chinese emissary, Tibetan Kanchung Sonam Gyatso, arrived at the Norbulingka with two cars. Thinking he had come to take the Dalai Lama, the crowd stoned Gyatso to death. So intense was people's anger that *ragyaba* refused to touch the body of the collaborator. Belts had to be used to drag the body through the streets back into Lhasa's center. Beijing radio later maintained that the pro-Chinese vice commander of Tibetan armed forces had also been wounded in this incident. Two of the *kaloons*—the six ministers who formed the Kashag, or traditional government of Tibet—were pro-Chinese. Both were injured as well.[23]

With his palace surrounded, it was clearly impossible for the Dalai Lama to leave—although he expressed a desire to do so in a letter he sent that day to the Chinese commander. The Dalai Lama maintained that, "Reactionary, evil elements are carrying out activities endangering me under the pretext of protecting my safety. I am taking measures to calm things down. In a few days when the situation becomes stable, I will certainly meet you."[24] Years later, the Dalai Lama recalled, "The crowd had already elected a kind of committee of sixty or seventy leaders, and taken an oath that if the Chinese insisted I should go, they would barricade the palace and make it impossible for me to be taken out. And the Cabinet told me the crowd was so alarmed and resolute that it would not be safe for me to go out. . . . I could hear what the people were shouting: 'The Chinese must go; leave Tibet to the Tibetans.'"

Apparently many of the leaders, including some who were armed, were women.[25] On March 11, Lhasa was engulfed in a sea of black flags acclaiming independence and support for the Dalai Lama. Thousands of women demonstrated and rallied the population of the city. They sent representatives to ask the Khampa fighters, by then with detachments only thirty miles away, not to bring the war into Lhasa. Tibetan soldiers threw away Chinese style uniforms and picked up their World War I weapons to defend their country. The Freedom Committee posted guards inside the summer palace to ensure his safety. They persuaded the remnants of the Tibetan army in Lhasa to open its arsenal, and arms were promptly distributed amid jubilation. Setting up barricades, they also fortified Chokpori Hill. Ordinary citizens of Lhasa armed themselves with shovels and farm tools, picks, swords, axes, and sticks to help defeat the Chinese. They set hundreds of goats free to ward off evil. They chanted and walked, prayed and talked.

Faced with an ultimatum by the Chinese to remove the barricades, the Dalai Lama summoned seventy leaders of the Freedom Committee and did his "best to dissuade them from their actions." On March 12, about five thousand women marched on the Indian consul-general's office and asked him to witness their planned talks with the Chinese foreign office. He refused. Nearly the entire population of Lhasa attended a meeting at Shol (under the graceful Potala).

Popular sentiment approved overwhelmingly the call to prepare formal documents of independence. Meetings in Lhasa were convened continually until March 17.[26] With Khampa fighters reported to be only twenty-five miles away, and Chinese aircraft landing nearby, no one knew what might come next. In the back

Thousands of women rallied the population to protect the Dalai Lama.
Photo by Associated Newspapers Ltd. in *Tibet Fights for Freedom: A White Book* (Bombay: Orient Longmans, 1960), 53.

streets of the Barkhor, singing could be heard of Tibetan King Gesar's victories over the Chinese around eight centuries ago. Amid great pride and happiness, lots of locally brewed *chang* was drunk.

Inside the Norbulingka, a decision was reached that the Dalai Lama should leave Tibet for his own safety. He consulted with popularly chosen leaders, who agreed.[27] On March 17, a disguised Dalai Lama slipped out of the Norbulingka undetected and made good his escape on the same day the Kashag repudiated the Seventeen-Point Agreement and formally declared independence.

The Chinese had carefully estimated Tibetan forces' strength. Cutting the city off from the Sera, Drepung, and Ganden monasteries, they isolated some four thousand fighters from Tibetan regiments ready to defend the city and surrounded thousands of people who remained encircled around the Norbulingka. Using heavy artillery and armored personnel carriers for five hours on the morning of March 19, the PLA was able to inflict enormous casualties on Tibetans without suffering many casualties of their own. When they tried to advance on the palace, however, they encountered unexpected resistance by the Dalai Lama's bodyguards and hundreds of resistance fighters who had infiltrated into the city. The heaviest fighting was in the two miles between the Potala and the Norbulingka. Launching counterattacks, Khampa fighters and Lhasa's citizens repeatedly stormed Chinese fortified positions at the cinema, radio station, and transport depot—only to be driven back with heavy losses.[28] That same day, Beijing radio formally declared the twenty-one-year-old Panchen Lama the new leader of Tibet. By the end of the month, on March 28, Chinese premier Chou En-lai ordered the government of Tibet dissolved.

On March 20, the day after Chinese artillery opened up on Norbulingka, they turned their fire on the Potala, the medical college on Chokpori hill, and other monasteries. During three days of savage fighting, two Chinese attempts were made to rush the summer palace, but Tibetans repulsed them from behind barricades with Molotovs against tanks. So many people were killed that corpses were stacked as parts of the barricades. On March 21, Khamba cavalry attacked Chinese lines but were driven back by Chinese armored personnel carriers. Seventy Khambas forced the Chinese to evacuate the cinema.[29] From the city's Muslim district, Tibetan mortars kept firing despite Chinese attempts to silence them.

Ultimately, heroism could not prevail against the technical superiority enjoyed by more than twenty-five thousand Chinese soldiers. Before dawn on March 22, defenders abandoned the Norbulingka, leaving behind piles of bodies. As Chinese soldiers entered the building, they inspected each of the hundreds of corpses to determine if one was the Dalai Lama. The Jokhang (Lhasa's main temple) was bombarded. That afternoon, as flames engulfed parts of the temple's domed interior, tanks rumbled up to its entrance. Khamba cavalry again charged and held them off for a time, even setting one tank on fire, but they were no match for twentieth-century weapons. Soon Chinese soldiers battered down the doors, and the voice of Ngabo, the same traitor who signed the Seventeen-Point Agreement, called upon those inside to surrender.

By March 23, with five thousand Tibetans killed and four thousand captured, the Chinese claimed to control the entire city. Other reports put the number killed in Lhasa at ten to fifteen thousand people with one-fourth of the city's population (about ten thousand) in prison.[30] Chinese sources claimed to have captured eight thousand small arms, eighty-one machine guns, twenty-seven mortars, and six mountain guns.[31] So many people were killed that it took at least two days to cremate or bury all the bodies.[32]

Outside Lhasa, fighting was reported in Gyantse. One dispatch maintained the city was in the hands of the resistance on March 22. Khampa soldiers and cavalry were said to control one-fourth of the countryside, where they disfigured and killed traitors.[33] By March 24, the *Hindustan Times* reported the revolt had spread to all parts of Tibet, and many sources indicated arms and equipment were being airlifted to Tibet by Chiang Kai-shek's U.S.-supplied air force. Among Muslims in neighboring Tsinghai (Qinghai) province, dozens of "counterrevolutionaries" were reported by China to have been executed or imprisoned in March, followed by an armed revolt in April.[34] By April 4, riots were reported in Xinjiang. In outer (Southwestern) Tibet, Khampa rebels received support from tens of thousands of monks. Reporters began speaking of a "national uprising," but in the same breath, they acknowledged the overwhelming force of China's army and air force. According to a secret 1960 PLA report, between March 1959 and October 1960, some eighty-seven thousand Tibetans were killed in Central Tibet alone.[35]

Exile and Occupation

From exile in Dharamsala, India, the Dalai Lama established a government-in-exile in September 1960. Elections were held for the Assembly of People's Deputies, and a new Tibetan constitution was approved in 1963, with a controversial clause allowing the removal of the Dalai Lama by a two-thirds vote. Most delegates were against the clause and were persuaded to pass it only when the Dalai Lama personally insisted upon it.

On May 1, 1960, a U-2 American spy plane was shot down over the Soviet Union, and direct U.S. air support for Tibetan fighters ended. Later that year, finding themselves under intense pursuit, Khampa resistance forces relocated to Mustang (a Tibetan part of Nepal) for easier supply. In February 1961, President Kennedy ordered new drops into Mustang.[36] In October 1962, war between China and India broke out along their border. Marginalized amid superpower rivalries, Tibetans suffered. Famine lasted into 1963 as the region reeled from the double whammy of their uprising's suppression and the aftereffects of the Great Leap Forward. The Sino-Soviet split, which caused Russia to cease its grain exports to China, dictated that Tibet's harvests were made to replace Russian grain. As a result of the subsequent shortages, Tibetans were compelled to eat cats, dogs, and anything they could find in order to survive. Disastrously, Chinese officials insisted Tibetans plant wheat rather than their traditional crop of barley. When the harvest failed to materialize, conservative estimates told of half a million Tibetans starving at the same time as their religious centers were decimated.[37]

Of 6,000 monasteries before the 1959 uprising, only about 370 remained open a year later.[38] Of 2,000 monks who had been living in the Sera monastery, a scant 50 remained. Mao may have promised to leave in twenty years, but Chinese troops were in Tibet to stay. During the Cultural Revolution, most remaining monasteries were destroyed, leaving only fifteen more or less intact.[39] "Superstitious" monks were forced to disrobe and marry. On August 25, 1966, Red Guards took over Jokhang Temple, desecrated its relics, burned precious manuscripts, and turned it into "Guest House Number Five" for their use.[40] If there is any doubt about the destruction of Tibetan Buddhist centers, Chinese statistics are equally disturbing:

TABLE 4.1 **Chinese Government Estimate of Tibetan Monasteries and Monks**

Years	Monasteries	Monks
Before 1959	2,700	114,000
1959–1966	550	67,000
1966–1983	8	970
1987	970 "religious centers"	1,500

Source: Tibet Autonomous Region report dated July 17, 1987 (prepared prior to German Chancellor Helmut Kohl's visit). See *Tibetan Review*, September 1990, 7.

While initially enthusiastic, JFK's support for Tibet's struggle dwindled after his ambassador to India, John Kenneth Galbraith, lobbied against it, calling Tibetans barbaric and "deeply unhygienic men."[41] Kennedy equivocated, but Nixon and Kissinger capitulated to Chinese demands. In 1969, a secret meeting between Mao and Kissinger took place that led to normalization of relations. Mao insisted above all that U.S. aid to Tibet (and diplomatic relations with Taiwan) must be cut off before China would restore diplomatic relations with the United States.[42] To help with demobilization of the Tibetan forces they had trained and equipped, the CIA spent millions of dollars to ease Tibetans into civilian lives, including the purchase of Annapurna Hotel in Pokhara, Nepal.[43] In 1974, Tibetan fighters in General Wangdu's detachment in Mustang refused to disarm. The Dalai Lama intervened and pleaded with them to lay down their arms. Unable to disobey but unwilling to surrender, many fighters committed suicide.[44]

With an end to armed resistance, China invited Tibetan representatives of the government in exile to return in 1978. When the first delegation from Dharamsala arrived, hundreds of thousands of people turned out to greet them with cries and wails about the misfortunes they suffered. In 1979, Deng Xiaoping permitted open cultural celebrations and a less restrictive environment, and a resurgence of public religious observances occurred.

The Late 1980s

As Han settler-colonialism increased the region's Chinese population, Tibetans spontaneously rose in opposition. Their poorly organized protests were suppressed by overwhelming force. In September and October 1987, a wave of discontent swelled in Lhasa and other towns at the same time as the Dalai Lama visited Washington, D.C., where he offered Beijing a five-point peace plan. Chinese television showed a brief segment of the Dalai Lama's visit, but only as a means to condemn him. As news traveled of their leader's initiative, twenty-one monks from the Drepung monastery met in a Barkhor teahouse on the morning of September 27.[45] (Three days earlier, more than fifteen thousand Tibetans had been compelled by work units and neighborhood committees to witness a mass sentencing at Lhasa sports stadium, where Chinese officials condemned eleven Tibetans, two to death.) At around 9:00 a.m. on the twenty-seventh, the monks unveiled a hand-drawn Tibetan flag and began to walk a circle around Jokhang Temple, shouting, "Tibet is Independent." Dozens of people joined them as they finished three circles. In the huge square in front of the Jokhang, all the monks and three others were taken into custody. (A subsequent Chinese account states that no clashes occurred.)[46]

On October 1, about forty monks (most from the Sera monastery) performed a similar circle of protest. This time, however, police arrived and beat many of them. More than sixty people were taken into a nearby police station. Soon a crowd of several thousand people converged and demanded the release of the protesters. After they forced police to retreat into the building, they set it on fire. One monk, Champa Tenzin, courageously ran inside and helped free monks being detained—but at least three were shot and killed as they attempted to escape. An eyewitness quoted by Chinese authorities claimed six people were killed.[47] Independent sources reported that a dozen people were killed and about four hundred arrested.[48] Police shooting from the rooftop of the burning building caused most of the casualties. Fights in the Barkhor continued through the night as people refused to be pacified. For his heroism, Champa Tenzin was lifted on the shoulders of the crowd—before melting away and making good his escape from Tibet.

The next night, soldiers surrounded Sera Monastery while police rampaged inside, arresting anyone they thought might have been involved in planning the

Champa Tenzin's heroism was greeted enthusiastically in the streets of Lhasa.
Photo by John Ackerly in *Tibet Since 1950: Silence, Prison or Exile* (New York: Aperture, 2000), 72–73.

demonstration. Three days later, on October 6, about fifty monks peacefully protested in front of the Tibetan Regional Administration office and asked for the release of the twenty-one monks from Drepung monastery who had mounted the first circle of protest on September 27.

For Tibetans, the circle of protest was more than a convenient way to picket. On any day, thousands of ordinary people can be seen circumambulating temples and holy sites, holding their prayer wheels and chanting. *Khorra* is a means of building up good karma—a way of being reborn in a better future life. Precisely because the protests used an ordinary means of religious expression, however peaceful, police felt the need to repress it as part of their struggle against "theism." Although monks simply walked peacefully on October 6, they were set upon by riot police, severely beaten, and arrested—even though they had not resisted, thrown stones, or even carried a flag.[49] Over the next several weeks, more than five hundred Tibetans were arrested, most taken from their homes around midnight, while the city slept. In late October, dozens of people were arrested in the Barkhor, and the army occupied the area.

Although brutalized and overwhelmed, Tibetans refused to remain quiet. The next spring, they rose again. On March 5, 1988, as the ten-day Monlam festival was finishing with a statue of the future Buddha circling the Jokhang, monks from Ganden monastery rushed the stage where Chinese officials sat. They demanded freedom for Yulo Dawa Tsering, a senior proindependence monk arrested months before and held without charges.

According to monks' testimony, a communist official told the protesters to shut up and threw a rock at them. After the rock was tossed back, gunfire rang out,

Monks initiated protests on March 5, 1988.
Photo from *Circle of Protest: Political Ritual in the Tibetan Uprising* (New York: Columbia University Press, 1994), 112–13.

and a Khampa fell dead. About two hundred monks picked up the dead body and walked clockwise around the Jokhang. Using their religion as a resource, protesters circumambulated the Jokhang with the corpse. By the third circuit, more than two thousand people had joined, and the crowd chased off Chinese riot police. Knowing too well that massive force would soon be used against them, monks took refuge inside the Jokhang's heavy doors. Behind a barrage of tear gas, police armed with iron bars and nail-studded clubs attacked. Once they got inside the temple, they killed many people and wounded dozens.[50] Many injured, limp bodies were thrown from the roof of the Jokhang onto the Barkhor plaza.

Street fighting went on into the night, and barricades were built to protect sections of the Barkhor. Monks changed clothes to avoid easy identification. Slingshots and stones were employed in battles all over Lhasa. One monk reported, "Tibetans said, 'Now we must chase away all the Chinese.' Then there were two groups of opinion. One group said we should not fight all the Chinese since they are human beings also. The other group said that as long as they are Chinese we must struggle against them."[51] Late that night, at least one Chinese restaurant and pharmacy were set on fire, apparently the first time protesters targeted Chinese businesses.

One Chinese policeman was killed and twenty-eight others admitted to hospital. Civilian casualties were more severe. One observer claimed sixteen dead. The next day, a street poster claimed twelve monks had been killed in one of the shrines inside the Jokhang. A subsequent account told of Chinese troops who beat twenty monks to death and dragged off two hundred others—who disappeared inside the iron cages of Chinese prisons in which thousands of Tibetans languish—and thousands more have expired.[52]

Conditions in prisons included beatings, electric shocks, injections of "truth" serums, ice water baths, hanging from ropes, and many other sadistic tortures. In July 1988, it was reported that dogs were set upon female prisoners in Gutsa prison.[53] Some nuns reported electric batons were thrust inside them.[54] In February 1990, Asia Watch called Tibet "a laboratory for torture techniques for the Chinese security forces."[55] Many prisoners never were granted trials at all, while others received only cursory judgments based upon poor evidence.

In the summer of 1988, while prisoner abuse and police brutality were rampant, Drepung monks (all veterans of the September 27, 1987, demonstration) used woodblocks to print an eleven-page manifesto, "The Meaning of the Precious Democratic Constitution of Tibet." Countering Chinese claims to have "helped" Tibet, the document sketched the outlines of an independent Tibet. The monks called for "political and social organization on the basis of cooperation and consent of the broad masses of Tibet . . . or by representatives whose powers are limited by the people." They did not want to return to the past: "Having completely eradicated the practices of the old society with all its faults, the future Tibet will not resemble our former condition and be a restoration of serfdom or be like the so-called 'old system' of rule by a succession of feudal masters or monastic estates." They advocated freedom for people with "different individual views" who should be "able to practice what they think without need of fear, hypocrisy, or concealment."[56] For writing it, one monk subsequently received a nineteen-year prison sentence. Others were denounced at a public rally called by the Communist Party and referred to as "scum of the religious circles" who had "thoroughly betrayed the religious doctrines and canons of Buddhism by their actions."[57]

On September 27, 1988, demonstrations broke out in response to renewed temple violations by Chinese police. The next month, a sixteen-year-old was shot and killed in Lhasa. Later in 1988 while in Strasbourg visiting the European Parliament, the Dalai Lama offered China control of Tibet's foreign policy. In 1989 he was awarded the Nobel Peace Prize. On December 10, 1988, the fortieth anniversary of Human Rights Day, protests—and hundreds of police—came to Lhasa. Mainly monks and nuns who met privately in small groups prepared the actions. That day, Chinese authorities refused to release many Tibetan children from school for fear they would join the protests, and Tibetans who worked for the state were not allowed to go home after work. With so many Chinese soldiers near the Jokhang, the monks changed the venue for the beginning of the protest to Ramoche temple. A small group of thirty to forty monks and nuns walked toward the Jokhang Temple led by a monk named Gyalpo carrying a flag.[58] When the group split in two, another flag emerged. Without warning, police ran toward the first group—by now about two hundred people—and the police chief opened fire, killing the monk with the flag. After using tear gas, the police opened fire upon the entire neighborhood with automatic weapons, killing and wounding many

118 | ASIA'S UNKNOWN UPRISINGS

others—including a Dutch tourist who lived to tell that she believed eighteen people were killed and seventy or eighty wounded.[59] Other estimates of casualties were lower—but all agreed the police fired without warning. According to an American tourist, "The demonstrators were completely non-violent—chanting, not carrying any kind of weapons or throwing rocks."[60] A week later on December 18, more than sixty Tibetan students protested in Beijing's Tiananmen Square.

On January 28, 1989, the Panchen Lama suddenly died of a heart attack a week after he had publicly criticized Beijing's policy and called for greater autonomy for Tibet. As rumors spread he had been murdered, a leaflet appeared in Lhasa signed by the "Independence Uprising Organization." The group questioned why Tibetans were not being allowed to view the Panchen Lama's body and announced it was sending a delegation to request a public viewing.[61] To stave off any great protest in Lhasa, authorities held a state funeral thousands of miles away in Beijing. Although religious leaders have traditionally determined the identity of successors, Chinese Premier Li Peng declared that the government would undertake the search for his replacement.

Sporadic protests and posters signed by the Independence Uprising Organization called for people to refrain from celebrating Losar (New Year) that March, the anniversary of the previous year's assault on the Jokhang. At the end of February, organized protests by monks and nuns, including a parade of 1,700 people, were broken up by hundreds of police. Nuns emerged as leaders of the movement.[62] On March 1, eight nuns marched; the next day, thirty-seven walked together; on March 4, a few monks and dozens of people joined some thirteen nuns. On Sunday, March 5, a small group began to circle the Jokhang, and it grew into a march of thousands of people, the biggest protest in thirty years.

As in so many other incidents when riots break out, police violence set off a reaction.[63] Around noon in the Barkhor marketplace around the Jokhang Temple, people were marching peacefully when Chinese police on nearby rooftops threw bottles at them. Without warning, police opened fire, killing at least two people. Around 3:00 p.m., people reassembled and marched again. Fighting back with stones against teargas, they were again fired upon by police, this time using automatic weapons.[64] One of the people killed was "guilty" of carrying a Tibetan flag, a "crime" for which he was shot dead. Dozens were wounded by gunfire. After soldiers destroyed a Tibetan restaurant, people attacked Chinese stores, burning them and setting alight bonfires of their goods in the streets. Furniture was piled into barricades, by now a familiar means of defense for citizens of Lhasa. The next day, renewed protests again brought police gunfire with more fatalities and injuries. Protesters attacked government offices even though rooftop police snipers continued to fire on them. Claiming Tibetans had used guns, Chinese troops withdrew from the center of the city.

The government response to the new wave of protests was to overrun temples, massacre as many as 250 protesters and finally, at midnight on March 8, 1989, to impose martial law for 387 days.[65] Chinese authorities ordered all foreigners out of Tibet. Two thousand heavily armed troops occupied Tibetan neighborhoods in Lhasa, and one thousand people were estimated to have been detained.[66] Notorious Drapchi prison was swollen with new arrestees. (While the government reported 16 citizens and 1 police officer killed in Lhasa, eyewitnesses claimed more than 60 and as many as 250 people were killed on March 5, 6, and 7. According to Chinese sources, in response to protests in towns and cities, police and military forces killed 600 people in the eighteen months leading up to the summer of 1989.[67])

Whatever their differences, Chinese leaders Zhao Ziyang and Li Peng—soon to be bitter rivals—saw eye-to-eye on Tibet. In February 1989, as tensions rose in Tibet following the death of the Panchen Lama, Zhao sent off a stern cable to Lhasa ordering officials to undertake "severe preventative measures." Only three months later, Zhao would be deposed for his sympathies for student protesters in Tiananmen Square, and martial law would be declared in Beijing in response to a student-led uprising that threatened to overthrow the government. Chinese citizens' silence during their government's repression in Tibet sealed the fate of their democracy movement. After a year of harsh martial law from 1989 to 1990, Tibet's Communist Party Secretary Hu Jintao praised troops for their "immortal deeds."[68] After his dutiful imposition of martial law in Tibet, Hu rose rapidly through the ranks and became paramount leader of China in 2002.

Continuing Resistance

With so many activists behind bars under abysmal conditions, it's not surprising that resistance inside Tibetan prisons became widespread. In 1992, about twenty-three women in Drapchi donned traditional clothing for Tibetan New Year, which fell on March 5 that year. Ordered to wear prison clothing, they refused. Beaten, kicked, and prodded with electric batons, the women persisted. They secretly recorded a cassette of themselves singing independence songs and smuggled it out. For singing on tape, many were again beaten, placed in solitary confinement, and had their sentences extended from five to nine years.[69]

Resistance continued with hunger strikes in 1993, 1996, 1997, and 1998. In 1998, prisoners were assembled inside Drapchi to dutifully observe International Workers' Day on May 1, but some persisted in shouting independence slogans. Gunfire, clubs, and electric batons were wielded against them. Three days later, a similar incident occurred, and deadly force was again employed. It appears the death toll may have been as high as eleven people: six nuns, four monks, and one other prisoner. Six nuns committed suicide on June 7, more than a month after the original incident.[70]

With sporadic episodes of protest, Tibetans continue to resist Chinese control. In May 1996, seventy Ganden monks were arrested and seven were believed to have been killed during a demonstration.[71] In 1997, many monks in Shigatse were forced to leave their monastery after they refused to cooperate with communist cadre who entered without permission. In March 1999, three monks were arrested in Barkhor for shouting independence slogans. In August 2007, dozens of people were arrested in Lithang (a town with many Tibetan residents in Sichuan) after someone took over the microphone at an annual horse festival and asked people if they wanted the Dalai Lama to return to Tibet. As people began to protest the detention of the man who asked the question, police were reported to fire into the air to disperse them. Some two hundred people were arrested. In October 2007, when the Dalai Lama was awarded a medal by the U.S. Congress, thousands of police confronted monks at Drepung Monastery who wished to celebrate.[72] All over Tibet, celebrations brought police attention—but were well attended nonetheless.

With the massive population transfer of Han Chinese to Tibet, some 7.5 million Han today outnumber the six million Tibetans. Tibetans' claims to special rights over their lands are rapidly becoming similar to those of Native Americans inside the United States. With flights and a direct rail link to China's East, tourism in Tibet accounts for an increasing part of its economy. Chinese vendors sell off precious temple artifacts in state stores. While ancient sites of worship are open, the number of monks is limited by the state, and modern conditions militate against religion's appeal. Beijing's third national forum on Tibet in July 1994 brought harsher supervision of monasteries and nunneries, purges of any Tibetan remotely suspected of nationalist sympathies, greater control over education of young Tibetans, increased population transfer of Han Chinese, and a campaign against the Dalai Lama.[73] In 1995, both the Dalai Lama and communist government chose different people to be the next Panchen Lama. The boy selected by the Dalai Lama disappeared.

Two discourses compete for hegemony today in Tibet. For Tibetans, March 10 is Tibetan National Uprising Day, the anniversary of the 1959 uprising in Lhasa, while Beijing celebrates "Serfs Emancipation Day" on March 28, to mark the abolition in 1959 of "slavery" and the theocratic rule of the Dalai Lama. In 2008, Chinese security teams canvassed monasteries and required monks and nuns to sign statements condemning the Dalai Lama—if they refused they were expelled from their monasteries and sometimes arrested. While the subaltern counter-narrative of Tibetan freedom may be censored inside China, Tibetans remain committed to their national identity and express it passionately—but without effective organization.

In the buildup to the 2008 Summer Olympics in Beijing, worldwide protests accompanied the journey of the Olympic torch from Greece, a dramatic show of how much China's Tibet policy costs its international image. On the anniversary of the 1959 uprising, hundreds of assembled monks in Lhasa called for release of imprisoned colleagues, including the Panchen Lama, and the Dalai Lama's return to Tibet. Police began to beat the monks, who retreated to the Drepung Monastery, where police surrounded them. The next day, more than six hundred monks from Sera and Ganden as well as nuns from Chutsang were prevented from demonstrating.[74] When monks were again assaulted, citizens spontaneously came to their aid. In the combat that day, at least one thousand Chinese-owned shops and dozens of cars were attacked—as were Han people caught in public. According to Chinese media, at least 19 people were killed and 325 injured in Lhasa, most of them Han Chinese. Protests rapidly spread into Sichuan, Gansu, and Qinghai provinces. All together, incidents of unrest occurred in some 177 places, making the 2008 uprising the largest and most widespread since 1959.[75]

Between March 10 and June 22, more than 125 riots were counted. Chinese authorities claimed 18 civilians and one police officer were killed, 382 citizens and 241 police injured, arson attacks on 120 houses and 84 vehicles, and looting of 1,367 small businesses.[76] Tibetan statistics were much higher: the Dalai Lama counted more than 80 people killed within the first week, and the Tibetan Government in Exile claimed 220 Tibetans had been killed and almost 1,300 wounded by Chinese forces by June 2008.[77] More than 4,434 Tibetans—the number claimed by China—and as many as 7,000 people—as stated by Tibetan sources—were rounded up. In Xiahe, 220 monks were arrested and beaten, and citizens responded by attacking Chinese-owned shops. Police killed several Tibetans.[78] In Beijing, Tibetan students conducted a candlelight vigil. In 2012, dozens of monks committed suicide.

The Dalai Lama is quite clear that force should not be used in the struggle for justice. He has frankly stated on a number of occasions that he was opposed from "the very beginning" to the use of arms. Given his status as god-king to so many Tibetans, his disapproval alone dooms in advance any resistance army or uprising involving force. As we saw in the case of Burma, leadership by one person—no matter how saintly—imposes strictures on the movement's unity and effectiveness.

The Tibetan government in exile in Dharamsala is democratically elected and includes only a minority of monks. The Dalai Lama has openly advocated more democracy, even hinting that his successor might be elected like a pope. He has also said he may choose the new Dalai Lama before he dies to ensure that the Chinese government does not usurp the religious authority for which they have shown so little respect. Although he has been incredibly flexible, requesting only more autonomy for Tibet, not full independence, within a context of China's control of military and foreign policy, he remains a pariah in the eyes of Chinese leaders.

The dispersal of Tibetans throughout China—and the world—provides an enduring stratum of resistance to the incorporation of noncapitalist Tibetans into the orbit of modernity. History works in mysterious and often invisible ways. The most significant Chinese popular movement in the latter part of the twentieth century followed the Tibetan Uprising of 1989. In the long run, Tibetans' history of having weakened the Mongols—then the world's most formidable military force—may prefigure their role in helping to create a world free of weapons of mass destruction, a world where all forms of life are respected.

NOTES

1   Dalai Lama, *My Land and My People* (New Delhi: Srishti Publishers, 1997), 69.

2   Ibid., 76.

3   Jamyang Norbu, *Warriors of Tibet: The Story of Aten and the Khampas' Fight for the Freedom of Their Country* (London: Wisdom Publications, 1986), 22–23.

4   Ibid., 52–53.

5   Mary Craig, *Tears of Blood: A Cry for Tibet* (London: HarperCollins, 1992), 15. See International Commission of Jurists, *The Question of Tibet and the Rule of Law* (Geneva, H. Studer, 1960), 132–33 for the estimate of the number of Tibetans who have died from Chinese attacks at 1.2 million. According to information compiled by the Tibetan

Administration in exile, over 1.2 million Tibetans died between 1949 and 1979. At least five hundred people in Eastern Tibet perished in 1956 as a result of Chinese insistence on replacing the region's traditional barley crop with wheat, which failed and caused famine to appear in Tibet for the first time. See Mikel Dunham, *Buddha's Warriors: The Story of the CIA-Backed Tibetan Freedom Fighters, the Chinese Invasion, and the Ultimate Fall of Tibet* (New York: Penguin, 2004), 5. Chinese government figures for both population and casualties are considerably lower.

6   *A Survey of Tibet Autonomous Region* (Tibet People's Publishing House, 1984).

7   Moreover, in his famous speech "On Contradiction" on February 27, 1957, Mao added, "It has now been decided not to proceed with democratic reform in Tibet during the period of the second Five Year Plan (1958–1962) and we can only decide whether it will be done in the period of the third Five Year Plan in the light of the situation obtaining at that time." See Raja Hutheesing, ed., *Tibet Fights for Freedom: A White Book* (Bombay: Orient Longmans, 1960), 20. The Dalai Lama was "convinced that Mao would never use force to convert Tibet into a Communist state. . . . I still find it hard to believe that these oppressions had the approval and support of Mao Tse-tung." He felt very differently about Chou En-lai. See Dalai Lama, *My Land*, 118.

8   William Blum, *Killing Hope* (Monroe, ME: Common Courage Press, 1995), 26; Dunham, *Buddha's Warriors*, 200–208, 365.

9   Jane Ardley, *The Tibetan Independence Movement: Political Religious and Gandhian Perspectives* (London: Routledge, 2002), 28–29.

10   "Work Report of the People's Council of the Tibetan Autonomous Chou of Kanze," *Kanze Pao* (Kangting) as quoted in Hutheesing, *Tibet Fights*, 23–24.

11   Dunham, *Buddha's Warriors*, 257.

12   Ibid., 256–59.

13   Hutheesing, *Tibet Fights*, 31.

14   Tashi Khedrup, *Adventures of a Tibetan Fighting Monk* (Bangkok: Orchid Press, 1998), 86.

15   Hutheesing, *Tibet Fights*, 28.

16   Dalai Lama, *My Land*, 134.

17   Khedrup, *Adventures*, 102; Craig, *Tears of Blood*, 97; Dunham, *Buddha's Warriors*, 263.

18   Hutheesing, *Tibet Fights*, 37; Dalai Lama, *My Land*, 168.

19   Hutheesing, *Tibet Fights*, 39.

20   Khedrup, *Adventures*, 89.

21   Hutheesing, *Tibet Fights*, 38; Dunham, *Buddha's Warriors*, 274.

22   Craig, *Tears of Blood*, 106.

23   Hutheesing, *Tibet Fights*, 17.

24   Ibid., 79.

25   Dunham, *Buddha's Warriors*, 272.

26   Hutheesing, *Tibet Fights*, 42.

27   Dalai Lama, *My Land*, 196.

28   Michel Peissel, *Secret War in Tibet* (Boston: Little, Brown, 1972), 143.

29   Ibid., 144.

30   Dunham, *Buddha's Warriors*, 326.

31   New China News Agency, March 25, 1959, as quoted in Hutheesing, *Tibet Fights*, 51.

32   An official act of the U.S. Senate Resolution 60, passed on March 9, 2000, cited Chinese statistics of eighty-seven thousand Tibetans killed, arrested, or deported to labor camps as a result of the March 10, 1959, uprising. The International Commission of Jurists estimated the number of people killed in Lhasa alone was placed at about twenty thousand, as reported in Hutheesing, *Tibet Fights*, 222.

33   Sadly for the resistance, these same fighters also seized the horses of monks fleeing

the fighting in Lhasa, whom they imprisoned. Some in the detachment of Khampa fighters with Chuzhi Gangdruk simply took flour, butter, and horses from poor farmers, but others also took Tibetan girls from their families. See Khedrup, *Adventures*, 98; Dunham, *Buddha's Warriors*, 241.

34   Hutheesing, *Tibet Fights*, 29, 45, 106.

35   *Xizang Xingshi he Renwu Jiaoyu de Jiben Jiaocai*, 1960, as quoted in http://www.tibet.com/WhitePaper/white5.html.

36   Dunham, *Buddha's Warriors*, 353.

37   Ibid., 5.

38   From India, the Dalai Lama claimed in June 1959 that over a thousand monasteries had been destroyed before 1958. See Ardley, *Tibetan Independence Movement*, 30; Dunham, *Buddha's Warriors*, 325.

39   Dunham, *Buddha's Warriors*, 372.

40   Craig, *Tears of Blood*, 167–68.

41   John Kenneth Galbraith, *A Life in Our Times* (Boston: Houghton Mifflin, 1981), 395, as quoted in Dunham, *Buddha's Warriors*, 356.

42   Dunham, *Buddha's Warriors*, 382.

43   Ibid., 383.

44   Ibid., 389.

45   Ronald D. Schwartz, *Circle of Protest: Political Ritual in the Tibetan Uprising* (New York: Columbia University Press, 1994), 22.

46   Qiogya, "What Really Happened in Lhasa," in *Tibetans on Tibet* (Beijing: China Reconstructs Press, 1988), 188.

47   Ibid., 189.

48   Melissa Harris and Sidney Jones, eds., *Tibet Since 1950: Silence, Prison or Exile* (New York: Aperture, Human Rights Watch, 2000), 146.

49   Schwartz, *Circle of Protest*, 26.

50   Testimony in ibid., 80–83.

51   Ibid., 83.

52   Lobsang Norbu, a monk arrested in 1959 who subsequently spent sixteen years in Chinese prisons, saw thousands of people die around him. Some even "cut their own throats" to escape the brutality of their daily conditions.

53   John Ackerly and Blake Kerr, "Torture and Imprisonment in Tibet," in *The Anguish of Tibet*, eds. Petra Kelly, Gert Bastian, and Pat Aiello (Berkeley: Parallax Press, 1991), 122–23.

54   Schwartz, *Circle of Protest*, 98.

55   Quoted in Craig, *Tears of Blood*, 18.

56   Schwartz, *Circle of Protest*, 126–27.

57   Ibid., 125.

58   See Amnesty International, report, "Repression in Tibet, 1987–1992."

59   Christa Meindersma, "Eyewitness Report: Tibet, December 10, 1988," in *Anguish of Tibet*, 245–47.

60   Schwartz, *Circle of Protest*, 140.

61   Although the Chinese government tried to use the Panchen Lama against the Dalai Lama, he refused to denounce the Dalai Lama in 1964, after which he disappeared for thirteen years. On March 28, 1987, he delivered a stirring appeal to a subcommittee of the National People's Congress in Beijing and referred to killings of civilians in Amdo by PLA troops as "atrocities." See http://www.tibet.com/WhitePaper/white5.html.

62   According to the Tibetan Information Network, February 21, 1992, nuns took part in fifteen of twenty-five demonstrations from September 1987 to September 1989, and were solely responsible for more than half of them.

63 Once again, a European tourist subsequently testified about these events. See Susanne Maier, "Impressions of Lhasa, March 1989," in *Anguish of Tibet*, 248–51.

64 Schwartz, *Circle of Protest*, 157.

65 Pico Iyer, "Tibet's Nobel Man," *Time* (Hong Kong) 173, no. 25–26 (June 29–July 6, 2009): 68. He counted 250 dead in Lhasa after the demonstrations in March 1989.

66 Amnesty International, "One Year after Martial Law: Update on Human Rights in Tibet," in *Anguish of Tibet*, 252.

67 *Tibet: The Lost Nation* (film, 1989).

68 Speech of April 30, 1990, as reported in *Tibet Review*, September 1990, 4.

69 Steven Marshall, "Prisons in Tibet," in *Tibet Since 1950*, 147.

70 Ibid., 144–49.

71 Ardley, *Tibetan Independence Movement*, 24.

72 "Tackling Tibet," *Time*, January 9, 2008.

73 International Committee of Lawyers for Tibet, *A Generation in Peril: The Lives of Tibetan Children under Chinese Rule* (Berkeley: International Committee of Lawyers for Tibet, 2001), 11–12.

74 Warren W. Smith Jr., *Tibet's Last Stand? The Tibetan Uprising of 2008 and China's Response* (Lanham, MD: Rowman & Littlefield, 2010), 2.

75 Free Tibet's website has an excellent BBC documentary available at http://www.freetibet.org/newsmedia/uprising-tibet-video-chronology.

76 Edward Wong, "China Has Sentenced 55 over Tibet Riots in March," *International Herald Tribune*, November 6, 2008, 6.

77 Taiwan Foundation for Democracy, *China Human Rights Report 2008* (Taipei, 2009), 11.

78 Nicholas Kristof, "The Terrified Monks," *New York Times*, May 15, 2008, A29; Smith, *Tibet's Last Stand*, 3.

CHAPTER 5

China

Let China sleep, for when she wakes, the whole world will tremble.
—Napoleon

Satellites Have Already Reached Heaven, but Democracy Is Still Stuck in Hell!
—Protest banner carried by researchers from Chinese Academy of Sciences

It's anarchy, but it's organized anarchy.
—Dan Rather, CBS News, May 1989

CHRONOLOGY	
April 15, 1989	Party leader Hu Yaobang passes away; within an hour, workers gather in Tiananmen Square
April 18	About two thousand students sit-in at Tiananmen Square; workers begin to discuss forming organization
April 19	Autonomous student union forms at Beijing University; ten thousand students in Tiananmen Square
April 19	125 students sit-in at elite housing at Zhongnanhai for two days until dispersed by police
April 20	Beijing Normal University Autonomous Union organized, calls for citywide student organization
April 21	Boycott of classes begins in response to police clubs breaking up Zhongnanhai sit-in previous night
April 21	Sixty thousand students gather in a soccer field, march to Tiananmen that night for Hu's funeral

April 22	At Hu's funeral, over a hundred thousand attend, chant "We Want Dialogue"; heavy protests in Xian April 22; after the funeral, students kneel, holding a petition; no one comes forward to accept it
April 24	Autonomous Student Federation founded in Beijing
April 26	People's Daily editorial condemns antistate turmoil and chaos
April 27	Despite police blockades, more than a hundred thousand students march to Tiananmen Square
April 27	Fourteen-hour march; over five hundred thousand citizens defy police in a carnival-like atmosphere
April 29	Officially recognized student group meets with government
May 4	Rally attracts over one million people for seventieth anniversary of 1919 student movement
May 8	Some students return to class, others favor a boycott
May 10	Over five thousand participate in bicycle-demonstration supporting journalists' call for press freedom
May 11	Over the heads of the autonomous student unions, celebrity movement leaders plan action
May 13	Hunger strike begins and soon is joined by about two thousand people
May 14	Because televised talks were being prerecorded, not broadcast live, some hunger strikers disrupt them
May 15	Gorbachev visits, but ceremony in Tiananmen replaced by airport ceremony
May 16	Three hundred thousand people march in sympathy with hunger strikers, occupy Tiananmen Square
May 16	On behalf of central committee, Zhao Ziyang calls protest "patriotic"; hunger strike continues
May 17–18	More than three thousand hunger strikers, some dramatically fainting; more than a million people protest in support on both days; media reports sympathetically on hunger strikers; workers congregate in square; journalists demand, "No more lies"; people sing "We Shall Overcome" for the foreign press assembled for the Gorbachev visit; singer Cui Jian joins protests
May 18	Li Peng sternly lectures hunger strikers in meeting in Great Hall of the People; Outside Secondary Schools Student Autonomous Federation formed
May 19	Early morning visit by tearful Zhao to Tiananmen calls for compromise; martial law declared; army mobilized; Beijing Workers Autonomous Union calls for general strike against martial law
May 20	Hundreds of thousands of Beijing citizens peacefully block

	the army for forty-eight hours and provide the troops with food, drink, and flowers; in more than eighty cities and at six hundred colleges and technical universities, protests involve more than 2.8 million people; "flying tigers" (citizens on motorcycles) report on troop movements; Zhao Ziyang out as Party general secretary; Premier Li Peng wins struggle; troops pull back
May 21	Television broadcasts from Beijing are suspended; more troops arrive; people continue to block them
May 23	Organization of all autonomous groups is formed; workers, students, intellectuals, and citizens meet at noon every day; unanimous decision to leave on May 30 (tenth day of martial law)
May 27	Millions of dollars raised in Hong Kong racetrack benefit concert; Central Art Academy students erect "goddess of democracy"
May 28	Attempted abduction of Chai Ling and Feng Congde (the "commanders") by other activists at 4:00 a.m.
May 30	Only ten thousand students still occupy the square
June 2	New hunger strike by four people has huge impact; square fills again
June 3	Army again tries to empty Tiananmen Square; buses stopped by crowds
June 4	At 2:00 a.m., army units begin fighting their way into the city; many soldiers killed; people gather at every intersection on Changan Avenue; disbelief that troops are using live ammunition; 4:45 a.m.: with the square surrounded, vote is taken and students leave square
June 5–6	Shooting continues in Beijing; casualties mount
June 8	Government spokesperson claims three hundred dead, seven thousand injured

IN 1989, STUDENT activists in China sparked a national uprising for democracy that was only brought to an end after a massacre in working-class suburbs around Beijing's Tiananmen Square.[1] Despite accounts linking it to reform-minded political leaders, the revolt in China originated outside the ranks of the Chinese Communist Party (CCP). Though it was widely portrayed as a student movement, workers were significantly involved—as was nearly the entire population of Beijing, especially after May 20, when hundreds of thousands of people successfully demobilized what seemed like an endless convoy of trucks bringing in army units to "sanitize" the protesters' base in Tiananmen Square. As we saw in 1980 in Gwangju, students initiated protests, but once dangers multiplied, they often took refuge in their homes and campuses, while working-class activists surged to the forefront of the movement and bore the brunt of the unleashed fury of the state.

Within the hallowed halls of the communist elite, as the global chain reaction of revolts against military dictatorships continued, significant support for reform emerged within the party. For sympathizing with protesting students, Hu Yaobang had been forced to step down as party general secretary in 1987, and two years later, Zhao Ziyang was similarly nudged from power. What distinguished the 1989 movement from previous episodes of dissent was the popular power wielded by spontaneously formed autonomous groups. No "commander-in-chief" or central committee controlled the whole movement, although several leaders claimed to do so. Rather, across the country, on university campuses and in workplaces, independent groups formed at the grassroots and united in action. Multiple and diverse tendencies simultaneously coexisted within the movement. While student leader Wuer Kaixi famously intoned his desire for Western consumerism and Nike shoes, the Beijing Autonomous Workers' Federation (BAWF), along with a dozen other such formations, advocated more democracy within a socialist framework.

A significant difference between the Chinese movement and simultaneously occurring ones in Czechoslovakia and much of Eastern Europe was the near absence of calls for a market-based capitalism among Chinese dissidents. Beginning in 1978, Deng Xiaoping had initiated a whole series of such reforms from the top and encouraged the emergence of a market-Leninist system within the state control-led economy so carefully nurtured from the 1950s to the 1970s. In December 1978, when the Central Committee ordered the dismantling of collectivized farms and authorized family farms to sell some goods on the market, one of the great accomplishments of the Maoist revolution was undone—and locally based party officials quickly enriched themselves. By 1980, Chinese citizens, if of any one opinion, were worried about high inflation and erosion in their standard of living that the new market-based reforms brought with them. "To get rich is glorious," Deng insisted, yet many workers found themselves less secure, while managers and the party elite become spectacularly wealthy. One of the world's most egalitarian societies became so stratified that the party eventually stopped releasing data measuring inequality.

The 1989 revolt was not limited to Beijing. By the time the insurgency had been brought to a bloody end, more than eighty cities experienced mobilizations of one kind or another involving millions of people as an eros effect swept the country. Years later, people spoke of a "Hundred Million Heroes" in reference to those who acted in 1989. Even though that is an astonishing number, it includes only about 10 percent of the country. When we consider four million out of Nepal's population of thirty million mobilized on the final day of protests in 2006 (more than 13 percent), and compare both those numbers with 300,000 of Gwangju's 750,000 citizens who mobilized on May 21 (or about 42 percent), we get a sense of the relative intensity of these mobilizations. While China's potential for political change was thwarted by overwhelming force in 1989 and blunted over subsequent decades by economic reform, the trajectory for China's future—as revealed in the actions and aspirations that emerged in the heat of events in 1989—provides a significant glimpse of the changing character of freedom in China.

While prolific, Western media coverage of the occupation of Tiananmen Square and subsequent reports on the Chinese democracy movement are suspect.

Many Western observers have framed the events in China with synchronous risings in Eastern Europe that overthrew Soviet rule in 1989 rather than in the context of Confucian culture and Asian politico-economic developments. The imposition of anticommunist Western ideology—so destructive in shaping U.S. interventions in Korea and Vietnam as means to "contain" communism—distorts Chinese history in 1989.

For decades, the United States has waged war on Chinese communism, our erstwhile ally during World War II. After the defeat of Japan, President Harry Truman ordered fifty thousand U.S. Marines to China to work alongside Japanese soldiers and fight on Chiang's side against communists. U.S. troops immediately looked askance at their officers for explanations about their mission. Around Christmas 1945, a U.S. lieutenant reported, "They ask me, too, why they're here . . . but you can't tell a man that he's here to disarm the Japanese when he's guarding the same railway with Japanese."[2] More than a hundred thousand U.S. soldiers and sailors were stationed in China by 1946.

During the subsequent bloody civil war, the United States aided Chiang Kai-shek and Kuomintang (KMT) while Western media vilified Mao Zedong and the Communist Party. After Chiang suffered ignominious defeat in 1949, the U.S. forces massively intervened in neighboring Korea's civil war the following year. As the war against communism intensified, McCarthyism polarized the United States, and U.S. planes repeatedly attacked China's side of their border with Korea. Finally the CCP authorized its army to drive back the United States. So badly did American ground forces fare that without air superiority and chemical/biological warfare, U.S. troops in all probability would have been overrun. From January to March 1952, a substantial body of evidence proves U.S. germ warfare against China "spilled over" from Korea—including testimony from thirty-eight captured U.S. Air Force officers and men and a six-hundred-page report coauthored by scientists from Sweden, Italy, Brazil, the Soviet Union, France, and Great Britain.[3] When the bloodletting ceased, Chinese casualties were estimated in the hundreds of thousands—including Mao's eldest son—while millions of Koreans were killed. It is no accident that both the Korean and Vietnam Wars were fought on China's borders.

Throughout the 1960s, U.S. forces aided Taiwan's shelling of the Chinese islands of Quemoy and Matsu. As a boy, I lived in Taiwan, and at night, from our home on the outskirts of Taipei, we could see the sky light up if we walked in the dark near the remote bomb shelter adjacent to our house. My father explained it was long-range U.S. artillery. As a fifth-grade student in 1959, I remember when one of my friends did not return to our school. I asked my father what had happened to him. His father and mine were both U.S. officers providing artillery support to Chiang Kai-shek's army. He told me my friend's father had been killed during his monthly rotation to the islands.

This "ancient" history has modern counterparts: In 1999, the Chinese embassy in Belgrade was intentionally targeted and hit by U.S. fighter bombers during U.S.-led NATO attacks on Serbia. At least three Chinese people were killed and the building set on fire. Today, it is no secret that U.S. world strategy continues to encircle China with American bases. Few if any of these dynamics have been reported in the U.S. media. At the same time, in one of his final books, Samuel Huntington calmly discussed the possibility of a future U.S.-China war.

The Cultural Revolution's Contribution to the Movement of 1989

Very often, the origins of social movements are understood retrospectively in unlikely and inauspicious events. This may well be the case of the seemingly insignificant appearance of people bringing white flowers to Tiananmen Square in April 1976, three months after the death of longtime leader Zhou Enlai. Within days of the first spontaneous commemoration of Zhou's life, thousands of people arrived to lay wreaths, leave poems, and otherwise mark the passing of a man whose significance the hard-line "Gang of Four" leaders sought to minimalize. Mourning Zhou was perhaps the only permitted public means of expressing displeasure with the continuing marginalization of conservatives like Zhou's protégé, Deng Xiaoping.

On Sunday, April 4, an estimated two million people visited the square.[4] The next day, police cleared away all the flowers and sanitized the memorial site, but people nonetheless returned. Ordered to disperse, the crowd fought back when police moved in with clubs, and in the ensuing scuffles, a police van was overturned. Soon a workers' militia arrived and broke up the assembly of mourners, but the damage had been done: the April 5 events were characterized as "counterrevolutionary." Deemed responsible for motivating the protests from behind the scenes, Deng Xiaoping was dismissed from all positions of responsibility, and Mao denounced Deng for a second time as an "unrepentant capitalist-roader." (The first time was in 1966 at the height of the Cultural Revolution, and Deng was banished for years to the countryside. Soon thereafter, radical Beijing University students incarcerated his eldest son. When Deng's son sought to escape by jumping from a fourth-floor dormitory window, he ended up paralyzed from the waist down—a tragedy for which Deng never forgave the student movement.)[5]

Western analysts have long assumed that Eastern European and Chinese activists may only have had experience with democracy before communist rule, that China has no civil society—or that it is born in the 1989 turmoil.[6] In doing so, they posit specific European and the U.S. models as defining civil society and ignore cross-cultural realities.[7] Chinese peasants' centuries of uprisings constituted a "dynastic cycle" (through which regimes came to power, increased their military budget to remain there, raised taxes to pay for the military, after which people revolted and overthrew the dynasty—leading to a reiteration of the cycle). Examples of more recent civil activities include the White Lotus rebellion from 1796 to 1801, the many public-minded literati networks in the late Ming dynasty, the Taiping rebellion of the 1860s, New Text Confucianism, the Reform Movement after the defeat by Japan, and the May Fourth uprising in 1919. Alongside this rich tradition, many examples of people's direct engagement with civil matters can be found since 1949. Through popular participation in movements of national political change—from the disastrous Great Leap Forward in 1957 to the Cultural Revolution a decade later—millions of Chinese people accumulated valuable experiences, as they drew upon previous history as a resource to mobilize.[8] The human costs were enormous, yet through these historical events, millions of people prepared themselves to take an active role in the country's political development.

In the Manichean world of U.S. anticommunism (including its Trotskyist wing that proved such a fertile recruiting grounds for neoconservatives in the Bush regime), the Cultural Revolution was purely an abomination. Mainstream historians in both China and the United States condemn it in no uncertain terms, yet it could also be viewed as "the history of Chinese youth gradually becoming enlightened about the nature of Chinese society."[9] Evidence persists that as a form of direct democracy—of people taking power into their own hands—it built a culture of resistance and became a source of encouragement for speaking out from the grassroots.[10] Mao's famous "Sixteen Points," the seminal document of the Cultural Revolution, promised more democracy. Mao advocated elections to replace officials, basing his ideas upon democratic currents in Marxism like the 1871 Paris Commune (where all elected delegates were subject to immediate popular recall). From this perspective, the Cultural Revolution was a mobilization of civil society against the state bureaucracy, and people's experiences during it became a resource to draw upon in the heated moments of 1989.

Since Mao's demobilization of the Red Guard in 1968 at the height of the Cultural Revolution, China's student movement slowly rebuilt itself. In both objective factors (number of students, their concentration on campuses, and the single-child policy of the government) as well as subjective factors (the quality of everyday experiences, legacy of past struggles, and desire for new forms of liberty), students were positioned for the leading role they would assume with great popular acclaim in 1989. In similar ways, the country's working class—officially acclaimed to be masters of the nation—was groomed to carry out a thorough and far-seeing transformation of the country.

In very specific ways, the Cultural Revolution schooled thousands of people in the ethics and etiquette of street protests. At one critical moment in 1989, only a day before the shooting began, soldiers and demonstrators who were locked in confrontation began a singing competition—a technique commonly used during the Cultural Revolution.[11] Another carryover came when workers issued a detailed expose of high officials' special privileges—from families' trips abroad to limousines and businesses—a direct descendent of antielitism and anticorruption campaigns during the Cultural Revolution. As one of their leaflets put it, "The bureaucratic cats get fat while the people starve."[12] Cultural Revolution experiences enriched centuries-old notions that the Emperor ruled through a mandate of heaven (which could be retracted if power was wielded in unjust ways), that the people have the right to petition for redress of grievances and officials a concomitant responsibility to respond intelligently, and that everyone has the right to rebel against unjust dictates.

Economic Reform
The month after Mao Zedong died on September 9, 1976, party conservatives moved quickly to remove from power the "Gang of Four" and hundreds of others

aligned with them. By November 1978, Deng Xiaoping had been restored to a high position, and the April 5, 1976, incident was reclassified as "revolutionary."[13] After the party recognized the righteousness of the 1976 events, the change in climate was immediate: wall posters began to appear in Beijing. The "Democracy Wall Movement"—as this spurt in spontaneous grassroots initiative became known in the Western media—was initially encouraged by top party leaders, but as it spread to other cities, many became worried they might again be targeted, especially since economic reforms began in earnest in December.

With the purge of the Gang of Four, hundreds of thousands of banished Red Guards returned to the cities after a "lost decade" in rural areas, and thousands of prisoners incarcerated during the Cultural Revolution were freed. Among those released from prison were three longtime democracy activists from Guangzhou known collectively as Li Yizhe, who had long advocated legal protection for individual rights. Radical factions from the Cultural Revolution that had been broken up in 1968 began to reconstitute themselves in the mid-1970s and organize against what they perceived as a restoration of capitalism by Deng and the new party elite. A legacy of the Cultural Revolution, this enduring culture of resistance appears to have been one of the key forces behind the 1978 movement, especially through groups like Hubei's Big Dipper Study Group and Yangtze River Commentary, Beijing's April 3rd Faction (which called for working people and not bureaucrats to be "masters of society"), and Hunan's Provisional Revolutionary Great Alliance Committee.[14]

In those heady days, a young electrician and former Red Guard, Wei Jingsheng, signed his name to a poster attacking Deng (then a party leader) and calling for democracy ("the fifth modernization"). Wei helped found one of China's first independent magazines, *Exploration*. Soon others published dissident poetry and essays in *Beijing Spring*, *Enlightenment*, and *Today*.[15] That winter, rural people streamed into the capital in a torrent of dissent. A ragtag assortment of peasants camped outside government offices to protest rapes, thefts, and even murder at the hands of powerful local communist authorities. One rape victim organized one of the largest marches. Unemployed young people militantly sought entry into Zhongnanhai—the exclusive compound where many of the party elite lived. On March 25, Wei called Deng a "fascist dictator." Having twice been purged in the past, Deng moved resolutely to prevent any new recurrence of his banishment. Within days, thirty activists had been arrested, and Democracy Wall was shut down.

In early 1979, as the official celebration of the April 5 Incident approached, Wang Xizhe (one of the three original Li Yizhe members) ended a rousing speech by calling on more than a hundred intellectuals and cadre to "grasp their pens and use them to struggle to bring real democratic rights to the masses."[16] Not one to let words alone speak, Wang helped organize a campaign against Deng's plan to abolish constitutional protections of the "Four Greats" (free speech, full articulation of viewpoints, public debates, and large character posters). Wang publicly encouraged opposition leaders to protest the detention of other dissidents, and he participated in an underground activist conclave in Beijing in June

1980 to discuss the need for a Chinese Communist League (to function as a "newly organized proletarian party").[17] In mid-1980, a national association of twenty-one autonomous magazines called for a mass democratic movement to counter the ensconced bureaucratic elite. Although Democracy Wall had been shut down, the current of resistance continued to flow.

Needless to say, the group soon drew the ire of Deng and top leaders. When the crackdown came in 1981, more than twenty activists were rounded up. Wang was subsequently sentenced to fourteen years in prison, and other leading advocates of democracy received similar rewards for their services to the people. Officials worried that if protesters in different parts of the country linked together, they might substitute themselves for the leading role of the party. In January 1981, party leader Hu Yaobang attacked the dissidents: "These illegal magazines and illegal organizations . . . have behind the scenes backers. . . . There are people within the party who . . . think some young people are so smart they can take over the country."[18]

No matter how much the government repressed small magazine publishers and isolated outspoken activists, democratic sentiments continued to be espoused. Within three years, calls for free expression were heard within the Party's Writers' Association, where some believed that "creation requires freedom."[19] The technical intelligentsia articulated the notion that "freedom of discussion is a prerequisite of the pursuit of truth." In many places, the need for academic freedom was discussed. In May 1985, the government granted Hefei's University of Science and Technology (UST) a measure of autonomy in its experiment with educational reform. Soon thereafter, a new wave of protests appeared on campuses at the forefront of reforms, around issues such as permitting faculty to select department heads and students to sit on presidential advisory boards. In July 1986, Li Honglin, president of the Fujian Academy of Social Science, called for concrete regulations to safeguard constitutionally protected rights. That fall, a Shanghai-based magazine published an exposition on two concepts of freedom: "If socialist society cannot offer the individual more and greater freedom, how can it display its superiority? . . . democracy and freedom very easily become derogatory words, associated with the bourgeoisie, as if our proletarians and communists did not want democracy or freedom, only dictatorship and discipline."[20]

On December 5, 1986, at Hefei's UST, students protested the closed process of nominations for the People's Congress. Within two weeks, protests in Hefei spread to more than a dozen other cities, bringing nearly a hundred thousand students into the streets of Shanghai.[21] After five days of public turmoil, student representatives from fifteen universities negotiated their demands with city leaders.[22] Wall posters at Beijing University read, "We want democracy, we want freedom, we support the university student movement in the University of Science and Technology." Among the list of complaints that arose across China were:

1. A ban on discussion of sexual liberation at Zhongshan University in Guangzhou
2. Beijing University's policy of lights out at 11:00 p.m.

3. Incompetent librarians who retained their positions only because of their connections to powerful party officials
4. Poor food service in campus cafeterias.

During six hours of negotiations with Shanghai Mayor Jiang Zemin, student representatives pressed four issues: democracy, recognition of their movement as benefiting China, no retribution against participants, and freedom to publish their own newspapers. Three years later, these would remain key issues for students who occupied Tiananmen Square.

Although the 1986 protests brought some reforms, especially electoral changes that opened the selection process for candidates to the People's Congress, the government again cracked down. The president of the Writers' Association lost his party membership. The president and vice president of UST were transferred to other posts and expelled from the party. Party General Secretary Hu Yaobang—who had opposed the 1980 upsurge—was linked to the new protests and forced to resign in early 1987—as were two other "leading lights of the party."[23] Hu's dismissal made him a hero to students and democracy activists—despite the fact he had opposed them a decade earlier.

At the same time as grassroots demands for more rights were being articulated, the government moved away from central economic controls. From 1979 to 1988, state planning's control of output declined from 77 percent to 47 percent of steel, from 85 percent to 26 percent of timber, and from 59 percent to 43.5 percent of coal.[24] As private industry was encouraged, many workers in state-owned enterprises faced hardship. In the spring and summer of 1988, factory layoffs affected four hundred thousand people in seven hundred Shenyang plants alone. White-collar workers were not directly benefiting from economic liberalization. The educated elite saw the country as increasingly mismanaged and corrupt. Work stoppages increased in the same period, as did the crime rate.[25] In early June, some two thousand Beijing University students protested in Tiananmen Square after one of their fellow students was murdered. They wanted the government to protect them from local criminals.

To be sure, between 1979 and 1984, people's standard of living improved. From the onset of economic reforms in 1978 to 1987, more than 38 times as many citizens owned televisions, more than 131 times more refrigerators were in people's hands, and about 5.7 million washing machines were in use—up from only about 1,000.[26] Urban workers' total compensation more than doubled. Yet by 1988, troubling signs appeared. Rather than "trickling down," wealth generated by new construction of hotels and capital investment schemes brought inflation. Almost unknown in previous decades, inflation grew from less than 3 percent before 1985 to more than 18 percent in 1988—some believed the actual rate was as high as 27 percent by the beginning of 1989.[27] With real wages stagnating, the cost of living rose, believed by many to be caused by officials who took their cut out of every transaction. In 1988, more than one in three urban families experienced a sharp decline in their earning power.[28] In the first four months of 1989, coal prices rose 100 percent, while food prices also rose significantly: vegetables went up 48.7 percent, for example.[29] A

TABLE 5.1 **Rates of Real Growth and Inflation, 1983–1991**

Year	Rate of Real Growth	Inflation of Consumer Prices
1983	10.9%	2.0%
1984	15.2%	2.7%
1985	13.5%	9.3%
1986	8.8%	6.5%
1987	11.6%	7.3%
1988	11.3%	18.8%
1989	4.1%	18.0%
1990	3.8%	3.1%
1991	9.2%	3.4%

Source: China Statistical Yearbook, 2002 as cited in China Institute for Reform and Development, ed., *Thirty Years of China's Reforms: Through Chinese and International Scholars' Eyes* (Beijing: Foreign Languages Press, 2008), 81.

populace used to decades of low and stable prices and nonexistent unemployment painfully experienced the insecurities of the "free" market.

To increase efficiency, the state implemented Taylorist production techniques and introduced piecework wages. When material incentives failed to provide the jump in labor productivity they sought, the party expanded management powers. A new 1987 law gave managers more power over workers without providing any simultaneous mechanism for workers to redress grievances. The new legislation also permitted layoffs that affected three hundred thousand workers by August 1988. Some fifteen to twenty million other workers classified as "underemployed" worried they, too, might be laid off. Suddenly, decades of rising expectations were dashed against the cold reality of insecurity and impotency—the very conditions sociologists identify as producing progressive social movements.

Simultaneously, the gap between elite and working people widened. For the elite, times had never been better. Party functionaries made huge profits on resale of commodities bought at low, state-mandated prices. They were able to buy luxury goods from abroad, send their families on foreign tours, and live in top housing. Party members received special consideration in courts if they were charged criminally.[30] Both Deng and Zhao's sons were thought to be engaged in corrupt practices. Last but not least, while all youth had to compete for scarce seats in higher education, top party members' children were granted special admissions.

The contradiction between the official ideology of equality and workers' subordination became unbearable. Nationalization of industry and property undermined economic equality—especially after the onset of Deng's reforms. Long nourished on a steady diet of government propaganda about the proletariat as the most advanced class, China's workers found that the reality of their everyday lives stood in sharp contrast to that of wealthy leaders whose slick suits and limousines were all too conspicuous signs of their rule over people who wore Mao suits and rode bicycles. China's economy was contained within social relations of a bygone era, the era of Maoist empowerment of peasants and proletarians. As workers took actions to improve their lot, strikes were increasingly their weapon of choice—officially counted at more than seven hundred in the first ten months of 1988—and not necessarily peaceful ones. Between January and July of that year, more than 297 managers were injured during 276 incidents of beatings meted out by angry workers. In Shenyang (Liaoning) three city managers were killed by subordinates.[31]

Like the proverbial genie that can't be put back in the lamp, China's culture of protest continued to grow. While in the United States and Europe, consumerism had tamed avant-garde art's subversive appeal by transforming it into another commodity, Chinese artists continued the rebellious antiestablishment upsurge.[32] Although many abandoned China when a campaign against "spiritual pollution" was waged, by the mid-1980s, a multifarious confluence of streams congealed as the New Tide movement. "Dada" performances were held in Xiamen and Beijing University in 1986. The new cultural opening included a television series, River Elegy, which emphasized the producers' desire to rid China of traditional civilization and become modern and westernized. A prominent magazine introduced a new series on "avant-garde art" in May 1988, and the opening of a "China/avant-garde" exhibition took place in early 1989. This "first modern art show" was brought to an early end after pistol shots were fired as part of a telephone booth installation piece. Officials punished the artists with a two-year ban on modern art, but the movement was about to emerge on a larger scale than anyone had dreamed possible.

The 1989 Crisis

On April 15, 1989, Hu Yaobang suddenly died from a heart attack. Within an hour, people began congregating near the revolutionary heroes' monument in Tiananmen Square, just as they had during the movement of April 5, 1976. That evening, as groups huddled together in animated discussions, many people decried inflation eating into their meager incomes. About 4:00 a.m., the first organized contingent marched in: twenty employees of the Ministry of Textiles placed a wreath at the base of the monument.[33] Not until more than twelve hours later did the first group of students arrive (late on the evening of April 16), when some three hundred from Beijing University brought eight wreaths to the growing altar dedicated to Hu. Thus, it was workers who initiated the autonomous commemoration of Hu and unleashed an escalating spiral of events that reached its bloody denouement forty-eight days later on June 4.

More than anyone else, students took the lead in provoking a confrontation with the government that would spark urban uprisings all over the country, but to characterize the movement of 1989 as a student movement fails to appreciate the popular character of the uprising. Chinese speak of "one hundred million heroes" when they describe the events, yet in 1988, the government counted only two million students (alongside 105 million workers—70 percent of the nonagricultural labor force).[34] Students first took decisive action on April 17, when more than a thousand people brought a petition criticizing officials' corruption to Zhongnanhai. During the next two days and two nights, no one would meet with students to accept their petition, so they remained sitting there.

At dusk on April 19, 1989, at Beijing University (Beijing Daxue or Beida, for short), hundreds of students shouted approval for formation of a planning committee to create an autonomous student union. Other campuses soon declared their own autonomous unions, and activists at each university selected a standing committee of five to seven members—which linked with other standing committees into a citywide coordinating group. Without knowing it, students had thereby passed a line of no return. By forming autonomous student unions parallel to government ones, they had unwittingly sown the seeds of a coming conflagration. During the same night that some students at Beida were organizing a new union, hundreds of other students were miles away, sitting in at Zhongnanhai. All over the city, groups were mobilizing. Workers were huddled in Tiananmen Square, and intellectuals associated with the World Economic Forum and *New Observer* magazine organized an academic forum to discuss a reevaluation of Hu Yaobang and to reverse the government's inclination to oppose political liberalization.[35]

The next morning at Beijing Normal University (*Beijing Shifan Daxue* or BeiShida), three activist friends resolved to create an autonomous union at their campus. Without elections, the three simply appointed themselves officers and called the dormitory residence of Wuer Kaixi their office.[36] Later that evening (April 20), police clubs put a brutal end to the two-day sit-in at Zhongnanhai, a drawing of first blood that propelled students at Beida to initiate a boycott of classes that would last for weeks and spread to many campuses.

The clusters of workers in Tiananmen Square were surprised to hear that students had been beaten at Zhongnanhai. They knew that students shared their frustration with officials, and their conversations quickly turned to the need for workers to form their own autonomous organization. Hearing about the bloody end to the students' peaceful sit-in, one worker among the two dozen people clustered in Tiananmen rose to his feet and roused the group with a fiery speech denouncing the violence. Two days earlier, the group had broached the idea of forming their own organization, and after the police action, they edged closer to it. The informal group published two leaflets exposing leaders' wealth, their families' corruption, and the shortsighted impact of their economic policies. How much money had one of Deng Xiaoping's sons bet at a Hong Kong racetrack? Did Zhao Ziyang pay for his golf excursions from his own pocket? How could he afford his fancy Western suits? How many villas did the party elite maintain for their private use? Alongside such questions, they provided their views of the problems caused by Deng's economic reforms—especially in the form of higher inflation. With these modest actions, the Beijing Autonomous Workers' Federation (BAWF) was born. The autonomous form of both students' and workers' organizations is of no small significance. This central characteristic of contemporary freedom—people's aspirations for self-government—is evident everywhere in insurgencies.

In the weeks of upheaval that followed, BAWF slowly moved from periphery to center of the protests. On April 20, they were seventy or eighty people—none of whom had activist experience. As soon as the group issued its first handbills that day, new faces surged forward to join, one of whom, Han Dongfang, became their most articulate spokesperson. As a means to continue, they resolved to meet every day in the northwest corner of Tiananmen Square. By the final phase of the insurgency, that is, after martial law had been declared and students melted away, the Workers' Federation continued to grow by leaps and bounds.

Students Take the Initiative

With Hu Yaobang's funeral scheduled for April 22, government leaders wanted Tiananmen Square kept clear, and they thought it would be a simple matter to do so. They planned to close the square before the funeral, but autonomously organized students outsmarted them. On the night of April 21, about sixty thousand students gathered on a Shida soccer field and marched to Tiananmen. While underway, the march from Shida was joined by contingents from Beida and the University of Politics and Law. The first group to arrive was from Qinghua University. Without a plan to do something once they got there, they sat down and rested. Soon the soccer field assembly, tens of thousands strong, marched in singing the Internationale and chanting, "Long Live Freedom!" and "Down with Dictatorship!"[37] At dawn, a meeting of representatives from each school was convened, and to everyone's surprise, nineteen colleges were present. The group approved a petition that included:

- Reassessment of Hu Yaobang
- Punishment for those responsible for the beatings at Zhongnanhai
- Permission to publish autonomous newspapers
- Publication of government officials' incomes
- Discussion of national education policy and fees
- Reconsideration of the "anti–spiritual pollution campaign"
- Accurate media portrayal of the new student movement.

As party leaders exited Hu's funeral in the Great Hall of the People, only a few even bothered to glance at the assembled students. Trying to get officials to meet them, tens of thousands of students marched around the square, chanting "We want dialogue," but they were ignored. A trio of Beida students knelt on the steps of the Great Hall and held the seven-point petition above their heads for about forty minutes. When there was still no response, many students began weeping in frustration.[38]

By themselves, the seven points were not revolutionary demands—indeed they were supplications to the government and recognized the power of the system. Yet by autonomously challenging the sole discretion of the party to make policy, students crossed a dangerous line. Furthermore, by honoring the long-standing Chinese tradition of petitioning authorities for redress of grievances, students acted within the set of values central to Chinese civil society. By ignoring them, officials' actions broke with people's expectations of proper behavior. Already enraged by a student sit-in at their elite housing complex, government leaders wanted nothing to do with upstart youngsters who dared reproach them. That same day, protests in Xian turned violent and many people were hurt. Some reports claimed eleven people were killed and hundreds injured amid a cluster of attacks on police.[39]

As early as 542 BCE, even before China became Confucian, student protests had occurred.[40] Over ensuing centuries, Chinese students played central roles in stirring the nation to act, resisting corrupt authorities, and supporting rulers they considered kind and just. Central to China's civil society and governing bureaucracy, scholars have long been held in high repute, and they have often reciprocated the public's esteem with concern for the well-being of ordinary people. A famous Song dynasty scholar, Fan Zhongya, is still remembered for his insight, "A scholar worries over the world before the world worries itself; a scholar is happy only after all of humanity has achieved happiness."

Seen in the best light, students acted in this tradition of generosity of spirit and high-minded fairness. They wanted an end to officials' corruption and greater opportunities for university graduates. Students felt excluded from positions they were most qualified to hold. One wall poster written in mid-April read, "The best and the brightest are refused party membership, while the dregs are admitted in droves. The party is being manipulated by a bunch of 'phonies.'"[41] Another decried party members lack of formal education: "Of the 47 million members of this 'vanguard,' as many as 75 percent have no more than elementary school education."[42]

Two days after Hu's funeral, about thirty-five students, including many of the activists who had stepped forward to formulate the seven-point petition, created the Autonomous Student Union of Beijing Universities and Colleges (ASU). With rotating delegates democratically selected from fifteen (and soon thereafter from forty-one) universities, the ASU reflected a bottom-up representative system. Not only did it have a much wider base of popular support than the government-sanctioned student union, it took actions mainstream organizations were afraid to undertake—or ones they thought were incorrect. At their first meeting, they elected Zhou Yongjun chairperson of the standing committee by a vote of nine to Wuer Kaixi's six. The ASU quickly became the "decision-making body that could work out an agenda and strategy for the movement as a whole."[43] Besides organizing demonstrations down to the finest details like slogans, times and places, it was viewed by student activists as their representative to the government.[44] The same night ASU was formally founded in Beijing, heavy protests turned into riots in Xian and Changsha, where shop windows were smashed and looting occurred.

For years, previous attempts to construct independent organizations were discovered and broken up before they could build a base. Within the newly liberated political space opened by the eros effect of 1989, many groups simultaneously mobilized, and the ASU was able to emerge as a major political player. During the next six weeks, much focus would be put upon obtaining government recognition of its right to exist. By the night of the group's second meeting on April 25, Central People's Radio read an editorial attacking autonomous unions as "illegal organizations" and promising to "stop any attempt to infringe on the right of legal organizations." Published the next day in *People's Daily*, this editorial became a major sore point for students—and an unveiled threat to them.

On April 25, Deng Xiaoping took to the airwaves and called for Chinese people to "prepare ourselves for a nationwide struggle and resolve to crush the turmoil." The following day, he warned Premier Li Peng that "this is not an ordinary student movement. . . . These persons have arisen to create turmoil after having been influenced and encouraged by liberalization elements in Yugoslavia, Poland, Hungary, and the Soviet Union. . . . The more the Poles gave in, the greater the turmoil became."[45] Deng was not entirely wrong: students had discussed the idea of naming their new organization "Solidarity" in honor of the Polish workers' movement.[46] Moreover, the ouster of Marcos from the Philippines and capitulation of Chun Doo-hwan in South Korea inspired people, while the transformation of Taiwan from a martial law garrison state to protodemocracy (see the next chapter) gave people reason to believe the time had come for China to open its political system. As one observer described the scene in Tiananmen Square, "Many emulated the white headbands worn by South Korean dissidents and flashed the V sign favored by anti-Marcos activists who fought for people's power in the Philippines."[47] Chinese people had assimilated a new tactic in the arsenal of insurgency: the massive occupation of public space as a means of rallying the population. While this tactic first appeared in the eros effect of the global movement of 1968, Filipinos used it to overthrow Marcos in 1986, and in 1987, South Korea's June Uprising compelled the dictatorship to grant democratic reforms.

It would be wrong however, to attribute the Chinese movement simply to spillover or "snowballing" from other countries. The simultaneity of China's movement and a dozen more in 1989 speaks to an occurrence of the eros effect, to the intuitive and spontaneous awakening of need for freedom. China's protests erupted months before the Berlin Wall came down, before Poland's Solidarity came to power, and before the Czech "Velvet Revolution"—all of which transpired in a process of mutual amplification.[48]

Chinese wall posters and placards drew inspiration from Martin Luther King Jr., Gandhi, and Abraham Lincoln; they mentioned Kent State and Gorbachev.[49] Inspired by King's speech, a Nanjing University student composed a poem, "I Have a Dream," which became a big character poster. *Eyes on the Prize*, an award-winning television series on the U.S. civil rights movement, had been available at her university.[50] Someone photocopied the *People Power* book from the Philippines and plastered it on a prominent situated wall. In the context of a worldwide continuation of 1968, with protests spreading in Hungary, East Germany, and many other countries, an editorial in *China's People's Daily* on April 26 condemned "anti-state turmoil and chaos," branding both students and workers in unsavory terms—a "conspiracy by a handful of unlawful elements" who had even taken over the broadcasting facilities of colleges and universities.[51] As in so many other revolts in this period—the media coverage in Gwangju and Thailand readily come to mind—protesters were deeply troubled by hostile and somewhat inaccurate media assessments of their movements and demanded retractions. The difference is that in China, they ultimately did receive a high-ranking leader's public praise as well as promises of no retaliation—but they came too late (on May 16) to change the trajectory of the protests.

Students Under Attack

Densely concentrated on campuses and afforded time and space to study, students mobilized quickly. Under attack on radio, television, and newspapers, students knew the state's iron fist was clenched and ready to strike. At their next meeting, the ASU hotly debated what course of action to take. With the Standing Committee unable to decide, they called a general assembly to vote. Nearly all of the forty schools present agreed to organize a major protest on April 27. With a class boycott already in place, students overnight became a powerful force that rivaled the party for people's loyalty. With Zhao Ziyang on a trip to North Korea, Li and Deng's hardline position clumsily handled the burgeoning movement. They brought heavy pressure to bear on ASU leader Zhou Yongjun, who evidently could not withstand it. On the night of April 26, he unilaterally called off the demonstration, but it was too late for one person to change anything. The next day, more than 100,000 students converged on Tiananmen Square. As they circumvented police blockades and marched in contingents, they were cheered on by hundreds of thousands of Beijing residents. As the seemingly endless procession passed, more than half a million citizens watched from sidewalks. The government's ban on protests became meaningless, and more than 150,000 people defied police by marching to Tiananmen Square, where they remained for some fourteen hours in "a carnival-like atmosphere." Cardboard boxes were filled with donations, and many workers mingled among the throng. Later one student leader called it "one of the greatest events in history."[52]

After witnessing the joyous civil disobedience of April 27, government leaders finally realized they needed to do something more creative than simply ignore or pressure protesters. On April 29, they held a widely publicized meeting primarily with members of the government-sanctioned student organization, thereby accomplishing two goals. The dialogue made it appear that the party was willing to talk and listen—which, it must be said, was remarkable when compared to dictators like Marcos in the Philippines, Ne Win in Burma, Chun Doo-hwan in Korea, King Gyanendra in Nepal, and Suchinda in Thailand—all of whom used bullets rather than words to respond to their youth.[53] Significant forces within the party's highest levels were listening, especially Zhao Ziyang, who sought to work with students in the reform process. The "dialogue" also split the ASU. Unable to reach a consensus on whether or not to attend, the group granted individuals autonomous discretion to decide whether or not to participate in the meeting.

After their successful mobilization on April 27, students reorganized themselves. Zhou Yongjun was forced to resign for his unilateral "cancellation" and Wuer Kaixi became the new president—but with a more limited set of powers. Two days later, Wuer failed to attend a meeting and was replaced by Feng Congde. Riding the enormous energy generated by the recent civil disobedience, the ASU decided to mount another protest on May 4, no easy task given the pressure on the newly formed organization. The government's official rally on May 4, the seventieth anniversary of the 1919 anti-Japanese protests, was dwarfed in size by the students' rally, which attracted 50,000 students and more than 250,000 others. More young workers than students were present. Once again, the autonomous marchers broke through police lines, this time while singing songs from the 1919 movement. The two dismissed former leaders of the ASU each made individual public statements as if they were still leaders: Zhou announced an end to class boycotts, and Wuer read a long declaration that few outside the media even heard.

Significantly, these individuals felt empowered to speak on behalf of the movement as a whole, and their words were taken by the media as representing the ASU. Such individualism would not be the last time organizations of the student movement were undermined by self-proclaimed leaders.

In the heady atmosphere following two successful massive protests, campus activists were uncertain how to proceed. On May 5, thousands of students at nearly all universities except Beida and Shida returned to classes. On many campuses, the ASU began to be viewed negatively—whether because of its internal power struggles or its changing positions on class boycotts. When campus representatives assembled on May 5, despair rather than optimism characterized the meeting. At least one standing committee member resigned, and many others were simply no-shows. The movement seemed stuck at a low point, and no one knew what to do next. By now, students' key demand was for dialogue with the government—a measure that carried within it implicit recognition of their autonomous organizations. To that end, they spun off a Dialogue Delegation and hoped to secure a positive response from the government.

While the ASU stagnated, students by the hundreds continued to hang wall posters, and other groups mobilized. On May 10, more than five thousand bicycle riders supported journalists' call for press freedom. Unlike 1960s movements in the United States, activist students had a core of older activists around them who could offer advice and provide insight into the character of the society they were attempting to change. Even more importantly, younger activists often listened to their elders. With experiences accumulated from years of struggle and analysis gleaned from study, a hundred flowers of ideas bloomed, some fragrant, others short-lived. One young teacher at People's University displayed a big character poster detailing continuity in the history of Chinese administrations by comparing the power structure in 1989 with that in China's feudal past. See TABLE 5.2. The political critique evident in the poster is incisive, but it does not represent growing public dissatisfaction with the deterioration of economic conditions.

The Hunger Strikers' Coup d'État

On May 11, a small group of celebrity activists including Wuer Kaixi and Wang Dan met at a restaurant to discuss the movement's impasse. Looking for a way to maintain momentum, they resolved to appeal to students to join a hunger strike without the approval of the autonomous student unions. None was a spokesperson for any organization, and they soon helped spawn a dynamic inside the movement through which the fruit of students' efforts—the autonomous unions for which they had so mightily sacrificed—was thrown to the wayside and replaced by the media appeal of leaders willing to "fast to the death"—as they insisted they would do.

On May 13, just before beginning their hunger strike, dozens of students gulped down a last lunch of beer and sausages. Gathering in Tiananmen Square before sympathetic media, they were quickly joined by hundreds more people. It was only two days before Russian leader Mikhail Gorbachev's historic visit marking an end to three decades of Sino-Soviet animosity was to take place. The

TABLE 5.2 **Comparison of the Present Power Structure and Feudal China's Power Structure**

	Feudal System	Present System
Control of state power	By single emperor	By single person
Ideology	One only: Confucianism	One only: Communism
Doctrine regarding source of power	Mandate of Heaven	Class struggle
Power base	Army	Army
System of officials	Appointed posts	Appointed posts
Principles of organization	Ruler guides subjects	The organization [the party] directs the individual
	Father guides sons	Higher levels direct lower levels
	Husband guides wife	The central committee directs the entire party
Political tactics	Highly sophisticated	Highly sophisticated
Assumption about human nature	Doctrine of inherent virtue	Doctrine of the perfect proletariat
Status of the individual	None	Extremely low

Source: Han Minzhu, *Cries for Democracy*, 155.

strikers realized they occupied a key strategic position from which they might win their demands—which included including two additional measures: repeal of the April 26 edict banning protests and televised talks between students and the government. Around 5:00 p.m., a slender psychology graduate student named Chai Ling led the crowd in an oath: "I swear, that to promote democracy, for the prosperity of my country, I willingly go on a hunger strike. I will not give up until I realize our goals."[54] Nearby, Wang Dan was using a bullhorn to hold a press conference. No organization existed to make decisions on behalf of the eight hundred hunger strikers milling around the Monument to the People's Heroes. Working now as celebrity activists, leaders wore shirts with their names written in large characters on them and moved around the square inside a phalanx of bodyguards, signing autographs as they passed through the crowd.

Communist leaders continued to seek ways to hear students' concerns—whether convinced by the sincerity of their hunger strike or troubled by the wide resonance and sympathetic media they enjoyed among citizens. Top leader Yan Mingfu, head of the CCP's united front department, sat down to meet with students on May 14. He promised there would be no "settling the account after the autumn harvest"—that is, that the regime would not retaliate against the students once their movement had died down. In the midst of the talks, hunger strikers—wearing hospital clothing and some with intravenous feeds attached to their bodies—burst into the hall and disrupted the conversation. They were angered because the televised version was being prerecorded, not broadcast live. Putting an end to the dialogue, they demanded to read their "last words" to their parents. Amid cries and weeping heard in all corners of the room, they proceeded to do so.[55] This charade took place *one day* after the beginning of the fast!

Massive media presence in Beijing stimulated activists to compete for fame.
Photographer unknown.

The hunger strike marked a turning point in the movement, a shift from righteous indignation to arrogant self-promotion. Among the public, the hunger strikers elicited great sympathy, but by undercutting students' autonomous organizations and seizing the center of attention for themselves, a few media stars emerged who drew the entire movement down the road to their stardom— and to the movement's demise. Later that day (May 14), twelve of China's most famous writers appealed to the hunger strikers to leave Tiananmen Square so that the grand ceremony honoring Russian leader Mikhail Gorbachev's visit the next day (the first by a Russian party leader since 1959) would not have to be cancelled. The intellectuals also called for the regime to recognize the autonomous student organizations, to consider protesters a patriotic, democratic contribution to society, and to take no action against them after the matter was settled. Nevertheless, students refused to budge. Gorbachev was met at the airport by senior Chinese leaders—and was never able to visit Tiananmen Square.

By circumventing the organizations their movement had only recently created, the hunger strikers set a dangerous precedent, one that ultimately doomed the movement to fall short of its possibilities. The autonomous unions did not agree to the hunger strike, and according to some sources, hoped it would fail.[56] When the ASU did not suit their agenda, its more famous members simply circumvented it. From that moment, it was only a short hop to the creation of a "Headquarters of Tiananmen Square" with a "commander-in-chief," who led the entire movement willy-nilly down the path of "holier-than-thou" radicalism and straight into a bloody confrontation on June 4. The strategy of escalation involved rejecting compromise, whether with Zhao and other moderates or with movement colleagues, and thereby doomed the movement in its arrogance to abject failure. The hunger strike was a great tactic in terms of gaining sympathy of people, in eliciting "an unprecedented outpouring of sympathy from the citizens of Beijing, young and old, rich and poor, highly educated and semi-literate," but since it cut the movement from democratic organizations, it was a huge strategic error.[57]

For three weeks, workers quietly organized and spread the word to large factories and offices. Only after hundreds of thousands of students occupied Tiananmen Square did the Workers' Federation (BAWF) feel safe enough to announce their presence publicly. On May 2, they had two thousand registered members. By May 13, when huge demonstrations were mounted almost every day, the clearly visible BAWF contingent marched prominently among many state-owned factories, which had also created their own autonomous worker federations.[58] Party leaders vainly sought to keep workers from joining the protests. In early May, the top party office in Beijing issued a directive to all factory managers instructing them to take all feasible steps to keep workers and students from coming together. On May 10, the Party Politburo received a report that a third of six thousands miners' families had taken part in the movement.[59] Three days later, both Premier Li Peng and Zhao Ziyang held special meetings with labor leaders, yet the outcome was not to their liking. On May 14, banners appeared in Tiananmen with the words one of the workers was rumored to have shouted during the meeting: "The party should sell off its Mercedes Benzes to pay off the national debt!"[60] On May 15, Beijing officials huddled in an emergency session devoted to the problem of how to "stabilize workers."[61]

Although considered an illegal organization by the authorities, BAWF continued to grow, both in numbers and in their systematic critique. On May 17, as martial law approached, they announced, "The people will no longer believe the lies of the rulers. . . . There are only two classes: the rulers and the ruled." In another public statement, they sounded a battle cry: "Ah, the Chinese! Such a lovable yet pathetic and tragic people. We have been deceived for thousands of years, and are still being deceived today. No! Instead we should become a great people; we should restore ourselves to our original greatness! Brother workers, if our generation is fated to carry out this humiliation into the twenty-first century, then it is better to die in battle in the twentieth!"[62] On May 17 and 18, workers flooded into the city to join the protests, at whose symbolic center sat several hundred hunger-striking students. From state-owned enterprises to collectively managed and privately owned ones, from large factories like the Capital Steel Corporation and Yanshan Petrochemical to small shops, they arrived in columns of trucks, cars, and buses, singing, drumming, beating gongs, and carrying enormous red flags and portraits of Mao. On May 18, the *New York Times* reported, "The demonstration today was the realization of one of the government's worst nightmares—organized worker participation in what began as student protests."

Unlike students, BAWF wanted a more democratic form of socialism. Their demands included price stabilization, the right to change jobs freely, and an end to hiring that discriminated against women. One BAWF activist subsequently declared: "In the factory, the director is a dictator, what one man say goes. If you view the state through the factory, it's about the same: one-man rule. . . . A factory should have a system. If a worker wants to change jobs, they ought to have a system of rules to decide how to do it. Also, these rules should be decided upon by everybody." Here in nutshell is a vision for a higher form of socialism, not a desire for consumerism. While many students criticized their exclusion from elite circles and demanded entry to off-limit state stores where Western goods were sold, workers sought to abolish the elite entirely and developed a vision for improving everyone's lives. "New hotels have gone up and changed the city's face, but the people still lack decent housing space," they wrote. "There's a craze for banquets at the top," they complained. As they organized, they articulated the belief that their autonomous organization represented workers better than the official All China Federation of Trade Unions (ACFTU) that they felt was controlled by the party, not the workers. Although many ACFTU members (including some officials) hung out at the BAWF convergence point in Tiananmen, the ACFTU refused to endorse the BAWF, whose stridency and independence threatened their complacency.

During the 1989 insurgency, students found a mentor and advocate in Zhao Ziyang, and like Zhao, many sought to play the role of loyal opposition. Many workers, however, tired of Zhao's fancy Western suits and matching policies, often shouted "Down With Zhao Ziyang!"[63] As the movement developed and workers increased their presence, they called for ordinary citizens to oversee officials and challenged the special privileges enjoyed by the communist elite. They sought to curtail arbitrary power of managers in factories and to stimulate autonomous unions that could help to formulate national policy and to craft specific agreements governing workplace relations. Far from rejecting the communist revolution, they sought to reenergize it on the basis of Marx and Mao. One of their wall posters was quite explicit: "We have calculated carefully, based on Marx's *Capital*, the rate of exploitation of workers. We discovered that the 'servants of the people' swallow all the surplus value produced by the people's blood and sweat. . . . But history's final accounting has yet to be completed."[64]

As the movement spread across China, preliminary assessments of the movement's scale indicated that of 434 big cities in China, 107 reported student protests, including thirty-two with participation of autonomous workers groups.[65] Years later, a more complete compilation counted demonstrations in 341 cities.[66] In Xian, one thousand hunger strikers sat down in New City Square.[67] Delegations traveled to nearby factories to gain support. As many as two thousand students rode trains to Beijing on May 18 and 19. In Chongqing, eighty-two students began a fast in front of City Hall on May 18, copying both the Beijing tactic and the demand for a dialogue with officials.[68] In Nanjing, tens of thousands of workers and students demonstrated, and some joined a hunger strike there.[69] A "Goddess of Democracy" was erected in Shanghai before art students did so in Beijing.

It appeared that everyone was pulled in by the "magnetic attraction" of the protests—even police officers, Foreign Ministry workers, bankers, and *People's*

Daily reporters.[70] One estimate said 10 percent of Beijing—about a million protesters—were in the streets every day during Gorbachev's three-day visit.[71] The city was so jammed that Gorbachev never made it to the Great Hall of the People, the Forbidden City, or even to the opera. In this "urban Woodstock" there was room for everyone, and hundreds of thousands of people streamed into Beijing from all parts of China. The Beijing Military Command sent over one thousand quilts, and state-owned pharmaceutical companies contributed to the square's medical tents. More than twenty-five hunger strikers came from the Central Academy of Fine Arts. Some established artists sold pieces to raise money.[72] Even the Communist Youth League sent over twenty cases of drinks. Modeling themselves on the Beijing scene, hunger strikers gathered in more than thirty other cities.[73] Beijing's festive "carnival" of protest remained peaceful, yet it had is downside. Walking through Tiananmen at 2:00 a.m. on May 19, Geremie Barmé observed, "The place stank, and there were piles of filth, decaying food, plastic and glass containers and all types of rubbish everywhere, with students huddled asleep all around the monument. Parents who had come to the square with their children had let them freely urinate around the place, and after some days of this, large parts of the plaza emanated a foul odour."[74]

For some people, the hunger strike also emitted a strange aroma. Many hunger strikers were observed eating secretly by foreign journalists who, while sympathetic to them, nonetheless subsequently reported these facts. One student openly admitted he was eating sweetened yogurt—claiming, "Snacking is okay. It's not really food."[75] Furthermore, it appears many of the students were on a relay hunger strike, fasting a day at a time after which someone else replaced them. For some unknown reason, Chinese people believed that the hunger strikers might die after seven days on a water-only diet, when in fact Dick Gregory is only one of many people who have fasted for many times as long.[76] As a democracy activist before he became president of South Korea, Kim Young-sam fasted twenty-three days on a water-only diet beginning on May 18, 1983, to express his support for Gwangju citizens' continuing struggle against the Chun Doo-hwan dictatorship.

Students' dignified role in the China—a society in which everyone worked incessantly for the nation to recover its greatness—meant they lived on a pedestal for most of the time—a position they demanded the government also accord them. The cream of the crop of a single-child nation, Beida students who spearheaded the hunger strike considered themselves the future leaders of the nation—as did the public that supported them. On the first day of their fast, some forty-one of China's future elite collapsed. Such theatrics, when not amusing, disguised a great deception. Tibetans' circles of protest were recreated around the water strikers' "altar." Without comprehending its Tibetan roots, Barmé described how, "As the space was a circle it immediately encouraged a type of circumambulation. Crowds of observers and delegations edged their way around it. People often burst into tears as they moved past the young water strikers huddled in the seats of the bus, sometimes raising their hands or flashing the V sign."[77]

"Commander-in-Chief of the Headquarters of Tiananmen Square"

On May 14, Chai Ling left the meeting with government officials due to "exhaustion," but at 8:00 a.m. the next morning, she announced the formation of a Hunger Strike Command with herself as chairperson. Her new position also brought her control of a broadcasting center in Tiananmen Square acquired with Hong Kong donations. Her husband and fellow activist, Feng Congde, personally refused to let ASU representatives have access to the station. Thus in a single evening, Chai Ling and her husband managed, in effect, a coup d'état that put her in the position she later called "Commander-in-Chief of the Headquarters for Defending Tiananmen Square." In her mind, the occupation of Tiananmen Square necessitated a new organization—the "Headquarters for Defending the Square" (HDS)—and it quickly constituted committees for finance, liaison, information, secretariat, and resources as well as action-teams for food and water distribution, medical care, picketing, and security.

Two of the original hunger strike conspirators, Wuer Kaixi and Wang Dan, were among the most upset by Chai Ling's ascendance to sole possession of such exalted status, particularly since they had not been present at that meeting. The next day, they insisted that leadership should be reconstituted. After a new standing committee again selected Chai Ling as chair, the first task they undertook was to set up a security perimeter. Activists cordoned off their inner circles, this time with transparent fishing line held by trusted students who kept even the most ardent citizen-supporters from reaching the increasingly isolated and arrogant leadership.

To counteract their marginalization, ASU representatives along with Qinghua University students set up a second broadcasting center (with its own security guards), "The Voice of the Student Movement." This new station's amplification was much more powerful and competed with HDS. Needless to say, the two had poor relations. More than $100,000 in donations had been raised to support the student movement, but Chai Ling controlled much of it, as did Beida's ASU, which had come to act independently of the citywide ASU.

On May 16, speaking on behalf of the party's Central Committee, Zhao Ziyang sought compromise and publicly called student protests "positive" and "patriotic." He promised no prosecutions if they would simply leave. Despite the government's generous offer, no one accepted it. On that fourth day of the hunger strike, about 200 of the 3,100 participants fainted.[78] Demonstrations continued and more than 300,000 people marched in sympathy. On both May 17 and 18, more than a million people attended protests. Hunger strikers continually fainted despite being fed intravenously. Unconstrained by party directives, media reported sympathetically at the same time that journalists publicly insisted, "No more lies." A rising number of workers congregated in the square. People sang, "We Shall Overcome" for the assembled throng of foreign reporters—as many as a thousand strong—who were in Beijing for Gorbachev's visit but spent the bulk of their time covering the "story of their lives" in Tiananmen Square. Whether delirious from the hunger strike or inspired to speak his true motivations, it was at this juncture that leader Wuer Kaixi uttered his most famous lines: "We want

Nike shoes, lots of free time to take our girlfriends to a bar, the freedom to discuss an issue with someone, respect from society."[79]

While no doubt most hunger strikers were sincere, Wuer apparently was not. Television reports later revealed footage of him eating at a Beijing Hotel, and AP reporter John Pomfret claims to have shared a meal with him during the hunger strike. Andrew Higgins of England's *Independent* saw him gulping down noodles in the back seat of a car, and Wuer told a friend he "needed to eat to conserve his strength because he was a leader and because he had a heart condition."[80] Sincere or not, reading the Beida manifesto in light of students' subsequent decisions to call off their strike leaves me skeptical of their commitment—if not their intentions: "We do not want to die; we want to live, for we are at life's most promising age. We do not want to die; we want to study, to study diligently. Our motherland is so impoverished; it feels as if we are abandoning her to die. Yet death is not what we seek. But if the death of one or a few people can enable more to live better, and can make our motherland prosperous, then we have no right to cling to life. As we suffer from hunger, Papa and Mama, do not grieve; when we part from life, Aunts and Uncles, please do not be sad."[81] This plea was not written in blood, although other oaths were.

Already elite and expecting to become powerful as they grew older, Beijing students excluded from their ranks in Tiananmen anyone not part of their campuses. Workers in particular were chased off as soon as they sought entry to the inner circles of power. In Beijing, students marched with hands linked to prevent ordinary citizens from joining their "pure" protests. Once they occupied Tiananmen, concentric rings of security prevented their inner circles from being reached by workers and other nonstudents. The Construction Workers Union and BAWF both sought to send delegations for discussions but student marshals chased them off. According to one worker-activist, students looked down on "construction workers from the villages, saying they're convict laborers."[82] To keep nonstudents out, students secretly told each other to wear sneakers or a black band or to pin a white flower and school emblem on their clothes.[83] They distanced themselves from any militant resistance—instead emphasizing nonviolence and legality. Some observers took the separation of workers to be of their own choosing, but in fact, they tried to access students leaders and were continually rebuffed, at least until late May.[84] Tuned into elite discourse, students struggled to ensure their status within it—and reproduced it within the movement.

From the workers' perspective, many of the same corrupt practices of the elite, such as secrecy, exclusivity, factionalism, struggles for power, and special privileges, could be found within the student movement, whose leaders reportedly had mattresses to sleep on and wads of cash from foreign donors in their tents. Student leaders took on absurd titles like "commander-in-chief" while workers remained opposed to hierarchy and let anyone join their meetings—including students. While workers considered themselves the "most advanced class," they had little of the cockiness students exhibited, and they worked with collective leadership rather than under "commanders" who seemed to multiply in student circles.

Most workers of China supported the seven initial student demands. Railway workers reportedly permitted thousands of students to ride the trains to Beijing without money so they could join the movement. During the hunger strike, as many as two hundred thousand students may have flooded into the capital to check on the scene.[85] So well did the population of Beijing come together during this episode of the eros effect that students easily found places to stay and food to eat. It was rumored that even the city's thieves had agreed to a two-day strike in support of students' hunger strike.[86] Crime rates for all types of offenses plummeted from mid-April to mid-May in an unprecedented drop.[87] Vegetable vendors kept prices down, despite the opportunity to charge more, because, "At such a time, everybody must have a conscience."[88] As one observer wrote, "The self-organization of the Beijing citizens, the establishment of committees that organized incoming supplies and saw to the housing of thousands of students and others from out of town, removed garbage, wrote, printed and distributed publications, not only exploded the fashionable Western myth that improvements in the Chinese standard of living had suddenly depoliticized the population, but also disproved, to the permanent discomfiture of our masters everywhere, that the population of one of the largest cities on the planet can organize its affairs without the interference of the government, the state, and any of its institutions."[89]

The students gave protests their start, and their courage inspired others to stand up, yet they were ultimately reform-minded. While students generally supported Deng's market liberalization and wished to see privatization proceed, workers opposed excessive marketization and worried they would lose their jobs and past gains from the planned economy. While people in the streets may have called for an overthrow of the bureaucracy, no major student organization did so. Rather, they wanted dialogue with and recognition from the government—which is why the designation student "rebellion" is appropriate. A rebel feels excluded from power and wants inside, while revolutionaries want to destroy the power structures themselves. Students wanted to be part of the reform process that Deng was leading, while workers marched with giant photos of Mao and wanted to oust Deng a third time. At best, students wanted reform; workers wanted revolution.

Farmers were never part of the movement in significant numbers—a reason why it cannot be said that the urban-based movement captured the overwhelming majority of Chinese citizens' loyalty. During the Great Leap Forward, farmers had resisted attempts at collectivization, resulting in severe shortages and famines that killed millions of people. In 1989, a material basis for farmers' political apathy can be found in benefits the countryside received during years of Maoist policy. While Deng's reforms would ultimately lead back to severe city-countryside economic disparities, in 1989 economic liberalization had yet to severely impact the countryside, and farmers did not rise up against Deng as workers did.

On May 17, believing Zhao's efforts at compromise had failed, Deng authorized martial law. Although Li Peng believed any further exhibition of regime weakness would have handed the country over to the students, he scheduled a meeting with students for May 18.[90] Only on that morning did students receive word that government officials would meet them at 11:00 a.m., and they hastily assembled a delegation that included many celebrity leaders. Televised live, the meeting in the Great Hall of the People provided de facto recognition of student autonomous organizations since Li Peng, the top government official, met face-to-face with student leaders. Nonetheless, the encounter failed miserably. Li Peng sternly lectured the hungers strikers and insisted the party "would not stand idly by." Although students finally got the nationally televised meeting they sought, Wuer Kaixi (who at that moment did not represent anyone but himself) took over the proceedings, castigated Li Peng for being late, and treated him with utmost contempt: "We don't have much time to listen to you. Thousands of hunger strikers are waiting. Let's get to the main point. It was *we* who invited you to talk, not you who invited us—and *you* were late."[91] Seconds later and plainly visible on camera, a medical team rushed in to rescue an apparently fainting Wuer as he grabbed his oxygen bag. Wuer apparently had a knack for "strategic fainting" in public, a talent he availed himself of more than once.[92]

At 5:00 a.m. on May 19, Party General Secretary Zhao Ziyang paid students an early morning visit. He tearfully called for students to evacuate Tiananmen, to no avail. That was the very last moment when a compromise could have been reached. After his visit, autograph hunters mobbed Zhao before he disappeared from public view. He did not comment on the events until his posthumous memoirs were published in 2009. Clearly a split in the party had occurred, but at the time, no one knew exactly why. In retrospect, Zhao Ziyang was forced to resign and Li Peng's hard line was upheld. Within a year, Jiang Zemin (who, as mayor of Shanghai, had skillfully defused protests in 1986 and subsequently purged the newspaper *World Economic Herald*) replaced Zhao on the standing committee of the Politburo and as general secretary of the central secretariat. By March 1990, Jiang was also chairperson of the Central Military Commission of the National People's Congress of the Central Committee.[93] The man who led the repression of the 1989 movement in Tibet, Hu Jintao, became general secretary in 2002.

From Martial Law to the Bloodshed of June 4

On the afternoon of May 19, as Beijing emptied of the foreign media that accompanied Gorbachev, word spread that a massive government crackdown was coming. Chai Ling called an emergency meeting of her headquarters in the command bus. While security prevented Wuer Kaixi from attending, the group voted to end the hunger strike, a message they broadcast without bothering to wait for hundreds of hunger strikers to discuss the matter. When hunger-striking students finally heard the announcement, they demanded reconsideration of the issue. Delegates from eighty schools gathered, and it took more than an hour for Chai Ling's security force to check their credentials. Finally, when the meeting was allowed to commence, some 80 percent voted to continue the strike. By that time, the vote of representatives didn't really make much difference. Chia Ling's headquarters had already announced an end to the strike. The democratic gathering of delegates insisted the strike would continue. The BASU called for unity, while the student leaders were split into bitterly divided factions. So frustrated were students from campuses outside Beijing by being excluded from decision-making in Tiananmen that they eventually called a meeting in front of the Museum of History and formed their own organization, the Outside-Beijing Autonomous Student Federation.

With martial law imminent, students began drifting away, but BAWF called for a one-day general strike to begin the next day. In a widely distributed handbill that first appeared at 9:30 on the morning of the May 19, BAWF exhorted workers to use "vehicles from every work unit to block main transportation arteries and subway exits, and to ensure the normal operations of the China Central Television and China Central Broadcasting stations."[94] Amazingly, they were able to persuade the All China Federation of Trade Unions, which had donated 100,000 yuan—about $25,000—to the protests, to join in the call for a general strike for May 20.[95]

On the evening of May 19, in a televised solo encore, Li Peng decried "chaos" in the capital and promised "resolute and decisive measures." The very next morning, with Zhao Ziyang unable to stop him, Li signed the martial law order and sent tens of thousands of troops into the city. It was one thing to declare martial law and another to enforce it. Party leaders ordered troops into Beijing, but the army refused to fire on mobilized citizens who peacefully blocked them with every available means. The army took over major media outlets like Central Television and Radio, *Xinhua* News Agency, and *People's Daily*, thereby ending mass media exhortation of people to resist martial law—and squelching reports of soldiers who promised not to use force. No more photos of conversing soldiers and citizens would be published in major media outlets. When soldiers tried to approach Tiananmen Square, however, they discovered that thousands of citizens had erected barricades all around its outskirts using everything from city buses and construction cranes to dumpsters and construction equipment. Responding to the call of BAWF, the people of Beijing had come to rescue their young people. As Jan Wong described the scene: "Elderly women lay down in front of tanks. Schoolchildren swarmed around convoys, stopping them in their tracks. After the first tense night, the soldiers began to retreat as the crowds cheered and applauded. Some bystanders flashed the V sign. Others wept, and so did some of the soldiers. One commander shouted, 'We are the people's soldiers. We will never suppress the people.'"[96] Subsequent reports told of the commanding general of the Thirty-Eighth Army refusing to obey orders to move on the capital, requiring Deng to summon the Twenty-Seventh Army from Hebei province.[97] Troops arrived in Beijing from Chengdu, Shenyang, and Jinan.

On May 20, popular forms of dual power emerged to contest the government's authority. Autonomously organized groups of protesters formed in factories and government work units, police precincts, hotels, law courts, CCP organs and youth groups, government ministries (including at least eight national government agencies), official media agencies, and university departments.[98] Contingents of "Flying Tigers" motorcyclists reported on troop movements. China's only two living Army Field Marshals praised publicly students' patriotism. Seven other generals—including a former minister of defense and a veteran of the Long March—circulated a statement that over one hundred senior officers

After preventing soldiers from reaching Tiananmen Square on June 3, Beijing citizens offered them food. Photo by Reuters/Bettman Newsphotos.

signed calling on the army not to open fire on people.[99] The National People's Congress Standing Committee circulated a petition for an emergency meeting to repeal martial law.[100] BAWF released a joint statement with hunger strikers and ASU that invoked the memory of the Paris Commune: "We members of the working class thank these students and think the Chinese nation should be proud of them. History will remember them. Tiananmen Square will be out battlefield. We will use our bodies to protect the students, hunger strikers, and sit-in protesters. We will build another Wall of the Communards with our life's blood."

For forty-eight hours, hundreds of thousands of Beijing citizens peacefully blocked the army. People fed the soldiers, passed them cases of liquid refreshments, sang songs for them, and bought them popsicles and flowers—as they implored them to be on the side of the people. A banner at the Chinese Academy of Social Science called on the government to resign and for an emergency session of the National People's Congress to be convened. In more than eighty cities at six hundred colleges and technical universities, protests involved more than 2.8 million students. In Shanghai, half a million people marched in support of the students, and in Xian some three hundred thousand people mobilized.[101]

With victory inspiring them and giving them new confidence, hundreds of thousands of Beijing's citizens remained at the barricades on May 21 and 22 and blocked renewed army attempts to reach Tiananmen Square. As Beijing held out, all over China, people mobilized, including four hundred thousand who marched in Hong Kong on May 21. TABLE 5.3 offers an indication of the national scope of the protests.

As people continued to block troops from entering the center of the city, BAWF distributed an open letter on May 21 calling for an indefinite general strike

TABLE 5.3 **Number of Protests, May–June 1989**

Date	Number of Cities with Protests
May 18	17
May 19	116
May 20	132
May 21–22	131
May 28	36
June 1	57
June 4	63
June 5–10	181

Source: Zhang, *Tiananmen Papers*, 214, 227, 243, 274, 316, 345, 392, and 398.

and insisting workers, "as the most advanced class," should form the "backbone" of resistance. So popular was their growing leadership that in the two weeks from May 20 to June 3, some twenty thousand Beijing workers signed their names to membership rolls.[102] With so many new recruits, the group spawned a new structure, with separate units for organization, logistics, and information (with daily broadcasts of news and a wildly popular evening free speech forum). They also set up an office to interface with factories, campuses, and grassroots groups. By the end of May, they had a printing press, broadcast station in the square, picket corps, four "dare-to-die" security brigades ready to fight police incursions, and a constitution specifying a general assembly, standing committee, and executive committee.

Beginning on May 20, they organized autonomous daily demonstrations and worked in tandem with the array of groups protesting martial law. They called for every work site to maintain its own self-organization, lest authorities invent a pretext to intervene by force. In Beijing, workers at Capital Steel Corporation, construction workers, Beijing Citizens Dare-to-Die Corps, and the Flying Tigers Motorcycle Brigade (with about three hundred members) formed. In China's northeast, the Manchurian Tigers Dare-to-Die Corps and Mountain Dare-to-Die Corps were similarly organized along autonomous lines. Among writers, the Beijing Union of Intellectuals was established, attributed by one Western observer to be the "first such autonomous sign of a civil society since the 1940s."[103]

On May 23, BAWF helped form a new confederation of all autonomous groups, including workers, intellectuals, citizens, and several student groups. As the student movement receded, workers took the initiative to form autonomous federations across China—in Shanghai, Wuhan, Canton, Xian, Nanjing, Hangzhou, Shenyang, Cumming, Lanzhou, Guiyang, Changsha, and Xining.[104] In this period, many other organizations formed, but none more potentially important than one formed on May 23, which sought comprehensively to unify all opposition currents. They called themselves the Joint Conference of All Persons of All Circles in Beijing and included about forty representatives of workers, intellectuals, and students. A series of meetings beginning on May 20 included BASU activists, members of the Outside Beijing Autonomous Student Federation, individual activists like Wang Dan, BAWF members, older intellectual-activists from the 1976 and 1978 movements as well as representatives of the Federation of Intellectuals. The group grew rapidly in size. On May 22, even representatives from the Hong Kong Student Union attended, but Chai Ling refused to come. By bringing together representatives of all autonomous groups, a potential Commune was created. The next day, the group resolved to meet daily at noon.[105] They asserted that everyone should obey the decisions of the Joint Conference, but many students thought of them more as advisors than leaders.[106] While they attempted to create a central clearinghouse and decision-making body, others talked of multiple centers transferring power and parallel "command" structures. Acting independently, Chai Ling helped set up a "student parliament" with representatives from each campus—and herself as chair.

As movement leaders huddled in seemingly endless meetings, three citizens arrived from Hunan, Mao's home province. As soon as they had a chance, they threw bags of ink at the Chairman's giant portrait. The Dare-to-Die Squad immediately grabbed the trio (a schoolteacher, a factory worker, and a town newspaper editor) and turned them over to police. (They later received sentences ranging from sixteen years for the worker to life in prison for the schoolteacher. By 2006, all were released after serving from ten to more than sixteen years.) Here is just one example of betrayal of the incredible sense of community in the movement. Yesterday "even the thieves were on strike for the common good," but today, the student security team turned overly freshly arrived activists to the police. "Betrayal" and "sabotage" emerged as words employed to describe fellow activists. Some students went to the train station and recruited new arrivals as soldiers under the orders of self-appointed commanders. Three or four "coups" per day took place at the loudspeaker broadcasting stations; at least one kidnap attempt was made on Chai Ling and Feng Congde by other activists; one student and his cronies tried more than half a dozen times to seize power. Referring to her rivals, Chai Ling declared: "I am the commander in chief. I must resist compromise, resist these traitors." She called for overthrow of the government. As we will see in Thailand in 1992, a single individual, Chamlong, was also able to take leadership of the movement out of the hands of a more democratic committee of organizational representatives. Like Chai Ling, Chamlong used a hunger strike to propel himself into the center. Circumventing and marginalizing democratic tendencies, these demagogical politicians turned personal charisma into media attention and made stardom into power.

Still the citizens of Beijing blocked the streets. Unable to deploy its military to clear the streets, the government hesitated. For a moment, it seemed as if anything was possible. On May 25, the Ministry of Foreign Affairs maintained that Zhao Ziyang was technically still general secretary of the Party's Central Committee. Some one hundred thousand workers and students in Tiananmen Square took to chanting, "Step down Li Peng!" That same day, the ASU completed its long process of reorganizing itself. Its massive student base had considerably dwindled, and the revived group worked in the shadows of the hunger strikers and media stars who made major decisions. For his part, Li Peng publicly predicted, "troops will successfully impose martial law."[107]

On May 26, BAWF wrote to all Chinese abroad: "Our nation was created from the struggle and labor of we workers and all other mental and manual laborers. We are the rightful masters of this nation. We should be, indeed must be, heard in national affairs. We absolutely must not allow this small handful of degenerate scum of the nation and working class to usurp our name and suppress the students, murder democracy, and trample human rights." Another of their public statements exhorted Chinese people to "storm this twentieth-century Bastille, this last stronghold of Stalinism!"[108] Immediately, international networks mobilized. Organizers in Hong Kong threw a racetrack benefit concert and raised millions more dollars on May 27. Tents and supplies arrived that very night in Beijing, along with wads of cash. Almost immediately, a dispute broke out among student leaders about who should control the funds. Finally agreement was reached to share them, with Chai Ling openly insisting she should control the largest share.

Chai Ling finally joined the daily meetings of the Joint Conference. On May 27, after an especially long discussion from 11:00 a.m. to 5:00 p.m., a unanimous decision was reached to leave Tiananmen on May 30, the tenth day of martial law. Delegates called a unified press conference and announced their decision to leave. Little did they know that Chai Ling's assembly of two to three hundred university representatives later voted at their nightly meeting by over 80 percent to stay. However painstakingly the Joint Conference decision had been made, it was overridden by Chai Ling's "student parliament." Once again, movement leaders released self-contradictory statements. While Wuer and Wang announced people's intentions to leave, Chai Ling insisted she had changed her mind, that the hunger strikers would stay. While many people may have thought about it, no one seriously proposed that their group abandon their comrades illegally occupying the square. Many individuals, however, simply voted with their feet and left. On May 29, some thirty thousand students departed by rail from Beijing while only 180 entered; by the end of the month, many campuses had returned to quiet.[109]

As the number of people remaining in Tiananmen dwindled, students sent outreach teams to recruit new constituencies. One of them went to Daxing County, where they were attacked and jailed by local police. Unable to get the arrestees released, students approached BAWF for help on May 28, and a contingent of workers consisting of at least six trucks and a motorcycle contingent was dispatched to Daxing. They confronted local officials, but were unable to get the students released, so they returned to Tiananmen. Two days later, police in Beijing responded to the incursion into Daxing by arresting three BAWF leaders, among them Shen Yinghan, and eleven Flying Tigers motorcyclists. Hearing the grim news, Han Dongfang and some thirty workers went to the Ministry of Public Security and demanded the prisoners be freed. Refusing to comply, the authorities insisted BAWF was an illegal organization and refused to negotiate with anyone other than students. Several thousand people gathered, yet officials would not relent. The next day, however, after BAWF organized a press conference for foreign media, a sit-in at the ministry, and a demonstration in Tiananmen, the police suddenly freed all the arrested. When we compare this treatment of workers with the fact that no students were arrested in Tiananmen Square from April 15 to June 4, we begin to get an understanding of the widening gulf between the two groups.[110]

Not only did the authorities see students and workers in different lights, within the movement, the line dividing them may as well have been written in indelible ink. The same day workers had been asked to help in Daxing, the BAWF expressed their desire to call for a strike, but students told them, "This is our movement, and you have to obey us." Without the consensus needed for action, some workers felt, "By the end, after 28 May, we didn't advocate sympathy for the students anymore. . . . We demanded to participate in the dialogue with the government but the students wouldn't let us. They considered us workers to be crude, stupid, reckless, and unable to negotiate."[111] Many individual campus activists did, in fact, reach out to factory workers. Shida sent as many as five teams to Capital Steel to encourage autonomous workers organizations, and ASU gave some funds to BAWF.[112] Student leaders, on the other hand, were reluctant enough to share the spotlight with each other—let alone with common citizens. After the Daxing action, as BAWF grew distant and the number of students declined, student leaders finally eased their prohibition on workers entering the main part of the square—a ban initially enacted to keep students' democracy movement "pure."[113]

Comparing the organizations of students and workers, many observers concluded that students were far more developed: "In contrast to students, workers were by and large unable to build effective autonomous organizations within their own factories. The newly formed municipal federations were at best small and skeletal, involving a small minority of workers."[114] Students enjoyed mobility facilitated by free train rides (courtesy of railroad workers) and they were also blessed with sympathetic media coverage that helped them spread their movement. Beijing students were sighted in universities and colleges in Harbin, Shanghai, Nanjing, Wuhan, Xian, and Changsha. Students also adapted new technologies like fax machines faster than the regime's repressive apparatus could control.[115] From 1978 to 1987, the number of urban telephone lines had more than doubled, and photocopy machines became widely available—at least to the strata of literati around universities.

Flush with funds, ASU members contacted students at Beijing's Central Academy of Fine Arts and commissioned them to create a statue by the demonstration scheduled for May 30. About fifteen undergraduate art majors agreed in principle, but they insisted on reworking the ASU proposal for a larger version of the Statue of Liberty in New York—as had been unveiled in Shanghai a few days earlier. Such a copy seemed too "pro-American." An additional objection was raised that a mere copy of an existing work did not resonate with artists' notions of creativity, so they proposed a more difficult figure, a statue with two hands holding aloft a torch. One of the students had fortuitously been working on adapting such a model based upon one produced by Russian female artist Vera Mukhina, whose monumental sculpture "A Worker and a Collective Farm Woman" had adorned the top of the USSR's pavilion at the 1937 Paris World's Fair.[116]

While the ASU worked on the statue as a means to draw people back to Tiananmen, Chai Ling scheduled a secret interview with journalist Philip Cunningham, during which she admitted, "What we actually hoped for was bloodshed. Only when the square is awash with blood will people open their eyes." Maintaining she "did not care if people say I'm selfish," Chai Ling called for people to "overthrow the illegal government of Li Peng."[117] On May 28, the World Bank suspended negotiations with China for further loans.[118] At dusk on May 29, fewer than ten thousand students remained in the square. No one could yet tell in which direction the country was headed. Some feared chaos, others authoritarianism.

On May 30, the arrival of the thirty-foot high Goddess of Democracy brought a fresh attraction to the square, enticing some three hundred thousand viewers to review the installation over the next forty-eight hours. Whether thought to be Guanyin, the Statue of Liberty, or a synthesis of the two, the sculpture enlivened the dismal scene and brought new hope to people. By Friday, June 2, the square seemed about to be abandoned, when a new hunger strike by four people, including rock star, Hou Dejian, had a huge impact, and Tiananmen again filled. The new hunger strikers released a statement that was highly critical of "internal chaos" of students' organizations. "Their theories call for democracy," they wrote, "but their handling of specific problems is not democratic."[119] The end was near, and even injecting new celebrity energy could not hold it off much longer.

During the night of June 2, troops began to infiltrate Beijing. Before dawn, people blocked troops and overturned trucks. Hundreds of soldiers were surrounded, some beaten and others arrested by people. A little after noon on June 3, troops used tear gas on protesters who had captured an ammunition truck near the southwest corner of Zhongnanhai, but the crowd refused to disperse. The army again tried to enter Tiananmen Square from the Great Hall of the People. Some came out of tunnels under the Great Hall, and engaged in a singing contest with demonstrators using versions of "Without the Communist Party, There Would Be No New China." At day's end, those troops went back into the Great Hall. While many people celebrated their victory, still believing that the People's Liberation Army (PLA) would not fire on people, a full-scale military assault was underway.

Around 5:00 p.m., BAWF started to distribute weapons (steel chains, clubs, cleavers, and sharpened bamboo poles). They organized people to break down a wall at a construction site in Xidan to take beams and bricks to use for self-defense.[120] That evening in the working-class area of Muxidi, west of Tiananmen, huge crowds blocked lightly armed troops who tried to advance. As stones flew, breaking some of their fiberglass helmets, heavily armed soldiers of the Thirty-Eighth Army behind them opened up with their AK-47s. In the ensuing confusion of battle, many people were killed, including soldiers of the Thirty-Eighth Army who were crushed to death by armored units of the Twenty-Seventh Army.

Resistance was massive and militant. Assaults were reported on seven separate troop formations during the night of June 3. As army units began fighting their way into the center of the city, people gathered at intersections on Changan Avenue. Amid disbelief that troops were using live ammunition, pitched battles involving barricades, stones, and Molotovs versus the armed military were fought all along Changan Avenue. Around 1:30 in the morning, fighting intensified as troops fired volley after volley. Ambulances raced to hospitals as quickly as they could, and pedicab drivers ferried many wounded as well. Around 2:30, someone tried to drive a bus into the assembled soldiers, only to be stopped by a volley of gunfire. Citizens swarmed hospitals to donate blood as soon as the call went out for donors.

As the soldiers reached Tiananmen Square, at least one report tells that their first assault was on the Western reviewing stand where the BAWF had its central meeting point.[121] About five thousand students, many of them crying uncontrollably, other singing, remained crouched around the Monument to the People's Heroes. Workers grew angry with students who broke captured guns and knives on the monument rather than use them to fight the military. Chai Ling was nowhere in sight, having left around 3:00 a.m.[122] At about 4:45 a.m., students took a vote and decided to leave. Twenty minutes later, they filed out peacefully along the southern side.

At dawn on June 4, Tiananmen was in the hands of the army. As the city awoke, outraged citizens took to the streets. Around 7:00 a.m., according to Beijing's mayor, "Rioters swarmed over military vehicles which had been halted at Liubukou and snatched machine guns and ammunition. From Jianguomen to Dongdan and in the Tianpiao area, martial law troops were cut off, surrounded, and beaten. On the Jianguomen flyover, some troops were stripped and others severely beaten." [123] The mayor went on to claim that soldiers were so badly beaten around Hufangqiao that some were blinded. "Mobs" attacked the Propaganda Department of the CCP Central Committee, the Great Hall of the People, the Ministry of Radio, Film, and Television, and two gates of Zhongnanhai, while the "Federation of Autonomous Workers 'Unions" urged people to "take up arms and overthrow the government." The mayor's report details "bestial" attacks on soldiers and police in five different locations. He claims submachine guns were taken in Hugosi. A police ambulance was stopped and one of the eight injured soldiers inside was beaten to death. The intensity of the fighting resulted in arson and damage to 1,280 police cars, military vehicles (including 60 armored personnel carriers), and buses. At Shuangjing intersection, insurgents took twenty-three machine guns from armored cars the crowd had stopped.[124]

Many reports of mutilations of soldiers' corpses were made, including to the east of Xidan intersection, where a soldier was killed and his body burned; in Fuchengmen, a soldier's corpse was hung in midair near where he was killed; in Chongwnemen, a soldier was burned alive and his corpse suspended from an overpass, while people cheered and described it as "lighting a heavenly lantern." Near the Capital Cinema on West Chang-an Avenue, platoon leader Liu Guogeng shot four people. The crowd beat him to death, burned and disemboweled his corpse, and hung him on a burning bus.

In many cities, people fought the military takeover. Despite the media blackout, reports filtered out of Beijing. Faxes from Hong Kong portraying the massacre were posted in several cities, including Shenyang and Shanghai.[125] In Chengdu,

Burning military vehicles reveal the intensity of the fighting in Beijing. Photographer unknown.

violent resistance was crushed. In Hangzhou at 2:00 p.m. on June 4, throngs attacked the railroad station and tied up traffic. Fighting there continued until June 7 as people put wood, rocks, and steel on the tracks to block traffic. Sit-ins at major intersections blocked traffic, and a contingent of art students lowered the national flag on the provincial government building.[126] Acts of heroism abounded, most famously by Beijing's anonymous "tank man"—a citizen who stared down a tank column and held them off on June 5. In Nanjing, ten thousand people marched to mourn the killings in Beijing. In Shanghai, after a train ran over protesters occupying the tracks, killing six people and wounding others, people set fire to train cars and tied up railway traffic for hours.

Overall, the army remained firmly under the control of the government, although in an unknown number of cases, soldiers refused to obey orders.[127] General Xu Qinxian, Commander of the Chinese Thirty-Eighth Army, was subsequently court-martialed for a failure to carry out martial law orders; on June 4, Beijing's deputy military commander was relieved of authority. On June 6 and 7, army units reportedly fought each other, but the government's forces overwhelmed and crushed all opposition.[128] More than one hundred PLA officers were later charged with having "breached discipline in a serious manner," and 1,400 enlisted men were found to have thrown their weapons and run away in the final hours.[129]

The Aftermath of the Uprising

Initial government reports about the crackdown maintained that a total of 300 soldiers and civilians were killed and seven thousand injured, yet over the years, estimates of the number of people killed ranged to 1,000 or more.[130] On behalf of the government, Beijing Mayor Chen Xitong counted several dozen soldiers and police killed and 6,000 wounded. Among civilians, he tabulated 200

Mutilated corpse of soldier Liu Guogeng. Photographer unknown.

killed—including 36 college students—and 3,000 wounded.[131] One of the mothers who lost her son to the violence, Professor Ding Zilin, spent years locating the closest relatives of deceased people. By mid-1995, her list included more than 130 names. At the end of June 2006, Ding and a group of relatives of the deceased named 186 people who had been killed. Although the government has yet to compensate the dead, Ding passed on financial help from abroad to bereaved families.

Hundreds of known activists were arrested in major cities as the crackdown proceeded step-by-step. By June 11, more than one thousand people had been taken into custody. Two days later, a wanted list for student leaders was released, yet for all the difficulties endured by student activists, the brunt of the state's repressive power came down on workers. On June 15, three workers convicted of damaging tools in Shanghai received death sentences, and on June 21, three who burned train cars were executed.[132] By July 5, the number of arrested reached 2,500. Two "rioters" in Chengdu were sentenced to death. Estimates were as high as ten thousand people being detained.

In video testimony from Hong Kong, Chai Ling told of tanks running over students sleeping in their tents in Tiananmen Square, after which troops doused them with gasoline and set them afire. The story was false.[133] Contrary to continual Western media reports, careful examination of video and eyewitness testimony reveals that no students were killed in Tiananmen Square.[134] Most of the killings took place in the working-class suburbs on the outskirts of Beijing. While many people blamed Li Peng, in a subsequent posthumous memoir, Zhao Ziyang maintained Deng Xiaoping ordered the crackdown on protesters without even taking a leadership vote.[135]

In the fall of 1989, a new law mandated that all Beijing University students must undergo one year of military training before entering college, and the entering class was cut from two thousand to eight hundred. All together in the country, some thirty thousand enrollments in humanities and social sciences were axed before the end of 1990.

One of the few surviving vehicles for public expression of protest sentiment was modern art, whose surge continued after 1989. With the success of Deng's market oriented reforms, commercialization tamed the art scene. Late in 1992, with market opportunities in Hong Kong, a third wave emerged.[136] Ironically appropriating socialist realist images and slogans, artists were able to subvert serious state art.[137] Mixing Cultural Revolution images with Western consumer script, Wang Guangyi created "political pop" art with Coca-Cola—fawning tribute to the accomplishments of the 1989 uprising.

China's Prosperity amid Repression

With the retrospective space of more than two decades, we can today appreciate how close China was to a revolutionary situation in 1989. No one applauds the application of state violence on citizens, yet the government has yet to apologize for its overwhelming use of force. Repression was its line of first defense, but the main thrust of government's two decade long response to the challenges posed by the uprising has been to provide unparalleled opportunities for prosperity and economic growth. Since 1989, evidence abounds of an increasing number of state-enterprise workers and university students becoming members of the CCP.[138] In the decade after the crackdown, ten times as many students joined the party as in the previous decade; in 2001, as many as one-third of all students applied for membership, only slightly less than the 28 percent of graduate students who were already members. More than 8 percent of all students were party members in 2007, compared with less than 1 percent in 1989.

Multiparty democracy and expansion of civil liberties are not yet on the horizon, yet the Chinese system has undergone significant reforms. Within academia, more room has opened for debate and airing of unpopular opinions.[139] Repression has certainly continued. In 2008, Wang Dan—by then a Harvard alumnus—counted three hundred thousand political prisoners in reeducation camps.[140] Compared with more than two million Americans who languish behind bars, China's poor human rights performance in the eyes of U.S. citizens is strongly indicative of the power of the mass media.

Many reforms have been made to soften the system. By the Sixteenth Party Congress in 2002, more than half of the Central Committee retired, and an important transition occurred. Officials are now rotated in an attempt to reduce corruption, mandatory retirement by age has been implemented for government

TABLE 5.4 **Rates of Real Growth and Inflation, 1997–2006**

Year	Rate of Real Growth	Inflation of Consumer Prices
1997	9.3%	2.8%
1998	7.8%	-0.8%
1999	7.6%	-1.4%
2000	8.4%	0.4%
2001	8.3%	0.7%
2002	9.1%	-0.8%
2003	10.0%	1.2%
2004	10.1%	3.9%
2005	10.4%	1.8%
2006	11.1%	1.5%

Source: China Statistical Yearbook, 2007 as cited in *Thirty Years of China's Reforms*, 91.

authorities, permission was given for entrepreneurs to join the party (resulting in one-third of China's richest citizens being CCP members), and professionals and intellectuals have been integrated into positions of power to provide expert advice to top officials. Despite efforts to curb it, corruption increased after 1989.[141] Consumer goods and travel options are more widely available, and the scope of political intervention and arbitrary intrusions in everyday life has decreased. In the 1980s, official clearance from work unit leaders was required to get married; travel privileges required approval from authorities; and even theater tickets were centrally allocated.

Of all the changes since 1989, the most significant may well be China's astonishingly constant economic growth rate. From 1980 to 1996, it was 9.6 percent, and even amid the IMF crisis of 1997, it remained robust at 9.3 percent.[142] As shown in TABLE 5.4, China's double-digit expansion from 2003 to 2006 has continued to propel the country forward. Now the world's second-largest economy, it is expected to reach the same level of output as the United States in 2035.

China is today regarded as another "miracle" in a string of Asian economic miracles. With WTO membership since 2001, the spectacular rise in living standards is due in no small part to export-oriented production for the U.S. market. From 2002 to the first half of 2006, China's foreign reserves increased by $654.7 billion.[143] From less than $17 billion in 1987, by June 2010 they approached $2.5 trillion.[144] So much money has flown into the country that real estate investment in Shanghai rose from $100 million annually in 1990 to $7.5 billion in 1996—a rise of 7,500 percent in just six years—before climbing to $11 billion in 2002.[145] In the country's 70 largest cities from December 2007 to April 2008, housing prices rose more than 10 percent *every month* before slowly decreasing to only a 5.3 percent rise in August 2008.[146]

In the process of this phenomenal growth, seven billionaires and more than three hundred thousand millionaires have been created—most either party members or government officials, or with close ties to them. By 2005, inequality has increased so rapidly that the government stopped releasing its calculation of the Gini Coefficient (a measure of inequality), but it did note that it was higher than for all developed countries and nearly all developing countries.[147] Before the reform, it stood at 0.20 in cities and slightly higher in rural areas, at 0.21–0.24. By 2002, the national figure had reached 0.454—one of the world's highest.[148] In 2002, the top 20 percent of the population held 59.3 percent of the country's wealth, while the bottom 20 percent possessed only 2.8 percent.[149] No significant middle class has yet to be built: the bottom 50 percent of economic strata held only 14.4 percent of wealth, and the bottom 70 percent less than 29 percent.

China's reputation as the "world's workshop" was built on the backs of a reserve army of labor of tens of millions—a floating population of more than a hundred million that brought tens of billions of dollars in investments by transnational firms bringing labor-intensive operations with workers paid the "China price."[150] With working conditions still rivaling those of any underdeveloped country, Chinese laborers suffered 14,675 workers killed on the job in 2003.[151] By contrast, only 1,456 workers were counted as killed on the job in the first nine months of 2008. Unskilled industrial laborers in China make a pittance. Even India paid 50 percent more to its workers than Chinese employers did in 1998—and the United States paid 47.8 times as much, South Korea 12.9 times as much.[152] While white-collar employees in large cities recorded significant gains in income, the unskilled suffered as the economy grew. Of all the secrets behind the Chinese miracle, the country's exploitation of her vast pool of semiskilled rural emigrants is at the top of the list. Others include imperial exploitation of Xinjiang and Tibet's vast mineral and oil deposits and their people's labor; state intervention in currency exchange, which limits international speculators' power; and an ideology of manufacturing's primacy, which orients all to production. By guiding investments, China provides another example of East Asian "developmental states"—precisely the kind of government dismantled by the United States in South Korea after the Gwangju Uprising. Finally, a unique feature of China's demographic transition from 1985 to 2007 was the decline in the number of young people, from a ratio of forty-five children (fifteen years old and younger) per hundred workers in 1985 to only fifteen youths per hundred workers in 2005.[153] The consequent freeing up of financial resources provides a boost to savings and capital outflows. Despite the small number of entry job seekers, in 2009, only half of all graduating college seniors were able to sign contracts for employment by May—meaning at least three million people remained looking for work after finishing college.

Continuing Resistance and State Incorporation

Alongside economic growth came a mushrooming of NGOs—or what should be called GONGOs (government-organized NGOs) because of funds received from and links to the state.[154] In 1994, the party granted legal status to private citizens' groups, and environment groups are one key focal point of those initially formed. While the national government formally calls on local groups to report environmental problems, local authorities are encouraged to accomplish high growth rates—a disincentive to maintain high standards for environmental protection.[155] From 1992 to 2007, more than three hundred thousand NGOs were registered. Unofficially, as many as two million may exist.[156]

Chinese people's culture of direct action and resistance to unjust authority remains a significant feature of the political landscape. TABLE 5.5 illustrates the increasing scope of unrest.

Other estimates of the number of protests are even higher.[157] Land is routinely usurped for development, whether for golf courses or power plants, a problem so glaring that the government acknowledges that the vast majority of grassroots conflicts involve land enclosures.[158] In 2006, police opened fire in Dongzhou (a coastal town outside Shanwei) and killed as many as thirty people— the bloodiest confrontation since 1989. This was the second time Dongzhou lands were taken, the first time for construction of a coal plant and the second for a wind power plant.[159]

Can China's central planning and control of finance capital keep its economy from the cycle of booms and busts that Western capitalism compels us to endure? That may well be the critical question determining the character of modern China. As economic prosperity quieted many voices from 1989, a major economic downturn could spark another movement for change. Some in the West delude themselves that China is close to collapse, a fate they similarly project onto North Korea. In 2002, for example, Gordon Chang predicted in *The Coming Collapse of China* that the "People's Republic has five years, perhaps ten, before it falls."[160] In 2008, it was Western capitalism that nearly collapsed.

China's Tibetan and Uighur minorities are also sources of instability, although in both cases, the overwhelming sentiment among the vast majority of Han Chinese favors the government's claim to these lands. The 1989 crackdown in Tibet began China's march toward repression and was many steps backward

TABLE 5.5 **Incidents of Social Unrest, 1993–2005**

Year	Number of Protests
1993	8,700
1994	10,000
1995	11,500
1996	12,500
1997	15,000
1998	24,500
1999	32,500
2000	40,000
2002	50,400
2003	58,000
2004	74,000
2005	87,000
2006	90,000
2008	100,000

Source: China Ministry of Public Security as reported in Andrew Mertha, *China's Water Warriors: Citizen Action and Policy Change* (Ithaca: Cornell University Press, 2011), 153. *Outlook Weekly* (Xinhua state news agency, January 2009) as quoted in "Chinese Question Police Absence in Ethnic Riots," *New York Times*, http://www.nytimes.com/2009/07/18/world/asia/18xinjiang.html?_r=1&ref=global-home; Yang Jianli, "Anti-Government Protests Every Day," http://roomfordebate.blogs.nytimes.com/2009/06/02/chinas-new-rebels/?hp.

on a path to democracy, but their hard lines also catapulted Tibet Governor Hu Jintao and Shanghai Mayor Jiang Zemin into positions of central importance by the beginning of 1990. (Jiang became general secretary of the CCP in June 1989 and Hu succeeded him in 2002.)

A different dynamic in the political relationship between Hong Kong, Taiwan, and the mainland may prove to be a future stimulus to progressive change. Both Taiwanese and Hong Kong activists played minor roles in the mainland's 1989 movement. Former National Taiwan University Professor Chen Ku-ying and legislative candidates Huang Hsun-hsin and Chang Chun-nan all found homes in China but left after the debacle of Tiananmen Square. Along with the Hong Kong representative to the People's Congress in Beijing, Huang was the only other representative to oppose the use of troops on students.

In 1989, repression was the result of the uprising inside China, but in neighboring Taiwan, Bangladesh, and Nepal, the next acts in the unfolding drama of regional democratic movements were sparked by people's resistance.

NOTES

1   Although the government claims far fewer, as many as seven hundred people may have been killed.
2   Blum, *Killing Hope*, 22.
3   Ibid., 26.
4   Roderick MacFarquhar, *The Politics of China: The Eras of Mao and Deng* (Cambridge: Cambridge University Press, 1997), 303.
5   Jan Wong, *Red China Blues* (New York: Anchor Books, 1997), 44.
6   See Mark Selden, "Limits of the Democratic Movement," in *Chinese Democracy and the Crisis of 1989*, eds. Roger Des Forges, Luo Ning, and Wu Yen-bo (Albany: SUNY Press, 1993), 112.
7   A good counterexample can be found in Jack Goody, "Civil Society in an Extra-European Perspective," in *Civil Society: History and Possibilities*, eds., Sudipta Kaviraj and Sunil Khilnani (Cambridge: Cambridge University Press, 2001). Besides pointing out the importance of guilds in medieval China and other specific examples of civil society, Goody also argues that "the rapacity and the despotism of Eastern rulers has often been exaggerated while that of the West has been underplayed" (155).
8   Frederic Wakeman insists these events left residues that persisted in the Cultural Revolution. "Boundaries of the Public Sphere in Ming and Qing China," *Daedalus* 127, no. 3 (1998).
9   Stanley Rosen, "Guangzhou's Democracy Movement in Cultural Revolution Perspective," *The China Quarterly* 101 (March 1985): 28.
10 Apparently even in China, the backlash against the Cultural Revolution was severe as well. Ten years after it ended, Shaoguang Wang interviewed eighty-five people in Wuhan and asked them if they would participate in another Cultural Revolution. All said no, but when he asked the same question about a movement against corrupt officials, all said yes. Shaoguang Wang, "From a Pillar of the Community to a Force for Change: Chinese Workers in the Movement," in *Chinese Democracy and the Crisis of 1989*, eds. Roger Des Forges, Luo Ning, and Wu Yen-bo (Albany: SUNY Press, 1993), 177.
11 Geremie Barmé, "Beijing Days, Beijing Nights," in *The Pro-Democracy Protests in China: Reports from the Provinces*, ed. Jonathan Unger (Armonk: M.E. Sharpe, 1991), 39.

12   Quoted in Andrew G. Walder and Gong Xiaoxia, "Workers in the Tiananmen Protests: The Politics of the Beijing Workers' Autonomous Federation," *The Australian Journal of Chinese Affairs* 29 (January 1993): 2, 19. Also available at http://www.tsquare.tv/links/Walder.html.

13   In a society where family honor is important, what is considered "just" and "unjust" are particularly significant. In the United States, such civil continuity is practically nonexistent. Few Americans know of the Bush's family's collaboration with Nazi Germany during World War II, a family legacy that would be politically disastrous if honor mattered.

14   Rosen, "Guangzhou's Democracy," 2.

15   Wong, *Red China Blues*, 188–89.

16   Rosen, "Guangzhou's Democracy," 14.

17   Ibid., 25.

18   *Freedom at Issue* 63 (November–December 1981): 24, as quoted in ibid., 31.

19   David A. Kelly, "The Chinese Student Movement of December 1986 and Its Intellectual Antecedents," *The Australian Journal of Chinese Affairs* 17 (January 1987): 132.

20   Quoted in ibid., 139.

21   Teresa Wright, *The Perils of Protest: State Repression and Student Activism in China and Taiwan* (Honolulu: University of Hawaii Press, 2001), 24.

22   Julia Kwong, "The 1986 Student Demonstrations in China: A Democratic Movement?" *Asian Survey* 28, no. 9 (September 1988): 970–72.

23   Kelly, "Chinese Student Movement," 127.

24   David Bachman, "Planning and Politics Since the Massacre," in *The Aftermath of the 1989 Tiananmen Crisis in Mainland China*, ed., Bih-jaw Lin (Boulder: Westview Press, 1992), 301, 305, 308.

25   Richard Baum, "The Road to Tiananmen: Chinese Politics in the 1980s," in *The Politics of China: The Eras of Mao and Deng*, ed. Roderick MacFarquhar (Cambridge: Cambridge University Press, 1997): 420–21.

26   Andrew G. Walder, "Political Sociology of the Beijing Upheaval," *Problems of Communism* 38 (September–October 1989), 33–34.

27   Inflation slowly rose from less 1 percent from 1951 through 1978, to less than 3 percent from 1979 to 1984, to between 6 percent and 8.8 percent from 1985 to 1987, before jumping to an official rate of 18.5 percent in 1988. See Calla Wiemer, "Price Reform Stalled: An Inherent Obstacle, A Missed Opportunity," *Journal of Asian Economics* 1, no. 2 (1990): 371.

28   Wang, "Pillar of Community," 184.

29   Bachman, "Planning and Politics," 303; Baum, "Road to Tiananmen," 420–21.

30   Han, *Cries for Democracy*.

31   Wang, "Pillar of Community," 186.

32   Ralph Crozier, "The Avant-Garde and the Democracy Movement: Reflections on Late Communism in the USSR and China," *Europe-Asia Studies* 51, no. 3 (1999): 483–513.

33   Walder and Xiaoxia, "Workers," 2.

34   Quoted in des Forges et al., *Chinese Democracy*, 180. Thompson, *Democratic Revolutions*, 145.

35   Orville Schell and David Shambaugh, eds., *The China Reader: The Reform Era* (New York: Vintage, 1999), 82.

36   Wright, *Perils of Protest*, 35–36.

37   Wong, *Red China Blues*, 227–28.

38   Wright, *Perils of Protest*, 38.

39   For details on events in Xian, see Joseph W. Esherick, "Xi'an Spring," in *Pro-Democracy Protests*, 83–91, and Han, *Cries for Democracy*, 100–101.

40 Karen Eggleston, "'You Are Dead, the Square Is Dead': The 1989 Chinese Pro-Democracy Movement," *Transactions of the Royal Asiatic Society* 64 (1989): 39.

41 Han, *Cries for Democracy* 37.

42 Ibid., 43.

43 Corinna-Barbara Francis, "The Progress of Protest in China: The Spring of 1989," *Asian Survey* 29, no. 9 (September 1989): 904.

44 Ibid., 903. The ASU was officially founded on April 26. The group's "highest platform" was the seven demands of the sit-in at the gated Zhongnanhai district (including freedom of the press and assembly, more funds for education, crackdown on corruption, release of income reports of high officials, and fair reappraisal of Hu Yaobang).

45 Lawrence Sullivan, "The Chinese Democracy Movement of 1989," *Orbis* 33 (Fall 1989): 565–66, as quoted in Eggleston, "Kwangju 1980 and Beijing 1989," 54–55.

46 Tang Tsou, "The Tiananmen Tragedy: The State-Society Relationship, Choices, and Mechanisms in Historical Perspective," in *The Roundtable Talks and the Breakdown of Communism*, eds. Jon Elster (Chicago: The University of Chicago Press, 1996), 221.

47 Walder, "Political Sociology," 32; Selden, "Limits," 127.

48 At the end of August 1989, a Solidarity-led coalition government was formed in Poland; the Berlin Wall was broken down on November 9, 1989; and Czechoslovakia's Velvet Revolution began three days later. Also see Rudolf Wagner, "Political Institutions, Discourse and Imagination in China at Tiananmen," in James Manor, ed., *Rethinking Third World Politics* (New York: Longman, 1991).

49 Walder, "Political Sociology," 32.

50 Han, *Cries for Democracy*, 318–20.

51 Tsou, "Tiananmen Tragedy," 216.

52 Wright, *Perils of Protest*, 48.

53 For a far-reaching and visionary explanation of the tendency of Marxist regimes to be open to reform, see Herbert Marcuse, *Soviet Marxism* (Boston: Beacon Press, 1958). Given their own self-understanding as products of revolution, communist regimes proved themselves particularly pliant in dealing with protest movements arrayed against them in comparison to their counterparts in the West or the South. In the USSR, the system was effectively overthrown in part because of the regime's ideology embracing social transformation and change as part of the historical process.

54 Wong, *Red China Blues*, 231.

55 Tsou, "Tiananmen Tragedy," 224.

56 Wright, *Perils of Protest*, 60.

57 Tsou, "Tiananmen Tragedy," 223–24.

58 See Teresa Wright, "Disincentives for Democratic Change in China," *Asia Pacific Issues* 82 (February 2007): 4.

59 Zhang Liang, *The Tiananmen Papers* (New York: Public Affairs, 2001), 133.

60 Barmé, "Beijing Days," 37.

61 Wang, "Pillar of Community," 178.

62 "Letter to Workers of the Entire Nation," quoted in Walder and Xiaoxia, "Workers," 8. Note here the call to "return to original greatness"—still a key part of Chinese Middle Kingdom identity, that is, that China is the center of the world.

63 Wang, "Pillar of Community," 179.

64 Dated May 17, as quoted in Walder and Xiaoxia, "Workers," 8.

65 Pik Wan Wong, "The Pro-Chinese Democracy Movement in Hong Kong," in *The Dynamics of Social Movement in Hong Kong*, eds., Stephen Wing Kai Chiu and Tai Lok Lui (Hong Kong: Hong Kong University Press, 2000), 58.

66 Zhang, *Tiananmen Papers*, viii.

67 Esherick, "Xi'an Spring," 92.

68 Anita Chan and Jonathan Unger, "Voices from the Protest Movement," in *Pro-Democracy Protests*, 114.

69 Eggleston, "You Are Dead," 52.

70 Wong, *Red China Blues*, 229.

71 Ibid., 232–24.

72 Crozier, "Avant-Garde," 504.

73 Wong, *Red China Blues*, 232. As it seemed like all of Beijing took to the streets in protests over which they alone took initiative, three thousand Muslims marched on May 12 to protest a recent book on sexuality that they felt degraded Islam. At the end of April, over twenty thousand Muslims had protested the book in Lanzhou, the capital of Gansu, and in the middle of May, a hundred thousand more Muslims demonstrated in Xining, the capital of Qinghai, with smaller protests in Urumqi, Shanghai, Inner Mongolia, Wuhan, and Yunnan. (See Dru C. Gladney, "The Social Life of Labels: State Definition, Religion and Ethnicity in China," AAA Paper, 1990.) These groups wanted the government to ban the book. The eros effect in that moment activated groups to articulate their own visions, even if they went against the grain of the majority's impetus.

74 Barmé, "Beijing Days," 54.

75 Wong, *Red China Blues*, 235.

76 Tsou, "Tiananmen Tragedy," 223.

77 Barmé, "Beijing Days," 52.

78 Zhang, *Tiananmen Papers*, 173.

79 Captured in the film *The Gate of Heavenly Peace*.

80 Wong, *Red China Blues*, 235.

81 Han, *Cries for Democracy*, 201.

82 Walder and Xiaoxia, "Workers," 24.

83 Francis, "Progress of Protest," 913.

84 See Selden, "Limits," 122.

85 Eggleston, "You Are Dead," 45.

86 Shen Tong, *Almost a Revolution* (Boston: Houghton Mifflin, 1990), 270.

87 "Crime in Beijing This Month Experiences Sharp Drop," *HuaQiao Ribao*, May 23, 1989, 6, as quoted in Francis, "Progress of Protest," 914. Beijing's Public Security Ministry reported that the rate of crimes, fires, and traffic accidents from May 1–21 was 33 percent lower than the year before (Zhang, *Tiananmen Papers*, 289).

88 *Reminin Erbao*, May 24, 1989, as quoted in Eggleston, "You Are Dead," 46.

89 Burt Green, "The Meaning of Tiananmen," *Anarchy: A Journal of Desire Armed* (Fall–Winter 2004–2005): 44.

90 *Huaqiao Ribao*, June 14, 1989, 4, as reported in Tsou, "Tiananmen Tragedy," 228.

91 Wong, *Red China Blues*, 234.

92 Joseph F. Kahn, "Better Fed than Red," *Esquire*, September 1990, 186–97.

93 Chu-Yuan Cheng, *Behind the Tiananmen Massacre: Social, Political and Economic Ferment in China* (Boulder: Westview Press, 1990), 41–42, 98.

94 Han, *Cries for Democracy*, 273.

95 Wang, "Pillar of Community," 179. Wang cites a Chinese scholar close to those who obtained agreement from the Council's leadership. He refers to the group as the National Council of Trade Unions. After June 4, one of its leading members, Zhu Houzhe, was forced to step down because of his involvement.

96 Wong, *Red China Blues*, 238.

97 Cheng, *Tiananmen Massacre*, 204.

98 Baum, "Road to Tiananmen," 452; Walder, "Political Sociology," 39.

99   Democratic Socialist Party of Australia, *The Class Nature of the People's Republic of China* (Newtown: Resistance Books, 2004), 21–22.

100 The *Asian Wall Street Journal* of May 23 reported that twenty-four members of the Standing Committee of the National People's Congress publicized their call for an emergency meeting to end to martial law.

101 Gene Sharp, *Waging Nonviolent Struggle: 20th Century Practice and 21st Century Potential* (Boston: Porter Sargent Publishers, 2005), 262.

102 Walder and Xiaoxia, "Workers," 9. Three years before Walder and Xiaoxia's study, Selden placed their membership at only three thousand ("Limits," 122).

103 Frederic Wakeman, "Items," *Social Science Research Council* 43, no. 3 (September 1989), 60, as cited in Karen Eggleston, "Kwangju 1980 and Beijing 1989," *Asian Perspective* 15, no. 2 (Fall–Winter 1991), 38. Of course, this discussion of civil society often has overtly Eurocentric overtones, by which certain specific kinds of European civil society institutions are projected as the only ones that count. So China's financial associations (so important as far away as Thailand and Indonesia) and the long-held capacity for petitioners to have their voices head, and hundreds of independent scholarly institutes are not included. See Tsou, "Tiananmen Tragedy," 220 and 234, for mention of "emergence of a civil society almost from scratch." Other scholars insist communism presented a "rupture" in traditional development of civil society, its suppression or disappearance, until its reappearance with economic reforms of 1978. See discussion in William A. Callahan, "Comparing the Discourse of Popular Politics in Korea and China: From Civil Society to Social Movements," *Korea Journal* 38, no.1 (Spring 1998): 281–82. Foucault considers China the "exotic East" [*History of Sexuality*, vol. 1 (New York Vintage, 1980), xv]; Afterward to Hubert Dreyfus and Paul Rabinow, *Beyond Structuralism and Hermeneutics* (New York: Harvester Press, 1982), 213.

104 Wang, "Pillar of Community," 179.

105 Wright, *Perils of Protest*, 83.

106 Ibid., 84.

107 Cheng, *Tiananmen Massacre*, 205.

108 Dated May 26, as quoted in Walder and Xiaoxia, "Workers," 12–13.

109 Zhang, *Tiananmen Papers*, 319–22.

110 Wright *Perils of Protest*, 94.

111 Walder and Xiaoxia, "Workers," 24.

112 Wright, *Perils of Protest*, 93.

113 Walder and Xiaoxia, "Workers," 15.

114 Selden, "Limits," 122.

115 After the uprising had been suppressed, the use of fax machines at Brandeis University in Waltham, Massachusetts was revealed. Chinese students would send reports from various cities to Brandeis and move their fax machines to a different location before police arrived. Once they had received a call from new locations, the Brandeis team of Chinese students would return reports they had compiled back to China.

116 Han, *Cries for Democracy*, 343–44.

117 The interview can be viewed in the excellent film *The Gate of Heavenly Peace*. When the military assault finally came, Chai Ling ultimately decided to leave the square on her own. See further clarification in Tsou, "Tiananmen Tragedy," 239.

118 Cheng, *Tiananmen Papers*, 205.

119 Quoted in Schell and Shambaugh, *China Reader*, 203.

120 Zhang, *Tiananmen Papers*, 367.

121 Green, "Meaning of Tiananmen," 44.

122 Baum, "Road to Tiananmen," 459.

123 A month after the assault, Shanghai mayor Chen Xitong wrote a lengthy and detailed

report, in which he compiled a list of the resistance that I relied on for this section. Chen Xitong, "Report on the Checking the Turmoil and Quelling the Counterrevolutionary Rebellion," in *The China Reader: The Reform Era*, eds. Orville Schell and David Shambaugh (New York: Vintage, 1999), 79–95.

124 Zhang, *Tiananmen Papers*, 384.
125 Unger, *Pro-Democracy Protests*, 77, 222.
126 Keith Forster, "The Popular Protest in Hangzhou," in *Pro-Democracy Protests*, 180.
127 Tsou, "Tiananmen Tragedy," 220.
128 Cheng, *Tiananmen Massacre*, 206.
129 Baum, "Road to Tiananmen," 469.
130 The toll ranges from 200–300 (government figures), to 400–800 by *The New York Times*, 1,000 (U.S. National Security Agency), and 2,600 (Chinese Red Cross). Marc Blecher puts the "best estimate" at around 1,000 in *China Against the Tides: Restructuring through Revolution, Radicalism and Reform* (London: Pinter, 1997). 108.
131 Schell and Shambaugh, *China Reader*, 92–93.
132 Cheng, *Tiananmen Massacre*, 207.
133 Jan Wong, *Red China Blues*, 257.
134 "The Tiananmen Square Confrontation Rewriting History for a new Generation," http://www.alternativeinsight.com/Tiananmen.html, accessed October 1, 2009.
135 *Prisoner of the State: The Secret Journal of Premier Zhou Ziyang* (New York: Simon and Schuster, 2009).
136 Crozier, "Avant-Garde," 498.
137 See Zhang Hongtu's *Last Banquet* in Crozier, "Avant-Garde," 492. Not only did the piece parody Mao by inserting him into Leonardo's Last Supper, but when it was exhibited in Washington, D.C., a conservative Congressman objected to its "sacrilegious" character.
138 Wright, "Disincentives," 4.
139 Interview with Professor Wu Jieh-min, Shanghai, August 15, 2009.
140 Wang Dan, "An Olympic Amnesty," *Washington Post*, June 3, 2008.
141 Han Dongfang interviewed by Feng Congde, "June 4th's Long-term Legacy," *China Rights Forum* 2 (2006): 75.
142 Yanqi Tong measured the 1997 growth rate at 7 percent. See "The Prospects of Democracy in China: Theory and Reality," in *Democracy and Human Rights in the New Millennium*, International Symposium on the 20th Anniversary of the Kwangju Uprising Program (Gwangju: May 18 Institute, 2000), 125.
143 China Institute for Reform and Development, eds., *Thirty Years of China's Reforms: Through Chinese and International Scholars' Eyes* (Beijing: Foreign Languages Press, 2008), 23.
144 State Administration of Foreign Exchange, People's Republic of China, http://www.chinability.com/Reserves.htm
145 Richard Walker and Daniel Buck, "The Chinese Road: Cities in the Transition to Capitalism," *New Left Review* 46 (July–August 2007): 48.
146 National Bureau of Statistics as reported in *China Human Rights Report 2008*, 112.
147 Taiwan Foundation for Democracy, *China Human Rights Report 2008* (Taipei: Taiwan Foundation for Democracy, 2009), 41.
148 China Institute for Reform and Development, *Thirty Years of China's Reforms*, 157–60.
149 Ibid., 167.
150 Walden Bello, "Asia: The Coming Fury," *Foreign Policy in Focus*, February 10, 2009.
151 *Asian Labour News*, May 8, 2004.
152 You Yongding, "The Experience of FDI Recipients: The Case Of China," in *Multinationals and Economic Growth in East Asia*, eds. S. Urata, C. Yue, and F. Kimura (London: Routledge, 2006), 436.

153 "China Is Rich Abroad Due to Worker Bulge," *China Post*, August 3, 2009.
154 See Mary E. Gallagher, "The Limits of Civil Society in a Late Leninist State," in *Civil Society and Political Change in Asia: Expanding and Contracting Democratic Space*, ed. Mutiah Alagappa (Stanford: Stanford University Press, 2004), 443.
155 Joseph Kahn, "In China, a Lake's Champion Imperils Himself," *New York Times*, October 13, 2007.
156 Howard French, "Citizens' Groups Take Root Across China," *New York Times*, February 15, 2007.
157 According to the Hong Kong Center for Human Rights and Democracy, large protests nearly tripled to 170,000 from 1998 to 2000. Cited in Green, "Meaning of Tiananmen," 47. Martin Hart-Landsberg and Paul Burkett reported 327,152 labor disputes in 2000 in *China and Socialism: Market Reforms and Class Struggle* (New York: Monthly Review Press, 2005), 82.
158 Taiwan Foundation for Democracy, *China Human Rights Report 2008*, 57.
159 Howard French, "China Covers Up Violent Suppression of Village Protest," *New York Times*, June 27, 2006.
160 Gordon C. Chang, *The Coming Collapse of China* (London: Arrow Books, 2002), book jacket.

CHAPTER 6

Taiwan

Every three years an uprising, every five years a rebellion.
—Qing dynasty saying about Taiwan

In 1947, the island greeted my birth with muffled echoes.
Looking back, my father said:
That wasn't the thunder of spring storms;
It was the elegy of a funeral procession.
The spring cultivation had yet to begin.
And weeds had overgrown the island's cemeteries.
In a quivering voice, Father said:
"An early harvest of death arrived in 1947."
—Chen Fang-ming

CHRONOLOGY	
1895	Japan gains control of Taiwan in Sino-Japanese War
1945	Allies award control of Taiwan to China
February 27, 1947	Police attack street vendor in Taipei and kill one citizen
February 28, 1947	228 Incident: "Tragedy in the Plaza"—at least two people killed
March 1, 1947	Meetings convened all over the island; at least 123 people killed in heavy fighting
March 1, 1947	Settlement Committee forms
March 2, 1947	Tainan citizens form Southern Alliance Association and arm themselves
March 2, 1947	Taipei Settlement Committee functions as government for one week
March 3, 1947	Uprising spreads to Kaohsiung

March 4, 1947	Armed conflicts in many places
March 5, 1947	Alliance of Youth for Self-Government forms; Settlement Committee issues 32 demands
March 6, 1947	General Peng's troops go on killing spree in Kaohsiung
March 8, 1947	Thousands of Kuomintang (KMT) troops arrive and massacre islanders
March 9, 1947	Martial law; over twenty thousand Taiwanese massacred by KMT
May 20, 1949	Martial law again declared as KMT loses Chinese civil war and evacuates to Taiwan
1949 to 1987	"White Terror": thousands killed, tens of thousands arrested
December 10, 1979	Kaohsiung Incident: protesters fight police; 183 police injured
December 1981	Taiwanese National University students seek direct elections for student government
May 19, 1986	Opposition stages twelve-hour rally; 1,500 riot police unable to stop it
September 28, 1986	Although illegal, opposition activists found Democratic Progressive Party (DPP)
July 15, 1987	Martial law lifted after thirty-eight years and two months— world record longest
May 20, 1988	Farmers militantly protest U.S. imports
April 7, 1989	Magazine editor Deng refuses to be arrested; commits self-immolation
March 14, 1990	Student protests break through police lines at KMT central offices
March 16, 1990	Students begin occupation of Chiang Kai-shek Memorial Hall
March 20, 1990	Occupation grows to over five thousand students in addition to many other constituencies
March 21, 1990	New president Lee Teng-hui meets with students and promises reforms
April 22, 1990	Constitution revised; elections planned
December 21, 1991	First full elections for National Assembly since 1947
March 18, 2000	Chen Shui-bian elected first non-KMT president
November 12, 2008	Chen arrested on corruption charges
September 11, 2009	Chen sentenced to life imprisonment

INTERNATIONAL DYNAMICS IN the twentieth century affected Taiwan as much as any part of Asia, yet the island remained relatively invisible, overshadowed by and subservient to its more powerful neighbors. Japan's military humiliation of China in 1895 resulted in its taking control of Taiwan (also called Formosa) from China's Qing dynasty. The Sino-Japanese War is primarily understood as having resulted in Japan's conquest of Korea, an indication of Taiwan's marginalization.

At the time, money extracted by Japan from China as war reparations—510,000,000 Japanese yen (more than six times annual Japanese government revenue)—was considered more significant than the value of Taiwan. Yet the island's strategically positioned naval ports, to say nothing of her bountiful provisions of food, timber, and "comfort women," made it a vital base for Japanese conquests in South Asia leading up to World War II.

At the end of World War II, the victorious Allies awarded control of Taiwan to China, then ruled by Chiang Kai-shek's National People's Party, the Kuomintang (KMT). A popular uprising sought to establish indigenous control after Japan's surrender, but Chiang ordered the massacre of thousands of Taiwanese, seized control of the island, and subsequently maintained the world's longest span of martial law. In 1949, Chiang and the KMT were defeated on the mainland in a civil war with the communists. With U.S. assistance, they took refuge on Taiwan, where they relocated the Republic of China.

Taiwanese resistance to the bloody imposition of Kuomintang rule, often mentioned in historians' accounts solely because of the KMT massacre of thousands of civilians, also revealed islanders' capacity for self-organization under extraordinarily difficult circumstances. While the decisions of "Great Men" like MacArthur, Mao, Chiang, and Churchill are the usual means to comprehend world events, ordinary people's ability to articulate their own needs revealed a collective intelligence far superior to that of any individual. On Taiwan as well as on Jeju Island in Korea, people's calls for self-government were answered by massacres perpetrated by U.S.-backed dictatorships. On both Korea's honeymoon island and China's "beautiful island," U.S. ships and American weapons became massive instruments of death. If the Americans had denied either of these vital logistically items, history would have been far different, at least for tens of thousands of people whose lives would have been spared.[1] American assistance was vital to the killings. As Assistant U.S. Naval Attaché George Kerr wrote: "It was apparent to all—including all Formosans—that the Nationalists were totally dependent upon the United States. They reached the island aboard American transports, and American arms and subsidies enabled them to stay."[2]

The poorly dressed mainland soldiers who began to arrive in increasing numbers appeared to be ignorant of local customs and envious of islanders' prosperity, while fifty years of Japanese rule left many Taiwanese unable to communicate in Chinese. Immediately after World War II, the KMT administration requisitioned fresh produce, rice, sugar, machinery, and coal purportedly for its troops, yet many goods ended up being sold on the Taiwanese black market at greatly inflated prices. Shortages on the island grew severe at the same time as corrupt mainland officials prospered. In 1946, when a cholera epidemic killed several thousand people, medicine was largely unavailable. In January 1947, KMT Governor-General Chen Yi created tax police to crack down on illegal sale of food and other commodities over which the state had declared its monopoly. As shortages grew, even rice was unavailable in local markets. When it was, inflation sometimes saw huge daily price hikes. Taiwan had two (sometimes three) annual rice harvests, yet widespread famine suddenly appeared imminent, and starvation began to kill people. Simultaneously, an unprecedented number of luxurious entertainment establishments catering to the KMT political elite opened.

The 1947 Uprising and Massacre

The events that precipitated brutal slaughters of otherwise peaceful islanders in both Korea and Taiwan began within a day of each other. Simply called "228," the massacre of over 20,000 Taiwanese began on February 28, 1947. The very next day about a thousand kilometers to the north, the first shots were fired into a peaceful Jeju crowd of over 50,000 celebrating the anniversary of the Korean independence movement of 1919. After U.S. soldiers ordered Jeju police to open fire, six people were killed and dozens wounded, setting off a spiraling set of reactions that propelled an island-wide uprising a year later. By the time the U.S. military government and its Republic of Korea successor had finished their military campaigns on Jeju, at least 30,000 of the island's 150,000 people lay dead—with tens of thousands more wounded or made into refugees.

Tensions on Taiwan grew slowly at first, but on the evening of February 27, an incident on Taipei's Taiping Street (now called Yenping North Road) led to anger "erupting like a flash fire."[3] Government tax police from the Monopoly Bureau sought to confiscate five boxes of contraband cigarettes from Lin Chiang-mai, a forty-year widow and street vendor. Lin protested and pleaded to keep the little money she possessed. With utter disdain for her fate, one agent cut a deep gash on her head with the butt of his pistol. As nearby people screamed at the police, another fired his pistol, killing an onlooker. In fear for their lives, the agents fled. The crowd burned their abandoned car and then went to report the murder to the city's police. Soon, over five hundred people converged on the police station and demanded swift punishment of the tax agents. Other locals went to the office of the *Taiwan New Life Daily* to demand the newspaper report what had happened. Beating drums as they scattered throughout the city, protesters stayed in the streets throughout the night, spreading the word that the time for action had arrived.

The next morning, workers and students declared a general strike, and hundreds of people gathered at Longshan Temple. On street corners, people called for Taiwan's six million people to rise against KMT corruption. The crowd grew to about two thousand people.[4] They moved through the area where the incident had occurred to the branch office of the Monopoly Bureau that had dispatched the agents the day before. Police were unable to stop them—even by firing into the air. As the throng attacked the office, people destroyed cases of wine and all the tobacco they could find inside. Some carried furniture and office equipment into the streets and burned it. Still not satisfied, they found two Monopoly Board police harassing a vendor in a side street and beat the agents to death.

Around 1:00 p.m., gongs and drums led a procession of hundreds of people on a circuitous route through the city. Along the way, thousands more joined, until the march occupied much of the center city. A small group took over the Taiwan radio station and broadcast a call for an end to state monopolies. As the marchers made their way to the Executive Office of the Taiwan Province (now the Executive Yuan), police opened fire without warning with a machine gun on the roof of the building. Indiscriminately aimed bullets swept the crowd, killing at least two people and injuring many more in what became known as the "Tragedy in the Plaza" or the 228 Incident.[5] With those shots, the crowd scattered and began to attack any mainland Chinese person they encountered. At the train station, arriving KMT soldiers were beaten, and hotels known to cater to mainlanders as well as businesses owned by them were targeted, their furniture and records burned in the streets. Despite the tumultuous reaction by thousands of islanders, there was no looting.[6]

"Let Taiwan Rule Itself!" people shouted. Over the occupied airwaves, an impassioned Taiwanese intoned: "They allow our rice to be sent abroad, so that people do not have enough grain and are dying of starvation. Since we are dying of starvation, why not rise up and survive?"[7] In nearby Keelung and Panchiao, people received the broadcasts and took to the streets, beating mainlanders, destroying their businesses and burning police dormitories. In Keelung, steve-dores attacked a police station and mainlanders, leading to days of turmoil. In Taoyuan more than seven hundred students met and exhorted citizens to attack mainlanders. In Taiyuan and Taiping, confrontations went on into the night. The government declared martial law, and armed patrols fired at will in the streets of Taipei. Although a delegation of local political leaders went to ask Governor Chen Yi to rescind his orders, he refused to meet them.

On the morning of Saturday, March 1, meetings were spontaneously con-vened all over Taipei. A delegation led by Huang Chao-Chin, speaker of the Taiwan Province People's Political Council, met with the governor and persuaded him to end martial law that evening. Political leaders (including national, provin-cial, and city officials) met at Jhongshan Hall and decided to form a Settlement Committee (ch'u-li wei-yuan-hui) to resolve the situation as peacefully as possi-ble. To quiet the situation, they publicly called for release of all those arrested and compensation for injured people. They asked for representatives of farmers, workers, and student associations to join the new Settlement Committee (SC), as well as for the abolition of the Taiwan Garrison Command (which had been responsible for much of the violence against people) and an end to press censor-ship. The governor approved the formation of the SC and announced the names of five officials who would sit on it as government representatives. He asked everyone to remain calm. That afternoon, Governor Chen and SC members met with hundreds of citizens and promised to resolve the situation peacefully. In a radio address, Chen promised to lift martial law and to compensate victims and their families.

Even with Taiwanese KMT officials meeting in emergency session, it was impossible to contain the explosion among starving Taiwanese after the "Tragedy in the Plaza." The wildfire of anger and righteous rebellion spread faster than offi-cials could contain it. While politicians sat in their meetings, throngs of people marched in the streets with large character posters calling upon people to "Use Guns against Guns!" They attacked the railway police station, and as many as 123 people were killed, with even more injured on both sides.[8] KMT soldiers used dum-dum bullets, causing terrifying wounds.[9] By word of mouth, news of the momentous events in Taipei spread throughout the island. In Taoyuan, about thirty militants from Taipei organized people to disarm railway police and use their weapons to control all the trains going into the capital. Public officials who did not take refuge in the police station were caught and held in Taoyuan's largest temple. Organizing themselves, armed citizens then assaulted the district government office while others attacked nearby Air Force warehouses. Fighting continued through the night.

On Sunday morning, Taipei's SC convened early in Jhongshan Hall and endorsed a broad notion of self-rule. At least one impassioned speech called for a self-defense force of one hundred thousand to be formed to prepare to confront an expected invasion from the mainland. They decided to form subcommittees for negotiations, relief and protection, and information. These politicians were not the only ones meeting that day. Throngs of students from various universities simultaneously arrived at the auditorium. By the time their meeting began, thousands congregated. Rather than advocating reconciliation, they called for self-rule and armed revolution. All over the island, people were animated by the need for economic and political reforms and organized to rule themselves.[10]

Alarmed by the character of the movement, Governor Chen and SC members met with hundreds of citizens that afternoon and promised to find a peaceful resolution. In a second radio address, Chen promised to lift martial law and to compensate victims and their families. Once again, however, while the governor acted in Taipei, people in outlying cities took matters into their own hands. In Taichung, radical communist Hsieh Hsueh-hung was elected chairperson of the town committee, and she urged the formation of a party capable of seizing power and consolidating democratic self-rule.[11] Insurgents captured town officials, and she made them line up in order of their rank, kneel to the crowd, and apologize for their ruinous governance. She then sanctioned the crowd to beat them. In Chiayi and Taoyuan, uprisings developed quite radically. Taoyuan activists formed a headquarters of paramilitary forces and organized to defeat provincial forces. When sixty Taipei citizens arrived in Tainan on March 2, they found citizens had already established the Southern Alliance Association and armed themselves with weapons abandoned by Taiwanese police. The next night, with the radio station and government offices under their control, a large meeting decided to fight for self-rule and to hold elections for local leaders. In Hsinchu, people tore up sections of railroad tracks to prevent troop movements. When the KMT attempted to move their soldiers by truck, barricades stopped ten truckloads from circumventing the railway damage.[12]

By Monday, March 3, calm had returned and shops reopened in Taipei, but the price of rice skyrocketed. Concerned students approached Taipei's SC to gain an audience with Governor Chen. Although he would not meet them, KMT officials agreed to student demands to stop armed patrols and to prohibit troops from firing at will, but they refused to abolish the hated Garrison Command. Agreement was reached that autonomous student and youth organizations would be empowered to preserve public order. Promises were made that transportation would be restored and military rice stores released to the public. Simultaneously, a "Loyal

Service Corps" was established by the SC, with a nucleus composed of Taiwanese police. Soon an All-Taiwan General Labor Union formed and voted to cooperate with the SC.[13] For the next week, the Settlement Committee "formed the effective government" of the island with sections coordinating general affairs, liaison, investigations, organization, public order, relief, finance, information, and food.[14]

Having received a secret cable informing him that KMT troops were about to be sent from the mainland, Chen ordered government officials to boycott the SC meetings. At 10:00 a.m., the SC met again and sought immediate freedom for the arrestees. Unaware of KMT maneuvers, they asked Hsu Te-hui to organize a Righteous Service Corps, a self-defense group entrusted with maintaining order that they felt hundreds of thousands of people from all parts of Taiwan would join. They also formed a Provisional Committee for Maintaining Order, a group aimed at organizing events to restore people's faith in governing bodies.

In Taichung, the SC under Hsieh took a totally different approach: they united all affiliated organizations to attack the KMT. Hsieh took command of forces and captured the Taichung Security Committee Headquarters along with thirty officers, three hundred soldiers, and an unknown number of officials. Citizens then attacked a firearms warehouse. After hours of fighting, activists won complete control of Taichung city, its surrounding suburbs, and the town's radio station. That night, Hsieh issued three principles of behavior:

1. Do not kill or wound mainlanders.
2. Do not burn or destroy public property.
3. Work to have all weapons placed in the hands of the people.

The next day, five hundred delegates, many of them self-appointed, convened in Taichung city auditorium. Representing popular organizations, they created a District Resolution Committee, agreed that Chuang Chui-sheng—not Hsieh Hsueh-hung—would be chairperson, and created bureaus for general affairs, security, information, and coordination. Many opposed Hsieh's radical tactics— to say nothing of her communist affiliation. Within the new district-level SC, they were able to subdue radicals much more effectively than any outside forces. Ultimately, as mainland troops arrived days later, the new district committee called on all fighters to disband.

On March 3, the uprising spread even further south to Kaohsiung, where citizens first took over city hall and then the entire city except for the Shoushan military base. General Peng Meng-chi ordered his artillery to shell the city, but the newly formed SC decided not to set fire to the nearby fortress, and instead sent three delegates to negotiate. General Peng quickly ordered the emissaries to be executed and launched a counterattack to retake the city. With heavy casualties on both sides, fighting continued until March 7, when government forces finally emerged victorious. In the northeast town of Yilan, students and youth formed armed squads on March 3 and attacked an Air Force warehouse, military camps, and weapons depots.[15] In Hsin-chu in the northwest, crowds set fire to the city hall, the Monopoly Bureau branch office, the courthouse, information office, and mainlanders' dormitories.

On Tuesday, March 4, Taipei's SC became increasingly assertive, while students resolved that they "should be organized into a large brigade for preserving public order." Upset that the SC included local gangsters and the Garrison Command, some forty student representatives met with Governor Chen directly to exchange views on the origins of the crisis. Chen agreed with them that some of his subordinates may not have understood his policies, but he also insisted that civilian responsibility for administrative issues were in no way a replacement for his directives.

In many other parts of the island, armed conflicts continued to escalate. Aboriginal groups descended from the mountains to fight the KMT. In Puli, several dozen students ferociously fought and defeated over seven hundred KMT troops.[16] Taichung students formed a student corps as well. Taiwanese organized the Twenty-Seventh Militia Corps, a fighting unit able to put four thousand fighters in the field—many of whom had served in the Japanese army.[17] Communist leader Hsieh Hsueh-hung was blamed (or credited) with being its commander—although subsequent testimony by the person who had so identified her revealed he—not her—was the unit's real commander. He had lied to KMT authorities to spare himself by throwing blame on the communists. (At the time, U.S. intelligence sources counted "fewer than fifty self-declared Communists on Formosa in a population exceeding six millions.")[18] While order was restored in Taoyuan, citizens in Hua-lien articulated revolutionary demands. At the same time, a loudspeaker truck in Taipei blared "The Star-Spangled Banner" as it called on citizens to resist.[19]

Evidently Taipei students remained unconvinced by Governor Chen's promises to improve the lives of ordinary people, for on Wednesday morning, March 5, the Alliance of Youth for the Self-Government of Taiwan was founded at Jhongshan Hall. Among other measures, the new group proposed elections, self-rule, the creation of new industry, and stabilization of the economy. With autonomous SCs in almost every county, the new student alliance, and KMT officials all claiming authority, Taiwan had three different forms of governing power, each seeking to assert influence over the island's increasing chaotic political life. In many places, KMT government forces relinquished their positions peacefully, as in Hualien. A native Taiwanese, who was deemed more able to control local people, replaced the police commissioner. By the evening of March 5, Taiwanese were in control of much of their island. Elementary schools reopened in the capital, and shops functioned as well.

The SC in Taipei sought agreement with the governor on thirty-two minimal demands, including political reform, dismantling of Garrison Command headquarters, and deployment of Taiwanese soldiers on the island. Governor Chen rejected their demands. In the swirl of events, rumors of all kinds circulated faster than anyone could verify them: Taiwan had won self-government; mainland troops were coming to restore KMT rule; communist forces would defeat the KMT and liberate the island. No one could be sure what would happen next. Only a coterie of KMT officials who huddled close to the governor knew that a large military force would soon arrive.

Unfortunately for Taiwanese, the uprising in Taiwan coincided with the breakdown of KMT-communist talks on the mainland. As the civil war began in earnest, Chiang Kai-shek decided on March 5 to send in the Twenty-First Division and make an example of Taiwan. That same day he had received a wire from his intelligence chief on the island that six hundred aborigines had surrounded and attacked a battalion of KMT troops. On Wednesday night, three KMT destroyers arrived in the port of Keelung, and on the mainland, Chiang Kai-shek readied the Twenty-First Division for deployment to Taiwan. As politicians continually caucused and sought to gently inform their mainland superiors of how far the uprising had progressed, there were reports of new violence in Kaohsiung and Keelung. On March 6, KMT General Peng Meng-chi's troops went on a killing spree in Kaohsiung, and the massacre continued unabated for days—earning him the nickname "Butcher of Kaohsiung."

The KMT hid its intentions to assault the rest of the island. On March 8, a KMT general assured the SC in Taipei that no military action would be taken against islanders, but in the stealth of that night and into the next morning, Nationalist troops arrived in force in Keelung port, more than ten thousand strong. Another three thousand put ashore simultaneously in Kaohsiung. Even before they landed, KMT troops were reported to have strafed the shoreline. When they came ashore in Keelung, they were "shooting and bayoneting men and boys, raping women and looting homes and shops. Some Formosans were seized and stuffed alive into burlap bags found piled up at the sugar warehouse and were then simply tossed into the harbor. Others were merely tied up or chained before being thrown from the piers."[20] When there were not enough bags, wire was strung through the palms of targeted individuals and they were collectively thrown into the harbor. One foreigner reported numerous castrations and other brutalities.[21] The troops swept into the city and occupied it quickly as most residents cowered in their homes in fear of their lives. Hundreds of activists attacked Keelung Garrison Command Headquarters but were thrown back with heavy casualties. Twenty vehicles packed with explosive were captured by the army before they could be detonated and destroy piers where KMT reinforcements were landing. At this decisive moment, the Taipei SC moderated its position. It called on students and workers to return to normal, and asked citizens to help "maintain law and order." That night, more militant citizens in Taipei attacked the Garrison Command office, banks, government offices, and police stations, but heavily armed troops repulsed them.

The next day, two additional KMT divisions arrived on the island. At 6:00 a.m. on March 9, martial law was again declared—and this time the KMT had sufficient forces in place to compel people to obey its dictates. In many places, indiscriminate killings began. KMT commander Ko Yuna-fen announced by radio that all public assemblies were banned and all SCs disbanded. An 8:00 p.m. to 6:00 a.m. curfew was imposed. From the mainland, Chiang Kai-shek blamed the uprising on Japanese and communists. He called the Taipei SC's thirty-two demands "irrational." Dismissing calls for more Taiwanese police, he ordered almost all suspended from duty. All student members of security patrols were ordered to

Thousands of native Taiwanese were massacred in 1947. Photographer unknown.

return their weapons. Near the Taipei airport on the night of March 9, about fifty students were reported killed, as were thirty more in Beitou.[22] By March 11, Tainan had been overwhelmed and its leaders executed. That night in Taipei, soldiers conducted a systematic search for middle school students. Near Taichung, Hsieh and approximately five hundred fighters resisted until the eleventh. Other reports have Taichung holding out until the seventeenth, the same day the KMT minister of national defense arrived with Chiang Kai-shek's son, Chiang Ching-kuo. By March 13, at least seven hundred students in Taipei had been arrested, as were two hundred more in Keelung. Also that day, the army overran Yilan. In the hills of central Taiwan, fighting continued until the twenty-first.

Around March 13, Wang Tien-teng, who had served as SC chair, was executed. On March 15, Governor Chen was replaced, and the terror was stepped up. Claiming two thousand rebels and communists had dispersed and continued to fight, KMT commanders launched an all-out war. In Chiayi city, corpses of students killed in the suburbs were trucked into the city and thrown into a fountain for the public to witness. In Kaohsiung, "Night and day the gunfire continued. On the streets and in the lanes and alleys there were dead bodies. Many bodies were already rotting, and blood still flowed from some. Nobody dared to go out and claim them. In this way, corpses were strewn as far as Kaohsiung Mountain, and blood flowed into nearby Lake His-tzu."[23] Both the Kaohsiung and Danshuei rivers were reported to be full of corpses.

By the time the KMT killing spree subsided, thousands of people had been massacred. No one will ever know exactly how many people were killed. Although conservative estimates are twenty to thirty thousand, others maintain more than a hundred thousand Taiwanese may have been killed (some insisted even more since the number of missing exceeded a hundred thousand).[24] Everyone agrees that the indigenous elite was especially targeted. Luminaries such as doctors, lawyers, businessmen, professors, journalists, and civic leaders were ruthlessly hunted down and murdered. In the aftermath of the uprising, the KMT's Counterespionage Bureau compiled a list of over a thousand "traitors" whom they marked for elimination.[25] For years, death squads operated with impunity—indeed, members were rewarded for zeal and efficiency. The hated Monopoly Bureau was restructured, and some state enterprises like the Match Company were privatized—as were mines and industry.

Chiang and the KMT had their way with Taiwan, but they were too corrupt and brutal to win the mainland war. To give a rough idea of how much KMT pillaging of wealth proceeded, U.S. General Wedemeyer estimated Generalissimo Chiang Kai-shek and a small coterie of his associates to have holdings of anywhere from from U.S. $600 million to $1.5 billion in 1948.[26] By 1949, their communist enemies had routed the KMT, and some two million KMT hangers-on scrambled to Taiwan, taking with them hoards of gold and a cache of national treasures. On May 20, 1949, martial law was again declared on the island, and in its first five years, some 5,000 to 8,000 people were executed.[27] In the "White Terror," the name given to the government's brutal campaign of suppression, one calculation placed the number of victims after the communists' victory (i.e., from 1949 to 1987) at 29,407 killed, imprisoned, or otherwise suppressed.[28] The civil service in Taiwan was purged as some 36,000 Taiwanese public officials lost their jobs, and KMT operatives eager to make up for their losses on the mainland by hunting Taiwanese communists replaced Taiwanese police. Hsieh Hsueh-hung made good an escape. In late 1947, she helped create the Taiwan Democratic Self-Government League in Hong Kong and later became an honored member of the PRC government. Governor Chen faced a firing squad on June 18, 1950, for consorting with communists.

Only after the death of Chiang's son and successor Chiang Ching-kuo did it become possible to speak publicly about 228. In February 1992, a "2.28 Incident Report" was published, and in 1997 (fifty years after the tragic massacre), a memorial to the victims was constructed. While often portrayed solely as a massacre (which it certainly was beginning on March 6 in Kaohsiung and March 8 in Keelung), the uprising spawned self-governing councils supported by armed militia groups that advocated Taiwanese self-rule.

From the "Silent Generation" to the Kaohsiung Incident

For thirty-eight years until it ended on July 15, 1987, Taiwan suffered the world's longest reign of martial law. Generalissimo Chiang Kai-shek ruled more than twice as long as Pinochet kept his grip on Chile and even longer than Generalissimo Franco's tenure as Spanish dictator. Many KMT criminal laws, gleaned from Nazi Germany, remain valid in the twenty-first century.[29] Even today, the legacy of decades of authoritarian KMT rule—imposed by the massacre of thousands in 1947—remains a blot on islanders' lives.

While much of the world was swept by youthful revolts in the 1960s, Taiwan's traumatization and White Terror so quieted people that youth in the 1960s were often called the "silent generation." As in South Korea, police routinely stopped young men with long hair and gave them haircuts. Even "strange apparel" was banned. Children who spoke Taiwanese in school were beaten, and parties where people danced were unlawful. The KMT strictly controlled television and domestic media, and its censors thoroughly processed foreign newspapers and magazines. Bibles translated into Taiwanese were banned. For almost half a century, privately owned radio stations were not permitted, and radios had to be registered with the government. Anyone discovered listening to "bandits' radio" from the mainland was immediately arrested. Dissidents were compelled to live in prisons or exile—if they survived. Despite a constitutional provision limiting the presidency to two four-year terms, in 1960, the National Assembly cleared the way for Chiang to remain president for life. When the editors of *Free China*, a biweekly magazine published since 1949, announced their intention to found a new China Democratic Party, they were promptly charged with sedition and their magazine closed.

The KMT hold on power was not solely based upon the might of police. While the government exercised extraordinary top-down control of civilian groups—including unions, farmers' organizations, and student groups—it permitted elections at the village level. A generous land reform program gleaned from failure on the mainland and strongly urged by the United States was enacted. In April 1949, the government reduced the rent that tenants paid to property owners to a maximum of 37.5 percent of harvest. Even more popular were subsequent measures allowing tenants to buy public land on favorable terms. In 1953, a "land to the tiller" program limited the amount of land any individual could own to about seven acres. Excess holdings were sold off on favorable terms to those who farmed it. Large landlords were compensated for the loss of their lands with stocks and bonds in Taiwan's biggest companies. Since farmers relied on the government for fertilizers, the state made huge revenues both from payments for lands they sold as well as from the sale of chemicals. Protests from the former landowning class were muted by their newfound wealth.

In 1962, Taiwan's GNP was a meager $162 but thirty years later, it passed the $10,000 mark.[30] For four decades from 1952 to 1991, average economic growth rate was an astonishing 8.7 percent, and exports grew from 8.6 percent of GDP to well over half of the island's total economic output. One key to Taiwan's growth—as was also the case for Japan—was the tragedy that befell Korea in 1950. As soon as the war began, U.S. President Truman promised to protect Taiwan with the Seventh Fleet. U.S. aid was stepped up, and long-term development projects were initiated, aimed especially at improving infrastructural needs that could prepare the ground for subsequent industrialization. U.S. aid had been cut off in 1949, but as soon as the Korean War began, American funding was massively restored. In the words of Minister of Economics Yin Chung-jung, "the timely arrival of U.S. aid was no less than a shot of stimulant to a dying patient."[31] Every year from 1950 to 1964, the government ran a deficit—and U.S. assistance covered them all even though the shortfall increased steadily from NT$466 million in fiscal 1951 to NT$3,195 million in fiscal 1964.[32] With the subsequent U.S. war in Indochina, once again Taiwan and Japan (as well as Thailand and South Korea) all reaped economic windfalls. American soldiers needed agricultural products and industrial goods, rest and recreation, and Taiwanese contractors found work in nearby Vietnam.[33]

Huge amounts of U.S. aid flowed into Taiwan until 1965. As in South Korea, economic policies designed to limit imports (and thereby save precious foreign exchange) were replaced under U.S. pressure by an export-oriented industrialization strategy. Coupled with generous access to U.S. markets, Taiwan embarked upon what Immanuel Wallerstein characterized as "development by U.S. invitation." In the 1950s, exports averaged between $100 and $125 million annually, but imports were nearly twice that. Again U.S. aid financed some 90 percent of the trade deficit. At the height of the Vietnam War, more than eight hundred thousand U.S. troops were in the region, and Taiwan's trade deficit had turned into a surplus.

From 1960 to 1970, grants and loans were 46.8 percent of Taiwan's 1965 GNP. For South Korea in the same period, they constituted an astonishing 139.1 percent of 1965 GNP. By the early 1970s, the percentage of aid was down to 18.3 percent for Taiwan's GNP (30.1 percent of Korea's); by 1980, Taiwan had zero external aid and grants, Korea only 1.4 percent of GNP.[34] From 1965 to 1970, the transition from import substitution to export-oriented development brought more than a million rural youth to the cities.

Unlike South Korea and Japan, where huge conglomerates were formed with government assistance, small businesses dominate the Taiwan economy. Fewer than 2 percent of all corporations are large, and it is estimated that one in eight Taiwanese is a boss of one kind or another.[35] In the 1990s, more than 85 percent of corporations had fewer than thirty employees—but employed 80 percent of the country's labor population.[36] Nearly half of all manufacturing corporations had fewer than a hundred employees and less than 24 percent had more than five hundred.[37] Under these circumstances, is it any wonder that Taiwan's automobile industry never took off like Korea's? In 1970, neither country produced fifteen thousand cars. In 1988, Korea sold over one million cars, while Taiwan managed barely more than one-fourth that number.[38] In both Korea and Taiwan, threats to withdraw U.S. aid resulted in regime compliance with export-led development.[39] While in Taiwan, civil organizations compliant with KMT policies helped maintain order, in Korea force was used to keep order, and large *chaebol* (giant family-owned corporations) were established to manage the economy.

With strong U.S. support, by the 1970s, manufacturing had mushroomed and output soared. High real wages, strong savings accounts, and a generally egalitarian distribution of the island's wealth ensured stability to the regime. Throughout the country small factories sprang up, and many homemakers converted their living rooms into piecework production sites. Only as international dynamics intervened did people begin to stir. The few antiregime actions that occurred were of necessity secretive. In New York, Peter Huang tried to assassinate President

Chiang Ching-kuo in April 1970, but his shot went wide. Provincial governor Hsieh Tung-min lost his hand when a mail bomb exploded, and other acts of sabotage were blamed on advocates of independence. With most people focused on working hard for future prosperity, the island was once again buffeted by international events. In 1971, the United States awarded Japan control of the Diaoyutai (Senkaku) islands—and Japan immediately banished Taiwanese from centuries-old fishing grounds. KMT rule suffered another major crisis when the mainland "bandit" regime was awarded China's UN seat in October 1971. Isolated and angry, the KMT government encouraged protests, but once people were in the streets, demands arose for reform within Taiwan, and the movement was quickly suppressed.

KMT police continued their strict supervision of young people. On February 5, 1972, more than 450 men with long hair, as well as 67 wearing bell-bottom trousers and 13 females in miniskirts, were rounded up. Off-campus youth were heavily monitored, and college students could not even choose their own campus governments. Outside the realm of government censorship, a vibrant literary movement blossomed, and the first modern Taiwanese dance group (Cloud Gate) began in 1973. The 1970s turned into a time of hopes and dreams for young people who emerged from the "cultural desert" of the 1960s. Music from the United States became popular, and well-known songs, including "We Shall Overcome," were sung in public. During a singing contest, one participant proposed that people write and sing songs of their own, rather than ones from records. As he sang his own composition, many people nodded their heads in approval, and a folk song–writing craze soon swept the campuses.

Throughout the decade a number of magazines crystallized dissent, and dozens of activists were sentenced to long prison terms for little more than writing or speaking in public. One collective that edited *The Intellectual* encouraged students and youth to speak out. In 1971, the magazine published a declaration decrying the fact that "people under forty-three years of age, who account for two-thirds of the population, have never had the opportunity to elect their own representatives at the central level." Debates were touched off on parliamentary elections, including a packed meeting at Taiwan National University (TNU) gymnasium.[40] The government targeted the TNU philosophy department and fired fourteen professors. A government "encirclement campaign" soon neutralized the magazine. Shortly thereafter, *The Intellectual* collective dissolved, and as more than one hundred associates split into various tendencies, subaltern discourse proliferated.

In the 1970s, ten major infrastructure projects were completed. As Taiwan industrialized, women's labor participation jumped from 33.1 percent to 43.5 percent in the two decades from 1969.[41] Often important to light industries in the first phase of export-led development because of their low wages, women made overall only 62 percent of male wages—even lower in places like the Kaohsiung Export Zone where thousands of young women found work. Working women began to vocalize demands for equal pay, while those who received college education in the United States formed early pockets of feminism. Influenced by

American feminism, a group of women including Annette Lu opened a women's center/teahouse, published dozens of books, and held public events, but the KMT forced their center to close in 1973.[42] Evidently, KMT flower arranging classes and pursuit of traditional maternal roles emphasized by its female branches, which extended even into small villages, were deemed appropriate, while autonomous discourse was not. Even among mainstream women, Lu was not always popular for her outspoken feminism. Under surveillance by secret police, feminists resorted to tactics like organizing a televised cooking contest for men on International Women's Day in 1976. In many cities, public events on "Love, Sex and Marriage" attracted over ten thousand people.[43] Women played prominent roles in demonstrations, sometimes standing in the front ranks with flowers. While the police on the street may have refrained from attacking them, KMT authorities came down hard on Lu, sentencing her to twelve years in prison after she gave a speech at an opposition rally in Kaohsiung in December 1979.

In August 1975, *Taiwan Political Review* formed and continued "criticizing the bureaucratic system"—the quasi-Leninist KMT. The magazine's fifth issue in November 1975 asserted that "the people of Taiwan had only two possible roads if they wanted to become 'masters of their own house'—to overthrow the KMT dictatorship by a popular, armed uprising or to united to struggle for early reunification with the motherland." The government quickly closed the magazine, but other magazines continually renewed the democratic impetus. *China Tide* was able to break ground by critically examining the U.S. imperial role, not only for its wars and support of dictatorships in South Korea and Chile, but also for the role of U.S. multinational corporations. As their publications were harassed and closed down, magazine editors turned into social activists. In 1977, a "native soil literature" controversy was touched off after publication of realist fiction addressing Taiwan's economic and cultural colonization.[44] Feminists like Li Yuan-chen participated and helped validate experiences of subaltern aboriginal groups and working-class people. Li also taught a class for teenage sex workers—many of them aboriginal girls sold by their impoverished parents.

For years, opposition candidates ran as independents in local elections. On November 19, 1977, people suspected the KMT of tampering with the results of a local election in Zhongli, and electoral fraud, already notorious in a 1975 special election, brought a violent reaction from thousands of people. They attacked police station, overturned antiriot vehicles, and set them on fire.[45] Police shot dead one university student. When the island's votes were tallied, non-KMT candidates running on non-partisan slates captured five mayoral seats and won twenty-one of seventy-seven seats in the Taiwan Provincial Assembly with over 30 percent of the votes. Moreover, after Zhongli, public protests became widespread, and opposition candidates continued to win elections.

In 1978, the KMT called off elections, ostensibly because of the crisis brought on by U.S. normalization of relations with the communist mainland. In response to the cancellation of elections, activists called *tangwai* (extraparliamentary—literally, "outside the party") organized a national conference at the Ambassador Hotel for December 25, 1978. KMT pressure on the hotel's owners compelled them to withdraw their contract, but *tangwai* activists, many of whom were non-KMT candidates, held the conference at their private offices and insisted elections go on as scheduled. Once again, international issues intervened. On January 1, 1979, the United States announced it would sever diplomatic ties with Taiwan and nullify the countries' mutual defense treaty by the end of the year. Angry protests erupted in the streets. That same afternoon, thousands of people assembled in front of the U.S. embassy, where some stomped on peanuts—President Jimmy Carter's cash crop—and screamed with anger at U.S. betrayal.

Opposition activists continued to demand elections, and on January 21, 1979, the government responded by arresting seventy-eight-year-old Yi Deng-fa, sparking one of the most notable demonstrations in decades. On January 27, a car containing a U.S. delegation led by Deputy Secretary of State Warren Christopher was surrounded near the airport. Stones and eggs broke a car window, reportedly wounding Christopher and the U.S. ambassador. In this climate, protests seemed to be mounting and public engagement took many forms. So much did patriotic sentiment grow in this period that when the government asked people to donate money, in ten days, enough was raised to buy eighteen F-5 jet fighters. The next few months came to be known as "Taipei Spring," an exciting break from the long winter of quietude and fear. A *tangwai* headquarters was created in May, and the height of public opposition was reached that summer. In August, *Formosa* magazine was founded, the first time anyone had attempted to speak for the entire opposition.

Crystallized from a flurry of undercurrents, *Formosa* peaked with a circulation estimated at one hundred thousand and with branch offices in eleven cities and a teahouse in Taipei.[46] The magazine organized a number of rallies, seminars, and public events aimed at the creation of a new political party. On December 10, 1979, activists chose Kaohsiung, Taiwan's second-largest city, to celebrate Human Rights Day. Although police tried to prevent the rally, activists persisted in holding it. The night before, police severely beat two organizers passing out leaflets. The day of the rally, with the riot squad out in force, hundreds of people assembled outside *Formosa's* branch office by 6:00 p.m. Surrounded by government forces, they sang "We Shall Overcome" (in Fujian dialect) among other songs.[47] Police entered the magazine's office and demanded the illegal rally cease. Organizers replied they would only agree after police who had beaten the leafleteers the night before apologized and their commanding officer resign. The crowd moved to a traffic circle two blocks away while *Formosa* leaders negotiated with the police. They asked for people who wished to join the rally to be permitted to pass unmolested through police lines. As they were talking, someone ordered the use of tear gas at the traffic circle. Protesters rushed to escape the gas, but police blocked exits. The crowd moved to leave to the south and regrouped at the *Formosa* office. Police again attacked, this time with tear gas and in force, causing the most injuries of the evening. People armed themselves with materials at a nearby construction site and fought back, injuring many police. A couple of hastily made Molotovs were ineffective. The government claimed 183 unarmed policemen were injured and insisted no protesters had been hurt. A subsequent report told of fifty citizens injured by police. The crowd size is also a matter of some dispute. An internal U.S. embassy figure put the number at 150,000, but Jaushieh Wu maintains only 100 people were present during the Kaohsiung Incident.[48] Eyewitness Michael Lin estimated the size at "probably two to three thousand, but certainly not over ten thousand."[49]

Whatever the crowd's size, the violence on December 10 was a watershed event, one the regime could not let pass without notice. The next night, the government arrested fourteen opposition figures, including most of the staff of *Formosa*, and within a few days, at least 152 people were rounded up. Eight defendants were selected to stand trial in military courts on sedition charges, where they were linked to communist subversion and terrorist attacks on government officials. In the middle of it all, on February 28 (the anniversary of the infamous 1947 massacre), defendant Lin Yisiong's mother and twin seven-year-old daughters were murdered by a knife-wielding assailant in their home. Despite twenty-four hour police surveillance on the residence, the police claimed they knew nothing about the murderer. On April 18, all defendants were found guilty and given long prison terms. Prosecuted under civilian law, thirty-two others also received time in prison.

Grassroots Protests and the End of Martial Law

With the Kaohsiung Incident, the movement had clearly passed an important milestone. Afterward, organizers were much more sure of themselves, and protests became highly orchestrated events such as sit-ins, rallies, and press conferences. In the somewhat exaggerated estimation of one observer, "Even Taiwanese activists without an anti-imperialist understanding (by far the majority) at that time saw the political question as one of armed revolution, like Iran or Nicaragua."[50]Although the opposition divided into moderates and radicals, Taiwan's movement remained very civil in character and it never became as militant as in many other countries. Literature, music, and dance were more important domains of resistance than street actions, and no well-organized armed campaign was ever launched. Writers continued to develop Taiwanese identity by improvising new expressive forms and appropriating Hokkienese, Japanese, and English into their stories.

As regime repression decimated opposition ranks, it also sparked widespread protests and international condemnation. In July 1981, Carnegie Mellon professor Chen Wencheng was visiting the island with his family. KMT officials denied him an exit visa, and Garrison Command officers took him in for questioning. The next day, his corpse was found. Few believed the military's claim that they had released him unharmed. In the subsequent outcry, U.S. Representative Stephen Solarz called for hearings into Chen's death. Investigations brought to light an extensive network of Taiwanese student spies on American campuses. Nonetheless, the regime simply denied any involvement in Chen's killing and insisted it had no spies on U.S. campuses.

The White Terror continued to claim victims. On October 15, 1984, U.S. citizen Henry Liu—author of a biography critical of Chiang and banned in Taiwan—was shot and killed in his California home. Subsequently the American FBI found evidence linking Taiwanese intelligence agents and Bamboo Union gang leader Chen Chi-li to Liu's murder.[51] Once again, international condemnation of the regime was loud—but this time there was a serious response. President Chiang set out to reform the secret police and promised no one in his family would seek election in the future. Despite the president's pledge to reform, the bureaucracy proved intractable. In November 1985, the wife of future president and then opposition political leader Chen Shui-bian was run over three times by a car, an attack blamed on KMT-hired gangs that left her permanently wheelchair bound.

Chafing at the government's control of everything, especially the student union, campus groups formed to agitate for direct elections of student government representatives at Taiwan National University. Rebuffed by the authorities, many moved off-campus and helped publish underground newspapers and journals. In 1982, a collective began to produce *Awakening*. Besides being the only feminist magazine in Taiwan at that time, *Awakening* organized events every March 8 and helped form an alliance of women's groups to decriminalize abortion. In 1984, after the government censored a campus newspaper, its editors distributed a blank newspaper—the "White Paper." Scattered protests were broken up, but the movement spread to many universities, where activists published an assortment of periodicals, the most famous of which was *The Love of Freedom*. Off campus, other activists formed the Taiwan Association for Human Rights in 1984—a clear challenge to the authorities, whose right-wing "human rights" association focused exclusively on the mainland.

Like his father before him, Chiang Chin-kuo's rule was autocratic and tolerated no dissent. Once the Generalissimo died in April 1975, Chiang Ching-kuo ruled for thirteen years until his death in 1988. Unlike his father, he integrated party positions with native Taiwanese, and in 1984, he was reelected along with Lee Teng-hui, a Taiwanese member of the KMT, as vice president. According to the constitution, a vote of the National Assembly, not a popular election, selected the president.

In three decades, Taiwan was transformed from an agricultural society into a modern industrial society. At the end of World War II, the majority of Taiwanese were farmers living in the countryside, but by 1986 only 17 percent remained involved in agriculture, and that sector's share of the economy was even lower, as shown in TABLE 6.1. In that same period of time, exports had increased from only 10 percent of GNP in 1952 to more than half of GNP by 1987.

After three decades of rapid economic expansion, one estimate placed Taiwan's middle class at 57 percent of the population (40 percent in terms of

TABLE 6.1 **Distribution of Gross Domestic Product**

Year	Agriculture	Industry	Services
1951	32.5%	23.6%	43.7%
1987	5.3%	52.0%	42.7%
1993	3.5%	40.6%	55.9%

Source: Taiwan government statistics in Wu, *Taiwan's Democratization*, 48.

TABLE 6.2 **Labor Disputes in Taiwan, 1965–1986**

Year	1965	1975	1980	1984	1985	1986
Number	15	485	700	1,154	1,622	1,458

Source: Hsu Cheng-Kuang, "Political Change and the Labor Movement in Taiwan, 1989 American Sociological Association paper, as cited in Walden Bello and Stephanie Rosenfeld, *Dragons in Distress: Asia's Miracle Economies in Crisis* (San Francisco: Food First Books, 1990), 224.

income and education, and 70 percent by subjective self-identification).[52] In the 1980s, the regime steadily adopted market liberalization policies. Although there was some disturbance of the equality fostered in the island's first thirty years, Gini coefficients remained low—and Taiwan remained one of the world's most equal places.[53]

At the same moment, the international organization, Committee to Protect Journalists, counted more imprisoned journalists in Taiwan from 1985 to 1986 than in any other noncommunist country.[54] The KMT controlled television and radio, so autonomous periodicals were dissidents' sole means of sending out their messages. As subaltern Taiwanese—some 85 percent of the population—sought to create a counterpublic discourse, all segments of the population were affected. From below, activists became increasingly bold in challenging the White Terror. An alliance of aboriginal groups destroyed Wu Feng's statue—a Han-invented deity believed to give Chinese power as they conquered the island. In the new aboriginal counternarrative, they insisted on being called "original inhabitants" (*yuanzhumin*) rather than the traditional Chinese word for "mountain people" (*shanbao*).[55] Even among *Hakkas* (Chinese people who had migrated to the Taiwan long before the KMT arrived), a surge of activism was generated by the *Zeitgeist* of change.

Inspired by *tangwai* political activists in the early 1980s, workers mainly concerned themselves with taking control of unions away from KMT, in struggles known as the "autonomous trade union movement."[56] The vast majority of labor disputes from 1982 to 1986—as many as 90 percent of them—were precipitated by companies' refusal to abide by existing labor laws.[57] In the 1980s, the vast majority of workers actions were organized directly by workers themselves—that is, without the "help" of yellow unions. Of 208 actions, unions led only 13, while blue-collar workers initiated 167.[58] TABLE 6.2 offers one indication of the increasingly restive character of civil society.

In the "overall rebellious *Zeitgeist* of civil society," a consumer movement mobilized and ecologists groups formed; in 1982, women mobilized, as did aboriginal human rights efforts from 1983.[59] A key dimension of the grassroots insurgency was in response to the degradation of the island's beauty. Beginning in March 1986, environmentalists staged months of protest in Lukang against U.S. Du Pont Corporation. In what became known as the Lukang Rebellion, the local elite united with grassroots and forced cancellation of a new plant.[60] Protests also focused on San Hwang chemical plant and Lee Chang-yong plant. In October 1986, the first anti–nuclear power protest occurred at Tai-Power Company's Taipei headquarters. In the six years from 1979 to 1984, there were only fifty-seven anti-nuclear articles in mainstream Taiwanese magazines, but in 1985 alone, sixty-one were published and in 1986, there were seventy-nine.[61]

Beginning in 1986, protests against Taiwan's martial law led to government promises to lift the decades-old state of emergency. Photograph by Sung Lung-Chyuan in *Witness: Taiwanese People's Power 1986.5.19–1989.5.19* (Taipei, 2004), 14.

Long before the lifting of martial law in 1987, pressure for democratization increased from below. As Yun-han Chu related: "Since 1979, the opposition has moved cautiously toward forming a quasi-party despite stern warnings from the government of its resolve to enforce the legal ban. . . . Beginning in 1984 the *tangwai* gradually stepped up their push for democratic changes in ways never before tolerated. They organized mass rallies, staged street demonstrations, and engaged in other kinds of confrontational strategies to undermine the political support of the KMT regime."[62] From only 175 incidents of protest in 1983, the number jumped to 1,172 in 1986.[63]

As ecological protests won victories, other activists targeted martial law directly. Galvanized in 1986 by the May 19 Green Action, over six months of street actions called for an end to martial law. Fearing the radicalization of large segments of the society, Chiang Ching-kuo announced he would lift martial law the following year. If the release valves had not been opened, no one knows how big the explosion might have been.

After the overthrow of Marcos, he saw the handwriting on the wall. Pressure from American Institute Director James Lilley helped to convince him that acceding to opposition demands was the best way to guide the country forward. He immediately sought to loosen restrictions on protests. The opposition *Tangwai* Research Association for Public Policy (TRAPP) was warned by Interior Ministry officials to disband, but Chiang directed his police to negotiate with the group. After two meetings seeking some sort of accommodation, however, five opposition politicians were taken into custody and prevented from participating in local elections. Around the island, thousands of people went into the streets, where speakers made recurrent references to "People Power" and the ouster of Marcos from the Philippines.[64] On May 19, 1986, more than 1,500 riot police failed to prevent a twelve-hour rally by the opposition.

Clearly, "People Power" was a significant force. Movement activist Wu Jieh-min told me, "We were inspired by People Power in the Philippines."[65] As another observer remarked, "In 1986 a ripple effect might have been felt in Taiwan as the rise of democracy toppled the neighboring autocratic regimes."[66] Such connections of movements inspiring each other across borders continually prove to be one of the most productive outcomes of activists' associations. Besides helping to stimulate Taiwan's movement, Taiwanese pastor C.S. Song played an important role in propagating *minjung* theology in Korea.[67] Anecdotal evidence tells of Taiwanese singing Korean democracy movement songs in the streets.[68] Reciprocal and simultaneous protests propel movements to ever-greater intensity and embolden activists to take steps thought to be impossible only a few months earlier. Without waiting for the government to authorize new parties, opposition activists founded the Democratic Progressive Party (DPP) on September 28, 1986. About 130 *tangwai* assented to a proposal made at the very end of their meeting to formally organize the DPP—even though it was still illegal to do so.[69] By illegally forming a new party in a one-party state, the opposition had finally cracked the regime's political monopoly, and by throwing the regime on the defensive, a whole new dynamic set in.

On November 30, 1986, in an action reminiscent of Benigno Aquino and Kim Dae Jung's returns from exile, some ten thousand supporters of opposition leader Hsu Hsin-liang, who had lived in the United States since the Kaohsiung Incident, flooded the streets around Taipei's international airport in support of Hsu's right to return. At the climax of a nine-hour confrontation with police, twenty-six police vehicles were overturned and many people on both sides injured.[70] Denied a seat on the flight, Hsu tried again on December 2. Once again, confrontations at the airport failed to win him permission to enter the country. In elections four days later, the opposition won 33 percent of the vote.

In January 1987, led by *Awakening* and the Presbyterian Church's Rainbow Project, a broad coalition of NGOs marched through Snake Alley—a notorious Taipei district owned by the KMT where many teenage prostitutes were for sale. This first protest against teenage prostitution quickly became the focal point of an island-wide movement to help these young girls. Students were centrally involved in the upsurge. Garnering supporters in the form of signatures on a petition for campus reform, some two thousand people signed on, and smaller group students marched to the Legislative Yuan in March 1987. Their candidate was elected chair of the student government, and he was able to institute direct elections for his successor.[71] On May 19, 1987, several thousand people occupied Longshan Temple for two days. When police surrounded them, supporters gathered outside police lines and threw bread and dumplings to the activists who called for lifting martial law.[72] Although the KMT likes to claim credit for ending martial law, clearly the pressures exerted from below were vital.

Democratization Upsurge

On July 7, 1987, the Legislative Yuan voted to end thirty-eight years of martial law, and on July 15, 1987, the White Terror officially came to an end. In the symbiotic relationship of civil society and social insurgencies, the sense of victory of opposition groups in stimulating an end to the world's longest running dictatorship opened the floodgates to a tidal wave of grassroots movements unlike anything Taiwan had experienced. Within a few months after martial law had been lifted, hundreds of protests by labor, farmers, teachers, veterans, and political victims transpired. Government data reported that between the end of martial law on July 15, 1987, and March 31, 1988, a daily average of five protests took place—a total of more than 1,408.[73] While the number of labor disputes from 1981 to 1988 was 1,305, in the first half of 1989 alone, some 1,009 took place as a "surge" followed the restoration of democratic rights.[74] No one knew it at the time but civil society proved to be a valuable resource that helped to transform Taiwan. In the 1970s, the *Zeitgeist* of change manifested itself as cultural energies, in the 1980s as social movements, and in the 1990s as constitutional and political transformations—all of which led to the opposition capturing the presidency in 2000.[75] Fan Yun expressed the significance of civil society: "Without an assertive and robust civil society, democracy may not have emerged and taken root in Taiwan."[76]

The White Terror may have ended, but Taiwan was still not a democracy—even by minimal standards of popular elections for president and parliament. The island remained governed by a National Assembly that had not stood in elections since 1947, and direct elections for president were not permitted but were left to that geriatric legislature. The ruling KMT ruthlessly clung to power and controlled the island's abundant natural resources along with many prosperous businesses. When martial law was annulled in 1987, Chiang Ching-kuo instituted a new National Security Law. People immediately rose against the new law in a campaign calling for a "100 percent abrogation of martial law." A long coming political change was needed, but no one seemed to know who could lead it. Once again, an insurgency in the streets provided the impetus to accomplish it step by step.

From 1986 to mid-1992, Taiwan experienced a veritable political renaissance. The number of parties mushroomed from three to sixty-nine. While magazines increased from 3,354 to 4,356, the number of newspapers grew by almost 800 percent—from 31 to 246.[77] As in Korea, Nepal, the Philippines, and Bangladesh, workers mobilized as soon as the insurgency won space for mobilizations to take place without severe repression. In Taiwan, at least seventeen types of social movements emerged along with the country's democratization, including among physically challenged people, anti–nuclear power, teachers' rights, and aboriginal rights.[78] On October 26, 1987, at the second conference of the Alliance of Taiwan Aborigines (originally founded December 29, 1984), a Manifesto of Taiwan Aborigines declared that lands should be returned to indigenous groups and administered autonomously.

In 1981, only 10 environmental demonstrations were reported in Taiwan's newspapers, while in 1991 at least 278 were counted—more than in the past twelve years combined.[79] In just three of those years (1988–1990) businesses paid $500 million (NT$12 billion) as a result of environmental lawsuits.[80] The mixture of modern ecology movements—as, for example, the example of the German Greens (which was widely discussed in the early 1980s)—with local Taiwanese customs reached a very interesting point in August 1987. Residents of Houjin were commanded by an omen during a temple ritual to form a committee to oppose a nearby naphtha cracking plant in a state-owned China Petroleum complex. Carrying their god to a string of protests, they were unable to close the plant but did win significant concessions. In 1988, after China Petroleum Company's refinery in Linyuan released thousands of gallons of wastewater and severely polluted surrounding farmlands, people surrounded the plant and closed it. Ultimately the government paid NT$1.27 billion in compensation. In March 1988, fishers created the locally based Yenliao Anti-Nuclear Self-Defense Association. For thirteen years, the group fought the nearby nuclear plant. On September 6, 1988, fishers from Kaohsiung protested in Taipei because of damage to their clams caused by water pollution.

Taiwan's dynamic economy could no longer be contained within the archaic authoritarian structures of KMT dictatorship. With businessmen needing to make decisions based upon global dynamics, with students involved in new industries requiring diversified interests and groups skills based upon open expression of ideas, with workers required to participate in production based upon intelligent decision-making, the old state-mandated system was in dire need of reform—or else it risked the prospect of revolutionary transformation. As with the demise of the "developmental state" in Korea and end of "crony capitalism" in the Philippines, Taiwan's system was about to be absorbed by global capital, which required new, more flexible structures to be put into place.

As in other countries where liberalization occurred, the United States demanded Taiwan lift tariffs—in this case on fruits, chickens, and turkeys, pressure intended to relieve U.S. balance of trade problems. Under AFL-CIO pressure, labor standards were upgraded (and thereby made Taiwanese goods more expensive on the international market). As Taiwan rushed headlong into the neoliberal era, its stock exchange boomed. Market capitalization reached twice GDP, and the daily volume surpassed all world exchanges besides in Tokyo and New York. The country's economic development had reached a stage where labor-intensive sectors like textile and shoe manufacturing began to be closed down and sent abroad. The onset of neoliberalism helped motivate more protests by workers and farmers.

In November 1987, families were allowed to visit the mainland—after forty years of separation. As newspapers were able to print previously restricted stories, public calls for parliamentary elections increased in volume. After President Chiang Ching-kuo died on January 13, 1988, bans on political parties, assembly, and the free press were rapidly removed. In December 1987, the DPP blocked traffic on Jhongwha Road in Taipei to dramatize their calls for parliamentary elections. The following spring in Dahu village on March 29, 1988, the DPP organized new protests near the homes of longtime members of National Assembly. In

February 1988, a five-day bus strike in Taoyuan signaled new labor militancy. On May 1, 1988, the Independent Alliance of National Labor brought together ten autonomous trade unions on the same day as 1,400 railroad workers went on strike. After months of no response from the government to their grievances, railroad workers mounted a one-day walkout. The government immediately responded by improving working conditions and wages. In July, oil workers went out on strike, and in August so did railroad workers in Miao Li. When a textile factory in Xin Guang closed, a massive movement to save the jobs emerged in which people blamed neoliberalism as the cause of the shutdown.

Perhaps the most militant of all insurgent forces against neoliberalism were farmers. On December 8, 1987, at least 3,000 farmers rallied in front of the Legislative Yuan to protest the fall in fruit prices caused by imported fruit.[81] Known as the "1208 incident," that initial protest was quickly followed by many smaller ones, as on December 18 when peanut farmers protested unfair competition of imported peanuts and oil as well as a Christmas protest of over ten thousand people. Farmers subsequently mounted large protests on March 16, April 26, May 20, and October 25. On April 26, 1988, hundreds of farmers drove more than 130 tractors to Taipei police station, and street conflicts tied up the area around KMT headquarters. With Taiwan-U.S. trade talks underway and the United States pressing for financial deregulation and trade liberalization, protests intensified.

The farmers' action on May 20, 1988, was the biggest confrontation in decades and involved as many as five thousand people. Protesters called not only for economic policies that would help—not hurt—farmers (including an end to opening of the local market to imports from the United States, health insurance, better association elections, and a Ministry of Agriculture), they also demanded new parliamentary elections and constitutional reforms. Street fights lasted through the night and into the next morning as farmers refused to submit. About 200 were injured and 122 arrested—of whom 68 were later convicted.[82] Many government officials supported the farmers, as did the Veterans Action League and Taiwan Human Rights Association.[83] Students intervened in the streets on the side of farmers. On May 29, conservative reaction set in as seventy-five KMT legislators requested a state of emergency, signaling a possible reinstatement of martial law. Sensing the possibility of reinstatement of the White Terror, the Farmers Association cancelled its next rally and apologized on June 16. More than a hundred professors and academics demanded fair trials for the arrested and for the government to take responsibility for its part in the violence. When the government failed to do so, professors formed an Autonomous Investigation Commission to investigate the 520 incident.

For the opposition DPP, the Lee Teng-hui administration's repression "killed hopes for a break with the past," but the street violence apparently persuaded authorities to initiate dialogue.[84] On July 4, 1988, the government announced a new health insurance program for farmers. On August 5, 1988, when banana farmers protested the monopoly by Japanese trading companies, they received an apology from the Executive Yuan, an acknowledgement of their difficulties caused by neoliberalism.[85] The South Korean Farmers' Union invited the Taiwanese

Farmers' Union to visit, and the chairperson of the Korean group came to the island to support the farmers in rallies that included professors, priests, women's groups, students, and the DPP.

In July 1987, an antipornography demonstration was organized at a Lion's Club convention that brought ten thousand males from all over the world. Feminists mobilized again on August 18, 1987, against the less than equal treatment of female workers at Sun Yet-sen Hall. An all-female union among educational institutions formed. In October, a Mr. Taipei beauty pageant was sponsored to protest the Miss Universe contest. On January 9, 1988, once again women mobilized against teenage prostitution when delegates of fifty-five groups marched in Taipei to dramatize that the continuing nature of the problem. Taiwanese women were greatly influenced by their U.S. counterparts. One writer quoted Jo Freeman's criticism of members of the American women's movement who took advantage of "power- and fame-hungry individuals for personal advancement."[86] Women's groups were successfully able to introduce eight major pieces of legislation. Gay Taiwanese became increasingly public in their identities and adopted the word *tongzhi* (comrades) to name each other. The term's usage originated in Hong Kong in 1988 and migrated to Taiwan, where its usage was unencumbered by previous associations with standard communist usage.[87] In 1993, a gay chat group was set up at TNU, and similar groups came into existence at several universities.

People took liberties months ahead of government authorization to do so. Just as the DPP was founded before the ban on political parties was lifted, so advocates of Taiwan independence, long a topic that brought arrest and punishment, began to raise the issue in 1989. Their sacrifices resulted in hard-won victories that opened Taiwan's discourse. Activist Deng Nan-jung, although of Chinese descent, led the movement's call for Taiwan independence. Using public rallies and a series of magazines he published (changing names as often as the military censors closed them down), Deng pursued what he called "one hundred percent freedom of expression." In 1988, when he published a draft of a constitution for a Republic of Taiwan by Hsu Shih-kai, the government filed sedition charges against Deng. Refusing to be arrested, he barricaded himself inside his magazine's office with three barrels of gasoline and held out for seventy-one days. Finally, on April 7, 1989, he set himself on fire rather than be arrested. As Deng's sacrifice refused to die, activist Chun Yi-hwa followed in his footsteps on May 19, 1988, and burned himself to death during a demonstration.

Although formal legalization of discussing Taiwan independence would not occur until 1992, Deng's sacrifice had won the substantive right to do so, and having won that right, the next step for the movement was democratic elections in which a proindependence party could compete. By the end of 1988, reform of the National Assembly became the movement's main goal. In this context, a newly formed Democratic Student Alliance from nearly all major universities arose to deal a final blow to the National Assembly's hold on power. On September 28, 1989, students organized a march of two thousand people to the Department of Education. Campus activists ultimately focused on political reform in the society— not simply on campus.

The Wild Lily Student Movement

A month before the naming of a new president scheduled for March 21, 1990, the country watched in amazement and disgust as conservatives inside the KMT attempted to give themselves veto powers (and voted themselves a huge pay raise to compensate for their "extra duties.") At that time, direct presidential elections were not allowed, and the National Assembly was full of "old thieves"—KMT representatives chosen in 1947 from districts of mainland China with practically no Taiwanese. (The KMT's official position was that it still ruled all provinces of China.) The overwhelming favorite to become the new president was Vice President (and Taiwanese) Lee Teng-hui. Much of the country objected to the continuing "service" of the old thieves, but students were the best positioned to lead the counteroffensive against them.[88]

In response to the continuing undemocratic character of the constitutional process, students mobilized in what became known as the Wild Lily Student Movement (also called the March Student Movement). Inspired by their counterparts in Tiananmen Square a year earlier (events covered profusely in Taiwanese media) students intervened to accelerate constitutional reform. On March 14, about a hundred students broke through police lines at KMT central offices. With remarkable patience and control, they avoided clashing with police as they created an energy center where some two hundred other students and numerous civil groups stopped by to show support and build strength for future actions. Two days later, students began a sit-in in the huge plaza outside Chiang Kai-shek Memorial Hall—the heart of the KMT. Their large character banners focused demands on dissolution of the National Assembly, new elections, and constitutional change. When police did not violently intervene, students spent the night. Sometime after midnight, they created an Intercampus Council composed of representatives from each of the thirty-five schools present. As television reported the occupation of the square, many organizations and thousands more students from around the country arrived to join the sit-in on March 17. Students' open mike led to discussions and disagreements, and they also sang "We Shall Overcome."[89] About a thousand citizens arrived to help protect the students' new space for political action and to raise funds for them. When the DPP held a rally not far away, students received a great deal of additional support and funds. On March 19—as in Tiananmen Square—a small group began a hunger strike. On March 20—the night before Lee Teng-hui was formally selected by the National Assembly as the next president—the number of students peaked at about five thousand.[90] Serenaded by pop stars and entertained by puppet theater, the Lily Student Movement mimicked the occupation of public space and hunger strike of their mainland comrades. They called for an island-wide school boycott on March 21, which they declared was "Democracy Shame Day" since the decrepit National Assembly still held the power to vote.

At the end of six days, some eighty-four civic groups had joined, but the core of the movement was students. Their internal organization was disciplined and orderly. To obstruct provocative behavior that might jeopardize their image in the media, they kept the main area they occupied confined to identifiable

Thousands of students occupied Chiang Kai-shek Memorial Hall plaza.
Photo by Tsai Wen Shiang in *The Age of Defiance 1988–1992* (Taipei: GA Design Corp., 2008), 169.

students. Within the ranks of students, they rotated leaders and maintained a security cordon around their representatives' meeting space. A Policy Group included a variety of key people who, in turn, selected a "Command Center" with three members who rotated their power every eight hours. Six departments were created to carry out tasks (finance, information, security, mobilization, general affairs, and conference). A "Square Bulletin" was published to keep everyone informed and to publicize the movement's structure of authority and rules of behavior. Their self-organization and collective discipline contrasts sharply with the individualism and power games of their mainland counterparts. Strictly safe-guarding their autonomy, Taiwanese students cooperated with professors and graduate students, even creating consulting groups for them to facilitate their participation. They remained in contact with police officials to prevent any mis-understandings from arising.[91]

Despite tremendous divisions in their ranks—which included many elected student government presidents who were openly pro-KMT—the group maintained a dignified process and was able to make collective decisions throughout the occupation. When a small group undertook the hunger strike on their own initiative, the larger group supported them despite the fact that the self-selected hunger strikers became the media focus and an autonomous equal partner of the Intercampus Council. No one individual clung to a position of power as in Tiananmen. When many people at the General Assembly complained that the Policy Group was making decisions in an undemocratic fashion, new members were rotated into it.

Within the Policy Group, some members advocated rushing the president's office, but the majority voted them down and instead renewed attempts to negotiate, through which they were able to secure agreement for a meeting with Lee. When the Inter-Campus Council reconvened, people expressed dissatisfaction with the Policy Group's decision to meet the president. The occupation's democratic process was noteworthy at this critical moment. Everyone agreed immediately to poll every campus and have a representative report back to the General Assembly. As the process unfolded, the Policy Group first apologized for its unilateral decision and offered their resignations as a group. When the campuses made their feelings known, twenty-two supported the meeting, seven were opposed, and six abstained. The assembly then decided each of the thirty-five schools should send a representative to meet president Lee and that previously selected Policy Group members and representatives of hunger strikers and professors should also be part of their delegation.

The day after his election, the first thing Lee Teng-hui did was to meet with the delegation. Once the large group convened in his office, Lee praised the students for their concerns for democracy. Mentioning the widespread prevalence of "materialism," Lee congratulated students on their ideals. He reminded them that he had no constitutional authority to abolish the National Assembly, but he promised to seek a conference on constitutional change within a month and to work for a more democratic system of representation and elections. Ten months earlier, Chinese Premier Li Peng had met with students but with disastrous result. Apparently Taiwan's students and political leaders had learned from China's failure, and there was no Wuer Kaixi in the room to disrupt the proceedings.

When student representatives returned to the square, they showed a videotape of their meeting to the sit-in's General Assembly, after which students caucused in campus groups. In the middle of the night, the Intercampus Council voted to leave the square, and by dawn a majority of students had packed and left. The hunger strikers voted to end their protest that same day. Before the Policy Group left, they announced the formation of a national student organization that would make sure the president remained true to his promise to work for change. Students cleaned the square. By 5:00 p.m. on March 22, the last of the protesters was gone.

Toward a Democratic Transition

President Lee's capacity to act as a go-between among so many different constituencies proved to be a difficult balancing act. On April 22, 1990, as promised, the constitution was revised and elections planned, but on May 1, angry demonstrations were called after Lee appointed active-duty General Hau Po-tsun to be his new premier. People felt that the military should not be involved in politics, and their sentiment resounded so widely that Hau himself agreed to resign permanently from the military. To placate protesters, President Lee Teng-hui granted amnesty to all *tangwai* activists on May 20, 1990, including the Kaohsiung defendants. In 1991, more than fifty thousand people assembled to rescue a small group being detained by Taiwan's CIA for studying Taiwanese history. The DPP's New Tide faction organized a rally for reforms that drew hundreds of thousands into the streets in April and May of 1991.

In December 1991 and early 1992, the National Assembly was elected for the first time since 1947. Although the KMT won an overwhelming majority of 71 percent of the vote against the DPP's 24 percent, it was an important beginning. In 1994, the first direct elections of governors took place, and in March 1996, the first time citizens voted for their president, Lee Teng-hui was elected. Taiwanese members of the KMT had risen from a paltry 6.1 percent in the early 1970s, to 19.3 percent in the early 1980s, 34.4 percent in the early 1990s, and 53.3 percent in the late 1990s.[92] Under Lee Teng-hui, political reform of the antiquated and authoritarian system proceeded step-by-step. In 1995, President Lee formally apologized to islanders for the 228 incident. In time, compensation was paid to victims and their families. Today dozens of memorials dot the island. Since 2001, February 28 is a national holiday, and after the government compensated victims of government terror, Taiwan became the only other place in Asia besides South Korea to do so. In 2000, Chen Shui-bian, the first non-KMT president, was elected.

Observers consider Taiwan's process of transformation one in which the elite changed itself to affect broad reforms.[93] By way of contrast, the Korean June Uprising compelled a democratic transition that combined actions of elite and opposition—a transplacement in which the old elite and opposition united to create a new system of governance. Such a contrast ignores Taiwanese grassroots pressure, the formation of the DPP as an illegal party, and its 2000 electoral victory. One residual effect of the grassroots insurgency was transformation of people's identity, a strengthening of the counternarrative through which people increasingly defined themselves as Taiwanese. In the 1990s, only about 20 percent of people selected Taiwanese when asked, "Are you a Taiwanese or Chinese?" That number rose to 36 percent in 2000 and to 60 percent in 2006.[94]

The role of the middle class was especially significant in Taiwan's democratization. According to Tien Hung-mao, "entrepreneurs, along with professionals, managers, and intellectuals, form a large new business class that has been at the forefront of democratic and social movement."[95] Hagen Koo noted that unlike in Korea, Taiwan's "intellectuals and new middle class avoided direct confrontation with authoritarian state power and instead chose the method of indirect pressure on state rulers to obtain a top-down process of transition."[96] In Hong Kong, pressure from professionals also resulted in greater freedoms after the 1997 transition. The continuing transformation of Taiwan meant increasing participation, evidenced by data showing at least fifteen thousand NGOs in 2001,

TABLE 6.3 **Growth of Civil Society Groups in Taiwan, 1980–2001**

Type of Group	Number in 1980	%	Number in 2001	%
Education and culture	541	13.7	2,801	15.2
Medicine and public health	48	1.2	526	2.8
Religious	64	1.6	725	3.9
Sports	50	1.3	2,098	11.4
Social welfare and charity	2,471	62.4	5,794	31.4
International	51	1.3	2,055	11.1
Business	–	–	1,943	10.5
Other	735	18.6	2,523	13.7
TOTAL	3,960	100	18,465	100

Source: Ministry of Internal Affairs, as cited by Yun Fan in *Civil Society and Political Change in Asia*, ed. Alagappa, 177.

a 400 percent increase since the lifting of martial law and more than a 50 percent increase in the decade from 1991.

The largest NGO in Taiwan was a largely female Buddhist charity, whose welfare allocations were greater than Taipei city's.[97] After surveying the data on NGOs, Michael Hsiao found that 31 percent of their "core leaders" were also government officials.[98] He subsequently developed data for "real" NGOs. Although much smaller in numbers, they experienced a similar mushrooming since the 1980s.

In 1991, nearly three thousand foundations existed, more than three-fourths of which were founded since the 1980s.[99] By 2004, twenty thousand membership associations were counted.[100] All together, more than 75 percent of all independent associations in 2000 began after 1980, showing once again that insurgent movements help foster social pluralization and horizontal political powers. Activists' mobilizing power also multiplied. On February 28, 2004, to protest China's aiming missiles at Taiwan, two million people joined hands from one side of the island to the other, a human chain that comprised the largest demonstration in Taiwan's history.

Round after round of constitutional reform resulted first in nonbinding referenda, which helped Houching residents opposed to a naphtha cracker plant in Kaohsiung. On May 6, 1990, two-thirds of those voting were against it, and the government promised to minimize pollution before starting the operations. Where the will of the people is so important, local governments jumped on the

TABLE 6.4 **Taiwan NGOs**

Year Founded	Associations	Foundations	TOTAL
Before 1949	13	0	13
1950–1959	7	1	8
1960–1969	14	2	16
1970–1979	18	6	24
1980–1989	39	23	62
1990–1999	103	24	127

Source: Hsiao, "NGOs," 47.

referendum bandwagon as a method to prove thirteen different projects' unpopularity to the central government.[101] So legitimate did referenda become that they have since been made binding.

Despite great progress, unresolved issues plague Taiwan's democracy. Within the opposition movement, sexual emancipation became a theme that drew extensive debate both within the movement, especially its feminist wing, and the society at large. The result was the marginalization of sex emancipation feminists, and their eventual exclusion from mainstream organizations. In May 1998, the Collective of Sex Workers and Supporters organized an international conference with sex-worker representatives from thirteen countries declaring, "Sex rights are human rights!" In the conference's aftermath, Awakening Foundation fired several activists who had supported prostitutes' organizing efforts.[102] As the split in the movement widened, two tendencies emerged: "civil society" vs. "people's democracy" with different views on the merit of freedom for minority lifestyles. As mainstream feminists were integrated into DPP government echelons, their aspirations for equality were increasingly channeled into the state, while more radical feminists criticized the mainstream turning into "a movement of neurotic hysterical mothers wielding the long arm of the law to eradicate anything vaguely sexual and thus maybe harmful to her child."[103] In the admixture of polarized opinions, erstwhile early feminist leader and former vice president Annette Lu claimed AIDS was punishment from God. Scholar-activist Josephine Ho was sued by thirteen conservative NGOs that brought charges against her for "propagating obscenities that corrupt traditional values and may produce bad influence on children and juveniles." Fortunately, Ho was found not guilty in 2004. In her view, "Asia's new democracies may be gradually liberalizing their political arena, yet with regard to other realms of social space, there has been an intensifying degree of surveillance and regulation, especially in regard to sexual matters."[104] Taiwan's 2008 gay pride parade attracted twenty thousand participants, Asia's largest gay event.

Elected as a minority president in 2000, Chen Shui-bian inaugurated Taiwanization even though the DPP had less than a third of the seats in Legislative Yuan. In his first term, state expenditures were nearly one quarter of GDP, while revenues never exceeded 13 percent—leaving a cumulative debt of 46 percent of GDP.[105] Nonetheless Chen nearly received an absolute majority in 2004, falling short by a slim margin of 48.8 percent. Chen welcomed international gay and lesbians NGOs and Taiwanese *tongzhi* activists in September 2000. His DPP administration's official policy affirmed multiculturalism as Taiwan's official policy, and he mandated gender training for all government workers. On his watch, nearly all unions were reclaimed by their members. Activists focused on revising the archaic and repressive Labor Law (promulgated in 1929) and countering the mainstream China Federation of Labor. A newly formed Taiwan Confederation of Trade Unions (TCTU) was inaugurated on May 1, 2000, with president-elect Chen Shui-bian in attendance—a sign of the DPP encroachment on the "autonomous" labor movement. The TCTU quickly became yet another mainstream union, and labor law revision has proven an elusive goal. As in South Korea with the election of

Noh Moo-hyun, mass protest actions largely ceased after the DPP came to power in early 2000.[106]

Progressive administrations in both Korea and Taiwan backtracked on central promises they made to the electorate. Noh Moo-hyun was unable to revise the National Security Law as he promised, and he became the foremost advocate of a highly unpopular Free Trade Agreement with the United States that half the electorate opposed. Chen and the DPP soon backtracked on their promise to close nuclear power plant number 4, which even President Lee Teng-hui had refused to endorse. Lee claimed to follow the ancient teaching from the eleventh century BCE, "Whatever the people desire, heaven must follow."[107] Yet his premier Hau claimed he would reestablish governmental authority by supporting the fourth nuclear power plant. On October 13, 1991, after Yenliao activists barricaded the construction site, a clash with police left one person dead and many injured. Courtroom proceedings found seventeen people guilty, and one was given a life sentence. As protests continued, Hau ultimately resigned early in 1993, and the plant did not open.

As happens in many situations, insurgent social movements embrace reform candidates, but once the candidates are integrated into the established system of government, they wean themselves from the very movements that brought them into prominence from obscurity. They gradually adopt precisely those positions of the erstwhile ruling party that they had opposed. "Reform" candidates thus use social movements to elevate their own personal agendas and careers. On October 18, 1996, a secret agreement was reached between the DPP and KMT, whereby DPP traded support for the nuclear plant for political concessions. Under pressure from Westinghouse Corporation, which was building nuclear plant 4, the American Institute in Taiwan also called secret meetings to advocate restarting plant construction.[108] In February 2001, the DPP decided to continue building it despite the controversy surrounding it.[109] In February 2002, more than twenty thousand antinuclear protesters rallied to criticize the DPP for its change in policy on nuclear power. From many people's perspectives, the DPP had used the ecological protests around nuclear power to gain power.[110]

The DPP's betrayal helped disappoint many people in the possibilities of "democracy." Doh Shin reported that support for democracy declined after 1993 (similar to findings in South Korea).[111] From 1998 to 2003, the percentage of people believing "democracy is always preferable to any other kind of government" declined from 55.5 percent to 42.2 percent in Taiwan. In Korea less than half—about 49 percent—expressed the same preference.[112] Although "democratic," both Korea and Taiwan have versions of laws requiring public employees to remain "neutral" and "nonpartisan" in public affairs, unfairly restricting their rights to freedom of expression.

Of course, the main disappointment of progressive administrations had been their corruption. Both Chen in Taiwan and Noh in Korea were publicly claimed to have accepted illegal monies. Similarities abound in the cases: relatively small amounts of money were involved when compared to the billions Marcos and Suharto absconded with or the hundreds of millions that Chun Doo-hwan is known to have pocketed; Chen and Noh's wives were involved centrally; and both Chen and Noh were convicted in the media long before any court action was taken. While Chen was imprisoned, Noh chose suicide to protest his unjust persecution orchestrated by the Lee Myung-bak administration. As symbols of the opposition, both former presidents' corruption was used to discredit the opposition movement as a whole. Chen and Noh both became the focal points for a reaction from the conservative establishments to the onset of political directions they did not control—toward independence in Taiwan's case and unification in Korea's. Surprisingly, Chen's former supporters, especially Shih Ming-teh, led the 2006 grassroots campaign against Chen's alleged corruption. Beginning on September 9, 2006, Shih led a series of self-described "People Power" rallies and sit-ins that peaked on September 15, when a crowd of more than three hundred thousand gathered.[113]

In an ominous sign of conservative rollback, the KMT won the 2008 elections with 71 percent of the seats (up from 35 percent in 2004), while the DPP's share declined from almost 40 percent to 24 percent. Soon thereafter newly elected President Ma Ying-Jeou's pro-unification policies began to undo the DPP's progressive steps toward autonomy. The unfair character of KMT persecution of Chen is clear to many observers. Although KMT leaders were found guilty of corruption—including President Ma Ying-jeou—none ever spent a day behind bars. From past confiscations of Taiwanese property, the KMT has a net worth in excess of U.S.$757 million. All other parties combined have a net worth of less than 1 percent of the KMT's.[114]

Taiwan and Korea have become significant self-financed consumers of the most important U.S. manufacturing industry—armaments. This third economic phase in bilateral relations (after U.S.-aided import substitution and export-led development) is a continuing and vital relationship. As a market for $18 to $24 billion of U.S. goods annually, Taiwan has huge foreign exchange reserves and claims the world's eighth largest economic relationship with the United States.[115] Pay-as-you-go deals with Taiwan made the island second only to Saudi Arabia as a buyer of U.S. weapons systems from 1993 to 2003. A $20 billion deal was arranged by George Bush in 2001—much of it high-technology weapons—after Taiwanese fears were stoked by carefully placed U.S. hints and callously made Chinese threats. Another similar U.S. warning was issued in Washington, D.C., in 2009 during a conference marking the release of a new Rand Corporation study on Taiwanese-China relations. Widely noticed in Taipei was one panelist's assertion that a DPP victory in the next presidential election might cause a Chinese military attack.[116]

If militarism continues to divert the island's resources, the tragic result would only further delegitimize "democracy" in a place where civil society and consensus have been so important to the transformation of one of the world's most repressive states. Taiwanese students' remarkable self-discipline and government civility during the 1990 takeover stand in sharp contrast to Tiananmen Square, where both protesters and authorities behaved with far less restraint and composure. Grassroots protests suffered enduring tragedies in Burma, Tibet, and

China, but Taiwan's successful transition provides an optimistic indication of a possible future of greater freedom. In 1990, their example helped pave the way for victorious uprisings in Nepal and Bangladesh.

NOTES

1   See *Asia's Unknown Uprisings Volume 1*, chap. 4 for discussion of events on Jeju.
2   George H. Kerr, *Formosa Betrayed* (Upland, CA: Taiwan Publishing Co., 2005; originally published in 1966), 76.
3   Lai Tse-han, Ramon Myers, and Wei Wou, *A Tragic Beginning: The Taiwan Uprising of February 28, 1947* (Stanford: Stanford University Press, 1991), 99.
4   Hung Chien-Chao, *A History of Taiwan* (Rimini: Il Cerchio Iniziative editoriali, 2000), 250.
5   Hung maintains at least four people were killed as does Kerr, *Formosa Betrayed*, 256. Others tell of dozens dead.
6   Ibid., 257.
7   Lai et al., *Tragic Beginning*, 107.
8   Hung, *History of Taiwan*, 251.
9   Kerr, *Formosa Betrayed*, 260.
10   Richard C. Kagan, *Chen Shui-bian: Building a Community and a Nation* (Taipei: Asia-Pacific Academic Exchange Foundation, 2000), 26.
11   Lai et al., *Tragic Beginning*, 125.
12   Kerr, *Formosa Betrayed*, 266.
13   Ibid., 273.
14   Ibid., 264, 274–75.
15   Lai et al., *Tragic Beginning*, 123.
16   *The Road to Freedom: Taiwan's Postwar Human Rights Movement* (Taipei: Taiwan Foundation for Democracy, 2002), 43
17   Lai et al., *Tragic Beginning*, 138.
18   Kerr, *Formosa Betrayed*, 233.
19   Ibid., 277.
20   Peng Ming-min, *A Taste of Freedom: Memoirs of a Formosan Independence Leader* (New York: Holt, Rinehart and Winston, 1972), 69–70.
21   Kerr, *Formosa Betrayed*, 301.
22   Hung, *History of Taiwan*, 253.
23   As quoted in Lai et al., *Tragic Beginning*, 157.
24   *The Road to Freedom*, 16–18. Decades later, a communist source on the mainland put the number at more than fifty thousand dead (Lai et al., *Tragic Beginning*, 158). In 1992, the *New York Times* reported twenty-five to thirty thousand out of a population of six million had lost their lives. Richard Kagan put the number of deaths at sixteen thousand to forty thousand, while Kerr insisted twenty thousand is a realistic estimate (Kagan, *Chen Shui-bian*, 26; Kerr, *Formosa Betrayed*, 310).
25   Chen Tsui-Lien, "Responsibility on the Part of Taiwanese Military and Political Authorities," in *Research Report on Responsibility for the 228 Massacre: A Brief Introduction* (Taipei: Memorial Foundation of 228, 2007), 30.
26   Kerr, *Formosa Betrayed*, 357.
27   Chen Chun-Hung, "Human Rights in the Process of Transition and Consolidation of Democracy in Taiwan," in *Colonialism, Authoritarianism, Democracy and Human Rights in South East Asia* (Conference book for the Second International Conference on the 1980 Gwangju Uprising) May 15–17, 2001.
28   Te-Lan Chu, "The White Terror in Taiwan: The Tsui Hsiao-ping Case," and Lai Jeh-hang,

"The State and the People: The History of Authoritarian Rule and Democratization in Taiwan, 1895–2000." Both articles are in *The Role of Jeju Island for World Peace in the 21st Century*, Conference Proceedings of the 2nd Conference on the Jeju April 3rd Uprising (Cheju National University, 2002), 62–63; 99.

29   June Teufel Dreyer, "Taiwan's Evolving Identity," http://www.formosafoundation.org/pdf/Taiwan's%20Identity%20(J_Dreyer).pdf.

30   Jaushieh Joseph Wu, *Taiwan's Democratization: Forces Behind the New Momentum* (Hong Kong: Oxford University Press, 1995), 46.

31   Quoted in Stephen Haggard and Chien-Kuo Pang, "The Transition to Export-Led Growth in Taiwan," in *The Role of the State in Taiwan's Development*, eds. Joel Aberbach, David Dollar, and Kenneth Sokoloff (Armonk: M.E. Sharpe, 1994), 60.

32   Hung, *History of Taiwan*, 271.

33   Thomas Gold, *State and Society in the Taiwan Miracle* (Armonk: M.E. Sharpe, 1986), 86–87.

34   Susan Greenhalgh, "Supranational Processes of Income Distribution," in *Contending Approaches to the Political Economy of Taiwan*, eds. Edwin Winckler and Susan Greenhalgh (Armonk: M.E. Sharpe, 1988), 80–81.

35   Robert P. Weller, *Alternate Civilities: Democracy and Culture in China and Taiwan* (Boulder: Westview, 1999), 68.

36   Walden Bello, *Dragons in Distress* (San Francisco: Food First Books, 1992), 219.

37   Fang-Yi Wang, "Reconsidering Export-Led Growth," in *Role of the State*, 28.

38   See Yun-han Chu, "The Automobile Industry in South Korea and Taiwan," in *Role of the State*, 125–26.

39   Haggard and Pang, "Transition to Export-Led Growth," 280.

40   Chen Guuying, "The Reform Movement Among Intellectuals in Taiwan since 1970," *Bulletin of Concerned Asian Scholars*, 14, no. 3 (July–September 1982): 34.

41   "The Feminist Movement in Taiwan: 1972–1987," *Bulletin of Concerned Asian Scholars* 21, no. 1 (January–March, 1989): 14–15.

42   U.S. feminism's influence was also noted in an interview with Sue Huang, Taipei, February 3, 2009.

43   Hsiu-Lien Annette Lu, "Women's Liberation: The Taiwanese Experience," in *The Other Taiwan: 1945 to the Present*, ed. Murray Rubinstein (Armonk: M.E. Sharpe, 1994), 294.

44   Chen, "Reform Movement," 32.

45   Ibid., 45.

46   John Kaplan, *The Court-Martial of the Kaoshing Defendants* (Berkeley: Institute of East Asian Studies, 1981), 14.

47   E-mail from Michael Lin, August 5, 2009.

48   Kagan, *Chen Shui-bian*, 64; Wu, *Taiwan's Democratization*, 63.

49   Michael Lin, interview in Taipei, August 10, 2009.

50   Linda Arrigo, "From Democratic Movement to Bourgeois Democracy," in *The Other Taiwan: 1945 to the Present*, ed. Murray Rubinstein (Armonk: M.E. Sharpe, 1994), 154.

51   See Mark O'Neill, "King Duck Goes to his Taiwanese Reward," *Asian Sentinel*, October 24, 2007.

52   Interview with Michael Hsiao, Taipei, February 3, 2009; James C.Y. Soong, "Explaining Taiwan's Transition," in *Institutional Reform*, 209.

53   Haggard and Pang, "Transition to Export-Led Growth," 320; From 1980 to 1991, the ratio of income of the top 20 percent to the lowest 20 percent of households in Taiwan was never more than 5.18 compared to 26.08 in Brazil, 8.90 in the United States and 9.59 in Australia. See Wu, *Taiwan's Democratization*, 52.

54   Denny Roy, *Taiwan: A Political History* (Ithaca, NY: Cornell University Press, 2003), 164.

55 Shih-Chung Hsieh, "Taiwan Aborigines in Transition," in *The Other Taiwan: 1945 to the Present*, ed. Murray Rubinstein (Armonk: M.E. Sharpe, 1994), 412.

56 Chen Hsin-Hsing, "State vs. Civil Society: Dynamics and Pitfalls of Social Movements in Taiwan since the 1980s," in Cho Hee Yeon, Lawrence Surendra and Eunhong Park, eds., *States of Democracy: Oligarchic Democracies and Asian Democratization* (Mumbai: Earthworm Books, 2008), 72.

57 Hsin-Huang Michael Hsiao, "The Labor Movement in Taiwan: A Retrospective and Prospective Look," in *Taiwan: Beyond the Economic Miracle*, eds., Dennis Simon and Michael Kau (Armonk: M.E. Sharpe, 1992), 159.

58 Ibid., 159.

59 Ming-sho Ho, "The Politics of Anti-Nuclear Protest in Taiwan: A Case of Party-Dependent Movement, 1980–2000," *Modern Asian Studies* 37, no. 3 (2003).

60 Wu, *Taiwan's Democratization*, 41, 67.

61 Ming-sho, "Anti-Nuclear Protest," 689.

62 Yun-han Chu, "Social Protests and Political Democratization in Taiwan," in *The Other Taiwan: 1945 to the Present*, ed. Murray Rubinstein (Armonk: M.E. Sharpe, 1994), 103.

63 Hung-mao Tien, "Taiwan's Transformation," 125. A more conservative counter nonetheless revealed the same trend when he reported that the number of reported incidents of social protests increased from 143 in 1983 to 676 in 1987. Chu, "Social Protests," 99.

64 Roy, *Taiwan*, 171.

65 Interview with Wu Jieh-min, Taipei, August 15, 2009.

66 Chin-Chuan Lee, *Sparking a Fire: The Press and the Ferment of Democratic Change in Taiwan* (Austin: Association for Education in Journalism and Mass Communication, 1993), 27.

67 Interview with Oh Choong-il, November 27, 2001, Seoul.

68 In an e-mail on July 31, 2009, Yun Fan confirmed that in the late 1980s, Taiwanese student activists read a translated history of the Korean student movement; interview with Jeon Seung-hee, Cambridge, Massachusetts, 2007.

69 Hung-mao Tien, "Taiwan's Transformation," in *Consolidating the Third Wave Democracies: Regional Challenges*, eds. Larry Diamond, Marc Plattner, Yun-han Chu, and Hung-mao Tien (Baltimore: Johns Hopkins, 1997), 123.

70 Alan M. Wachman, *Taiwan: National Identity and Democratization* (Armonk: M.E. Sharpe, 1994), 145.

71 Wright, "Disincentives," 99.

72 Interview with Frank Chen, Taipei, August 10, 2009.

73 *Central Daily News*, April 20, 1988, 2, as quoted in Wu, *Taiwan's Democratization*, 60.

74 Hsiao, "The Labor Movement in Taiwan," 157.

75 I am indebted to Michael Hsiao for this insight.

76 Yun Fan, "Taiwan: No Civil Society, No Democracy," in *Civil Society and Political Change in Asia: Expanding and Contracting Democratic Space*, ed. Muthiah Alagappa, (Stanford: Stanford University Press, 2004), 185.

77 John Minns, *The Politics of Developmentalism: The Midas States of Mexico, South Korea and Taiwan* (New York: Palgrave, 2006), 219.

78 Hsin-Huang Michael Hsiao, "Emerging Social Movements and the Rise of a Demanding Civil Society in Taiwan," *The Australian Journal of Chinese Affairs* 24 (July 1990).

79 Weller, *Alternate Civilities*, 7, 122.

80 Ibid., 110.

81 Hsin-Huang Michael Hsiao, "Political Liberalization and Taiwan's Farmers' Movement," in *The Politics of Democratization: Generalizing East Asian Experiences*, ed. Edward Friedman (Boulder: Westview Press, 1994), 205.

82 Roy, *Taiwan*, 178.
83 Hsiao, "Political Liberalization," 213–15.
84 Ibid., 207.
85 Ibid., 215.
86 "The Feminist Movement in Taiwan: 1972–1987," in *Bulletin of Concerned Asian Scholars* (January–March, 1989), 12.
87 Jens Damm, "Tongzhi in Contemporary Taiwan: Successful Only on the Surface? From a Promising Start to the Abuse of a Multiculturalism Policy?" unpublished manuscript.
88 June Teufel Dreyer, "Taiwan's December 1991 Election," *World Affairs* 155 (1992).
89 Interview with Yi-Cheng Jou, Taipei, August 6, 2009.
90 Yun Fan estimated the number in the tens of thousands in Alagappa, *Civil Society*, 164–90.
91 See Wright, *Perils of Protest*, 106–25 for more details on the Lily Student Movement of 1990.
92 Hung-mao Tien, *Taiwan's Electoral Politics and Democratic Transition* (Armonk: M.E. Sharpe, 1996) as quoted by Yun-han Chu, "Taiwan's Unique Challenges" in *Democracy in East Asia*, eds., Larry Diamond and Marc Plattner, (Baltimore: Johns Hopkins University Press, 1998), 138.
93 Wright, *Perils of Protest*, 114.
94 Tu Cheng-sheng, *Educational Reform in Taiwan: Retrospect and Prospect* (Taipei: Taiwan Ministry of Education, 2007), 17.
95 Tien, "Taiwan's Transformation," 17.
96 Hagen Koo, "Globalization and the Asian Middle Classes," in *The Changing Faces of the Middle Classes in Asia-Pacific*, ed. Hsin-Huang Michael Hsiao (Taipei: Center for Asia-Pacific Area Studies, 2006), 16.
97 Weller, *Alternate Civilities*, 17.
98 Hsiao, "Civil Society," 217.
99 Hsin-Huang Michael Hsiao, "NGOs, the State, and Democracy under Globalization: The Case of Taiwan," in *Civil Life, Globalization, and Political Change in Asia*, ed. Robert P. Weller (London: Routledge, 2007), 45.
100 Hsin-Huang Michael Hsiao, "Civil Society and Democratization in Taiwan, 1980–2005," in *Asian New Democracies: The Philippines, South Korea and Taiwan Compared* (Taipei: Center for Asia-Pacific Area Studies, 2006), 212.
101 Yung-Ming Hsu, Chia-Hung Tsai, and Hsiu-Tin Huang, "Referendum: A New Way of Identifying National Identity," in *Asian New Democracies: The Philippines, South Korea and Taiwan Compared* (Taipei: Center for Asia-Pacific Area Studies, 2006), 274.
102 Josephine Ho, "Sex Revolution and Sex Rights Movement in Taiwan," *Berliner China-Hefte/Chinese History and Society* 32 (2007): 130.
103 Ibid., 135.
104 Ibid., 123.
105 Chu, "Taiwan's Unique Challenges," 51.
106 Chung Hsiu Mei, et al., "Towards Flexibility and Dynamism: Taiwan's Social Movements," in *The Disenfranchised: Victims of Development in Asia*, ed. Urvashi Butalia (Hong Kong: Arena Press, 2004), 209.
107 Lee Teng-hui, "Chinese Culture and Political Renewal," in *Consolidating the Third Wave Democracies: Regional Challenges*, eds. Larry Diamond, Marc Plattner, Yun-han Chu, and Hung-mao Tien (Baltimore: Johns Hopkins, 1997), 196.
108 Interview with Congresswomen Tien Chiu-Chin, Taipei, February 4, 2009.
109 Ho, "Politics," 684–85.
110 Resource mobilization theory feeds this co-optive use of reforms to bring social movements into becoming a form of system maintenance. As Ming-sho Ho put it from his

analysis of the DPP's abandonment of the antinuclear movement, "External elite sponsorship lessened the dire deprivation of indigenous resources and lowered the threshold of initial mobilization," ("Politics," 688).

111 Doh C. Shin, *Mass Politics and Culture in Democratizing Korea* (Cambridge: Cambridge University Press, 1999), 260.

112 Chu Yun-han, "Taiwan's Struggling Democracy," in Cho et al., *States of Democracy*, 49.

113 Keith Bradsher, "Protesters Fuel a Long-Shot Bid to Oust Taiwan's Leader," *New York Times*, September 28, 2006, A3.

114 Jerome Keating, *Taiwan: The Search for Identity* (Taipei: SMC Publishing, 2008), 15; also see Jerome Keating, "Chen's Gone, the System Lives on," http://en.taiwantt.org.tw/index.php/editorials-of-interest/15-taipei-times/256-chens-gone-the-system-lives-on.

115 John Tkacik, "Reflected Reflections: Elections in the U.S., Taiwan, and Japan, and How They Influence U.S. Policy-Making," in *The U.S.-Japan-Taiwan Trilateral Strategic Dialogue* (Washington, D.C.: Heritage Foundation, 2003).

116 William Lowther, "Study Warns PRC Patience May Be Tested," *Taipei Times*, September 25, 2009.

CHAPTER 7

Nepal

We can convert the palace
Into a deserted grave
We will knock the cruel system down
And end all black law in smoke.

—Ramesh, Volcano of Revolution

CHRONOLOGY

August 15, 1947	India's independence proclaimed
February 18, 1951	Formal end of 104 years of Rana family rule in Nepal: "Democracy Day"
December 15, 1960	King Mahendra imposes direct royal rule
April 1979	Student protests; the king announces referendum on royal *panchayat* (assembly) system
May 2, 1980	National referendum approves *panchayat* system
March 23, 1989	India closes all but two border crossings
August 1989	Radical Maoists (CPN-ML) agree to work for parliamentary democracy
January 15, 1990	Formation of United Left Front
January 18, 1990	Nepali Congress Party holds convention
February 18, 1990	People's Uprising (*Jana Andolan*) begins: fifty days of protests
March 30, 1990	Patan's liberation
April 6, 1990	Half a million people march in Kathmandu
April 6, 1990	Dozens of protesters killed near the royal palace in Kathmandu; curfew declared
April 8, 1990	Royal ban on political parties lifted
April 9, 1990	Nepali Congress Party and ULF call off further demonstrations; negotiations with the king

April 16, 1990	*Panchayat* system dismantled
April 19, 1990	Interim government sworn in
April 23, 1990	Police, *mandales* (hired thugs) lynched
May 7, 1990	Interim government formed
June 30, 1990	Buddhists lead demonstration for a secular state
November 9, 1990	New constitution proclaims Nepal a "Hindu, monarchical state"
May 12, 1991	Elections held
May 29, 1991	Congress Party government sworn in
April 5, 1992	Police open fire on protest in Kathmandu; kill seven people
February 13, 1996	Maoist armed struggle launched
June 1, 2001	Palace massacre: King Birendra and family slain
May 22, 2002	Gyanendra dissolves parliament
October 4, 2002	King Gyanendra dismisses prime minister and seizes power
February 1, 2005	The king declares martial law
May 2005	Seven Party Alliance (SPA) formed
November 22, 2005	Maoists and opposition parties reach twelve-point agreement to restore democracy
April 6, 2006	Uprising begins; *Loktantra Andolan* or *Jana Andolan* 2: nineteen days of protests
April 20, 2006	Three killed, more than a hundred wounded in Kalanki
April 21, 2006	King asks opposition leader to become prime minister; SPA refuses
April 22–23, 2006	Millions of people protest
April 24, 2006	Twelve killed, hundreds wounded; the king reinstates parliament
May 1, 2006	Confederation of Nepalese Professionals calls for "total democracy"
May 18, 2006	Monarchy abolished by interim parliament: "Democracy Day" proclaimed
November 21, 2006	Maoists and SPA sign Comprehensive Peace Accord
April 10, 2008	Maoists win elections with 217 seats in the new 601-member constituent assembly
2008 to 2011	Continuing discussions and debate but no new constitution

THE UNFOLDING OF contemporary history rarely creates situations in which people must choose either to rise up against their government or to let it run roughshod over them, to break through to greater freedom or to endure odious forms of domination for decades to come. When people do stand up, their courageous actions become mythologized in song, dance, poetry, prose, and theater. If, however, they acquiesce in the face of arrogant power, nowhere are they celebrated—except in the inner sanctums of victorious tyrants.

Seldom does history impose twice on the same people to make such a heartfelt choice. Almost never have people's uprisings recorded successive victories over brutal power. In both Burma and Tibet, the state's iron heel has continually crushed people's freedom dreams and destroyed thousands of lives. Yet in Nepal, a fifty-day uprising in 1990 won a multiparty parliament and reduced the king to a constitutional monarch. Royal machinations and political power games intervened to restore the king's power, and the monarchy bloodily sought to make its rule absolute. In 2006, people once again flooded the streets and refused to permit usurpation of their human rights. A second heroic uprising was crafted by hundreds of thousands of people who again braved police batons and bullets, flooded the streets with their bodies, and improvised new forms of resistance. In nineteen consecutive days of actions, they finally threw their king, the "reincarnation of Vishnu," onto the dustbin of history and proclaimed a secular, democratic republic.

In contrast to any palace revolution (like that of 1950 that overthrew more than a century of rule by the country's Rana oligarchy), hundreds of thousands of ordinary people became the driving force of the 1990 and 2006 people's uprisings (or *jana andolan*). More than any other forces, people's unity and courage made the democratic breakthroughs possible. A unique blending of more than fifty different ethnicities and ninety-two known languages, Nepal is also divided by caste, yet the country forged a new unity and identity through struggle against the monarchy. As in Korea, people's incredible unity stands as the chief reason for the movement's success.

The 1990 uprising flowed from a vibrant civil society with deep roots in Nepal's past, which in turn helped to foster new grassroots initiatives that are so vital to a free citizenry. In the uprising's aftermath, labor militancy became strident, women mobilized to fight patriarchy, minorities actively struggled for autonomy, and the number of autonomous media mushroomed. This mutually reinforcing relationship of uprisings and civil society is a pattern already discerned in civil uprisings in South Korea, Taiwan, and the Philippines.

Nepali Civil Society

A diverse and complex web of civil relationships dating back centuries remains the foundation for Nepali everyday life. In ancient Vedic society, *dharma* simultaneously nurtured just rulers who cared for their people's well-being and a citizenry who observed established laws. So long as the king ruled kindly, people welcomed his authority, and priestly *rishis* helped rulers observe appropriate behavior. In the country's far west (outside the zone of kingdoms in the Gorkha highlands or Kathmandu valley for millennia), a *badghar* ("big house") system facilitated election of village guardians. By custom, people selected would politely refuse to serve until pressured to do so, and direct democratic norms existed even within family disputes. In times of crisis, all residents gathered to find communal resolutions. Through a *parma* system of voluntary labor exchange among members of rural communities, social relations were strengthened, a cooperative banking system (*dhukuti*) involved groups in which individuals made small regular deposits and were permitted occasional larger lump sum withdrawals—sometimes with interest.[1]

More than six hundred years ago, medieval guilds (*guithis*) were "more comprehensive than the [European] guilds in their scope and regulated not only the profession or occupation but also the social and religious life of their members. . . . The system of sixty-four occupational castes such as *chitrakara* (painters), *taksakara* (carpenters), *silpokara* (craftsmen) etc., each with a guild or *guithi* of its own . . . indicates a fairly advanced level of economic and social activity with a large variety of specialized functions performed by a number of occupational castes."[2] Within some *guithis*, participatory forms of decision-making existed, and families cooperated on a variety of projects, such as to build small dams and accomplish other communally beneficial tasks.

Often still intact, these cultural forms (including odious caste identities) remain very real forces in contemporary Nepal. Many different religious practices and culturally specific beliefs pattern everyday life. There are still people who believe the king is the incarnation of Vishnu, others worship a cluster of young "living goddesses," and a few observe Buddhist or Christian rituals. So real are past events in people's memories that one analyst thought the Gorkha conquest of the Kathmandu valley more than two centuries ago might help explain the 1990 uprising against the monarchy.[3]

Sandwiched between India and China, tiny Nepal must tread carefully or get squashed, as has often been repeated, like "a yam between two stones." Bordering the world's two most populous countries, Nepal (with less than thirty million people) is heavily impacted by its neighbors. Its geographic isolation makes the roads from India of utmost importance. Even in times of good relations with India, Nepal's economy has never brought prosperity to its people, and it remains one of the world's poorest countries. As many as half of all children suffer from malnutrition. Nine million people (about 35 percent of the population) live on less than $1/day. The upper third control over 75 percent of wealth and income; the country's Gini coefficient increased to 0.47 in 2008 (South Korea's was 0.31). For two centuries following the Gorkha conquest, royal governments ruled by high-caste people made only sporadic and halfhearted attempts to alleviate the squalor and poverty afflicting the country's vast majority in the countryside. After the restoration of monarchical power in 1950, all-powerful kings paid lip service to "liberty, equality, and fraternity" while squandering the national patrimony.

So great was the king's loyal following and so strong his military power that Nepal's revolutions of 1951 and 1990 were both linked to India's government. The more recent Maoist rural insurgency owes a great debt to India's Naxalites—and to China's revolutionary past. Shortly after the 1949 communists' victory in the Chinese civil war, Tibet was invaded, a momentous event for the Himalayan region—even if the rest of the world scarcely seemed to notice at the time. China's conquest of Tibet precipitated India's heavy-handed treatment of Nepal. On November 10, 1950, a small contingent of forty to fifty armed Nepali Congress Party members were permitted to cross over from India and attack Birganj, setting off fighting across the country and massive demonstrations in Kathmandu against the Rana oligarchs. While the army mainly remained loyal to the regime, Indian support for the rebels compelled the Ranas in January 1951 to accept the "suggestion" that Nepal have elections for a Constituent Assembly (with Tribhuvan remaining king). On February 18, 1951—a date that would be celebrated as Democracy Day in Nepal for more than half a century—a coalition government was established.

Having overseen a palace revolution and transition to Nepali democracy in 1951, India was understandably unhappy in 1962 when Tribhuvan's son, King Mahendra, instituted the royal *panchayat* system and banned all political parties, including the Congress Party (Nepal Congress or NC), then a weak counterpart to India's ruling party of the same name.[4] When a border war broke out between India and China that same year, India's relations with the Nepali monarchy suddenly improved. In 1972, Bahendra replaced his father as king, and the NC briefly resorted again to armed insurgency, but without India's support, it was quickly abandoned. Stability characterized Indo-Nepali relations until 1989, when a new window of opportunity to overthrow the Nepalese royal family opened.

As in so many of the countries where uprisings changed the course of political history, students and intellectuals played a vital role in sparking movements and providing them with continuity during quiet times. With less than half of Nepal's people literate, intellectuals are not only enormously important, they take their responsibilities seriously. In 1979, writers in Kathmandu gathered on street corners, recited their poems, and demanded an end to the *panchayat* system. Later dubbed the Street Poetry Revolution, at its climax the campaign involved as many as two hundred poets.[5] Many writers traveled to meet their countryside peers, so the movement spread to as many as fifty other towns.

After writers agitated, students began to mobilize, pressing for reforms in the universities. Crushed mercilessly by the police in Kathmandu, the student movement spread to other parts of the country. The demand for independent student unions united the many different factions in the movement. On May 23, 1979, townspeople joined student demonstrations, and the crowd converged on the royal palace, setting ablaze selectively targeted government buildings—including newspaper offices—within sight of the king.

Having perceived first-hand the threat to his power, King Birendra surprised the nation the next morning when he announced on Radio Nepal his decision to hold a national referendum for people to choose between the *panchayat* system and multiparty democracy. He lifted his royal ban on political parties, ended censorship, freed prisoners (some of whom had been in jail for as long as twenty years), and permitted public debate on political questions. The movement's outburst and the king's generous response ushered in a year of political freedom, but when the referendum's results were tallied, a slight majority (54.7 percent) was counted as having voted in favor of retaining the royal *panchayat* system.

Appearing magnanimous in victory, King Birendra decreed on December 15, 1980, that a nonpartisan parliament would be elected. Despite the appearance of democratic reform, political parties were again banned, and elected officials remained powerless. Royal appointees ran both the new parliament and, most importantly, the National Sports Council (which trained police, the army, and paramilitary *mandales*). If there was any doubt about the king's absolute political power, none remained after palace cronies summarily dismissed the first parliament's elected prime minister. Hopes for at least a façade of democracy were quickly dashed as corruption scandals and intimidation of independently minded political figures continued to plague political appointees. In the mid-1980s, the NC initiated a nonviolent campaign against the government (*satyagraha*), and communists mobilized their own "fill the jails" movement. After a series of mysterious bombs exploded in five places around the royal palace on June 20, 1985, all protests were called off. It didn't matter that word on the street blamed the bombs on Prince Gyanendra (who went on to seize power in 2002). The royal family blamed an opposition politician and quickly sentenced him to death, leaving the opposition to beat a hasty retreat.

In 1986, several progressives, including communists, were elected in nonpartisan votes, but their opposition to *pancha* authorities landed them on a revolving door between prison and parliament. Nevertheless, by dramatizing the king's inability to rule justly, electoral activism helped build the movement. When the NC organized publicly in defiance of the king's ban on political parties, he had hundreds of their leaders rounded up. At the same time, shortages of fuel and food sapped people's good will toward the crown. As inflation grew, even the Hindu faithful's sense of the king's divinity—his status as the contemporary reincarnation of Vishnu—waned.

Despite the royal family's political domination of the country, students' militancy had helped unleash powerful forces. New press freedoms in the early 1980s led to the nation's first autonomous newspapers. So great was people's thirst for information that the number of the country's newspapers, anywhere between twenty-seven and eighty-four between 1960 and 1980, grew fivefold from 1980 to 1990.[6] Roads and telephone services were greatly improved, facilitating communication among disparate parts of the country (and among movement activists). The literacy rate reached 40 percent in 1989 (up from 5 percent in 1952), and higher education was expanded enormously, as TABLE 7.1 indicates. In less than a decade from 1984, the number of students enrolled in postsecondary institutions doubled, providing the opposition with a potent constituency for change.

With the expansion of educational opportunities, the seeds of a cultural revolution against the caste system were sown. While still a major force in Nepali society, caste no longer plays the rigidly paramount role it did for centuries in structuring relations of everyday life. Ethnic and caste groups began to assert their human rights. Also significant were the growth of a new professional middle class and increasing opportunities for women to work outside the family. Educational

TABLE 7.1 **Enrollment in Secondary and Higher Institutions**

	1950	1961	1970	1984/85	1989/90	1991/92
Secondary School	1,680	21,115	102,704	216,473	364,525	421,709
Higher Institute	250	5143	17,200	55,560	95,240	110,329

Source: Martin Hoftun, William Raeper, and John Whelpton, *People, Politics and Ideology: Democracy and Social Change in Nepal* (Kathmandu: Mandala Book Point, 1999), 95.

reforms were rapid and helped amalgamate promising new dynamics in civil society, but they fell short of desired results. Even today, Nepal still struggles to spread literacy and educate its young. Too many children endure lives of forced labor and servitude. UNICEF estimates that malnutrition affects more than half of the country's young.

As Nepal modernized in the early 1980s, cinemas opened, and television became wildly popular soon after being introduced. By the end of that decade, when news of Asian and European uprisings for democracy was broadcast, people flocked to any set they could find.[7] As with so many uprisings, events in distant parts of the world have profound consequences on people who long for freedom in their own. In 1986, when the People Power revolution in the Philippines overthrew Marcos, people rejoiced, many openly musing that the king should—and even more importantly, could—be driven from power. During the Eastern European revolutions of 1989, especially during the fighting in Romania (whose president Ceausescu had recently visited Nepal), people followed the uprising closely and longed to imitate it. Ganesh Man Singh, considered the "supreme leader" of the 1990 Nepalese democracy movement, related that "With Gorbachev's announcement of *perestroika* and *glasnost* something like this became possible even in Nepal."[8] By contrast, the Tiananmen protests in China were hardly covered due to the country's delicate relations with its northern neighbor.

Preparing the *Jana Andolan*

As 1990 opened, neither the king nor the opposition knew what to expect for the coming year. Soon after New Year's celebrations had ended, King Birendra and the royal family left Kathmandu for their annual tour of rural areas. A week later, on January 10, seven communist parties formed a United Left Front (ULF) and agreed to work with the Congress Party. Together, they formed the Movement for the Restoration of Democracy (MRD). Seven more radical communist parties organized themselves into the United National People's Movement (UNPM). While they agreed with the MRD on the short-term goal of multiparty democracy and constitutional monarchy, they also remained autonomous in order to plan their own actions.

Encouraged by the wave of insurgencies sweeping the planet, Nepal's main opposition parties agreed to cosponsor mass protests scheduled to begin on February 18, 1990. As in Burma, a carefully selected date was chosen for protests to commence: February 18—officially "Democracy Day" marking the anniversary of King Tribhuvan's commitment to a multiparty system in 1951. Meeting secretly, they came to agreement on their goals: a one-person, one-vote multiparty constitutional monarchy, a change that would involve the dismantling of the *panchayat* system and transformation of absolute royal powers into a parliamentary framework.[9] Although many militants were ready to begin the protests as soon as possible, activist leaders delayed them.

Many people predicted the movement would begin on January 18, when some four thousand people assembled at the plush Thamel home of Ganesh Man Singh for a national conference of the NC, but the opposition wanted to give the king time to submit to its demands. The Congress Party also needed time for its organizers to prepare their actions. Leaders postponed demonstrations for a month, formed a secret coordinating committee with the ULF on January 30, and made elaborate plans for a popular insurgency that could win. The day after the opening of actions on February 18, there was supposed to be a general strike; the ULF would organize a "black day" on February 25; and another general strike was scheduled for March 2. Even before the movement took to the streets, the president of NC, Krishna Prasad Bhattarai, predicted, "This time we are going to win. We will force the king to be constitutional. If everything goes well, only a few weeks, and we will be in power. If things go wrong, I and my colleagues might end up in jail, but that's not a threat—we know that if this happens, it can only last a few months and then we will win."[10]

Parliamentary representatives from India's Congress Party were sent to the January 18–20 convention of the NC and helped initiate Nepal's democracy movement. Chandra Shekhar—a leader of India's Janata Party and later Indian prime minister—told amazed Nepalese that all Indian political leaders supported Nepalese democracy and that they "should take courage from the overthrow of tyrants like Ceausescu, Marcos and the Shah of Iran."[11] While a number of forces converged to create conditions for the uprising's success, one key factor was a trade embargo imposed by India after the countries' bilateral Trade and Transit Treaty expired. In late 1989, twelve of fourteen border crossings were closed, and on February 15, 1990, All India Radio announced that two remaining roads into Nepal would be closed on February 18—the same day the democracy movement's actions were scheduled to commence. India's blockade of traffic put landlocked Nepal in an untenable position, and India promised that no new protocol would be agreed until "an understanding about democracy in Nepal" had been reached.[12]

Nepalis immediately began to suffer dwindling supplies of necessities— shortages it could ill afford given its economy's already precarious condition. In 1990, the World Bank's conservative estimate was that at least seven of the country's nineteen million people lived in absolutely impoverished conditions.[13] Between 1970 and 1990, grain production had dropped by almost 50 percent, the number of animals had declined by half, and a day's hard work in the fields did not even produce enough to feed a family—let alone provide one with housing and clothing.[14] While 90 percent of the country's people lived in impoverished rural areas, rampant corruption in the palace, although widely ridiculed, continued unabated. After inflation doubled in the 1970s and doubled again between 1980 and 1987, the IMF imposed a structural adjustment package on the country, a notorious "solution" well known across the world for intensifying the plight of the poor.

Although limited, Nepal's new freedoms and educational opportunities won through the struggles of 1979 were of most significance to the growing number of upwardly mobile, urban citizens. Their rising expectations, fueled by envisioned membership in global consumer culture made familiar through television advertising, were a key driving force in the movement of 1990. A poll published at the

beginning of 1990 indicated that 73 percent of middle-class respondents supported the democracy movement, and 25 percent said they would participate.[15]

The seven-week struggle for democracy erupted on February 18 and lasted
until victory on April 9—fifty days of courageous resistance to brutal attacks.
Dozens of people were killed, hundreds wounded, and thousands arrested.
Nevertheless, tens of thousands of people continued to go into the streets and
demand democracy. More than any others, students were in the forefront of initial
street actions, and they suffered the most from the police violence. Imprisoned,
beaten, tortured, and even killed, they refused to submit. The king closed all universities—as well as secondary and primary schools in the capital—but protests
spread. Although most intense among Newaris in the Kathmandu valley and
professionals (teachers, doctors, and lawyers), the *jana andolan* came to involve
all of the country's ethnic groups and castes, workers and students, farmers, and
unemployed youth.

An empirical analysis of the 1990 uprising helps shed light on the conscious-
ness-in-action of hundreds of thousands of people—the most significant defining feature of Nepali society at that time. By looking specifically at the form
and content of people's actions, we can gain insight into their aspirations, their
autonomy amid unity, and the international networks from which they drew
inspiration. A closer examination of the uprising's specific character reveals the
intelligence and innovation of ordinary people.

Political Parties and People's Movement

Political parties may have initially called for the protests, but people's actions
far surpassed politicians' wildest dreams. Beginning in the Kathmandu valley,
the uprising drew the entire country into it, creating a centripetal force whose
irresistible power ultimately compelled the monarchy to relent.

When students mobilized before the date agreed by the MRD, the king
ruthlessly crushed their protests. In Pokhara on February 12, with the king and
queen nearby, more than five hundred young students were brutally arrested
when they formed a peaceful procession celebrating the release from prison of
Nelson Mandela. Many of the females were stripped of their clothing, and one of
them, Laxmi Karki, was terribly mistreated. When news of the tragedy in Pokhara
spread, public outrage grew—as did momentum for the uprising.[16]

Since everyone knew of the plans for the coming uprising, the government
arrested nearly all known activist leaders. By February 10, some 500 arrests had
been made; by February 13, about 1,500 people had been rounded up; and by
February 18, as many as 5,000 political leaders had been indefinitely detained.[17]
Those fortunate enough to elude the police were compelled to go underground.
Beginning on February 15, the authorities also began to confiscate privately
owned newspapers and arrest journalists by the dozens. None of these measures, not even the detention of most opposition leaders by February 18, was
able to stop the eruption of the popular movement. Painted on walls across the
country, "Do or Die for Democracy!" became the rallying cry for thousands of
ordinary citizens.

On February 18, as protests began in concert, writers released a new book of poems, *The Search for Spring*. One poem in particular, "Once Fists Are Clenched" by Vinay Raval, called people to action:

> Once fists are clenched,
> Even the Berlin wall falls down;
> Once fists are clenched,
> The events of Tiananmen Square take place,
> Once fists are clenched,
> Even Mandela is freed . . .
> Why are we the only ones
> Who do not clench our fists,
> And seek to be prisoners of history?
> Has the man inside us died? [18]

On February 18, thousands of riot police lined all major thoroughfares and prevented people from assembling in the streets or spilling into nearby parade grounds. The first few brave souls who unfurled banners were quickly hauled away, but people continued to arrive, until at least ten thousand people were able to form a procession in the streets of central Kathmandu. Simultaneously, the government's planned Democracy Day commemoration was assembling with prominent *panchas* in its front ranks. Police tried to disperse protesters by using sticks and tear gas, but the crowd refused to be beaten into submission. Some began to march, while others, notably students from Trichandra College, defaced the statue of King Mahendra, founder of the *panchayat* system. As the throng moved away from police attacks, they collided with the official Democracy Day celebrations. Throwing stones, they chased off government ministers at the head of the official procession. For the rest of the day, police, and demonstrators clashed in many parts of the capital.

That evening Radio Nepal reported unrest all over the country. In over forty places, district headquarters were the scene of protests.[19] One report told of police opening fire in Chitwan killing four people, after five thousand people tried to unarrest two movement leaders.[20] In Hetauda, a policeman was stoned to death and many cars torched. In the first three days of the uprising, as the king's police used violent means across the country, a dozen participants were killed in Bharatpur, Bhaktapur, and Janakpur—a total of twenty-four in all of Nepal.[21]

On February 19, the MRD's call for Nepal's first general strike met with great success in urban areas. Shops in the capital were closed and traffic minimal, but police again used deadly force. In the Newari town of Bhaktapur near Kathmandu, police used dum dum bullets on crowds that included women and children, killing six and injuring twenty-five.[22] In Kirtipur, people set a police station afire. Dispatches from Jadukuha, Narayanghat, and Hetauda all reported killings of protesters. Police violence also reached intolerable levels in the Southern Terai.

In response to state violence, the Lawyers' Association called for a general strike on February 20. On February 23, the country's medical doctors went on a two-hour warning strike. The entire staff of Maharajganj Teaching Hospital mobilized to stop police from stealing corpses. One eyewitness account recorded how, "About two or three hundred police arrived to steal the bodies from the mortuary. The nurses came first and lay down on the ground in front of the cars carrying the dead bodies. And the doctors, and even the patients and their relatives surrounded the police vehicles. So the police were forced to negotiate."[23] Time and again, police sought to steal corpses, not from any sadistic pleasure they might derive from denying the bereaved the chance to mourn their dead, but from the monarchy's embarrassment and shame at having to kill its own subjects. There is, perhaps, no more damning indictment of a Hindu monarch than killing, rather than protecting, his own people. In Nepal—as in Gwangju and in Burma—the government sought to hide the corpses of its victims in a vain effort to forestall popular revenge for elite violence.

By the end of the first week, movement sources reported thousands of arrests and at least forty dead. As the daily protests and police attacks continued, NC totals placed the number of arrests at 7,045 on March 3. By mid-March, the Forum for the Protection of Human Rights announced that besides 5,000 people in custody since February 18, another 20,000 had been temporarily detained. Unlike the government, people's actions were primarily directed against property, not human beings: when the government tallied its casualties from February 18 to March 4, it counted the number of buses damaged by "disruptive elements" at thirty-three.

In the first month of the uprising, censorship was strictly imposed. Television did not mention the protests, but instead fed people daily scraps of scenes from the royal family's visit to Western Nepal. The country's two most significant independent newspapers had been closed down. Although BBC, India Radio, and Voice of America radio broadcasts were still available, the movement was compelled to rely on its own underground networks, improvised media, and word of mouth to spread news of its events and to announce future actions. Beginning on February 21, NC published an underground *Jana Andolan Samachar* (People's Movement News) that was sold secretly for one rupee, but before the end of the month, police raided its offices and closed it down. From February 26 until the last days of the uprising, the CPN (ML) published a daily *Sangharsha Bulletin* (Struggle Bulletin) on A4 paper, but its daily print run was a meager five hundred.[24]

Black became the symbol of people's anger and hope. Even before "Black Day" on February 25 when organized groups wore black armbands and carried black flags of protest, people spontaneously adapted the color to their needs. In Biratnagar on February 22, women with black strips over their mouths staged a mute protest. In broad daylight, they also carried lanterns—as Diogenes had done in ancient Greece—to dramatize their search for truth. On February 26, thousands of teachers and professors—many wearing black—went on strike. The second Nepal *bandh* (general strike) on March 2 again revitalized the struggle. The next day, artists tied black scarves around their mouths and sat down in the streets near Tricandra College in the capital. Soon black scarves, long a symbol of Nepali independence, were worn everywhere. In Biratnagar, donkeys, dogs, and cats were adorned with black scarves and democratic slogans and unleashed to run through the streets.

The people of Patan took down the sign in front of the district court and held their liberated turf for days. Photo by Thomas Bonk.

People unfortunate enough to be grabbed by police were jammed together in filthy cells, many without access to toilets or water. Many were beaten, smeared with feces, and subjected to electroshocks.[25] On Black Day alone, more than a thousand people were taken away. In Biratnagar, a large women's protest was assaulted by police and dozens of women taken into custody. When protests appeared to lose momentum in early March, government employees took initiatives for new actions. On March 8, International Women's Day, hundreds of women carrying black flags and wearing black armbands gathered at Padma Kanya campus in Kathmandu, where female leaders discussed women's roles in changing society.[26] On March 20, Nepal's leading intellectuals called for a public meeting at a university to discuss the country's situation. Halfway through the meeting in Kirtipur, police arrived and arrested 700 people. That same day at Pokhara's forestry campus, some 320 students were arrested. The mass arrests only further inflamed the country's indignation with the king's arbitrary actions.

March 23 was "People's Unity Day" and political parties prepared feverishly for it for over two weeks. NC and ULF planned separate marches, and the parties believed more than twenty thousand people would assemble in Kathmandu alone. Nonetheless, when the appointed time arrived, there were more police than people at the gathering points. The parties' best efforts were a dismal failure.[27] Once again, spontaneous mobilizing power of ordinary people proved a much more potent weapon than that of centrally organized parties.

Various groups autonomously took imaginative forms of action, instituting a variety of tactical innovations, spontaneously creating insurgent means of communication, and calling continually for the end of the monarchy. Under the auspices of the Nepal University Teachers' Association (NUTA), hundreds of lecturers launched a "pen down" strike. University officials were sometimes surrounded by dozens of enraged employees who demanded justice. The movement spread to high schools and even to twelve and thirteen-year-olds. On March 27, NUTA launched a boycott of classes and sit-ins to protest the arrests and dismissals of teachers who had participated in the movement.

On March 28, the opposition called on citizens to withhold payment on taxes, water, electricity, and telephone bills as a means to bankrupt the government, a tactic reminiscent of the Philippines four years earlier. The Nepal Medical Association held its first emergency meeting and released a statement condemning the state's violence. Two days later, the Nepal Engineers' Association also issued a proclamation of dissent. On March 31, housewives formed a kettledrum procession outside Padma Kanya University, using their pots and pans as instruments of political expression. Soon thereafter, pots and pans began to be heard at protests around the country.

Blackouts became one of the movement's most important daily rituals, bringing many people into action who feared doing anything more than turning their lights out. Without anyone ordering it, they originally began in the town of Narayanghat in the Terai, and the tactic quickly diffused to Kathmandu and other towns. Beginning on March 29, blackouts became more systematic. Across Kathmandu, people plunged their neighborhoods into darkness for ten minutes every evening beginning at 7:00 p.m. It was a heartening show of solidarity and resolve—although houses that did not respect the blackout often had their windows broken. Soon the blackouts spread across the country. One movement leader later remarked, "It was during these evening hours we finally knew that a victory was imminent."[28]

The masses of people were far ahead of the parties and their secret "Joint Coordination Committee." At the very beginning of the popular upsurge, on February 18, "It was clear that the extent of the mass support for the revolution came as a surprise to the opposition leaders as much as to the *panchayat* government."[29] While many histories treat prominent leaders and political parties as the main force of the uprising, time and again the leaders of the movement expressed surprise at the extent of the popular mobilization. It is difficult to gauge the coordinating committee's influence on people in the streets, but one foreign observer who was present tells us, "The MRD was expressly non-violent in character, as demanded by the NC-ULF alliance."[30] Yet he described how "some activists battled against the police with rocks and streets stones. . . . The public contestation of space inscribed upon Kathmandu a mosaic of signs which speak of the ferment in its streets: broken windows of government offices and shops; burnt-out skeletons of government buses; torn-up street stones, used in battles with the police, lay strewn across streets and sidewalks; prodemocracy and political party slogans began to appear on the walls of the city and its temples. . . . Once on the streets, people set fire to car tires to act as temporary barricades across the narrow streets, and pitched battles between armed riot police and stone-throwing demonstrators ensued, the incendiary of protest lighting up the darkened city."[31]

Liberated Patan

At the end of March in the Newari town of Patan (just across the river from Kathmandu), the uprising reached its highest level of expression when people took over the town and held it for a week. More than any other single battle, Patan's full-fledged popular uprising spelled the end of Birendra's reign as absolute monarch.

After horrific state violence had antagonized Patan's residents for weeks, youths attacked the local *panchayat* office at Mangal Bazaar. Before police could assemble to stop them, they emptied the building of desks, chairs, and files and set the heap on fire. When riot police arrived, their tear gas failed to drive the protesters out of Patan's narrow and windy maze of streets. People continued to regroup and were able to launch another attack on the *panchayat* office. As fighting continued into the afternoon, police resorted to their firearms and shot dead at least two people in the bazaar in the center of town.

The next day, Saturday, March 31, a large contingent of police arrived and began systematically searching for suspects—kicking down doors of homes and

In liberated Patan, citizens spoke freely about strategy and tactics.
Photo by Min Bhajracharya in *Dawn of Democracy: People's Power in Nepal* (Kathmandu: Forum for the Protection of Human Rights, 1990), 49.

brutalizing anyone they found. That evening, as lights went out and the blackout spontaneously continued until dawn, activists went door-to-door in their neighborhoods (*tols*) and mobilized people to end the bloodshed by seizing control of the streets. According to two youthful participants, "During the night, we went from *tol* to *tol*, block to block, telling people that they should defend their brothers and sisters, daughters and sons, of whom some had already been killed and injured by the police. The people came out with knives, spears, and rods and whatever they could find in their household, both women and men, young and old. The activists really started at Chyasal Tol where the people all belonging to the same caste which practiced intermarriage were the most unified block in Patan. But from there it spread to all other *tols* and areas."[32] After parading though the town with their weapons, people's spirits were lifted. Activists called upon them to make the town a liberated area. Soon hundreds of people helped to dig trenches and build barricades to protect Patan from further attacks.[33]

Liberated Patan, declared a "Zone of Democracy" and "Free State" by its people, held out for a full week. On April 1, as police were unable to enter the town, some fifty thousand people assembled, shouting slogans opposed not only to the *panchayat* system but also to the monarchy. They tried to march across the river to nearby Kathmandu to encourage people there to follow their example, but massed police formations halted them. The procession retreated back to Patan, where people reinforced the barricades of the seven roads leading into it and deepened the trenches on their defensive perimeter.

Within liberated Patan, nearly every neighborhood had its own autonomously organized self-defense force. "The Committees consisted of between fifty and a hundred people armed with *khukris* (curved knives), tools and sticks, who staffed the barricades around the clock. All those entering the town were checked."[34] Using garden tools, broom handles, and kitchen knives, women stood resolutely determined to protect their families and town. Whenever temple bells warned of government intrusions, residents converged on the barricades to defend their *tols*. In one case, when the government sent in a bulldozer to clear barricades, the driver was quickly removed and his vehicle torched. Patan's narrow streets made massed police formations impossible; simultaneously the back streets continued to provide activists with a safe route between neighborhoods—even as far as Kathmandu and back.

People surrounded Patan's main police station at Mangal Bazaar with 128 policemen inside. In addition to building barricades around it, deep trenches were dug to prevent vehicles from driving in. When the trapped police tried to evacuate, they were stoned from nearby rooftops. After they retreated back into their station, they were offered the choice to remain in the building with their safety guaranteed and sufficient food and water, or to leave without any promises of their safety. They chose to stay.[35]

Daily rallies continued, although it is unclear whether people were able to craft town-wide participatory rallies as activists did in liberated Gwangju. The vast majority of these rallies—if not all of them—were unidirectional: leaders spoke to masses rather than facilitating horizontal lines of communication. On

April 2, underground leaders of illegal political parties publicly appeared for the first time. Sundhara Square was jammed with people. As the rally ended, a white helicopter's hovering noise drowned out the speaker.[36]

On the positive side, for the first time, liberated Patan provided movement leaders with the only public space where they could address thousands of people. When politicians came with megaphones, large assemblies paid close attention to their speeches. Yet when amplification equipment and prominent leaders were absent, a continual public discourse transpired in small groups. People exchanged stories of their experiences in the uprising with each other and proffered advice on how best to proceed. As someone present later explained to me, "Neighborhood districts spontaneously organized themselves. In the main square, non-amplified meetings continued constantly. When political parties arrived, they set up speakers. While there, some expressed disagreements, it was because some people said things like, 'We should be nice and not throw stones.'"[37]

On April 2, eighty thousand people demonstrated in the liberated town. Time and again, radical activists stressed the need to expand the Patan Commune to other towns, yet police had strict orders to prevent crowds from entering or leaving Patan. "The rulers feared marches towards the capital, towards the Palace. Activists had to calm down the crowd to avoid further bloodshed."[38]

In Kirtipur, only a few miles from the center of Kathmandu, people soon joined Patan in seizing control of the town center. The struggle developed when women led assaults on the police station in attempts to free their arrested sons. They were greeted with massive quantities of tear gas—including from the same white helicopter that had earlier disrupted the rally in Patan. When tear gas failed to disperse the crowd, police used their guns and killed four people. That night, residents dug trenches and built barricades on the main roads entering the town. After the funeral procession for one of the victims, people assembled at Bagh Bhairab temple for a rally. Everyone applauded the decisions made by eight *panchayat* officials when they announced their resignation from the "arrogant establishment."[39] From his hospital bed, Ganesh Man Singh compared heroism there to that in Timisoara in Romania, where armed freedom fighters had only recently defeated the Ceausescu's troops.[40]

Patan's Commune inspired people across the country. Following Patan's example, *panchayat* buildings were set ablaze in many towns and villages. Among urban professionals, even the pilots of the Royal Nepal Air went on strike. While in other places, police gunfire killed people, no one was killed in liberated Patan. Tensions inside the town increased as supplies of fresh food, kerosene, and cooking oil ran low. After a week, the government finally sent in the army to retake Patan. Rather than fight a suicidal struggle, people let the soldiers in. They knew military force could control the streets during the day—but that people would regain supremacy at night.

When the government unleashed its hired thugs (*mandales*) to beat peaceful demonstrators, new strata of the population became involved in the movement. On April 1, television broadcasters, emboldened by demonstrators' courage and enraged by state violence, broadcast news of the unrest in Kirtipur and called

on the government for dialogue. During a subsequent *bandh* against the government on April 2, estimates placed the number of teachers involved at fifty to sixty
thousand and workers at thirty to forty thousand.[41] In succeeding days, thirty
thousand rallied in Patan on April 3; on the following day, dubbed "Condolence
Day" in honor of the uprising's martyrs, while many memorial services were
being held, tanks entered the capital. All fifty-five pilots of Royal Nepal Airlines
conducted a half-day strike that grounded all domestic flights; on April 5, many
ministries experienced a "pen down strike," and electrical and telephone workers
joined the strike movement. As the ranks of protesters continued to expand, even
the country's foreign minister protested the repressive measures.

The movement spread by less conventional means than might be expected:
besides word of mouth, well-known folk songs were changed so that the melodies conveyed insurgents' acts and dreams. Poetry conveyed the aspirations of
the movement; leaflets with extracts of the moral code from Hindu epics like
the *Mahabharata* were juxtaposed with the king's unjust rule; and photo displays in public squares dramatized torture and repression. In Patan, the movement's intelligence meant some people eavesdropped on government FM airwaves and informed neighborhoods in advance of police actions. Photocopy and
fax machines were used to distribute autonomously produced daily reports both
inside Nepal and internationally. A huge network of couriers conveyed verbal
messages.

As the whole society became politicized, the unleashed energies and imaginations of ordinary people became the greatest force in all of Nepal. As one poet
expressed the newfound end to compartmentalization of dreams:

> Now poetry's not found in solitude,
> You meet it in demonstrations.
> Now poetry isn't written on paper,
> You find it running down the street.
> —Julusma Kavita, "Poetry in Processions"

The "backbone" of the prodemocracy movement in 1990 was the new professional
middle class—a group whose activism also animated movements in Thailand,
Korea, and the Philippines.[42] Michael Hutt observed, "What was new was the
way in which the movement snowballed, involving not only students, but also
the new professional classes, and ultimately, ordinary people."[43] The new middle
class may have been the "backbone" of the movement, but it drew in the working
class, peasants, and urban poor. Within a few short weeks, the uprising found
support among many sectors of the urban population: doctors,[44] lawyers, journalists, housewives, trade unionists, artists, the urban poor, and truck drivers.
Women were especially active in the valley towns outside Kathmandu, where
female factory workers were well organized and played significant roles in the
mobilizations.[45]

One analyst bemoaned the participation of the poor and uneducated,
because, in her view, their more passionate and diffuse protests meant that "the
aims of the campaign became confused."[46] Since writers of history often come

Women armed with farm tools took to the streets.
Photo by Angelika Appel-Schumacher in *Dawn of Democracy*, 51.

from the new middle class, they tend to exaggerate the relative importance of that group. In Nepal—as in Korea—it seems fair to say that the middle class was of great significance in originating the movement, while urban poor and working-class people were of more importance in sustaining it when government repression became extensive. Some trade unionists participated in the movement under the aegis of the newly formed General Federation of Nepalese Trade Unions, but many workers were involved as individuals. Workers' strikes were often political in nature among the new working class—teachers, journalists, doctors, medical professions, lawyers, and government workers. On the morning of April 15, Bir Hospital medical staff initiated a relay hunger strike (each participant took a twelve-hour period without food) to demand the removal of the king's newly appointed home minister as they were "disenchanted with the indecent way" he treated them on bloody Friday, April 6.

Of course, from another perspective, it is unfair to divide the working class by occupation or economic status. Any empirical history of the 1990 uprising reveals that proletarianized professionals and white-collar employees, no less than their colleagues in factories and fields, comprised a new class-for-itself, a fused group of insurgents whose unity-in-action went beyond academic attempts to categorize class solely on the basis of "objective" data (like occupation or payscale). The more active group engagement of proletarianized professionals reveals their significance in the contemporary process of social transformation, a new dynamic incomprehensible to leftists mired in economic categories of the nineteenth century.

In a country where eight in ten people lived in rural areas, the leadership of urban professionals was noteworthy. Of course, the vacillating character of "middle classes" makes their allegiance problematic—but no less so than that of their blue-collar or rag-tag (lumpen) comrades. The participation of activists who had helped overthrow Rana rule in the palace revolution of 1951 was also a double-edged sword for the movement, since they provided many of the movement's public spokespersons and gave it great respectability. Later, however, they would quiet the movement and lead it to a negotiated settlement with the king that was far from satisfactory.

Of all the remarkable characteristics of the 1990 *jana andolan*, the unity of so many different kinds of people and parties was most salient. Except for rural landlords and *panchas*, the movement successfully created a new national identity and forged a unity that became a huge future resource.

The Uprising's Climax

The seven most radical communist parties, organized under the umbrella UNPM, called for a new nationwide *bandh* on Friday, April 6. Faced with the unstoppable force of popular mobilization, King Birendra rose early that day. At 6:45 a.m. on Radio Nepal, he announced his dismissal of the government and the formation of a new cabinet led by former prime minister Lokendra Chand. By appearing to grant some changes, the king raised people's expectations, but by stubbornly attempting to keep his government in power through reshuffling positions among his hated *panchayat* administrators, his obstinacy further enflamed people.

Later that morning, people spontaneously decided not to go to work but instead began to converge on the heart of the capital. Fittingly enough, the march downtown was spearheaded in Patan by a gathering of ten thousand female factory workers. From all directions, demonstrators swarmed into the center of the city, joining together at Tundikhel parade grounds—a scant few hundred meters from the royal palace. Police did not intervene—in all likelihood they could not have stopped the huge throngs from converging near the palace. Variously estimated to have involved anywhere from one hundred thousand to five hundred thousand people, the huge rally (the largest in all of Nepal's history) soon began to chant antimonarchist slogans. Everywhere illegal party flags were proudly carried. A popular refrain went, "Thief Birendra, Leave the Country!" Others insulted the queen, while still more simply said, "We want democracy!" From a distance, one observer noticed: "A sea of humanity . . . marched endlessly, peacefully and unarmed. . . . They were clapping their hands above their heads as they chanted their slogans, and from a distance they looked like participants in a sort of ballet as they waved their arms in the rhythm of their chanted demands. People in Bagh Bazaar houses were sprinkling water on them from first- or second-story windows: it was a very warm afternoon, and this was the women's way of cooling the marchers."[47]

At the mass rally—the first democratic mass meeting in decades—the amplification equipment was limited to a few megaphones, so not many people could hear what the politicians were saying. While speakers followed one another in calling for a restoration of multiparty democracy, from the grassroots, calls to abolish the monarchy grew louder—as did suggestions to march on the palace.

Instead of attacking nearby government offices, the crowd surged in the direction of the palace. At least two lines of police were broken through peacefully as people reached to within three hundred meters of the royal residence. Suddenly at 4:00 p.m., police whistles signaled a massive assault on the crowd. Everywhere, police batons rained down with force on people's heads. Stones and bricks were thrown in answer.

Accounts vary as to what exactly happened next. As police pumped in volumes of tear gas, more militant members of the throng broke shop windows of a store belonging to the king's brother-in-law. People began to deface King Mahendra's statue—the same one students had attacked on February 18. One young man climbed up and grabbed the scepter from the statue's arms. He was quickly shot dead. The army then opened fire from rooftops, shooting many people in the back as they scrambled for cover. In a few minutes of bloody gunfire, the government killed more people (perhaps as many as one hundred) than in the previous seven weeks of protest.[48] Hundreds more were wounded. All over Kathmandu, people built barricades out of tires, bricks, large stones, trashcans, and anything else they could find to disrupt the police and army vehicles. Bonfires lit up the night as savage fighting continued until morning. At 4:00 a.m., gunfire was widely heard as troops entered liberated Patan.

After the killings on April 6, two days of curfew were imposed. Telephones were out of order and supplies of food and fuel ran low all over the city. In the intervening forty-eight hours, opposition leaders began to be released from prison, but the army seemed to be everywhere. The uprising had evolved through two stages: the buildup—leading up to February 18 and continuing for at least a month afterward; and the climax—when initiative shifted from the political parties to more revolutionary actors, the "crowds" whose initiatives now determined the course of events.

"The second stage of the revolution could be termed the 'climax.' This began when the crowds erupted into the streets. The sheer volume of the crowd rendered the opposition leaders temporarily impotent. They had to act quickly to regain the initiative. During this period it was the mood of the crowd, not the time-table of the opposition leaders, which dictated events."[49]

Not only did the size of mobilizations grow, but also people's stated aspirations went far beyond those of the political parties in the MRD. The mood of the country had changed, and people now demanded an end to the bloody monarchy. In this period of time, "The movement, then onwards, gained a revolutionary character that never flagged . . . the movement assumed a new shape: a true people's movement. . . . Since the movement was moving toward revolutionary resolution in terms of popular participation and the style of agitation, King Birendra was compelled to realize the limitations of his options."[50]

In a move that probably saved both the monarchy and moderate opposition leaders from being swept away by the forces in the streets, four central MRD figures (NC leaders K.P. Bhattarai and G.P. Koirala as well as ULF leaders Sahana Pradhan and R.K. Mainali) agreed to go the palace for direct talks with the king. Apparently, when police opened fire and killed dozens of people on April 6, it was not only the king who panicked at the thought of the crowd overrunning his royal residence. Political parties, only too eager to become legalized and handed a modicum of power, also grew alarmed.

By the time the four politicians left the palace, the king had agreed to lift the curfew as well as his twenty-nine year ban on political parties. Although the king failed to order the *panchayat* government to cease operating, he had appointed a new prime minister and opened consultations with the NC and ULF. That was enough for the four opposition leaders to announce publicly that the movement was "categorically called off."[51]

Negotiations and Compromise

By having further protests cancelled, the newly established alliance between the palace and the NC/ULF short-circuited a revolutionary process, and the uprising entered a third phase: consolidation of a new order. To regain control of the explosive situation, opposition leaders needed to control the crowds. Although people in the streets and more radical Left groups continued to demand an end to the monarchy—or at least the king's unconditional surrender—moderate forces remained committed to the minimal objective of a multiparty constitutional monarchy agreed upon before the revolutionary situation. They focused on negotiating a new interim government and a permanent end to the *panchayat* system. Muffled were people's cries for an end to the monarchy—to say nothing of justice for dozens of people killed by the king's men, for hundreds wounded, thousands imprisoned, and countless incidents of brutality.

Through "constructive" talks with the king and armed forces, the NC salvaged the king's position by buttressing up their own.[52] With negotiations between the moderate opposition and entrenched *panchas*, an elite-led transition to a formal democratic government was accomplished, a process Huntington referred to as "transplacement."[53] One report told how the United States encouraged NC to "agree to a compromise with the palace and to a constitutional monarchy in order to prevent the growth of the Left in Nepal."[54]

At that time, few realized that the movement had been prematurely brought to an end. Stopping the bloodshed pleased everyone, and on April 9, the day after the announcement of the agreement between the king and MRD, joyous throngs appeared in the streets in Kathmandu. Hundreds of thousands of people again surged into the streets and converged in a carnival of democracy at Tundikhel parade grounds. Almost all those arrested during the movement were released. Everywhere red flags were waving and vermillion powder (*abir*) was in the air. In what was an ecstatic moment for many people, "All felt how strong and deep-rooted was the desire for liberty in human beings. People forgot for the moment that Nepal is one of the poorest countries in the world."[55]

Among the hundreds of thousands of people, some guessed that their leaders had already decided to save the king. They refused to believe the party representatives who spoke from the stage and promised that the movement would not end—that it was simply "changing form." People's desire for something more than what their leaders were ready to give them was evident when many people booed G.P. Koirala, general secretary of NC, as he hailed the victory of "both the people and the king." After the loud chorus of shouts and whistles subsided, people on the stage had to act quickly to stave off a physical assault on him by the crowd.[56]

Although the radical UNPM openly criticized the MRD for giving up without finishing off the *panchayat* system, they did not want to split the movement or to see bloodshed continue. Their public statements called MRD actions "an act of treachery against the people of Nepal" but they were at a loss to do anything about it. People's autonomous mobilizations still occurred, but with the uprising's coordinating committee negotiating with the king, possibilities for independent actions were restricted. In dozens of cities and towns, the Left held mass meetings to celebrate "liberation" and organized condolence meetings to mourn martyrs.

To their credit, MRD leaders refused to join the new *panchayat* government appointed by the king and insisted on a new government. As the crown continued to oppose a multiparty parliamentary system, people refused to stand by. On the night of April 15, as opposition politicians and members of the royal government remained secluded in talks at Royal Academy Hall, thousands of people surrounded the building. They demanded dissolution of all officials appointed by the king and the immediate formation of an interim government. To make sure they made their point, they padlocked the entrances into the hall. At 3:00 a.m., when the interim prime minister tried to leave, the crowd destroyed his car. He finally did manage to leave—and drove straight to the palace and resigned. The next day, the king proclaimed an end to the *panchayat* system.

On April 19, formal agreement was reached for an interim government, and NC leader K.P. Bhattarai was sworn in as prime minister (the first "democratic" prime minister since his elder brother had held the same position almost thirty years before.) The new government's other ten ministers included representatives from the ULF as well as royal appointees. For politicians and parties, this was a great day, but for many others, little had changed.

Unfinished Character of *Jana Andolan* 1

As most people had adhered to the wish of the political parties to refrain from using arms, bloodshed during the *jana andolan* was far less than during European insurrections of the nineteenth and early twentieth century. Nonetheless, human rights groups counted at least five hundred people killed in the course of the national uprising—a number also used by Krishna Prasad Bhattarai, the new prime minister. Others put the number at twice that, but when the official commission of inquiry reported a year later, it established only sixty-two deaths.[57] While the majority of those killed were Newaris (the traditional inhabitants of the Kathmandu valley), everyone suffered from the government's repressive measures. Three-fourths of those killed were less than twenty-five years old. One book published the names and addresses of 1,307 people who had been wounded.[58] In addition to the deaths, somewhere between eight and twenty-five thousand people had been arrested.[59]

While for some, the revolution may have ended in early April, for many others, the gains made then were only the first taste of victories they expected were yet to come. Once political parties had been legalized, politicians sought to stop spontaneous mobilizations. Workers striking for decent wages were not supported, parents whose children had been killed or wounded by the king's police found no one listening to their justified complaints, and poverty remained a problem. People wanted justice, and neither the king nor the new government would give it to them.

A marked increase in crime led many neighborhoods to strengthen their own autonomous security networks, (much like in Burma, where high rates of criminal activity, sometimes involving the police, made many people feel unsafe after the movement's initial upsurge). Vigilante groups, composed of young men armed with lengths of pipe or wooden poles, patrolled neighborhoods throughout the capital, including Dilli Bazar, Asontole, Naya Bazar, Lainchaur, Jyatha, and Thamel.[60] Police and *mandales* continued to be involved in thefts, burglaries in homes and businesses, and attacks on individuals. In other places, the power vacuum allowed old political rivalries and long-held grudges to get settled. The country was spinning out of anyone's control. While communists posted hit lists in public places naming those who had murdered demonstrators, police refused to cooperate with the commissions investigating the dozens of deaths—or even to help find more than a hundred missing persons.

As police continued to brutalize and arrest activists, people finally took matters into their own hands. In Patan, police were thought to be behind the arson of some sixty houses on April 17, and the situation grew especially tense.[61] On April 23, nearly a dozen *mandales* driving police cars were captured by people in Teku and taken to the center of Kathmandu. Denounced at an open-air meeting, at least six were then executed. One account says they were beaten to death.[62] Others claim they were lynched.[63] Although the general inspector of police and home minister arrived and pleaded for the release of the remaining hostages, angry people quickly surrounded (*gheraed*) them. Later that day, the minister was compelled to go to a crowded theatre and promise he would fire the police chief.

Elsewhere in the capital, a parade of people carried police corpses along with wounded officers and shouted antimonarchal slogans. After being identified as *mandales*, these "people's prisoners" were tried, and some were executed.[64] The new government ordered police to intervene. When the procession approached Hanuman Dhoka, one of the main temples of Kathmandu, police on rooftops opened fire, killing two demonstrators and wounding more.[65] In many parts of the capital, the situation appeared to spin out of anyone's control. A crowd gathered outside the office of a zonal administration.[66] After cars were set ablaze, police opened fire. Near Dilli Bazaar, a crowd set fire to the house of a *mandale* leader. There were further reports of selected lynchings of *mandales* and police.[67] A rumor with wide currency had the queen shooting—and possibly killing—the king for his refusal to sign a check. Meanwhile, on the same day in nearby valley towns, another six policemen were beaten to death, and police gunfire killed about a dozen people.[68]

On April 25, hundreds of police carried the bodies of their slain colleagues in a public procession aimed at fomenting counterrevolution. Shouting "blood for blood" and promising to restore the *panchayat* system, they torched a government office. Rumors swirled of a coming palace coup, of Indian troops massing on the border, and of the water supply being poisoned. The new government appealed for calm. Prime Minister K.P. Bhattarai threatened to resign unless the king offered his public support. Once he received the royal nod, he ordered a nighttime curfew for Kathmandu, later extended it to Patan and Kirtipur, and called upon the army to enforce it. The former opposition leader had few qualms using force to maintain order. The army remained in the streets of Kathmandu until May 9 and Patan until May 14. Universal fear of crowds notwithstanding, both the entrenched royal power and the opposition parties were clearly overwhelmed by the popular impetus.

Undeterred by threats of a royal coup—or should I say because of them?—mobilizations intensified. In the six months between formation of the interim government and the proclamation of a new constitution of November 9, the country was the scene of enormous social struggles. In Pokhara on April 30, only police gunfire that killed five protesters saved a high official whose home was surrounded by hundreds of people who believed he had set fire to the local *panchayat* office to destroy documents linking him to police atrocities.

Called "chaos" by some, people's creativity continued alongside more violent actions. In Ramechap at the end of September, a large crowd gathered and packed up all the papers and documents of their district headquarters and moved it to what they considered a more suitable location. (In Denmark, antiapartheid activists used this same sort of action, which they called "compulsory relocation," against South African businesses.)[69] In this Nepalese case, fighting broke out with a rival group, and police reinforcements were called in. The "anarchy and chaos" made some remember the *panchayat* system fondly. One former minister remarked, "In the name of democracy, mob-ocracy has been established!"[70] He complained, "People cannot wear their jewelry or other valuables. You are afraid to walk in the streets and people no longer let the traffic pass easily."

For some people, democracy (*prajatantra*) was little more than another word for crime, but for the less privileged, the new opening gave them hope for change.[71] Landless Shukumbasis blocked roads and surrounded the district government building on February 4, 1991. When an expected visit from the prime minister failed to materialize, two hundred police attacked. People fought back, forcing the police into their station house. The crowd refused to disperse, and police opened fire, killing at least three people. (According to activists, three others were also killed, but the police hid their bodies.)

The Uprising's Renewal of Civil Society

As in South Korea where the victory of democratic forces in the June Uprising of 1987 led to a tidal wave of industrial strikes, workers immediately mobilized after the democratic breakthrough in Nepal. On April 20, workers demanded higher wages and better working conditions, and strikes hit all Kathmandu Valley factories.[72] Groups of office workers occupied government buildings. At the same time, organized relay hunger strikes and *gheraus* (encircling a person and publicly humiliating them) broke out. A former *pancha* observed, "Nobody is working. You go to some offices and people only come once a week to do their attendance and get their pay. The lower staff isn't obeying the senior staff. The senior staff cannot handle the situation and find it impossible to give orders. Everywhere employees bang tables against their chiefs. The workers are always on strike."[73]

In May, professors' demand for the dismissal of *panchayat* era administrators was granted; in June, a hunger strike by the Nepal Teachers' Association ended only after all their demands were met; in August, a hunger strike by journalists brought sympathetic government intervention. In September, radical writers and artists protested the newly reconstituted Royal Nepal Academy because of its domination by male, pro-Congress members.

Between 1951 and 1979, only 74 strikes had been recorded (fewer than three a year over nearly three decades), yet from 1991 to 1992, 128 strikes were reported. The following year, twenty-five strikes broke out—more than eight times the previous average.[74] (The main reason for strikes was wage grievances, but a few were called for shorter workweeks and better conditions.)

Alongside workplace struggles, religious, cultural and social conflicts were visibly intensified. Indeed, "it seemed as if every caste, linguistic group, or ethnic community raised its voice in one way or another in the six months between the end of the revolution and the announcement of the new constitution."[75] For the first time, Buddhists became a visible political force. On June 30, 1990, the Nepal Buddhist Association led some twenty thousand people in Kathmandu on a show of support for a secular state. Although a tiny minority, Christians also advocated a secular state. With thirty different ethnicities and almost a hundred languages, Nepali society is far from uniform. If the king's autocratic rule had made the country seem unified, democracy exposed deep social divisions. Since the eighteenth century, high-caste Hindu rule had rested upon religious and linguistic grounds. Suddenly, all that seemed solid vanished. Tibeto-Burmese Newaris, whose uprisings in Patari, Bhaktapur, and Kirtipur were central to the 1990 revolution, joined with Mongol, Tamang, and Magar to demand greater autonomy. One analyst concluded, "The 1990 movement gave women, Dalits, and other low caste groups—ethnic groups as well as regional, linguistic, religious, and a plethora of other groups—the legal and political voice required to resist the old legitimacy of ascription, oppression and discrimination."[76] So rapidly did ethnic/caste identities develop in this dynamic period that the government's Central Bureau of Statistics had counted fifty-nine groups in 1991, a number that nearly doubled to a hundred in 2001.[77]

Women mobilized as never before. Some immediately began agitating for equal property rights for women. In 1992, a large protest was mounted in the Terai city of Butwal. By 1995, the All Nepal Women's Association passed a "Women's Rights Charter" that formally recognized females' equal rights to family property.[78] One of the groups that grew out of the uprising, the Feminist Dalit Organization (FDO), reveals the extent to which Nepali society was transformed after 1990.

Formed in 1994, activist women in FDO sought to counter the two dimensions of oppression they suffered: patriarchal values that discriminate against women, and the caste system that places all Dalits in conditions of extraordinary hardship. At least 14 percent of Nepal's people are Dalits—80 percent of whom live below the official poverty line.[79] They are not allowed to enter many temples and routinely face discrimination in jobs and payscales. In the countryside, many Dalits are landless sharecroppers; in the cities, it is estimated that 80 percent of sex workers are Dalits.

Participation of women in the movement led to many families experiencing changes in everyday power relations. Yet the status of women remains greatly suppressed. Women's life expectancy is shorter, literacy rates far below that of men (65.1 percent of men were literate in 2001 compared with only 42.5 percent of women). Estimates reported that from seven to ten thousand women and children were sold every year into the sex trade in India. Another estimate reported nearly ten times that many—about a hundred thousand Nepali girls every year—being delivered to prostitution houses in India, and as many as twice that number working there at any given time.[80] Bonded child labor was common, since rural families often needed cash. Children lucky enough not to be sold as indentured servants were often compelled to work at home since they were needed to contribute to the house and the farm from an early age. Deprived of an education, many children became lifelong illiterates—a large majority of them female. In 1992, a Bonded Laborers Liberation formed; eight years later, legislation passed outlawing such forms of slavery.[81]

The uprising not only gave new impetus to insurgent workers, women, bonded laborers, and ethnic minorities, it also energized activists in a diversity of efforts. In 1974, only 15 registered NGOs could be counted in all of Nepal.[82] In 1977, with the queen as chair, 37 social service organizations formed a national council that by 1990 grew to include 219 groups. Seven years after the 1990 uprising, the number of NGOs had mushroomed to 5,128 that were registered with the national Social Welfare Council. In the same year, another estimate counted more than twenty thousand.[83] Another analyst claimed there were at least six thousand voluntary NGOs, not including "political parties, their frontal vocational or class organizations, trade unions, student organizations and the network of quasi-governmental local and municipal organizations."[84] The number of formally organized cooperatives also skyrocketed after the uprising: from a total of 850 prior to 1992, in 1997 nearly four times as many (3,200) existed.[85] Most significantly, new found freedoms won and energies generated by the *jana andolan* impelled a huge expansion of autonomous media. From far fewer than 400 newspapers in 1990, their number more than doubled to over 874 in 1996.[86]

Nepal's vibrant civil society helped to produce the 1990 civil uprising. In turn, the *jana andolan* strengthened many sources of civil society: independent media, cooperatives, progressive NGOs, minority movements, feminism, and workers' movements. Today, as Nepal continues to seek a new constitution, the capacity of its people to create new forms for action, central to the victorious uprising of 1990, remains one of the country's great resources. Understanding the mutually

reinforcing relationship of civil society and popular uprisings is key to comprehending a secret to movement building: long-term organizing efforts and sporadic
insurgencies can be additive and complementary. Often portrayed in either/or
terms, such a dichotomy more often than not privileges patient and quiet activism over militant confrontation politics. Nepal's 1990 uprising provides a vivid
and instructive example of how popular insurgency can help amplify strengths
of civil society.

The Interim Government

In January of 1990, few people could have guessed that before the end of the year
(on November 9, coincidentally exactly a year to the day after the fall of the Berlin
Wall), King Birendra would be proclaiming a new democratic constitution. Yet the
people's uprising left him no other choice—short of complete abdication. During
times when people mobilize in extraordinary ways—as they do during popular
uprisings—time becomes so compressed that what normally takes years can be
accomplished in a few days.

While people in the streets called for an end to the monarchy—a cry echoed
by more radical communists—mainstream politicians would hear nothing of
it. From the start, politicians were clear that the MRD's goal was constitutional
democracy. At the NC conference on January 18, 1990, so strong was monarchist
sentiment among the NC elite that the party's "supreme leader," Ganesh Man
Singh, clearly stated that "abolition of the monarchy is tantamount to the end of
democracy in Nepal."[87]

Assured by the NC that he would remain on the throne as a constitutional
monarch, the king finally ordered the end of the *panchayat* system on April 27.
Dissolution of village and town *panchayats* meant that for the first time in over
thirty years political parties were legal, freedom of expression and association
had been won, and people would be voting for a parliament. Despite political
reforms, of course, everyday life was large unaffected. Traditional feudal relationships in the countryside remained intact—the old *panchas* retained power, and
caste continued to delimit the meager life-possibilities for much of the country.
Instead of justice, people encountered corruption, discrimination, lack of
accountability, and extortion by police and local officials. As inflation increased
sharply, it became clear the new regime had failed to ameliorate economic hardships afflicting so many people.

When the *panchayat* system was abolished in favor of a representative
democracy, months passed before anyone felt secure under the auspices of the
new regime. The king remained in the palace—albeit as a constitutional monarch
rather than an absolute one. Practically none of the administrative positions of
the bureaucracy changed. Many former *panchas* simply joined the NC, some even
running for office as part of the party's slate. During the early 1990s, NC strategy
for democratic consolidation was to integrate traditional elites into its ranks. The
steady flow of *panchas* into NC soon saw members of the old regime outnumber-
ing Congress's old guard by the time the new constitution was in place.[88] To top
it off, nepotism with the NC remained overt. When the party's list of candidates

in Kathmandu was announced, people were shocked to learn that longtime activists had been passed over in favor of the wife and son of Ganesh Man Singh, the "commander" of the democracy movement.

Radical opposition forces, afraid of a split in the movement, only insisted upon a minimal program—not on a complete surrender by the palace as many ordinary Nepalis hoped. In the interim government dominated by the NC, old *panchas* held positions of power, and they permitted no punishment of past abuses. Despite dozens—if not hundreds—of state-sanctioned killings during the uprising, no one was ever held responsible. Subsequent commissions ultimately named police and high officials responsible and even recommended criminal charges, but none were ever brought.[89] In February 1991, five high-level officials were dismissed, but further punishment was never meted out. No "truth and reconciliation commission" as in South Africa or trials as in South Korea were ever established.

Caught in a vise-grip between a mobilized citizenry who demanded immediate changes and a king who dragged his feet on agreeing to a new constitution, the interim government rushed the process of constitutional revision. The NC was unable even to summon the will to override the palace's insistence that the king was the "incarnation of God."[90] Despite widespread sentiment for a secular state, high-caste Brahmins who controlled the country's major institutions refused to budge. To many people's relief, months of wrangling over the constitution ended in November, and elections were scheduled for May 12, 1991. The new constitution named Nepal a "Hindu, monarchical kingdom." Although caste discrimination was officially made illegal, demands for school education to be held in some of the thirty-eight mother tongues of different ethnic groups were rejected. Both Congress and the ULF supported "equal rights for women," and the new constitution called for 5 percent of all candidates for any party to be women.[91] Nonetheless, their differences on the retention of the monarchy—even a constitutional one— were quite large. Once the 1990 victory was won in April, radical communists lobbied intensively for the new constitution to give the people the right to abolish the monarchy through a popular vote.[92] They were also in the forefront of many *bandhs* (shutdowns of businesses and traffic in urban areas) and championed the rights of minorities. While the political elite clumsily compromised on a constitution swearing the king's divinity, many activists turned away from traditional forms of politics and focused on changing everyday lives as a fundamental of social change. Ethnic groups' autonomy, women's liberation, and caste discrimination all became thematized and helped guide grassroots political initiatives.

In the months before elections in May 1991, the World Bank, the United States, Japan, and India all expressed concern about repression. The government may have stabilized the situation, but its failure to punish—or even remove from positions of authority—those officials responsible for killing demonstrators further enflamed an already volatile situation. Perhaps most significantly, the IMF structural adjustment regime remained firmly in place, bringing with it increased poverty and hardship for the poorest of the poor. The demise of planned economies in Eastern Europe abetted international capital's increasing penetration of Nepal's economy. With the rest of the world, soon to include liberated South Africa and democratic South Korea, joining the global chorus singing hallelujahs to neoliberal hymns, tiny Nepal could not radically depart in the direction of autonomous economic development.

As the elections approached, differences between parties became more pronounced. The ULF and NC ultimately parted ways in January 1991, largely because of ULF objections to the growing royalist presence inside the NC. Subsequently, communist groups realigned: the ULF split, and two of its members, the moderate Communist Party of Nepal (Marxist) and Communist Party of Nepal (Marxist-Leninist), merged to create the Communist Party of Nepal (Unified Marxist-Leninist). The most radical communists formed a new United People's Front (UPF). In the spirited election campaign, marked in many outlying areas by fisticuffs, students played central roles. They demanded a month-long furlough to travel back to their homes to participate, and the interim government immediately agreed.

Despite violent confrontations that resulted in six deaths, the voting itself was orderly, and in a country with only 40 percent literacy, some 65 percent of those eligible voted. The election was widely regarded as fair and its results accepted by all parties—even by the far Left and the remnants of the *panchas*. Although the Anglo-American winner-take-all system favored the larger parties, communists won a surprising victory, receiving 36.6 percent of the vote (only slightly less than the Congress Party's) and some eighty-two seats in the new parliament.[93] They swept Kathmandu, defeating the interim prime minister as well as the wife and son of Ganesh Man Singh. The NC was the only party that ran a national slate with candidates in nearly every district, and they won a majority of the seats. The most radical party, the UPF, won a surprising nine seats, while parties associated with the old *panchayat* system garnered only four seats (and 12 percent of the vote), as can be seen in TABLE 7.2.

Although the elections dealt monarchists a severe blow, Brahmin domination of the new government was an ominous sign. It was only a matter of time before the country lapsed into intense new struggles. Strikes, walkouts, protests, and demonstrations greeted the new NC government even before it was worn in. Immediately after the elections, civil servants went on strike for their third time since the democratic breakthrough; they "paralyzed the new government in its first two months in office."[94] As inflation continued to rise, economic collapse was a constant fear. The government seemed powerless, and corruption continued to plague it. The monarchy slyly bided its time before it could "save the country" and become the solution to the disintegration of Nepalese society.

While politicians vied for positions of power, radical communists took direct action. Less than two years after the election, on April 5, 1992, the Joint People's Agitation Committee called for thirty minutes' lights-out in Kathmandu. Violence broke out outside Bir Hospital when activists tried to enforce the blackout by attacking cars. The next day, the government used force to prevent an open-air meeting in the center of Kathmandu. After police attacked, some in the crowd tried to burn down the Nepal Telecommunication building. Police opened fire, killing at least seven (some counted fourteen dead) and wounding dozens more.[95]

The *Guardian* opined that a "a wave of popular discontent is threatening to derail the country's infant democracy."[96]

In 1994, when the NC narrowly garnered more votes than the CP-UML (33.4 percent to 30.9 percent), a minority coalition formed led by self-described Marxist-Leninists, making Nepal a rare example of a communist monarchy. Between 1995 and 1999, half a dozen coalitions alternated in power, until the 1999 elections gave Congress an absolute majority. By 2002, twelve years of multiparty parliamentary democracy had produced ten governments, none of which proved able to move the country forward. Low-caste people, ethnic minorities, and women remained underrepresented in the parliaments. (Women were never more than 5.6 percent of elected representatives.)[97] As the country's economy faltered, more than two million young people left Nepal in search of jobs elsewhere. With the increasingly repressive rule of parliamentary governments, many Left activists became prepared to fight them with arms.

In the estimation of Maoist leader Barburam Bhattarai, the upper class that had supported parliamentary reform in 1990 gradually returned to the monarchist camp while the lower class and a section of the middle strata was won over to people's war.[98] Because the two key components of power—the army and national sovereignty—remained in the hands of the king, the 1990 constitution was fatally flawed.[99] More, corruption among the political elite was so endemic that even U.S. senator Patrick Leahy expressed disappointment with the country's 1990s governments: "The leaders of the country's political parties distinguished themselves by amassing personal fortunes and doing little for the people."[100]

The Maoist Impetus

As early as 1972, Nepali opposition politics, divided into Left and democratic tendencies, was fragmented as in few other countries. Even Nepal's communists were organized into no fewer than fourteen parties that varied widely on interpretations of revolutionary theory and ways to implement it in practice. All agreed on the need to fight the monarchy, and their unity was an important driving force

TABLE 7.2 **National Election Results, May 1991**

Party	Seats won	% total seats	% of the vote
Nepali Congress	110	53.65	37.75
Communist Party of Nepal (Unified Marxist-Leninist)	69	33.66	27.98
National Democratic Party (Chand)	3	1.46	6.56
National Democratic Party (Thapa)	1	0.49	5.38
United People's Front	9	4.39	4.83
Nepal Sadbhavana Party	6	2.93	4.10
Communist Party of Nepal (Democratic)	2	0.98	2.43
Nepal Workers' and Peasants' Party	2	0.98	1.25
Independents/other parties	3	1.46	9.72
TOTAL	205	100	100

Sources: Hutt, *Nepal*, 78; Hoftun et al., *People, Politics and Ideology*, 183.

behind the broader movement's mobilizations. Before 1990, communists had no real power in the country, but as people awakened, their clear positions against monarchy, caste rule, class domination, and patriarchy won them many new supporters. Groups that espoused notions of federalism immediately found they had many members drawn from ethnic minorities. Nepalese communism's consistent focal point was economic inequality—a scar on society that no other parties seemed able to prioritize, let alone to impact. Communists' prominent role in the 1990 uprising encouraged them to take new autonomous initiatives and brought them unanticipated electoral victories.

In the Nepali context, communism's unique appeal needs to be understood through the prism of cultural traditions. As longtime activist Tulsi Lal Amatya, communist leader in Patan, explained: "In our ancient days, our Hindu sages (*rishis*) used to recite a saying which went like this: 'Let us live together, let us eat together, let us work together, let our intellect grow, and let us not be envious of each other. Let us live together like friends, as a family.' And this is what we mean by communism . . . let nobody suffer under the system because they are all human beings. . . . Buddha said that the principle of the ruler is that there should be nobody in this kingdom who has tears in their eyes. And what the Buddha stands for is also what we communists stand for."[101] Amatya continued: "Communist ideas of equality go hand in hand with a Buddhist concept of compassion and of the righteous Newar king." (Crucial to the success of the 1990 revolution, the mass uprising in Patan also grew from the ethnic solidarity of the town's Newaris.)

After the 1990 revolution, communists remained in the forefront of rural struggles. While the mainstream political parties entered the new government in Kathmandu (and failed for the most part to build democratic forms of popular participation), leftists moved into the countryside, filling a vacuum left by the demise of the *panchayat* apparatus. The dire situation of the rural poor—a great portion of the population—had hardly changed with the new government.

The most radical communist group, the Communist Party of Nepal (Maoist), failed to win a single seat in the 1994 general election and was excluded from the subsequent UML government. Launching a people's war in February 1996, the small party of only 85 cadre and leaders grew into a People's Army of anywhere from five thousand to nineteen thousand armed combatants in a few years. Like the uprising of 1990, the armed rural insurgency gained supporters faster than anyone—including its leadership—had expected.[102] In at least twenty-one districts, they formed people's governments through direct elections in which everyone except "feudal elements" and "comprador and bureaucratic capitalists" participated.

The Maoist parallel judicial system won wide support among the rural poor.[103] Their redistribution of wealth at the village level endeared them to many whom they freed from generations of servile existence. They burned bank records of farmers' debts and assaulted tax collectors and moneylenders who charged up to 60 percent annual interest to beleaguered villagers. In many cases, if these moneylenders had compelled families to sell their children into sexual slavery in order to pay off their debts, communist justice imposed a death sentence. The

Maoists redistributed land, promoted women to positions of leadership, formed all-female fighting units, and lent money to needy individuals at normal rates of interest. They banned dice, cards, and alcohol and strictly enforced a prohibition on male violence against wives. They compelled schools to stop teaching the arcane Sanskrit texts the monarchy had imposed on ethnic minorities and lowered the fees for private schools so that not just the children of the rich could attend.

Although they spoke on behalf of ordinary Nepalis, Maoists remained a force above the people. On the back cover of a Maoist journal, party leaders were pictured as successors to Shah monarchs.[104] The people's movement of 1990 had spread outward from Kathmandu, but the Maoists strategy was to invert that direction, building up rural base areas and surrounding the capital. In May 2002, official estimates put Maoists in control of 25 percent of the country.[105] By 2003, they had captured nearly all big property owners' land, but the Royal Nepalese Army (RNA) prevented people from farming it. By 2006, Maoist adaptation of the Chinese path to power (prolonged people's war from secured base areas) was so successful that they controlled more than half the countryside and seemed poised to bring their armed campaign to the capital—where it was said they had already their own tax system on many businesses.[106] By 2005, the United Revolutionary People's Council was believed to be the embryo of a new government, and many expected the Maoists to seize power. The United States was worried, and on May 2, 2002, President George W. Bush instructed Prime Minister Deuba, "Go get them, fight them, and finish them."[107] The United States provided more than $20 million in military aid and an additional $40 million in development aid to support the war effort.

The specific precursor of the Maoist insurgency, like so many other political tendencies in Nepal, can be traced to India—in this case to the Naxalbari outbreak of armed struggle against landlords in 1967. Nepal's first Naxalite inspired action came in 1971, in the area around Jhapa in Nepal's Southeast, where seven "class enemies" were eliminated before the insurgency was suppressed.[108] Over the course of the Maoist campaign beginning in the mid-1990s, estimates put the number of people killed at more than thirteen thousand—eight thousand at the hands of the RNA and police and five thousand by Maoists.[109] Another five thousand were missing. The U.S.-trained RNA repeatedly perpetrated human rights abuses against the population as they killed thousands of "suspected Maoists." Human rights organizations counted about two thousand people victimized by government extrajudicial killings in only a "fraction of the cases" between 2001 and 2004.[110] The World Bank estimated destruction of property caused by the war at $300 million between February 1996 and May 2002, and the country's GDP shrank from 2001 to 2002.

October 4, 2002, Royal Coup d'État
In a bloody palace massacre on June 1, 2001, King Birendra and all of his immediate family were slain, and Gyanendra was proclaimed the new monarch. (Although one of the princes was blamed for the slaughter, many people believe the new

king was responsible, motivated by his predecessor's secret dialogue with the Maoists and failure to permit the army to take decisive action against the guerrillas.) The Achilles heal of the 1990 constitution was Article 115, which granted the king power to declare a state of emergency. On May 22, 2002, King Gyanendra dissolved the parliament, and a few months later, on October 4, he seized absolute power. In addition to enforcing strict media censorship, his government banned any kind of gathering, procession, sit-in, and rally in and around the capital city and other districts. Once the king had abrogated freedom of assembly in Kathmandu, the movement against his autocratic rule spread to other cities. New restrictions prevented people from traveling to protests elsewhere. As arbitrary arrests and the use of plastic bullets became everyday events, professionals—especially health care workers—overwhelmingly joined the movement. Many of the protests were led by the All Nepal Free Student Union, whose red, blue, and yellow flags often became the assembly point for those brave enough to risk police brutality and arrest by going into the streets.

On February 1, 2005, the king declared martial law using the pretext of the threat from the Maoist rebels in the countryside. Telephone lines were cut, and the prime minister and other political leaders were detained. Satellites were shut off, media censored, and airports closed. Three days later, army helicopters fired on protesting students in Pokhara, wounding fifteen people. Within ten months, over six thousand people were summarily arrested, many held without medical treatment at undisclosed detention centers. Luckier activists fled to India and regrouped. The country seemed headed for catastrophe, caught between the king's iron heel and the Maoists' iron fist.

To lead the country out of the clutches of a looming disaster, a Seven Party Alliance (SPA) formed.[111] Since it was again illegal in Nepal to belong to a political party, Gyanendra ordered countless raids on homes and businesses in attempts to locate members of the SPA. Suspects were beaten and tortured to elicit information on movement plans and membership. On November 22, 2005, encouraged by Indian officials, the SPA and Maoists signed an agreement to unite against the monarchy. The parties promised to hold elections for a constituent assembly with power to revise the constitution, and the Maoists promised to respect multiparty democracy and freedom of speech.

An opposition-called *bandh* brought Kathmandu to a standstill on January 24, 2006.[112] Withdrawing their unilateral ceasefire in January 2006, the Maoists insisted on another *bandh*, this one for a week, at the end of February and used their military strength to cut off Kathmandu, crippling transportation from March 14. On the 19th, they agreed to the SPA's request to lift the blockade and also joined the SPA's call for a four-day *bandh* beginning on April 6.[113] Boycotting scheduled municipal elections in February, they prepared for a new people's uprising. On January 19, 2006, the day before planned protests against the king's municipal elections, police rounded up over one hundred activists.[114] A series of confrontations lasted into mid-February in which hundreds more people were arrested, and police routinely opened fire on people bold enough to protest in public. Many activists were killed or wounded. The Asia Human Rights Commission (AHRC) documented at least eight hundred cases of torture between March 2005 and April 2006.[115]

Jana Andolan 2—The 2006 *Loktantra Andolan*

On April 6, exactly sixteen years after the first *jana andolan* according to the Nepali Calendar, the leadership of the democracy movement again mobilized massively. Although they did not initially call for another prolonged popular uprising, autonomous grassroots initiatives transformed their planned four-day countrywide general strike into *Jana Andolan* 2—a nineteen-day uprising that finally drove the monarchy from power. As in 1990, people courageously took the streets despite great danger, and many were beaten and arrested—twenty-one were killed. Once again, ordinary people's visions for what was needed were more radical—and accurate—than that of the leading parties. This time the Maoist armed struggle supplemented the unarmed insurgency. More than any other factor, thousands of people's stubborn refusals to submit to overwhelming state power carried the day. A nationwide *bandh* brought traffic to a standstill and transformed the entire country. At its high point, five million people were involved, while millions more watched with passionate hope.[116] On the monarchy's side, there was no lack of will to employ violence to maintain the king's rule. All together, alongside the 21 martyrs of *Jana Andolan* 2, 18 others disappeared, more than 3,723 were wounded, and 2,979 arrested.[117]

During the first days of the protests, only a few thousand people appeared in the streets, but their numbers grew rapidly as the uprising unfolded. On April 5, security forces rounded up nearly all major party leaders—some fifty in all—and government forces killed Darsan Lal Yadav as he peacefully protested in Saptari. The next day, the first in the planned general strike, over 450 people—including at least 17 journalists—were arrested in Kathmandu. Where mass arrests failed to deter protests, police used clubs and mercilessly beat unarmed people. When beatings failed to quiet the streets, bullets were used—but nothing could contain people's yearnings for freedom.

Unlike the 1990 uprising, when the unarmed people's movement faced the army alone, the 2006 *jana andolan* intimately intertwined the Maoist-led armed struggle in the countryside with vibrant popular mobilizations. The unity of these two disparate strands of opposition gave the Nepalese movement strength and resiliency unknown in countries where social movements remain bitterly divided (and sometimes even antagonistically pitted against each other). On April 3, Maoists announced a unilateral ceasefire in the Kathmandu valley. Enforcing a blockade of roads leading into the capital, elsewhere they launched a military offensive. During the night of April 6, they overran the town of Malangawa and freed 197 prisoners. A government helicopter equipped with special night vision capability crashed—the RNA claimed technical problems, while Maoists insisted they had shot it down. On April 8, thousands of guerrillas attacked in Butwal and Kapilvastu, freed more prisoners, and destroyed police posts as well as army barracks. "Without the armed struggle, there would have been no victory in 2006," Maoist leader Shalik Ram Jamkattel told me in Kathmandu.[118]

The movement's coordinated military offensive and general strike presented the monarchy with a qualitatively higher order of threat—and the king responded with a greater level of violence against street assemblies. On April 7, medical personnel joined the protests as did bank and telecommunication workers. Taxis that violated the *bandh* were vandalized. On April 8, the king ordered a curfew from 7:00 to 8:00 p.m. and insisted protestors would be shot on sight. Mobile phone services were cut off. Despite heavy police presence, protesters defied the curfew in many locations, and dozens were injured. In Pokhara, at least one person was shot dead and two more injured. Three women sitting in their veranda were wounded by police gunfire in Bharatpur. In Chitwan, more than fifty thousand demonstrators took over government offices and held them for hours.

The next day, the SPA promised that protests would continue indefinitely and called on people to refuse to pay taxes. In Banepa, one person was killed when police opened fire and three others were wounded. In Janakpur, almost a thousand workers in a cigarette factory walked off the job to support the general strike. In Parasi, telecommunications, banks, electrical workers, and other state employees all joined the protests. Security forces opened fire in many parts of the country, including Pokhara and Synagja, killing three people and wounding at least twenty-six more.[119] As the wounded poured into hospitals, medical workers organized protests at hospitals in many districts.

As the government curfew was extended—and people continued to remain in the streets—police began invading homes. In Pulchowk, they opened fire on a peaceful rally by the Engineers' Association. In Pokhara, university and school-teachers defied the curfew to protest the many injuries, and dozens were arrested. Journalists throughout the country marched against the lack of press freedom and imprisonment of dozens of their colleagues. For their efforts, many were severely beaten. In Kathmandu, five hundred doctors rallied—as did physicians in at least nine other districts.

On April 11, the sixth day of protests, the SPA called for an indefinite general strike, while the king extended the curfew. More than two dozen people were wounded by gunfire in Gongabu.[120] In Lalitpur, residents chased away security forces after they opened fire. In Pokhara, police again opened fire on a rally of thousands. In Thamel, nine tourists who called for restoration of democracy were arrested. Police opened fire on a poetry reading in the Baneshwar district of Kathmandu.[121]

As professionals continued to mobilize on April 12, police arrested dozens of professors, journalists, teachers, and lawyers. In Pokhara, a rally by the Professionals' Association for Peace and Democracy resulted in 239 arrests. On the thirteenth, lawyers who peacefully assembled were fired upon with rubber bullets, and three were wounded. Many more were injured when police charged with clubs, and seventy were arrested at the rally of a thousand attorneys organized by the Nepal Bar Association.

As the protests built momentum from April 9 to 21, the numbers of people in the streets increased to three hundred thousand (some claimed half a million). On April 10, the day of Birkham Sambat (Nepal's New Year), massive crowds flooded the capital's streets, and protests occurred in hundreds of towns throughout the country. The next night, as more people were killed and wounded, soldiers mercilessly beat students in a medical school dormitory. Despite the king's heavy hand, people refused to stay home. The army shot dead one protester in Pokhara and their bullets hit many others. Ambulance and health care workers were denied permits to pick up the wounded, but they braved army reprisals to care for them. Barricades and burning tires seemed to be everywhere in the capital. On its outskirts, people torched a government revenue office. Journalists were again rounded up; many reported being kicked and punched while in custody.

Even more than in 1990, people from all walks of life mobilized: farmers and workers, the urban poor, women's groups, cultural workers, students, professors, engineers, lawyers, accountants, bank employees, transportation and government office workers. Their participation in the uprising gave it a new character and was a significant force making it a people's movement, not just an instrument of political parties based upon different sectors of Nepal's urban elite. Peasants traveled from their villages to towns and cities to demonstrate. Actors performed antigovernment plays, musicians sang familiar melodies with new movement-inspired lyrics, comedians used laughter and irony as weapons, and poets inspired through words. When people were not allowed to protest outdoors, they occupied government offices. Besides marches and rallies, other tactics included strikes, sit-ins, and vigils. Everywhere vehicular traffic was halted, bringing the country to a standstill—one within which everything changed—or so it seemed.

Having accumulated experiences in the 1990 uprising, people well understood the need to keep fighting until victory. Prakash Man Singh described the 2006 uprising, as "sustained and durable: 'This should be the last uprising against the king!' was something we all agreed."[122] Knowing that they could prevail against the army and police even with the ban on protests being enforced by bullets and clubs, the opposition was determined to make every arrest and casualty count.

On Thursday, April 13, 2006, about 1,500 lawyers conducted a peaceful vigil near Kathmandu. Police fired at the rally, critically wounding two and injuring

Table 7.3 **Comparison of *Jana Andolan* 1 and 2**

Jana Andolan 1 (1990)	*Jana Andolan* 2 (2006)
Mainly urban	Not limited to main cities—also rural areas. Massive involvement of people
Middle and lower-middle class	Unprecedented numbers
Political change effected: absolute monarchy to constitutional monarchy	Political change effected: constitutional monarchy to republic
Unitary system	Federal system
Hindu state	Secular state
49 days	19 days
Panchayat system toppled	Monarchy ended

Women brought flowers to help persuade security forces to be gentle. Photo by Shruti Shrestha in Kunda Dixit, *A People War: Images of the Nepal Conflict, 1996–2001* (Kathmandu: Jagadamba Press, 2006), 186.

fifty others. They then arrested seventy-two legal workers while firing tear gas to drive off remaining protestors. In response, the Nepali Bar Association resolved to boycott all court cases in the country until prisoners were released and police involved in the firing were punished. Later that day, around a hundred people were arrested at a stadium where NGO activists had gathered. When two hundred journalists protested the censorship, the police attacked their peaceful rally, arresting twenty and injuring many others. After six days of protest, Reporters Without Borders counted ninety-seven Nepali journalists who had been arrested and twenty-three injured.

Mass arrests continued on April 14 and 15, especially in Baglung Municipality and Biratnagar. When political parties convened a peaceful demonstration in Lalitpur, police opened fire, wounding over a hundred people.[123] On April 16 as protests continued unabated, police resumed firing on peaceful rallies, while the SPA called on Nepalis to refuse to pay taxes and to boycott all businesses belonging to the royal family. Thousands of women paraded with musical instruments in Gaighat, and at least five thousand people rallied at the end of the procession. In Tanse, as well, thousands of women marched. In Thamel, thousands of workers and entrepreneurs in the tourism industry protested government repression. In Chitwan, over twenty thousand people attended the SPA rally.

The next day, security forces injured over a hundred people all over the country. Over a hundred bullets were fired in Nijgadh of Bara when people burned the king in effigy. Many were injured and one man killed. In Kathmandu, dozens were wounded when police opened fire in the late afternoon. In Chuchchepati

(Kathmandu), about three dozen women brought flowers and food to security personnel to ask them to stop using force.

Meanwhile in Chitwan, dozens of people were injured when police opened fire. In Kavre, women rallied, while in dozens of other places, people took to the streets and were met with fierce repression. Gunfire in Tanahun and batons in Damauli wounded five people. In Kathmandu, Supreme Court workers sat-in for an hour and wore black armbands. Bank workers protested. The BBC reported crowds of more than a hundred thousand people in Butwal, Nepalganj, and Bhairawa.[124]

On April 18, one person was killed and over a hundred injured. Some thirty-six protesters were wounded by police gunfire in Savagriha Chowk. As protests moved into their third week, torture was reported at Morang prison. Rubber bullets continued to be used alongside live ammunition, and the number of people injured rose dramatically.[125] Although the media were increasingly restricted, dozens of rallies took places throughout the country.

As in 1990, the uprising started as a vehicle for political parties to become legalized and grew into a people's movement. Along with Dalits, tourism workers, teachers, doctors, engineers, disabled people's groups, civil servants, Supreme Court staff, and lawyers all joined the protests. As participation in the movement expanded in ever wider circles of protesters, people's dreams and aspirations grew. "The future agenda to liberate Dalits, women and ethnic groups was set by the people in the streets. Parties did not spearhead that effort."[126]

Unlike in 1990, the police and army fought resolutely to prevent people from going into the streets. In many cases the forces of order chased people inside and beat them for having dared to protest publicly. On April 19, police went as far as breaking into a medical dormitory and violently beating students whom they had observed at protests earlier that day. In Jhapa, two people were shot to death and hundreds more were wounded before the RNA was able to enforce quiet. In Banke, one person was killed. Radio Nepal staff joined the protests. In Nepalganj, a woman was killed after she was hit in the face by a tear gas canister when police attacked a rally of over a hundred thousand.

The next day, in defiance of the extended curfew, an estimated one to three hundred thousand demonstrators gathered peacefully in response to the SPA's call to encircle Kathmandu by massing on Ring Road, the four-lane street around the city.[127] Outside the area where the king had banned gatherings, without provocation, police and soldiers opened fire in Kalanki, killing three people and wounding at least a hundred, nearly a dozen critically. The next day, the victims' families reported that security forces tried in vain to force them to acknowledge that their victimized loved ones were Maoists. In response, massive protests called for the corpses to be released from police custody.

From the Kalanki massacre onward, the size of protests expanded even more dramatically. On April 21, a "human sea poured in the capital."[128] According to the *New York Times*, "Hang the King!" became a popular mantra of many demonstrators. Sources claim that a million people participated in the demonstrations despite the curfew.[129] In Pokhara, nearly a hundred thousand people joined in

Madhav Kumar Nepal addressed people in Kalanki. Photo by Bimal Chandra Sharma.

the protest march. That evening, after a meeting with a special envoy from India, King Gyanendra appeared to relent. In a televised address, he announced he would permit parliament to reconvene. He asked Krishna Prasad Koirala of the SPA to become new prime minister (to replace the one he had dismissed more than four years earlier). The palace wanted the royal family to keep their position according to the 1990 constitution (which held the king and his family above the law). Fully aware of the king's sleight of hand, the SPA insisted on a full return of parliament, an interim government, and an assembly to lay down the framework of a new constitution before they would agree to call off further protests. Maoists in particular insisted on nothing short of a constitutional assembly empowered to abolish the monarchy. Slogans in the streets called for "complete democracy" and warned leaders not to compromise.

Many people thought the time had come simply to act autonomously of any agreement with the palace. Madhav Kumar Nepal, leader of UML, called for the SPA to think about simply reinstalling the old parliament since the king did not realize that "the people's power has been shown." In contrast to the 1990 uprising, this time the rural armed struggle meant a blockade of the capital and shortages of fuel and food. The *New York Times* reported:

> Schools have been closed. Offices have been shut. Shops have opened and closed at unpredictable hours. Kerosene has become so scarce that a mother in the central city said Monday that she planned to serve the local equivalent of potato chips for dinner. The produce markets have opened at the whim of the palace curfew—begun at 2:00 a.m. one day and 11:00 a.m. another. . . . Fuel trucks have not been able to enter the capital because of the general strike, which prohibits the movement of vehicles. At the few

open gas stations, long lines snaked into the streets early each morning. The price of tomatoes quadrupled in three weeks because the strike also makes it impossible to ferry goods from the countryside. A daily laborer at the city's wholesale vegetable market said he could no longer afford to eat two meals a day.[130]

Despite the hardships endured by citizens, they were in no mood to let the palace and political parties end their uprising prematurely. On April 22 and 23, millions of Nepalis went into the streets to protest. Madhav Kumar Nepal estimated that five million Nepalis (out of a population of less than thirty million) protested on April 22 alone. In an interview in Kathmandu on April 12, 2009, he described people's overwhelming support: "Out of a population of twenty-five million, five million people were in the streets, another five million cheered from rooftops, and ten million more were hoping the movement would be successful." He also remembered pressure from India, the United States, China, and Europeans to compromise with the king at that decisive moment, but "We refused to stop until the king bowed down before us."[131] As the whole country seemed to be in the streets, a notable contingent was one hundred thousand women in Chitwan, the largest exclusively female march in Nepal's history.[132] It was revealed that on Sunday, April 23, Gyanendra had dispatched his army chief and foreign minister to ask the Indian ambassador for approval for a massive military intervention to forestall "chaos and anarchy." Not only did the Indians turn Gyanendra down, they reprimanded him for even considering that option.[133]

The capacity of ordinary people to understand that the monarchy would resort to any means to save itself did not stop them from marching. At this high point of the uprising on April 22, over two hundred protesters were wounded by gunfire. Heroic actions tipped the balance in favor of democracy. On April 23, knowing full well the risks involved, people marched on the palace. When police attacked with bullets and tear gas, at least twenty-three people were critically injured, and hundreds more wounded were rushed to hospitals. Word of mouth told to regroup and promised that two million people would storm the king's palace two days later.[134] On the evening of April 24, more than a million people converged in the streets. Again targeting the monarchy, thousands of voices chanted "Hang the King!" and "Burn the Crown!" That night, Maoists attacked government facilities including a telecommunications tower in Chautara, a scant seventy-five miles north of Kathmandu.

Finally, late that night, after more demonstrators were killed and hundreds wounded, King Gyanendra relented, agreeing to reinstate parliament (which he had dissolved in 2002) and to permit a referendum on the constitution. After the king's proclamation on April 25, people ran into the streets cheering wildly for their hard-won victory. While people continued to chant slogans warning leaders not to accept compromise with the king, the SPA called off the general strike. Victory rallies celebrated for weeks.

Before the king publicly admitted defeat, representatives of three of the seven parties in the SPA had met with U.S. ambassador James Moriarty in a meeting

Maoist victory rally in Kathmandu, June 2, 2006. Photo by Narendra Shrestha in *A People War*, 204.

described as "very positive" by a Western diplomat. The United States classified the Maoists as "terrorists" and worried that Gyanendra's brutal intransigence would only bring them more supporters. After his April 25 proclamation, the U.S. State Department called on the king immediately to hand over power to the parliament and to assume no more than a ceremonial role in governing the country. The SPA chose frail octogenarian Girija Prasad Koirala, youngest son of K.P. Koirala, to lead the new government, but the Maoists demurred, saying a new parliament would only restore the unacceptable status quo ante. The Maoists released a statement asserting that "by accepting the so-called royal-proclamation the leaders of these seven parties have once again made a blunder." They vowed to fight on and press for a Constituent Assembly with a blockade of Kathmandu.

As Nepal struggled to find a new equilibrium, foreign influence remained a factor of intense scrutiny. Although China supported the monarchy, they provided very little support for Gyanendra. Sensing that he was soon to lose his throne, they knew that by withholding aid to the king, it would be very easy for them to form an allegiance with whatever party took control. The United States initially supported the king and warned the SPA to act cautiously. The United States wanted to keep their access to Nepal's market and maintain their strong military influence in the country. When it became clear the people's movement was not to be stopped, the United States changed its stance and warned the king to allow parliament to take charge. India continues to view Nepal as a junior sibling. By 2003, it had supplied Nepal with $25.8 million toward arms and planned to spend an additional $12.9 million in arms dealings. As home for many Nepalese refuges, India benefits from their status as underpaid factory workers.

No one was sure whether people would accept the king's promise as sufficient grounds to cease massive protests. An article in the *Washington Post* noted that the mainly youthful demonstrators had gone further than the political parties by demanding an end to the monarchy and creation of a republic.[135] An online report on April 25 put it this way: "Officially the general strike has been lifted by the SPA. . . . But everything is still not 'normal' in the streets. Fully aware of the past, thousands are still chanting slogans cautioning the SPA leadership that it's not just *Prajatantra* (democracy) they want now; they want *Loktantra* (true democracy)."[136] Crowds continued to chant, "Burn the Crown!" and "Hang the King!" One protester warned, "We are here not just to celebrate the king's defeat, but also to warn the leaders that if they betray the people, this very crowd will not leave them alive."[137] The mood in the streets was euphoric. Ram Chandra Poudel, a central committee member of NC, understood, "This is a victory for people on the street." That same day, the SPA promised elections for a Constituent Assembly, and the Maoists declared a three-month ceasefire and lifted their blockade of the capital.

On April 27, hundreds of thousands of people filled the streets of Kathmandu in an enormous, celebratory rally called by the SPA. After nineteen consecutive days of illegal demonstrations, people had won a great victory. At the same time, they remained vigilant lest political parties squander another uprising's gains. At the giant victory rally, some threw rocks at the stage when a Congress spokesperson appeared in place of new Prime Minister G.P. Koirala, eighty-four years old, who was too ill to attend—or to be sworn in days later when parliament convened for the first time in four years. On May 1, the Confederation of Nepalese Professions called for a Constituent Assembly and "total democracy." The next day, students rallied against the "reemergence of the old practice" of political leaders competing for personal power. People wanted punishment of those responsible for the shooting of protestors—to say nothing of the arrests and years of indignities people had suffered. The new government had to act quickly or lose control of the situation. On May 12, four royalist ministers were arrested, and an investigation was ordered into human rights abuses during the uprising. Four arrests were not enough to appease people. They wanted an end to the monarchy itself for giving orders to kill so many citizens. After parliament failed to act decisively, protesters burned cars and demonstrated against the politicians.[138]

At last, in a momentous act passed unanimously by the interim parliament, the king was stripped of all his powers. Called a "Nepalese Magna Carta," the act made Nepal a secular republic and ended the world's last Hindu kingdom. All the king's powers were taken over the parliament; command of the army was designated to the prime minister; the word "royal" was deleted in reference to the army and airline; and, for the first time, the government announced it would tax the monarchy. May 18, the day on which the interim government acted, is now called Democracy Day (*Lokantrik* Day). Quietly passed at the same time was a bill banning demonstrations near Kathmandu's government buildings and royal palace—essentially a carbon copy of the king's previous ban.

A Difficult Harvest

In this dynamic period, people felt they had won a spectacular victory. Nepal's Hindu Kingdom had lasted 238 years, until it was toppled by the power of the people that swept though every part of the country. On November 21, with the euphoric victory still fresh, the Maoists and SPA signed a peace treaty ending the armed struggle in the countryside. Since the twelve-point agreement a year earlier (which had provided the basis for united resistance to the monarchy), some 1,380 people had been killed in armed conflicts, 70 percent by Maoists. With an interim constitution, a new coalition government formed that included the Maoists. Among the agreements reached were a provision for direct elections for a Constituent Assembly and formation of a Truth and Reconciliation Commission within sixty days to make known the fate of the missing, to investigate crimes against humanity, and to give relief to families.

As had happened in the aftermath of *Jana Andolan* 1 in 1990 (as well as in many other countries' postuprising surges), NGOs mushroomed—stimulated by movements in the streets. Collective Campaign for Peace (COCAP), an imaginative network of forty-four peace and human rights NGOs formed in 2001, was greatly strengthened. During the uprising, they had fifty full-time volunteers living in their office. Using five thousand e-mail identities to avoid government censors, they were able to update activists and networks—except during the final week when all Internet connections, cell phones, and landlines were shut down.[139] After the victory over the monarchy, their momentum carried over, and COCAP continued to grow. In 2009, they sponsored a nationwide bicycle ride for the disappeared from the civil war, conducted gender workshops, and mobilized more than three hundred groups working for violence-free elections. Another NGO center, Informal Sector Service Center (INSEC), sponsored a human rights radio show that led to grassroots formation of over five thousand listeners' clubs by 2009.[140] After young girls protested publicly for the right to go to school, INSEC helped them organize a children's march. They declared children a "Zone of Peace" and assembled a children's parliament, whose new laws were passed along as suggestions to the Constituent Assembly.

The uprising had transformed many people's "normal" everyday lives. Bonded laborers mobilized and won legislation freeing them from servitude. Maoists had played a huge role in ending it in areas they controlled. Although illegal, bonded labor is nonetheless still prevalent.[141] As people's identities were transformed after the uprising, mini-movements in the Terai militantly arose among ethnic groups who demanded greater participation within a federal structure. More than two million Nepalis instituted forms of direct democracy in community-owned forests.

So great was the postuprising surge that many people felt overwhelmed by the popular mobilization. As late as 2009, continuing *bandhs* in the Terai by minority groups seeking autonomy and a federal structure caused long lines of cars and motorcycles waiting for fuel to appear in Kathmandu. As Professor Lok Raj Baral described the situation: "Sometimes we feel there is no state. *Bandhs* take place everywhere. Factories are closed. Exports have ceased. Billions in rupees have been collected in tax revenues but no one can spend it. Every party wants a share. The educational system has collapsed except for private schools."[142] Roads remained abysmally pot-holed and unsafe. Electricity in the capital was available for only part of the day, sometimes only a few hours. As people enforced their own laws, neighborhood residents charged for safe parking and enforced other regulations without wide discussion.

Continuing politically motivated killings and attacks constituted a major problem for postmonarchist Nepal. In the first twelve months after the democratic breakthrough, human rights groups claimed government forces killed thirty-four people, while Maoists were held responsible for forty-six others in that same period.[143] Police remained on the force, although they had been heavily involved in repressing the protests in 2006. Indeed, the specific men implicated in the shootings at Kalanki got promotions.[144] For many the army is little better. In 2009, twenty-six of the top thirty army commanders were from the intermarried Rana and Shah clan groups, which have ruled the country for centuries.

Initially, the interim government proved utterly indecisive. The report of the commission to investigate human rights abuses reportedly found two hundred people (including Gyanendra) responsible for the killings, but the report was not made public despite repeated requests. On the first anniversary of the king's reinstatement of parliament, protesters demanded the report be made public and that Gyanendra be jailed. Carrying placards depicting the king in a prison cell, protesters screamed, "People's Movement is Still On" and "Down with the Royal Regime!" When a senior member of the NC, Ram Chandra Poudel, rose to speak at the first anniversary of the people's victory, he was booed and hit with empty water bottles.[145]

On April 1, 2007, eight political parties (including the Maoists) formed an interim government, but barely a quorum of representatives even bothered to show up for weeks at a time. After months spent scheduling elections for the Constituent Assembly, the vote was twice postponed because of "irreconcilable differences" among political parties as to how to measure their outcome. In fairness, the Maoists made reasonable demands as preconditions for participation in the elections, especially the declaration of a secular republic and a proportional system of representation. As one observer noted, however, the highly visible squabbling led to widespread popular disillusionment with parties: "The Nepali people today have become disillusioned with the multi-party dispensation that virtually swept the country off its feet with the success of the movement for the restoration of multiparty democracy in 1990. In just a span of some seventeen years this aversion towards the most popular and coveted form of governance came about primarily because of democratic norms and values being thrown to the winds by the new leadership."[146]

With the king deposed, no one could speak for the entire country. One expert claimed more than 70 percent of Nepalis wanted to maintain a monarchy—but not in the person of Gyanendra (who remained in Kathmandu gathering supporters). In early July 2006, one hundred thousand people honored the king in the streets. In February 2007, however, a crowd attacked the king's motorcade with stones as he sought to visit a pilgrimage site in Kathmandu. If anything is clear, it is that the revolt spread far and wide and would not easily be quieted. A newfound empowerment of ordinary people prevailed. Kanak Dixit, editor of *Himal* magazine, put it this way: "Our people power is unique, it comes from the grassroots and rural people. They are not only the middle class, as in Thailand. They are the vanguard of democracy here."[147]

The much-anticipated elections took place on April 10, 2008. When the final tallies were compiled, the Maoists had won a spectacular victory. Gaining more than 3.1 million votes, they won 229 seats, while the Congress Party garnered about 2.3 million votes but only 115 seats, closely followed by CP-UML with 108 seats. All together twenty-four parties were represented in the Constituent Assembly, one-third of which was female and also included the first openly gay member of parliament. (In previous legislatures, less than 5 percent of the delegates were women.)

During its first session on May 28, the Constituent Assembly voted to declare Nepal a federal democratic republic and thereby abolished the monarchy by a vote of 560 in favor and 4 against. On August 15, Maoist leader Pushpa Kamal Dahal (Prachanda) was selected as prime minister, with the backing of CPN (UML) and twenty other parties.

The nebulous character of the new secular republic left a precarious peace in place. As the Constituent Assembly drafted the constitution, they solicited people's input in a variety of forums, including thousands of written suggestions that were diligently compiled for lawmakers. Much of the country cried out for a federal structure so that its various ethnic groups and regions could manage their own affairs. The unresolved issue of the country's devolution of power to local groups remained the source of great conflict. Yet for others, fear of Nepal's devolution and even annexation by India—as occurred in Sikkim in 1974—were

TABLE 7.4 **2008 Election Results for Constituent Assembly (Top 12 of 55 Parties)**

Party	Votes	% of Votes	Seats	% of Seats
Communist Party of Nepal (Maoist)	3,145,519	30.52	229	38.10
Nepali Congress	2,348,890	22.79	115	19.13
Communist Party of Nepal (Unified Marxist-Leninist)	2,229,064	21.63	108	17.97
Madhesi Jana Adhikar Forum, Nepal	634,154	6.15	54	8.98
Tarai-Madhesh Loktantrik Party	345,587	3.35	21	3.49
Rastriya Prajatantra Party	310,214	3.01	8	1.33
Communist Party of Nepal (Marxist-Leninist)	168,196	1.63	9	1.50
Sadbhavana Party	174,086	1.69	9	1.50
Janamorcha Nepal	136,846	1.33	8	1.33
Communist Party of Nepal (United)	39,100	0.38	5	0.83
Rastriya Prajatantra Party Nepal	76,684	0.74	4	0.66
Rastriya Janamorcha	93,578	0.91	4	0.66

Source: Nepal Election Commission, http://www.election.gov.np/reports/CAResults/reportBody.php?selectedMenu=Party%20Wise%20Results%20Status(English)&rand=1260333150.

dominant concerns. As Nepal's government remained in limbo, many groups vied for immediate justice.

Divided by significant matters, political parties seemed endlessly to boycott parliamentary sessions, leaving the government less than able to cope with urgent popular needs. Dozens of people were killed in protests in the southern part of the country as minority groups used strikes, transportation disruptions, and demonstrations to dramatize their demands for autonomy and adequate representation in the government. Three years after the victory of *Jana Andolan* 2, Durga Sob, chairperson of the Feminist Dalit Organization, claimed Dalit women were "accused constantly of practicing witchcraft" by high castes. "Dalit women cry for equal representation," she said.[148] In 2009, the Committee to Protest Journalists and Reporters Sans Frontiers ranked Nepal below Sudan in terms of attacks on journalists and denial of press freedom. In August 2009, citing "a sharp and sustained decline in food security," the UN World Food program reported that more than three million Nepalis were endangered. The agency estimated that 48 percent of children under five were chronically malnourished—as many as 60 percent in mountainous regions. As young people left the country to find work, at least 17 percent of GNP was due to remittances from abroad (some say the figure was closer to 25 percent).

A positive note could be found in workers' increasing self-consciousness of their significance as a class. In May 2009, a Joint Trade Union Coordination Centre was created that includes unions affiliated with six parties (including United CPN-Maoist, NC, UML, and Rashtriya Prajatantra Party). Along with the Confederation of Professionals–Nepal, an invigorated General Federation of Nepalese Trade Unions also emerged.

Who's in Power?

Looking back at the two uprisings, one cannot help but be struck by the incredible heroism of ordinary people. At the same moment, the failure of political parties to act swiftly and with resolve is evident. Although almost all citizens happily bade farewell to King Gyanendra, some favor restoration of the monarchy. Former prime minister and NC founder K.P. Bhattarai publicly called abolishing the monarchy "sheer stupidity" and a "mistake."[149] Kamal Thapa, chairperson of the Rashtriya Prajatantra Party, has long advocated restoration of the monarchy to uphold Nepal's territorial integrity and preserve national unity. At least one newspaper, *People's Review: A Political and Business Weekly*, openly called for a referendum on restoring the monarchy.

Overwhelmingly on the side of the Maoists, the urban and rural poor, or lumpen, continue to fight for justice with impunity—as does the army that opposes them. In political conflicts during one year from mid-2007 to mid-2008, more than six hundred people were killed and many more beaten or threatened.[150] With thousands of PLA fighters semiconfined to cantonments with UN observers, the Maoists retained a force of considerable strength. In addition, they have slowly built a paramilitary Young Communist League alongside the PLA. Of hundreds of cases of their forces attacking rival political groups or demanding extortion money, one became nationally prominent. A PLA commander, Bibidh, on the run for murdering a businessman, was arrested in 2009, but released on the order of the Maoist home minister. Subsequent revelations in the press announced that Bibidh had been sheltered from police in a PLA camp and promoted to the powerful Central Secretariat level in the Unified CPN (Maoist).

In mid-2009, control of the national army became the country's key political issue. According to previous agreements, the PLA was to be integrated into the country's military force, but top military commanders refused to comply, citing the fact that even a few Maoists within the ranks would probably subvert the entire one-hundred-thousand-strong armed forces, 95 percent of whom were lower-caste. For his refusal to comply with political directives to integrate the military, the Maoists called for the resignation of top General Rookmangud Katawal in April—only a few months before his mandatory retirement in August. According to the interim constitution, however, the president, not the prime minister, controls the army. When President Yadav refused to fire Katawal, Maoist Prime Minister Prachanda resigned in protest, and the Maoist-led government collapsed. Katawal was certainly no saint—and neither was his second-in-command, whom Maoists nominated as his replacement. The CPN-UML (Unified Marxist-Leninists) proposed firing all three top generals and bringing in a completely new army leadership, but the Maoists rejected that offer and instead created the crisis leading Prachanda to resign and the government to fall. Once Prachanda stepped down and the government they led fell, Maoists revived "parallel governments" in rural areas and stepped up protests in the capital.

The Maoists made great contributions to ending of the monarchy and to liberating hundreds of thousands of poverty-stricken people from the throes of feudal bondage and crass capitalist exploitation. They spearheaded the liberation of women and the struggle for national independence. They organized village councils and patiently participated in a government of national unity. Yet their sectarianism remained an obstacle to their own realization of the creation of a unified hegemonic bloc capable of leading the whole society. The prime minister who replaced Prachanda, Madhav Kumar Nepal of the CPN-UML, was a former Maoist ally and staunch anti-imperialist. Yet they could not work with him properly, not because of reactionaries and foreigners, but because they and their foreign "comrades" stoked the fires of sectarian struggles in Nepal as a means to initiate conflict, which they hoped would result in their sole possession of state power.[151]

The controversy was further enflamed when Nepali television released a video of a Prachanda speech at a Chitwan gathering of PLA fighters in January 2008 in which he said that the Party had purposely deceived the UN into believing PLA strength was thirty-five thousand, when in actuality the number was between seven and eight thousand. (Inflating the number was supposed to give the Maoists greater leverage within the integrated army.) In the same video, Prachanda also promised that future government reparations to martyrs would help fund implementation of a "good battle plan" for the "ultimate revolt."[152] Nepalese Maoists' commitment to the peace process and multiparty democracy has been significant, yet the sad legacy of Pol Pot hangs over them. Their own hard-liners call for over-throwing the government—duplicating the success of the two Russian Revolutions of 1917 (when the Bolsheviks seized power from a "democratic" government after first aligning with a broad coalition to overthrow the Czar).

The remarkable unity of 95 percent of the people of Nepal in defeating the monarchy is one of their great resources. While Nepal's (and Burma's) upris-ings were planned in advance and organized from the top-down, the Gwangju Uprising was a spontaneous reaction to military violence and was structured from the bottom up. The violence among people in Nepal and Burma stands in sharp contrast to the Korean situation. In Nepal, political differences often remain the source for altercations, and physical confrontations—even killings—are common. The roots of such violence can be found even during optimistic moments of peo-ple's uprisings. More than one account tells us that during the "voluntary" black-outs in 1990, houses which did not turn off their lights had their windows broken, after which their inhabitants were told that if they continued not to comply with the blackout that their houses would be burned down.[153] In Gwangju, insurgent forces treated even captured enemy soldiers humanely; some were released back to their units, and at least one even given back his M-16 (but not his bullets) so his officers would not punish him for losing his weapon. When the police chief in Gwangju refused to order his men to open fire on protesters, he was taken away and relieved of his command. Reports indicate that many Korean police changed clothing and joined the insurgents. Nepal's rigid lines of division remain an obsta-cle to the country's progress.

Despite the great victories won in 2006, political parties again showed them-selves incapable of consolidating the gains won by the sacrifices of people in the streets. The monarchy has been abolished, and newfound liberties greatly improved people's everyday lives and increased political parties' powers. The royal family's former central residence in Kathmandu was turned into a museum, which tens of thousands of ordinary Nepalis stood in long lines for the chance to glimpse. Yet in five years of parliamentary wrangling, little has been accom-plished in the way of instituting a new constitution, which has yet to be revised. The Maoist armed forces have not been integrated into the Nepalese Army (largely because of fears they would easily subvert the entire military). As rivalries and foreign intrigue mount, no one can predict the country's future.

Neighboring Bangladesh also totters between civil strife and military force, yet in 1990, its people, like their Nepali counterparts, united to overthrow their dictatorship.

NOTES

1   Interview with Professor Kapil Shrestha, Tribhuvan University, Kathmandu, April 26, 2009.
2   Rishikesh Shaha, *Ancient and Medieval Nepal* (New Delhi: Manohar Publishers, 2001), 105.
3   Kanak Mani Dixit, foreword to Kiyoko Ogura, *Kathmandu Spring: The People's Movement of 1990* (Lalitpur: Himal Books, 2001), x.

4   See Jagadish Sharma, *Nepal: Struggle for Existence* (Kathmandu: 1986), 37–49. Ostensibly a form of "direct democracy" overseen by the palace, the *panchayat* system aimed at creating a "classless society" although most of the *panchas* were not elected directly by people. Theoretically, the system was based on direct democracy: grass-roots village councils were directly elected; they selected district councils which in turn selected zonal councils which selected the 140-member *Rastriya Panchayat*, the national assembly that also included royal appointees. In theory, the system itself was described by the king as "an administration, which rises from below and rests on popular consent as well as on the active co-operation of the people, and aims at the creation of a society which is democratic, progressive and free from exploitation." See King Birendra, *Proclamations, Speeches and Messages 1972–1981* (Kathmandu: Royal Government of Nepal, 1982), 7.

5   Michael Hutt, ed., *Nepal in the Nineties* (New Delhi: Oxford University Press, 1994). The roots of the writers' movement can be traced to publication in 1968 of the "Rejected Generation" and the 1974 "Boot Polish" demonstrators, who gathered under the *pipal* tree on New Road to protest censorship.

6   G. Pokhrel, "Media Perspective," in *The Role of Civil Society and Democratization in Nepal*, ed. Ananda P. Srestha (Kathmandu: Nepal Foundation for Advanced Studies, 1998), 84.

7   William Raeper and Martin Hoftun, *Spring Awakening: An Account of the 1990 Revolution in Nepal* (New Delhi: Viking, 1992), 24, 76, 86, 97, 108, 214.

8   Ibid., 97.

9   Present in Nepal at the time, Paul Routledge portrays the leadership of the movement as having great control over the popular upsurge. See "Backstreets, Barricades and Blackouts: Urban Terrains of Resistance in Nepal," *Journal of Environment and Planning* 12, no. 5 (1994): 559–78.

10   Raeper and Hoftun, *Spring Awakening*, 103.

11   Saubhagya Shah, "A Himalayan Red Herring?" in *Himalayan People's War: Nepal's Maoist Rebellion*, ed. Michael Hutt (Bloomington: Indiana University Press, 2004), 203; also see Martin Hoftun, William Raeper, and John Whelpton, *People, Politics and Ideology: Democracy and Social Change in Nepal* by (Kathmandu: Mandala Book Point, 1999), 117.

12   Raeper and Hoftun, *Spring Awakening*, 123. Even after the king's April proclamation legalizing political parties, India refused to negotiate a new treaty. While restoring the one that had expired, they insisted they would wait until after elections in Nepal to conclude a new agreement.

13   World Bank, *Nepal: Poverty and Incomes* (Washington, D.C.: World Bank, 1991), xii.

14   Alan Macfarlane, "Fatalism and Development in Nepal," in *Himalayan People's War: Nepal's Maoist Rebellion*, ed. Michael Hutt (Bloomington: Indiana University Press, 2004), 108.

15   Tribhuvan University survey, January–February 1990, quoted in Hoftun et al., *People, Politics and Ideology*, 118.

16   Rishikesh Shaha, *Politics in Nepal: 1980–1990: Referendum, Stalemate and Triumph of People Power* (Kathmandu: Manohar, 1990), 188; *Dawn of Democracy: People's Power in Nepal* (Kathmandu: Forum for the Protection of Human Rights, 1990), 24.

17   *Dawn of Democracy*, 118.

18   Hutt, *Nepal*, 90–91.

19   Ogura, *Kathmandu Spring*, 33.

20   Hoftun et al., *People, Politics and Ideology*, 120.

21   Krishna Hachhethu, "Mass Movement 1990," *Contributions to Nepalese Studies* 17, no. 2 (July 1990): 180; *Dawn of Democracy*, 26.

22 Raeper and Hoftun, *Spring Awakening*, 56.

23 Ibid., 57.

24 Ogura, *Kathmandu Spring*, 74–75.

25 *Dawn of Democracy*, 26.

26 Saroj Pant, "One Step toward a Brighter Future," http://www.asmita.org.np/Women_ Subject_Category/social_movement.htm.

27 Ogura, *Kathmandu Spring*, 86–88.

28 Raeper and Hoftun, *Spring Awakening*, 109.

29 Ibid., 106.

30 Routledge, "Backstreets," 565.

31 Ibid., 568.

32 Raeper and Hoftun, *Spring Awakening*, 110.

33 Ogura, *Kathmandu Spring*, 114–17.

34 Routledge, "Backstreets," 570.

35 Ibid., 570.

36 Ogura, *Kathmandu Spring*, 123.

37 Anonymous interview at the interviewee's request, Patan, April 14, 2009.

38 *Dawn of Democracy*, 30.

39 Ogura, *Kathmandu Spring*, 131.

40 Hoftun et al., *People, Politics and Ideology*, 129.

41 Routledge, "Backstreets," 567.

42 Raeper and Hoftun, *Spring Awakening*, 79.

43 Michael Hutt, "The Blowing of the April Wind: Writers and Democracy in Nepal," *Index on Censorship* 8 (1990): 8.

44 See Vincanne Adams, *Doctors for Democracy: Health Professionals in the Nepal Revolution* (London: Cambridge University Press, 1998).

45 David Seddon, "Democracy and Development," in *Nepal in the Nineties*, ed. Michael Hutt (New Delhi: Oxford University Press, 1994), 137.

46 T. Louise Brown, *The Challenge to Democracy in Nepal: A Political History* (London: Routledge, 1996), 134.

47 Shaha, *Politics in Nepal*, 208.

48 See Seddon, "Democracy," 138; Routledge, "Backstreets," 573; Hoftun et al., *People, Politics and Ideology*, 132; *Dawn of Democracy* reports fifty dead at Bir Hospital and more than a hundred more buried in a mass grave at Sundharijal (34); Hisila Yami, *People's War and Women's Liberation in Nepal* (Kathmandu: Janadhwani, 2007) reports that over two hundred were killed in the shootings (191).

49 Raeper and Hoftun, *Spring Awakening*, 112.

50 Hachhethu, "Mass Movement," 181.

51 Hoftun et al., *People, Politics and Ideology*, 134.

52 Raeper and Hoftun, *Spring Awakening*, 113.

53 Huntington, *Third Wave*, 151–61.

54 Brown, refers here to an interview with D.R. Pandey (*Challenge to Democracy*, 139). At the start of the uprising, the U.S. State Department issued a statement encouraging the government and opposition to negotiate and expressed "support for human rights, including the freedom of expression." Three congressmen, including Stephen Solarz— who had played a prominent role in the Philippine transition from the Marcos regime to the Aquino regime—as well as Senators Kennedy, Pell, and Moynihan sent a letter expressing concern about mass arrests, but on March 6 the U.S. assistant secretary of state, John H. Kelly, testified before a House subcommittee and praised the government's "restraint." Kelly told Congress, "Nepal has its own system of government which certainly has many attributes of democracy" (Shaha, *Politics in Nepal*, 194).

55   Pant, "One Step," 2.
56   Brown, *Challenge to Democracy*, 143.
57   Raeper and Hoftun, *Spring Awakening*, 113; Routledge, "Backstreets," 573; Hutt, *Nepal*, 29. The Mallik Commission found that only forty-five people were killed between February 18 and April 13 (Brown, *Challenge to Democracy*, 148).
58   Narayan Prasad Sivakoti, *Jan-Andolan ra Sahidharu* (Kathmandu: Bhisma Kadariya, 2047 V.S., 1990).
59   Amnesty International reported over eight thousand arrests in a 1992 report. See T. Louise Brown, *The Challenge to Democracy in Nepal: A Political History* (London: Routledge, 1996), 123. The number of arrests varies from source to source, but nearly everyone reported widespread abuse and torture of detainees.
60   Shaha, *Politics in Nepal*, 220.
61   Richard Burghart and Martin Gaenszle, "Martyrs for Democracy," *European Bulletin of Himalayan Research* 2 (1991): 13.
62   Shaha, *Politics in Nepal*, 221.
63   Burghart and Gaenszle, "Martyrs," 14; *Dawn of Democracy*, 38.
64   Brown, *Challenge to Democracy*, 145.
65   Hoftun et al., *People, Politics and Ideology*, 138.
66   Brown maintains this action was undertaken by *mandales* wishing to destroy evidence of their misdeeds (*Dawn of Democracy*, 38) also attributes this action to *mandales*.
67   Hoftun et al., *People, Politics and Ideology*, 374; Shaha, *Politics in Nepal*, 220–21.
68   Hutt, *Nepal*, 32.
69   See *Subversion of Politics*.
70   Raeper and Hoftun, *Spring Awakening*, 137.
71   Martin Hoftun, "The 1990 Revolution," in *Nepal in the Nineties*, ed. Michael Hutt (New Delhi: Oxford University Press, 1994), 19.
72   Shaha, *Politics in Nepal*, 219.
73   Hoftun et al., *People, Politics and Ideology*, 158.
74   Pushkar Bajracharya, "Trade Union Perspective," in *The Role of Civil Society and Democratization in Nepal*, ed. Ananda P. Srestha (Kathmandu: Nepal Foundation for Advanced Studies, 1998), 20–21.
75   Raeper and Hoftun, *Spring Awakening*, 171–72.
76   Chaitanya Mishra, *Essays on the Sociology of Nepal* (Kathmandu: Fine Print, 2007), 29.
77   Santa B. Pun, "How 'Inclusive' Nepal's Institutions?" in *Peace Building Process in Nepal*, eds. Ananda P. Srestha and Hari Uprety (Kathmandu: Nepal Foundation for Advanced Studies, 2008), 89.
78   Gabriele Beisenkamp and Thomas Beisenkamp, *Women of Nepal March Forward* (Kathmandu: Jana Shikshya Griha, 2007), 31.
79   Yami, *People's War*, 141; The 2001 census counted 13.8 percent of population as Dalit, but most people think this is far below the true number. Prakash A. Raj, *The Dancing Democracy: The Power of the Third Eye* (New Delhi: Rupa and Co., 2006), 57.
80   Yami, *People's War*, 188; Sumon Tuladhar, "Gender and Social Change in Nepal," *Society and Education* 1 (2007): 99.
81   Interview with Subodh Raj Pyakurel, INSEC, Kathmandu, April 13, 2009.
82   D. Chand, "NGO Perspective," in *The Role of Civil Society and Democratization in Nepal*, ed. Ananda P. Srestha (Kathmandu: Nepal Foundation for Advanced Studies, 1998), 49.
83   Ibid., 50; similar numbers can be found in Jan Sharma, "Nepal's Faltering Peace Process: Civil Society, Media and International Community," in *Peace Building Process in Nepal*, eds. Ananda P. Srestha and Hari Uprety (Kathmandu: Nepal Foundation for Advanced Studies, 2008), 61. Sharma counted 221 international NGOs in 1990, 3,284 in 1995, and about 21,000 in 2005.

84 Pokhrel, "Media Perspective," 84.

85 *The Kathmandu Post*, February 22, 1997.

86 G. Pokhrel, "Media Perspective," 86.

87 Hachhethu, "Mass Movement," 182.

88 Hutt, *Nepal*, 19. Also see Hutt, *Himalayan People's War*, 61, and Hoftun et al., *People, Politics and Ideology*, 169.

89 In April, the king's government had promised to provide Rs. 15,000 to every family of someone killed in the movement, Rs. 5,000 to persons seriously injured, and Rs. 2,000 to those slightly wounded. The death benefit was raised to Rs. 25,000 by the interim government.

90 Krishna Hachhethu, "Transition to Democracy in Nepal: Negotiations Behind Constitution Making, 1990," *Contributions to Nepalese Studies* 21, no. 1 (January 1994): 124.

91 In 1991 and 1994, women accounted for between 5 and 6 percent of all candidates and 4 percent of the members of the lower house; there were not more than three women in the upper house of parliament. Moreover, as one analyst summarized their role, they were "allowed" only one specialty—women's issues. See Stephanie Tawa Lama, "Women and Politics in Nepal: Small Actors, Big Issue," *European Bulletin of Himalayan Research* 11 (1996): 4–7.

92 Raeper and Hoftun, *Spring Awakening*, 188.

93 John Whelpton, "The General Elections of May 1991," in *Nepal in the Nineties*, ed. Michael Hutt (New Delhi: Oxford University Press, 1994), 71.

94 Raeper and Hoftun, *Spring Awakening*, 216.

95 Hoftun et al., *People, Politics and Ideology*, 189.

96 *Guardian*, April 27, 1992.

97 See Birendra Prasad Mishra, *Rebuilding Nepal* (Kathmandu: Bhrikuti Academic Publications, 2007), 176–84.

98 Barburam Bhattarai, *Monarchy vs. Democracy: The Epic Fight in Nepal* (Noida, India: Samkaleen Teesari Duniya, 2005), 5.

99 Ibid., 43.

100 Patrick Leahy, Speech to the U.S. Senate, September 18, 2007, as quoted in Srestha and Uprety, *Peace Building Process in Nepal*, 1.

101 As quoted in Raeper and Hoftun, *Spring Awakening*, 92–93.

102 Interview with Shalik Ram Jamkattel, Kathmandu, April 12, 2009.

103 See Sudheer Sharma, "The Maoist Movement," in *Himalayan People's War: Nepal's Maoist Rebellion*, ed. Michael Hutt (Bloomington: Indiana University Press, 2004), 43–47.

104 Marie Lecomte-Tilouine, *Hindu Kingship, Ethnic Revival, and Maoist Rebellion in Nepal* (New Delhi: Oxford University Press, 2009), 219.

105 Arjun Karki and David Seddon, eds., *The People's War in Nepal: Left Perspectives* (New Delhi: Adroit Publishers, 2003), 43.

106 Raj, *Dancing Democracy*, 22.

107 Bush quoted in Jan Sharma, "Nepal's Faltering Peace Process: Civil Society, Media and International Community," in *Peace Building Process in Nepal*, eds. Ananda P. Srestha and Hari Uprety (Kathmandu: Nepal Foundation for Advanced Studies, 2008), 70.

108 Deepak Thapa, "Radicalism and the Emergence of the Maoists," in *Himalayan People's War: Nepal's Maoist Rebellion*, ed. Michael Hutt (Bloomington: Indiana University Press, 2004), 33.

109 Interview with Professor Lok Raj Baral, Kathmandu, April 15, 2009.

110 Human Rights Watch, "Between a Rock and a Hard Place: Civilians Struggle to Survive

in Nepal's Civil War," October 2004, http://www.hrw.org/reports/2004/nepal1004/nepal1004.pdf.

111 The SPA included the NC, Nepali Congress (Democratic), the Communist Party of Nepal (Unified Marxist-Leninist), Nepal Workers and Peasants Party, Nepal Goodwill Party, United Left Front, and People's Front.

112 Ayaz Muhammad, "Nepal: *Jana Andolan* and Its Challenges," *Nepali Journal of Contemporary Studies* 6, no. 2 (2006): 4.

113 Mishra, *Rebuilding*, 168.

114 Asia Human Rights Commission, *The State of Human Rights in Eleven Asian Nations—2006* (Hong Kong, 2006), 133.

115 Ibid., 139.

116 Roshan Chitrakar, "Education for Social Transformation," *Society and Education* 1 (2007): 10.

117 Kundan Aryal and Upendra Kumar Poudel, *Jana Andolan II: A Witness Account* (Kathmandu: INSEC, 2006). These are minimal numbers; others report twenty-two people killed and more than four thousand seriously injured. See Anirban Roy, *Prachanda: The Unknown Revolutionary* (Kathmandu: Mandala Book Point, 2008), 135.

118 Interview with Shalik Ram Jamkattel, Kathmandu, April 12, 2009.

119 Asia Human Rights Commission, *State of Human Rights*, 146.

120 This is a minimal number. Other sources reported two hundred wounded. See Poudel, *Jana Andolan II*, 1.

121 Raj, *The Dancing Democracy*, 31.

122 Interview with Prakash Man Singh, Kathmandu, April 12, 2009.

123 Poudel, *Jana Andolan II*, 75.

124 Raj, *The Dancing Democracy*, 32.

125 Asia Human Rights Commission, *State of Human Rights*, 147.

126 Interview with Professor Lok Raj Baral, Kathmandu, April 15, 2009.

127 Poudel, *Jana Andolan II*, 49.

128 Ibid., 2.

129 Ibid., 130.

130 Somini Sengupta, "In a Retreat, Nepal's King Says He Will Reinstate Parliament," *New York Times*, April 25, 2006.

131 During my interview with Madhav Kumar Nepal in Kathmandu on April 12, 2009, he related to me with great acclaim that he had visited Gwangju before *Jana Andolan 2* and was "inspired by people's heroic struggle."

132 Ameet Dhakal, "Triumph of People Power," *Republica*, April 24, 2009, 1.

133 Ibid., 3.

134 Roy, *Prachanda*, 135.

135 John Lancaster, "Bowing to Protests, Nepal King Reinstates Parliament," *Washington Post*, reprinted in the *Boston Globe*, April 25, 2006.

136 Akhilesh Tripathi, editor of Kantipuronline, as quoted in "Nonviolent Uprising Restores Democracy in Nepal" by Alyson Lie, http://www.peaceworkmagazine.org/node/94.

137 See the article by Nathalie Hrizi, "Mass Uprising in Nepal Forces King to Grant Concessions," *S&L Magazine*, June 2006.

138 Somini Sengupta, "Nepal Legislators Move to Curb the King's Powers," *New York Times*, May 19, 2006, A14.

139 Interview with Deepak Kumar Bhattarai, Gopi Krishna Bhattarai, Bishnu Khatri, Pawan Roy, Punya Bhandari, and Bhawana Bhatti, Kathmandu, April 11, 2009.

140 Interview with Subodh Raj Pyakurel, INSEC, Kathmandu, April 13, 2009.

141 Interview with Madhav Kumar Nepal, Kathmandu, April 12, 2009.

142 Interview with Professor Lok Raj Baral, Kathmandu, April 15, 2009.

143 Liam Cochrane, "A Year after Uprising, Nepal Takes Halting Steps toward Peaceful Republic," *World Politics Review*, April 25, 2007.

144 Interview with Bimal Sharma, Kalanki, April 17, 2009.

145 Somini Sengupta, "New Conflicts Accompany Nepal's Efforts at Democracy," *New York Times*, April 29, 2007. The report was finally made public, but no high-level official has yet been made to bear responsibility for the killings. In addition, the former king's control of uncounted millions of dollars in assets has yet to be challenged.

146 Srestha, *Peace Building*, v–vi.

147 Quoted in Bill Weinberg's blog entry "Nepal: 'Light at End of Tunnel'—for Tribal Peoples Too?," World War 4 Report, http://ww4report.com/node/2184.

148 *Himalayan Times*, May 2, 2009, 2.

149 *People's Review*, April 30–May 6, 2009, 1.

150 Interview with Sudip Pathak, Human Rights Organization of Nepal, Kathmandu, April 24, 2009.

151 See "Who Is Endangering Civil Peace in Nepal?" http://links.org.au/node/1050, December 10, 2009. The article's very title indicates that a constitutional crisis is being used as a pretext to blame foreigners and reactionaries for the looming possibility of renewed civil war. In the rarified world of left sectarian politics, Afghan communists took the Maoist government to task for permitting the United States to recruit Gorkha soldiers to fight alongside the United States in Afghanistan.

152 The video is available at http://www.nepalnews.com/archive/2009/may/may05/news12.php#1.

153 Routledge, "Backstreets," 568.

CHAPTER 8

Bangladesh

In no country in the world was student activism in the 1950s
and 1960s of greater intensity, continuity and concern than in
Bangladesh. . . . Use of students as party cadre was also more
necessary in Bengal than in other Muslim majority provinces,
primarily because there the main politically relevant sections—
lawyers, doctors, businessmen and landlords—were almost entirely
dominated by Hindus.

—Talukder Maniruzzaman

The discontent against parliamentary democracy is due to the
realization that it has failed to assure to the masses the right to
liberty, property or the pursuit of happiness. . . . Parliamentary
democracy took no notice of economic inequalities and . . . has
continuously added to the economic wrongs of the poor, the
downtrodden and the disinherited class.

—Babasaheb Ambedkar

CHRONOLOGY	
March 1, 1971	Pakistani martial law authorities refuse to convene National Assembly
March 25, 1971	"The Black Night": Pakistani tanks appear in Dhaka
March 26, 1971	Bangladesh independence from Pakistan proclaimed
December 16, 1971	Independence War victorious after more than one million deaths
August 15, 1975	President Mujibur and family murdered during military coup
November 3, 1975	Countercoup by supporters of Mujibur

November 7, 1975	Soldiers' coup overturns government
April 21, 1977	General Ziaur Rahman becomes president
May 30, 1981	President Zia assassinated
March 24, 1982	General H.M. Ershad seizes power
November 8, 1982	Police attack Dhaka University; students liberate it for three months
November 21, 1982	Organization for Student Struggle formed
December 22–23, 1984	Workers-Employees Unity Council organizes two-day *hartal* (general strike)
January 1988	Dozens killed during protests in Chittagong and Dhaka
November 10, 1989	Protesters set fire to Home Ministry near Nur Hussain Square
August 1990	Government agrees to enhanced IMF structural adjustment program
October 10, 1990	All Party Students' Union formed
November 19, 1990	Three alliances announce united front against Ershad
November 22, 1990	Dhaka University attacked by government forces
November 25, 1990	Government goons (*mastans*) defeated after pitched battle at Dhaka University
November 27, 1990	Curfew enacted; spontaneous resistance, Dhaka University becomes liberated territory
December 4, 1990	Ershad agrees to leave office
December 6, 1990	Parliament dissolved as Ershad hands over power to caretaker government
December 27, 1990	Fire kills twenty-five children and female textile workers
January 2, 1991	March of twenty thousand textile workers; union formed
February 27, 1991	Elections held by caretaker government; Bangladesh Nationalist Party wins majority
October 1991	Sex workers organize
March 26, 1992	People's Tribunal finds Muslim fundamentalists guilty of collaboration with Pakistan
February 1993	Feminist writer Taslima Nasrin forced into exile
April 26, 1994	Textile workers erupt in protests; Dhaka shut down
December 7, 1998	Female NGOs attacked by religious fundamentalists in Brahmanbaria
May 20, 2006	Wildcat strikes engulf some four thousand factories
June 12, 2006	Tripartite memorandum of understanding signed by workers, employers, and government
January 11, 2007	"Stealth Coup" in which military seizes power
December 29, 2008	Awami League sweeps elections
February 25, 2010	Twenty-two workers perish in fire at Gazipur factory manufacturing clothing for H&M
December 14, 2010	Twenty-six textile workers burned to death in factory fire on the outskirts of Dhaka

EIGHT SHORT MONTHS after the absolute monarchy was overthrown in Nepal, democratic forces in Bangladesh were able to topple the military dictatorship of General Muhammad Ershad. Again, students were in the forefront of the movement for democracy—although in Bangladesh, they functioned even more as a vanguard for several reasons, chief among them because the country's major political parties were incapacitated by their own leaders' personal bickering. Attacked by the regime for their continuing opposition, students responded by leading the whole society forward.

Bangladesh's Bloody Birth

When British colonialism retreated from South Asia after World War II, Pakistan was created as a Muslim country with two separate geographic areas separated by a thousand miles and enormous cultural differences. After decades of tenuous coexistence, the rift between the two sides ruptured in 1970, when Bengali-speaking East Pakistan's Awami League won a majority of seats in national elections. Despite the people's vote, entrenched leaders in West Pakistan refused to relinquish power. On March 2, 1971, the day after Pakistani martial law authorities refused to convene the new National Assembly, students raised a new flag of Bangladesh at a huge rally, setting the nation on course for independence. Within weeks, Pakistani tanks appeared in Dhaka on "The Black Night." The next day, March 26, 1971, Bangladesh independence from Pakistan was proclaimed. In the ensuing bloodbath, Pakistani troops slaughtered over a million people in a vain attempt to maintain control. All together, as many as three million people may have been killed and tens of thousands of women raped during the nine-month war that gave birth to Bangladesh.

Once independence was won and the Pakistani ruling class was driven from power, a unique situation arose in which the middle class—using the vehicle of the Awami League (AL)—became the most powerful force in the new country. In the absence of any significant rural landlord class or entrenched power elite, social capital (educational credentials, degrees, and a capacity to network with global financial institutions) became keys to success. As might be expected, lawyers dominated the AL, and urban professionals, especially teachers and doctors, were also of great importance.

In the new nation, short-lived governments alternated with periods of military rule. Even after independence, violence continued. In 1974, some forty-six million people (out of a total population of seventy-four million) were living below the poverty line. At this time, when the price of rice increased by a factor of ten, an astonishing 78 percent of the population survived on less than 1,935 calories per day—defined as the level of absolute poverty by the International Labor Organization.[1] Floods inundated more than two-fifths of the country, and famine set in.[2] President Mujibur Rahman ("Father of the Country") visited Washington in September, but he was refused U.S. aid. By the end of October, at least fifty thousand people had starved to death. Mujibur was compelled to accept harsh terms from a consortium led by the World Bank in exchange for credits in international financial markets. He was forced to devalue the new nation's currency by 50 percent, denationalize state-owned industries, liberalize restrictions on imports, adopt new rules aiding foreign investments, and fire his finance minister.[3] In November, when U.S. Secretary of State Henry Kissinger arrived in Dhaka on a brief visit, he met with Mujibur for two hours. The country reeled from politically motivated murders. In 1974, some four thousand AL members (including at least five members of parliament) were murdered.[4]

At that time—as today—U.S. security interests privileged Pakistan—a status then denied the newly emergent country of Bangladesh (famously called a "basket case" by Kissinger). Within a year of Kissinger's visit, on August 15, 1975, President Mujibur and forty members of his family were murdered in a military coup. The men who seized control of the country's intelligence apparatus were among more than forty Bengali officers who had been trained in Washington, and evidence subsequently emerged that the United States had discussed the coup in advance with its promulgators.[5]

On November 3, 1975, supporters of Mujibur overthrew the new military rulers, and four days later, rank and file soldiers successfully seized control of the government. The radical socialist organization, *Jatyo Samajtantrrik Dal* (JSD), emerged as leadership of the nation in this period. The JSD had held rallies of one hundred thousand and led two general strikes. Troops had opened fire on one of their marches on the home minister's residence, killing at least eight people (thirty by doctors' reports). The party offices had been ransacked, its leaders arrested, and newspaper closed down. By November 7, when the JSD launched its successful national uprising, some ten thousand of its members were in prison. Although they seized power, the radical potential of their program was never realized, in large part because their leaders, including war hero Colonel Abu Taher, freed General Ziaur Rahman from prison and positioned him to become the country's next president. Zia turned on Abu Taher and had him executed after a secret trial marred by irregularities.

Under Zia's post-1977 regime, far-reaching Islamization of government was instituted. Whatever their ideology, all governments of the new republic constricted people's rights, Zia's perhaps most of all. Nor was Mujibur an exception. He had enacted a Special Powers Act and constitutional amendment that introduced one-party rule, and his elite paramilitary force, although intended to curb the power of the military establishment, committed massive violations of human rights including torture.[6] The country's parliament was enervated by unending turmoil between the two main political forces: the AL (which dominated the government immediately after independence) and the Bangladesh Nationalist Party (BNP), which had won 207 of 300 seats in 1979 parliamentary elections. Frustrated with their lack of influence once the BNP assumed the reins of power, the AL had organized a ten-party alliance in 1980 that embarked on an extraparliamentary campaign of *hartals*, demonstrations, and continuing agitation against the elected BNP government.[7]

After surviving at least twenty coup attempts, on May 30, 1981, President Zia was assassinated. In the continuing context of assassinations of top political leaders, parties were unable to stop the military from seizing power again on

March 24, 1982, when General Muhammad Ershad proclaimed himself dictator. As with the country's body politic, opposition to Ershad was weakened by rivalry between the AL and BNP, whose differences are often personalized by the women who lead both. AL's leader Hasina Wajed blames the BNP for the 1975 assassination of her father, Sheikh Mujibur, the "founding father" of the country. On the other side, when BNP leader President Zia was assassinated in 1981, his widow Khaleda Zia inherited that party's mantle—as well as unending enmity toward the AL, whom she blamed for her husband's murder.

Students to the Fore

With political parties incapacitated by factional strife, autonomous, extraparliamentary forces had to become activated in order for democratization to succeed. Students in Bangladesh have a long history of leading the nation forward. In the estimation of Talukder Maniruzzaman, "In no country in the world was student activism in the 1950s and 1960s of greater intensity, continuity and concern than in Bangladesh."[8] During decades known internationally for unparalleled student engagement, Bangladesh's campus movement stood tall among many noteworthy cases. Historically low rates of matriculation and the country's high poverty rate made students especially privileged and destined to become part of the political elite, and they responded with heroic leadership based upon the nation's universal interests.[9] When the region was known as East Pakistan, students played leading roles in antidictatorship struggles against Ayub Khan's rule. In late 1969, they formulated an eleven-point program and initiated an antigovernment movement that sustained wide support—including large-scale worker actions. In March 1971, as they mobilized Bengalis for independence, they coordinated a huge non-cooperation movement at which "even Gandhi would have marveled."[10]

The pattern of events in the unfolding of Bangladesh's democratization is familiar. After a dozen coups d'état in the first decade of the country's existence, General Hussain Muhammad Ershad consolidated power after 1982 by increasing both the size and power of the military. Active or retired members of the military headed fourteen of the country's twenty-two large corporations and a third of all embassies abroad.[11] On the same day of Ershad's coup, student opposition to his autocratic rule began.[12] Within a month after Ershad's seizure of power, student opposition was answered with violence, beginning a cycle of repression and resistance that led to widespread public sympathy for the student movement.

When students protested, some were killed. Lawyers and trade unionists then mobilized against the regime, which escalated its intimidation tactics. Seeking to undermine the constituency for campus opposition, the regime developed a plan to restrict higher education. When that plan only intensified campus opposition, police and paramilitary forces invaded Dhaka University in November 1982, where they mercilessly attacked students and faculty. After dozens of people were savagely beaten, the student government united a plethora of twenty-four groups to create the Organization for Student Struggle. With two representatives from each organization and a rotating chair, forty-eight floating members (including less than a handful of women) were able to formulate the movement's objectives. Their three primary demands were:

1. An immediate end to martial law and implementation of full democracy and respect for human rights
2. Cancellation of the new proposed education policy
3. The release of all political prisoners and an end to repression

On February 14, 1983, thousands of students marched on the Ministry of Education, where police and paramilitary forces opened fired, killing at least four people. The event was doubly frustrating for rank and file students since they had attempted to march from Dhaka University on the education building a month earlier (on January 11), only to have their initiative sapped by a last minute veto by political parties (including communists, socialists, the Workers Party, and the Awami League). On the night of February 13, when it appeared that the parties were once again going to block the action, hundreds of student activists compelled their leaders to pledge in writing not to change the plan to march. The next day, students took the initiative to target the Ministry of Education, only to be met by deadly gunfire.[13]

At a time when top leaders of the AL and BNP would not meet in the same room or speak from the same platform, autonomous student leadership was required to bring coherency and unity to the movement for democracy. Unafraid to speak truth to power, youthful students shamed the divided political parties into action. As a result of students' heroic sacrifice, nineteen political parties issued a unified statement supporting them, and Bangladesh witnessed the birth of unified antiregime actions. In the mid-1980s, the opposition was "diverse and diffuse, offering a thousand points of resistance,"[14] but students retained a leadership role for two reasons: besides the unending AL-BNP rivalry stood the completely unreasonable way the authorities treated protests. Even when students took to the streets in peaceful processions, police opened fire on them and killed many. When student leaders publicly spoke out, they were arrested. Not content to promulgate nationalist demands alone, students publicly proclaimed their solidarity with movements for democracy in Nepal, Burma, Korea, and Palestine.[15]

Alongside students, lawyers became activated in response to regime repression. In June 1982, when the Ershad regime reconfigured high court venues, lawyers launched a national boycott of the Supreme Court and demanded Ershad step down. Associations of doctors, engineers, teachers, and trade unions also arose to challenge Ershad. Spurred by grassroots activism in the 1980s, a fifteen-party alliance against Ershad formed, and united actions included another coalition of seven parties. Time and again, the Ershad regime answered protests with gunfire. On November 28, 1983, when opposition alliances organized thousands of people to stream into the Secretariat (the seat of government), police killed a number of protesters.[16] The following March, the opposition so successfully boycotted local elections that the government cancelled them. In 1984, a two-day *hartal* called by the Workers-Employees Unity Council (known by the acronym, SKOP and representing more than fifteen national union federations) demanded the government implement an existing agreement to legalize trade unions, a reform that the employers' association had blocked by claiming it would devastate their businesses. During the *hartal*, two people were killed, and 772 arrests were made in two days in Dhaka. Angry groups of protesters smashed rickshaws and buses that did not observe the *hartal*, and at least one shop that remained open was attacked. During a solidarity action by the Student Action Committee at Rassahi University, leader Shah Zahan Shilas was killed by police gunfire.

Despite the regime's violence, government sponsored elections consistently gave Ershad mandates to rule—at the same time as people's common sense understood that his regime was widely unpopular. While many claimed electoral fraud, another reason for Ershad's political prowess was isolation of the country's population. In 1986, it was estimated that the country's mainstream media only reached some 4 percent of the population (or four million people)— that is, those who had access to one of four hundred thousand television sets, each of which cost the equivalent of six months of a bank branch manager's salary. While radio reached a daily audience of some thirty to forty million (as much as 40 percent of the population), newspapers' combined circulation was little more than 580,000. Traditional methods of communication like storytellers, traveling theater troupes, word of mouth at festivals, market gatherings, and buses were used by the democratization movement to energize opposition, but these arenas do not have the synchronicity and broad audience of mass electronic media. Despite the shortcomings of traditional media, they are more polycentric and participatory than centralized ones, and the insurgency's use of them help to build a vibrant civil society—which in turn contributed to the movement's success.

Opposition umbrella alliances managed to work together until 1985, when disagreements about whether or not to participate in new elections emerged. When the AL broke its promises to oppose elections, almost all other parties, including the BNP, boycotted them. Ershad's seizure of power in 1982 had effectively caused the BNP to lose control of the government, but it also provided an opportunity for the AL to enter into a coalition with him. In an election described as a "tragedy for democracy" by a British team of observers, Ershad's party won a majority, but mass protests caused the new parliament to be dissolved.[17]

With political parties still divided, subaltern forces were compelled to regroup and take the lead against Ershad's "martial democracy." By 1986, some seventeen peasant and agricultural workers' unions, associations of journalists, lawyers, teachers, doctors, and cultural workers joined urban workers and students to propel forward demands for democracy. Centered in Dhaka, the movement spread to other cities, but there appears to have been few actions in rural areas, as activists did not make serious attempts to bring the movement to the countryside. Students, urban professionals, and government workers were in the forefront of the movement, a fact so obvious that one observer labeled it "revolt of the urban bourgeoisie."[18] Autonomous of the established political parties, these sectors' spontaneous capacity for self-organization was an important resource that helped bring the anti-Ershad movement to victory.

In 1987 and 1988, three alliances united to organize *hartals* to demand Ershad's resignation and fair elections. In the country's two largest cities, Dhaka and Chittagong, thirty-eight people were killed during opposition rallies.[19] The 1987 uprising was particularly intense. Although it was unsuccessful in dislodging Ershad, it was powerfully important in shaping the opposition's capacity to unseat him in 1990. At the same time as Ershad built up the army, putting retired top commanders in positions of power and wealth, doubling officers' pay, and swelling the number of troops, he positioned the country increasingly closer to the United States. He agreed to send 2,300 troops to Saudi Arabia to help with the first U.S. Gulf War, an act of "solidarity" for which the country received over $350 million—more than 40 percent of its foreign earnings. In August 1990, the IMF negotiated an enhanced structural adjustment program. Needless to say, both these initiatives were highly unpopular.

Bangladesh is heavily dependent upon global financial institutions for loans and grants. Between independence and democratization (i.e., from 1971 to 1991), foreign aid totaled something like $33 billion, almost equally divided between grants and loans. A new comprador ruling class was subsidized by such aid, and it actually exported capital, especially to the Middle East, where rates of return on investments were higher than in domestic endeavors.[20] While the country's constitution promised equality and people's expectations for prosperity rose, the reality of repression and misery led to a willingness to act against the regime.

As opposition to his rule mounted, Ershad sought constitutional reform to enable him to serve a second term as president. Political parties responded with a sit-in at the Secretariat on October 10, 1990, but once again, antagonism between the AL and BNP bitterly divided the movement.[21]

Bangladeshi Student Power

More than any other force, students came together to lead the country forward. The country's political parties were of little use to the movement since they could not find ways to cooperate with each other. When they were not simply shunning each other, they argued endlessly about tactical differences. The AL and its alliance of eight parties called for a *hartal*; the BNP and seven other parties advocated a huge rally; and a left-wing five-party coalition called for a *ghrao*—surrounding television stations to call attention to the pro-Ershad bias of the country's media.

On the campuses, a diverse spectrum of groups coexisted, until 1990, when the Nationalist Student Party (loosely affiliated with the BNP) won student government elections in 270 of the country's 350 colleges. Parties' squabbles had long hindered student efforts to unify, but with a large majority from the BNP, students were able to overcome their differences.[22] On October 1, 1990, more than 2,700 student leaders answered the call of Dhaka University's Central Students' Union. The assembled students agreed that they should take unified action to compel the resignation of the Ershad government, after which a neutral caretaker regime could sponsor elections. They organized a militant protest on October 10 that "was not only against the regime but against the opposition leadership as well."[23] During this autonomously organized demonstration, at least five people were

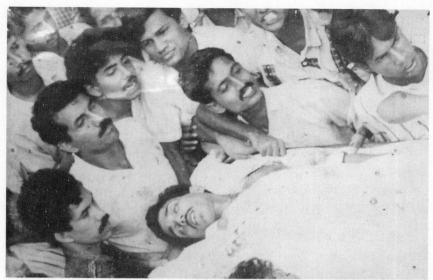

Student Jahad's corpse was carried back to Dhaka University. Photographer unknown.

killed and hundreds wounded when police attacked the gathering. Infuriated by the regime's continuing violence, students carried the corpse of BNP student leader Jahad back to Dhaka University. Rallying around a platform where his body lay, tens of thousands of students raised their right hands to swear they would not return home until Ershad had been forced to resign.[24]

Two days later, the movement was again viciously attacked, and many leaders were wounded. With prominent individuals being targeted, some twenty-two student organizations formed the All Party Students' Unity (APSU), a coalition that would take responsibility for daily participatory meetings and demonstrations. By October 15, the group also functioned as a liaison committee linking the three alliances of the country's political parties.

Since politicians failed to lead the popular movement, autonomously organized activists became the main facilitators of protests, public funerals, and meetings. Within a month, students had stimulated district committees of all the major parties to work together. Finally, by November 19, the three alliances, shamed by the unity of their grassroots groups, signed a Joint Declaration and agreed to cooperate with each other. They announced a united front against Ershad and endorsed the process of democratic transition laid out by students. Despite the announced unity of the parties, Sheik Hasina continued to refuse to speak from the same platform as BNP leader Khaleda Zia.

By the end of the year, mobilized students were able on several occasions to cut off communications between the central government in Dhaka and the rest of the country by using the tactic of *ghraos* of television and radio stations, encircling them or occupying them and refusing to leave or to let the managers exit until their demands were met. In this period, the movement also instigated several *hartals*, and more than one large student demonstration led to

Students played a major role in uniting and leading the Bangladeshi movement in 1990.
Photographer unknown.

street fights with police and paramilitary thugs. In a cynical attempt to remain in power, Ershad's forces organized attacks on Hindu businesses—hoping to fan the flames of ethnic conflict. As grassroots activists continued to pressure Ershad, the regime developed a new tactic, similar to one used in Burma: a host of hardened criminals was released from prisons and sent to attack protesters in the streets. On November 20, *mastans* (government-empowered paramilitary forces) nearly killed student leader Nazmul Haq, and the next day, they injured dozens more students. Emboldened by the free hand granted them by the regime, on November 22, they launched an armed attack on the Dhaka University campus. In response, the APSU organized a huge demonstration on November 25, and when *mastans* attacked as expected, students were ready for them—a few carried arms to counter those of the *mastans*. In a campus battle that lasted for hours, *mastans* were soundly defeated and fled in government vehicles.

With his paramilitary forces in disarray, Ershad invoked emergency legislation and proclaimed a curfew on November 27, but people continued to resist. The residents of Mohammed Pur in particular took great pains to remain outdoors. During the protests, Dr. Milan (a key APSU leaders in 1982) was shot dead as he crossed a street. The Journalists Union had promised that if the regime declared an emergency, they would not publish newspapers, and they remained true to their promise.[25] Students organized illegal demonstrations, and the entire faculty at Dhaka University resigned. As the strike spread, artists and workers at television and radio stations refused to participate in programming beginning on

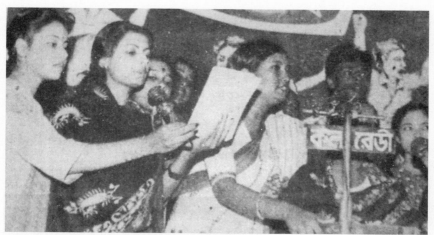

Women television stars led a celebration after Ershad was overthrown. Photographer unknown.

December 1. Three days later, government workers declared a strike until Ershad left office—effectively paralyzing the country's civil administration.

Hundreds of demonstrations, spontaneous rallies, and a wide variety of protests took place throughout the capital. Student liaison committees functioned daily on district levels to coordinate actions. Surreptitiously meeting, the APSU coordinating committee articulated continuing national protests. As Fazlul Haque Milan told me: "Our main weapon was our mental edge. We didn't care if we got killed, and a huge number of students were in the streets. Most people in Bangladesh supported us. That was out main strength." It even appeared that some sections of the military sided with students.[26] Inside army cantonments, anti-Ershad sentiment widely appeared.[27] After November 27, so great was the disaffection among the regime's armed forces that where paramilitary forces operated barricades, people were able to stream through without violence.

With the country clearly against him, Ershad proposed a way out of the crisis: he would select a vice president, subject to approval by all three opposition alliances, and call new elections. But people refused to call off their protests, since they were unwilling to let Ershad choose his successor. In this decisive moment, the activated populace had an intelligence and unity that surpassed the regime's elite—as well as that of the opposition parties. In the words of Alam, "The masses sensed the crumbling of the regime and remained vigilant so that no opposition leader would be able to make a backdoor compromise with the regime."[28]

Faced with the continuing mobilization of tens of thousands of citizens, Ershad agreed to leave office on December 4. Behind the scenes, he nonetheless attempted to assemble a fresh martial law regime, but top generals refused to support him. Despite the magnificent victory won by the movement in the streets, the opposition parties could not agree on a leader for the caretaker government. Autonomous political activists, led by the APSU, set a deadline of 6:00 p.m. on December 5 for the parties to reach some agreement. On December 6, parliament was dissolved, and Ershad handed over power to a caretaker government. As news spread of Ershad's demise, celebrations animated Dhaka throughout the night. After midnight, residents in Mohamed Pur paraded with flowers, and the next day thousands of people attended a victory rally at Purano Paltan. In front of the National Press Club, people thronged the square. Flowers appeared everywhere.

The Democratic Breakthrough

It was a costly victory. From 1982 to 1990, over a hundred people were killed and thousands more were wounded in the struggle against Ershad.[29] Along with ten of his ministers, Ershad was later punished for corruption—but not for the murders committed at his behest. The former dictator spent more than five years in prison, but he never returned any of the $100 million he is thought to have embezzled. Along with the end of the dictatorship, major gains in civil liberties were won: trade unions were legalized, minorities won more rights, freedom of expression and press freedom were extended, and relatively clean elections were held. As we have seen elsewhere, with the expansion of freedom, the GNP grew at unprecedented rates.

In almost every country, world events provide an important context for comprehending people's mobilizations, and Bangladesh is no exception. Her membership in the cluster of nations that underwent popular upheavals at that time remains a source of national pride. As S.M. Shamsul Alam put it, "Given the extent of mass participation in antiauthoritarian social agitation, Bangladesh proudly stands with countries like the Philippines, Haiti, and many other socialist and nonsocialist countries."[30] Leading up to the People Power uprising that ended Ershad's regime, movements in the Philippines, Burma, and Tibet provided inspiration and convinced people that in Bangladesh, too, ordinary citizens could determine their society's direction.[31]

Uprisings—especially victorious ones—energize people, spurring them on to change more dimensions of life than simply the character of regimes or the names of men and women at the top levels of power. We can witness similar generalized unleashing of pent-up aspirations in Korea and Nepal, where in the weeks after the democratic breakthroughs of 1987 and 1990, workers mobilized to demand better wages and working conditions, and women insisted upon greater life possibilities and more liberty in everyday life. In Bangladesh, as in Korea and Nepal, among the most significant immediate gains in the struggles in the afterglow of political democratization were the formation of unions that could advocate the long-term rights of working people and the mobilization of women for their liberation.

As in Nepal and Korea, democratic breakthroughs also lead to autonomous mobilizations of subaltern groups seeking to overturn long-held patterns of discrimination against them. Uprisings tear apart long-held prejudices and lead people to challenge afresh even the most deeply ingrained patterns of behavior. As in these other cases, workers, women, and other oppressed groups gained increased social visibility as a result of their participation in the democracy movement. Simultaneously, the number of NGOs multiplied, as professional activists rose to prominence within these new grassroots initiatives.

TABLE 8.1 **Officially Registered NGOs in Bangladesh, 1990–2006**

Year	Local	Foreign	Total
1990–1991	395	99	494
1995–1996	887	134	1021
2000–2001	1500	171	1671
2005–Jan. 2006	1807	190	1997

Source: Farida Chowdhury Khan, Ahrar Ahmad and Munir Quddus, eds., *Recreating the Commons? NGOs in Bangladesh* (Dhaka: The University Press limited, 2009), 10.

National elections at the end of February 1991 were inconclusive: no party received even one-third of the popular vote, although the AL and BNP each received over ten million of the thirty-four million votes cast. Out of 300 seats, the BNP finished with 141, the AL with 44, and the Nationalist Party (headed by deposed dictator Ershad) with 35 seats. Whatever their differences, each of these three major parties counted more than 70 percent of their elected officials as lawyers, businessmen, and industrialists. The other major component of the new government's elected representatives were urban professionals (doctors, professors, teachers, journalists, and student activists against Ershad), who comprised a scant 17 percent of the new legislature. In September, when a parliamentary system was formed with Khaleda Zia as prime minister, more than three-fourths of her ministers were lawyers and businessmen. Women held only a handful of seats.[32] So divided was the opposition, even journalists and women's groups remained formed along party lines.

The democratically elected parliament could barely claim legitimacy in the eyes of many people. Although about forty-eight former student activists got elected, some of the new parliament's 311 members were known to be smugglers of human beings, while as many as thirty of the more respectable ones were owners of garment factories (notorious for inhumane treatment of their workers), and another sixty were connected to or related to such owners. As one human rights defender put it, "Elected governments are not necessarily democratic."

While formally "democratic," a succession of governments remained deadlocked and ineffective, while an activated civil society arose from the broader impact of freed Bangladeshi imaginations and will. A groundswell of sentiment to prosecute leaders who had actively aided Pakistan's army in their murderous incursion of 1971 led on March 26, 1992, to a public people's tribunal. The "Coordinating Committee for Elimination of Collaborators and Assassins of 1971" sponsored an autonomous public court and found Muslim fundamentalist leader Golum Azam guilty of collaboration with Pakistani massacres. While the "public court" sentenced him to death, the government only agreed to look into his possible crimes.

For twenty years, no Bangladesh government had summoned the will or had the vision to hold collaborators with Pakistan responsible for the horrendous massacres, but autonomously organized civil activists—galvanized in the struggles of 1990—compelled the government to act. This particular issue dramatizes the incapacity of elected governments to act: in 2011, the government continues to contemplate prosecutions of individuals involved in atrocities in 1971.

The Bangladeshi case portrays how professional associations (especially doctors, journalists, teachers, and lawyers) can become parallel political forces that wield significant power from outside the party system. Yet it also illustrates the incapacity of these groups to sustain the struggle, in part because of their own inferiority complex. As one former activist remembered, "We, the students who struggled from 1982, should have taken over the caretaker government. Instead, as soon as elections were called, corruption set in. Industrialists and the rich used their money to become candidates and ministers."[33] Dr. Beena Shikdar echoed that sentiment: "It was the students, then lawyers, then workers who revolted but the parties stole the fruits of our labor."

While the quantity of activist groups and a modicum of democratic rights were won in struggles against Ershad, the country remains stuck in a bitter cycle of repression and resistance to unjust authority. Despite many gains, a lasting effect of Ershad's corruption was its trickling down to other levels—including into the student movement, which no longer seems motivated by universal interests. The top-down character of the new democratic regime is reflected in the movement's key decisions being made by its leaders, in the increasing power of the military and expansion of corrupt bureaucracy while poverty and illiteracy remain rampant.

Women's Movement

In the immediate aftermath of the democratic breakthrough, women's roles in a predominantly Muslim society became a focal point for great tensions. In October 1991, Islamic fundamentalists mounted a campaign against Dhaka's red light district. Prostitutes organized counterprotests, sometimes with the help of Women's Side, an autonomous organization of women, and were able to keep their space. In February 1993, feminist novelist Taslima Nasrin was targeted by male, Islamist anger. A *fatwa* accusing her of blasphemy was issued, and on September 2, 1993, an obscure religious group put a price on her head equal to more than ten times per capita GDP. As other groups called for her assassination, she fled to India, where she also drew calls for her assassination from Muslim leaders, causing her to take refuge in Sweden.[34] Nasrin's case helps illustrate the precarious position of women in Bangladesh.

Since the leaders of the two major political parties are women, it is sometimes stated that women in general have somehow been liberated from the yoke of patriarchal control. In the first place, Zia and Wajed are the widow and daughter of assassinated former presidents. They derive their power from men to whom they were related by blood or marriage—not from their status as individual women. Furthermore, the practice of these two women leaders has been nothing different than typical male political behavior. Rather than uniting, they have continually fought, sometimes over issues that seem of little consequence. In the mid-1990s, their inability to work together left the government deadlocked for years and resulted in outbursts of violent confrontations among their supporters. Better indications of women's status were revealed in a 2003 female literacy rate of only 29.3 percent as against 52 percent for men. The female labor force participation rate stood at only 14 percent in 1996.[35]

Despite the transition to democracy, Islamic patriarchy remains entrenched, and many people felt women's status has improved little with liberation from the Ershad dictatorship. Indeed, a steep rise in reported crimes against women was reported, particularly in rural areas where traditional justice was severely meted out. In 1993, several women accused of adultery were killed by stoning, and another was burned to death.[36] Islamic clergy forcibly dissolved dozens of marriages and ostracized the families of some five thousand female NGO workers.

Nonparty affiliated women's groups had long been active in autonomous protests against male violence and for improvements in rural women's lives. Self-help campaigns for prostitutes as well as in the ongoing struggle for fair wages and safe conditions for factory workers were continually being generated. In the 1990s, women's movements arose calling for an end to domestic violence, rights for sex workers, and recognition of household work.[37] On December 7, 1998, when NGOs rallied over eight thousand poor women and men in Brahmanbaria, clergy from the local Islamic schools (*madrassah*) led a violent assault with knives and axes. For three days, widespread looting of NGO offices and schools took place, and twenty-six houses belonging to NGO members were burned. Local women associated with NGOs were publicly stripped of their clothing and humiliated, while many NGO leaders fled in their imported SUVs to find refuge in Dhaka, where they used the event to raise new funds from foreign donors.[38] In 1999, a significant jump in violence against women was recorded, with the number of registered attacks increasing from 1,705 to 8,710 in a five-year period.[39] As women mobilized for greater rights, they won a significant victory in 2001, when the country's highest court ruled that all religious verdicts (*fatwas*) were illegal.

Class Struggles of Garment Workers

As post-Ershad Bangladesh enjoyed a surge in economic output, those at the top enriched themselves and answered expressions of discontent with violence. Simultaneously, a great number of people were uprooted from their traditional dwelling places in the countryside and forced into cities, where, at best, many found only transitory work. From about 285,000 garment workers in 1969, one 2006 estimate counted about 2,500 factories that employed 1.8 million garment workers—90 percent of whom are women.[40] "Floating urban workers" endure impoverished lives at the margins of society, where conditions compel them to accept any job at any price. Paid barely enough to survive (minimum wage is $14 per month), workers are often forced to work a seven-day week twelve hours per day without holidays or sick leave.

Women workers in Bangladesh are doubly (or even triply) oppressed. Since their families depend upon them both for household chores and income, they are compelled to take low-paying jobs. For years, workplace safety problems plagued them but little was done to provide for their well-being. Factory owners blocked unions from forming, and armed thugs (*mastans*) used force to keep female laborers compliant. Only a few weeks after the victory over Ershad, on December 27, 1990, a horrific fire killed twenty-five women and children in a factory called Saraka on the outskirts of the capital. The popular mobilizations of the democratic breakthrough had barely come to an end, so people were able to use the space opened by the democracy movement to mobilize for economic justice. On January 2, 1991, some twenty thousand women garment workers marched in Dhaka to demand compensation for the dead and wounded, a proper government investigation, and improved safety measures at work.[41] Perhaps the most significant outcome of the women's protests was their formation of an inclusive union, the United Council of Workers and Office Personnel in Garments.

In the early 1990s, employer attempts to divide workers between Hindus and Muslims failed as workers' united in demonstrations and strikes. In 1993, workers blocked highways during a union-led general strike, and at least four universities were shut down as well. As the movement deepened, it succeeded in shutting down Dhaka on April 26, 1994, and strikes continued into June.[42] With the plight of workers unresolved, farmers burned much of the jute crop in October. In December, wildcat strikes and violence continued, and even lower-level police and militias joined. After rank and file dissidents took some twenty-two officers hostage when they occupied their headquarters in Dhaka, Elite Special Forces were called in. At least four people were killed and fifty wounded before the government could regain control. Nonetheless, garment workers continued to strike in January 1995. Protests became especially intense in the port city of Chittagong. By the end of 1995, trains, buses, ships, and airplanes were all brought to a halt.

After the wave of intense protests in the early 1990s, it took another decade before the next widespread class confrontations reached a boiling point. In the interim period, the country continued to have more than its share of brutality with which to contend. In 2002, army, police, and border guards were mobilized for eighty-six consecutive days during which over eleven thousand people were arrested and at least fifty-eight died in prison—all from "heart attacks" according to authorities' medical experts.[43] In 2004, a Rapid Action Battalion was created; soon a new plague of extrajudicial killings, torture, and other crimes broke out.[44]

In response to the shooting death of a worker in May 2006, workers burned down seven factories in and around Dhaka, blocked highways, and clashed with police for several days.[45] When a spiraling wave of strikes and violence could not be contained, a caretaker government was installed, but wildcat strikes rolled across some four thousand factories from May 20 to 24. Workers in nearby districts blocked highways, and the government responded with gunfire and clubs. In the first week, at least three workers were killed, three thousand injured, and thousands arrested. Protests escalated on May 20 as a workers' sit-in calling for the release of their imprisoned colleagues was answered with a lock-in—with no drinking water in sweltering heat. Police and thugs then attacked the massed workers—shooting twelve and beating many more. By the end of the day, as workers blocked traffic and continued to resist, more than eighty had to be treated for gunshot wounds. At least one worker was killed in front of FS Sweater Factory. Two days later in Savar EPZ, workers who insisted upon receiving their back pay were attacked by private security guards—but protesters went from neighboring factory to factory, where others joined them until twenty thousand were marching. Once again, bullets were indiscriminately fired, and this time hundreds were injured. Violence spread to the capital, where heavy protests closed a downtown industrial area. Some workers were reported to have been attacked for not joining in protests.[46]

The next day, May 23, Dhaka's industrial suburbs were closed down by a general strike. Workers' committees demanded holidays, an end to repression, release of arrested protesters, higher wages, and overtime pay for extra work. Again, highways were blocked. Seven factories were set afire. That evening, the Bangladesh Rifles—army forces entrusted with border protection—were called upon to restore order. Nonetheless workers continued to shut down the factory districts on May 24. Finally, the Minister of Labor coordinated an agreement whereby workers won many of their demands, but factory owners refused to honor the minister's promised reforms. On May 29, a new round of resistance and repression occurred. Hundreds more workers were wounded by gunfire, and at least one was killed.

The brutality of the paramilitary Rapid Action Battalion made it possible for factories to reopen on June 8—after nearly three weeks of struggles. Factory owners submitted a claim for losses to the government totaling $70 million. As a compromise was reached, workers, employers, and the government signed a tripartite Memorandum of Understanding on June 12, 2006 that mandated a minimum wage, rights to unionize, and release of all arrested workers in exchange for a return to work. Nonetheless, the vast majority of factory owners refused to honor the agreement.[47] As a result, again in October 2006, widespread work stoppages, highway blockades, and state violence plagued garment workers. Security guards brutalized workers in Uttara Syntax Sweater Factory, but many people immediately objected. When police attacked with sticks, workers drove the police back to their station, then broke all its windows and destroyed seven police vans parked outside. A week later in Dhaka, clashes began and quickly spread to Uttara, Abdullahpur, Tongi, Mirpur, Pallabi, and Savar. Dozens of factories reported sabotage, and three shopping malls were attacked.

After three months of upheaval in which sixty-four people were killed and the country's economy nearly collapsed, the interim caretaker government was replaced in October 2006. According to the constitution, elections were supposed to be held within ninety days, and the Awami League's *Mohajote* (grand alliance) was expected by many to emerge victorious.[48] Months passed during which rival groups violently fought each other. During this period, it was uncommon for a week to pass without a nationwide strike of one kind or another.[49] Elections in 1991, 1996, and 2001 formalized the democratic transition, but the two major parties effectively monopolized political debate. Each party resorted to *hartals* and blockades to enforce their will on the country when they could garner a majority. One observer called the process of deterioration "The Funeral of Democracy under Democratic Leadership."[50]

With violence and sectarianism rampant, the military declared a State of Emergency and took over power in what has been termed a "Stealth Coup" on January 11, 2007. Basic rights were suspended. Police detained over two hundred thousand people and turned houses and offices into "subjails." Sixty deaths in custody were reported in seven months of the decree—all reminiscent of 2002 "Operation Clean Heart" in which at least fifty-eight people died in detention after mass arrests had been made.[51] With China, India, the United States, and UN supporting the military government, the military was able to create its own rules and enforce them bloodily.[52] Even the nation's top political leaders were included in the sweeps. Sheikh Hasina was arrested on July 16, 2007, and Khaleda Zia on September 3. While they ruled in the name of combating corruption, military men staffed the country's ministries, where they enriched themselves at public expense. Army officers routinely monitored courtrooms and were given the official responsibility to prepare voter lists. At least 160 newspapers and a television station were closed down. From January 11, 2007, to the end of 2008, half a million people were arrested or detained.[53]

Although elections were supposed to take place and emergency rule was constitutionally limited to a maximum of 120 days, for more than two years, the military simply remained in power without elections. During this time, citizens' rights shrank. On July 31, 2007, four jute mills were closed by the military without paying six thousand workers their back pay. Another fourteen thousand workers were expecting a similar fate in eighteen other mills. The next month, nearly a hundred students and teachers were wounded in protests against the occupation of Dhaka University by the army. A few days later, on August 23, 2007, at least twelve journalists were arrested for covering the fights between students and the military.[54] In 2008, nearly three hundred factories, among them twenty-one in the Savar Export Processing Zone, were badly damaged in a new round of violence in which dozens of workers were severely injured and hundreds arrested.

Corruption is considered by the World Bank to be Bangladesh's main impediment to development. Transparency International ranked Bangladesh at the very bottom of its list of world corruption from 2001 to 2005, after which it was ranked third from the bottom in 2006 and seventh from the bottom in 2007.[55] (One should question World Bank conclusions, since it paid bribes in 1974 worth $4 million for an irrigation project—at the same time as it imposed one of its infamous structural adjustment programs on the starving new nation.)[56] Amid daily reports of corruption, politicians and business leaders were permitted by military leaders to enrich themselves at the same time as millions of ordinary citizens were reduced to semistarvation. With the press muzzled, the military arrested almost twelve thousand people in an anticorruption campaign in 2008.[57]

When elections were permitted in 2008, the AL swept back into power. The BNP barely won 10 percent of the seats in parliament, and its leaders were again subjected to political persecution. Khaleda Zia was evicted from her family mansion. Under restored democracy, the police routinely mistreat BNP members. While many see the AL as the sole perpetrator of abuse, others point to the role of deposed former dictator Muhammad Ershad, who was back in government. After serving nearly five years in prison for his crimes while military ruler, Ershad was elected to parliament five times and his party became one of those governing with the AL after the 2009 elections. Talukder Maniruzzaman referred to him as "Machiavelli incarnate."[58] Although the economy is growing at 6 percent per year, poverty is entrenched and inequality grows. Activist Anu Muhammad summarized the country's dilemma: "Although the major political parties of the country had opposed the autocratic government and its policies since 1982–1983, and that government was overthrown through a mass uprising in 1990, as soon as they got elected these parties, one after another, became busy in implementing the same policies formulated under the military regime. So, elected and non-elected, military and non-military governments made no difference in the realm of government policy because ultimately all those governments represented the same class and imperialist interest."[59]

Not only are the established political parties part of the systematic problems plaguing the country, but NGOs also feed into the very system of exploitation they criticize. In the view of one activist:

Beneficiaries of the poverty alleviation programs, or microcredit etc., are not the poor, but a section of the middle class and the wealthy. In fact, with a few exceptions, creating an NGO has become a good way of earning money in the name of the poor, the environment, gender equality and/ or human rights. That has also led to a spread of a begging culture. This growth of NGOs is also a neoliberal phenomenon, where the state's responsibility towards its citizens is thoroughly reduced and the market is given full authority in every sphere of life. In this model, the NGO is a supplement to as well as an instrument of market economy.[60]

Despite people's best efforts to break free of the spiral of dictatorship and emerge from its clutches, real democracy has yet to be realized. The prophetic words of Babasaheb Ambedkar ring as true for Bangladesh as for India: "the discontent against parliamentary democracy is due to the realization that it has failed to assure to the masses the right to liberty, property or the pursuit of happiness. . . . Parliamentary democracy took no notice of economic inequalities and . . . has continuously added to the economic wrongs of the poor, the downtrodden and the disinherited class."[61]

In 2010, workers' grievances and employer intransigence again resulted in widespread struggles for justice. The garment industry had grown to constitute more than three-fourths of Bangladesh's foreign exchange earnings and 40 percent of the industrial workforce. Although sixteen recognized trade unions existed, a small unionization rate and fragmentation of the labor movement sapped workers' power. Denied representation in parliament, workers finally expressed their outrage, but their cries were answered by violence, rather than compassion and reform. In February, at least twenty-two workers perished in a factory fire in Gazipur at a plant manufacturing clothing for H&M. Protests from June to August compelled the government to enact a minimum wage of barely $40 a month in November 2010. The new wage regulation was enforced scantily—if at all—and the average pay received was $29 a month. Workers had set $73 as their goal but faced severe legal obstacles. In response to their campaign for implementation of the legal wage structure, dozens of labor leaders were imprisoned, and nearly twenty-one thousand workers had cases filed against them.

Protests reached a peak from December 7 to 12, when strikes broke out in four cities: Dhaka, Chittagong, Narayanganj, and Gazipur. The focal point became the factory of South Korean YoungOne Corporation in the Chittagong Export Processing Zone, a company that accounted for nearly 5 percent of the total export earnings of the apparel industry.[62] At least four people were killed, twenty factories damaged, and a hundred vehicles vandalized. The entire EPZ had to be closed down. On December 14, a fire broke out in a ninth floor of a factory that manufactured garments for Gap, JC Penney, and Van Heusen. At least twenty-six workers perished—most of them unable to escape because of locked doors. Clean Clothes Campaign estimated that 200 workers have been killed in factory fires in the garment industry over the past five years.[63] The Bangladesh Fire Service and Civil Defense Department put the number at 414 garment workers killed in 213 factory fires between 2006 and 2009.

Despite its status as a "democracy," Bangladesh continues to convulse in violence. In the month of October 2010, a total of 24 people were killed and 770 injured in political violence. In 2010, WikiLeaks released cables proving that Rapid Action Battalion (RAB) received training from the British government in "interviewing techniques." Torture has been widely documented by human rights groups. RAB was held responsible for more than 1,000 extrajudicial killings since 2004.[64] In the decade to 2010, every four days, one citizen was killed in political violence—a total of 853 as tabulated by the human rights monitoring group Odhikar.[65] Although problems of violence and poverty continue to weigh heavily on Bangladesh, its people made important steps forward twenty years ago. Their continuing struggles can find in the victory of 1990 a source of pride and inspiration from which people can draw nourishment for the future.

Bangladesh's successful overthrow of Ershad in 1990 contributed to the international wave of uprisings against dictatorships. Soon thereafter, the people of Thailand grew restive under their own military rulers, and in 1992, Thais won democracy.

NOTES

1   Lawrence Lifschulz, *Bangladesh: The Unfinished Revolution* (London: Zed Press, 1979), 44–45, 109, 139.
2   Anthony Mascarenhas, *Bangladesh: A Legacy of Blood* (London: Hodder and Stoughton, 1986).
3   Lifschulz, *Bangladesh*, 140–41.
4   Al Masud Hasanuzzaman, *Role of Opposition in Bangladesh Politics* (Dhaka: The University Press Limited, 1998), 60.
5   Lifschulz, *Bangladesh*, 100–119.
6   Interview with Md. Shariful Islam, Dhaka, December 22, 2010.
7   Hasanuzzaman, *Role of Opposition*, 99. A *hartal* (or *bandh*, as the phenomenon is known in Nepal and Burma) is more than a general strike, which it encompasses and surpasses. Everyone is supposed to stop business as usual: not only do businesses close, schools are adjourned, and offices are emptied; while normal services like water and electricity function, transportation facilities close. *Hartals* are not media events but movement building gauges of strength. The word *hartal* is derived from the Sanskrit word for market (*haar*) and the Hindu word for lock (*tal*). See Robert

S. Anderson, "Stop Everything in Bangladesh: Communication, Martial Law and National Strikes," *Canadian Journal of Communication* 13, no. 5 (1988): 85.

8   Talukder Maniruzzaman, *The Bangladesh Revolution and Its Aftermath* (Dhaka: The University Press Limited, 1988), 53.

9   Bazlul M. Chowdhury, *Class and Social Structure of Bangladesh* (Dhaka: Ankur Prakashani, 2008), 66.

10   Talukder Maniruzzaman, "The Fall of the Military Dictator: 1991 Elections and the Prospect of Civilian Rule in Bangladesh," *Pacific Affairs* 65, no. 2 (Summer 1992): 3, 63, 80–82.

11   Ibid., 203–24.

12   Interview with Amirul Haque Amin, Dhaka, May 10, 2010.

13   Ibid.

14   Anderson, "Stop Everything," 67–86.

15   Interview with Dr. Mushtuq Husain, Dhaka, May 10, 2010.

16   Hasanuzzaman, *Role of Opposition*, 109.

17   *Far Eastern Economic Review*, May 22, 1986.

18   Badruddin Omar as quoted in S.M. Shamsul Alam, "Democratic Politics and the Fall of the Military Regime in Bangladesh," *Bulletin of Concerned Asian Scholars* 27 (1995): 36.

19   Maniruzzaman, "Fall," 206.

20   Ibid., 218.

21   Hasanuzzaman, *Role of Opposition*, 133.

22   Interview with Adilur Rahman Khan, Dhaka, May 11, 2010.

23   Alam, "Democratic Politics," 33.

24   Interview with Fazlul Haque Milan, Dhaka, May 11, 2010.

25   Interview with Ataur Rahman, Dhaka, May 11, 2010.

26   Interview with Ashim Kumar Ukil, Dhaka, May 10, 2010.

27   Interview with Amirul Haque Amin, Dhaka, May 10, 2010.

28   Alam, "Democratic Politics," 34.

29   Interview with Gopal Chandradas, Dhaka, May 11, 2010.

30   Alam, "Democratic Politics," 28.

31   Interview with journalist Aini Elias, Dhaka, May 9, 2010.

32   Interview with Dr. Beena Shikdar, Dhaka, May 10, 2010; Hasanuzzaman, *Role of Opposition*, 209.

33   Interview with Amirul Haque Amin, Dhaka, May 11, 2010.

34   For Alam, "Islam in Bangladesh and in other Islamic countries reproduces at the level of civil society the modern conditions of authoritarian and patriarchal frameworks of kinship, village and religious communities at a time when such communities are dispersed and loosened by the socioeconomic process of modernity" ("Democratic Politics," 39).

35   Imtiaz Ahmed and Binayak Sen, "The Case of Bangladesh," in *The Disenfranchised: Victims of Development in Asia*, ed. Urvashi Butalia (Hong Kong: Arena Press, 2004), 221, 245.

36   Lamia Karim, "Democratizing Bangladesh: State, NGOs, and Militant Islam," in *Recreating the Commons? NGOs in Bangladesh*, eds. Chowdhury Khan, Ahrar Ahmad, and Munir Quddus (Dhaka: The University Press limited, 2009), 149.

37   Amena Moshin, "The Nation State and Its Limits: Reflections from Bangladesh" in *Nepal: New Frontiers of Restructuring the State*, ed. Lok Raj Baral (New Delhi: Adroit Publishers, 2008), 209–11.

38   Karim, "Democratizing," 169.

39   Ahmed and Sen, "Case," 243.

40 Chowdhury, *Class and Social Structure*, 93.

41 Alam, "Democratic Politics," 41.

42 Kasimere Bran, "Setting Hell on Fire: Solidarity and Destruction in Bangladesh," *A Murder of Crows* 20 (March 2007): 6.

43 Asia Human Rights Commission, *State of Human Rights*, 19.

44 Ibid., xix.

45 "Workers' Uprising in Bangladesh," http://www.infoshop.org/inews/article. php?story=2006052417570713.

46 Ibid.

47 J. Hasan, *Labour Rights in the Readymade Garment Industry in Bangladesh* (Dhaka: Odhikar, 2008), 15–18.

48 Moshin, "Nation State," 201.

49 Rater Zonaki, "The Misrule of Law in Bangladesh," *Article 2* 6, no. 4 (August 2007): 38.

50 Md. Shariful Islam, "Democratization and Human Rights in Bangladesh: An Appraisal of the Military-Controlled Fakhuddin Interregnum," *Article 2* 7, no. 4 (December 2008): 27.

51 Other reports put the number of deaths in detention during the first seven months at 126.

52 Interview with Subodh Raj Pyakurel, INSEC, Kathmandu, April 13, 2009.

53 Asian Human Rights Commission, "Insidious Militarization and Illegal Emergency," 21.

54 Asian Legal Resource Center, "Bangladesh's State of Emergency is a State of Lawlessness," *Human Rights Solidarity* 17, no. 5 (September 2007): 3.

55 Iftekharuzzaman, "Corruption, Human Insecurity and Democratization in Bangladesh," in *Breaking the Barriers*, eds. Mohiuddin Ahmad and Cho Hee-Yeon (Dhaka: Nabodhara, 2008), 170–71.

56 "Letter from London," *Far Eastern Economic Review*, February 7, 1975.

57 Somini Sengupta, "Nearly 12,000 Are Arrested in Roundup in Bangladesh," *New York Times*, June 5, 2008.

58 Interview with Talukder Maniruzzaman, Dhaka, December 20, 2010.

59 Manoranjan Pegu, "Development, Capitalism, NGOs and People's Movements in Bangladesh: An Interview with Anu Muhammad," http://links.org.au/node/2075.

60 Pegu, "'Development.'"

61 Babasaheb Ambedkar, "What Congress and Gandhi Have Done to the Untouchables," (1946).

62 Mubin S. Khan, "Wage Wars," *New Age Extra*, December 17, 2010, 11.

63 Amy Kazmin and Jonathan Birchall, "Brands on Safety Push after Bangladesh Fire," *Financial Times*, December 20, 2010.

64 "UK Aids Dhaka Death Squad, Cables Show," *South China Morning Post*, December 23, 2010, A8.

65 Interview with Adilur Rahman Khan, Dhaka, May 11, 2010.

CHAPTER 9

Thailand

In Thailand, for the most part, the corpses of political victims have lent their evocative power to realizing the transformation toward a liberal free-market politics in step with the values of global capitalism.

—Alan Klima

CHRONOLOGY	
October 5, 1973	Eleven political activists demand a democratic constitution by December 10
October 9, 1973	Hundreds of people hold meetings around the Bo tree at Thammasat University
October 10, 1973	Thousands gathered, so meeting moves to Thammasat's football field
October 11, 1973	More than 70 percent of Bangkok's colleges closed by student strike
October 12, 1973	More than one hundred thousand people at Thammasat
October 13, 1973	Largest protest in Thai history—about five hundred thousand people—leaves Thammasat
October 14, 1973	Military fires on student protesters, killing seventy-three people; buildings burned; Thanom resigns
October 15, 1973	Fighting continues, spearheaded by "Yellow Tiger" engineering students
October 15, 1973	Thanom and top generals go into exile
November 1973	Postuprising surge begins: workers, farmers artists, women, students mobilize
1974	New constitution
1975	Investment strike as capital moves out of Thailand

April 30, 1975	Saigon taken as Vietnam is liberated; Laotian and Cambodian royal families overthrown
May 1, 1975	Mayday rally of 250,000 workers in Bangkok
1975	Right-wing vigilantes murder dozens of farmer activists
September 19, 1976	Thanom returns from exile and is visited by king and queen
October 4, 1976	Seven thousand people assemble at Thammasat University, create a "base" to expel Thanom
October 6, 1976	Police and vigilantes massacre students at Thammasat University: forty-one killed
October 6, 1976	Military seizes power and imposes harsh dictatorship
1976	Three thousand student activist join armed struggle in countryside
1979	Amnesty offered to student activists; elections held, neoliberalism implemented
February 23, 1991	Military coup d'état
April 19, 1991	Campaign for Popular Democracy calls for democratic constitution
April 7, 1992	General Suchinda Kraprayoon becomes prime minister
April 8, 1992	Chalard Worachat begins hunger strike to compel Suchinda to step down
April 20, 1992	One hundred thousand rally to support Chalard and ask Suchinda to step down
May 4, 1992	Bangkok mayor and former general Chamlong begins hunger strike
May 6, 1992	Huge crowd gathers at parliament; Chamlong moves them to Sanam Luang
May 8, 1992	Rally moves to Rajadamnoen Avenue
May 9, 1992	Leaders decide to suspend rallies until May 17
May 14, 1992	Confederation for Democracy reorganizes, chooses seven new leaders
May 17, 1992	More than three hundred thousand rally at Sanam Luang
May 17, 1992	Troops stop protesters from marching over Phan Fa Bridge
May 18, 1992	Troops open fire after midnight, killing dozens of people
May 18, 1992	Government buildings burned; army continues killing; people fight back
May 19, 1992	Troops rampage in makeshift hospital in Royal Hotel
May 20, 1992	Protests spread throughout Thailand
May 20, 1992	King orders Suchinda and Chamlong to settle differences; army withdraws
May 22, 1992	Confederation for Democracy demands Suchinda step down
May 22, 1992	Death toll counted at fifty-two with three hundred still missing; protesters demand punishment
May 24, 1992	King grants blanket amnesty to all involved in protest; Suchinda steps down

September 13, 1992	Pro-democracy parties win enough seats to form new government
1997	People's Constitution takes effect: best in Thai history; IMF Crisis
2001	Thaksin's *Thai Rak Thai* Party wins first election 2001, wages "war on drugs"
2006	Peoples Alliance for Democracy (Yellow Shirts) protests against Thaksin
September 19, 2006	Military coup against Thaksin
November 2008	Yellow Shirts end occupation of airports after courts dissolve pro-Thaksin government
April 13, 2009	Violent confrontations in Bangkok between Red Shirts and army
April to May 2010	At least ninety people killed and 1,800 injured as army clears central Bangkok of Red Shirts

LIKE THE PEOPLE of Nepal, Thais have twice massively protested and laid down their lives by the dozens in successful uprisings for democracy, only to have their heroic sacrifices squandered by political leaders, swept aside by dictators, and made into profits for global corporations. Unlike Nepalis, Thais have not abolished their monarchy, but rather revere the royal family with a fanaticism that borders on the extreme. A rich history of uprisings in the late twentieth century crystallized among ordinary citizens a lasting comprehension of the power of people taking control of public space. Ongoing battles between Red Shirts and Yellow Shirts are but the most visible indication of this consciousness.

In October 1973, hundreds of thousands of militant protesters led by students overthrew the military dictatorship—but only after the army killed seventy-one people and left scores of others missing, wounded, or traumatized. The military's humiliation at the hands of smiling youth in 1973 led to a counterattack of enormous proportions three years later. On October 6, 1976, paramilitary and police units assaulted Bangkok's Thammasat University, killing at least forty-one people—including many who were grotesquely disfigured, burned alive, or hanged from trees. The land of smiles revealed a ghastly underside. In the aftermath of the 1976 massacre, the military ran roughshod over the labor movement and curtailed civil liberties as neoliberalism was bloodily born. Renewed protests for democracy galvanized a massive base in May 1992, and once again, the army and police reacted violently to peaceful protesters who asked for rights taken for granted in Europe and the United States. At least forty-four people were killed and thirty-eight others remain missing, minimal numbers that belie enormous violence inflicted on citizens during three days of unbridled military mayhem. The insurgent energies unleashed in 1992's uprising helped propel a broad democratic offensive whose shining culmination occurred with the 1997 inauguration of a participatory constitution and Bill of Rights.

The new electoral system opened the door for billionaire CEO tycoon Thaksin Shinawatra become president. Like former Philippine president Fidel Ramos,

Thaksin served on Carlyle Asia's advisory board—yet another link in the chain of global domination by transnational capital as it sweeps aside "crony" (read "local") economic control. To his credit, Thaksin brought schools and hospitals to rural areas that had long been impoverished. He built roads and assisted farmers who had long been marginalized. As his popularity grew to rival that of the king, however, the monarchy helped engineer protests that drove him into exile. The new military dictatorship threw out the 1997 constitution—one of the best in Asia's long history. Divided since 2008 into competing camps of Red Shirts and Yellow Shirts, Thais continue to contest the precious political fruits of their democratic uprisings.

Nation, Religion, King

From the outside, Thailand remains a happy and tranquil society, one of the few countries in Southeast Asia to somehow avoid the scourge of European colonization. For having escaped such a fate, most Thais credit their monarchy—as they do for saving the nation from Burmese occupation in the sixteenth century. As a result, not far beneath the surface of the land of smiles, brutal authoritarianism and harsh punishment await anyone—foreigner and Thai alike—who violates unquestioned reverence for the royal family.[1] Unlike any of the countries discussed in this book, and, for that matter, perhaps more than anywhere else in the entire world—in Thailand, the king holds the status of demigod, and people's allegiance to the royal family is one of their most defining cultural characteristics. With the king's blessing, the military plays an inordinate role in economics and politics.

Since 1946, Thailand has experienced no fewer than eighteen military coups and fifteen constitutions—but only one king. With military dictators at the helm for decades, civilian governments have remained marginalized despite popular insurgencies seeking to limit the power of generals. It is no accident that King Bhumibol also happens to be the world's richest monarch, with wealth estimated in 2008 at $35 billion, well ahead of UAE Sheik Khaifa ($23 billion) and Saudi King Abdullah ($21 billion).[2] As a constitutional monarch, the king only wields moral authority and not legal power, yet he has continually imposed his rule without legal challenge. Hierarchical client-patron relationships patterned the traditional organization of Thai society. In comparison to Chinese and Korean mutual help associations built from the bottom up, Thai networks ascend from the top down.[3] Seventeenth-century palace law forbade high officials from meeting secretly or forming close associations with anyone except the king.[4] In clear vertical lines, all wealth and rank flowed through the king.

For centuries, a tradition permitted petitions for justice to be honored by the royal family. In the thirteenth century, Thai people were permitted to ring a bell outside the palace to request resolution of a grievance. A stone tablet in Sukothai reads, "If any commoner in the land has a grievance . . . King Ramkhamhaeng, the ruler of the kingdom, hears the call. He goes and questions them and examines the case, and decides it justly." King Bhumibol invokes this tablet as a symbol of Thai traditional democracy.[5] Bhumibol's grandfather, Chulalongkorn, made famous by the movie *The King and I*, prevented Thailand from falling to European

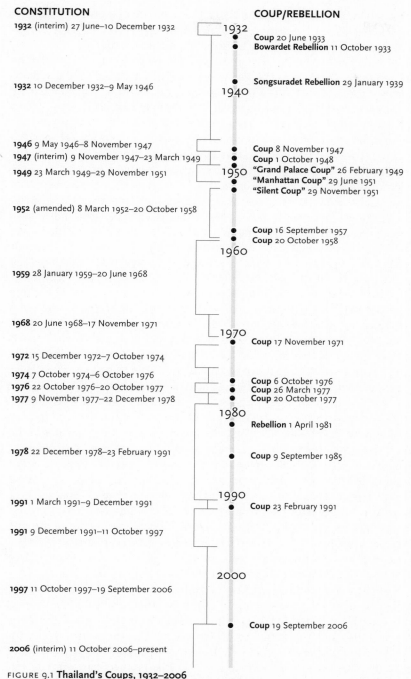

CONSTITUTION

1932 (interim) 27 June–10 December 1932

1932 10 December 1932–9 May 1946

1946 9 May 1946–8 November 1947
1947 (interim) 9 November 1947–23 March 1949
1949 23 March 1949–29 November 1951

1952 (amended) 8 March 1952–20 October 1958

1959 28 January 1959–20 June 1968

1968 20 June 1968–17 November 1971

1972 15 December 1972–7 October 1974

1974 7 October 1974–6 October 1976
1976 22 October 1976–20 October 1977
1977 9 November 1977–22 December 1978

1978 22 December 1978–23 February 1991

1991 1 March 1991–9 December 1991

1991 9 December 1991–11 October 1997

1997 11 October 1997–19 September 2006

2006 (interim) 11 October 2006–present

COUP/REBELLION

1932

Coup 20 June 1933
Bowardet Rebellion 11 October 1933

Songsuradet Rebellion 29 January 1939
1940

Coup 8 November 1947
Coup 1 October 1948
1950 **"Grand Palace Coup"** 26 February 1949
"Manhattan Coup" 29 June 1951
"Silent Coup" 29 November 1951

Coup 16 September 1957
Coup 20 October 1958
1960

1970 **Coup** 17 November 1971

Coup 6 October 1976
Coup 26 March 1977
Coup 20 October 1977
1980
Rebellion 1 April 1981

Coup 9 September 1985

1990 **Coup** 23 February 1991

2000

Coup 19 September 2006

FIGURE 9.1 **Thailand's Coups, 1932–2006**
Source: *Article 2 of the International Covenant on Civil and Political Rights* 6, no. 3, June 2007 (Hong Kong: Asian Human Rights Commission), 12.

colonization at the same time as he opened educational opportunities for girls and abolished slavery (thereby weakening any nobles who vied with him for power). His administrative reforms helped cement national unity.

University education in Thailand owes its origins to the king, when by royal command in 1916, the Civil Servants School was renamed Chulalongkorn University. In 1933, a year after a bloodless coup ended the absolute monarchy, what later became Thammasat University ("university of moral science") was founded to represent the liberal ideals of the new government. Thai people's strong moral compass led them to form a peace movement in 1950 against the Korean War. Over one hundred thousand people signed petitions opposing the war, despite the fact that the country's economy was profiting from it.[6]

During the Vietnam War, the country's military profited so handsomely from U.S. payments that Thailand became a giant staging area for the American war on nearby Vietnam, Cambodia, and Laos. Round the clock aerial bombardment from Thai bases went on for more than a decade. Estimates attributed half of the growth in Thai GNP between 1966 and 1968 to contracts with Washington, and top military commanders gorged themselves at the ox of U.S. taxpayers.[7] By 1968, 48,000 American troops were stationed inside Thailand. U.S. airbases in the northeast—many of them secret—required huge expenditures for construction, to say nothing of five-star hotels for top brass, support services for the troops, or the deluge of American soldiers granted leave from Vietnam to enjoy themselves during their "rest and recreation." Annually an additional $53 million in aid flowed into the country, helping build up an indigenous military of over 260,000. So top heavy was the Thai brass that there was one general for as few as three hundred men, compared to a ratio of one to three thousand or more in Western militaries.

As in the case of Korea, the U.S. war in Indochina produced an enormous boom in Thailand's economy. U.S. airbase construction alone was said to have injected more than $2 billion into Thailand. An undercurrent of opposition to the country's servicing the American war machine found expression in a statement by Buddhist activist Sulak Sivaraksa, who reminded people that the pursuit of material wealth undermined foundations of Thai culture. Alongside U.S. dollars, Americanization of Thai culture and institutions—especially educational and business—caused severe dislocations. More than half of all Thais lived in poverty, millions of children were chronically malnourished, tens of thousands of young girls and boys were compelled to find employment as sex workers to feed their families, and tens of thousands of teenagers were addicted to narcotics. As late as 1992, one estimate had eleven million children forced into one form of labor or another.[8]

A wealthy comprador class, largely grafted onto the military, meant the estates of top generals grew ever larger, as did their political ambitions. As generals became the most powerful group after the monarchy, their power struggles for seats on corporate boards and government offices cost the country dearly. On November 17, 1971, a faction within the military seized power. Supreme military commander Thanom Kittikachorn and Police Chief Prapas Charusathiara executed a coup, hoping to create a political dynasty that would continue through Colonel Narong Kittikachorn, Thanom's son as well as Prapas's son-in-law. A year later, in December 1972, Thanom announced a new interim constitution that provided for an appointed parliament with a majority from the military and police. It didn't take long for people to mobilize against the two families running the country.

The 1973 Student Revolution
From 1961 to 1976, national development plans provided more than 30 percent of all government funds to education, and the number of university students increased from eighteen thousand in 1961 to one hundred thousand in 1972. Poised to lead the country forward, these "Young Men and Women of the New Generation" embraced an idealism that would shake the military's hold on power.

The global wave of youth protests in 1968 greatly affected Thais. Music, art, philosophy, news reports, and books all brought to Thailand new ideas for the young generation. Already in South Korea, students had successfully overthrown the Rhee dictatorship in 1960. Students returning from studies abroad became especially important in protests. Some spent time in the United States and had been affected by the student movement there. *Ramparts* magazine, Herbert Marcuse's writings, and translations of article about the Black Panther Party helped inform the new generation's sensibility.[9] Jean-Paul Sartre's writings and understanding of the May 1968 near revolution in France also infused people's consciousness with the power of activism. Another intellectual precursor of the student revolt was in the earlier generation of Thai leftist intellectuals whose books were reproduced and studied. A synthesized amalgam of royal-democratic-nationalism served both as a means of legitimacy and critical force in confronting the military dictatorship.[10]

By 1968, student-led illegal demonstrations in Bangkok succeeded in getting martial law lifted in the capital.[11] In 1969, students won a brief struggle against a hike in bus fares, and representatives from Thammasat, Chulalongkorn, and Chiang Mai universities formed a National Student Council. The next year, thousands of students mobilized to observe voting in national elections, and a series of intercampus meetings resulted in the formation of the National Student Center of Thailand (NSCT) with two members from each of eleven institutions.

In the summer of 1972, hundreds of students at Chiang Mai University gathered for Hyde Park–style free speech rallies to discuss campus issues.[12] Thailand's economy began to experience inflation and declining standards of living, and a strike wave swept the country. Many people blamed the greed of the military-business complex for the country's problems. Unapologetic corruption went hand-in-hand with easily visible U.S. and Japanese domination of the economy. In November, alarmed by the increasing trade deficit with Japan, the NSCT organized an "anti-Japanese goods week" and also presented a ten-point plan for economic revival to the government. Out of such humble beginnings, a movement for a democratic constitution swept the country.

By calling for an elected parliament and a new constitution, the student movement politicized workers' economic struggles. Beginning in May 1973, students and workers rallied in the streets for a democratic constitution and parliamentary elections. In this early stage of the movement, the rector of Ramkamhaeng University miscalculated: he expelled nine students for publishing a satirical magazine criticizing top Thai military officials. (Officers had used a helicopter to ferry them and their movie-star girlfriends to a hunting expedition in Thung Yai nature preserve.)[13] As soon as the semester began on June 20, campus rallies called for reinstatement of the "Ramkamhaeng Nine." The very next day, campus security assaulted students, injuring many. Eighty-two professors from five institutions signed an open letter supporting the students. On the evening of June 21, ten thousand students from all of Bangkok's universities rallied at Democracy Monument—the mammoth structure downtown commemorating the peaceful 1932 overthrow of the absolute monarchy. As many as five thousand people remained throughout the night, surrounded and cut off by five hundred police. The government ordered all major universities in Bangkok closed, but the next morning, thousands more students joined the demonstrators.

One leaflet produced by the camp-in at the monument reflected a new mood: "Now these incidents have indicated that we are ruled by tyrants." Students' demands escalated to include a democratic constitution within six months, and the numbers supporting them swelled to fifty thousand by midday on June 22. Citizens donated food, drinks, and money. Students' loyalty to the king was evident as they periodically turned toward the palace and sang the King's Song.[14] As the crisis spiraled out of control, Prime Minister Thanom consulted his cabinet in emergency session. Meeting with student representatives, they agreed to reinstate the nine students, to investigate the rector who had expelled them, to make those who had assaulted students stand trial, and to reopen all universities. The issue of the constitution was avoided—for the moment.

The U.S. embassy followed these events closely, noting with concern that U.S. military presence "did appear in one brief satirical skit. . . . This is by all accounts the largest demonstration of its type ever held in the kingdom. Observers have noted that this is also the first time that students have been united on a national basis. Heretofore most student issues have flared on a campus-to-campus basis. . . . A good percentage of the demonstrators were girls. . . . It is clear that the speed and organizational skill with which the students called in their compatriots, including from up-country campuses, caught the government by surprise."[15] The embassy concluded that students "would be back again" but that they had no idea how much their return would change the country.

Energized by their June victory, the NSCT set out on a campaign to revise the nation's constitution. Their leaders were ecstatic over their victory. A paper written by Theerayut Bunmee, "The Students Begin to Find the Target," noted that "student activism can change society as witnessed in Indonesia, Turkey, France, Japan, USA and in other countries. We study and understand what has happened in other countries."[16] Simultaneously, a wave of wildcat strikes broke out. In the first nine months of 1973, at least forty strikes occurred, including a victorious one at Thai Steel Company.[17]

On October 5, 1973, eleven political activists called a press conference to demand a democratic constitution by December 10—Thailand's Constitution Day.

The next day, they were all arrested as they handed out antidictatorship leaflets calling for a democratic constitution, even though they had quoted the king in their criticisms. As police searched their homes and offices, activists' posters seemed to be going up everywhere. Another student was arrested, bringing the number of imprisoned to twelve. On Sunday, October 7, the NSCT released a public statement, saying, "No governments in the world suppress their citizens demanding civil rights and liberties except fascist and communist dictatorships."

For their part, the military publicly called the protesters communists, while in private meetings, they agreed some students "should be sacrificed for the survival of the country." Thammasat University's student union called an emergency meeting, and an open mike around the Bo tree in the back courtyard began a public conversation on October 5. The participatory meeting in which people could respond to each other spawned many ideas and actions, including an initiative by sixty faculty representatives to visit the twelve detained students. When professors arrived at the jail, however, they were turned away by authorities but did not leave before signing their names in the visitor's log and adding, "We Shall Overcome!"

For days, people remained peacefully in conversation around the Bo tree. Like the gatherings around the fountain in front of Province Hall in Gwangju, the site became a place where deliberative democracy encouraged popular actions. By October 9, as many as two thousand students got involved in the discussions on how to overturn the military dictatorship. As they conversed and disagreed, argued, and came to agreement, their participation helped fuse many different streams of thought into a unified movement. Only a few dozen people had been present initially, but like the Berkeley Free Speech Movement, the gathering mushroomed in size.[18] As people freely took turns speaking, all perspectives were treated with respect. At least four streams flowed together to create the student upsurge: New Left, royalist, liberal, and nationalist. Their combined calls for reform affected their professors, the Bar Association, and high school students from rural areas—all of whom arrived to participate in the meetings at the Bo tree. Eight neighboring colleges of education declared strikes, and high school and vocational students announced a boycott of classes. Statements of support from campus after campus arrived—as did contingents of hundreds of people from many places in Bangkok. That afternoon, the Thammasat Student Legislative Body approved four points of action: nonviolent protests; appointment of ten representatives to negotiate the release of the detainees; sending letters to all universities calling for support; and, "If the government still refuses to release the twelve after all these nonviolent protests have been made, the students voted to resort to violence in the form of demonstrations and bloodshed."[19]

By October 10, the meeting grew so large that it was moved to the nearby football field. Although normally considered conservative and royalist, Buddhist monks arrived as part of a continuing stream of thousands of people who wanted to support the students. From everywhere, food and support flowed in. A seventy-vehicle caravan from Kasetsart University brought four thousand students. Jantakesam Teachers' Training College students organized a thirty-three-vehicle

The gathering at Thammasat University grew beyond anyone's expectations.
Photographer unknown.

caravan. Thai students studying in Australia, Germany, and the United States sent in letters of support. A skit parodying Deputy Prime Minister Prapas as "The Godfather" drew laughs and hoots. Given the significance the gatherings carried, the NSCT took over coordination from the Thammasat Student Union.

On October 11, student activists closed more than 70 percent of all Bangkok campuses. Offering food to the monks at Thammasat, speakers announced a hunger strike by the imprisoned detainees. Prapas met with student representatives, but he refused to release the arrested activists. Thinking he could cajole students into dispersing, he promised a new constitution within twenty months. As the frustrated representatives returned to Thammasat, they found the rally had swelled to more than fifty thousand people. The next day, bolstered by the postponement of examinations at most major universities and the indefinite closure of all Bangkok schools, the assembly doubled in size to more than a hundred thousand people. Over Thammasat's football field, a sea of posters and banners hung in the air. Throughout the city, contingents of students marched, sang, and collected donations for the movement—including a hundred thousand bag lunches.[20] The NSCT issued a twenty-four-hour ultimatum for noon the next day, calling on the government to free the detainees or to face "decisive measures."

With so many students mobilized, the NSCT reorganized itself as shown in FIGURE 9.2. Various subgroups played important logistical roles, but the final decision-making body was the general assembly—a form of direct democracy that would also emerge in liberated Gwangju in 1980. After days of heady meetings, a new unity of students had been achieved. By autonomously organizing themselves, they revealed their own capacity to manage society far better than

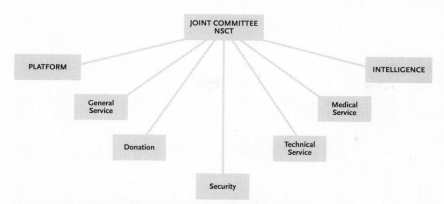

FIGURE 9.2 **Organization of the National Student Center of Thailand**
Source: Ross Prizzia and Narong Sinsawasdi, "Evolution of the Thai Student Movement: 1940–1974" *Asia Quarterly* 1 (1975): 37.

the generals who had usurped power. That is one reason why so many different segments of society joined them.

Print media relayed news of student demands for a constitution, and provincial protests at universities were autonomously organized at many places, including Chiang Mai University, Songkhla Nakharin University, and Khonkaen University.

Although the imprisoned activists were offered bail, they refused, insisting they be unconditionally set free. Expelled from Bang Khen Detention Center, they remained on the grass outside the building. For hours, debate among thousands of people at Thammasat University transpired about the proper course for the detainees to take. Finally a majority of those present voted to reject the bail offer. The assembly's decision was transmitted to the released detainees, who then refused to sign the documents acknowledging their temporary release. A delegation from the campus went to the palace to seek an audience with the king. Throughout the night, people rallied, made speeches, sang songs, and read poetry to keep spirits high, while the NSCT checked and double-checked its plans for the next day. As thousands of people attended an all-night meeting to prepare for the next day's march, their Intelligence Section reported a strengthening of police presence.

Throngs of people continued to arrive as noon approached on October 13, the deadline given to the government. Finally, exactly at noon, NSCT representatives led people in praying, singing the National and Royal Anthems, and swearing allegiance to the Nation, Religion, King, and Constitution.[21] Marching peacefully out of the university, the huge crowd was immaculately organized. Scouts were sent ahead to clear the route. At the front were "commando units" with grappling hooks followed by an all-female contingent carrying flowers, Thai flags, and a Dharma Chakra banner—all in organized in rows five abreast. The procession included groups clustered by school as well as by function—first aid, food, coordination, and commando. Thousands of smiling young students, many carrying portraits of King Bhumibol—made this remarkable display of unity a "Day of Joy," as organizers referred to it.

Smiling young people with portraits of the king and queen led the "Day of Joy."
Photographer unknown.

People armed themselves with a variety of weapons, including bags of chili pepper to deal with police dogs and ropes to remove barricades. The Welfare Committee's contingent loaded trucks with food, water, and towels for protection against tear gas. Heading to Democracy Monument, the largest demonstration in Thai history had a "command center" that was protected by thirteen small pickup trucks, including an electrical truck. Engineering students carried wooden and iron bars, while others held thick sacks to throw on barbed wire or dogs. Vocational students formed ten security teams with names like Bear, Elephant, Yellow Tiger, and Vishnu. Alongside and behind students were disciplined and smiling contingents of citizens with Thai flags, flowers, and portraits of the king and queen. All together, the crowd was estimated at five hundred thousand people. Their smiles and resolve drew the sympathy and support of the entire country—except for the generals in power. One report told of a majority of bus drivers passing regular stops or only picking up people going to the protests. One driver explained, "We are all fighting for the Constitution."[22]

As people marched, the government scrambled to placate them. At 4:20, NSCT leaders received assurances from Prapas that the arrested students would be released and a new constitution would be in place within a year. A delegation of nine NSCT representatives met with the king, who also promised a new constitution within a year. After their meeting with Bhumibol, protest leaders called for an end to the demonstration when they addressed the crowd and returned to Thammasat University to celebrate. Many people in the streets, however, either did not hear—or did not heed—their leaders' decision to end the protest. For days during the general assembly at Thammasat, people had democratically deliberated. Now the central group's unilateral decision, made on the basis of

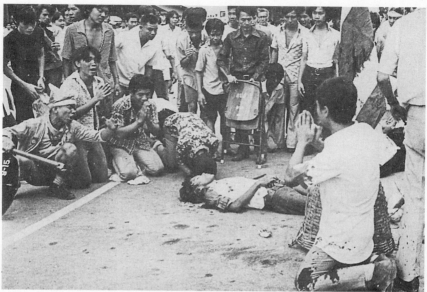

Many people were shot dead in the streets. Photographer unknown.

a meeting with the king and Prapas's promise, proved insufficient to convince hundreds of thousands of people to disperse. Repeated loudspeaker announcements also failed to work. At 5:30 p.m., the leader of the Demonstration Action Unit instructed people to move from the Democracy Monument to the parade ground by the statue of King Rama V. At 8:00 p.m., government radio announced acceptance of the group's demands. Nonetheless, many people still remained in the streets two hours later. Rumors spread that nothing had changed, that their leaders had been killed—or fooled. Around midnight, the crowd moved near Jitlada Palace in the hopes that the king would protect them if police moved in.

After a peaceful night in the streets, a representative of the king again called on protesters to disperse around 5:30 a.m. Many people sang the national anthem and prepared to go home. At 6:00 a.m., vocational students from the Dare-to-Die Unit laid down their arms and destroyed their Molotovs. They called on others to follow their example, but as they tried to leave, police commandoes blocked people's exits. In the ensuing scuffles, food was thrown at police who then opened fire with tear gas and bullets. People responded with Molotovs. As attacks and counterattacks ensued, some people were pushed into canals, while others climbed nearby walls into the zoo. Machine-gun fire scattered the crowd. Protesters scurried out of harm's way, and many swam the moat around the palace and begged for royal intervention. Royal pages opened the palace gates to give students refuge on palace grounds.

Others stayed in the streets and fought back. At about 8:00 a.m., a fire engine near Thammasat University was commandeered, and Metropolitan Police Headquarters on Rajadamnoen was attacked. As citizens joined students, the government brought in the army with tanks to assist the police.

Tanks were ordered to disperse crowds in Bangkok. Photographer unknown.

For thirty-six hours, fighting raged in the streets. Some people already had pistols and used them. People took over buses and used them to charge police positions. Small groups of demonstrators carefully selected symbolically significant structures to attack, like the Public Relations building (believed to have created false media reports about the protests). People swarmed into the building, took firearms, and set it on fire. At 11:45 a.m., the Revenue Department building was burned down, as was the National Lottery a few hours later. (The lottery was widely believed to be fixed by the two families.) Narong's Anti-Corruption Center was also set to the torch.

The army attacked again with tanks and helicopters. At 3:30 p.m., they took control of Thammasat University. Hundreds of fleeing students jammed the Pran Nok landing on the opposite side of the river. As others fleeing the fighting near Thanom Luang arrived on the campus, rooftop snipers and soldiers in helicopters gunned them down.[23] Citizens continued to surge into the streets to support students, and some four hundred thousand people gathered. About 5:30, as people refused to submit, the government withdrew its soldiers from Rajadamnoen Avenue—but not before dozens of people had been killed.

Only too happy to be seen as the nation's savior, King Bhumibol summoned Thanom to the palace, went on the airwaves to announce Thanom's resignation, and promised a new constitution. Thais' joy turned into sadness as the king announced that a hundred people had been killed. He requested an end to the violence and appointed the rector of Thammasat University and president of Thailand's Buddhist Association, Sanya Thammasakdi, as the new prime minister. On October 14 at 6:10 p.m., Thanom Kittikachorn officially resigned. Still, people in the streets refused to go home.

As army attacks continued, small groups set fire to symbolically significant targets.
Photographer unknown.

At 11:00 p.m., the king's mother broadcast an appeal for calm, and Sanya promised a new constitution within six months. Although he had officially resigned, Thanom also took to the airwaves, but his message carried sinister undertones: he called on all "responsible officials to do their duties." Thanom and hardliners within the military were attempting to override the king's authority, but were stymied by opposition within the military—especially from army commander (and U.S. favorite) General Kris Sivara, who refused to send additional troops to Bangkok.[24] The Royal Thai Navy openly supported the students, as did some army and air force officers.[25] Once again, NSCT leaders pleaded with protesters to go home, but people angrily denounced Thanom (who remained supreme commander of the armed forces) and Prapas (still director-general of the police). Attack teams formed to assault police headquarters. A new battle ensued, and fighting lasted from late on October 14 into the following afternoon. Led by a group of engineering students with Molotovs and wearing yellow headbands—the "Yellow Tigers"—repeated assaults were launched on police headquarters. By now, NSCT leaders were marginalized and unable even to gain accurate information. On the night of October 14, activists established a new "Thai People's Center" to coordinate actions. Throughout the night, attacks on the police station continued. At 1:00 a.m., about four hundred engineering students fought their way to Pan Fah Bridge, but they were driven back by machine-gun fire. The bloodiest fighting took place in front of Chalerm Thai Theatre. All the while, some thirty thousand people huddled around Democracy Monument.

The next morning, at least five gun shops in Wangburapa district were raided by students who rammed buses through the iron bars covering their doors. Using commandeered buses and trucks, others built barricades and organized resistance. A notice appeared from the "Students and People Coordination Unit" calling for a general strike against "the two tyrants bearing the two family names" and for the liberation of the country from the "barbarians." At Don Muang airport, air force personnel put out a leaflet calling for police, soldiers, and government workers to walk out in peaceful protests. At 8:15 a.m., Prime Minister Sanya announced a three-day work release for all government workers. Banks and government offices were closed. As students in outlying areas mobilized, localized uprisings broke out.

In Bangkok, police stations continued to be attacked while soldiers rounded up and brutalized anyone they could find. Elsewhere in the capital, students and boy scouts directed traffic. At noon, ten thousand demonstrators at Democracy Monument divided themselves into two groups—one calling for nonviolence and the other vowing to fight on. Soon thereafter, with police again firing wildly on them, the Yellow Tigers used a captured fire engine to set afire the police station at the Phan Fa Bridge.[26] Crowds cheered the engineering students as they blew a stream of gasoline into the building and set it afire. As police continued to shoot from upper stories, another fire engine was hijacked and more gasoline pumped into the building.

As the fighting raged on, Bhumipol demanded Thanom, Prapas, and Narong leave Thailand. With troops running low on ammunition and reinforcements unavailable because of Sivara's opposition to Thanom, the three ruling generals decided to exit. Prapas and Narong left at 8:45 p.m. for Taiwan; Thanom left for Boston on a TWA flight the next day under the name of Smith. At 9:00 p.m., it was announced that the hated dictators had left the country, and NSCT leaders televised yet another appeal to stop the violence. Sivara publicly backed the new government. Most importantly, government forces withdrew. Not a single uniformed police officer or soldier could be seen on Bangkok streets. A palpable sense of victory was felt everywhere. Students directed traffic as people came out in droves to sweep the streets and clean up the mess left by the fighting. When the shooting finally stopped, at least 77 citizens had been killed and 857 wounded.[27] Dozens more were missing and would never be found. The order to shoot on October 14 had been given by Thanom in what many people called an act of premeditated murder.[28] Although people continued to demand he be punished, nothing ever came of it. Failure to hold Thanom accountable would have disastrous consequences three years later.

The Postuprising Surge

A turning point in Thailand's political development, the democratic breakthrough of 1973 gave birth to one of the nation's most free periods of time. The rights to demonstrate, to peacefully assemble, and to speak dissonant words in public were won. Political parties were able to campaign and meet openly; business leaders gained more power in the political structure.[29] Ross Prizzia and Narong Sinsawasdi noted, "The psychological barrier which had kept thousands of Thais submissive to military authority for over five decades was seriously impaired if not altogether broken."[30] For the next three years, in Benedict Anderson's view,

"Thailand had the most open, democratic political system it has experienced, before and since."[31]

Thai students electrified insurgent movements all over the world. A month after the uprising, Greek students rose against the Papadopoulos dictatorship at Athens Polytechnic. As in Thailand, the military mobilized tanks against students, and thirty-four were killed on November 15. Thai activist heard that Greek students had chanted praise of their success overthrow of the dictatorship.[32] The U.S. antiwar movement drew inspiration, while the U.S. government worried that Burmese students might become activated. On November 7, 1973, the U.S. embassy in Rangoon sent a cable to the secretary of state in Washington. The top-secret cable concluded that the "success of Thai students, however, could help make Burmese students forget the lesson they were taught in 1962 when GUB (Government of the Union of Burma) forces mowed them down."

Ji Ungpakorn understood that the 1973 "mass uprising against the military dictatorship in Bangkok shook the Thai ruling class to its foundations. It was the first time that the *pu-noi* (little people) had actually started a revolution from below. It was not planned. . . . It was not just a student uprising to demand a democratic constitution. It involved thousands of ordinary working class people and occurred on the crest of a rising wave of workers' strikes. Success in overthrowing the military dictatorship bred increased confidence. Workers, peasants, and students began to fight for more than just parliamentary democracy. They wanted social justice and an end to long-held privileges. Some wanted an end to exploitation and capitalism itself."[33]

While students were the main force, urban workers mobilized as never before. The nonagricultural labor force had grown from two to over three million in the decade to 1970. Workers eked out a bare subsistence, unprotected by unions or legislation. As unions were illegal from 1958 to 1972, only about twenty strikes per year occurred. Once the uprising helped lift restrictions on workers' collective actions, in two months after it, more than 300 strikes—many of them wildcat— took place. All together, the number of strikes grew from 34 in 1972 to 501 in 1973 (some 73 percent of which occurred after the October uprising).[34] In the midst of economic hardship caused by the 1973 hike in oil prices, strikes involved 177,807 workers.[35]

As we have seen repeatedly in this study of uprisings, new grassroots organizations form in the wake of popular mobilizations. Along with teachers' groups, workers' associations mushroomed after the uprising.[36] The number of registered labor associations tripled from 60 in early 1974 to 185 in late 1976. By October 1974, some 154 new unions had been organized, and at the end of 1975, they united in the Federation of Labor Unions of Thailand (FLUT).[37] As they formed a central trade union federation, workers also struck against corrupt officials in state enterprises.[38]

In June 1974, huge strikes drew participation of about twenty thousand textile workers in six hundred factories. With student support, strikers succeeded in more than doubling the daily minimum wage to $1.25. At one point, thousands of farmers converged on Bangkok to show support for textile workers.[39] In 1975, two thousand female textile workers at Standard Garment factory in Bangkok led a prolonged strike for pay raises. Women at Hara Jeans occupied their worksite and ran it as a workers' cooperative. At the same time, new groups like People for Democracy and the Union for Civil Liberty advocated greater public rights like freedom of assembly. On May 1, 1975, some 250,000 workers in Bangkok rallied, and the next year, half a million joined a general strike against inflation.[40]

Autonomous farmers' groups emerged, calling for land reform and tax relief. Rural poverty nagged at the country's fragile stability. A 1974 survey in Chiang Mai of over 1,400 households determined 37 percent were landless.[41] In May 1974, soon after freedom of assembly became constitutionally protected, hundreds of farmers took to the streets in public protests against usurious interest rates that had led moneylenders to seize their lands. For the first time, thousands converged on Bangkok's Thanom Luang park to call for land reform, tax relief, and lower rents. The next month, a new government committee formed to investigate farmers' grievances was deluged with 10,999 petitions—and the number grew to 53,650 three months later. Spurred on by these mobilizations, the Farmers' Confederation of Thailand (FCT) was created on November 19, 1974. The group successfully pressured the government to impose rent ceilings and allocate funds to rural areas. As with workers, student activists formed an alliance with rural farmers.

During the postuprising surge, as hundreds of thousands of workers and farmers mobilized, many student activists remained intensely involved in democratic struggles. Immediately after the October victory, the NSCT attracted thousands of nonstudents to its events and became a leading group, but it was limited since its members were chairpersons of student associations at various campuses, a highly centralized group that included jocks and popular students rather than politically astute ones. Within a month after the uprising, activists within it resigned and formed the Federation of Independent Students of Thailand (FIST). So powerful was the student movement in this period that five thousand carefully selected students were dispatched by FIST to rural areas to listen to villagers' concerns and help address them. Spokesperson Theerayut Boonme studied the Vietnam Communist Party and concluded "the study of the brave Vietnamese struggle, the transformation and revolution of Vietnamese society is worthwhile so we can adapt their methods to use in Thai society."[42] FIST's guidelines included "preservation of democracy, the country's religion, and the king."[43] The group advocated "Buddhist socialism" and hurriedly called actions, leading to criticisms of its "news snatching" and a "personal rulership" that mirrored larger society.

On October 21, within days of the breakthrough in Bangkok, thousands of students demanded and received the resignation of a corrupt governor in Lamphun province—part of the generalized rural upsurge that followed the movement's victory in the capital. Students mobilized on a variety of issues: against school administrators deemed unfair, against biased newspapers, and against the U.S. ambassador and military personnel. Anti-U.S. mobilizations lasted into the next year. In an enormously important incident, the Internal Security Operation

Command (ISOC), a military intelligence unit created by the CIA, massacred dozens of villagers.[44] While originally blamed on communists, student activists brought survivors to Bangkok where they testified about ISOC perpetrators, and a subsequent inquiry by the Ministry of Interior confirmed the government's responsibility for a number of massacres.

In November 1973, two events of note transpired. Students at Chulalongkorn University launched protests against newly appointed U.S. Ambassador William Kinter: Their leaflet made clear their view that "American intervention in Indochina has caused adverse effects on Thailand. Support for the previous military government has led to the decay of democracy in Thailand, and American bases here have tarnished the good image of Thailand as an independent country."[45] Students' anti-U.S. campaign received unexpected bolstering when a CIA blunder exposed the agency's bungling. The CIA had sent a phony letter purportedly from a communist guerrilla leader to Thailand's prime minister. It was already no secret that U.S. Ambassador Kinter had worked for the CIA for two years and that hated dictator Thanom Kittachorn had an exceptionally close relationship to his CIA mentors. In early January, activists put a wreath with a note reading "Ugly Americans, go home" at the U.S. embassy. The government finally ordered CIA field offices in Thailand closed, thereby threatening one of the largest CIA bases of operations. At Mahidol University, students published a book specifying that a U.S. political, military, and economic invasion had already occurred. With eleven bases and operational areas along the border, the United States had advisors with many units from the Army Department even down to the battalion level.

A month after the uprising, the Dean of the School of Public Administration was forced to resign after he gave a speech in Tokyo that students felt misrepresented the 1973 movement. In the wake of the uproar, the selection process for the school's rector and deans was democratized so that faculty could vote for deans who in turn would select a rector. During this same period of time, Japanese Prime Minister Tanaka's Bangkok hotel was surrounded with buses by angry students who demanded modification of the terms of Japan's loans to Thailand as well as a lifting of Japan's import quotas on Thai goods. When Tanaka was finally permitted to exit, students surrounded his car and banged on it as they shouted, "Japanese Go Home!"

With the student revolution's success, artists enjoyed more freedom of expression than in decades. The Coalition of Thai Artists held a street exhibition of people's art on Rajadamnoen Avenue in October 1975. From the grassroots, initiatives like "theatre for the people," "Art for Life's Sake Theatre," "songs for the people" (often substituting Thai lyrics to Western folk songs), and "literature for the people" were launched. One exhibition entitled "Burning Literature" condemned "feudal" interests as part of a campaign against elitist education. Many artists—like other activists—were greatly influenced by Maoist socialist realism. Others responded with conceptualism, surrealism, and other forms of experimentation—including transformation of traditional forms that were rejuvenated as well.[46]

Student union elections were overwhelmingly won by left-wing candidates supported by autonomous parties, such as Moral Force Party at Thammasat University, the Moral Truth Party at Ramkhamhaeng University, and the People's Morals Party in Chiang Mai. The publishing industry flourished. Hundreds of Marxist books and pamphlets were translated and sold openly. U.S. imperialism and Japanese neocolonialism became common topics of discussion, and indigenous Thai theories and history suddenly were republished and gained new readers. The new turn to humanistic values led to the suspension of the Miss Thailand beauty pageant in 1973.[47] Educational reforms opened new opportunities in rural areas. Inequalities in education were finally addressed, and curricula opened. Seeking to transform cultural values, students launched a *lang kru* campaign—literally meaning to "clean up" teachers whose archaic style reflected authoritarian practices.

A new constitution was drafted by a wide array of citizens' groups, including the women's movement, which emerged from with the democratization impetus as well as from Maoist influences.[48] Approved in 1974, the new constitution addressed gender issues and contained an equal rights protection clause for the first time in Thai history. Sweeping changes were promised in women's opportunities to become judges and prosecutors, and equal wages were promised for equal work. The new constitution was needed to incorporate the burgeoning social movement stimulated by the success of the 1973 uprising.

In January 1974, the NSCT was replaced by the National Coalition Against Dictatorship as the leading force in the movement, an umbrella organization of more than twenty groups that united workers, farmers, and students in a Triple Alliance. The influence of the Communist Party of Thailand (CPT) grew even in the cities. Already, their guerrilla forces included some seven thousand fighters and a hundred thousand supporters.[49] In neighboring Indochina, Saigon was taken over on April 30, 1975, and the Cambodian and Laotian royal families were overthrown.

Economic problems began to mount. From less than 5 percent in 1972, inflation jumped above 15 percent in 1973 and rose to 24.3 percent in 1974. Real wages declined by 3.8 percent in 1973 and 8.8 percent in 1974.[50] With the upsurge in Thai civil society and falling dominos in nearby Indochinese neighbors, foreign investors became so frightened that an investment strike was the result. Japan's share, long the country's highest among foreign investors, fell from $749.6 million in 1974 to $423.6 million the next year. In January 1975 elections, left-wing candidates won thirty-seven seats in parliament, and in the next eight months, net capital outflows amounted to $59.9 million—more than double the $27.7 that went abroad in the previous year's first eight months. New Prime Minister Kukrit explained that "investors were particularly frightened by some groups which uncompromisingly oppose foreign investment."[51] On December 3, 1975, the *Bangkok Post* quoted the U.S. ambassador, Charles Whitehouse: "As viewed from the United States, Thailand's investment climate has deteriorated during the last two years."

Even more disturbing in the top echelons of power was the military's loss of major sources of incomes. Generals' power rested upon enormous payments they made to each other and came primarily from three sources: U.S. aid, the drug trade, and industry—the latter through membership on corporate boards.[52] After 1973, generals' income from these domains declined precipitously, and the loss of status of the military—with a simultaneous outpouring of public support for students—constituted a double humiliation. The 1975 Kukrit government promised to oversee the withdrawal of all U.S. troops from Thailand, a prospect that angered key military leaders for many reasons, not least because it would mean the end of a very profitable relationship. Social movement theorists have long noted that right-wing movement are spawned under conditions of declining status, and Thailand was no exception. With the decline of the military, a desperate response was prepared.

The 1976 Massacre of Students

Given the country's sudden openness and rapid changes, it is not shocking to encounter violent counterrevolution, yet the grotesque nature of the assault on Thammasat University (TU) on October 6 in which at least forty-one people were murdered continues to repulse and disgust. If that massacre had been the first attack against the movement, it would have been surprising, but the deterioration of Thai civil peace occurred step by step. On July 3, 1974, when people converged on Plabplachai Police station to protest U.S. interference in Thailand, police opened fire and killed peaceful demonstrators. Between March and August 1975, at least twenty-one leaders of the Farmers' Confederation (FCT) were murdered.[53] On September 24, 1976, two weeks before the massacre at TU, two students caught postering in Bangkok were garroted, their bodies discovered the next day by horrified colleagues.

Several different networks of right-wing vigilante groups were at work, one rumored to have close ties to U.S. intelligence: Nawaphon, the group behind murders of FCT leaders and anti-Vietnamese pogroms in the country's northeast. *Nawaphon* is the Sanskrit word for "ninth power"—a reference to king Bompibhol, the ninth rule of the Chakri dynasty. A leading Buddhist monk affiliated with Nawaphon, Kittiwutho, publicized the merit of killing communists. By the end of 1975, the organization boasted a membership of more than 150,000, including large landowners, provincial governors, and village heads organized into a cell structure. The Red Gaurs was another group that attacked peaceful protests. Described by Benedict Anderson as "high school drop-outs, unemployed street-corner boys, slum toughs, and so forth" who responded to "promises of high pay, abundant free liquor and brothel privileges," they were among the most vengeful assailants at Thammasat University on October 6.[54] Many were drawn from the ranks of the vocational students who had been the shock troops of the 1973 uprising; others were out of work mercenaries left over from the U.S. war on Laos. In December 1975, the king warned his Royal Guard that the country had been targeted by an "enemy" and told them to "prepare your physical and mental strength and be ready to cope with an emergency."[55] In a highly symbolic event at the beginning of 1976, he personally test fired weapons at a Red Gaur camp. On March 21, 1976, Red Gaur were spotted when grenades were lobbed into a demonstration of thirty thousand people advocating withdrawal of U.S. troops from Thailand.

As street protests and strikes became commonplace, parliament was unable to muster its political will. When the government raised the prices of rice and sugar, the Labor Federation (FLUT) called for a general strike in January 1976. Kukrit rescinded the price hikes, but his legitimacy among even his supporters eroded to such a low point that on January 12, the day after one hundred leading officers called for his resignation, he dissolved parliament. As new elections approached in April, student leaders and a prominent Socialist Party politician were assassinated—as were about twenty more FCT leaders. The nation's supreme military commander warned of Vietnamese sappers in Bangkok. Voter turnout was an abysmal 29 percent in Bangkok and 46 percent nationally, and on April 23, democracy advocate General Kris Sivara—who had outmaneuvered Thanom in 1973 and forced him out of power—suddenly died of a heart attack. As the nation looked for signs of its future, the United States announced that its military aid for fiscal 1977 would be increased by over 900 percent from that of 1975—a clear signal where Washington's wanted the country to go.

Apparently, Thailand's monarch, so passionately a defender of democracy in 1973, had a change of heart as he witnessed the fall of the Lao and Cambodian royal families. Convinced that communism, not his rivals in the military, was the main threat to his unbridled power, Bhumibol patronized a range of ultra-right paramilitary groups, including the Village Scouts. Under royal patronage, recruitment into the Village Scouts soared. In Bangkok alone, some 19,828 members were enrolled and actively campaigned for right-wing candidates in new elections of April 1976 (during which more than thirty people were killed).

As right-wing mobilizations progressed, Thanom and Prapas—the generals who had been forced into exile in 1973—publicly expressed their desire to return home. Shortly thereafter, Prapas returned to Thailand from exile in Taiwan. The families of people killed and missing from the 1973 uprising were angered and renewed their call for punishment of those responsible. Their protests resulted in the government chartering a special plane to return Prapas to Taipei, but a few days later, Thanom announced he, too, wished to return. Accompanied by Interior Minister Samak Sunthornvej at the king's request, Thanom was readmitted to the country on September 19.[56] Both the king and the queen visited him in the monastery where he took refuge. On October 1, the crown prince returned from his studies at Duntroon Military Academy in Australia, and he also visited Thanom.

Relatives of those killed in 1973 called for Thanom's prosecution. They gathered outside the prime minister's office and began a hunger strike on October 3. After police harassed them, they accepted the hospitality of the Buddhist Association of Thammasat University and moved to sanctuary inside the campus. On October 4, some seven thousand students congregated at Thammasat University, and they declared it would serve as their base to expel Thanom.[57] On October 5, a few thousand people (including rickshaw drivers and workers[58]) gathered inside Thammasat for a rally and theatre performances. One of the plays reenacted the recent garroting of two activists, but the media twisted it into an alleged portrayal of the crown prince being lynched, inflaming the Red Gaurs. An already ugly mood among the hostile crowd in Thanom Luang Park

Mobs of police, soldiers, and civilians attacked Thammasat University students in 1976.
Photographer unknown.

adjacent to TU grew murderous as photos of the alleged performance of the crown prince's murder were circulated. Army-controlled radio called for people to overrun the campus at the same time as police blockades prevented anyone from leaving the university. That same day, Village Scouts mobilized hundreds of their most ardent members to Government House to demand the resignation of three progressive cabinet members. Successful in ousting government officials, they would change Thai history the next morning with their violent rampage at Thammasat University.

Around four on the morning of October 6, 1976, when the national anthem blared from loudspeakers, police opened fire on the assembly inside Thammasat University from behind the walls dividing the campus from the National Museum. Inside the university, a theatre collective was performing a play about the lives of impoverished urban dwellers when the first shots were fired. Overwhelmed by machine guns and M79 rocket launchers, lightly armed student security teams fell back as the first contingents of some six thousand police, right-wing gangs, and soldiers clamored over walls. For at least four hours, shooting continued. Around 7:00 a.m., a student with a bullhorn emerged in front of the campus and solemnly surrendered. He was cut down by automatic weapons fire. At 8:15 a.m., a massive new attack was launched, again with bazookas. Unlucky souls who tried to escape through the front gate were dragged out and lynched from nearby trees. Others were burned alive in front of the Ministry of Justice. One woman— already shot dead—was sexually violated with a piece of wood. Another man had a wooden spike driven through his body. As one man urinated on some of the corpses, others danced around them, while still more watched and cheered.

Horror-stricken students who had taken cover in buildings around the football field were forced back out to the field, made to remove their shirts and lie face down in the mud. Uniformed police fired heavy machine guns over their heads. Some were able to escape through the back gate of the university, where merchants hid them. Dozens tried to swim to safety across the river. While many drowned, coast guard boats rescued the lucky ones. The route to the river was also the scene of grisly murders and deadly shootings. A lynch mob carried out a massacre in plain view of hundreds of spectators. Many photos were published of the macabre event, but police never prosecuted anyone. Student leaders arrived in an ambulance at the prime minister's house, but he refused to see them. At 6:00 p.m., the crown prince arrived and asked the mob to disperse. When the carnage ended, at least forty-one people had been killed, hundreds injured, and 3,037 arrested. The Chinese Benevolent Association, which cremated the corpses, maintained that more than one hundred people were killed.[59] That same night, the military seized power in the name of the National Administrative Reform Council—appropriately enough called NARC.

Was the king a hidden force behind the slaughter on October 6, 1976?[60] Why had Bhumipol called the crown prince back home at the beginning of October? Why did he issue a royal proclamation ending initiations of new members into the Village Scouts a little more than month after the massacre? The border police units involved in the Thammasat massacre were known to be among the king's favorites. In a New Year's message on January 1, 1977, Bhumipol referred to the October 6 coup as "a manifestation of what the people clearly wanted."

Abrogating the democratic constitution of 1974, the military abolished parliament on the same day that the orgy of violence took place. They instituted repressive measures befitting a Pinochet, whose bloody U.S. sponsored coup on September 11, 1973, murdered at least two thousand victims. Hundreds of student activists and labor leaders were rounded up, and eighteen students identified as leaders spent more than two years in prison. All together, at least six thousand people were arrested, more than twenty newspapers shut down, over two hundred books banned, all political parties dismissed, meetings of more than four people prohibited, strikes outlawed, and the constitution revoked. The junta that came to power has been called "the most repressive government in Thai history."[61] Sulak Sivarak's Buddhist bookshop was ransacked and over a hundred thousand books burned.[62] Similar book burnings, reminiscent of Nazi ones, occurred after many university libraries were purged. With NARC in power, foreign investors overnight ended their strike and workers' actions faded into the past. In 1976, 133 strikes were counted. After the massacre and coup, only seven occurred in all of 1977, and workers remained quiet for years, as TABLE 9.1 shows. In February 1977, when workers in a small Bangkok factory asked for a raise, the owner fired them all. Throughout the country, labor leaders were assassinated while investor confidence rose.

Some three to four thousand student activists escaped and sought refuge in rural areas, where most joined Maoist guerrillas of the CPT. From only 75 attacks in 1975, the group claimed 717 battles in which 1,475 enemy troops were killed during the year after the October 6 massacre. By 1979, they fielded battalion-sized combat units in many parts of the country and claimed ten thousand armed combatants.[63]

TABLE 9.1 **Strikes in Thailand, 1972–1980**

Year	Number of Strikes	Workers Involved
1975	241	9,474
1976	133	65,342
1977	7	4,868
1978	21	6,842
1979	62	15,638
1980	18	3,230

Source: Thai Ministry of Interior as quoted in Andrew Brown, "Locating Working-Class Power," in *Political Change in Thailand: Democracy and Participation*, ed. Kevin Hewison (London: Routledge, 1997), 171.

Many people were convinced that armed revolution was the only viable option to oppose the dictatorship, but Maoists proved unable to integrate the new recruits. They considered students "petty bourgeois" and treated them miserably. In the words of one longtime activist, Comrade "Sung," "If we had questions about politics, we seldom received answers."[64] While praised for their sacrifices, they were not permitted to publish much of what they wrote and were "told to deal only with local issues and not think about major problems."[65] Communists' authoritarian behavior contrasted sharply with the egalitarian norms and autonomous organizing capability of students—attributes that had helped them mobilize the country so successfully in 1973. In some areas, CPT leaders adapted Pol Pot and the Khmer Rouge's quota system of killing enemies. In late 1980, Sung remembered, "The old comrades looked at us October 6th students as though we were the enemy. Many times they would take off the safety catches on their weapons or brandish knives in our faces to show us if we did not obey the Party or insisted on asking questions of Organising Comrades [leaders], how they would deal with us."[66] One activist "found it so threatening that they wanted us to kill each other like that—to meet a quota."[67] Although CPT leaders subsequently acknowledged their mistake, the guerrilla movement was already a dismal failure. Within a decade, the CPT collapsed.

Neoliberalism's Thai Face
By the late 1970s, as the armed insurgency approached its high point, many officers within the Thai military began to advocate a new approach to undermine the guerrillas. Offering amnesty to activists who turned themselves in, a new regime emerged that changed the constitution and permitted elections in 1979, 1983, 1986, and 1988. Many student activists took advantage of the offer to return to their urban homes and reconstruct their lives. Thailand returned to normalcy, but it did so without any left-wing organizations within its political system. Before the massacre of October 6, socialist parties had received about 15 percent of votes, but the massacre of 1976 marked the bloody birth of pro-American neoliberalism in Thailand. As brute repression of 1976 gave way to greater prosperity in the 1980s, the number of strikes annually never exceeded seven from 1985 to 1991.

In 1982, an IMF structural adjustment agreement was concluded, bringing economic liberalization that opened the way for transnational capital to capture much of Thailand's economy. Liberalization of banking rules permitted foreign investors to penetrate Thailand's markets, marginalizing the Thai financial elite, long controlled by a few wealthy Chinese-Thai families.[68] Foreign investment flowed into South East Asia, especially from Japan and South Korea. Japan alone sent $24 billion in investments in five years from 1987 to 1991.[69] From 1988 to 1993, another $40 billion was invested by Japan in Asia-Pacific—one of the largest outflows in history. Thailand received $5.3 billion in Japanese investments from 1988 to 1993—nearly 500 percent of what had been invested in the previous thirty-seven years.[70]

As the economy expanded from the influx of capital, the phrase "Asian Miracle" was increasingly bandied about. Long reclusive, the few Chinese families who controlled Thailand's banking system were drawn into the global system. Neoliberal economic reforms in the 1980s brought a modicum of prosperity to the country. The number of workers in manufacturing grew to 2.4 million by 1988, nearly five times as many as in 1961.[71] An urban middle class emerged as Thailand's economy was transformed from import-substitution and export of foods to export-oriented industry, with an emphasis on textiles and electronics. In 1980, three-fifths of exports had come from agriculture; by 1995, more than four-fifths were produced by manufacturing sector.[72] A similar process had led to South Korea and Taiwanese "miracles," but in those countries, a national developmental state financed the industrial transition. In Thailand, private sources of capital—especially a large sum from the royal family's Siam Commercial Bank—dominated the economy.

So successful was Thailand's performance in the 1980s, that in 1991 the World Bank and IMF began to refer to it as "Asia's fifth tiger." Thailand's economy was among the world's fastest growing with a rate averaging 10 percent between 1985 and 1995. In that decade, per capita GDP doubled to about $1,000 (from a scant $200 in 1960), but distribution of wealth became even more skewed. In 1975, the upper 20 percent of the society owned 49.3 percent of wealth, a number that increased to 54.9 percent in 1987, while the share of the bottom 20 percent decreased from 6.1 percent in 1975 to 4.5 percent in 1987. Between 1975 and 1992, the bottom 80 percent of the population's income share dropped as the top 20 percent's rose—an obvious "benefit" of neoliberalism.[73] In Thailand, as in Chile, South Korea, and Turkey, military dictatorships ran roughshod over their citizens without care for how much blood they spilt in order to implement neoliberal policies benefitting global capital.

TABLE 9.2 **Foreign Direct Investments (in million U.S.$)**

	1980	1985	1990	1995	1997
Indonesia	180	310	1,092	4,346	4,677
Thailand	189	164	2,562	2,068	3,626
Philippines	-106	12	550	1,459	1,249

Source: UNCTAD, as quoted in Dae-oup Chang, "Neoliberal Restructuring of Capital Relations in East and South-East Asia," in *Neoliberalism: A Critical Reader*, eds., Alfredo Saad-Filho and Deborah Johnston (London: Pluto Press, 2005), 254.

Alongside polarization of wealth and poverty, pollution increased. In Bangkok, the number of automobiles on the city's streets nearly doubled in six years to more than one million. Today the city is known as having one of the world's worst traffic congestion problems. Overwhelmed by the country's rapid change, ecologists successfully fought the construction of a huge dam at Nam Choan in 1988. As Thailand moved from being the "rice bowl of Asia" to the world's leading exporter of rice, regional income distribution became increasingly skewed. Bangkok residents' disproportionate share rose from five times that of people living in the northeast in 1960 to nine times national per capita income in 1987.[74] The overwhelming majority of economically active people (64 percent) was involved in the primary sector—agriculture and fishing in 1990.[75] In 1991, agriculture accounted for 11.8 percent of GDP, industry 40.4 percent (manufacturing 26.6 percent), and trade and services 47.8 percent.[76]

While much the rest of Asia was modernizing, Thailand remained mired in structures some considered neofeudal. The country's economy became globalized, but its archaic political structures remained frozen in the poisoned period iced by the 1976 massacre. From 1987 to 1990, real economic growth in Thailand was 36 percent—the world's highest.[77] In the 1960s and 1970s, the economy had steadily grown by 5 to 6 percent, when Thailand was known to have "the most stable currency and least inflation of any developing nation in the world."[78] As export-oriented diversification of the economy produced startling expansion, new prosperity fueled rising expectations, especially among ascendant professionals and educated workers. Higher education expanded rapidly between 1987 and 1994, with total enrollment in postsecondary institutions growing from 364,000 to 659,000.[79] Per capita income increased to nearly $1,500 by 1992. Basic indicators like the sharp decrease in infant mortality and child malnutrition only told half the story. More homes than ever had electricity, life expectancy was rising, and real wages were up. Although they increased only 1.4 percent annually from 1982 to 1989, wages shot up at the rate of 8.2 percent per year beginning in 1990.[80] The number of workers in state enterprises rose steadily from 137,437 in 1973 to 433,649 in 1983, and their unionization rate was far greater than among private sector employees. In 1983, some 323 unions in the private sector contained only 81,465 members, while ninety-one state enterprise unions had 136,335 members.

The impact of the 1986 People Power overthrow of Marcos and the 1987 demise of Chun in Korea was profound, especially on professionals. Many observers commented on the mobilizing impact on medical students and doctors.[81] Despite the clear signs of change, in 1989 Larry Diamond, a U.S. expert in democracy studies, advised that democratic forces in Thailand should "have a longer-term strategy." In his view, "By pragmatically conceding for a time military preeminence in security matters and participation in politics, committed democrats may find the space to build the infrastructural base for future democratization."[82] Like Huntington, Diamond was unable to anticipate the enormous force of popular insurgency and the rapid transformation such movements make possible.

In 1991, the military conservatives again seized power. Business was receptive to the military's role after the coup of February 23, 1991, especially when the president of the Federation of Thai Industries, respected technocrat Anand Panyarachun, was appointed prime minister. Reacting to the coup, the director of the American Chamber of Commerce, Thomas A. Seale, called it a "great leap forward to a better, Thai-style democracy" that would "make Thailand a less expensive place to invest."[83] The Anand government pushed through more legislation in a year than the previous government had done in three. On the heels of a spike in strikes for wage increases in April 1990, the new government banned unions in state enterprises—in one stroke, sending the number of state sector unions from 130 to 36 and halving the total number of labor union members, from 336,061 to 162,424.[84] The Thai Trade Union Congress lost eighteen of its governing council's thirty-nine members, including its president and four vice presidents. A subsequent law instituted in 1991 by the new junta banned strikes and unions in state enterprises altogether—a key point of organizing for unions since no more than 5.6 percent of 4.5 million workers in the private sector were organized.[85] On June 19, 1991, labor leader Thanong Pho-an, president of the Labour Congress of Thailand, mysteriously disappeared. He was widely assumed to have been assassinated.[86]

No political party emerged to challenge the military's preeminent role. Rather, extraparliamentary forces came together to mount opposition. About a month after the coup, democratic activists revitalized a network known as the Campaign for Popular Democracy (CPD) that had helped spearhead previous attempts to promulgate democratic constitutions.[87] On April 19, 1991, their coalition of nineteen organizations (including labor, farmers, students, women's groups, slum community organizers, academics, teachers, NGOs, and human rights groups) began organizing public events to criticize the new government's constitution as it was being drafted. The regime sought to bypass the House of Representatives to write their new constitution, but the CPD convened a meeting of a broad range of representatives chosen in local and regional meetings to write a constitution from the grassroots. Later in 1991, the Student Federation of Thailand (SFT) was also revived. Two intergenerational meetings with twenty activists from 1991 and an equal number from 1973 took place. (Older activists remembered that 1973 was not as nonviolent as its memory indicated. They also emphasized the importance of paying attention to every detail of protests.) After these preparatory consultations, student unions in twenty-four of twenty-five states joined together.[88] The SFT joined with the CPD to organize the People's Congress on the Constitution, comprised of representatives of rural forums and urban middle-class activists. After much debate and deliberation, the group hammered out key points for a new constitution, which they publicly presented on the anniversary of Thailand's first constitution. They insisted that the prime minister had to be an elected member of parliament, that parliamentary meetings should be broadcast live, and that the role of the appointed Senate should be reduced. From these meetings, they then embarked on a campaign to gather one million signatures in support of their proposal.[89]

Despite the unpopular character of trade liberalization measures, market-based reforms, and cancellation of public sector unions, Anand's government narrowly won the March 1992 elections. With little opposition inside the government, protests began to mount. On November 19, 1991, more than seventy thousand people responded to a joint call from the SFT and CPD—after which five political parties promised to help press for constitutional reform. In the process of building their organizations, the groups mobilized a broad cross section of Thai society—from farmers and workers to academics and youth—organizing efforts that help to explain the broad multiclass alliance that emerged to confront the dictatorship.

In response to people's resistance, commander of the armed forces General Suchinda Kraprayoon promised not to become prime minister. After the March 1992 elections, Suchinda submitted a list of 270 senators to the king, with 147 drawn from the army, air force, and navy—more than 50 percent of the total, making the list in violation of Article 94 of the constitution. Nonetheless, all nominees received royal appointment from the king.[90] Anand initially remained prime minister, but on April 7, 1992, Suchinda took over—despite his promises not to do so—"for the sake of the nation." He immediately appointed his buddies from Class Five at Chulachomklao Military Academy into lucrative positions of power. The next day, retired naval officer and former member of parliament Chalard Worachat announced he would fast to the death unless Suchinda stepped down. The stage was set for another bloody contestation of power.

1992 "Black May"

On April 8, 1992, hunger striker Chalard Vorachad sat down near the parliament building and vowed not to begin eating until a civilian prime minister blessed Thai politics. This solitary action by a minor politician resonated among many people. Soon office workers and business people began to arrive after work, park their cars, and congregate outdoors to show their support for democracy. As crowds swelled, they moved to Sanam Luang, where food vendors and hawkers provided for fun-loving gatherings accompanied by a steady stream of speakers and entertainers. Government-controlled media, including all television stations, failed to report Chalard's fast, but independent print media covered it extensively. For his paper's accuracy, the *Nation*'s publisher, Suthichai Yoon, had his car windshield smashed, and Democratic Party leader Chuan Leekpai repeatedly received death threats. Inside parliament's opening session on April 16, opposition MPs wore black armbands "to mourn the death of democracy in Thailand."[91]

After twelve days of his hunger strike, about fifty thousand people assembled at Royal Plaza as Chalard sat outside parliament next to a portrait of Gandhi. On April 25, day seventeen of his fast, the SFT, CPD, and four opposition parties—now dubbed "angel" parties—organized another rally, this time financed by General Chavalit of the New Aspiration Party.[92] As many as a hundred thousand people, many of them office workers and middle-class professionals, sang the Thai Royal Anthem. Demonstrators formed a candlelight process to "dispel the political darkness that had overtaken the nation" through the power of "devil parties." On May 1, two separate workers' day celebrations took place: the official rally at Sanam Luang and another organized by autonomous unions at parliament, where workers presented thousands of roses to hunger strikers who had joined Chalard. Banners read, "Workers Will Endure if the Tanks Don't Interfere" and "Labor Must Have Freedom, People Must Have Democracy."[93]

On day twenty-four, Chalard collapsed and was taken to hospital, but his daughter took up his fast—a heroic example that helped spark a huge rally on May 4 at which more than a hundred thousand people gathered.[94] Two labor leaders were among the many speakers. While the stock market declined precipitously and tourists headed home, the movement picked up momentum. The hunger strike was joined by several more people, most famously by Chamlong Srimaung, popular two-term former mayor of Bangkok, devout Buddhist (member of the highly ascetic Santi Asoke sect), and leader of the Village Scouts in 1976. (Chamlong was rumored to have been involved in the 1976 massacre of students.)[95] Known as "Mr. Clean," Chamlong and his Power of Virtue Party (Palang Dharma Party or PDP) had just won thirty-two of Bangkok's thirty-five seats in parliament. On May 4, he declared he would "fast until death" unless his former military colleague Suchinda resigned as self-appointed prime minister. Among others joining the fast were slum activist Prateep Ungsontham, student leaders like Parinya Tevanarumitrakun, labor activists, and NGO members like Dr. Sant Hathirat.[96]

More than anyone else, the media focused on Chamlong and propelled him into leadership of the movement. Giving orders as if he were still in the military, Chamlong led five thousand marchers to parliament when he began his hunger strike. Insisting he would only drink water and refuse glucose, saline injections, and medical attention, Chamlong dramatically predicted that he would die within seven days—unless Suchinda resigned. Remarkably, he thereby used exactly the same tactic which hunger-striking Chinese students had used to seize control in Tiananmen Square in 1989. Using the threat of death from a hunger strike to elicit broad popular support, he circumvented the authority of grassroots groups—the kernel of a new democratic government—and instead substituted his own charisma and decision-making. In both cases, individual leaders made decisions outside the democratic structures created by the movement—and in both cases, acts of individual heroism mobilized thousands of people.

On May 6, at least 150,000 people surrounded parliament. The crowd cheered opposition MPs who walked out when Suchinda arrived. By then, their numbers had swelled to nearly 200,000—the largest protest since October 14, 1973. Since they had outgrown the space around parliament, the assembly needed to move. In this critical moment, Chamlong and his coterie of followers moved the huge crowd to Sanam Luang despite objections from the coalition of protest organizations coordinating the actions (including CFD and SFT). The following day, when the military ordered protesters to disperse, Chamlong moved people back to Royal Plaza. That night, demonstrators around parliament were surrounded by hundreds of police, and barbed wire barricades kept others from joining them. Around 9:00 a.m., workers pushed a car through one of the barricades. Soldiers melted away, and the crowd surged through to Sanam Luang.

In intense heat on May 8, tens of thousands of people continued to hold the site at Sanam Luang. On the fourth day of his hunger strike, Chamlong collapsed.

The *New York Times* reported that the four main opposition parties had written to the king asking for royal intervention. That evening, as the crowd swelled to as many as two hundred thousand people, for the first time, it occurred to student leader Parinya Thevanaruemidkul that protesters might win.[97] A government plane flew overhead and dropped leaflets urging people to leave. Heavy rain began, but people stayed. Military radio claimed the crowd was intent on disrupting the annual Buddhist plowing (*Makha Bucha*) ceremony. Organizers huddled to decide what to do and differing opinions emerged. Many people wanted to remain, but a revived Chamlong unilaterally decided to move the entire group to Rajadamnoen Road. By the end of the day, everyone joined his contingent. TV and radio congratulated Chamlong on "preserving peace and unity in the nation." Chamlong's personal appeal in the media as well as his charisma at the rallies left organizers in a relatively powerless position.

Early on the morning of May 9 at Democracy Monument, Chamlong asked the few thousand people who had remained overnight for their "permission" to end his fast so he could continue to be their leader. The crowd cheered and praised Chamlong's decision since "democracy needed his leadership more than his martyrdom." Rallies continued around the clock on Rajadamnoen Avenue. Contingents of rail workers and their families were roundly cheered as they entered. Together with students from working-class Ramkhamhaeng University, unionists provided a security force for the rallies. As labor leader Somsak Kosaisook recalled,

> I shall remember those nights on Ratdamnoen Avenue until the very end of my life. Those who gathered loved democracy, they possessed a strong ethical stance and exhibited admirable self-discipline. They cared for and supported each other. They sang together and clapped to the rhythm of the music and this helped to create an atmosphere, which strengthened their resolve to continue the struggle. All this stimulated in me an even greater faith in democratic ideology, faith in a society marked by equality, freedom and fraternity where people would live as brothers and sisters. The demonstrators came from all walks of life but there were no differences, just a feeling of warmth and cooperation. Although the period was short, the atmosphere on Ratdamnoen Avenue provided me with the happiest moments of my life. It left me with the dream that perhaps one day both Thai society and world society would be truly democratic. That humanity would cease the endless competition among themselves, cease the hate and violence.... The events demonstrated that people who love democracy possess peaceful ethics, despise exploiting others, think of the majority rather than themselves, use reason instead of force and are able to distinguish between right and wrong. This is the democratic society we dream of.[98]

Speakers were polite, nonviolent, and mixed satire with jokes and serious commentary, music with Chinese opera. Student read articulate statements and comedians did stand-up political routines. Four labor leaders addressed the gathering. Yet there were no open mikes, no public deliberations of strategy and tactics. In Alan Klima's view, "The demonstration was a market, and the protest stage was the mass media. Students, politicians, public celebrities, and articulate members of the public gave speeches, alternating with performances by musicians, including the rock star Aed Carabao, who played his banned tunes about democracy."[99]

Characterized by a cynicism befitting American academia, Klima's prose was also imbued with the erotic energy of the nightly rallies. The crowd divided into thirds to synchronize the pounding of their plastic water bottles on the street, creating a cascading roar that organizers called "people power." Klima described the emotions surging through the crowd:

> Those were the good days. I regret that I can only describe them in rose-colored language. It seems that in times like these the best side of people comes out. Within the temporary community of the protest, people were incredibly nice to each other. They wanted justice, morality, and truth to prevail. . . . They sat peacefully for hours and hours listening to talk of right and wrong, justice and injustice, and received hour after hour of education into social values and the noble methods to achieve a better society through nonviolent struggle. It was very much like listening to a sermon in a temple. The stage was like an altar, and the audience was like the laity, the way they sat politely on the ground, enduring the same painful aching and sleeping limbs that one endures through a long sermon. Only this was bigger, much bigger, than any temple—any temple so far.[100]

Two things stand out here: first, the eros effect, the emotional bonding and love among strangers. Secondly, one must note the one-way character of the communication. The spatial relationship of audience to stage on Rajadamnoen Avenue mirrored the one-way mass media, unlike the Bo tree meetings at Thammasat University in 1973 or at the fountain in front of Province Hall in 1980 Gwangju, where speakers communicated with—rather than simply spoke to—tens of thousands of people.

People's transcendental energy was so powerful that even when the army deployed into Bangkok on May 9, a peaceful sea of red, white, and blue Thai flags calmed everyone. Huge celebratory rallies continued, folk singers, and rock 'n' roll bands serenaded the streets. Finally, the government promised to change the constitution so no nonelected person could be prime minister—a change that would end Suchinda's tenure.

As soon as the Speaker of the House of Representatives promised democratic constitutional reform, the small group coordinating protests met. Many people wanted to remain in place. Once again, Chamlong's personal decision-making and media appeal held sway. At 9:00 a.m. on May 10, organizers attempted to end the rally, but the crowd howled them down. Many workers and students cried as Chamlong appealed for protests to be suspended until May 17, when people could again mobilize if the government failed to keep its promise to amend the constitution. No one wanted a breakdown of solidarity among the protesters, and with Chamlong insisting on the temporary suspension, everyone again went along with him.

Suchinda accused protesters of being communists and, worse, disloyal to the royal family. Bolstered by media fabrications, he claimed that people in the streets violated the sacred trinity of "Nation, Religion, and King" so cherished by the vast majority of Thais. Few among the insurgents failed to show reverence for the king and his family. Indeed, they took great pains at all points to hold his portrait. No event proved the loyalty of demonstrators to the royal family more than on Sunday May 10, when Princess Maha was scheduled to host a public Buddhist Week ceremony at Sanam Luang. Since the previous Friday, Rajadamnoen Avenue had been flooded with protesters—whom the state media insisted were intent upon disrupting the ceremony. Showing discipline and wisdom (but not necessarily a decisive break with inherited values), thousands of people opened a path for the royal procession and lined Rajadmnoen Avenue with Thai flags. When the motorcade took a detour, it was because of the military blockade at Phan Fa Bridge—not because of people blocking the streets. On Thursday, May 14, when the royal plowing ceremony took place, people in the streets were solemnly tranquil as the royal family observed the rituals at Thanom Luang. Two days later, when the king and his entourage went to the Temple of the Emerald Buddha in the Grand Palace, demonstrators seemed to have completely vanished.

During the respite in protests, activists deepened their organizational structures. On May 14, about 125 people from twenty-six groups (including the SFT, CPD, unions, poll-watching volunteers, NGOs, and opposition parties) gathered at the Royal Hotel. Their four-hour meeting established the Confederation for Democracy (CFD), a broad multiclass alliance with a seven-person leadership— a majority of whom was loyal to Chamlong. Besides Chamlong, slum activist Pratheep, and labor leader Somsak, student leader Parinya Tevanarumitrakun, Jittravadee Worachat (as representative of her father Chalard), academic Sant Hathirat, and Weng Tojirakan (representative of the 1973 generation) became the publicly recognized heads of the movement.[101] Separately, the labor movement gathered union leaders from both the private sector and state enterprises on May 15. All present joined the call for renewed protests if the government failed to act. On May 16, the unionists held a press conference at Bencha Temple—where Chalard continued his hunger strike. They called for people to gather at 5:00 p.m. the next day to compel Suchinda to step down.[102]

During uprisings and similar crises of enormous magnitude, at the same moment as erotic bonds emerge from the grassroots, the veil normally covering significant forms of social stratification is removed, laying bare the ugly reality of violence and corruption at the heart of major institutions. Thailand's military would soon embark on another of its infamous killing sprees, bringing tanks into Bangkok to battle against ordinary citizens. Even institutions normally considered neutral and truthful, such as the media, also revealed a seamy side in 1992. While broadcast media overwhelmingly took the military's side and barely mentioned the protests (or, when they did, greatly distorted events), some print media courageously supported democracy and sought a truthful accounting of events for the first time in the history of antigovernment protests. People's experience of outright lies of the most transparent variety led to a widespread questioning, "Who Controls the Media?" When the facts became known, they revealed that the government controlled 100 percent of national and regional television and 82 percent of the nation's 484 radio stations.[103]

Showdown on May 17

On Sunday, May 17, more than three hundred thousand protesters assembled at Sanam Luang. Some estimated the crowd at half a million people, equaling the largest in Thai history. From the speakers' platform, one person after another denounced Suchinda and the government for failing to keep promises to amend the constitution. During the rally, the leadership group polled the crowd to ask whether people thought it best to remain at Sanam Luang or move.[104] They made a decision to move outside the office of Prime Minister Suchinda so he could see hundreds of thousands of people when he arrived at work the next morning. (They did not know Suchinda was not even in Bangkok.) Around 9:00 p.m., Chamlong spoke and led people in a pledge not to end their protests until Suchinda had stepped down. About five hundred workers were crowded near the prime minister's office, holding the ground in preparation for the arrival of the main rally. CFD leaders informed the rally of their decision to move to the prime minister's office, and people roared their approval. Tens of thousands of people headed toward Government House. They divided into three contingents, preceded by a hundred motorcycles. Nonviolent activists included Chamlong. Coordinating group member and student leader Parinya Thevanaruemidkul remembered that Chamlong moved the demonstration "like soldiers in the army."[105] Concerned that people's lives would be endangered, the SFT had decided not to endorse night rallies, yet the situation was now out of their control as CFD leaders voted to follow Chamlong. Touring the country's North, Suchinda promised to suppress the riots and resolve the crisis that very night.

The peaceful crowd was "a cross-section of Bangkok: poor workers, middle-class civil servants and shop owners, and wealthy yuppies."[106] Faced with a barbed wire barricade dubbed the "Berlin Wall" at the Phan Fa Bridge, people remained in the street. When the advance contingent broke through the barbed wire, Chamlong ordered them to return, but they continued to press ahead. Chamlong called on riot police to arrest them.[107] Soon the police used water cannons to disperse the crowd. As people surged on the truck shooting water, police clubs greeted them. Militants were able to destroy the barbed wire fence and put at least one fire engine out of action. Others near the bridge listened to speeches. Soon explosions could be heard, and a fire engine was set in flames along with Nareung Police Station and Youth Welfare Building. From his position in the final car of the procession, SFT leader Parinya saw the police station on fire and knew trouble would follow. Stones and Molotovs flew from the crowd. In addition to the police station and welfare building, about ten vehicles and Phukhaothong fire station were also set afire.[108] By midnight, a state of emergency was declared, and the army was mobilized. Soldiers took up positions away from the Phan Fa Bridge on Rajadamnoen, the same venue where fierce fighting had raged in 1973. Many people stayed in the streets by the bridge. Referring to protests that night, CNN described an "army of motorcycles" against the mobilized armed forces.

May 18, 1992, was one of the bloodiest days in modern Thai history. Around 1:00 a.m., tanks arrived. Many people were clustered near Democracy Monument, some singing and a few sleeping. About 2:00 a.m. Prateep addressed forty thousand or more people there.[109] An hour later, thousands of troops arrived, carrying live ammunition and orders to fire on "anti-Buddhist communists." Protest leaders gave speeches to troops surrounding them, and some people handed flowers to soldiers. About 3:30 a.m., while student leaders addressed the crowd from atop a van, soldiers opened fire. For hours, intermittent shooting continued. Around 4:00 a.m., the military swooped back onto the peaceful assembly, shooting as they arrived, leaving dead and wounded as they left. Even when people tried to sing the King's Song at Democracy Monument around 5:30 a.m., soldiers opened fire. To make sure they did not fraternize with citizens, fresh troops from the Burmese and Cambodian borders were rotated every three hours. One eyewitness recalled, "Every time the soldiers stopped shooting, people brought them food and water and put flowers into their guns."[110] The majority of those killed were shot in the back as they ran away. Others were reportedly executed at point-blank range. Doctors who treated the wounded were beaten.

In response, the crowd attacked carefully selected buildings. In a seesaw battle, people pushed the police back and retreated when police charged. Many citizens were forced into the canals, some jumping off the Phan Fa Bridge. As truckloads of demonstrators arrived to reinforce those fighting back, the street actions included more and more workers.[111] Once the shooting started, protest leaders became irrelevant, and students and middle-class people melted away. With no central leadership, polycentric sites of contestations permitted multiplication of actions. In the era of the cell phone, protesters communicated among themselves, horizontally coordinating their attacks and regrouping as they found space to do so. Thousands soon gathered at working-class Ramkhamhaeng University on the outskirts of the city.

As dawn broke, some ten thousand troops controlled Rajadamnoen Avenue. Still people remained in the streets. Around two thirty that afternoon, the army dragged off Chamlong. Troops burst into Majestic Hotel looking for other leaders, but Somsak and Prateep escaped with the crowd's help. Hundreds were arrested, many of them stripped of their shirts and hogtied. Nonetheless, thousands of people refused to give up. As William Callahan found, "Actually the mass protest blossomed after Chamlong (along with thousands of others) was arrested and Rajadamnoen Avenue was cleared by the army."[112] About 6:00 p.m., fifty thousand people assembled in front of the notorious Public Relations building. After physicians and nurses turned the lobby of nearby Royal Hotel into a field hospital, police erected barricades on Rajadamnoen Avenue. Around 9:30 p.m. troops, still numbering around ten thousand, fixed bayonets. An hour later, protesters pushed two buses into the barbed wire barricades, and soldiers opened fire. For

An "army of motorcycles" swept through the streets. Photographer unknown.

the next half hour, firing continued, reaching a "relentless thunder" for twenty minutes.[113] Again, many people were shot in the back as they fled. From rooftops, army sharpshooters picked off selectively targeted individuals. Most of the killings occurred between 10:20 and 10:40 p.m.

As in Gwangju, the broadcast media's false reporting—calling democracy protesters "rioters" and ignoring casualties—enraged people who were witnessing their friends being brutalized and murdered. People dubbed the Public Relations Department, home of state-run Radio Thailand, the "Department of Lies" and set fire to the building.[114] That fire spread to the Revenue Office—not coincidentally two of the same buildings torched in Gwangju—while hundreds of working-class motorcyclists roamed the city pursued by "headhunters," military agents who arrested or murdered them. Somsak Kosaisook counted about two thousand motorcycles.[115] All together, seven carefully targeted buildings were torched.

Within hours, magazines appeared with images of the dead and injured. By the next morning, tapes of CNN and BBC broadcasts were offered for sale by street vendors. Although Thai television had not covered the protests, autonomous productions of civil society—not corporate or state—were raw and unedited, giving them the aura of authenticity and the feel of real experience. Leaflets announced thousands of dead. Places where people had been gunned down became shrines of democracy. At one point, a procession of people all wearing black clothes, carrying black banners, and holding black wreaths, surged pass Democracy Monument to the Royal Hotel. Hundreds of doctors and nurses formed a notable contingent in the solemn march, whose final stragglers were thousands of people huddled in "hundreds of discussion groups mixing in the avenue's heat, dust, and noisy sidewalk vendors."[116] They left wreaths at both Democracy Monument and Royal Hotel, and soon lotus flowers and incense engulfed the monument. The next day, dozens of monks prepared a formal ceremony for the dead.

Soldiers stripped and tied up thousands of people. Photographer unknown.

All the while, the army continued to brutalize people. For three days, the killings continued. One witness told of soldiers near the Chao Phraya River placing bets on which of their prisoners would pass out first as they kicked them in the head.[117] The government banned gatherings of more than ten people, closed all schools, and enacted restrictions on the print media. The crematoria burned unidentified bodies as rumors spread of mass graves and helicopters taking away corpses. On May 19, troops entered the Royal Hotel, site of a makeshift emergency room and morgue, and mercilessly beat medical doctors and nurses treating the wounded. Television footage aired abroad showed troops firing at unarmed people, bludgeoning them with gun butts, kicking, swearing, and stepping on prostrate people. They forced about three thousand people to take off their shirts, crawl outside at gunpoint, and wait outside for hours on their hands and knees before being taken away.

Schools, offices, hospitals, and stores closed down, and even the city's buses stopped running. In Bangkok's East at Ramkhamhaeng University, tens of thousands of protesters established a liberated territory and barricaded the campus against a military assault.

Protests spread throughout the country—to the North's Chiang Mai, Khon Khen, and Nakhon Ratchasima; to the South's Nakhon Srithammarat, Songkhla, Krabi, Trang, and Pattani provinces. In the country's South, the state enterprise confederation and students, teachers, and NGOs organized rallies of 30,000 in Hat Yai; in Nakhon Srithammarat, some 60,000 joined, as did 30,000 in Surat Thani. Tens of thousands demonstrated in provincial capitals, including Songkhla, Krabi, Trang, Pattani, Ratcharim, and Khon Kean. Some 10,000 gathered in Chiang Mai.[118] All together, the unprecedented rural mobilization involved at least 186,000 demonstrators in twelve provinces as shown in TABLE 9.3. The awakening of the rural population may well be one of the most significant lasting effects of the 1992 uprising.

TABLE 9.3 **Rural Protests, May 20, 1992**

Region	Province	Participants
Northeast	Nakhon Ratchasima	20,000
	Khon Kaen	30,000
	Ubon Ratchathani	20,000
Central	Nakhon Panthom	30,000
	Kanchanburi	1,000
South	Songkhla	30,000
	Phatthalung	5,000
	Trang	10,000
	Nakhon Srithammarat	10,000
	Surat Thani	10,000
	Yala	10,000
North	Chiang Mai	10,000
TOTAL		186,000

Source: *Bangkok Post*, May 21, 1992.

At ten o'clock on the morning of May 20, railway workers voted to strike. Sporadic fighting continued for the fourth day despite mobilization of forty thousand troops.[119] Suchinda declared a curfew for Bangkok from 9:00 p.m. to 4:00 a.m. As the country teetered on the brink of civil war, the rich abandoned their posts. Crown Prince Vajiralongkorn left for South Korea and was seen off by Japanese Ambassador Okazaki.[120] In Paris, Princess Maha Chakri Sirindhorn happened to catch the French broadcast of horrific footage of troops gunning down people. Frantic at the disaster befalling her country, she attempted to reach her father. Unable to get through, she released a statement calling for an end to the violence. That afternoon, Princess Sirindhorn finally spoke with the king, who had already decided to handle the crisis directly. Suchinda and Chamlong were summoned to the palace. Kneeling before the king, Suchinda promised to accelerate reform, and Chamlong urged people to stop the protests. The meeting was telecast around 10:00 p.m. on May 20.

The two men were well acquainted with each other. "Brothers" at the Chulachomklao Military Academy, both had received training in the United States and served together for years. They did their best to turn a social crisis into a personal feud. On May 18, Suchinda referred to the entire crisis as "my conflict with Major-General Chamlong," and Chamlong wrote a public appeal to Suchinda that addressed the dictator as "older brother." The king further personalized the struggle, telling Chamlong and Suchinda publicly, "I would like both of you to talk face-to-face, not to confront each other."

While the carnage continued, the government of Japan—Thailand's largest foreign aid donor and leading economic power—formally announced it would not press for the government to stop its harsh repression. While officially not involved with Thailand's military, U.S. servicemen secretly trained the soldiers doing the shooting on the streets of Bangkok up to the last moment before their deployment from upcountry camps.[121] The Thai business community insisted that

Suchinda had to go. After the May 18 murders, a statement calling for him to step down was endorsed by Business Society for Democracy, the Industrial Federation of Thailand, the Thai Chamber of Commerce, and Bankers' Association. At many hospitals, banners prominently insisted that Suchinda resign, and automobile owners began to drive with their lights on during daylight hours as a signal for him to leave office.[122]

On May 21, the crisis continued. Thousands of people assembled at Democracy Monument, where Chamlong threatened new protests if promised constitutional reform again failed to materialize. Many people in the streets expressed dissatisfaction with the deal worked out by the king between Chamlong and Suchinda. They angrily called for punishment of Suchinda and others responsible for ordering the shootings. Sites where people had been killed were made into altars of democracy, as people created monuments to honor the martyrs of May. Thousands brought flowers to Democracy Monument.

On May 22, the CFD demanded punishment of officials who ordered shootings as well as Suchinda's immediate resignation as prime minister and supreme armed forces commander. As people tried to make sense of the wanton violence, they could not believe the statistics that became public: 52 people had been killed, 293 were missing, and more than 505 wounded. Immediately after the events, diplomats and medical workers reported again that unidentified bodies had been removed to crematoria by the military, and the public filed more than 1,000 missing persons reports. The Relatives Committee of the May 1992 Heroes subsequently put the number of missing at around 300.[123] Calls for punishment resonated widely, as did the far less radical call for Suchinda to step down. Hundreds of workers at the Thai Foreign Ministry wore black to protest the crackdown, and the foreign minister himself called for the Suchinda to resign.

On May 24, as Suchinda continued to bargain, the king granted amnesty to anyone found to have done wrong during the protests. While many people breathed a sigh of relief that they would not be punished for participating, their emotions turned to anger when they realized that the king's amnesty was prepared primarily for Suchinda—not for ordinary Thais. With a royal pardon in hand, Suchinda finally stepped down. As his forty-eight-day dictatorship ended, tens of thousands of Thais took to the streets and gathered at Democracy Monument to call once more for Suchinda and his cronies to be punished. Some opposition parties declared they would seek to overturn the royal proclamation of amnesty. The king had no constitutional authority to grant anyone amnesty, and even though political leaders swore to uphold the constitution, none of them would—or could—stand up to the king.

At dawn the next day, thousands of people—many living in poverty—rose to offer alms to Buddhist monks in honor of the May martyrs. So many gifts were showered on bewildered monks, they had to call for taxis and at least one pickup truck to carry them. That same day, parliament convened, and thousands of people's chants could be heard inside. A large banner in front of the building read, "No Peace for Mass Murderers!" Suchinda's whereabouts remained a public mystery. The House of Representatives approved constitutional amendments specifying that the prime minister must be selected by them, not by the military-appointed Senate.

As long as political parties bickered about the royal pardon's constitutional character (or lack thereof), a new government could not be formed. From a secure and secret position, the new army commander announced he would not tolerate any government that sought even to investigate—let alone to punish—those responsible for the bloodshed.[124] On May 31, the *Bangkok Post* published a list of 979 missing people, while the Interior Ministry and police claimed the number was about five hundred. Unlike in Nepal, where the opposition movement decided on the new prime minister after overthrowing the dictatorship, neither the CFD nor street protests made any attempt to do so. On June 10, in a move that all but formalized their powerlessness, the Thai parliament accepted the recommendation of the king to reappoint Anand Panyarachun as new prime minister, a move that only further emasculated parliament. On June 17, the army and air force commanders justified the killings, saying it was the only appropriate response to the uprising. No one was ever punished for the killings.

The Outcome of Black May

For the second time in twenty years, Thailand's courageous citizens sacrificed their lives and safety to overthrow military rulers. Once Suchinda had been deposed, the people's movement completed the grassroots initiative to write a new constitution, producing one that was ratified in 1997. Along with the fall the Suchinda government, top military officers were fired, including Army General Issarapong, brother-in-law of Suchinda, who was also compelled to step down as chair of the Telephone Organization of Thailand. Driven on the defensive, the military lost political hegemony to parties representing business interests and the urban middle class. Many state owned enterprises were demilitarized, and military men chairing the national airlines, communications authority, and State Railways Authority were removed. Civilian cabinets began routinely to reject increases in the military budget. Financial liberalization reduced the power of the Bank of Thailand and expanded the role of international investors.[125]

Media reform proceeded with vigor. Private licenses were granted for the first time, and UHF channels were opened. Print media's truthful reporting led to their enhanced legitimacy and a new dynamic involvement in Thai politics.[126] Along with media reform, decentralization of power was effected through elections of municipal leaders and enhanced power at provincial, village, and district levels. Corruption was temporarily reduced and people's participation in government increased.

Former Chief Justice Sophon Rattanakorn was empowered to lead an investigation into Black May, and his committee's report was released on September 25, 1992, before new elections were held. He determined that the military government had decided to use force against protesters as early as May 7 and had foreclosed peaceful solutions to the crisis. The report counted fifty-two people killed and over 3,500 arrested—many of who were tortured. Besides those killed (including one foreigner), they found 36 others who had been "crippled," 120 more seriously injured, and 115 confirmed missing. At least 207 others were on the Interior Ministry's list of missing. Eighty-eight police received outpatient hospital care, four soldiers were seriously injured, and 192 sustained minor injuries. Besides the human casualties, seven buildings were destroyed by fire, and total property losses were estimated at 1,508 million baht (then about $60 million at the exchange rate of 25:1).[127] The Sophon report recommended that the Defense Ministry be required to consult with the Cabinet before using force—even in emergencies—and they also called for tough penalties for anyone leading future military coups. The Ministry of Labor and Social Welfare issued figures of 44 deaths, 42 missing, and 292 injured.[128]

Evidently, democracy is good for growth as the country's economy continued to expand, posting positive rates of 7.6 percent in 1992, 8.1 percent in 1993, and 8.5 percent in 1994.[129] In elections three months after the uprising, "angel and devil" parties vied for power, and prodemocracy parties won enough seats to form a new government with one of the highest nationwide voter turnout ever: over 62 percent.[130] The new prime minister was Chuan Leekpai, a "champion of democracy." On October 7, the new parliament unanimously rejected Suchinda's amnesty, but he was never held accountable for his crimes.[131] For his part, the king invited 256 recently appointed generals and colonels to visit him. Assuaging their bruised egos, he refuted foreign critics who pointed out the top-heavy character of Thailand's military. While many foreign observers praised the king for his intervention to stop the violence during Black May, the king showed a more accurate portrait of himself during a meeting with eight Nobel laureates in February 1993. To people's amazement, Bhumibol openly condemned Aung San Suu Kyi in neighboring Burma for marrying a foreigner. In his view, she was therefore not representative of Burmese culture, and he insisted she should abandon her struggle and return to England.

The movement continued to agitate mildly—for example, by organizing an exhibition of political art entitled "Ratchdamnoen Memory" in late November at the Imperial Queen's Park Hotel in which more than 120 pieces in a variety of media reconsidered the movement and the massacre.[132] In 1995, the Relatives Committee filed a lawsuit against five military leaders who ordered troops to shoot in 1992, but the defendants maintained the royal pardon exempted them from penalties. Although no cabinet approved the royal pardon and the king did not have the constitutional authority to exempt anyone from civil or criminal prosecution, the courts threw out the lawsuit. Private fundraising efforts secured some monies for bereaved families—especially for those whose main breadwinner had been killed. Many people continued to demand an independent fact-finding commission, a memorial, and designation of May 17 as a national "Democracy Day." One mother who mourned for her twenty-year-old son donated all of her compensation money (100,000 baht, about $3,000) to establish a foundation for the education of poor children.[133] Although the government maintains only thirty-eight people had disappeared, relatives of about a hundred missing organized the Black May Relatives Committee to continue the search for the location of their loved ones' bodies. In March 2001, the Relatives Committee continued to insist that the number of missing stood at over a thousand.[134]

"Cell Phone Mob"

As the term "People Power" became the defining label for the 1986 Philippines overthrow of Marcos, the "cell phone mob" came to be associated with Black May. The media pronounced that label and maintained yuppies had been the mainstay of protests. Similarly cynical labels were echoed in the Western media. To be sure, urban professionals participated widely in the initial protests of November 1991, when the military's draft constitution was first made public. The media's focus on the "cellular phone revolution" drew attention to "designer clothes and expensive watches," to Mercedes and BMWs parked by protesters as they arrived from work.[135] For days, articles with similar intonations ran in major media with Western reporters attributing the nickname to the protesters themselves.[136] In the intervening years, these tales have been repeated in academic treatises and magazine retrospectives.

The mobilization of the middle class, a constituency whose ranks had greatly expanded during the decade of strong economic growth in the 1980s, was noteworthy. Teachers, academics, doctors, nurses, businesspeople, and other professionals played significant roles in the protests. Unlike in Eastern Europe, where protests began because the system could not deliver the goods, rising expectations fueled the Thai movement in 1992.

During the peaceful phase of demonstrations, the Social Science Association of Thailand was able to poll protesters and ascertained most were married and white-collar. They found that some two-thirds had an academic degree, 40 percent worked in the public sector, and 86 percent had incomes in excess of 5,000 baht per month (and half of this group more than double that).[137]

Workers' significant role in the protests remained hidden, largely because privately owned media overemphasized the role of middle-class businesspeople and simultaneously minimized the coverage of workers' participation. Many observers commented on the absence of organized labor from the protests, although evidence to the contrary merits examination. Kevin Brown argues persuasively that working class participation was robust—although not in the ideal-typical imagery of industrial workers wearing overalls and carrying hammers and sickles.[138] In a 2008 interview, Somsak Kosaisook reminded me that three thousand security people who managed security at the protests were all trade unionists and farmers, and that nearly all those killed were "labor and grassroots people, not students or middle class."[139] Another eyewitness, Alan Klima, speaks of an "army of pushcart vendors" that backed the protests and tells us "most of those killed were urban and rural poor."[140] The working-class "army of motorcycles" provided invaluable intelligence and mobility to militants who remained in the streets after most middle-class people returned home. One Thai observer found 45.5 percent of demonstrators were "middle-class," but noted that those who remained to fight after the shooting started were overwhelmingly working-class: "In truth, workers and lower class people were part of the movement, but more important than that, it is this group's refusal to retreat and run away in the hour of danger that kept the movement going for so many days."[141] *Thai News* reported that the arrested were made up of low-ranking civil servants, public enterprise workers, manual workers, university and school students, teachers, and health workers. An eyewitness who was a student at working-class Ramkhamhaeng Open University could only find the names of a few university students who were hit by gunfire. In her view, "The heroes of the May events were all nameless people, good 'followers.' None came from the upper classes or middle classes. All were people from the bottom of society who came to demand democracy and justice with a pure heart."[142]

Manual workers' participation may not have been immediately apparent because of several factors. Labor unions did not march in organized contingents. Fragmentation of the Thai labor force and the small size of firms in the private sector meant workers could not cluster in large contingents, as they had three years earlier in Beijing. (As previously noted, even then, widespread participation of workers was marginalized in media coverage, which routinely referred to the movement as "student protests.") In addition, approximately 25 percent of the workforce was self-employed and another 14 percent made their living as household workers. Another factor is divisions among labor unions. A few years after Black May, eight national trade union centers and eighteen registered trade union federations were counted.[143] Key to the mobilization in 1992 were Thai NGOs and informal, autonomous organizations, not unions or political parties.[144]

The 1997 People's Constitution

With its power increased and the role of the military reduced, Thailand's business class oversaw rapid economic expansion after the uprising, as international investors lined up to profit from the country's new dynamism. As we have seen in many cases, successful uprisings and democracy are good for business, and Thailand was no exception.

In 1993, legislation encouraged trade liberalization, eased restrictions on flows of finance capital, and reduced the number of regular workers, leading to layoffs and strikes. As in so many other cases, labor unrest mushroomed after the 1992 uprising.[145] Thai textile workers protested for five days and nights at the Government House and won a struggle to end unjust terminations. Foreign Direct Investment (FDI) rose a whopping 80 percent from 1995 to 1997, expanding from just over $2 billion to $3.6 billion. In 1996, Asia's share of FDI into South East Asia was $52 billion, up from $11.4 billion in 1990, an indication of Japan's consolidation of its control of Thailand's domestic automobile market. So rapidly did Asia-Pacific's domination by Japanese capital occur that in 1993, for the first time in half a century, Japan's profits in Asia were higher than those of the United States.[146]

Continuing development of export-oriented production brought the percentage of workers employed in manufacturing from 7.1 percent in 1981 to 13.4 percent in 1995. Already at astronomical figures, on the job injury rate skyrocketed from 32 per thousand workers in 1988 to 44.4 in 1995. South Korea's notoriety in this regard was discussed in *Asia's Unknown Uprisings Volume 1*, yet its injury rate of 15 per thousand workers makes Thailand seem barbaric—as it should. Occupation deaths rose from 282 in 1988 to 927 in 1996.[147] On May 10, 1993, at least 189 workers were burned to death at Kader Toy Company in one of the worst factory fires of all times. Significantly, this same Hong Kong company employed Chinese women in Guangdong, many only twelve years old, to work fourteen-hour days and seven-day weeks, for about $21 a month. A Kader executive told how in Guangdong, "We can work these girls all day and night, while in Hong Kong it would be impossible."[148] At that time, NGOs estimated more than half a million children under twelve were working in factories or in commerce.

After the uprisings, NGOs also mushroomed—including groups like Businessmen for Democracy that endorsed democratically minded candidates, and MPs Watch, a group that publicly monitored records of politicians. In 1995, at least ten NGO coordinating bodies existed, one of which—on rural development—had 220 affiliated organizations.[149] By 1999, 18,000 NGOs were registered in Thailand. So many collaborationist NGOs took part in military governments or otherwise worked against democracy that some people referred to two different kinds of NGOs: "collaborationist and autonomist." As the middle class gained in status and money after 1992, the working class and farmers saw their incomes deteriorate as a result of intensified neoliberal policies. A vast gulf opened between former erstwhile allies.

Working to craft a constitution worthy of the sacrifices made by people in the 1992 uprising, activists worked tirelessly for the 1997 "People's Constitution." Written by an elected assembly with ninety-nine members, it institutionalized visionary reforms, facilitated broad citizen participation in government, and self-consciously sought to move the country beyond representative to "participatory" democracy. Seventy-six elected representatives and twenty-three experts drafted the document after consulting with hundreds of grassroots groups. Throughout the process, lively debates aided deliberations and brought people to fine-tune their views. The CFD and other organization active in the 1992 uprising helped coordinate the efforts to involve more than 147 groups in the "People's Draft."[150] Dr. Thanet Aphornsuvan believed, "The whole process of constitution writing was also unprecedented in the history of modern Thai politics. Unlike most of the previous constitutions that came into being because those in power needed legitimacy, the Constitution of 1997 was initiated and called for by the citizens who wanted a true and democratic regime."[151] For the first time, citizens were declared "innocent until proven guilty."

Women's groups were especially active in advocating gender equality, protection of women from domestic violence, extension of maternity leave from thirty to ninety days, and tougher laws regulating prostitution—including punishment for perpetrators of child prostitution.[152] Thai women's groups had opposed antiprostitution laws in the 1970s since the laws criminalized women—even those forced into sex work—but granted customers impunity and pimps light sentences.[153] Yet with Thailand becoming "the brothel of Asia," new concerns began to be raised as estimates told of more than a million sex workers. Thailand's democracy may permit dissent, but it exports hundreds of thousands of women to serve as sex workers in Japan, keeps another million as tourist inducement to foreigners, and ignores the nation's AIDS crisis. With women's labor force participation rate exceeding 76 percent, Thai women are among the world's most economically active and are concentrated in key manufacturing sectors—95 percent of textile workers, 100 percent of leather goods, and 79 percent of footwear and garments.[154] Women were more than half of all professional and technical workers but only about 10 percent of elected representatives.[155]

From the grassroots, a diverse range of movements mobilized—again in autonomous forms outside the realm of political parties. In the 1990s, a Gay, Lesbian, Bisexual, and Transgender Movement (GLBT) slowly emerged, and in 2000 health professionals and NGO activist formed Rainbow Sky. One of the most significant groups to emerge was Assembly of the Poor (AOP), part of an international network of NGOs in eight other countries and regional coordinator of Via Campesina.[156] Refusing to call itself an organization but preferring the term "network" in which decision-making and power are decentralized, the Assembly of the Poor formed in December 1995 in simultaneous gatherings at Thammasat University and in Khong Chiam (Ubon Ratchathani Province). Born in the middle of "war" over natural resources between the state, businesses, and villagers, the group became an autonomous means for grassroots concerns to be articulated and empowered. While many members of the "October Generation" (former student activists who drew their life-forming identities form the 1973 insurgency) had moved into comfortable professional positions, others were involved in groups like the AOP—especially those who had fled the cities to find refuge in the CPT's armed struggle after the 1976 massacre. Final decision-making authority inside the AOP rests with the *pho khrua yai* ("head chefs")—a variable number of village representatives, normally composed of about 260 people. No one holds a "central" position such as secretary-general—making it difficult for state repression (or cooptation) to have significant impact. The group's first leaflet illustrated their own organizational structure. See FIGURE 9.3.

Soon after their formation, they had some 180,000 people organized into problem groups (such as dams, forests, alternative agricultures, and slum communities).

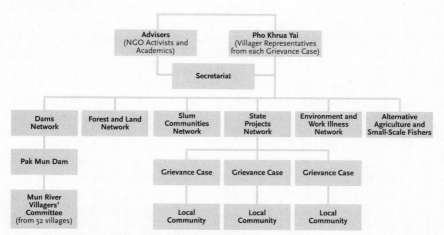

FIGURE 9.3 **Structure of Thailand's Assembly of the Poor**

In April 1996, the AOP brought more than 10,000 people to Government House, where they camped out for five weeks and insisted the government make good on some 100 broken promises. Again on January 25, 1997, AOP brought thousands of villagers to Bangkok, where urban slum dwellers joined the gathering, swelling its numbers to 25,000.[157] For ninety-nine days, a "Village of the Poor" witnessed speeches and performances. Carrying large photos of the king and Thai flags, the group nonetheless insisted on collective leadership and internal democracy. NGO members spread throughout the city to give talks and explain the reason for the occupation. During these times, the group had thirty-eight meetings to negotiate with the authorities, until finally, the government made "unprecedented concessions" by meeting all 122 grievances and compensating nearly 7,000 families hurt by dam construction.[158] The cost was high: ten people were killed and two more committed suicide.[159]

As the "Thai Miracle" continued into 1997, the official poverty numbers tallied only 13 percent of the population.[160] No one seemed to believe that neoliberal policies and export-oriented production would stop producing growth and prosperity. Yet in July 1997, a financial meltdown left the economy in ruins and quickly spread through East Asia. The Suharto dictatorship fell in neighboring Indonesia, and Malaysia's stability was called into question.

The 1997 IMF Crisis

Financial crises are powerful means of wealth redistribution and an essential part of capitalism's life cycle. Since they result in the "survival of the fittest" as part of an inherited structure, they are an entirely different kind of crisis than those produced by popular will in the form of uprisings, revolutions, and political change. In the case of the 1997 IMF crisis that swept through East Asia, international financial investors in currency and loan markets, as well as decisions made by the IMF itself, played prominent roles in setting off and accelerating the region's tailspin. Former IMF chief economist Joseph Stiglitz is among those most critical of the IMF role. George Soros in particular profited enormously from the Thailand's misery. His notorious Quantum Fund rode the upswing of Thailand's economic expansion, but on May 14 and 15, 1992, he initiated a massive sell-off, essentially placing a huge bet on devaluation of the baht. Soros flooded the market with Thai currency, dumping it as quickly as he could before its value plummeted, a process that brought him hundreds of millions of dollars overnight while ruining Thailand's economy and sending ripples throughout the region that engulfed neighboring countries. A million Thais were pushed below the poverty line. (At one point, Soros was actually indicted in Thai courts for his malicious greed, but evidently his violation of moral and ethical codes did not hold up to Thailand's flexible legal interpretations of law—particularly after he had visited the king.)

When the baht lost more than half its value, stocks fell even more—as much as 75 percent—and property values plummeted. In 1997, as the economy contracted, hundreds of thousands of urban dwellers returned to their villages, and more than six hundred thousand foreign workers were sent home. In 1998, economic performance was even worse, declining by more than 10 percent.[161] The government sold off banks and commodities to foreign investors—especially from Japan—at bargain prices, draining domestic holders of wealth and further integrating Thailand's economy into the world system (increasing its future vulnerability). Three years later, GDP remained 2.3 percent below precrisis level.[162] By 2003, GDP still had not climbed back to its level of 1996.[163] Where the United States held a slight lead over Japan from 1970 to 1986, Japan's direct investment in Thailand was more than three times that of the United States from 1997 to 2006.[164] As domestic retail and production firms were driven out of business, European firms Tesco, Carrefour, and other supermarkets increased their outlets from 18 in 1996 to 58 in 2000 and to 148 in 2006.[165]

Overnight, the Bank of Siam teetered on the brink of survival, and the Crown Property Bureau (CPB) lost 75 percent of its income—compelling the royal family to seek loans to cover their living expenses.[166] The CPB's income is tax-free and its assets are kept secret—an easy task considering it is not required to file annual reports. Through its subsidiary, Siam Commercial Bank, it is the country's largest investor, and through Siam Cement Group, it maintains strict control of all building. Its landholdings in Bangkok are enormous. Estimated at about $40 billion in 2005, its net worth accounts for some 40 percent of Thailand's GNP.[167]

With international bond credit ratings sinking from AA+ to DD—junk bond status—and with more than half of foreign debt of $89 billion due in just a few months, Thailand's bankruptcy meant the country's only recourse was an IMF structural adjustment bailout to the tune of more than $17 billion. Key components of the IMF's conditions—called a "slave contract" by labor—were maintenance of high interest rates, budget cuts, privatization of state enterprises, tax increases, and opening of the financial sector even more to "foreign capital injection."[168] Thailand's response to the crisis was predictable: rely even more heavily on those that had caused it—foreign investors. In 1997, foreign companies were granted the rights to own a majority of shares in some firms. Two years later the list of open targets was expanded. As downsizing of government programs occurred, market forces were introduced into state enterprises, universities, and health facilities. The AOP's agreement fell by the wayside, as did Thailand's previous resistance to foreign ownership of land and ban on 100 percent foreign ownership of financial institutions.

Billionaire telecommunications tycoon Thaksin Shinawatra came to the rescue of Siam Commercial Bank and the king, buying a bankrupt television station at an overvalued price. It wasn't charity but ambition that drove the sale: Thaksin soon turned the station into a vehicle for the promotion of his political career. Changes in the character of the investment regime governing Thailand's major industries were accompanied by political transformations. Facilitated by the 1997 constitution, the country's business class came to preeminent power over the military. Thaksin built a support base in the country's northeast that assured him continuing success in democratic elections. He was elected prime minister in 2001 and again in 2005. Voter turnout in 2001 of 69.95 percent was highest in Thai history. So popular was Thaksin that he was seen as Bhumibol's competitor in the hearts of many people. Thaksin built hospitals and schools for the rural poor, instituted universal health care, completed road construction in rural areas, funded financial relief for farmers in the northeast, and redistributed wealth from the nation's urban middle class to rural areas.

Yet there was a harsh side to Thaksin's rule. Beginning in February 2003, more than two thousand people were killed in his "war on drugs." Massive repression of the Muslim south was unleashed. On October 25, 2004, at Takbai, some ninety Muslim young men were massacred—an action compared by many to the 1976 massacre at Thammasat University. Alongside Muslims and drug peddlers, massive police force was used to disperse street vendors, anti-IMF protesters, farmers, and pipeline opponents. The Assembly of Poor had 560 members charged and 118 warrants for arrest. Farmers' protests were broken up with massive police force. A massive movement of two hundred thousand electrical workers opposed Thaksin's privatization plan. Thaksin somehow believed he had the king's blessing, perhaps because he had helped Bhumipol during the IMF crisis. He could not have been more mistaken.

Red Shirts and Yellow Shirts

When the floodgates of opposition to Thaksin opened, a counteroffensive by the monarchy and military was unleashed. The strange admixture of monarchy, nationalism, and democracy that characterized uprisings in 1973 and 1992 was suddenly burst asunder. Former allies became enemies, and the country convulsed in continuing street battles as Yellow Shirts attacked Thaksin and Red Shirts defended him. By April 2006, protests organized by the anti-Thaksin People's Alliance for Democracy (PAD), a popular front of twenty-three organizations also known as Yellow Shirts, grew into mammoth rallies of more than a hundred thousand people. Founded in 2005, they are held together by a core leadership that includes Chamlong Srimaung and Somsak Kosaisook, major figures of the 1992 uprising. Yellow Shirts believe Western-style democracy encourages corruption. In their view, Thaksin is a corrupt billionaire, who sought to supplant the king as the nation's leader and bought the voters of rural areas through hospitals, schools, and roads. They believe that "Dhammocracy"—the rule of Buddhist precepts like *dharma* (righteous rule), selflessness, asceticism, compassion, and sympathy for all who suffer—is superior to electoral democracy. For Dhammocracy to work, the wisdom of the king is paramount, and Yellow Shirts have requested that the monarchy appoint the majority of parliament. Reviving a proposal Suchinda made for a nonelected parliament, the Yellow Shirts proposed that only 30 percent of representatives in parliament's lower house be elected. The irony of "democratic" activists fighting for the proposal made by Suchinda is not lost on their opponents.

On September 19, 2006, as the country became more polarized than in recent memory, a military coup d'état occurred when Thaksin was in New York preparing to address the United Nations. Covered sympathetically by the Western media, this eighteenth coup since the end of World War II not only overthrew a democratically elected prime minister, it also abolished the best constitution in Thailand's history. The newly installed prime minister was a military commander in charge of the 1992 shooting down of unarmed protesters. The junta carefully selected a group to draft a new constitution and forbade public criticism of its features before a 2007 referendum that approved it.

With every new election under the revised constitution, Thaksin supporters emerged as winners, but their Yellow Shirt opponents would not accept the results. In August 2008, tens of thousands of them surrounded Government House, effectively closing the new prime minister's compound, but army commander General Anupong Paochinda refused to do anything even after the prime minister declared a state of emergency. On the fifth day of protests, many observers noted a carnival atmosphere. On August 30, 2008, the Associated Press reported, "The crowd included stockbrokers, financial analysts and entrepreneurs, many carrying expensive cameras and mobile phones. And nearly all of them wore yellow to honor Thailand's wildly popular king, Bhumibol Adulyadej. 'This is democracy in action,' said Amorn, the chemical company owner. 'We have come together to show our people power. This scene may seem strange to Westerners, but it's normal to us.'" Finally on September 10, the Constitutional Court ruled that the prime minister' receipt of money for his popular television cooking show constituted a conflict of interest, thereby removing him from office.

Since pro-Thaksin forces still held power in parliament, PAD protests continued. In early October 2008, riot police using Chinese-made tear gas against Yellow-Shirt protesters killed at least two people and maimed several others, whose limbs or feet were cut off from the explosions during clashes between the police and demonstrators.[169] Despite their Hippocratic oaths, some doctors in Bangkok hospitals reported they would refuse to treat wounded police officers that fought against Yellow Shirts. A Thai Airways pilot similarly would not fly three members of parliament from the pro-Thaksin People Power Party. Encouraged by support from the queen and the military's reluctance to intervene, the Yellow Shirts went on to close Phuket and Bangkok's airports, precipitating a major crisis for the country. By taking sick leave, hundreds of railroad workers forced cancellation of dozens of trains. Finally, protests ended in December 2008 after the Constitutional Court dissolved the pro-Thaksin government, paving the way for a new prime minister loyal to the king, Abhisit Vejjajiva, who ruled until new elections in 2011. Human Rights Watch named Abhisit "the most prolific censor in recent Thai history" as he arrested opposition leaders for their opinions, shut down websites, and closed radio stations.

After Thaksin was found guilty of violating conflict-of-interest law, his passport was revoked, much of his wealth was frozen, and he was sentenced in absentia to two years in prison. In August 2009, the Red Shirts, or United Front for Democracy against Dictatorship (UDD), gathered over five million signatures on a petition asking the king to grant Thaksin royal clemency. The king refused their request. As they were increasingly frustrated in their attempt to win democratic reforms, Red Shirts occupied downtown Bangkok, insisting that the non-elected Abhisit government was illegal and should step down. For nearly two months beginning on April 10, 2010, Red Shirts occupied much of the central city, including its commercial core. As the government teetered on the brink of violence, Army General Kattiya Sawatdipol, one of the most significant Red Shirt allies, was assassinated with a single shot to his head during an interview with the *International Herald Tribune*. On May 19, the military moved in force to evict the Red Shirts, who responded by setting fire to luxurious shopping malls and downtown commercial buildings. According to government statistics, at least eighty-four civilians and seven soldiers were killed in the violence of April and May 2010; more than 1,800 others were wounded; besides the thirty buildings that were torched, there were sixty-two bombings.[170] As we saw in the Philippines, poor protesters involved in People Power 3 were handled with far greater violence than more acceptable middle-class participants in People Power 1 in 1986 or People Power 2 in 2001.

In Thailand, middle-class vacillation in support of democracy is revealed in their changing position: for it in 1973, against it in 1976, for it in 1992, against it in 2008.[171] The media have labeled Yellow Shirts as middle-class and as "a diverse mix of royalists, military officers, business owners, social activists, students and middle-class homemakers."[172] The reality is far more complicated. In my experience in 2008 when I twice visited the Yellow Shirt occupation of Government House, their working-class component is significant. Trade-union security forces guarding the leadership's convergence area wore Che Guevara T-shirts. No clear middle-class label is appropriate unless the "labor aristocracy" is considered middle-class. (In a later chapter, I discuss the role of the middle class in civil uprisings.) As speaker after speaker addressed several thousand people gathered in their tented assembly space outside the prime minister's office, vendors hawking their wares in the encampment's winding passageways, constructed to frustrate police or soldiers who might invade, included sizeable amounts of left-wing paraphernalia, from Zapatista videos to Palestine buttons. Yellow Shirt spokesperson Suriyasai Takasila is a former student activist who was also head of the CPD.[173]

Red Shirts clearly include more poor people than do their opponents, but one need always remember that they work in support of Thaksin, a corporate billionaire with a neoliberal agenda. As the UDD struggle progresses, their distance from the royal family may well increase—even to the point of rupture, which would be a revolutionary development. True to longstanding tradition, however, a continuing pattern of hierarchical politics can be observed in the influence of Thaksin on the Red Shirts and the monarchy on the Yellow Shirts. Thailand's future is being written in backroom deals rather than through transparent and egalitarian relationships. While bosses wield tremendous power from behind the scenes, ordinary citizens are far more capable of democratic deliberation and governance.

The past years of ongoing conflicts speak volumes to the popular consciousness produced by Thailand's history of uprisings. Before the army's violence in 2010 against the Red Shirts, student leader Parinya Thevanaruemidkul remembered that during the 1992 uprising there were three major rallies in two weeks, and that during eighteen hours in 1973, two rallies took place. In 2008, in more than a hundred days, Yellow Shirts held twenty rallies, and no one was killed.

"The Thai nation has learned the power of non-violence. Even though we are divided as in 1976, we have learned how to express our differences."[174] The space for public contestation in the streets is a fruit of people's sacrifices over the years. With so many popular mobilizations, people have internalized a belief in their power and may yet come to enjoy the kinds of freedoms they have already twice won.

NOTES

1   The Thai legal system ratchets up pressure against anyone even vaguely truthful about the role of the king in keeping Thailand in a state of impoverished smiles. Australian writer Harry Nicolaides, author of a self-published novel that sold fewer than a dozen copies, received a prison sentence of three years under Thailand's tough lèse-majesté laws. The court found Nicolaides's book "suggested that there was abuse of royal power." In April 2008, a Thai citizen was arrested after he remained seated in a movie theater when the royal anthem played before a film. When a colleague wore a shirt saying "Not standing up is not a crime," she was summarily fired, and her union subsequently refused to support her. With dozens more such cases awaiting trial in 2008, professor Ji Ungpakorn left the country rather than submit to the arbitrary judgments being levied against him. Hundreds of websites were closed down. After Buddhist activist Sulak Sivaraksa raised doubts about lavish celebrations of the Bhumibol's reign, he faced charges under lèse-majesté.

2   "Thai King Is World's Wealthiest: Forbes," *Korea Times*, August 23–24, 2008, 5.

3   See Prudhisan Jumbala, "Toward a Theory of Group Formation in Thai Society and Pressure Groups in Thailand after the October 1973 Uprising," *Asian Survey* 14, no. 6 (June 1974): 537.

4   Yuangrat Wedel, with Paul Wedel, *Radical Thought, Thai Mind: The Development of Revolutionary Ideas in Thailand* (Bangkok: Assumption Business Administration College, 1987), 6.

5   Ian Buruma, "All the King's Men," *New York Review of Books*, October 11, 2006, 44.

6   Ji Ungpakorn, *The Struggle for Democracy and Social Justice in Thailand* (Bangkok: Arom Pongpangan Foundation, 1997), 20.

7   J. Stephen Hoadley, *Soldiers and Politics in Southeast Asia: Civil-Military Relations in Comparative Perspective* (Cambridge: Schenkman Publishing, 1975), 32; Surachart 1985, 152–55).

8   Van Erven, *Playful Revolution*, 207.

9   Interview with Prajak Kongkiriti, Bangkok, October 28, 2008.

10   E-mail correspondence with Prajak Kongkirati.

11   Ross Prizzia and Narong Sinsawasdi, "Evolution of the Thai Student Movement: 1940–1974" *Asia Quarterly* 1 (1975): 3–54.

12   Ruth Inge-Heinze, "Ten Days in October—Students vs. the Military," *Asian Survey* 14, no. 8 (June 1974): 491.

13   Jumbala maintains the group was founded in 1969 ("Group Formation," 540); others state the date at 1970. Charnvit Kasetsiri, ed., *From October 14, 1973 to October 6, 1976: Bangkok and Tongpan's Isan* (Bangkok: Foundation for the Promotion of Social Science and Humanities Textbooks, Thai Year 2549), 94.

14   Prizzia and Sinsawasdi, "Evolution," 26.

15   U.S. Embassy Confidential Memorandum, June 23, 1973 (BANGKO 09756 231325Z).

16   As quoted in Prizzia and Sinsawasdi, "Evolution," 29.

17   Giles Ji Ungpakorn, *A Coup for the Rich: Thailand's Political Crisis* (Bangkok: Workers Democracy Publishing, 2007), 71.

18   Interview with Prof. Naruemon Thabchumpon, Chulalongkorn University, Bangkok, October 29, 2008.

19   Quoted from Prizzia and Sinsawasdi, "Evolution," 32.

20   Inge-Heinze, "Ten Days in October," 497.

21   Kasetsiri, *From October 14*, 108.

22   Inge-Heinze, "Ten Days in October," 499; Prizzia and Sinsawasdi, "Evolution," 38.

23   Inge-Heinze, "Ten Days in October," 501.

24   *Far Eastern Economic Review*, October 22, 1973, and October 29, 1973.

25   Prizzia and Sinsawasdi, "Evolution," 44.

26   Ungpakorn, *Coup for the Rich*, 72.

27   Haggard and Kaufman say that nearly eighty were killed (*Political Economy*, 104). Norman Peagam, "A Cinema Review of *Tongpan*," uses the figure of seventy-one in Kasetsiri, *From October 14*, 168. The remarkable video, *October 14, 1973 Student Uprising* (with English subtitles by Benedict Anderson) gives the figures I use above.

28   See Terence C. Lee, "The Causes of Military Insubordination: Explaining Military Organizational Behavior in Thailand," Paper presented at the Annual Meeting of the International Studies Association Honolulu, Hawaii, March 2005.

29   Interview with Somchai Homlaor, Bangkok, October 28, 2008.

30   Prizzia and Sinsawasdi, "Evolution," 44.

31   Quoted in Somchai Phatharathananunth, *Civil Society*, 55.

32   Interview with Prof. Ji Ungpakorn, Chulalongkorn University, Bangkok, October 30, 2008.

33   Ji Giles Ungpakorn, *History and Class Struggle in Thailand*.

34   Katherine A. Bowie, *Rituals of National Loyalty: An Anthropology of the State and the Village Scout Movement in Thailand* (New York: Columbia University Press, 1997), 104; David Morell and Chaianan Samudavanija, *Political Conflict in Thailand: Reform, Reaction, Revolution* (Cambridge, MA: Oelgeschlager, 1981), 188–89.

35   Walden Bello, Shea Cunningham, and Li Kheng Poh, *A Siamese Tragedy: Development and Disintegration in Modern Thailand* (Oakland, CA: Food First Books, 1998), 75.

36   Jumbala, "Group Formation," 542.

37   Marian Mallet, "Causes and Consequences of the October '76 Coup," in *Thailand: Roots of Conflict*, eds., Andrew Turton, Jonathan Fast and Malcolm Caldwell (Nottingham: Spokesman, 1978), 1082.

38   Ungpakorn, *Struggle for Democracy*, 91.

39   Bruce D. Missingham, *The Assembly of the Poor in Thailand: From Local Struggles to National Protest Movement* (Chiang Mai: Silkworm Books, 2003), 24.

40   Ungpakorn, *Coup for the Rich*, 73.

41   Bowie, *Rituals*, 101.

42   Quoted in Wedel, *Radical Thought*, 145.

43   Inge-Heinze, "Ten Days in October," 505.

44   Harold Stockwin, "The Unholy Gross," *Far Eastern Economic Review*, November 5, 1973, 45.

45   *Bangkok World*, November 18, 1973, as reported in Prizzia and Sinsawasdi, "Evolution," 47.

46   Luis Camnitzer et al., *Global Conceptualism: Points of Origin, 1950s–1980s*, (New York: Queens Museum of Art, 1999), 144.

47   Callahan, *Cultural Governance*, 47.

48   See Virada Somswasdi, "The Women's Movement and Legal Reform in Thailand," April 1, 2003, Cornell Law School, http://lsr.nellco.org/cgi/viewcontent.cgi?article=1001&context=cornell/biss.

49   Inge-Heinze, "Ten Days in October," 506.

50 World Bank, IMF, Haggard and Kaufman, *Political Economy*, 92.
51 Mallet, "Causes and Consequences," 86.
52 Alex Hang-Keung Choi, "Non-Governmental Development Organizations (NGDOs) and Democracy in Thailand: The 1992 Bangkok Uprising," unpublished thesis (Queen's University, 2001), 45–46.
53 Bowie, *Rituals*, 102. Between 1974 and 1979, forty-six leaders of the FCT were killed. "People's Progress: 30 Years On," Special Supplement to the *Bangkok Post*, October 14, 2003.
54 Benedict Anderson, "Withdrawal Symptoms: Social and Cultural Aspects of the October 6 Coup," *Bulletin of Concerned Asian Scholars* 9 (1977): 19–20, from Bowie, *Rituals*, 106.
55 Mallet, "Causes and Consequences," 85.
56 Suthachai Yimprasert, "The Coming of 6th October 1976 Suppression in Thailand," *Colonialism, Authoritarianism and Human Rights of South East Asia*, conference book (Gwangju, South Korea: May 18 Institute, 2001).
57 Frank C. Darling, "Thailand in 1976: Another Defeat for Constitutional Democracy," *Asian Survey* 17, no. 2 (1977): 127.
58 Puey Ungpakorn, "Violence and the Military Coup in Thailand," *Bulletin of Concerned Asian Scholars* 9, no. 3 (1977): 5.
59 Ibid., 8.
60 See Bowie, *Rituals*, 128 for discussion of academics' views on the role of the monarchy in the October 6, 1976, bloodbath.
61 See Bowie, *Rituals*, 115.
62 Ungpakorn, *Coup for the Rich*, 84.
63 P. de Beer, "History and Policy of the Communist Party of Thailand," *Journal of Contemporary Asia* 8, no. 1 (1978): 148–49, in Bowie, *Rituals*, 137.
64 Comrade "Sung," "Looking Back to When I First Wanted to Be a Communist," in *Radicalizing Thailand: New Political Perspectives*, ed. Ji Giles Ungpakorn (Bangkok: Institute of Asian Studies, 2003), 172.
65 Wedel, *Radical Thought*, 163.
66 Comrade "Sung," "Looking Back," 179–80.
67 Wedel, *Radical Thought*, 183.
68 See Dae-oup Chang, "Neoliberal Restructuring of Capital Relations in East and South-East Asia," in *Neoliberalism: A Critical Reader*, eds. Alfredo Saad-Filho and Deborah Johnston (London: Pluto Press, 2005), 252; Joseph Kahn, "Thai Troubles Drive a Dynasty to Sell Its Crown Jewel Bank," *New York Times*, April 16, 1998, A1.
69 Bello, "Asia."
70 Bello, Cunningham, and Li, *Siamese Tragedy*, 66.
71 Ibid., 74.
72 Pasuk Phongpaichit and Chris Baker, eds., *Thailand's Boom and Bust* (Chiang Mai: Silkworm Books, 1998), 4.
73 Bello, Cunningham, and Li, *Siamese Tragedy*, 37.
74 Gerald W. Fry, "Saturday 'Surprise,' the February 23, 1991 Coup in Thailand: The Role of the Military in Politics," Georgetown University School of Foreign Service, Case 353, 1992, 12.
75 *Statistical Yearbook*, Thailand, 1992.
76 Kevin Hewison, ed., *Political Change in Thailand: Democracy and Participation* (London: Routledge, 1997), 140.
77 Fry, "Saturday 'Surprise,'" 3.
78 Ibid.; Larry Diamond, Juan Linz, and Seymour Marin Lipset, eds., *Democracy in Developing Countries: Asia,* (Boulder: Lynne Rienner, 1989), 329.

79 Phongpaichit and Baker, *Boom and Bust,* 147.

80 Ibid., 97.

81 Scott Bamber, "The Thai Medical Profession and Political Activism," in *Political Change in Thailand: Democracy and Participation*, ed. Kevin Hewison (London: Routledge, 1997), 240.

82 Larry Diamond, "Introduction," in *Democracy in Developing Countries: Asia*, eds. Larry Diamond, Juan Linz, and Seymour Marin Lipset (Boulder: Lynne Rienner, 1989), 44.

83 *New York Times*, February 27, 1992, as quoted in Physicians for Social Responsibility, "Bloody May: Excessive Use of Lethal Force in Bangkok: The Events of May 17–20, 1992, October 1, 1992.

84 See Andrew Brown, "Locating Working-Class Power," in *Political Change in Thailand: Democracy and Participation*, ed. Kevin Hewison (London: Routledge, 1997), 172.

85 Bello, Cunningham, and Li, *Siamese Tragedy*, 77.

86 See Somsak Kosaisook, *Labour Against Dictatorship* (Bangkok: Friedrich Ebert Foundation, Thai Labour Museum, and Arom Pongpangan Foundation, 2004), 87–89 for discussion.

87 Formed in 1979 to amend the constitution, the group formed again in 1983 when military control of the office of prime minister was imminent. Its third incarnation was in 1991. Interview with Professor Naruemon Thabchumpon, Chulalongkorn University, Bangkok, October 29, 2008.

88 Interview with Parinya Thevanaruemidkul, Bangkok, October 30, 2008.

89 Choi, *NGDOs and Democracy*, 306, 316.

90 Khien Theeravit, *Thailand in Crisis: A Study of the Political Turmoil of May 1992* (Bangkok: Thailand Research Fund, 1997), 20.

91 Surin Maisrikrod, *Thailand's Two General Elections in 1992: Democracy Sustained* (Singapore: Institute of Southeast Asian Studies, 1992), 29.

92 Tatsuya Hata, *Bangkok in the Balance: Bangkok's 'Slum Angel' and the Bloody Events of May 1992* (Bangkok: Duang Prateep Foundation, 1996), 178.

93 Kosaisook, *Labour*, 98.

94 Alan Klima, *The Funeral Casino: Meditation, Massacre, and Exchange with the Dead in Thailand* (Princeton: Princeton University Press, 2002), 96.

95 Interview with Prof. Vipar Daomanee, Thammasat University, Bangkok, October 28, 2008.

96 Hata, *Bangkok*, 251.

97 Interview with Parinya Thevanaruemidkul, Bangkok, October 30, 2008.

98 Kosaisook, *Labour*, 109–10.

99 Klima, *Funeral Casino*, 101–2.

100 Ibid., 108–9.

101 Choi, *NGDOs and Democracy*, 350; *Thai NGOs: The Continuing Struggle for Democracy* (Bangkok: The NGO Support Project, 1995), 130.

102 Kosaisook, *Labour*, 117–18.

103 Public Relations Department, 1990, as reported in Ubonrat Siriyuvasak, "The Development of a Participatory Democracy: Raison d'Être for Media Reform in Thailand," *Southeast Asian Journal of Social Science* 22 (1994): 105.

104 Kosaisook, *Labour*, 117.

105 Interview with Parinya Thevanaruemidkul, Bangkok, October 30, 2008.

106 Paul Handley, *The King Never Smiles*, as excerpted in *Asia Sentinel*, September 8, 2006.

107 Kosaisook, *Labour*, 123.

108 Physicians for Social Responsibility, "Bloody May," 8.

109 Hata, *Bangkok*, 189.

110 Quoted in Stan Sesser, "The Course of Corruption," *Mother Jones*, May–June 1993.

111 J. Ungpakor, *The Struggle for Democracy and Social Justice in Thailand* (Bangkok: Arom Pongpangan Foundation, 1997), 108–12.

112 William A. Callahan, *Imagining Democracy: Reading "The Events of May" in Thailand* (Singapore: Institute of Southeast Asian Studies, 1998), 86.

113 Physicians for Social Responsibility, "Bloody May," 9.

114 Siriyuvasak, "Development," 107.

115 Kosaisook, *Labour*, 128.

116 Klima, *Funeral Casino*, 138.

117 Philip Shenon, "Military Crackdown in Thailand Blunts Protest Against Army Rule," *New York Times*, May 20, 1992, A1.

118 Choi, *NGDOs and Democracy*, 332.

119 Hata, *Bangkok*, 235.

120 Ibid., 215

121 Klima, *Funeral Casino*, 9.

122 Interview with Prof. Naruemon Thabchumpon, Chulalongkorn University, Bangkok, October 29, 2008.

123 The Thai Interior Ministry claims forty-four dead, thirty-eight disappeared, eleven disabled, and over five hundred wounded. Human rights activists have noted that hundreds were killed or disappeared. No Thai government has ever been held responsible for massacres of prodemocracy demonstrators in 1973, 1976, or 1992.

124 Philip Shenon, "Thai Coalition Struggles to Form a New Government," *New York Times*, May 29, 1992, A7.

125 Xiaoke Zhang, *The Changing Politics of Finance in Korea and Thailand: From Deregulation to Debacle* (London: Routledge, 2003), 128.

126 See Thitinan Pongsudhirak, "Thailand's Media: Whose Watchdog?" in *Political Change in Thailand: Democracy and Participation*, ed. Kevin Hewison (London: Routledge, 1997), 217.

127 Maisrikrod, *General Elections*, 37; Theeravit, *Thailand in Crisis*, 58.

128 Reported in Surichai Wun'gaeo, "Human Rights and Democracy in Thailand," in *Democracy and Human Rights in the New Millennium*, International Symposium on the 20th Anniversary of the Kwangju Uprising Program (Gwangju: May 18 Institute, 2000), 155.

129 Jacques Bertrand, "Growth and Democracy in Southeast Asia," *Comparative Politics* 30, no. 3 (April 1998): 369.

130 Maisrikrod, *General Elections*, 1.

131 "Ousted Thai's Decree for His Own Amnesty Is Reversed," *Boston Globe*, October 8, 1992.

132 See Callahan, *Imagining Democracy*, 145–48 for discussion.

133 Wun'gaeo, "Human Rights," 157.

134 The Relatives Committee of the May 1992 Heroes, "The Status of the Missing as a Result of the May 1992 Political Crackdown," (Pathumdhani: March 2001), 73.

135 Philip Shenon, "Mobile Phones Primed, Affluent Thais Join Fray," *New York Times*, May 20, 1992, A10.

136 Philip Shenon, "The 'Mobile Phone Mob' Faces Guns and Tanks," *New York Times*, May 24, 1992, E3.

137 Kevin Hewison, "Thailand" in *The New Rich in Asia: Mobile Phones, McDonald's and Middle-Class Revolution*, eds. Richard Robison and David Goodman (London: Routledge, 1996), 138; Phongpaichit and Baker, *Boom and Bust*, 238.

138 Andrew Brown, "Locating Working-Class Power," in *Political Change in Thailand: Democracy and Participation*, ed. Kevin Hewison (London: Routledge, 1997), 162.

139 Interview with Somsak Kosaisook, Bangkok, October 31, 2008.

140 Klima, *Funeral Casino*, 9, 159.
141 Anek Laothamatas, *The Mobile Phone Mob: The Middle Class and Businessmen and the Development of Democracy* (In Thai) (Bangkok: Matichon Publishing, 1993) as quoted in Ungpakorn, *Struggle for Democracy*, 111.
142 As quoted in Ungpakorn, *Struggle for Democracy*, 112.
143 Bello, Cunningham, and Li, *Siamese Tragedy*, 80.
144 Callahan, *Imagining Democracy*, 109.
145 Phongpaichit and Baker, *Boom and Bust*, 141.
146 Bello, Cunningham, and Li, *Siamese Tragedy*, 66.
147 Ibid., 83.
148 *Business Week*, October 31, 1988.
149 Amara Pongsapich, "Strengthening the Role of NGOs in Popular Participation," in *Thai NGOs: The Continuing Struggle for Democracy* (Bangkok: The NGO Support Project, 1995), 30.
150 Kosaisook, *Labour*, 226.
151 Asian Human Rights Commission, "Thailand: The Return of the Military and the Defiance of Common Sense," *Article 2 of the International Covenant on Civil and Political Rights* 5, no. 5 (October 2006): 4.
152 Somswasdi, "Women's Movement." As the author pointed out, the new constitution nonetheless retained less than progressive features of the old order: to marriage and family life are still there. Women "can still be bought by the man who wishes to engage with her. . . . He is entitled to decline to marry her if she is raped or has consensual sexual affairs with another man, not vice versa. He can file for a divorce for a single act of extra marital affairs. But, the only divorce ground for her is to prove that he openly recognizes the other woman (women) as his wife (wives) and/or financially supports her (them). In addition, marital rape is not punishable and not deemed a ground for divorce. Children have to carry the father's last name unless the man is unknown." In addition, laborers complained about the provision requiring people to return to vote in their home villages—a hardship for migrant workers—and the requirement prohibiting candidates without a university degree (Kosaisook, *Labour*, 226–27).
153 Yuki Fujime, "The Prohibitionist System and Feminism in Thailand and the Philippines," in *Contemporary Women's History in Asia* (Osaka: Association for the Study of Contemporary Asian Women's History and Gender, 2005), 29.
154 Bello, Cunningham, and Li, *Siamese Tragedy*, 81.
155 Juree Vichit-Vadakan, "Women in Politics and Women and Politics in Thailand," in *Women and Politics in Thailand: Continuity and Change*, ed. Kazuki Iwanaga (NIAS Press, 2008), 28.
156 Somchai Phatharathananunth also locates the AOP's birth in an international meeting of NGOs from ten countries at the same time. In a nicely crafted study that supplements Missingham's pathbreaking analysis, he also frames AOP's emergence in the history of organizing efforts in rural areas and the centralization of previous efforts (*Civil Society*, 143–44).
157 Missingham, *Assembly of the Poor*, 121.
158 See Pei Palmgren, "Claims to Globalization: Thailand's Assembly of the Poor and the Multilevel Resistance to Capitalist Development," *The Resistance Studies Reader 2008*, ed. Christopher Kullenberg and Jakob Lehne (London and Gothenburg: Resistance Studies Network, 2009), 34–60. Also see Phatharathananunth, *Civil Society*, 161.
159 Phongpaichit and Baker, *Boom and Bust*, 207.
160 World Bank, Thailand Country Brief, September 1997.
161 Pasuk Phongpaichit and Chris Baker, eds., *Thai Capital After the 1997 Crisis* (Chiang Mai: Silkworm Books, no date), 9.

162 Stiglitz, *Globalization*, 97.
163 Peter Brimble, "The Experience of FDI Recipients: The Case of Thailand," in *Multinationals and Economic Growth in East Asia*, eds. Shujiro Urata, Siow Yue Chia, and Fukunari Kimura (London: Routledge, 2006), 354.
164 Phongpaichit and Baker, *Boom and Bust*, 24.
165 Ibid., 92–93.
166 Ibid., 168.
167 "The Crown Property Bureau in Thailand," Talk at Harvard University, Southeast Asia Workshop Series October 4, 2007.
168 Bello, Cunningham, and Li, *Siamese Tragedy*, 45.
169 Seth Mydans, "In Thai Heartland, Anger over Protests," *New York Times*, October 13, 2008.
170 Seth Mydans, "Conflict in Thailand Shifts from Protests to Politics," *International Herald Tribune*, June 2, 2010, 8.
171 Thanks to Ji Ungpakorn for helping to formulate this insight.
172 Mydans, "Thai Heartland," *New York Times*, October 13, 2008.
173 Giles Ji Ungpakorn, *Thailand's Crisis and the Fight for Democracy* (London: WDPress, 2010), 61.
174 Interview with Parinya Thevanaruemidkul, Bangkok, October 30, 2008. He also expressed his view that another pole is needed since neither red nor yellow represent the poor and working-class.

CHAPTER 10

Indonesia

Indonesia has achieved a remarkable economic development
success over the past decade and is considered to be among the
best performing East Asian economies.
                                    —World Bank, September 1997

As the stricken economies registered negative growth rates and
record unemployment rates in 1998, and over one million people
in Thailand and 21 million in Indonesia fell below the poverty line,
the IMF not surprisingly joined corrupt governments, banks and
George Soros as the villains of the piece in the view of millions of
impoverished Koreans, Thais and Indonesians.
                                    —Walden Bello

CHRONOLOGY	
December 7, 1975	Indonesia invades East Timor; thousands killed
November 12, 1991	Dili Massacre: at least 273 unarmed East Timorese killed
July 27, 1996	Thousands of people confront police barricades in Jakarta
January 9, 1998	IMF Crisis: rupiah falls from 2,400 to 10,000 to the dollar, then to 17,000
January 12, 1998	U.S. official Lawrence Summers in Jakarta; pressures Suharto to sign IMF accord
February 9, 1998	Food riots in many cities
March 10, 1998	Legislature grants Suharto a seventh term as president
May 12, 1998	Four students shot to death by police at Trisakti
May 12, 1998	Bloody riots break out in Jakarta; hundreds killed and raped
May 13–15, 1998	Riots spread to many cities; hundreds more killed and raped

May 18, 1998	Tens of thousands of students take over parliament building
May 20, 1998	One hundred thousand students rally in the parliament complex
May 20, 1998	More than one million citizens march in Jakarta
May 20, 1998	Parliamentary leaders call for impeaching Suharto
May 20, 1998	U.S. Secretary of State Madeleine Albright also calls for him to step down
May 21, 1998	President Suharto resigns
May 22, 1998	Army gently expels two thousand remaining students from parliament building
November 12, 1998	More than a hundred thousand students protest military's influence in politics
November 13, 1998	Hundreds of thousands of workers and urban poor also mobilize
November 1998	Soldiers shoot dead five people near Atmajaya University, sixteen people killed
August 30, 1999	East Timor overwhelmingly endorses independence in a referendum
August 30, 1999	Before and after referendum, Indonesian militias kill over a thousand Timorese civilians
September 7, 2004	Activist Munir poisoned to death aboard an Indonesia Airways flight

ALREADY IN POWER for more than three decades, Indonesia's Suharto regime might have survived the wave of uprisings that swept Asia if not for the 1997 IMF crisis, which devastated the country like nowhere else. When the financial storm struck, more than twenty-one million Indonesians were swept below the poverty line, and food riots broke out all over the country. President Mohammed Suharto was compelled to sign an IMF agreement that brought billions more dollars back into the country, but protests led by students in 1998 spiraled in size. Invoking the memory of the overthrow of Marcos in the Philippines twelve years earlier, Indonesian students called for a "People Power Revolution" and occupied the parliament building after the army let them cross their lines. Opposition legislators moved to impeach the president. Reluctantly, Suharto left office, leaving the door open for constitutional reform.

Suharto first came to power in 1966, aided in no small part by the student movement. That year, their "Three Demands of the People" had called for resignation of President Sukarno, liquidation of the Indonesian Communist Party, and lower prices on basic goods. Suharto had much more powerful friends, among them the United States, whose war in Indochina was going badly. With U.S. knowledge and support, Suharto's regime massacred an estimated five hundred thousand "leftists" within first four years of coming to power. So closely did Suharto follow U.S. leads that the CIA and State Department drew up death lists to target opposition leaders.[1] International investors flocked to the country as Suharto "purified" it.

By 1971, after the horror of the killing fields subsided, students turned against the regime. They launched a blank ballot campaign, asking people to abstain from voting to protest unfair elections. Although heavily repressed, student unrest continued. In January 1974, demonstrations against a visit by Japanese Prime Minister Tanaka embarrassed Suharto, since such a prominent symbol of the country's domination by foreign capital was attacked under his rule.[2] Artists also turned against the regime's corruption and favoritism. In the Black December Incident, many contested the jury selection process for the 1974 Jakarta Biennale. Soon an Indonesian New Art Movement announced its formation.[3] Challenging the system of art education, their manifesto called for subversion of aesthetic hierarchies and advocated assemblage, happenings, and found objects. In 1978, the New Art Movement's third exhibition contained montages that directly criticized President Suharto and performance pieces that parodied his authority. Although harshly repressed, Indonesia's student movement continually revitalized itself and employed different forms of resistance to congeal opposition around a variety of issues.[4] At Bandung Institute of Technology in 1978, four years after their protests against Tanaka, students challenged the People's Consultative Assembly—the mainly appointed legislature that selected the president. They chose the "Day of Heroes," named in honor of anticolonial fighters, to go into the streets with elaborate slogans like "People who once fought for independence now fight for wealth."[5]

Enticing giant multinationals with lucrative offers, Suharto built a substantial empire for his family, and at the same time, his regime reduced poverty from more than half the population in the 1960s to about 12 percent in 1996.[6] Decades of steady 7 percent annual growth helped produce a small middle class. A gay movement, a rarity for Islamic countries, appeared in the late 1980s. With the declining price of oil, the regime made significant transitions in this period: market orientated policies catered to foreign investors, and the regime shifted economic output from import-substitution to exports. Agriculture tailed off, as rice output in particular declined, and the country began to import more food. The manufacturing sector of the labor force expanded from 9.1 percent in 1980 to 25 percent in 1997, and a labor movement came to life in the mid-1990s at the same time as direct foreign investment grew over 400 percent from 1990 to 1997.[7]

During thirty-two years of Suharto's regime, Indonesia bloodily intervened against independence movements throughout its archipelago, especially in Christian East Timor, only recently freed from Portuguese colonialism. The military killed at least one hundred thousand people after an invasion in 1975. The day before the invasion, Suharto got a green light in a personal meeting with Henry Kissinger and U.S. President Gerald Ford in Jakarta on December 6, 1975.[8] During these consultations, they discussed insurgencies in Thailand and Malaysia, and Ford mentioned the "severe setback of Vietnam." Ford promised to be an "enthusiastic" supporter of a plan to build an M-16 manufacturing facility in Indonesia. This modern equivalent of the Taft-Katsura Treaty, of countries secretly dividing territories to promote their own narrow interests, indicates how little U.S. policy in Asia changed in seventy years. As Timorese casualties mounted in the late

On July 27, 1996, thousands of Indonesians rose against the dictatorship. Photo by Robinsar VDN, in *The Long Road to Democracy: A Photographic Journey of the Civil Society Movement in Indonesia, 1965–2001* (Jakarta: Yappika Publishers, 2002), 33.

1970s during the era of President Jimmy Carter's "human rights" policy, American aid to Jakarta continued to flow, and the United States blocked UN attempts to stop the slaughter. Weapons sales to Suharto's regime passed the billion-dollar mark under the Reagan administration from 1982 to 1984.[9] Massacres in East Timor continued for twenty years. On November 12, 1991, at least 273 unarmed East Timorese were slaughtered in Dili.

In this same period, dozens of democracy activists throughout the country were abducted by the military. People's tolerance finally reached their limits on July 27, 1996, when government thugs attacked and occupied the offices of the leaders of the Indonesian Democratic Party (including Megawati Sukarnoputri, the daughter of Suharto's predecessor as president). Going into the streets, thousands of people confronted military barricades, as shown in the photo above.

So concerned was Washington that Suharto might become an ever-larger problem that the United States secretly spent $26 million between 1995 and mid-1998 to fund Suharto's political opponents in the hopes of helping facilitate a democratic transition that would inject a more pro-U.S. business environment.[10] Like Marcos in the Philippines, Suharto's regime in Indonesia became what Max Weber would have called "sultanist," one led simply by the ruler, his family, and a tight circle of friends. Lacking legitimacy, sultanist regimes are vulnerable to uprisings precisely because there is no other way to remove them from power.[11] Democratic regimes—that is, ones based upon modest distribution of individual wealth and voting legitimation rituals—are much more difficult to transform.

Early in 1998, Forbes magazine estimated Suharto's wealth at $16 billion, making him the world's sixth-richest man.[12] Others guessed even more—anywhere from $30 to $40 billion.[13] His family's businesses stretched from hotels to satellites and proudly claimed partnerships with the likes of Lucent Technologies, General Electric, Hyatt Hotels, and Hughes. Over his thirty years of rule, the World Bank supported him, delivering over $30 billion in loans. For decades, according to many reports including one of its own, the World Bank "tolerated corruption, accorded false status to false government statistics, legitimized the dictatorship by passing it off as a model for other countries, and was complacent about the state of human rights and the monopolistic control of the economy."[14]

Western reporters at the time loved to castigate Suharto's cronyism and called for an end to "kleptocracy." The word applies very well to subsequent measures of war-profiteer Dick Cheney and the billions of dollars in no-bid contracts the Bush administration awarded to Halliburton/Blackwater. Like the fixed 1987 elections in South Korea that were replicated in Florida in 2000, Indonesian cronyism and economic crisis in 1997 would migrate from periphery to center and strike full force in the United States in 2008. As was said with regard to Indonesia might just as well have been written about the United States: "The whole basis of cronyism—the awarding of contracts without bidding, the amassing of huge wealth—all this will be affected by the economic crisis."[15]

IMF Crisis
The torrid pace with which the IMF crisis of 1997 engulfed Indonesia left many experts looking embarrassed, but the rapid deterioration overnight condemned millions of people to dire conditions of existence. Shortly after the value of the Thai baht plummeted in July 1997, the contagion spread to Jakarta. International speculators began selling off Indonesian stocks, and the market's value was cut in half. Its currency fell more than 70 percent. Riding to the rescue—or so it proclaimed—the IMF floated a U.S. $43 billion bailout in October. In exchange, Suharto had no choice but to agree to sell off public enterprises and open the gates to more foreign investments. The IMF directive also stipulated that sixteen local banks had to close, causing a run on remaining financial institutions. From a July level of 2,400 rupiah to the dollar, by January 9, it fell to the 10,000 mark.[16] Within two weeks, it reached 17,000 to the dollar. As even more money left the country in panic, calls for Suharto's resignation became increasingly vocal.

To pressure Suharto to comply, the IMF structural adjustment package delayed installment payments until Suharto also agreed to shut down state monopolies, to cancel the development of indigenous automobile and aircraft industry, and—as in all IMF "assistance" programs—to cut government subsidies that kept the price of basic foods low. Refusing to submit to the dictates of international investors, Suharto stunned the country—and much of the world's press—on January 6, 1998, when he announced an overall 32 percent increase in government spending that included major hikes in subsidies for the cost of necessities like rice and fuel. Despite a phone call on January 8 from U.S. President Clinton, Suharto stubbornly resisted. On January 12, Deputy Treasury Secretary Lawrence Summers (who was later to become President Obama's treasury secretary) visited Jakarta to pressure Suharto to sign the IMF agreement. On January 12, German Chancellor Helmut Kohl, Japan's Prime Minister Ryutaro Hashimoto, and

IMF Director Michel Camdessus watched as Suharto was compelled to sign an agreement.
Photographer unknown.

Australian Prime Minister John Howard all called to urge imposition of the IMF austerity package. Unable to hold out any longer, on January 14, Suharto reluctantly agreed, but when he faltered on implementing it, U.S. President Clinton sent in former vice president Walter Mondale to keep up the pressure. On January 17, *The Economist* blared, "Step Down, Suharto."

International investors and American politicians imposed their ideas of what was best for the country's people, but all their pressure backfired when a photograph was published showing IMF Director Michael Camdessus standing sternly with folded arms behind Suharto as he finally signed an interim agreement on January 15. Ordinary Indonesians were angered to see their leader treated so desultorily by a representative of international capital. When food riots broke out on February 9, many citizens blamed foreigners who had forced starvation wages upon the population. Their president, Asia's longest serving head of state, was seen by many as a hero for refusing to implement IMF terms. Since the IMF withheld a $3 billion installment, it was seen as causing the economy's freefall. On March 10, the People's Consultative Assembly granted Suharto a seventh term as president.

With an estimated $70 billion in foreign loans already made to Indonesian businesses, international officials were desperate to keep the economy afloat. In April, a third rescue package was signed, permitting the government to delay the unpopular end to subsidies on gasoline and food (blamed by many for antigovernment protests). In May, as the number of kidnapped democracy activists rose to at least fourteen, the United States and IMF promised to continue their aid programs. "Our national interest is seeing the economic reforms go forward," a White House official intoned to the *New York Times* of May 9 while announcing a billion-dollar U.S. loan guarantee made with no considerations of human rights guarantees. Nearly all the country's corporations were in a technical state of bankruptcy, and price inflation led to food riots, especially bloody in Medan, Surabaya, and Jakarta. Indonesia, long an exporter of food, needed to import rice from Vietnam.

The 1998 Student Uprising

On dozens of campuses in March, daily protests were organized as the upsurge against Suharto built momentum. Students used the Internet to built a national network and passed along stirring accounts of the 1986 Filipina People Power uprising (after which they modeled their revolt). Text messages helped them share intelligence on police and army movements as well to coordinate demonstrations. Aware that secret agents of the government heavily infiltrated all their meetings and public groups, students responded by rotating their leadership and changing the office location every week of one of their key organizations, City Forum. The tactic succeeded in creating difficulties for any individual—police agent or not—to assert dominance of the movement.[17] Drawing in representatives from local groups across the country, they developed a decentralized coordinating structure. The role of women at demonstrations was often to form a line between armed soldiers and protesters. On more than one occasion, as people had done at the 1967 Pentagon march and in the streets of Prague during the Russian invasion of 1968, they put flowers in the barrels of guns pointed at them. At the end of April, housewives in the small city of Semarang joined a march of two thousand female students.[18]

While peaceful protests by students continued, everywhere there was talk of "People Power." Nonetheless, on May 1, Suharto insisted there could be no political reform for five more years and flatly refused even to discuss selling off his family's businesses. That same day, representatives of more than thirty Jakarta-based workers' groups arrived at the University of Indonesia campus in Depok and met for four hours with student activists.[19] In Bandung and Surabaya as well, students and workers met to develop joint actions. On May 12, a peaceful march of about ten thousand students sang songs and spilled off campus from elite Trisakti University onto a major highway. Suddenly police attacked, fearing the march was headed toward the parliament in Jakarta. After a barrage of teargas, police snipers shot four students to death.[20] The country's shock quickly turned into anger. In a number of cities, students fought back. Very quickly, the capital was overcome with bloody riots.

From May 13 to 15, devastating riots quickly spread to other cities, especially to Solo, Ugung Padang, Jogjakarta, and Palembang. What began as student protests turned into looting by the urban poor—and then into a more deadly set of attacks

The army cooperated with students as they took over parliament. Photographer unknown.

involving gang rapes, arson, and slaughter. In Jakarta, hundreds of people were killed—more than one thousand in all parts of the country—as crowds singled out Chinese-Indonesians and their businesses.[21] Many stores with "Muslim-owned" signs were spared from destructive power of the crowd violence. (A small fraction of Indonesia's population, Chinese-Indonesians control as much as 75 percent of the country's wealth.) As many as 468 women, nearly all of Chinese descent, were gang-raped in just a few days in fifteen places. More than one thousand houses were set afire; some 1,604 shops were damaged, as were 40 shopping malls, 12 hotels, 11 police posts, and hundreds of cars.[22] At Yogya Plaza in East Jakarta, a grisly scene of with 174 charred bodies was found. Many people saw the dark hand of Suharto and his son-in-law, General Prabowo Subianto, behind the shootings of the Trisakti students and attacks on women.[23] These actions were similar to the anti-Chinese pogroms that had swept Suharto into power in 1965 when nearly half a million Chinese Indonesians were slaughtered, and their 1998 duplication was thought to be designed to spread panic at the thought of his departure.

On May 18, tens of thousands of students wearing their brightly colored college jackets marched on the country's parliament building and occupied it. They called for "reformation in the political, economic and legal fields" and vowed to remain until Suharto resigned from office.[24] As in China and Taiwan, students insisted on maintaining their "purity" and prevented nonstudents from participating in the movement.[25] Parallel support groups demanding Suharto's resignation were composed of poets, writers, and professors. For four hours, soldiers guarded the entrance to the building and prevented students from entering, but after Speaker of the House Harmoko called for Suharto's resignation, they stood by while thousands of students took over the building.[26] Carrying roses (which they presented to soldiers), the students remained inside for days. That night, the army isolated the building and deployed tanks throughout Jakarta, but students were soon joined by thousands of their campus colleagues.

The student movement self-consciously identified with the global People Power's incarnations.[27] Interviews conducted by an American correspondent at the universities in Indonesia determined that their "People Power" identity was adopted from the Philippines, as was the tactical innovation of the occupation of public space. In this moment of the eros effect, students could have become masters of the political system and led their country forward. They enjoyed widespread support among the army and the people. Senior military officers from Suharto's generation called on him to resign and publicly declared their support for the students occupying parliament.

On May 20, the country's National Day of Awakening commemorating their anticolonial struggle against the Dutch ninety years before, some one hundred thousand students rallied in the parliament complex, while more than one million citizens marched in nearby Yogyakarta. Swarming over the domed roof and grounds of the legislature, students made merry, turning the scene into an "Indonesian version of Fort Lauderdale, Florida, during spring break." Inside, people congregated in the marble hallways, while in the main chamber, leaders debated, made speeches, and parodied politicians and generals, in what was described as a "spontaneous shadow government." One American reporter described the scene less optimistically: "Students in khaki uniforms from the Indonesian Maritime Academy sprinted around the room on the desktops. Others heckled the speakers by tossing wads of paper at them. And the unofficial leaders sitting on the rostrum elbowed each other out of the way as they tried to get a turn at the podium."[28] Instead of such a farce, students could have organized a general assembly involving tens of thousands of people. But in the seductive halls of parliament, the semblance of power turned the proceedings into a circus. When we contrast the proceedings with the seriousness of students in 1980 Gwangju, at Thammasat University in 1973, or in the occupation of Chiang Kai-shek Square in March 1990, a wide gap opens between these other occupations and their Indonesian counterpart.

Until the very end, the United States supported Suharto, as did the World Bank and IMF. So unpredictable are uprisings that in April 1998, only days before the end of Suharto, one observer predicted, "Despite the pressures of some, however, the prospects for democratization in the near future are slim."[29] Only when people rose up and insisted Suharto leave did his international benefactors support "democracy."[30] On the same day that students occupied parliament, political leaders called for a special session of the electoral commission to annul its March reelection of the president and, instead, to impeach him. U.S. Secretary of State Madeleine Albright also called for him to step down and ensure a democratic transition. The next day, May 21, 1998, President Suharto finally resigned and handed over power to his handpicked second in command, Vice President B.J. Habibie.

With no organization or charismatic leader, the opposition stood by while their overthrow of Suharto led to a succession of established political leaders moving up to claim their turn at the highest levels of national power. On the morning of May 22, more than thirty thousand students still occupied parliament, but their antics left them in no position to provide leadership to the country. Students were far from unified, having already divided between those who supported Habibie and his "Reform Cabinet" against others who insisted on democratic elections. Late that night, soldiers gently moved in and expelled the two thousand remaining students from the building they had occupied for five days.

The *Reformasi* Era

Indonesians won the right to go down the road to *reformasi*, which many hoped would lead to a complete restructuring of society. Instead they got old wine in new bottles, Suhartoism without Suharto—a new version of the military-dominated system they had been fighting, one that benefited disproportionately a few families at the top and was based upon the subordination of two hundred million people spread across a wide swath of ocean to the dictates of Jakarta's political-military elite.

Before Habibie could even speak of a "honeymoon," the nation's economic crisis continued to intensify. Nearly 15 percent of all employed men lost their jobs by August 1998. GDP fell 13.1 percent in 1998.[31] Poverty afflicted forty to fifty million people—one-quarter of the population—at the end of 1998.[32] So severe was the plight of the poorest that up to 170,000 children starved to death every year, or 465 every day of the year. From $1,155 in 1996, GDP per capita fell to $449 in 1998, rising only to $720 in 1999.[33]

While Indonesians suffered, foreign companies bought the country's assets at fire sale prices. The IMF structural adjustment program forced the closure of more than sixteen banks, and the government's largest bank, PT Bank Madri Tbk, its second-largest telecommunications firm, and hundreds of private companies were sold to foreign investors at bargain basement prices. With the skewed exchange rate, acquisitions were incredibly cheap. Later that year, the government announced plans to sell off many of its state-owned enterprises. As occurred in South Korea and Thailand, the IMF crisis and "democratization" led to privatization and greater penetration by global corporations.

Within months, civil society's changed character was evident. Many groups mobilized in the months after Suharto's fall. Almost immediately, displaced farmers occupied his massive ranch at Tapos.[34] Some two thousand farmers in Medan demonstrated for return of their lands. Transport workers and teachers both protested for better working conditions and higher wages.

After the overthrow of Suharto, teachers massively called for improved working conditions and higher pay. Photo by Vitasari/Antara in *The Long Road to Democracy.*

In August 1998, a bank workers' declaration led to the formation of white-collar unions that provided office workers in more than dozen banks with job security and better wages.[35] Soon media workers, teachers, civil servants, service workers, pharmacy workers, and others also organized themselves. The Alliance of Independent Journalists, long active in the anti-Suharto movement, played a key role in leading people. Labor experts from the U.S. embassy, the AFL-CIO, and other U.S.-backed international labor groups helped to reorganize Indonesian unions, breaking them away from government control and setting up an American-style labor federation in August 1998.[36]

In 1999, the number of NGOs mushroomed to an estimated seven thousand.[37] Among the new groups were victims' associations like the Indonesian Association of the Families of the Disappeared, formed on September 17, 1998. KontraS (Commission for Involuntary Disappearance and Victims of Violence) was set up on March 20, 1998, successor to a long line of human rights watchdog groups. New NGOs also included a number of conservative groups, like the Islamic Defenders Front that formed on August 17, 1998. Advocating *sharia* (or Islamic law) for the whole country, they formed their own militia and investigations bureau. They discovered that the murder of hundreds of so-called practitioners of "black magic" in Java were actually attacks on Muslims.[38]

As before the overthrow of Suharto, students remained in the movement's forefront. Student demands focused on the creation of a transitional government to hold elections and end the military's role in political decision-making. Once again, their movement found wide resonance among the populace. Neighborhood residents plied student marchers with money, refreshments, and verbal support. When hundreds of army-paid thugs attacked the students, poor people rushed to their defense and compelled the thugs to retreat. On November 10, tens of thousands of students massed at the parliament building and demanded Habibie immediately step down and transfer power to a transitional presidium of five *reformasi* leaders, including Nobel laureate Bishop Carlos Belo.[39] Student protests reached their peak in a pitched battle around the parliament on the night of November 12. In other cities as well, students remained active. In Solo, they took over the local government building, and in Yogyakarta, they occupied a state radio station.[40] When the People's Consultative Assembly (still comprised mainly of Suharto appointees) reconfirmed the military's paramount political role, more than a hundred thousand students demonstrated on both November 12 and 13. In addition, hundreds of thousands of workers and urban poor mobilized. In dozens of cities, people supported a three-day general strike after soldiers shot dead five people near Atmajaya University, close to the parliament building. Reports of two killed in Aceh and a total of sixteen people in all of Indonesia surfaced as violence reached its most intense level since May. Television aired footage of the crowd beating bloody an isolated policeman, whose life was saved only when marines intervened.[41]

Years of struggle ensued as people sought to "cleanse" the ranks of government officials of corrupt individuals left over from Suharto's New Order, but results were few. Regional autonomy remained elusive for ethnic minorities. Teachers' salaries were still less than $50 per month in 2004—one tenth of the pay of teachers in Malaysia and half of those in the Philippines.[42] Three years after the "end" of the crisis, the country's GDP remained 7.5 percent lower than in 1997.[43] On June 9, 1999, new elections were finally held, and in July 2001, Megawati was selected president by the new House of Representatives. In 2004, the president was directly elected for the first time. In the post-Suharto era, a modicum of decentralization of power took place, and some transparency and accountability was instituted in policymaking. Government reforms included the creation of a National Human Rights Commission, Police Commission, and Corruption Eradication Commission. Police and military functions were separated from each other, but torture remains a routine part of police practice.[44]

Most significantly, independence was won by East Timor. The new *reformasi* regime permitted a referendum, and islanders overwhelmingly endorsed independence in August 1999. Almost immediately, militias supported by the Indonesian army went on a killing spree. More than a thousand innocent civilians were massacred and some three hundred thousand refugees driven into West Timor, where Indonesia continues to rule. While East Timor was able to break from Jakarta's grip (and encounter its own set of seemingly intractable problems) Aceh and West Papua have not been so lucky. Devastated by a tsunami in

December 2004, Aceh's people failed to achieve their goal of independence—at least in this generation. In fact, in Aceh after "liberalization," incidents of torture, extrajudicial murder and disappearances more than doubled on an annual basis, as shown in TABLE 10.1:

In 2002, the former governor of East Timor was found guilty of crimes against humanity and given a three-year jail sentence for failing to halt the killing spree by militias after the independence referendum in 1999.[45] Two years late the verdict was overturned, and no one was ever punished for any of the atrocities committed by the Indonesia government. In May 2007, relatives of those killed in 1998 repeated their call for full investigation of who was responsible.[46] As Ricky Gunawan expressed it, "Indonesia's failure to break the chain of impunity creates a notion that human rights abuses are tolerated. Repeated impunity makes the criminal justice system vulnerable and if that happens, it is like a house of glass that can shatter sooner or later."[47] Human rights violations continue to plague even the mildest forms of dissent. On September 7, 2004, activist leader Munir was poisoned aboard a Garuda Indonesia Airways flight to Amsterdam and died— one of eight murders of human rights activists in a two-year period.[48] Although one individual was subsequently found guilty in Munir's case, the masterminds— thought to be high-ranking government officials—remain at large.

International connections among grassroots groups are another significant legacy of the 1998 uprising. Leading up to the 2004 general elections, KontraS launched a campaign against "Bloody Politicians" (which they announced was a direct way they had learned from South Korea to target and defeat reactionary parliamentary candidates). Of eighty-six such candidates, fifty-nine were defeated. As the Indonesia movement was influenced by People Power in neighboring countries, its influence was felt in Malaysia. On March 8, 1998, Deputy Prime Minister Anwar Ibrahim's sacking led to an outburst of discontent that turned into a self-described "*reformasi*" movement. Citizens mobilized for months against the paternalism of the Mahathir government. Protests reached their peak when Queen Elizabeth visited on September 20.[49] Tens of thousands of people gathered at the national mosque and marched to the prime minister's house.

Whether or not individual instances of civil insurgencies are successful or not, they blaze the trail for future movements. In so doing, their contributions to humanity's freedom are lasting. In the following chapters, I trace continuing influences and implications of Asian uprisings.

TABLE 10.1 **Violence in Aceh, 1999–2002**

Year	Extrajudicial executions	Torture	Capture/ detentions	Forced disappearances	TOTAL
1999	421	802	293	101	1,617
2000	524	549	419	140	1,632
2001	1,014	768	578	110	2,470
2002	1,307	1,860	1,186	377	4,730
TOTAL	3,266	3,979	2,476	728	10,449

Source: Database KontraS, 2002

NOTES

1 Blum, *Killing Hope*, 194.

2 Yayasan Penguatan Partisipasi Inisiatif dan Kemitraan Masyarakat Indonesia, *The Long Road to Democracy: A Photographic Journey of the Civil Society Movement in Indonesia, 1965–2001* (Jakarta: Yappika Publishers, 2002), 33.

3 Queen's Museum of Art, *Global Conceptualism: Points of Origin, 1950s–1980s*, (2000), 144.

4 See Mikaela Nyman, *Democratising Indonesia: The Challenges of Civil Society in the Era of Reformasi* (Copenhagen: Nias Press, 2006), 64–68.

5 "The White Book of the Indonesian Student Movement," *Ampo* 10, no. 1–2 (1978): 30.

6 Irwanto, "Indonesia," in *The Disenfranchised: Victims of Development in Asia*, ed. Urvashi Butalia (Hong Kong: Arena Press, 2004), 31.

7 Ibid., 19.

8 For related documents, see http://www.gwu.edu/~nsarchiv/NSAEBB/NSAEBB62/#doc4, December 9, 2009.

9 Boggs, *Crimes*.

10 Tim Weiner, "U.S. Has Spent $26 Million Since '95 on Suharto Opponents," *New York Times*, May 20, 1998, 11.

11 Thompson, *Democratic Revolutions*, 114.

12 Mydans, "Suharto and Co."

13 Nicola Bullard with Walden Bello and Kamal Malhotra, "Taming the Tigers: The IMF and the Asian Crisis," in *Tigers in Trouble: Financial Governance, Liberalisation and Crises in East Asia*, ed. Jomo K.S. (London: Zed Books, 1998), 95.

14 Walden Bello, *Deglobalization: Ideas for a New World Economy* (Manila: Ateneo de Manila University Press, 2006), 70.

15 Muthiah Alagappa quoted in the *New York Times*, May 20, 1998.

16 See Bullard "Taming the Tigers," 93–96.

17 Jorgen Johansen, "Waves of Nonviolence," 37.

18 Nicholas D. Kristof, "Students in Struggle to Topple Suharto," *New York Times*, April 29, 1998, A1.

19 Margot Cohen, "Indonesia: To the Barricades," *Far Eastern Economic Review*, May 14, 1998, 22.

20 Descriptive analysis of these events appeared in a *Washington Post* article by Keith Richburg on June 8, 1998, and was reprinted in Edward Aspinall, Herb Feith, and Gerry Van Klinken, *The Last Days of President Suharto* (Clayton, Australia: Monash Asia Institute, 1999), 45–50.

21 At the time, the military counted 499 killed in Jakarta and the police claimed a far lower number of 293, but a Jesuit investigation on May 18 determined that 1,188 people were killed in Jakarta and Tangerang. See Gerry Van Klinken, "The May Riots," in *The Last Days of President Suharto*, ed. Edward Aspinall, Herb Feith and Gerry Van Klinken (Clayton, Australia: Monash Asia Institute, 1999), 50; Asia Human Rights Commission also maintains that one thousand people were killed (*State of Human Rights*, xvi).

22 Van Klinken, "May Riots," 50–51.

23 See Susan Berfield and Dewi Loveard, "Ten Days that Shook Indonesia," *Asiaweek*, July 24, 1998 as reprinted in *The Last Days of President Suharto*, ed. Edward Aspinall, Herb Feith, and Gerry Van Klinken (Clayton, Australia: Monash Asia Institute, 1999), 53–64.

24 Seth Mydans, "Suharto Reverse Hike in Fuel Price Demanded by I.M.F.," *New York Times*, May 16, 1998, A1.

25 Nyman, *Democratising Indonesia*, 77.

26 Seth Mydans, "In a Suharto Fief, 'Hang Suharto!'" *New York Times*, May 19, 1998, A10.

27 See Cohen, "Barricades," 21–22.
28 Mark Landler, "Joyfully, Indonesian Students Thumb Noses at Authority," *New York Times*, May 20, 1998, A10.
29 Jacques Bertrand, "Growth and Democracy in Southeast Asia," *Comparative Politics* 30, no. 3 (April 1998): 369.
30 Thomas Carothers, "The Sequencing Fallacy," *Journal of Democracy* 18, no. 1 (January 2007): 21.
31 Dae-oup Chang, "Neoliberal Restructuring of Capital Relations in East and South-East Asia," in *Neoliberalism: A Critical Reader*, eds. Alfredo Saad-Filho and Deborah Johnston (London: Pluto Press, 2005), 252.
32 These are World Bank numbers. Chris Manning and Peter Van Diermen, present evidence that the number of people living in poverty had decreased from more than 54 million in 1976 to 22.5 million in 1996. See *Indonesia in Transition: Social Aspects of Reformasi and Crisis* (London: Zed Press, 2000), 151. Dan La Botz cites much higher figures. See *Made in Indonesia: Indonesian Workers Since Suharto* (Boston: South End Press, 2001), 37.
33 Irwanto, "Indonesia," 57.
34 Anton Lucas and Carol Warren, "Agrarian Reform in the Era of *Reformasi*," in *Indonesia in Transition: Social Aspects of Reformasi and Crisis*, eds. Chris Manning and Peter Van Diermen (London: Zed Books, 2000), 228.
35 Donni Edwin, "The White Collar Movement," in *Indonesia's Post-Soeharto Democracy Movement*, eds. Stanley Adi Prasetyo, A.E. Priyono, and Olle Tornquist (Jakarta: Demos, 2003).
36 La Botz, *Made in Indonesia*, 174–75.
37 See Philip Eldridge, "Nongovernmental Organizations and Democratic Transition in Indonesia," in *Civil Life, Globalization, and Political Change in Asia*, ed. R.P. Weller (London: Routledge, 2005), 149.
38 Jajang Jahroni, *Defending the Majesty of Islam: Indonesia Front Pembela Islam, 1998–2003* (Chiang Mai: Silkworm Books, 2008), 25.
39 David Bourchier, "Habibie's Interregnum," in *Indonesia in Transition: Social Aspects of Reformasi and Crisis*, eds. Chris Manning and Peter Van Diermen (London: Zed Books, 2000), 19.
40 John Percy, *Green Left Weekly*, November 19, 1998, http://www.mail-archive.com/leftlink@vicnet.net.au/msg00262.html.
41 *Albion Monitor*, November 15, 1998, http://www.monitor.net/monitor.
42 Irwanto, "Indonesia," 25.
43 Stiglitz, *Globalization*, 97.
44 Asian Human Rights Commission, "Torture, Killings Continue Despite 10 Years of Reforms" *Hong Kong* 7, no. 4 (December 2008): 94.
45 Jane Perlez, "Indonesia Convicts an Ex-Governor in East Timor Killing Frenzy," *New York Times*, August 15, 2002.
46 "May 1998 Riots Remain a Mystery: Indonesia," http://www.planetmole.org/daily/may-1998-riots-remain-a-mystery-indonesia.html.
47 Ricky Gunawan, "Indonesia can learn from Korean uprising," May 20, 2009, http://www.upiasia.com/Human_Rights/2009/05/20/indonesia_can_learn_from_korean_uprising/7836/.
48 Impartial Indonesian Human Rights Monitor, *Test of Our History? A Thick Wall on the Murder investigation of Munir* (Jakarta, 2006), 3.
49 Liew Chin Tong, *Speaking for the Reformasi Generation* (Kuala Lumpur: Research for Social Advancement, 2009), xiii and 17.

CHAPTER 11

People Power and Its Limits

> The struggles of people in the Philippines, South Korea, Bangladesh and many other countries including my own [Sri Lanka] were not struggles for People Power. They were for the ending of oppressive structures, for creating possibilities of a more sophisticated form of the development of the relationship between power and freedom, and for the possibilities of expanding the area of freedom and lessening the area of power.
>
> —Basil Fernando

> By their very nature, humans are destined to be free.
>
> —G.W.F. Hegel

AMERICAN POLITICAL SCIENTISTS teach that participatory democracy is the province of the distant past, a relic of ancient Greece or New England town meetings, but Asian uprisings at the end of the twentieth century provide contemporary proof of its existence. Modern forms of participatory democracy embody humanity returning to our natural inclinations for equality and consensus. Social uprisings since 1968 involve activated democracy, not a passive and much-abused representative system of choice between Tweedledum and Tweedledee. They remind us that human beings remain capable of changing the planetary structures that condemn millions of people to living hell at the periphery of the world system—and involve all of us in continual wars and destruction of the planet.

As we have seen in the preceding case studies, ordinary people's capacity to govern themselves during uprisings consistently produced democratic forms of deliberation that made intelligent and reasonable decisions. The wisdom of ordinary people may surpass that of any elite, but the rich and powerful are often able to use uprisings to consolidate their hold on people's lives and resources. In the name of individual liberty and "neoliberalism," billionaires appropriate as their private property the vast social wealth produced by generations of laborers. In the name of democracy, politicians make militarized nation-states into provinces of power that stand above ordinary citizens, and sometimes destroy human lives by the thousands. As political leaders pontificate "solutions" like cutbacks of funds for education and pensions, they squander precious resources by waging "just" wars and "saving" giant corporations. The corporate mass media's constant messages of fear serve to discipline us to accept wars as necessary (even "humanitarian"), while billions of dollars of advertising seek to channel our life-forces into consumer choices.

Uprisings are powerful vehicles for overthrowing entrenched dictatorships, and they are also useful to global elites whose interests transcend nations. The eros effect is clearly effective in overthrowing existing regimes, but the system has become adept at riding the wave of uprisings to stabilize its operations. The wave of People Power uprisings helped to incorporate more of the world into the orbit of Japanese and U.S. banks. The South Korean working class's heroic struggles for union rights became useful to neoliberal economic penetration of the country.[1] In democratic South Korea and Taiwan, as in the Philippines after Marcos and elsewhere, newly elected administrations accelerated neoliberal programs that permitted foreign investors to penetrate previously closed markets and to discipline workforces of millions of people in order to extract greater profits.

Humanity's unending need for freedom constitutes the planet's most powerful natural resource. In the struggle to create free human beings, political movements play paramount roles. Uprisings accelerate social transformation, change governments, and revolutionize individual consciousness and social relationships. Most popular insurgencies result in expanded liberties for millions of people; when they are brutally repressed, the regime's days are numbered. Uprisings' enormous energies transform people's everyday existence and continue to energize long past their decline. The postuprising surges uncovered in the empirical cases in the Philippines, Taiwan, Nepal, Bangladesh, and Thailand reveal the same phenomenal activation of civil society and mobilization of subaltern groups, whether working class, students, minorities, or women. After uprisings, autonomous media and grassroots organizations mushroom, feminism strengthens, and workers strike. Even among nonparticipants, bonds are created through powerful erotic energies unleashed in these exhilarating moments. These instances of what Marcuse called "political eros" are profoundly important in rekindling imaginations and nurturing hope.

The twentieth century will be remembered for its horrific wars and mass starvation amid great prosperity. It will also be known as a time when human beings began a struggle to transform the entire world system. Uprisings at the century's end reveal people's attempts to enact global justice. From the grassroots, millions of people around the world in the past three decades have constituted a protracted people's uprising against capitalism and war. Without anyone telling people to do so, millions of us in the alter-globalization movement have confronted elite meetings of the institutions of the world economic system—practical targets whose universal meaning is profoundly indicative of people's yearnings for a new world economic system. No central organization dictated this focus. Rather, millions of people autonomously developed it through their own thoughts and actions. Similarly, without central organization, as many as thirty million people around the world took to the streets on February 15, 2003, to protest the second U.S. war on Iraq. As the global movement becomes increasingly aware of its own power, its strategy and impact are certain to become more focused. By creatively synthesizing direct-democratic forms of decision-making and militant popular resistance, people's movements will continue to develop along the historical lines revealed in 1968 and subsequent Asian uprisings: within a grammar of autonomy, "conscious spontaneity," and the eros effect.

As we move into the twenty-first century, the Arab Spring provides empirical evidence of the growing consciousness of ordinary people who go into the streets to change history. In 1968, "the whole world was watching." Today, it is increasingly the case that the whole world is awakening. The stabilization of Egypt without Mubarak is another example of how dictatorships in danger of being toppled—and possibly taken out of the orbit of the United States—can be salvaged by deposing a few men at the top while retaining the core of the system. Egypt's military leaders enforced Mubarakism without Mubarak, as a more stable repressive regime consolidated itself. As we saw in the Philippines without Marcos, Korea without the military dictatorship, and Taiwan without the White Terror, unstable countries were turned into fertile grounds for U.S. and Japanese banks and corporations. An end to "crony" capitalism meant the expansion of transnational corporate markets and profits.

The key problem here is for social movements to continue pushing society forward without their energies being co-opted by entrenched economic and political elites. All too often, great expectations, when disappointed by failure to materialize dreams in one fell swoop, produce bitterness and despair. Even the great Simón Bolívar was not immune. After he witnessed the wave of Latin American struggles lift the yoke of Spanish domination only to be replaced by usurious national elites, he remarked that, "Those who made the revolution have ploughed the sea."

Uprisings' usefulness to the rich and powerful is due in part to the fact that people who have suffered long years of suppression and media manipulation are not accustomed to freedom. Even when they gain freedom through their own insurrections, they often do not know what to do with it. People who habitually work all the time do not know how to make use of free time when it becomes available. Like prisoners so accustomed to incarceration they cannot deal with being released, people who are used to having decisions made for them are unaccustomed to making substantive choices. This problem of freedom remains particularly acute in societies where severe oppression was the normal way of life. People who live for centuries under forms of local oppression often are deprived of many capabilities, such as capacity of the intellect that comes with the ability to read, to write, and to analyze and understand situations.

They can be denied other kinds of cultural capacities to communicate and be unable to develop their own forms of ongoing protest against their own everyday oppressions.

After victorious uprisings, decades-old habits formed within people do not disappear overnight. The underdevelopment of the intellect does not vanish with political change—nor do the competitive and hierarchical values that have been inculcated into us by capitalist relations. Definite measures must be taken to improve people's capacity to communicate their own creativity, for them to be able to learn to read and write and to express themselves, to become literate in the sense that they could express their own concerns in a deeper manner—and to become capable of forming nonhierarchical, cooperative relationships. In the Philippines and Bangladesh, people who suffered from centuries of oppression rose against a particular regime, demolished that regime, but then the advantage was taken by an elite few. The people were again pushed back to an inarticulate situation, and they are again oppressed by new regimes.

While elites are often ruthless in pursuit of their domination, forms of inarticulateness and timidity of the oppressed remain operative. While economic and political gains may be won, inner cultural forms of oppression continue to deny people the capacity to attain the kinds of freedoms they most desire—at least for the present. The love of freedom is not merely expressed in uprisings aimed at bringing down particular regimes; it is a love for the total transformation of human beings, especially of the most oppressed, in order for them to become articulate, to express themselves fully, and to overcome their own cultural inhibitions inherited from centuries of local oppression.

In Basil Fernando's view, "The coinage of the term 'People Power,' while it was meant to be something positive, has created limitations on proper thinking in the process of seeking liberation from the oppressive actions of the state. Regimes that came to power as a result of People Power were not necessarily better states . . . the achievements were partial because many aspects of that oppressive structure still remain and are being utilized by the very people who came to power through what was called 'People Power.'"[2] Successful uprisings may have brought down the most immediately odious dimensions of oppressive systems, but in so doing, they shored up elite domination and capitalist relations at their core.

Uprisings expand moral capacities of people, create new avenues for creativity, and foster new forms of expression even when people's innermost aspirations remain unfulfilled. What people desire—as expressed through their courage and sacrifices during uprisings—is not power, but freedom. The ultimate aim of people's uprisings is to put down structures of oppression and to expand the space for freedom. People wish to see a lessening of the power of the state, while governments and political parties seek greater control. What people want is various dimensions of freedom: freedom from hunger, freedom from ignorance through the benefits of education, freedom from patriarchy and dictatorships of any kind, freedom from drudgery, freedom against the definition of their lives as work.[3] People want freedom to control the products and process of production, freedom to live in a clean and safe environment, and freedom in artistic fields; they want to be left alone to pursue their lives without interference and freedom to express themselves as they choose.

The Global Imperative

It is no accident that social movements after World War II were strongest in Korea, Vietnam, and other regions of Asia, not only in militant tactics and numerical support, but also in the internal strength of the movement. One could look in vain for a recent European or American equivalent of the kind of loving portrayal of Yoon Sang-won in Korea (hero of the Gwangju Uprising) or Nguyen Van Troi in Vietnam (who was executed for trying to assassinate U.S. Secretary of Defense Robert McNamara in 1964). In both cases, U.S. wars caused millions of deaths—and conditioned movements whose communal cultures sustained resistance. A country with a citizenry deeply sensitive to issues of war and peace, Korea has a voice that speaks passionately to activists everywhere through sacrificial actions such as farmer Lee Kyung-hae's 2003 suicide at WTO protests in Cancun. In December 2005, dozens of Korean farmers swam Hong Kong harbor to bring their protest to the meeting site of the WTO.

In the array of vehicles to loosen the grip of psychic prisons in which people's desires for freedom are confined, past examples of others rising up remain a powerful force. If we look at history, the global movement of 1968 was largely unconscious of its world-historical character. The new alter-globalization movement that first emerged in the 1990s not only understands itself as international, it has significant characteristics that might enable it to break the systematic character of unending wars and poverty. To create global justice and reasonable forms of democratic deliberation, insurgent movements need to develop a new relationship between spontaneity and consciousness, to synchronize actions and goals internationally. Increasing the self-consciousness of civil society, stimulating its inner blossoming, is a process already at work in uprisings, as can be traced in their empirical history, especially in South Korea (whose rich history of modern social movements I portrayed in Volume 1).

Betrayals within the movement as well as self-defeating behavior (or "psychic Thermidors," as Herbert Marcuse named this phenomenon) internally sap the strength so badly needed to defend people's gains won through uprisings. Yet there are also structural reasons why even great victories—like the breakthrough of Vietnam's national liberation struggle—become insidiously subverted by corporate globalization and the power of capital. The global antiapartheid struggle brought Nelson Mandela out of decades of imprisonment on Robbin Island and into the highest seat of power in South Africa, but he, too, was compelled to implement neoliberal economic policies that further plagued the poor. Similarly, East Asian uprisings against dictatorships, even when they included significant forces against capitalism, enabled the IMF and World Bank to broaden their powers.

The history of modern revolutions reveals that the world system cannot be transformed unless its strongest links are broken. Previous revolutions have only streamlined and thereby strengthened capitalism, not transformed it. From the

French and American revolutions to the Russian and Chinese, the system drew strength and expanded its domain. Even as the system destroys many of its own accomplishments, its collapse is not the same as its transformation. Freedom worthy of the name requires subversion of politics as we know it—not simply reforms in existing structures nor collapse of giant capital formations. In subsequent chapters, I discuss forms of avant-garde organization that are alternatives to hierarchical, centralized parties as well as structural imperatives of global capitalism that make its transformation necessary. Before doing so, I analyze the growing international capacity for self-organization during episodes of the eros effect since 1968.

From 1968 to Uprisings 2.0

In the dialectical process of revolution, dynamics continually change—as does the meaning of freedom. Globally aware movements already helped to defeat U.S. imperialism in Vietnam, to end apartheid in South Africa, and to reform East Asian dictatorships. By building on the legacy of these struggles, we can continue to create a world fit for human beings and for all forms of life—but only if we carefully evaluate our victories and defeats.

Citizens have watched as revolutions atrophied, or even turned into their opposite (as happened in both the United States and the USSR). Alongside participatory currents, the history of social movements is also the history of popular insurgencies being placated, accommodated, and sold out by parties and organizations that grew out of past progressive movements—whether French or Italian communists, Czech or Bangladeshi democrats, or Korean or French trade unions. Ritualized protests organized by top-down groups with leaders who give orders no longer suffice to bring the "masses" into the streets. Apparently entrenched elites, like Leninist-style parties, are no longer needed to transcend the reformism of spontaneously formed movements since these movements are themselves capable of developing a universal critique and autonomous capacities for self-government. The series of uprisings in East Asia in the last three decades validates the capability of people to organize themselves directly without the "leadership" of professional politicians.

In the twenty-first century, as society's velocity of change accelerates, so too do people's capacities to assimilate tactics of recent struggles and to adapt new technologies to changing circumstances. Since 1968, the global movement's mobilizations have changed from unconscious and spontaneous to a form of "conscious spontaneity" during alter-globalization protests from 1999 to 2001. During the Arab Spring, the chain reaction of uprisings spread from Tunisia to Egypt, and then to Yemen, Bahrain, Syria, and Libya, turning into a veritable tidal wave. Millions of ordinary people demonstrated the growing consciousness that by going into the streets they could change regimes. The increasing sophistication of protesters' use of social media (Facebook, Twitter, YouTube, SMS) and the cross-border speed with which the revolt spread offer a glimpse of People Power's potential in the twenty-first century. What some have called Uprising 2.0 refers to people's use of the Internet to quickly propagate news from one part of the world to another, to coordinate actions in real time, and to directly have a global voice.

Synchronicity facilitated by social media grew in a fertile environment, for movements had already been accumulating the capacity for international simultaneity since 1968, when the global movement emerged with spontaneous coincidences, with international harmonization from people's intuitive identification with each other. Four years later, as people around the world united to support Vietnam's struggle for independence, a significant portion of the worldwide movement came together under central leadership. In February 1972, the Vietnamese organized an international conference in Versailles, France, and peace movements from more than eighty countries dispatched representatives. Delegates agreed upon an action calendar designed to coordinate international demonstrations to show the world how unpopular the U.S. war was. Something was supposed to happen around Easter in Vietnam, followed by demonstrations from east to west—from Moscow to Paris to New York and finally to San Diego, where U.S. President Nixon was due to be renominated at the Republican National Convention in August. All over the world, people were amazed when the Easter Offensive in Vietnam that led off the planned global peace offensive involved, for the first time, tanks appearing among the arsenal of guerrilla forces in southern Vietnam. Vietnamese military forces had disassembled them, carried them south, and then reassembled them without being spotted. In coordination with the global political movement, Vietnamese resistance forces simultaneously announced the formation of Provisional Revolutionary Government, with a capital at Quang Tri. The U.S. response was increased destruction. Photos of Quang Tri after U.S. bombing show scarcely a building's wall left standing. It was said at the time that more destructive force was used on the city than on Hiroshima or Nagasaki in 1945.

Despite horrific brutality inflicted against its land and people, Vietnam prevailed, reunified itself, and today is increasingly prosperous. In 2001, Vo Nguyen Giap, military commander of Vietnamese forces against the French and Americans, summarized the reasons why the Vietnamese were able to defeat the United States. The antiwar movement inside the United States was a prominent part of his list. For years, Vietnamese leaders cultivated the U.S. movement until it grew into a force with which they were able to coordinate their battlefield tactics.[4] Yet the battlefield victories soon gave way to unbridled repression from the top. As Vietnam entered the WTO and World Bank, its revolutionary ideals were sacrificed on the altar of economic prosperity—still an elusive goal for many people there.

These instances of the spread of movements across borders, involving a process of mutual amplification and synergy, are significant precursors for future mobilizations. In the period after 1968, as the global movement's capacity for decentralized international coordination developed, five other episodes of the international eros effect can be discerned:

1. The disarmament movement of the early 1980s
2. The wave of East Asian uprisings discussed in this book

3. The revolts against Soviet regimes in Eastern Europe (see chapter 1)
4. The alter-globalization wave and antiwar mobilizations on February 15, 2003
5. The Arab Spring in 2011 and the Occupy Movement

In 1972, the Vietnamese centrally orchestrated global actions, but no single organization has been responsible for more recent waves of "conscious spontaneity."

After the apparent decline of the New Left, a massive peace movement was ignited by the United States and USSR continuing their escalation of the Cold War. The two superpowers stationed intermediate range Pershing and SS-20 nuclear missiles in Europe, making it possible that the USSR and United States could have fought a "limited" nuclear war in Europe without Russia or the United States being directly attacked. At this key moment, protests spread rapidly, simultaneously bringing hundreds of thousands of people into the streets of many cities. All together, millions of people took to the streets of Paris, London, Rome, Brussels, and Bonn. From a handful of nuclear disarmament protesters in the 1970s, an enormous peace movement changed world history in the early 1980s, helping end the Cold War and alter the global balance of power. On June 12, 1982, almost one million people converged on New York to call for a nuclear-free planet. That fall, more than eleven million Americans voted for a freeze on nuclear weapons. These grassroots mobilizations convinced Gorbachev he could relax control of Eastern European buffer states without fearing another invasion by Germany. In this same era, the wave of Asian uprisings broke down repressive Cold War regimes and amplified indigenous resistance in Eastern Europe.

As a peace dividend with the end of the Cold War failed to materialize and global capitalism was strengthened, millions of people "spontaneously" chose to challenge giant corporations and the WTO-IMF-WB axis. Without any central group deciding the focus of people's mobilizations, people themselves made the global capitalist system the focal point of protests. All over the world, grassroots movements for global economic justice and peace confronted elite summits in the 1990s, making such demands as canceling the national debt of the world's poorest countries and abolishing the WTO, IMF, and WB. In dozens of countries, local revolts against IMF structural adjustment programs occurred. In Berlin in 1988, tens of thousands of people militantly confronted the global financial elite gathering and compelled the world's bankers to adjourn a day earlier than planned. Huge confrontations of attempted imposition of corporate domination arose in Caracas (1989) and Seoul (1997).

Beginning with "global carnivals" in 1998 and 1999, activists in dozens of countries synchronized actions to protest elite meetings. In 1999, Seattle's exhilarating victory in halting WTO meetings broke new ground when Teamsters and Turtles, workers and ecologists, Lesbian Avengers and Zapatista partisans all converged for unified action. The worldwide coordination of protests that day involved actions in dozens of other cities around the world.[5] After Seattle, ordinary people in places such as Cochabamba, Bolivia (2000), and Arequipa, Peru (2002) fought back against attempted privatization of communal natural resources and won significant victories. All over the world, whenever elite summits took place, so did tens of thousands of protesters, including at meetings of the:

1. World Bank in Washington, D.C. (April 2000)
2. Asian Development Bank in Chiang Mai, Thailand (May 2000)
3. World Economic Forum in Melbourne, Australia (September 2000)
4. World Bank and IMF in Prague (September 2000)
5. World economic elite in Davos (January 2001)[6]
6. Summit of the Americas in Quebec City (April 2001)
7. European Union summit in Gothenburg (June 2001)
8. G-8 meetings in Genoa (July 2001)

As a result of popular opposition to their rule, world elites were compelled to schedule meetings in remote places, far from people's capacity to travel, such as the Qatar WTO ministerial in November 2001, or the G-8 summit in 2002 in the high Rockies.

Al-Qaeda's attacks on the World Trade Center in September 2001 significantly undercut this grassroots alter-globalization upsurge. Nonetheless, the global movement reached a new level of synchronicity on February 15, 2003, as the United States prepared to attack Iraq for the second time. A call for antiwar demonstrations was issued in the fall of 2002 at the European Social Forum in Florence. With no central organization, as many as thirty million people around the world took to the streets on February 15 to protest the U.S. war on Iraq, even though it had not yet started.[7] People in eight hundred cities and sixty countries mobilized from the grassroots to protest the war.[8] From Damascus to Athens, Seoul to Sydney, New York, Rome, and Buenos Aires, millions constituted a global civil society that the *New York Times* named a "Second Superpower." In London 1.4 million took to the streets in the biggest demonstration in that city's two thousand years of history.[9]

People's aspirations for peace were remarkably similar in every part of the world—another example of the wisdom of ordinary people in comparison to the elites that compel warfare and demand corporate profits. As the movement took many directions, actors staged performances of Aristophanes's antiwar play, *Lysistrata*. By March 3, 2003, more than a thousand productions were counted in all fifty U.S. states and in at least fifty-nine other countries. A year later, on March 20, 2004, centrally organized antiwar protests took place in more than seven hundred cities, and participants were estimated at two million.[10]

Although the summit confrontations and mobilizations failed to end the war or overnight alter capitalism, they prepared the ground for the Arab Spring and future transnational mobilizations. Leading up to the 1986 uprising in the Philippines, to the 1987 Korean June Uprising, to Nepal's 1990 *jana andolan*, and to Thailand's 1992 overthrow of Suchinda, there were countless demonstrations. Precursor mobilizations schooled people and organizations, built up practical experiences step by step, and taught invaluable lessons that crystallized in large-scale uprisings. Beatings, shootings, and prison only steeled the resistance.

Millions of people learned how escalating confrontations spread like a wave in a stadium, intuitively mobilizing sister movements in other places, until finally, a crescendo of protests erupted, after which dictatorships could no longer be maintained.

Cycles of revolt developed in relation to each other through the eros effect. From the global eruption of 1968 to the string of Asian uprisings after Gwangju, from Eastern Europe in 1989 to the alter-globalization confrontations of elite summits, ordinary people gleaned the lessons of history. The wave of popular insurgencies in the Arab world is an indication that ordinary citizens everywhere are prepared to act.

The Arab Spring

During the six-year period of 1986 to 1992, Asian uprisings overthrew seven dictators, an astonishing feat that largely went unnoticed because of their spatial and temporal dispersion. During the Arab Spring, movements erupted within weeks of each other rather than the years it had taken in Asia, and everyone noticed. Although few victories can be counted because of bloody resistance from entrenched elites, the upheavals already had global repercussions. Around the world, people enthusiastically embraced the "Egyptian Revolution"—the astonishing victory won by the historic eighteen-day People Power Uprising in Cairo. A few months prior to his ouster, the prediction that Hosni Mubarak would be compelled to end his pharonic rule over Egyptians would have been regarded as ludicrous—or wishful thinking. Yet Mubarak was not only driven from power, thousands of people refused to be quieted until he was put on trial for corruption. It is another question whether anyone will be punished for the 846 people killed by his forces of order when he ordered them to suppress the protests.

Mubarak's decades-long stranglehold on power was broken by a chain reaction of events set off by the suicide of Mohamed Bouazizi, a rural vegetable vendor in neighboring Tunisia, where a popular uprising quickly sent that country's long entrenched dictator into exile (along with his powerful wife and as much of the country's wealth as they could ferret onto a plane). Bouazizi's and at least eight other self-immolations in Algeria, Mauritania, and Egypt caused a powerful grassroots response, prompting Yemen's president Ali Abdullah Saleh, in power for more than three decades, to promise to leave office. As the wave of popular uprisings spread within weeks to Bahrain, the Palestinian territories, and Syria, hundreds of people—possibly many more—were killed. A civil war erupted in Libya as regime opponents, backed by Europe and the United States, attempted to overthrow Gaddafi. Suddenly, throughout the Arab world, even in Saudi Arabia, dictators rushed to implement preventative reforms.

While grassroots power of the people finally arrived in the Arab world, to limit comprehension of the phenomenon that swept the region to its own parochial history would constitute a misreading of recent history, as well as a limitation of the movement's potential. Certainly pan-Arab sentiments were a driving force, yet they were not essential. At first glance, the current revolt appeared to be confined to the Arab world, but it spilled over ethnic boundaries and was embraced by Spanish and Greek "indignants." Soon its impact was evident in Gabon, Iran, China, and Israel. Workers in Wisconsin, who were fighting cutbacks in their standard of living, expressed admiration for the Egyptian uprising. Asking if America is ripe for a Tahrir Square moment, protesters occupied Wall Street to fight back against bankers' greed. People feel in their bones that change is possible.

If we look at other recent examples of People Power Uprisings suddenly ending the reign of longstanding authoritarian regimes, I am especially struck by parallels with Korea's 1987 June Uprising, when for nineteen consecutive days, hundreds of thousands of people illegally went into the streets and battled tens of thousands of riot police to a standstill. On June 29, the military dictatorship finally capitulated to the opposition's demands to hold direct presidential elections, thereby ending twenty-six years of military rule. As in Egypt on February 11, 2011, the man who made the announcement in Seoul on June 29, 1987, was none other than the dictatorship's second in command. Roh Tae-woo went on to become the country's new president after elections marked by both a bitter split between rival progressive candidates and widespread allegations of ballot tampering. People's high expectations and optimism after the military was forced to grant elections turned into bitter disappointment.

As it seems that Korea's democratization might hold possible lessons for Egypt, so might the Philippines in 1986. Less than a year after the first "People Power Revolution" sent longtime dictator Ferdinand Marcos into exile, Corazon Aquino's new government shot to death twenty-one landless farmers who marched in Manila to demand she keep her promises for land reform. The Philippines today is plagued by increasing hunger, and more than three million children are underweight and underheight. In 1973, students in Thailand overthrew a hated military dictatorship after seventy-seven people were gunned down in the streets of Bangkok. After a two-year hiatus, one of the most free periods in the history of Thailand, the military bloodily reimposed dictatorship and killed dozens of students. In Nepal in 1990, fifty days of popular protests during which sixty-two citizens were killed won a constitutional monarchy, but within a few years, the royal family again seized absolute power. A nineteen-day People Power Uprising in 2006 ended the monarchy altogether, but only after twenty-one more unarmed civilians had been killed by the forces of order.

Rapid and unanticipated political change is increasingly a fact of life in the twenty-first century. In the past fifty years, high-tech media have united the planet as never before, and people have come to realize the power of synchronous popular action to overturn governments. By occupying public space without anyone telling them to do so, people have launched revolts that have spread from one city to another and from country to country.

While the stories in the mainstream media after Mubarak was toppled mainly involved the machinations of Obama and the military rulers of Egypt, the real story was the transformation of Egyptians from passive recipients of dictatorial commands to active creators of momentum for change. The handwriting is on the wall. The multitude of Cairo appropriated the lessons of Bangkok's Red Shirts and Yellow Shirts, of Manila's yellow confetti that toppled Marcos. It is nothing new that the United States chose to sacrifice yet another of its pet dictators on the altar of "progress" or that Syria's Assad bloodily clings to power.

What is newsworthy now is that People Power has been embraced by the Arab masses. Beginning in 1987, the first Palestinian Intifada paved the way for people in the region to comprehend the power of mobilized citizens.[11] Whether or not the wave of protests sweeps the region clean of dictators, the emergence of an activated citizenry poses the question not of whom is in power but the form of power itself. The ultimate goal of People Power is the institutionalization of popular forms of decision-making—taking power from elites and reconstituting it into grassroots forms. In 1980, the people of Gwangju beautifully came together while surrounded by murderous military forces to govern themselves peacefully through direct democracy. This radical potential of the movement is precisely why the political elite today scurries to implement the appearance of change—not system transformation, but only rotation of personalities at the apex of power.

The young activists in Cairo understood Mubarak's ouster as their starting point, but what they want is a wholly new form of justice, recovery of the people's wealth that has been so scandalously appropriated by the rich, and punishment of those responsible for decades of torture and dictatorship, to say nothing of the recent slaughter of 846 unarmed citizens in the streets. It remains unclear who will emerge victorious in Egypt—whether peaceful protesters will hold sway and move the society to a higher level of democratization, or, as seems more likely, that American and Egyptian politicians (Islamic or not) will continue to have their way. If the latter remains the case, the current possibility for a leap into substantive democracy would have been missed.

No one can predict with certainty the outcome of what has been set in motion in the Middle East, but historical antecedents may provide insight into possible outcomes. Will the blood of murdered citizens in the Middle East, like the hundreds of martyrs of the 1980 Gwangju Uprising, water the tree of liberty? Or will their sacrifice grease the wheels as U.S. banks and global corporations rush to replace "crony capitalism" with ever more profitable arenas for wealthy investors? No doubt, both will occur, but the balance between them depends vitally upon the continuing participation of citizens in the struggle for freedom. In Asia, the wave of uprisings accelerated a period of unprecedented economic expansion, and it seems very likely the economies of both Egypt and Tunisia will grow robustly in the decades ahead. In the year before Mubarak was overthrown, Egypt (with a population of eighty million) produced less than Costa Rica (whose citizens number only eight hundred thousand). With new opportunities already open in high-tech and communications, Egypt's future is far more promising.

Revolutions and popular uprisings have unexpected results—and not necessarily immediate ones. Even generations later, people's memories and psyches assimilate lessons from previous waves of struggles. The courage of Iranians in 1979, their withstanding of ferocious repression by the Shah and his forces, was evident for people all over the world, and inspired Haitians and Filipinos to overthrow their dictators. In 1987, I wrote, "In the epoch after 1968, popular movements have internalized the New Left tactic of the occupation of public space as means of social transformation, and this tactic's international diffusion led to the downfall of the Shah, Duvalier, and Marcos . . . the significance of the eros effect and the importance of synchronized world-historical movements will only increase."

The Arab Spring indicates that synchronicity of revolts and occupations of public space (tactics that emerged in 1968) are being embraced in continually widening circles. While now seemingly marginalized, the global movement today involves more activists than at any other point in our species' historical evolution. As the multitude animates our own dynamic, the tendency we can project into the future is for the activation of a global eros effect, in which synchronous actions erupt across the world and unify people across borders of nationality, age, gender, and race.

Revisiting the Eros Effect

Since World War II, humanity's increasing awareness of our own power and strategic capacities has been manifest in sudden and simultaneous contestation of power by hundreds of thousands of people. A significant new tactic in the arsenal of popular movements, the eros effect is not simply an act of mind, nor can it simply be willed by a "conscious element" (or revolutionary party). Rather it involves popular movements emerging as forces in their own right as ordinary people take history into their own hands. The concept of the eros effect is a means of rescuing the revolutionary value of spontaneity, a way to stimulate a reevaluation of the unconscious.[12] Rather than portraying emotions as linked to reaction, the notion of the eros effect seeks to bring them into the realm of positive revolutionary resources whose mobilization can result in significant social transformation. As Herbert Marcuse understood, Nature is an ally in the revolutionary process, including internal, human nature.

Despite his conservative political orientation, Carl Jung also recognized ways that instinct makes rebellious actions necessary on our part: "The growth of culture consists, as we know, in a progressive subjugation of the animal in man. It is a process of domestication which cannot be accomplished without rebellion on the part of the animal nature that thirsts for freedom. From time to time there passes as it were a wave of frenzy through the ranks of men too long constrained within the limitations of their culture."[13] For Jung, these internally necessary drives for change manifested themselves in the European Renaissance and other forms of cultural expression. Under certain conditions they could produce social eruptions: "Separation from his instinctual nature inevitably plunges civilized man into the conflict between the conscious and unconscious, spirit and nature, knowledge and faith, a split that becomes pathological the moment his consciousness is no longer able to neglect or suppress his instinctual side. The accumulation of individuals who have got into this critical state starts off a mass movement."[14]

Humans' instinctual need for freedom—something that we grasp intuitively— is collectively sublimated through the eros effect. Although contemporary rational

372 | ASIA'S UNKNOWN UPRISINGS

choice theorists (who emphasize individual gain as the key motivation for people's actions) cannot comprehend communal motivations, even George Kennan, who famously started the Cold War with an essay written under the pseudonym Mr. X, found the antinuclear wave of protests in the early 1980s to be an "expression of a deep instinctual insistence, if you don't mind, on sheer survival. . . . This movement is too powerful, too elementary, too deeply embedded in the natural human instinct for self-preservation to be brushed aside."[15]

The instinctual basis for action was also gleaned by social scientist Choi Jungwoon in reference to the Gwangju Uprising. As an established scholar unfamiliar with what had transpired in 1980, Choi was subsequently approached by his professional academic association to investigate the uprising. After extensive research, he concluded that Gwangju citizens had crystallized an "absolute community" in which all were equal and united by bonds of love. For Choi, "it was not 'mobs' of cowardly people hoping to rely on the power of numbers. The absolute community provided encounters among dignified warriors. The absolute community was formed only from love. . . . In Western Philosophy, reason is derived from solitary individuals. However the Gwangju uprising demonstrates that reason was achieved by human beings who were conscious of being members of a community. Reason was the capability of the community, not that of individuals."[16]

So impressed was Choi with the solidarity he uncovered in Gwangju, he believed, "The most basic human values travel beyond history and culture; they began with the birth of humankind and will continue into the unknown future. . . . The term to refer to this primeval instinct has not been found in South Korea's narrow arena for political discourse and ideology." The empirical history of crowd behavior in the late twentieth century—most clearly in Gwangju—demands a reevaluation of the frozen categories of crowds, through which they are viewed as emotionally degraded, when Gwangju's people were passionately intelligent and loving.

Is the eros effect an analytical concept as well as a tactic for a better world? The sudden emergence of people massively occupying public space; the spread of the revolt from one city to another and throughout the countryside; the intuitive identification with each other of hundreds of thousands of people and their simultaneous belief in the power of their actions; the suspension of normal values like regionalism, competitive business practices, criminal behavior, and acquisitiveness: all these dimensions of the eros effect were present in Gwangju.

The connective threads running through grassroots movements around the world are often intuitively woven together in innumerable strands of what might seem like very different struggles. In the 1970s, Italy's Metropolitan Indians, the most spectacular of dozens of autonomous groups that constituted Italian Autonomia, adopted very similar notions to Yippies and Black Panthers, the Dutch Provos, and Christiania's communards before them.[17] No organizational means of communication tied together these three communities of struggle; rather, intuition and common sense made the same conclusions flow naturally from people's hearts.

When the eros effect is activated, humans' love for and solidarity with each other suddenly replace previously dominant values and norms. Competition gives way to cooperation, hierarchy to equality, power to truth. During the Vietnam War, for example, many Americans' patriotism was superseded by solidarity with the people of Vietnam, and in place of racism, many white Americans insisted a Vietnamese life was worth the same as an American life (defying the continual media barrage to the contrary). According to many opinion polls at that time, Vietnamese leader Ho Chi Minh was more popular on American college campuses than U.S. President Nixon. Moments of the eros effect reveal the aspirations and visions of the movement in actions of millions of people, a far more significant dimension than statements of leaders, organizations, or parties.

The Marxist notion of the circulation of struggle and the concept of diffusion are valuable because they show that struggles impact each other. Diffusion—what Samuel Huntington called "snowballing"—can help us to trace how one event causes another, which causes another in turn. But neither theory allows us to comprehend the simultaneity of struggles that occurs during moments of the eros effect. It's not simply a chain reaction, not just that A causes B which causes C. Events erupt simultaneously at multiple points and mutually amplify each other. They produce feedback loops with multiple iterations. To put it in terms of a mathematical analysis, we could say that diffusion and the circulation of struggles describe the process of movement development geometrically, while the eros effect describes these same developments in terms of calculus.

Samuel Huntington used the notion of "snowballing" as an explanatory metaphor for the emergence of so many movements in a short period of time.[18] Snowballing is a postmodern version of "Domino Theory" that guided American anticommunism in the 1950s. Based upon the assumption that there is a single point of origin for insurgencies, his concept expressed the paranoid fears of a center for social control that perceives itself to be surrounded by enemies, not the wondrous joy at the simultaneous emergence of freedom struggles. Tied as he was to Washington policymakers, Huntington could not comprehend the emergence of polycentric grassroots movements. Observing these events as an outsider, he believed, "Whatever economic connections may exist between them, the fundamental cultural gap between Asian and American societies precludes their joining together in a common home."[19]

What Huntington called snowballing has been described by others—even by progressive academics in what Barbara Epstein dubbed the "social movement industry"—through terms like demonstration effect, diffusion, emulation, domino effect, and contagion. The sheer number of labels is one indication of the phenomenon's recent emergence as a significant variable. Leaving aside the difference in values embedded in disease-laden labels like "contagion" and less pejorative terms like "diffusion" and "demonstration effect," they all assume a single, external point of origin. None of these concepts comprehends the simultaneous appearance of insurgencies among different peoples, even across cultures. While the influence of one event upon another is no doubt substantial, to comprehend movements as externally induced—much as a collision of bowling balls—is to miss something essential about their inner logic and meaning. Simultaneous emergence and mutual amplification of insurgencies are alternative understandings, ones embedded in the notion of the "eros effect." Rather than a simple monocausal process of protest, the eros effect provides a way to comprehend the polycentric—indeed decentered—source of movements' energies. For Huntington, simultaneity was "impossible," and he excluded it in advance.[20] The distance between his theory and law enforcement officials is not great. As the U.S. civil rights movement accelerated in the 1960s, sheriffs and police continually blamed Martin Luther King or Malcolm X for their own city's problems, and campus administrators often insisted that "outside agitators" caused university protests.

Out of a series of struggles in France, activists developed a very similar notion to the eros effect: "Revolutionary movements do not spread by contamination but by resonance. . . . An insurrection is not like a plague or a forest fire—a linear process which spreads from place to place after an initial spark. It rather takes the shape of music, whose focal points, though dispersed in time and space, succeed in imposing the rhythms of their own vibrations, always taking on more intensity."[21] In many places, grassroots activism made possible "discoveries" of this same phenomenon with a simultaneity and autonomy that defied "scientific" understanding.

Long before the introduction of social media, simultaneous tactical innovations occurred in different places. To name just one example, in May of 1970, after the United States invaded Cambodia and killed college students on its own campuses, activists from all across the country simultaneously blocked highways. There was no central organization directing people to do so. People didn't obstruct highways simply because they heard that people elsewhere in the country were doing it but because people thought they should do so to stop a society destroying hundreds of lives every day in Vietnam and elsewhere. Without direct lines of communication, activists on the West Coast clogged Route 5 while, at the same time, activists in other parts of the country stopped traffic on nearby roads. Tactics may move in a line from point A to point B through a process of diffusion, but we can't ignore how tactical innovations can also happen simultaneously.

For Carl Jung, synchronicity was so abstract and "irrepresentable" that he insisted we abandon completely the notion that the psyche is connected to the brain.[22] Instead, through archetypes, he understood that unconscious impulses could influence consciousness. Such instinctual impulses originate in the deep layers of the unconscious, in what Jung called the "phylogenetic substratum."[23] They function to return to consciousness our unknown lives from a distant past— from the world of communalism at the dawn of human existence (what has been called "primitive communism.") For Jung, "in addition to memories from a long-distant conscious past, completely new thoughts and creative ideas can also present themselves from the unconscious—thoughts and ideas that have never been conscious before. They grow up from the dark depths of the mind like a lotus and form a most important part of the subliminal psyche."[24] The unconscious may not be rational, but it can certainly be more reasonable than rational thought. Consider the intuitive revulsion everyone feels for the wanton destruction of Nature caused by "rational" industrialization.[25]

When the unconscious is aroused, it flows toward consciousness, a psychic process very similar to what I understand as the eros effect.[26] Jung refers us to something that "indwells in the soul" and has the power to transform things, especially in moments of "great excess of love or hate."[27] We should note that by love, he meant Eros in all its forms, not simply sex. According to Jung, Freud attempted to understand the inner erotic necessities emanating from our instincts according to that one dimension. Freud sought to "lay hold of unconfinable Eros within the crude terminology of sex."[28] In our age, when reversal of commodification of the life-world is paramount, can we reclaim Eros from the throes of its reification as sex? For Marcuse, political Eros was "Beauty in its most sublimated form."[29] The eros effect emanates from the instinctual reservoir, the collective unconscious, and is a form of sublimation of instinctual drives into erotic channels of solidarity and love.

The eros effect rests on intuition, an unquantifiable quality that may make its simultaneity impenetrable to the social control center (the police)—as well as impossible to "scientifically" verify. For Jung, synchronistic phenomena are akin to magic, and are not statistically verifiable.[30] "Meaningful coincidences" cannot be explained by rational cognition but to recall them is to prepare the ground for their future recurrences. Just as keeping a dream journal enhances remembering dreams, so recalling instances of the eros effect prepares the ground for further episodes. Revolutionary spirit for Jung would arise outside the realm of sense perception: "The hallmarks of spirit are, firstly, the principle of spontaneous movement and activity; secondly, the spontaneous capacity to produce images independently of sense perception and thirdly, the autonomous and sovereign manipulation of these images."[31]

When time and space are drastically altered in moments of the eros effect, explanations that assume linear conceptions cannot comprehend what is happening. Thus, the cause of the eros effect may not be capable of being understood within the framework of academic social science. As Jung describes such moments: "There I am utterly one with the world, so much a part of it that I will forget all too easily who I really am. 'Lost in oneself' is a good way of describing this state. But this self is the world, if only a consciousness could see it."[32] Time does not exist in the unconscious, which may help us understand why outbursts of insurgencies take past identities. Being "one with the world" implies bonding with those around us, a process similar to what Gaetano Mosca conceived as a human "instinct" for "herding together" that underlies "moral and, sometimes, physical conflicts."[33] Such smart group behavior—containing no centralized control yet eliciting appropriate responses to local situations—is present already among caribou, birds, bees, and ants. Swarm theory seems an appropriate means to comprehend Seattle protests in 1999 where cell phones, texting, Internet, and people's common sense created a "smart mob" that came together, dispersed, and reformed "like a school of fish."[34]

In a later chapter, I discuss whether or not mainstream social science offers satisfactory explanations for the eruption of Asian uprisings. I find none of their explanatory variables universally robust (middle-class threshold, J-curve, religious similarities, repression index, etc.). Rather, it would appear that the simultaneity and relationships of uprisings to each other are more significant. None of the mainstream explanations anticipated anything like the Arab Spring, while the eros effect's formulations of periods of accelerated and simultaneous uprisings does. While political leadership based upon authoritarian models of organization has withered among freedom-loving movements, the power of example and synchronicity of uprisings are increasingly potent—especially when their promulgators are among the poorest inhabitants of a world capable of providing plenty for all.

Activating the Eros Effect

Future global upsurges will pick up from the international synchronicity and expanding popular involvement of movements since World War II. The next generations of protests—drawn from the trajectory of Chiapas, Caracas, Gwangju, Berlin, Seattle, February 15, 2003, and the Arab Spring—will surpass these other waves in a cascading global resonance. As the global tendencies of the world system intensify in their impact on millions of people's everyday lives, internationally coordinated opposition is more and more a necessity. For the eros effect to be activated, thousands and then millions of people who comprise civil society need to act—to negate their existing daily routines and break free of ingrained patterns. This process is not simply enacted by the will power of a small group—although some may help spark it. Without help from anyone, the global movement is building toward a protracted people's uprising that breaks through regional cultures and confronts the planetary constraints on people's freedom. As the target is fixed, its bull's-eye will be reached: the hundred billionaires who greedily hoard humanity's collective wealth, an even smaller number of gigantic global banks and corporations, and militarized nation-states armed with weapons of mass destruction.

Based upon recent historical experiences, I see possibilities for how the eros effect might be activated through conscious decision. When the Zapatistas used the Internet to call for demonstrations against neoliberalism during the summer of 1999, activists in several cities responded. London experienced its largest riot in at least a decade after a Zapatista *encuentro* (international gathering of activists) in the jungle called for internationally synchronized actions. Proposed initially at such an *encuentro*, People's Global Action (PGA) formed in February 1999 and organized an International Caravan of Solidarity and Resistance that sparked sixty-three direct actions before culminating in big actions at Birmingham's G-8 meeting and Geneva's WTO assembly.[35] PGA's founding statement called for a clear rejection of capitalism and all systems of domination—including patriarchy and racism—and advocated confrontational direct actions organized by autonomous groups.[36] A few months later, PGA brought together a second "carnival of resistance" with actions in forty-three countries (including prominently in London). In Europe, they helped inspire actions like Reclaim the Streets, Carnival Against Capitalism, and EuroMayday. The global action-calendar's third day of resistance culminated in N30—best known for the now mythologized protests against the WTO in Seattle.[37]

These examples provide an indication of the effect that the Zapatistas in Mexico had around the globe. People used to think that it took a vanguard party to provide this kind of coordination, but these actions prove otherwise. The multitude has its own intelligence, an intelligence of the life-force, of the heart. The eros effect is not an intelligence of Cartesian duality, yet is a moment of extraordinary reasonability. How did three thousand poorly equipped, mainly impoverished Native American guerrillas gain the support of people in Mexico City, New York, London, Paris, Toronto, Madrid, Milan, and Sydney? Corporations' global quest for complete control and domination, to break down indigenous cultures and local autonomy, finds its most articulate negation in the Zapatista movement for dignity for the peoples of Chiapas. What began as an insurrection on January 1, 1994, the same day that the North American Free Trade Agreement (NAFTA) went into effect, was turned into a worldwide focal point for grassroots actions against neoliberal capitalism's systematic injustices. For this method of international mobilization to succeed, the group(s) initiating the call must be a socially legitimate leadership in the hearts of many people and must wisely wield broad hegemonic authority. Besides the Zapatistas, Gwangju might increasingly play such an international role. Like the Battleship Potemkin, Gwangju's actions might again signal the time for uprising—and not only in Korea.

No one could have guessed that the suicide of a vegetable vendor in a small Tunisian town would set off the Arab Spring. Not even Mohamed Bouazizi himself had any idea that his solitary act of despair and anger would resonate among so many people. It appears that leaderless conjunctures most often produce the eros effect. Like falling in love, enacting the eros effect is a complex process. Can we make ourselves fall in love? Can we simply will ourselves to remain in love? If the eros effect were continually activated, we would have passed from the realm of prehistory, to the realm in which human beings for the first time are able to determine for themselves the type of society in which they wish to live.

NOTES

1   See Loren Goldner, http://libcom.org/history/korean-working-class-mass-strike-casualization-retreat-1987–2007.

2   Thanks to discussions with Basil Fernando for the above insights.

3   Many contemporary theorists fail to comprehend this basic dimension of freedom and instead advocate new mechanisms for collective control of the individual.

4   We all owe Vietnam a great debt, for their sacrifice and resistance preserved the idea of national independence. Resistance to the war inside the United States helped preserve principles of individual liberty and prevent direct U.S. military intervention in Central America and Africa in the 1980s. If the truth about U.S. massacres during the Korean War had been known, how many Vietnamese lives would have been saved?

5   See Mark Laskey, "The Globalization of Resistance," in *Confronting Capitalism: Dispatches from a Global Movement*, eds. Eddie Yuen, Daniel Burton-Rose and George Katsiaficas (New York: Soft Skull Press, 2004).

6   Some twenty thousand people simultaneously gathered in Porte Alegre, Brazil for the first World Economic Forum.

7   See Barbara Sauermann, ed., *2/15: The Day the World Said NO to War* (Oakland: AK Press, 2003).

8   Studying the contours empirically of both these mobilizations, developing more precise numbers, areas of greatest impact, forms of action, organizations involved, could yield a wealth of data.

9   Joss Hands, "Civil Society, Cosmopolitics and the Net: The Legacy of February 15, 2003," *Information, Communication & Society* 9, no. 2 (April 2006): 225–43.

10   John Berg, "Waiting for Lefty: The State of the Peace Movement in the United States," in *Tamkang Journal of International Affairs* 12, no. 4 (April 2009): 77–101.

11   The Palestinian people have inspired international solidarity actions by groups such as the BDS (Boycott Divest Sanction), whose "organized spontaneity" in actions like dance protests in supermarkets that carry Israeli products attracts increasing support. See http://www.youtube.com/watch?v=y6dO9eVOY2I&feature=player_embedded.

12   For an earlier theoretical formulation, see my 1989 paper at http://eroseffect.com/articles/eroseffectpaper.PDF.

13   Carl Jung, "The Eros Theory," in *Collected Works*, vol. 7 (Princeton: Princeton University Press, 1966), 19.

14   Carl Jung, *The Undiscovered Self* (New York: Signet, 2006), 79.

15   George Kennan, "On Nuclear War," *The New York Review of Books*, January 21, 1982, as quoted in Marc Nerfin, "Neither Prince Nor Merchant: Citizen—An Introduction to the Third System," *Development Dialogue* (1987), 175.

16   Choi, *Gwangju Uprising*, 134.

17   See Mary Anne Staniszewski, Dara Greenwald, and Josh MacPhee, eds., *Signs of Change* (Oakland: AK Press, 2010).

18   Huntington, *Third Wave*, 46.

19   Samuel Huntington, *The Clash of Civilizations and the Remaking of World Order* (London: Simon and Schuster, 1996), 307.

20   Huntington, *Third Wave*, 33.

21   The Invisible Committee, *The Coming Insurrection*, http://www.bloom0101.org/thecominginsurrection.pdf, 6.

22   Carl Jung, *Synchronicity: An Acausal Connecting Principle* (Princeton: Princeton University Press, 1973), 89.

23   Carl Jung, *The Archetypes and the Collective Unconscious* (Princeton: Princeton University Press, 1990), 286.

24   Carl Jung, "Approaching the Unconscious," in *Man and His Symbols* (New York: Dell, 1968), 25.

25   Teodros Kiros considers a "rationality of the heart" an antidote to contemporary civilization's misuse of reason. See *Zara Yacob: Rationality of the Human Heart* (Trenton, NJ: Red Sea Press, 2005).

26   Jung, *Synchronicity*, 30.

27   Ibid., 32. As Jung notes, the concept is originally Avicenna's. Three hundred years later, Ibn Khaldun similarly discussed forms of cognition outside the realm of rational thought. See my essay, "Ibn Khaldun: A Dialectical Philosopher for the New Millennium," in *African Philosophy: Critical Interventions*, ed. Teodros Kiros (New York: Routledge, 2000).

28   Jung, "Eros Theory," 28.

29   Herbert Marcuse, *The Aesthetic Dimension: A Critique of Marxist Aesthetics* (Boston: Beacon Press, 1978), 64.

30   See Jung, *Synchronicity*, 95, 103, 106–7.

31   Jung, *Archetypes*, 212.

32   Ibid., 22.

33   Gaetano Mosca as quoted in Mancur Olson, *The Logic of Collective Action: Public Goods and the Theory of Groups* (Cambridge: Harvard University Press, 1971), 17.

34   For more on swarm theory, see Peter Miller, "Swarm Theory: Ants, Bees and Birds Teach Us How to Cope With a Complex World," *National Geographic*, July 2007, 146.

35   See Amory Starr's inspiring book, *Global Revolt: A Guide to the Movements against Globalization* (London: Zed Press, 2005), 26–27. Activists appear to be far ahead of the 1960s in at least one admirable and crucial dimension: the apparent lack of sectarian troubles between ideological poles. Movement activists themselves are more attuned to dangers of true belief and as a result are self-organized.

36   For an earlier Zapatista version, see Markus S. Schulz, "Collective Action across Borders," *Sociological Perspectives* 41 (Fall 1998): 3.

37   See Yuen, et al., *Confronting Capitalism*.

CHAPTER 12

The Commune: Freedom's Phenomenological Form

> In its struggle against the revolution, the parliamentary republic found itself compelled to strengthen, along with the repressive measures, the resources and centralization of governmental power. All revolutions perfected this machine instead of smashing it.
>
> —Karl Marx

> The popular masses, insensible to the bourgeois ideal of a municipal council, were bent on the Commune. . . . What did they care for a council, even elective, but without real liberties and fettered to the state—without authority over the administration of schools and hospitals, justice and police, and altogether unfit for grappling with the social slavery of its fellow-citizens?
>
> —Lissagaray

DURING UPRISINGS, PEOPLE in struggle create new organizational forms of action that prefigure a free society. Spontaneously created organizations and improvised takeovers of space led to forms of direct democracy at Bangkok's Thammasat University in 1973, in liberated Gwangju in 1980, in Tiananmen Square in 1989, in Patan (Nepal) in 1990, and Taipei's Chiang Kai-shek Square in 1990. Like the function of the liberated Sorbonne in Paris during the events of May 1968, such temporary autonomous zones provide for deliberative democracy in moments when civil society engulfs politics and supplants the state. Within them, everyone seeks to guide action in certain directions—political parties, unions, subaltern groups, collectives, and individuals all smell the changes in the air and sense the time has finally come. The form of the Commune is the revolutionary umbrella of all these concerns, not the monolithic imposition of a leading party (no matter how correct), as when Soviet Communists sought to substitute themselves for the will of the people.

In moments of crisis, liberated spaces can be decisive in determining whether the movement will continue—or if the forces of order will restore quiet. In moments when the eros effect is activated, such spaces become key to formulating and implementing the popular will. They are sites to develop forms of direct democracy through which the movement can continue to develop its vision and tactics. As the Egyptian movement's return to Tahrir Square months after overthrowing Mubarak illustrated, continuing occupation of public space can rejuvenate subaltern groups' counterpublic discourse and challenge the system's cooptative forces. When movements are victorious, these liberated spaces give birth to the Commune—the phenomenal form of freedom. The Commune is the form of freedom that breaks through the illusion of contemporary "democracy" offered by ritualized elections between candidates of the ruling elite.

Governments recognize the threat posed by liberated spaces—even in quiet moments. Uprisings since 1968 would have been impossible to create without the safe haven of refuge offered by countercultural spaces at the edges of the commodity system. From Chiapas to Christiana, Oaxaca to Gwangju, and Brixton to Kreuzberg, many people are able to live significantly freer lives than their counterparts in more mainstream places. The example set by the liberation of public space is subversive—it ripples outward and has influence far beyond the immediate place where people gather. In free spaces, people can also experience, however temporarily, a break from the sometimes overwhelmingly incessant imposition of cash connections and instrumental relationships. While they may seem marginalized and otherworldly, insignificant and even comical, these liberated spaces—themselves often enclaves left as residue after the high tides of insurgencies recede—can be incredibly significant facilitators of people's capacity to envision their lives in new terms. We should not underestimate the significance of every space in which people can deliberate about substantive issues, every space of autonomy for women, of psychological independence for youth, and of feelings of empowerment for subaltern groups. Do such subversive effects explain why Christiania suffered continual threats from police invasions, and why Ungdomshuset, a Copenhagen movement center for decades, was violently evicted on March 1, 2007?

Free deliberation of significant problems has defined the human condition since the dawn of time—and will continue to be the case no matter how much contemporary civilization limits people's autonomy and choices. From the Athenian polis to American town meetings, forms of democratic governance by an activated citizenry flourished. People made informed decisions for themselves, not by electing representatives. In the nineteenth century, Alexis de Tocqueville noted carefully that, "local assemblies of citizens constitute the strength of free nations. Town meetings are to liberty what elementary schools are to science; they bring it within the people's reach." In his view, a pillar of American democracy was that, "in the townships . . . the system of representation is not adopted . . . the body of the electors, after having designated its magistrates, directs them in everything that exceeds the simple and ordinary executive business of the State."[1]

Based upon more recent experiences, in 1957, Cornelius Castoriadis posited the deliberative decision-making in Hungarian workers' councils as models for democratic governance. Castoriadis perceived that politicians had monopolized public terrain, whereas the proper space for solving political problems was "the workers' councils and the general assemblies of each particular enterprise, the vital collective setting within which there can be a confrontation of views and an elaboration of informed political opinions. They will be the ultimate sovereign authorities for all political decisions."[2] Within U.S. radical movements, two separate strands of radical democratic thought came to very similar conclusions: both Black Panther leader Huey Newton, who advocated "revolutionary intercommunalism," and anarchist Murray Bookchin, who proposed "municipal socialism," defined the political form of freedom as direct democracy and local control.

In the past two millennia, governments in Europe and Asia have taken control of free, commonly owned arenas. From rivers and lands to intimate relationships, governments have come to license and control our everyday lives, to establish "full spectrum domination." Cultural colonization destroyed natural democratic forms based upon consensus and direct democracy, subsumed them under the rubric of voting as "democracy," with the result of less popular control. The fetishization of voting mirrors the commodity form in the life-world of the abstract individual: voting satisfies freedom and democracy, while sensuality is reduced to consumerism, and Eros diminished to sex. Reversing this colonization of the life-world, breaking routine acceptance of everyday power relations, requires inordinate effort and energy.

In the twenty-first century, social media give citizens even more capability for direct and immediate communication, for direct-democratic governance on a scale never before possible. The solitary subject, whether seen as individual or organization—has been superseded by a diverse plurality of subjects. Today's capacity to author documents on Google Docs will tomorrow help enable new forms of consensual democracy. Philosophically, the new possibility of the subject-object duality that has characterized Western political existence since Descartes may be resolved through the emergence of the people as a unified subject-object. Within new technologies, "collective intelligence" has become a new force in creations like Wikipedia, where producers of information are simultaneously consumers of it and vice versa in a seamless tapestry of yin and yang. Web 2.0 gives humanity the chance for "a new modality of organizing production: radically decentralized, collaborative and nonproprietary, based on sharing resources and outputs among widely distributed, loosely connected individuals who cooperate with each other without relying on either market signals or managerial commends."[3]

Two previous Communes that sprang to life during the 1871 Paris Commune and 1980 Gwangju Uprising reveal in concrete experience the capacity and needs of people for direct political engagement. The communal forms of freedom during these historical experiences provide optimistic grounds to project the future of politics.

From the Paris Commune to the Gwangju People's Uprising

Two events in modern world history stand out as unique beacons of the spontaneous ability of hundreds of thousands of ordinary people to govern themselves:
the Paris Commune of 1871 and the Gwangju People's Uprising of 1980. In both
cities, an unarmed citizenry, in opposition to their own governments, effectively
gained control of urban space despite the presence of well-armed military forces
seeking to reestablish "law and order." Hundreds of thousands of people created
popular organs of political power that effectively and efficiently replaced traditional forms of government; crime rates plummeted during the period of liberation; and people felt new forms of kinship with each other.

There are remarkable ways in which the two events converge. Within these
liberated territories, a number of similar dynamics arose:

> Spontaneous emergence of popular organs of democratic decision-making
> Emergence of armed resistance from below
> Attenuation of criminal behavior in the cities
> Existence of genuine solidarity and cooperation among the citizenry
> Suspension of hierarchies of class, power, and status
> Appearance of internal divisions among the participants

Like the Paris Commune, Gwangju's historical significance is international. Its
lessons apply equally well to East and West, North and South. The 1980 people's
uprising, like those earlier revolutionary moments, continues to have worldwide
repercussions. As a symbol of struggle, Gwangju continues to inspire others to
act. An example of ordinary people taking power into their own hands, it was a
precursor of events that followed in East Asia. In 1996, activist Sanjeewa Liyanage
of the Asian Human Rights Commission in Hong Kong expressed this dimension
of the uprising when he wrote:

> The "power of people" is so strong that it just cannot be destroyed by
> violent suppressive means. Such power, from the people, spreads a spirit
> that will last for generations. Gwangju is a city full of that "people power."
> What happened in 1980, in Gwangju, was not just an isolated incident. It
> has brought new light and hope to many people who are still suffering from
> brutally oppressive regimes and military-led governments.... The strength
> and will of people of Gwangju to carry on their agitative actions was very
> impressive.... Today many look up to them, paying tribute to what they
> have achieved.... I was inspired by their courage and spirit. Gwangju
> remains a unique sign that symbolizes a people's power that cannot be
> suppressed. That sign is a flame of hope for many others.[4]

The most important historical legacy of these uprisings is their affirmation of
human dignity and prefiguration of a free society. Like the Paris Commune, the
people of Gwangju spontaneously rose up against insuperable forces. Like the
long tradition of Parisian insurrections, the people of Gwangju have repeatedly
signaled the advent of revolution in Korea—in recent times from the 1894 Farmers'
War and the 1929 student revolt to the 1980 uprising.

Both uprisings were produced by the accumulation of grievances against injustice and precipitated by extreme events. The Paris Commune arose in 1871 as the victorious Prussians moved to seize the capital of France at the end of the Franco-Prussian War. The French government's complete capitulation to the Prussians angered Parisians, and on March 18, the National Guard of Paris seized control of the city in a relatively bloodless coup d'état. Despite their own government attacking them, the Communards held out for seventy days against French troops armed and aided by their Prussian conquerors. The Communards established a functioning government that coordinated defense and met the daily needs of Parisians. Twice elections were held, and chosen delegates sought to govern the liberated city in a robustly democratic manner. Finally, on May 28, overwhelming military force crushed the uprising, and thousands were killed in a "Bloody Week" of urban warfare.

Over a century later, the Gwangju People's Uprising occurred at a time when the firepower of militaries was multiplied by several orders of magnitude. There was no conquering foreign army advancing on the city, but the citizenry rebelled nonetheless against their own government's military dictatorship (which was aided and abetted by the United States).[5] After horrendous barbarity was inflicted on the people of Gwangju by elite paratrooper units, thousands of people bravely fought the military and drove them out of the city. They held their liberated space for six days, a far shorter period than the Paris Commune. Inside liberated Gwangju, daily citizens' assemblies of tens of thousands of people gave voice to years-old frustrations and pent-up aspirations of ordinary people. Local citizens' groups maintained order and created a new type of government—one of, by, and for the people. On May 27, 1980—almost on the same day that the Paris Commune was crushed 109 years earlier—the Gwangju Commune was overwhelmed by military force.

In order to contain the uprisings and prevent them from spreading, the established governments isolated both cities. Cut off from the provinces, the Paris Commune nevertheless found many supporters, and similar communal experiments erupted in many cites, from Marseille to Tours. In Paris, Communards flew balloons filled with letters to the provinces to try to spread the revolt,[6] and circulars for farmers were dropped successfully.[7] In Gwangju, the revolt spread to at least sixteen neighboring sections of South Jeolla province. Many people were killed attempting to break out of the military cordon around Gwangju to spread the revolt, and dozens more died trying to get into Gwangju to help in its defense.

As in Paris, where Courbet participated in an artists' group that supported the Commune in many ways—most remembered for tearing down the Vendôme column—artists in Gwangju also played vital roles. Clown theater group (Kwangdae) took a central role in organizing the rallies; Hong Sung-dam and visual artists made posters for the movement and helped with the daily newspaper.

In both cities, traitors to the uprisings and people who supported the government (including spies and saboteurs sent inside the Communes to disrupt and destroy them) were quite numerous. In Gwangju, government agents took the detonators from the basement of Province Hall, thereby rendering useless the dynamite brought there by Hwasun coal miners. During the Paris Commune, the decision by a small group of Communards to leave their post guarding one of the forts overlooking the city led to the loss of a most strategic position—one the reactionary forces soon used to bombard the city with artillery. Paris was "full" of internal enemies, and there were riots at Vendôme Place and the Bourse, instigated by "loyal" citizens in constant contact with Versailles. In Gwangju, the "poison needle incident" is but the most famous in a series of internal problems.[8]

The liberated realities of the Communes in Paris and Gwangju contradict the widely propagated myth that human beings are essentially evil and therefore require strong governments to maintain order and justice. Rather, the behavior of the citizens during these moments of liberation revealed an innate capacity for self-government and cooperation. It was the forces of the defeated state, not the autonomously governed people, which acted with great brutality and injustice. Reading the following description of state brutality, it is difficult to tell whether it occurred in Paris or Gwangju:

> You shall perish, whatever you do! If you are taken with arms in your hands, death! If you beg for mercy, death! Whichever way you turn, right, left, back forward up down, death! You are not merely outside the law, you are outside humanity. Neither age nor sex shall save you and yours. You shall die, but first you shall taste the agony of your wife, your sister, your mother, your sons and daughters, even those in the cradle! Before your eyes the wounded man shall be taken out of the ambulance and hacked with bayonets or knocked down with the butt end of a rifle. He shall be dragged living by his broken leg or bleeding arm and flung like a suffering, groaning bundle of refuse into the gutter. Death! Death! Death![9]

In both 1871 and 1980, after the halcyon days of liberation were bloodily brought to an end, brutal repression remained the order of the day. Estimates of the number of people executed in the aftermath of the Paris Commune reach to thirty thousand, a number that does not include thousands more who were summarily deported to distant Pacific holdings of the French Empire.[10] In Gwangju, far fewer people were killed, testament to the declining power of governments to murder its own citizens. Although today's official count of the dead hovers around two hundred, most people then believed that as many as two thousand died in the uprising, and hundreds disappeared. Even after the Gwangju Commune had been ruthlessly crushed, the news of the uprising was so subversive that the military burned an unknown number of corpses, dumped others into unmarked graves, and destroyed its own records. To prevent word of the uprising from being spoken publicly, thousands of people were arrested and hundreds tortured, as the military tried to suppress even a whisper of its murders. At least a dozen people committed suicide as they proclaimed the truth of the massacre. Despite repression, the people of Gwangju continued their uprising in new forms, and they ultimately led Korea to overthrow the U.S.-backed military dictatorship.[11] In France as in Gwangju, years of repression sought to suppress the truth. Police harassed funerals, refusing to allow the somber burial of anyone publicly associated with the movement. This practice continued as late as 1887,[12] and in South Korea until at least 1987.

Both uprisings took place after many years of economic growth. Although repressive, the yushin system of Park Chung-hee galvanized great gains in the Korean economy in the 1970s, albeit at the price of super exploitation of the working class through long workweeks, low wages, and systematic suppression of people's basic rights. In France, output had expanded during the Second Empire of Louis Napoleon. Between 1853 and 1869, agricultural output grew 78 percent, industry grew 53 percent; building increased by 106 percent; and exports rose 164 percent.[13] Between 1860 and 1870, national income rose 24 percent, and real wages increased 20 percent from 1852 to 1869.[14] Similarly in Korea, Between 1968 and 1979, agricultural output increased 82 percent, industry grew 746 percent, building construction more than tripled, exports skyrocketed, and national income rose significantly. The regions around Gwangju in 1980 and Paris in 1871 underwent similar transitions from agriculture to industry, a trend resulting in great migration from the countryside to the cities. The 1872 census put the number of industrial workers in France at 44 percent of the workforce, but there were probably no more than fifteen factories that employed more than a hundred workers each, and an additional hundred factories employed between twenty and fifty workers.[15] Similarly, Gwangju in 1980 was the site of many small factories, a feature typical of the transition to higher forms of industrialization. In 1866, 49.8 percent of French people worked in the primary sector, 28.9 percent in secondary (manufacturing), and 21.3 percent in services.[16] In 1975, 45.9 percent of Korean people worked in the primary sector, 19.1 percent in secondary, and 35.0 percent in services.[17]

During both uprisings, women played significant roles, although in both cases they organized themselves to contribute within domains considered traditionally female in the patriarchal division of labor. Strong feminist sentiment emerged in Paris, particularly within the ranks of the International Workingmen's Association (IWA). Elisabeth Dmitrieff, a young member of the Russian section of the IWA, helped found the Women's Union for the Defense of Paris and Care of the Injured. The IWA demanded gender equality and the abolition of prostitution. The Women's Union took part in many of the Commune's action-committees and also organized work cooperatives, like the restaurant La Marmite, which served free food for indigents. Although barred from voting in initial elections, women were enfranchised by the newly constituted regime. In Gwangju, high school girls took care of the many corpses and helped care for the wounded. Although a few men were involved in cooking communal meals in Province Hall and around the city, it was predominantly women who took care of making sure everyone had food. While only a few women carried arms during the Gwangju Uprising, a separate female battalion of the Parisian National Guard fought to defend Place Blanche when the Prussians and their French allies attacked.

Differences Between the Two Uprisings

Differences between these two historic events are quite apparent. As previously mentioned, the Paris Commune lasted some ten weeks from the insurrection of March 18 to the final suppression on May 28. The Gwangju People's Uprising held liberated Gwangju for only six days: May 22 to 27. For such political events, however, time is not a key variable—at least not as we ordinarily measure it.

Like the insurgents of the 1789 Revolution, Communards considered the church enemy territory. In the first week of April, more than two hundred priests were arrested, mainly through grassroots initiatives.[18] Without anyone telling them to do so, people took over many neighborhood parishes and turned them into community centers, orphanages, and family refuges, places where the city's poor could rest. Neighborhoods convened in them to discuss communal grievances. In Gwangju, by contrast, churches played a significant role in support of the uprising. Many churches voluntarily became meeting places for their parishioners to discuss the insurgency and to decide what their roles in it should be. Catholic priest Jo Bi-ho spent much time with the young fighters on the front lines, and the YMCA and YWCA were organizing centers for some of the most radical insurgents. No one was executed in liberated Gwangju. In Paris, as the city was about to fall, the Archbishop of Paris and a handful of priests were executed.

The Paris Commune included people of many European nationalities. Italian, Polish, German, Swiss, and even Russian expatriates participated as equals. For a time, the commanding general in charge of the city's defense was Jarosław Dombrowski, a Pole, and Leo Frankel, a Hungarian, was elected to the government and became minister of labor. While in Gwangju few foreigners were positioned—geographically or linguistically—to participate in the movement, Korean xenophilia welcomed journalists and even missionaries, who were applauded and aided in public and private.

A more significant difference is that in Gwangju, no preexisting armed force like the Parisian National Guard led the assault on power. Liberated Gwangju was organized without the contrivance of governments or planning by political parties. Rather a spontaneous process of resistance to the brutality of the paratroopers threw forward men and women who rose to the occasion in the concrete context of unfolding historical events. Many had little or no previous political experience. Some had little or no formal education, although military service was then mandatory for every male. In the latter part of the twentieth century, the Gwangju Uprising is one indication of the capacity in millions of people to govern themselves far more wisely than military dictatorships or tiny elites. People's capacity for direct self-government (as well as the deadly absurdity of elite rule) is all too evident in the events of the Gwangju uprising.

Not only was there no preexisting organization to stage a coup d'état, but known leaders of the movement were either arrested or in hiding when the uprising began. On the night of May 17, military intelligence personnel and police raided homes of activists across the city, arresting the leadership of the movement. Almost all of those not picked up left the city and went into hiding. Nonetheless, first students and then the entire city organized spontaneously, drove the military out, and then peacefully governed themselves. Their capacity for direct democracy was evident even in the midst of tremendous bloodshed. On May 20, tens of thousands of people had gathered on Kumnam Avenue and sang, "Our wish is national reunification." Paratroopers' clubs dispersed the singing throng, but a group of five thousand was able to reassemble and sat-in on a road. They then *selected representatives* to try and split the police from the army.[19]

Daily rallies of tens of thousands of people in Gwangju provided a forum for direct democracy where differences of opinion could be aired and free-ranging perspectives expressed. People from all walks of life were able to address the entire city—including leaders of criminal gangs who promised solidarity. Shoeshine boys, prostitutes, and people normally considered to be at the "bottom" of society participated as equals in the liberated city. Whereas in Paris elected leaders made decisions for people and issued proclamations, in Gwangju people made decisions directly. Two significant such determinations were *not* to surrender to the military (as many people advocated) and to give the military hundreds of weapons in exchange for the release of dozens of prisoners. When citizens vocalized needs that required action, groups immediately formed to take appropriate measures.

Unlike Gwangju's general assemblies and direct democracy, a variety of representative authority structures existed in Paris. During the war against Prussia, the French government on August 11, 1870, had organized 200 new National Guard battalions from the poorer classes to fight alongside the 60 battalions already drawn from the propertied classes. When the newly elected National Assembly of February 8, 1871, voted for France to surrender to Prussia, the people hated it, and the National Guard became the sole source of national pride. On March 15, some 215 battalions held a general assembly at the Vauxhall and proclaimed Garibaldi commander-in-chief of the National Guard. At the same meeting, thirty elected neighborhood delegates presented themselves to the group.[20] With the support of at least 215 of the existing 260 National Guard battalions, their leaders seized power on March 18. The Central Committee (CC) of the National Guard, composed of three representatives from each of the twenty *arrondissements* (districts) of Paris, effectively became the new government. Paris was full of already-constituted organizations and parties, such as the IWA, the International Workingmen's Association to which Marx belonged. At the beginning of March, their Parisian branch still had no definite political program.[21]

To legitimate the new political system, elections were held on March 26, in which 287,000 men voted (women were not yet enfranchised). Ninety members of the Commune were elected—but they included fifteen government supporters and nine citizens against the government but also against the March 18 "insurrection."[22] The next day, two hundred thousand people attended the announcement of the results and installation of the new government at the Hôtel de Ville (City Hall). Unlike the free flowing gatherings at Democracy Square in Gwangju when everyone had a voice, the crowd in Paris watched as their representatives were sworn in, after which they simply left. The newly elected government proclaimed the enfranchisement of women, separation of church and state, no more night work in bakeries, no back rent for the poor, the arrest of reactionary priests, the reopening of abandoned factories, and abolition of fines against workers—the last measure permitting workers to reclaim their tools from the city's pawnshops.

The elected representatives, however, were not the only power with which to be reckoned. "The republican Central Committee [based upon neighborhood associations from which the National Guard was drawn and favoring democracy rather than monarchy or elite rule] acted as a shadow government."[23] Along with the IWA and the Federal Chamber of Workingmen's Societies, three separate groups each convened initially at the Place de la Corderie, sometimes issuing manifestos together and at other times in opposition to each other.[24] In many *arrondissements*, separate subcommittees formed and issued their own instructions to citizens. In addition, National Guard commanders also gave independent orders to their units. Within the cacophony of directives, officers in the field sometimes received three sets of conflicting orders. Elected parliamentarians' orders were often reversed by one of the other groups claiming authority—the CC or the Republican *arrondissement* associations. As a result, the elected government was practically powerless, rivaled in military affairs by the CC and diminished in political power by autonomous *arrondissement* associations. The new government created nine commissions to manage Paris, the most radical being for Labor and Exchange, yet these commissions were unable to act effectively. A grassroots Committee of Artillery argued with the government's War Office about how to deploy cannons; each group controlled big guns in different locations.[25]

Tragically, the elected government was also mired in personal antagonisms among its members and depleted by elected representatives who refused to serve or resigned. Most significantly, it was weakened internally by those loyal to the old government, the bitter enemy of the Commune. Distracted by significant issues like cutting the budget for public religious ceremonies, the government ignored urgent military matters requiring immediate attention. Their commanding generals did not even bother to inform the sitting representatives of detailed military information.[26] While the CC leaders heard of the fall of the fort at Mont-Valerien—a strategic position believed by Communards to be in their hands—the CC did not inform the public, and many brave Communards died after exposing themselves to fire from what they thought was a friendly position.

Bad decisions—or lack of any decision at all—soon became commonplace. Just one example gives an indication of how reliance upon representatives was inferior to people governing themselves: of 1,200 cannons in Paris, only 200 were used by the Communards, and of 2,500 experienced artillerymen, only 500 were kept busy with their work.[27] Finally, as the representative system collapsed, on May 1, by a vote of 34 to 28, the government created a Committee of Public Safety "having authority over all the Commissions."[28]

It appears that ordinary Parisians were not in favor of representative government, preferring instead direct democracy. As Lissagaray tells us, "the popular masses, insensible to the bourgeois ideal of a municipal council, were bent on the Commune. . . . What did they care for a council, even elective, but without real liberties and fettered to the state—without authority over the administration of schools and hospitals, justice and police, and altogether unfit for grappling with the social slavery of its fellow citizens? What the people strove for was a political form allowing them to work for the amelioration of their condition. They had

390 | ASIA'S UNKNOWN UPRISINGS

seen all the constitutions and all the representative governments run counter to the will of the so-called represented elector, and the state power, grown more and more despotic, deprive the workman even of the right to defend his labour, and this power, which has ordained the very air to be breathed, always refusing to intervene in capitalist brigandage."[29]

Here we see the most significant dimension of Paris and Gwangju: by posing the demand for substantive democracy—a far more empowering system than mere elections that choose the next rulers—the people of Paris and Gwangju reveal the trajectory of future forms of freedom. While elections were eventually held in Paris and led to increasing centralization of power in the hands of the Committee of Public Safety under wartime conditions, in Gwangju—despite the imminent threat of invasion—people resolutely maintained the communal form of deliberative democracy. Even when the military's threats mounted and the final days of liberation approached, a new structure to facilitate the rallies and resistance was created, with separate sections for many nearby towns. The new leadership saw itself as a means of facilitating the general assembly's decisions, not making decisions in place of it.[30]

The Role of the Military

Both Communes were ultimately overwhelmed by military force. During the Paris Commune, whole units of the regular army went over to the side of the Commune (although most remained faithful to the government and fought on the side of the Prussians). Those military units that sided with the Commune were at times undisciplined. According to one observer: "The artillery battalions were in effect more completely a law unto themselves, having their own *arrondissement* committees, which refused to merge with the main National Guard Central Committee."[31] Even though the Commune had at its disposal something like sixty thousand fighters, nearly two hundred thousand muskets, more than a thousand cannons, five forts and enough munitions for years, confusion and polycentric patterns of authority made decisive action difficult to take.[32] Despite the presence of as many as three thousand Blanquists in 1871, no attempt was made to seize the Bank of France.[33] Louise Michel tells us that fifteen thousand people stood up to clash with the army during the final Bloody Week, but when the Versailles army first broke into the city on May 21, there were large crowds listening to a concert in the Tuileries Gardens.[34] Indeed, one strategically placed unit guarding the heights overlooking the enemies' entryway to Paris decided to abandon their position, leaving the door to Paris ajar for the deadly final assault.

In Gwangju, as in Paris, soldiers and police sometimes sided with the insurgents. General Chung Oong, commander of the Thirty-First Provincial Division (composed mainly of South Jeolla natives) and Yoon Hung-jong, the province's martial law commander, were both sacked for refusing to follow orders.[35] During a battle near the train station, troops of the Thirty-First announced through loudspeakers, "We are not harming you people. We are just moving out. Please make way!" They were allowed to depart without incident—as the crowd's wisdom understood the sincerity of the soldiers. Later it was learned that Special Forces parachuted into the unit's headquarters and detained their commander, Chung Oong, for bravely refusing to order the killing of innocents. The police chief in Gwangju, cognizant of the death sentences meted out to police officers who ordered the deadly shootings on April 19, 1960 (when dictator Syngman Rhee was overthrown in a student-led revolution), also refused to participate in the slaughter. Many individual police officers helped wounded citizens and cooperated with the new civil authority once Gwangju had been liberated. Some even took off their uniforms and fought alongside insurgents to drive the military out.

Although secret U.S. documents charged Gwangju insurgents with executing captured enemies, no one was ever executed in liberated Gwangju. In Paris, a limited number of executions did take place. At the very beginning of the Commune on March 18, General Lecomte, who had thrice ordered his troops to open fire, was swept away and executed by mutinous soldiers sympathetic to the crowd's mobilization for a Commune. Although officers tried to stop them, twenty soldiers lined up, and their muskets quickly finished off the general and one of his associates without a trial. At the end of May, with Paris burning during intense fighting and hundreds of captured Communards already summarily executed, the Public Safety Commission ordered the execution of six prominent prisoners, including Archbishop Darboy. Volunteers rushed forward to carry out the punishment.[36] Reactionary newspapers were also suppressed, and a total of some eight hundred arrests were made. Even more indicative of the lack of unity in Paris was a poster of the Central Committee of the National Guard: "Death for Looting, Death for Stealing."[37] In liberated Gwangju, by contrast, incidents of looting or stealing were practically nonexistent.

Insurrections in the early twentieth century—in St. Petersburg and Moscow in 1917, Budapest and Bavaria in 1919, or Hamburg, Canton, and Shanghai in 1923—were led by centralized organizations intent on seizing power, such as Communist Parties. This earlier wave of insurrectionary uprisings necessitated creating Red Armies that could decimate enemy troops and establish a new government, and in this sense they were closer to the American and French revolutionary wars than they were to wave of the civil uprisings at the end of the twentieth century, which were not directed by centralized organizations. In China, Korea, and Vietnam, protracted wars led by centralized parties were vital to national liberation. European communist insurrections and Asian wars of national liberation are different from more recent civil uprisings in more than simply tactical dimensions. Civil insurgencies emanate from civil society—not from the state or political parties—and their aspirations and results are far less clear, and therefore more difficult to attain, than in winner-take-all battles of armed forces. While popular support for contemporary movements may mitigate overt government repression, it is by no means certain that states will refrain from massacring their own citizens in order to preserve themselves.

The Paris Commune's Role in the Gwangju Uprising

Often unnoticed, one of the greatest accomplishments of uprisings is to thoroughly transform ordinary people. Once they have tasted the exhilaration of freedom and experienced their power to change society, people are prepared again and again to go into the streets to claim their rights. This helps explain why the Philippines had two subsequent People Power uprisings after 1986, why Korea's 2008 candle-light protests were so massive, why Burma's 2007 Saffron Revolution caught on so quickly, why Tibet's 2008 protests were its most widespread, why Nepal's second people's uprising in 2006 abolished the monarchy, and why Thailand's Red Shirts and Yellow Shirts remain locked in combat. Freedom struggles condition subse-quent uprisings, a phenomenon not contained within boundaries of space and time. Historic events in one part of the world can inspire and motivate people across continents and centuries. It is no accident that German revolutionaries of the early twentieth century called themselves Spartacists, nor that the memory of the nineteenth-century Paris Commune inspired activists in Gwangju in 1980 as well as in Beijing in 1989 (as noted in chapter 5).

In the course of dozens of interviews with former fighters in Gwangju, I found many people for whom the historical memory of the Paris Commune pro-vided inspiration. Of the twenty-nine interviews I conducted in 2001 with partici-pants in the uprising, many indicated that they had been part of study groups that for a time focused on the Paris Commune before the Gwangju Uprising. Moreover, one person remembered that Yoon Sang-won, martyred symbol of the uprising, had attended a 1976 speech given by poet Kim Nam-ju at Nokdu bookstore in which he discussed the Paris Commune.[38] During the uprising, Yoon Sang-won spoke publicly at least once about the Paris Commune in his discussions with other leading activists.[39]

A history major in his undergraduate years at Chonnam National University, Lee Yang-hyun read about the Paris Commune in the 1970s. From his readings, he recalled "three to four-year-old kids threw rocks at the French Army." Though he thought that was an exaggeration, he observed his own three-year-old son throw rocks at the police during the Gwangju Uprising.[40] During high school, Lee and his classmate Jung Sang-yong (also a prominent participant) were part of a book club that focused for a time on the Paris Commune. Kim Jong-bae reported that Jung Sang-yong, Yoon Gang-ok, Kim Young-chol, Yoon Sang-won, and Park Hyo-son were all members of a Paris Commune study group prior to the upris-ing.[41] Yoon Gang-ok described the group as "loose-knit"—meaning anyone could join—and recalled the key role of Professor Lee Young-hee. Kim Hyo-sok read about the Paris Commune during one of the meetings of his "good book club" at the YWCA.[42] Organized by Jang Du-sok, Yoon Young-kyu, and Song Gi-suk, these clubs attracted a wide following. According to Yoon Young-kyu, at least eighteen readers' clubs were organized in Gwangju in the late 1970s. Bringing together high schoolers, college students and professors, these groups included "opinion leaders" and leaders of illegal organizations. Many books were available about the Paris Commune, all illegal and many of poor quality printing.[43]

Chong Sang-yong remembered reading about the Paris Commune before the uprising in a group called *Gwang Rang* (Gwangju Young Men), which had been created after the overthrow of Syngman Rhee on April 19, 1960.[44] As he recalled, in 1966 the texts were read in Japanese by older college colleagues who then presented summaries in a group of about twenty people—several from each grade level. These people then, in turn, discussed the subject with their own colleagues, a structure that facilitated learning by a large number of people. Kim Sang-yoon remembered a study group in 1978 that focused on the Paris Commune. "At most, five people would study together. Each member would then form another group on almost the same topic. Kim Nam-ju got a Japanese book about the Paris Commune."[45] While Lee Chun-hee read intensively about the Paris Commune after the uprising, she recalled that during the uprising, leading people talked about the Paris Commune at the YWCA, along with the significance of Che Guevara.[46]

According to Kim Jang-gil, the Paris Commune and Gwangju Uprising were similar in their community spirit, in the ways people "lived and struggled together" under difficult circumstances. As in the Paris Commune, there were many calls for an uprising before the actual event transpired. Kim recalled how he, Kim Nam-ju, and Park Sung-moo called for an uprising in 1972. They secretly threw leaflets from the roofs of the administration and law school buildings at CNU on December 8, after which they repeated their action at Gwangju Ilgo and a girls' high school.[47] He also mentioned other calls for an uprising long before 1980.

Others felt the two events were not so similar. In a series of interviews, Lee Jae-eui, author of the definitive narrative history of the Gwangju Uprising,[48] offered penetrating analysis of the differences and similarities between the Paris Commune and Gwangju People's Uprising.[49] "During the Paris Commune, they had enough time to organize elections and set up an administrative structure. But in Gwangju, there was not the time for the leadership to get authority from the people." Lee continued: "In response to the situation, I suppose it's very similar. Even though there were so many differences—ideological, historical, social, cultural—human beings respond to protect their dignity and existence."

Yoon Han-bong felt the Paris Commune and the Gwangju Uprising were not similar because the Paris Commune was more "systematic and ideological."[50] In his view, Gwangju was more "voluntary." "People's level of democracy was very low here," he said. "They believed U.S. ships were coming to help them, showing they had no understanding of international political dynamics." Yoon felt that the workers of the Paris Commune had a high consciousness but that in Gwangju the workers were not educated. The Gwangju Uprising was "moral"—stores and banks were not robbed. "If they had some conception of class consciousness, they would have redistributed these goods and funds to the poor." When I interjected that the Bank of France had also been left alone during the Paris Commune—indeed guarded by the Communards—we decided to continue the discussion at greater length another time. Unfortunately, Yoon passed away before we were able to continue.[51]

These direct connections between the Paris Commune and the Gwangju Uprising illustrate how the legacy of uprisings, whether in Paris or Gwangju, is to empower other humans to struggle against oppression. In the wake of both Paris and Gwangju's heroism, people were empowered, consciously or not, and educated in preparation for future freedom struggles. Even when an uprising is brutally suppressed—as in both cases here—its being experienced publicly creates new desires and new needs, new fears and new hopes in people's hearts and minds. In 1987, when South Koreans rose up in their historic nineteen-day June Uprising, "Remember Gwangju!" was a key rallying cry. Two years later, on May 20, 1989, Chinese workers and students occupying Tiananmen Square invoked the memory of the Paris Commune in a joint statement in which they proclaimed, "We will build another Wall of the Communards with our life's blood."[52]

Uprisings have historically been fountainheads of revolutionary theory, but in the twentieth century, after communist parties aligned with the Soviet Union proclaimed Russia the motherland of the revolution, defamation of "spontaneity" reached such extremes that any popular movement outside the control of the Soviet Communist Party was categorically excluded from the realm of revolutionary action. In France and May 1968 and Italy in 1977, communist parties opposed insurgent movements and sided with government. Looking at the history of uprisings in the eighteenth and nineteenth centuries, one discerns a far different orientation of revolutionaries.[53] Both Marx and Lenin enthusiastically embraced the Paris Commune as the embodiment of their aspirations. While Soviet communist theory came to vilify spontaneity and reify organization, anarchist thinking remained more tied to insurgencies. The contributions of Peter Kropotkin especially lend themselves to be extrapolated into our own time. With regard to the fate of the Bolshevik revolution, such a task is straightforward. While remaining friendly to it, Kropotkin was able to analyze its development and regression at a very early date. It is quite a bit more difficult to apply Kropotkin's thinking to the development of revolutionary movements in the latter half of the twentieth century.

Peter Kropotkin and People's Uprisings

We must forgive Kropotkin for many things. At the top of that list is his support for Germany during World War I in the hope the Kaiser would end the Czar's reign. Somewhere else in this list is his Eurocentric bias.[54] A kind and gentle soul, Kropotkin was a benevolent man-child, the best of the Russian aristocracy, passionate in his commitment to revolutionary change. He was, if anything, an internationalist. Considering the role of *Le Revolte*, the Swiss paper he edited, he wrote: "To make one feel sympathy with the throbbing of the human heart, with its revolt against age-long injustice, with its attempts at working out new forms of life—this should be the chief duty of a revolutionary paper. It is hope, not despair, which makes successful revolutions."[55]

Alongside the Russian revolution and his experiences in England and the United States, Kropotkin developed his analysis of revolutions mainly in relation to movements in France, especially the Revolution of 1789 to 1793 and the Paris Commune of 1871. For Kropotkin, the free commune became the ends and means of genuine revolution. He detested representative government and those bureaucrats who sought to take upon themselves the responsibilities and rights of the people. More than once, he blasted those who would sit, like generals from afar, and give directives to movements in the streets.[56] One can only imagine what he would have to say about those who sit home today during demonstrations and tomorrow write "handbooks" full of advice for activists. In his own day, he participated in armed demonstrations and thematized on the necessity of overcoming cowardice inside the movement.[57]

Kropotkin's faith in ordinary people was boundless. Admiring the "spontaneous organization shown by the people of Paris" in the French Revolution, he noted that each section of the city appointed its own military and civil committee, but "it was to the General Assemblies, held in the evening, that all important questions were generally referred."[58] Over time, observed Kropotkin, these sections were transformed into arms of the Committee of Public Safety (i.e., into instruments of the state). As forty thousand revolutionary committees were swallowed by the state, the revolution was killed.[59]

The sacrifices of thousands of people who lost their lives in revolutionary movements revealed to Kropotkin the form in which a genuine revolution would appear: the "independent commune." Throughout his writings, Kropotkin understood democratic republics and representative governments as fulfilling the ambitions of middle-class radicals, of those who wanted reform of the existing system in order to improve their individual lot rather than to revolutionize all of the existing social order.[60] "Representative government has accomplished its historic mission; it has given a mortal blow to court-rule."[61] "Absolute monarchy corresponded to the system of serfdom. Representative government corresponds to the system of capital-rule."[62]

Developing his thoughts in relation to the Paris Commune of 1871, he wrote: "The uprising of the Paris Commune thus brought with it the solution of a question, which tormented every true revolutionist. Twice had France tried to achieve some sort of socialist revolution by imposing it through a central government more or less disposed to accept it: in 1793–1794, when she tried to introduce *l'égalité de fait*—real economic equality—by means of strong Jacobinist measures; and in 1848, when she tried to impose a "Democratic Socialist Republic." And each time she failed. But now a new solution was indicated: the free commune must do it on its own territory . . ."[63]

The political form of a free society, for Kropotkin, clearly was the independent commune. "This was the form the social revolution must take—the independent commune. Let all the country and all the world be against it; but once its inhabitants have decided that they will communalize the consumption of commodities, their exchange and their production, they must realize it among themselves."[64] In his understanding of the Paris Commune and the Cartagena and Barcelona Communes that followed on its heels, Kropotkin fleshed out the meaning of the Commune as a political form, projecting it into the future:

> If we analyze not only this movement in itself, but also the impression
> it left in the minds and the tendencies manifested during the communal
> revolution, we must recognize in it an indication showing that in the future
> human agglomerations which are more advanced in their social develop-
> ment will try to start an independent life; and that they will endeavor to

convert the more backward parts of a nation by example, instead of imposing their opinions by law and force, or submitting themselves to majority-
rule, which always is a mediocrity-rule. At the same time, the failure of
representative government within the Commune itself proved that self-
government and self-administration must be carried further than in a mere
territorial sense. To be effective they must also be carried into the various
functions of life within the free community.[65]

In a later work, Kropotkin proclaimed that after 1871, "The free commune would
be henceforth the medium in which the ideas of modern Socialism may come to
realization."[66] Further, in *Mutual Aid*, he traced the form which communal cooperation has taken in evolution and in history.

After 1917, he moved back to Russia. Although critical of the Bolsheviks,
he published only two short statements about the revolution, mainly aimed at
undermining the counterrevolutionary, foreign armies sent into Russia. He did,
however, indicate again support for the free commune: "All efforts to reunite
under a central control the naturally separate parts of the Russian Empire are
predestined to failure. . . . I see the time coming when each part of this federation
will be itself a federation of free communes and free cities. And I believe also that
certain parts of Western Europe will soon follow the same course."[67]

In relation to all the revolutions of his time, he established the goal of
genuine freedom as the independent commune. But how were people to accomplish this goal? What means were to be used? For Kropotkin, the answer was clear:
uprisings would prepare the ground. Uprisings and the free commune were essential to Kropotkin because he believed the people themselves must make their own
revolution—not a vanguard party or any otherwise organized small group. For
popular mobilization, nothing was more important than a central meeting place,
as for example, the Palais Royal during the French Revolution: "The Palais Royal,
with its gardens and cafes, had become an open-air club, whither ten thousand
persons of all classes went every day to exchange news, to discuss the pamphlets
of the hour, to renew among the crowd their ardor for future action, to know and
to understand one another."[68]

One example of the importance of meeting places for popular mobilization
was on June 10, 1789. After learning that eleven soldiers had been arrested and
imprisoned for refusing to load their muskets to use against the citizens of Paris,
some four thousand citizens went immediately from the Palais Royal to rescue
the soldiers. Seeing such a large force, the jailers complied, and the dragoons,
riding at full speed to stop the crowd, quickly sheathed their sabers and frater-
nized with the people.[69] Admiring the spontaneous militancy of people in the
streets, Kropotkin noted that thievery ended—that crowds in control of shops did
not loot—but only took what was necessary for their collective nourishment and
defense.[70] As the revolt spread from one city to another—from Paris to much of
France, "All Europe was moved to enthusiasm over the words and deeds of the
revolution." Kropotkin traced how the revolts unified France in ways previously
not imagined.[71]

There are three principal ways in which the Gwangju Uprising illuminates and verifies Kropotkin's framework of analysis:

1. The independent commune and free distribution of commodities
2. General assemblies at Democracy Square, not representative government, was the highest decision-making body
3. Spontaneous organization

After the Paris Commune of 1871, when similar uprisings occurred in Cartagena and Barcelona in Spain, he came close to understanding that uprisings themselves inspired others to rise up—a phenomenon I understand as the eros effect. Kropotkin noted that uprisings, while often the product of desperation, were essential to revolution: "They also rebelled—sometimes in the hope of local success—in strikes or in small revolts against some official whom they disliked, or in order to get food for their hungry children, but frequently also without any hope of success: simply because the conditions grew unbearable. Not one, or two, or tens, but *hundreds* of similar revolts have preceded *and must precede* every revolution. Without these no revolution was ever wrought."[72]

He later proclaimed uprisings to be not only the means but also the key to determining the ends of the revolution: "And it may be stated as a general rule that the character of every revolution is determined by the character and the aim of the uprisings by which it is preceded."[73]As the global revolt of 1968 prepared the ground for the epochal events of 1989 in Russia and Eastern Europe, so the Paris Commune paved the way to the Gwangju Uprising, and Gwangju for subsequent waves of insurgent movements. Today, these Communes stand as concrete embodiments of the evolving form of freedom. They continue to provide all of us with a palpable feeling for the dignity of human beings and the necessity of intensifying the struggle for liberation.

NOTES

1   Alexis de Tocqueville, *Democracy in America*, vol. 1 (New York: Colonial Press, 1899), 60–61.

2   Cornelius Castoriadis, *Political and Social Writings 1955–1960: From the Workers' Struggle Against Bureaucracy to Revolution in the Age of Modern Capitalism* (Minneapolis: University of Minnesota Press, 1988), 140.

3   Yochai Benkler, *The Wealth of Networks: How Social Production Transforms Markets and Freedom* (New Haven: Yale University Press, 2006), 60.

4   Sanjeewa Liyanage, "Gwangju, The Flame of People's Power," *International Youth Net* 1 (1996): 29.

5   For details on U.S. involvement in the suppression of the Gwangju Uprising, see the PowerPoint at my website, http://eroseffect.com/powerpoints/NeoliberalismGwangju.pdf. For a graphic comparison of Gwangju and the Paris Commune, see http://eroseffect.com/powerpoints/518ParisCommune.pdf.

6   Louise Michel, *The Red Virgin: Memoirs of Louise Michel* (Tuscaloosa: University of Alabama Press, 1981), 65.

7   Eugene Schulkind, ed., *The Paris Commune of 1871: The View from the Left* (New York: Grove Press, 1974), 152.

8   See *Asia's Unknown Uprisings Volume 1*, chap. 6.

9   Quoted in Peter Kropotkin, "The Commune of Paris" which first appeared in English as *Freedom Pamphlets* 2 (London: W. Reeves, 1895).

10   Louise Michel put the number at thirty-five thousand killed (*Red Virgin*, 67 and 168). Stewart Edwards tells us the number was twenty-five thousand (*The Communards of Paris, 1871* [Ithaca: Cornell University Press, 1973], 42). Patrick Hutton estimates twenty-five thousand were executed at the wall after the suppression of the Commune (*The Cult of the Revolutionary Tradition: The Blanquists in French Politics, 1864–1893* [Berkeley: University of California Press, 1981], 96). Roger L. Williams estimates that between seventeen and twenty thousand were killed, "many of whom had been given no quarter but simply butchered" (*The French Revolution of 1870–1871* [New York: W.W. Norton, 1969], 151). In addition, of the 46,835 cases heard in trials from 1871 to 1875, 24,000 were acquitted. Of the nearly 13,000 convictions, 110 were sentenced to death—of which 26 were actually executed (Williams, *French Revolution*, 152).

11   See Na Kahn-chae, "A New Perspective on the Gwangju People's Resistance Struggle: 1980–1997," *New Political Science* 23, no. 4 (December 2001); reprinted in *South Korean Democracy: Legacy of the Gwangju Uprising* (London: Routledge, 2006), 165–83.

12   Hutton, *The Cult*, 127.

13   Alain Plessis, *The Rise and Fall of the Second Empire 1852–1871* (Cambridge: Cambridge University Press, 1987), 69. The increases in output cited were measured in constant francs.

14   Ibid., 68, 115.

15   Edwards, *Communards of Paris*, 15.

16   Plessis, *Rise and Fall*, 96.

17   The Bank of Korea, *Year Book of Economic Statistics* (1981), 132, 142, 178–79, 206, 288.

18   Hutton, *The Cult*, 81–82.

19   Lee Jae-eui, *Gwangju Diary: Beyond Death, Beyond the Darkness of the Age* (UCLA Asian Pacific Monograph Series, 1999), 64.

20   Prosper Olivier Lissagaray, *History of the Paris Commune of 1871* (St. Petersburg, FL: Red and Black Publishers, 2007), 68–69. Originally published in 1876.

21   Schulkind, *Paris Commune*, 294.

22   Plessis estimates the number of voters at 230,000 out of 470,000 who were registered (*Rise and Fall*, 171).

23   Williams, *French Revolution*, 90, 122, 130.

24   Lissagaray, *History*, 47, 6.

25   Ibid., 177–78.

26   Ibid., 137.

27   Ibid., 171.

28   Ibid., 198–99.

29   Ibid., 80.

30   See *Asia's Unknown Uprisings Volume 1* for more details.

31   Edwards, *Communards of Paris*, 32.

32   Lissagaray, *History*, 183.

33   Hutton, *The Cult*, 30; Williams, *French Revolution*, 138.

34   Michel, *Red Virgin*, 67; Edwards, *Communards of Paris*, 40.

35   Lee, *Gwangju Diary*, 70.

36   Lissagaray, *History*, 75, 280.

37   Schulkind, *Paris Commune*, 136.

38   Interview with Kim Jang-gil, November 7, 2001.

39   Interview with Lee Yang-hyun, June 22, 2001.

40   Ibid.

41   Interview with Kim Jong-bae, November 27, 2001.

42   Interview with Kim Hyo-sok, November 6, 2001.
43   Interview with Yoon Young-kyu, April 10, 2001.
44   Interview with Jung Sang-yong, October 17, 2001.
45   Interview with Kim Sang-yoon, April 15, 2001.
46   Interview with Lee Chun-hee, December 21, 2001.
47   Interview with Kim Jang-gil, November 7, 2001.
48   Translated into English as Lee Jae-eui, *Gwangju Diary: Beyond Death, Beyond the Darkness of the Age* (UCLA Asian Pacific Monograph Series, 1999).
49   Interview with Lee Jae-eui, March 17, 2001.
50   Interview with Yoon Han-bong, October 29, 2001.
51   These preliminary remarks point in the direction of future work that could be done to further illuminate the similarities and differences between the Paris Commune and Gwangju People's Uprising. Among empirical endeavors are studies of crimes statistics before, during and after the uprisings; spatial dynamics comparing the Province Hall and Hotel de Ville in their relationship to the rest of the city; comparison of higher education and religious sectors; developing a chart of the authority structures of the Paris Commune to compare with Gwangju; a fuller comparison of Paris in 1870 and Gwangju in 1980; and documents' comparison.
52   Zhang, *Tiananmen Papers*, 236.
53   See W.J. Fishman, *The Insurrectionists* (London: Methuen and Co., 1970).
54   See *Asia's Unknown Uprisings Volume 1*, chap. 1.
55   Peter Kropotkin, *Memoirs of a Revolutionist*, (New York: Dover Publications, 1971), 418.
56   See for example, Kropotkin, *Memoirs*, 282.
57   Ibid., 419.
58   *The Great French Revolution* (New York: Vanguard Press, 1929), 313.
59   Ibid., 532.
60   See, for example, *The Conquest of Bread*, (London: Chapman and Hal, 1906), 44, 213–14.
61   "Anarchist Communism" in *Kropotkin's Revolutionary Pamphlets*, ed. Roger Baldwin (New York: Dover Publications, 1970), 68.
62   Ibid., 52.
63   "Modern Science and Anarchism," in *Kropotkin's Revolutionary Pamphlets*, ed. Roger Baldwin (New York: Dover Publications, 1970), 164.
64   Ibid., 163. Italics in the original.
65   "Anarchist Communism," 51–52.
66   Page xiv of the 1906 preface to *The Conquest of Bread*.
67   "Letter to the Workers of Western Europe," *Kropotkin's Revolutionary Pamphlets*, ed. Roger Baldwin (New York: Dover Publications, 1970), 254. Originally published in English July 20, 1920.
68   *The Great French Revolution*, 61.
69   Ibid., 69.
70   Ibid., 75, 106.
71   Ibid., 95, 177.
72   "Modern Science and Anarchism," 190. Italics in the original.
73   Ibid., 191.

CHAPTER 13

Organizations and Movements

We, the artists, will serve as the avant-garde: for amongst all the arms at our disposal, the power of the Arts is the swiftest and most expeditious. When we wish to spread new ideas amongst men, we use in turn the lyre, ode or song, story or novel; we inscribe those ideas on marble or canvas. . . . We aim for the heart and imagination, and hence our effect is the most vivid and the most decisive.
—Henri de Saint-Simon

The autonomy of art reflects the unfreedom of individuals in the unfree society. If people were free, then art would be the form and expression of their freedom.
—Herbert Marcuse

WITH GROWING INTERNATIONAL recognition by ordinary people of their capacity to flood the streets in order to effect political change, the ability of organizations and groups to spark popular uprisings is of no small interest. The considerable impact of social media in catalyzing the Arab Spring has accorded them considerable praise (or blame, depending on one's perspective), even to the point of ascribing to them the principal explanation for uprisings. Optimistic readings of Facebook, YouTube, and Twitter confuse resources that may help mobilize the populace with the real driving force of contemporary social movements— people's self-understanding that history is, to some large degree, of their own making. Without this consciousness, the social media are shells of interaction whose content devolves to the level of disembodied personalized networking. In the context of an activated populace, social media strengthen links between imagination and action, and create public space more real than the vacuity of many American cities.

Uprisings enrich our understanding of the possibilities of revolutionary change—and of the obstacles to it. They break out with unexpected speed and proliferate rapidly once the eros effect is activated. The acceleration of this dynamic is conditioned by past experiences. Lubricated by the social media, people's intuitive impulse to act becomes ever more immediate. While the bureaucratic Left argues for centralized parties, experiences indicate time and again their betrayal of popular movements. Like no one else, groups inside the movement have the capacity to frustrate citizens' radical aspirations.

What is most important during crises (and in preparation for them) is for activists to give the populace self-confidence in their capacity for self-governance, to construct spaces for self-rule, and to strengthen the organs of popular power, especially general assemblies. Even when the military is called out to occupy public space, what is most urgent is to build the Commune, if not in physical space then in virtual realities, in cyberspace or civil society. Contemporary forms of avant-garde revolutionary organizations empower people directly, making even more insightful Rosa Luxemburg's belief that, "Historically, the errors committed by a truly revolutionary movement are infinitely more fruitful than the infallibility of the cleverest Central Committee."

During moments of political crisis, small groups can wield enormous influence, as with Facebook partisans in Egypt and Action-Committees in May 1968 in France. Unlike vanguard parties, decentralized avant-garde groups develop according to a grammar of autonomy, equality, decommodification, and solidarity ("eros effect"). Direct-democratic forms of decision-making and militant popular resistance are intimately woven together within movements based upon self-organization.

Normally considered outside the realm of politics, the world of art provides robust forms of accomplishing long-lasting transformations of consciousness. In the struggle to create human beings freed from narrow limits of perception, Cubism, Dada, and Surrealism have contributed mightily. Although each began with a tiny number of practitioners, they eventually had wide cultural impact, ultimately challenging and altering the form of aesthetic expression—a precursor of alternative political and economic domains. In this chapter, my focus is the capacity of groups to lead movements and transform consciousness. For future revolutionaries, artists' movements like Dada and Surrealism might be better models than vanguard parties.

Aesthetic Avant-Gardes

For most of the twentieth century, the term "avant-garde" was widely used to define groups that forged new dimensions in perceptions and relationships in the world of art. Yet the term originated at the intersection of art and politics, and it is there that its most explosive interpretations can be found. While many people recognize labor as a species-constitutive action, revolution and art are also means through which the species builds itself from naturally given existence to social being. At its best, art is a form of production entirely controlled and managed by its producers.

What is called "avant-garde art" today is often completely depoliticized, a facet of modernist discourse through which "aesthetic" concerns replace spiritual and religious structuring of emotional experience with a secular equivalent: "art." Depoliticization of the concept of the avant-garde is part of the process through which art has become a commodity (for sale on the art market), a fate suffered by all human relationships in capitalist society. Soviet Marxism stridently attacked "avant-gardism" as "saturated with capitalist and petty bourgeois individualism" and simultaneously reified social realism, turning art into a means of glorifying the party and the state.[1]

Within avant-garde movements from nineteenth-century France to the contemporary period, considerable tension between political and aesthetic domains related to avant-garde praxis is evident.[2] Over the last two centuries, groups seeking to transform aesthetics and politics have sometimes been entwined together in complementary relationships, and at other moments in separate and even antagonistic strands. In the nineteenth century, when the term "avant-garde" was first used in relation to artistic movements (i.e., before both Soviet communism and the "modernist" period), such movements were thought to be forces that would propel society forward, and not simply within the realm of aesthetics.

The notion of an avant-garde emerged in France from the intersection of the milieu of revolutionary politics and opposition to art's domination by the Academy. In 1825, Henri de Saint-Simon is thought to have made the first use of "avant-garde" in his book *Literary, Philosophical and Industrial Opinions*.[3] Painters such as Gustave Courbet, Honoré Daumier, and Jean François Millet were some of the earliest advocates of the idea that art could play an emancipatory role in society. Courbet's monumental canvas, *The Stonebreakers*, painted in 1849—one year after the failure of continent-wide revolutionary movements—centrally portrayed ordinary workers, not the wealthy or powerful.[4] During the Paris Commune, Courbet was one of the chief organizers of the Federation of Artists and helped carry out the destruction of the Place Vendôme column originally erected to honor Napoleon's battlefield victories. Although he survived the slaughter during the "Bloody Week" at the end of the Commune, Courbet was imprisoned and his work barred from exhibition. Financially ruined, he went into exile in Switzerland, where he died a few years later.

Although largely absent from French art in this period, the defining event of that epoch was the Paris Commune's bloody suppression at the cost of more than fifteen thousand lives. We are well familiar with the gay Parisian scenes painted after the Commune by Toulouse-Lautrec, Monet, Renoir, and Degas, images highly valued in today's art market. Painters of the pleasures of Paris in the period after the Commune call on us to enjoy ourselves in the midst of barbarism—despite all the insanity around us. In this transitional period, Impressionism arose as the defining genre of art despite being initially regarded as scandalous. (The French legislature even considered a bill to bar public funds from helping its exhibitions.) Impressionism evokes memories of a belle époque before dwellers of twentieth-century cities turned inward because of crime, prior to automobiles' deleterious effects on the urban landscape and industries making waste of Nature.

Impressionism's sensuous play with light and color provides immediate satisfaction of the senses, and its contemporary popularity can be understood by locating its context in a society based on consumerism and individual gain.

An alternative stream of artistic production that emanated from France after the Commune can be located in the paintings of Édouard Manet. Although his most famous painting, *Le Déjeuner sur l'herbe*, is often regarded as a portrayal of gay Parisian life, a different reading is possible: Manet painted the woman in the foreground staring directly at the viewer, thereby giving her a subjectivity normally reserved for men. Commonly understood as an early modernist, Manet's canvases contain more social content than immediately apparent. In *Rue Mosnier with Flags* (1878), the urban landscape is almost deserted. In the foreground, a one-legged man with his back to the viewer makes his way on crutches up a colorless street. French flags hang eerily overhead, as much a menacing accoutrement as patriotic celebration. By contrast, Claude Monet's *Rue Montorgueil, Festival of 30 June 1878* renders Paris after the Commune as a gallant and happy nation, crowded by a patriotic procession and countless flags, including one miraculously fluttering in midair in the very center of the painting. Seldom mentioned in the art world's valorization of Manet is his service in the Parisian National Guard during the Commune, no doubt a crucial factor in his subsequent compositions of *The Barricade* and *Civil War* (both from 1871).

Camille Pissarro, Paul Signac, and self-described anarchist painters among the Postimpressionists sought to integrate artistic and political concerns. For Signac in particular, it was radical techniques like pointillism through which artists "contributed their witness to the great social process which pits the workers against Capital." Signac inveighed against the reduction of radical art to its content (as advocated by political activists like Proudhon), arguing instead that the revolution "will be found much stronger and more eloquent in pure aesthetics . . . applied to subjects like working-class housing . . . or better still, by synthetically representing the pleasures of decadence."[5] At a moment when history denied the possibility of social engagement, artists like Signac propagated new ways of seeing as a means to continue the project to restructure the social world.

Despite hundreds of volumes of art history, the role of anarchists in creating avant-garde is seldom mentioned. Among many others, Picasso emerged from the anarchist circles of Barcelona, whose sister free spirits in Paris gave him refuge in Montmartre after fascism had subjugated Spain. So connected were anarchism and art that in 1908, British writer G.K. Chesterton observed, "an artist is identical with an anarchist."[6] Whether one considers the *Fauves* ('the wild beasts'), who exhibited at the Salon of Autonomy in 1905, or the "anarchic threat to cultural values"[7] posed by the ostensibly nonpolitical work of Henri Matisse (whose Blue Nude was burned in effigy by students at the Art Institute of Chicago in 1913), the political threat posed by avant-garde art was considered quite real.

Of utmost significance in this regard is Cubism, which radically deconstructed the one-point scientific perspective that had dominated European art for over five hundred years. Cubism invented a cerebral art that eclipsed Impressionism's preoccupation with the tactile world of sensory delight, thereby providing a significant example of how artists are able to transform the grammar of visual expression and consciousness. Like Impressionism, Cubism was initially greeted with shock and abhorrence. One must think in order to understand cubist art, a development that liberated composition from the realm of the senses. Picasso's *Les Demoiselles d'Avignon* is today regarded as one of the greatest paintings of the first half of the twentieth century, yet Picasso himself was so afraid of what he had produced that he kept it hidden for years in his bedroom closet. Looking back at Cubism nearly a century after its inception, we can see that its impact has continued to spread. Is there a logic to this process of changing consciousness that political movements can appropriate?

After the carnage of World War I had decimated Europe and revealed the barbarism of its political institutions, art turned against the orderly mentality that had produced such bloody results. With Dada came the ultimate revolt against bourgeois orderliness. Play, randomness, chaos, and spontaneity become enshrined as the avant-garde's new core values. Instead of being confined to the canvas, Dada used all available media to express its repulsion with the "civilized barbarism" of European culture: collage, music, film, photography, sculpture—and these media were turned against themselves. "Down with Art!" they screamed. "Dada is on the side of the revolutionary Proletariat." They called for destruction of the "aggressive complete madness of a world abandoned to the hands of bandits."[8] As the movement spread throughout Europe, it was increasingly intertwined with radical communism, at one point being called "German Bolshevism."

During the Russian revolution and the civil war that followed on its heels, the new language of abstract art was mobilized in the struggle to defeat the counterrevolution. Closer to engineering than to any other avant-garde form of art, Constructivism emerged as an artistic movement aligned with the building of a new society. It was undermined from two different sources. On the one side, its transmutation into the Bauhaus idea of "form following function" reduced it to a purely utilitarian endeavor, sanctioned by authorities as the revolution was consolidated—or turned into its opposite. As the Soviet Union's initial revolutionary impetus, so vibrant in the first decade of the revolution, turned into counterrevolution and old Bolsheviks were liquidated in Stalinist purges, social realism became the only acceptable form of art. Soviet authorities condemned all forms of avant-gardism. In 1932, all autonomous arts groups were legally dissolved, and a repressive system of censorship reigned supreme.

In the capitalist West, Surrealists negated the anti-individualism of Dada, although here too, radical political thought informed their aesthetics. The first Surrealist journal was *The Surrealist Revolution* and the second, *Surrealism in the Service of the Revolution*. Strongly affected by Freud's discovery of the continent of the unconscious, the Surrealists painted dreams and fantasy as a means of distancing themselves from consumerist cultural commodification and conventional notions of personal identity. Like Surrealism, Dada and Constructivism attempted to integrate aesthetic innovation with a radical critique of the social order. They sought "the destruction of art as an institution set off from the praxis of life"—a break with "high modernism." Emerging from within circles of revolutionary activists, Dada, Surrealism, and Constructivism were able to reinvigorate the relationship between political engagement and aesthetic innovation.

With Pop Art, Minimalism, Abstract Expressionism, and Action Painting, the distance between aesthetic formalism and political engagement widened. The prices offered for such paintings on the New York art market after World War II soared. Seldom did art that had anything to do with overtly radical themes fetch dealers' attention. Comparing the aesthetic and political engagement of Dada, Surrealism, Constructivism, and Futurism (in both its right-wing Italian and left-wing Russian versions) with the consumerist appeal of post-1945 New York art provides striking evidence of the colonization of both imagination and art by advanced capitalism.

At a time when consumerism envelops the continent of Desire and weapons of mass destruction destroy the foundations of the Beautiful, art's own autonomous logic might be its salvation. The resolution of this apparent contradiction is the understanding that within art's formal aesthetics, a truth is contained that transforms society. For Marcuse, "Art can express its radical potential only *as art*, in its own language and image. . . . The liberating 'message' of art . . . is likely to persist until the millennium which will never be, art must remain *alienation*. . . . Art cannot represent the revolution, it can only invoke it in another medium, in an aesthetic form in which the political content becomes *meta*political, governed by the internal necessity of art."[9]

The call for art to obey the dictates of the political struggle would mean "the imagination has become wholly functional: servant to instrumentalist Reason."[10] Especially in an era when the system delivers the goods so that people live to work in order to buy into consumerism, art's role may even become that of "An Enemy of the People" as it seeks to change the world.[11]

Political Avant-Gardes

While revolutionary political organizations are commonly regarded as qualitatively different from aesthetic movements, the very success of contemporary consumerism has created the preconditions for the aestheticization of everyday life. As Marcuse posed the contradiction, "The autonomy of art reflects the unfreedom of individuals in the unfree society. If people were free, then art would be the form and expression of their freedom."[12]

As artists distanced themselves from overtly political concerns, movement activists after World War II simultaneously became autonomous of political parties and integrated dimensions of artistic avant-gardes into their practical attempts to transform everyday life. Originating with modernist musicians who breathed fresh life into Dadaist notions of indeterminacy and chance, Fluxus reinvigorated the art world at the same moment as it breathed life into political groups like the Provos, the Orange Free State, and Kabouters in Holland, the Situationists in France, Subversive Aktion in Germany, and the Diggers and Yippies in the United States. In many countries, politically engaged groups used the streets of major cities to paint on the canvas of everyday life. Seeking to transform the grammar of people's existence and to change the aesthetic form of life, Yippies threw money onto the floor of the New York Stock Exchange, a Dadaist action par excellence that not only succeeded in halting trading as brokers scurried for dollar bills but also brought wide publicity to young people's rejection of the rat race. By running a pig for U.S. President in 1968, Yippies forever changed the calculus of politicians' images, not only in the United States. As Stew Albert recalled, the Yippies bathed in the global counterculture of the 1960s:

> In 1971 in Germany, Jerry Rubin, Phil Ochs and I hung out with Daniel Cohn-Bendit for a few days. Very friendly. He loved the fact that I had run for sheriff and kept pretending we were all in a Western. Kabouters? We did spend a few days with them and Indonesian grass in Amsterdam. They were talking about creating an Orange Free State—sort of their Woodstock Nation. Jerry and I were influenced by the Provos.
>
> The Yippies had many other influences, ranging from *Mad* magazine, Artaud, Jean Shepherd, and *Dr. Strangelove* to Dada and Surrealism. We had a sense of putting things together, arranging them in unusual and illogical ways, to shock, get attention, and make points.
>
> We realized that TV had become an extension of consciousness—was now part of the communal human brain. Our object was to create images (throwing money at millionaire stock brokers, running a pig for president) so different and entertaining that they would be shown on television and overthrow addicted patterns of mass thought. We turned the streets and its objects into unbounded outdoor props for the creation of TV images.[13]

Yippies helped inspire the notion that small direct actions might be more appropriate vehicles for the transformation of modern societies than political parties. In May 1968 when a student rebellion spread throughout France, a small group of older activists suddenly occupied the Sorbonne, thereby creating a central meeting place for the movement as well as a place where workers could come to join. The liberated Sorbonne became a direct democratic forum where people from different occupations and classes spoke freely. Soon ten million workers were on strike and France was on the brink of revolution. This is one example that we can point to in the late twentieth century when small-group avant-garde actions instigated larger shifts and movements.

Besides being a model for strategic action, art can also provide tactical innovations. At the World Bank protests in 2000 in Washington, D.C., where riot police in full battle gear lined up and prepared to disperse thousands of protesters who refused to obey their orders to leave, someone in the crowd had the presence to turn on a boom box at full volume and play the theme from *Star Wars*. At that moment, no better vehicle could have been used to disarm the riot police, who stepped back and laughed at their own inane attire.

Artists are also central figures in the construction of identity of movements—particularly during insurgencies' occupation of public space. In liberated Gwangju, members of Clown theater group (Kwangdae) took the lead in organizing and stage-managing the daily rallies. Artists like Hong Sung-dam created wood-block prints that came to represent the movement's aspirations. In Tiananmen Square, art students created a Goddess of Democracy, the most enduring symbol of the uprising. A diverse group of artists have turned more than a hundred miles of the illegal wall Israel built to cordon off and annex Palestinian lands into a giant gallery space to register their opposition.[14]

As Marx expected the dull discipline of factory life to help shape the emancipatory proletariat, so we can observe today that consumer society's spectacles, like the Olympics and World Cup (despite the nationalist wrappings in which they are packaged) help craft an international identity of humanity. Around the world, people identify more closely with each other than ever before. Diffusion of uprisings via the eros effect is one robust indication of such a universal identity and so is the reproduction of tactical innovations across borders. An approach to demonstrations that became realized globally in the late twentieth century was the Black Bloc (BB), a militant alternative to both parliamentary and guerrilla tactics. At key demonstrations, activists disguised themselves by wearing black, formed radical contingents, and attacked targets that clearly indicated the movement's message. From confronting U.S. President Reagan's visit to Berlin (when the United States escalated the nuclear arms race) to helping defeat the Wackersdorf nuclear reprocessing plant in Southern Germany (which would have provided Germany with weapons grade plutonium), the BB opened resistance to the rottenness of the existing global system *as a whole*. The conscious spontaneity of the Black Bloc relied on popular participation and people taking to the streets, not on the armed actions of a handful of people.

A continuing series of confronting illegitimate power brought cycles of ever-larger mobilizations, a vital dimensions of awakening popular upheavals. While academic and professional activists emphasize organizational efforts and resource accumulation as central to movement building, confrontation politics unleashes popular will and imagination like nothing else. The international networks forged in the crucible of street actions and confrontations in the 1980s became the seeds of the alter-globalization movement and opposition to the control of humanity's wealth by giant transnational corporations. The spontaneous agglomeration of activists from many language groups and cultures at international protests were all means of constructing a global civil society. The forging of political identity in moments of confrontation politics indicated vitality in the creation of long-lasting social movements. The fact that so many youth became activated over many decades shows confrontation politics' tactical resonance, its capacity to renew protests from generation to generation.

Militant street confrontations are a crucible of psychic reworking of needs and desires, a theatre of reality with enormous transformative value. After Genoa, one Black Bloc participant told me his experiences "changed me more in a few days than in the preceding years of meetings." Another person called it the "most important experience" of her life. If we accept that consumer culture is a form of colonization, then the Black Bloc's destruction of McDonald's, Nike outlets, and banks are a concrete decolonization—a freeing of space from corporate control and creation of autonomous zones not controlled by the police. As Fanon long ago discovered, violence plays an essential role in decolonization movements. The controlled violence of the Black Bloc is not only a psychic reworking of individuals in the streets, it is a moment of opposition to the system as a whole. By making concrete people's desires to be free, decades of deadening consumerism and debilitating comfort can be thrown off overnight. By calling into question the reasonability of the existing global system, militant confrontations can have significant long-term impact.

Despite the subversive character of militant actions, they can rapidly lose their relevance when frozen into ritualized repetition of once vibrant actions. Even previously vibrant groups like the Situationists, for example, when frozen into ideological sects, evoke nostalgia more than movement. As Jacques Rancière observed, "The trajectory of Situationist discourse—stemming from an avant-garde artistic movement in the post-war period, developing into a radical critique of politics in the 1960s, and absorbed today into the routine of the disenchanted discourse that acts as the 'critical' stand-in for the existing order—is undoubtedly symptomatic of the contemporary ebb and flow of aesthetics and politics, and of the transformation of avant-garde thinking into nostalgia."[15] Combined with the problem of ritualization of militancy, the BB was also heavily infiltrated by police, whose agent provocateurs attacked protesters, making it appear that demonstrators were turning against each other.

Middle-class elements within the movement scandalously vilified militancy of all varieties. Bifurcation of demonstrations into militant street confrontations alongside large, peaceful protests is a reflection of contemporary movements' diversity, of the autonomy and variety of groups who combine themselves into protests against commonly perceived problems. Yet some groups seek to impose monolithic control. Some "pacifists" imposed "discipline" in Seattle in 1999 by physically restraining and unmasking more militant protesters (even helping police to arrest them). A better example of vibrant diversity can be located in 2000, when the alter-globalization movement gathered in Prague for protests at a summit of the World Bank and IMF. Unity of a diverse range of tactics reached a high point with color-coded contingents that converged in different parts of the city. Many bankers were unable to get through the crowded streets to reach their convention, and the meetings had to adjourn early. Diversity and improvisation within the movement were key to sparking the successful resistance. Clearly, no one tactic or organization is the solution—nor the problem—despite the black-white lines often laid down on all sides.

Uprisings 2.0: Building the Virtual Commune
Building waves of popular protests should not simply be understood as a question of will. Historical developments and the system's power as an alien force out of human control precondition possibilities for action. We may not be able to make the future according to conditions of our own choosing, but we do have choices in key moments, as is clear during recent uprisings. In Latin America as well as Asia, the wisdom of crowds has been an ascending dynamic during protests. In 2001, after economic crisis struck like a thunderbolt, and overnight, Argentina's

economy collapsed, autonomous grassroots mobilizations were visionary. As during subsequent candlelight protests in South Korea in 2008, people tolerated no leaders: "The few political leaders who tried to join the crowd were rejected."[16] People refused to submit to IMF/World Bank impoverishment, and they mobilized to sweep out collaborationist presidents. Self-managed workers' councils and forms of direct democracy blossomed all over the country. Such participatory forms of governance—similar to those revealed in Asian uprisings—are significant indications of people's capacity and yearning for direct democracy. Demanding jobs, food, and education, young *piqueteros* organized street blockades. Insisting they would not send representatives to negotiate with the government, they demanded that all decisions occur at roadblocks so that everyone could participate. On June 26, 2002, the government warned it would tolerate no more blockades, and thousands of people mobilized—as did hundreds of police. Using pickup trucks and rifles, police hunted *piqueteros* throughout Buenos Aires, wounding over a hundred people and arresting at least 160 others.[17] Workers took over factories, hotels, and offices and ran them more productively than capitalists were able to do. Hundreds of popular neighborhood assemblies formed and held weekly meetings to determine future actions and policies.

Similar dynamics emerged in Mexico in 2006. What began as a teachers' strike led to the liberation of Oaxaca—and government assaults against it. After teachers demanded such outrageous items as shoes for their pupils, they drew in the city's populace, long angered by marginalization of Oaxaca at the hands of elected governments in Mexico City. A grassroots epicenter, APPO (Popular Assembly of the Peoples of Oaxaca), grew from the continuing mobilization of citizens fighting for control of their city. As the struggle matured, they declared APPO the governing authority. A popular, participatory council became the city's de facto government for months—the same direct-democratic communal form as in Gwangju. Despite a bitter struggle marked by murders and ongoing physical attacks by thousands of police that recaptured the city, APPO continues to resist—although its influence is greatly reduced.

From the Zapatistas to the communards of Arequipa (Peru), people's daily lives are being bettered in Latin America through ballots, protests, and all kinds of political activism—including elections and popular insurrections. In Venezuela, "All Power to the People!", a slogan coined by the Black Panther Party, is used by Chávez's Bolivarian government to encourage popular action from below. The Chávez government has instituted a Bank of the South, whose goal is to dislodge the IMF and WB's predatory hold on the region's economies. They nearly paid off Venezuela's entire foreign debt and lent other countries vast sums at reasonable rates of interest to get global institutions off their backs. They sent oil to Cuba in exchange for medical specialists, and as a result, many people in Venezuela have seen doctors for the first times in their lives. Although this movement owes much to Chávez, it is not confined to him or to Venezuela. In Bolivia and Ecuador, elected leaders reflect the grassroots movements' widening base. Latin American social movements promised to thoroughly undermine centuries-old relations of dependency and hierarchy. As popular mobilizations intensified, center-left regimes arose, which then contained and dissipated movements in the streets. Soon thereafter, indications of residual popular gains were diminished, while the region's traditional forms of subservience, such as its role as commodities exporter and subservience to elite rule, began to be restored.[18] Nonetheless, because these movements are not composed of a single leader or party, they continue to animate grassroots change. Roger Burbach was one of the first to portray their extraparliamentary base: "the new model of state transformation in South America is rooted in building a broad political coalition based on a complex mixture of progressive social actors and movements. The very role of political parties in this process is the subject of intense debate. Many reject the centrality of parties, arguing that they are inherently hierarchical (and often patriarchal) and thus antithetical to authentic popular participation. Others assert that 'parties of a new type' are needed, like Bolivia's Movement Toward Socialism, which defines itself as a 'party of social movements.'"[19]

Such massive outpourings of self-conscious autonomy are not confined to Latin America. From South Korea in 2008 to the Arab Spring in 2011, demonstrators used decentralized organizations as well as the Internet, especially Facebook, to organize and aid each other. Tunisians posted phone numbers to call if hurt by police so other activists could come help, and the locations of police formations were uploaded in real time so activists would know which areas to avoid. Wherever alternative perspectives are denied access to mainstream media, the Internet has become an invaluable means of mobilization and information (at least until the authorities choose to shut it down). "Smart crowds" use cell phones even more efficiently for real-time mobilizations.

As we've seen, Thai protesters in 1992 adapted cell phones, and Chinese students in 1989 used a portable fax system to communicate. In the Philippines in January 2001, text messaging helped mobilize millions of people and depose president Joseph Estrada. Burmese activists in 2007 adopted videophones and blogs to communicate with the outside world. Moldova's youth in 2009 employed new communications technologies to gather together. In fact, Natalia Morar, one of the initiators of ThinkMoldova, characterized the organizations behind the first protest of fifteen thousand people as "six people, ten minutes for brainstorming and decision-making, several hours of disseminating information through networks, Facebook, blogs, SMSs, and e-mails." Using Twitter and Facebook to tell people to recongregate the following morning, thousands again mobilized, but this time, fights with police broke out and government buildings were attacked. After 193 arrests, Twitter carried hundreds of stories of the protests. The government promptly shut down the Internet.[20]

Looking at the "candlelight revolution" in Korea—the wave of protests in 2008 against newly elected conservative president Lee Myung-bak and U.S. beef—we can observe similarly innovative forms of organization and action: open mikes at rallies that brought participants from all walks of life, rotation of leadership, and emergence of new sectors of the population (middle school girls and female netizens who initiated and led the protests in their early stages). Widely appreciated among Koreans were the "festival-like" atmosphere and "leaderless" movement. By dubbing the president "2 Megabyte" (a play on his initials), teenage girls humorously altered the country's lexicon and the political standing of its most powerful politician. An article in Hangyoreh newspaper caught the sense of the uprising: "Seoul Plaza became a venue of a festival filled with games, satires and laughter. . . . Solemn resistance toward the government has disappeared and anger has been channeled into satires. Families, college students, and company workers who took part in the 'festival' became one even if they didn't know each other. . . . New friendships between citizens became cemented through the sharing of food."[21]

Numbers of people in the streets skyrocketed, and the police response was to attempt to cut off the protests. Police buses and cargo containers were suddenly piled into enormous blockades of key streets. Immediately, someone posted an on-line request for rope to pull the buses aside, and within minutes, rope arrived, people pulled aside the blockades, and the crowd surged forward. As high school students handed roses to riot police, couples were making dates to meet at the protests. When the conservative media fanned the flames of protesters' "violent" tendencies and distorted beyond recognition the protests' overwhelmingly peaceful character, netizens began to broadcast their own accounts of "Protests 2.0." Without anyone authorizing them to do so, "embedded" citizens turned into journalists by adapting their own laptops to broadcast real-time reports, while hundreds of others blogged and chatted. Using YouTube to post reports, activist websites also sprang up, as many people did what Hans Enzensberger had advocated decades earlier—turn every receiver into a sender. Soon mainstream media began to quote netizens.[22] By June 10, 2008—the anniversary of the June 1987 Uprising—so many people gathered that it became the largest demonstration in Korean history.[23] The mini-TV stations that emerged in both Seoul's citizen journalists during the candlelight protests had parallels in Burma's brave reporters who risked their lives to smuggle out video footage, photos, and accounts of their uprising in 2007.

The diversity and proliferation of websites and Internet communications contributes to movements' decentralization and rejection of ideological uniformity. In this sense, the social media indicate a reduced need for a "conscious element" over and above the people. Social media are a resource to multiply collective intelligence; they are tools for participatory democracy that catalyze grassroots participation and control. Collective intelligence of Web users has helped make people aware of newfound popular power. Korean protesters' capacity to rename the president as 2MB is but one indication of how people can use irony and playful criticism to transcend powers-that-be. By connecting us to each other in new and yet to be colonized ways, new technologies help form unsupervised collectivities whose intelligence and capacity for direct action reshape the phenomenal forms of insurgencies.

The problematic of avant-garde groups is not to lead the people but to preserve their energies and spark imaginations. Looking at the uprisings in East Asia, that insight is gleaned by comparison between Gwangju and Burma: decentralized grassroots insurgencies have greater impact than top-down ones. The weakness of centralized leadership, especially when based upon charismatic single leaders, is all too evident in the crushing defeat endured by generations of Burmese since 1988.[24] People today know they are more intelligent than rulers of any kind, whether self-appointed or democratically elected. In South Korea, one of the world's most wired societies, netizens have played a huge role in the country's political life. The promise of direct democracy using the Internet is widely discussed:

> The ideal of electronic democracy that they predicted was to achieve essential participatory democracy in which all citizens take part freely and equally, instead of an elite-led representative democracy. In electronic democracy, citizens do not stick to the traditional participation method of selecting their representative through elections. They prefer direct participation in their daily lives to indirect participation through political mediums such as parties, votes, or interest groups. The model of political participation has changed from group-based to network-based individuals, and from indirect participation focused on election of representatives to direct participation that comprises the establishment of agenda, mobilization of public opinion, and decision-making. This direct everyday political participation method has presented the possibility of 'rule by the people,' which is the core of the democratic political system.[25]

Modern technology can facilitate deliberative democracy and autonomy on scales never before possible. Years ago, Paul Mattick argued convincingly that popular citizens' councils need to control production—not a national state or even workers' self-management. More than ever before in history, it is possible—and even necessary—for all people to decide what to produce in a free society.

The Role of NGOs

Even when unsuccessful, uprisings stimulate the formation of new groups and spark people's desire for greater freedoms. In every case discussed in this book, a mushrooming of NGOs, civic organizations, autonomous media, and other institutions of civil society transpired in the afterglow of the popular insurgency. Because an aura of progressive activism often encapsulates them, many key personnel of NGOs have been lured from poorly paid and risky social movement activism into the well-heeled world of professional management of subaltern needs. Paid by their benefactors to live at the standards of prosperity enjoyed by the majority in the industrialized North, former activists become alienated from their social bases and aligned instead with international elites who need indigenous allies to assist them in controlling potential opposition groups.[26] U.S. agencies have funded NGOs in targeted countries to build indigenous leadership strata friendly to U.S. interests and willing to serve as sub-elites in a global corporate system. As James Davis quipped, "NGOs are to imperialism what artist bohemians are to urban gentrification."[27]

Officially recognized as nongovernmental organizations (NGOs) when the UN formed in 1945 and wanted to include consultants that were neither member states nor governments, NGOs today are neither small in number nor marginal in influence. The first major surge in their numbers took place after the global revolt of 1968. In 1985, the *Yearbook of International Organizations* noted the existence of 7,109 NGOs.[28] Writing in 1999, James Petras counted more than 50,000 NGOs in the Third World alone that received at least $10 billion from global financial institutions.[29] Another estimate a year later uncovered two million NGOs in the United States and more than one million "grassroots groups" in India. Between 1988 and 1995, about 100,000 NGOs were initiated in Eastern Europe. According to the Red Cross, the world's NGOs in 2000 "disburse more money than the World Bank."[30]

Internationally, there has been enormous growth in the number of NGOs. To give numbers for just one domain in the past decades, a phenomenal growth of more than 500 percent in international NGOs (INGOs) has occurred, as revealed in TABLE 13.1. The below numbers are minimal ones. *The Economist* guessed the number of INGOs at 26,000 in 1996 (up from 6,000 in 1990), and the UN put the figure at 37,000 INGOs in 2002.[31]

Made glamorous by pop star Bono, NGOs follow in the historic footsteps of missionaries whose function was to work with the established imperial system to soften native resistance. Just as trade unions became vehicles for delivering a compliant working class to corporations, NGOs provide a mechanism for mitigating the system's worst excesses—or appearing to do so. After neoliberalism uprooted vestiges of the welfare state, NGOs have become a way to privatize the delivery of social services. According to *The Economist*, "The principle reason for the recent boom in NGOs is that Western governments finance them. This is not a matter of charity but of privatization."[32] As governments and business increasingly intervened in global civil society, NGOs became instruments for their penetration of the formerly autonomous sphere that unfolded from citizens' movements. During the 1990s, corporate giving doubled to nearly $385 billion.[33] The World Bank has aggressively pursued NGOs participation through a network led by over eighty Civil Society Country Staff, and the World Trade Organization's 1994 Marrakesh Agreement opened the door for "consultation and cooperation with NGOs."[34]

Once "cronies" have been overthrown and replaced by more "efficiently" functioning global banks and corporations, NGOs play a vital role in privatizing subaltern needs and thereby demobilizing resistance movements. By incorporating progressive activists into his administration, for example, progressive Korean president Noh Moo-hyun dampened street protests, and activist memberships

TABLE 13.1 **Number of Transnational Social Movement Organizations, 1973–2003**

Year	Number
1973	183
1983	348
1993	711
2000	959
2003	1011

Source: Jackie Smith and Hank Johnston, eds., *Globalization and Resistance: Transnational Dimensions of Social Movements* (Lanham: Rowman and Littlefield, 2003), 32.

in progressive organizations plummeted. With the conservatives back in power, protests were renewed and resistance again regained vitality. Compared to dictatorships, democratic governments, like countercultural spaces, also contain greater freedoms and new opportunities for subaltern groups—for women, for minorities, for gays, and for youth. Popular victories in achieving democracy in Korea, ending apartheid in South Africa, mitigating U.S. racism and sexism, and promoting expanded rights for subaltern people all create the staging grounds for professional activists to advance their careers. More often than not, professional activists and specialized groups have the effect of dampening systematic challenges, not only because of the material rewards received by self-proclaimed leaders from international funding, but through the framing of people's needs into manageable reformist avenues. Popular intuition of the need to forge a new international civil society that can delegitimize militarized nation-states and socialize predatory transnational corporations is contradicted by the logic of NGOs professionals who insist that the system is working. Professional activists may speak a language of fundamental change, but as Immanuel Wallerstein reminds us, they use "slogans that emerged from antisystemic movements—a green universe, a multicultural utopia, opportunities for all—while preserving a polarized and unequal system."[35]

Returning from international conferences where they rub shoulders with members of the global elite, NGO activists encourage accommodation with neoliberalism as they talk the language of "progress" and "enlightenment" in phrases like "sustainable development" and "gender equality." Seldom are internationally funded NGOs democratically structured; even more rare is for them to oppose corporate globalization. By reinforcing fragmentation of subaltern groups, NGOs often become obstacles to clear-sighted critiques of the whole system. They are often means of co-opting insurgencies into the existing system, of channeling radical desires into reformist results.

In this context, the term "civil society" has become a means of obscuring class divisions, a cover for international capital and its institutions like the WB and WTO to infiltrate and utilize grassroots energies for their own ends. As James Petras found, although NGOs cultivate a public image of themselves as a "Third Way between authoritarian statism and savage market capitalism," they are far from their claim to be the "vanguard of civil society." Rather, NGOs often obscure inequalities that are more profound today than ever. As Petras reminds us, "Most of the greatest injustices against workers are committed by the wealthy bankers in civil society who squeeze out exorbitant interest payments on internal debt; landlords who throw peasants off the land and industrial capitalists who exhaust workers at starvation wages in sweatshops."[36]

Lest anyone doubt the potential power of such organized small groups, let's consider how the CIA and international investor George Soros have used them.

NGOs and the Changing Character of U.S. Intervention
The relationship of the United States to the wave of democratic insurgencies is a topic scarcely revealed in existing studies. The more insidious and furtive

interventions of the CIA, the National Endowment for Democracy (NED), and the promulgation of corporate interests by George Soros are relatively untouched areas of research.[37] As we saw with the suppression of the Gwangju Uprising, the United States imposed economic liberalization without supporting political liberalization, and it suffered consequences of anti-Americanism for decades to come. Worried that the anti-American impetus threatened its huge investments in South Korea in the 1980s, the United States began to ride the wave of democratic uprisings to expand the capitalist world market and penetrate economies closed off by "crony" regimes.

The Philippines is another case on point, although there were many reasons for U.S. intervention—especially Marcos's faltering war against communism. In the early 1980s, the Communist New People's Army had thousands of men and women under arms and had liberated vast swaths of the countryside, while the Philippine army did without proper medical care and boots. Helicopters provided by the United States to fight the war were denied to troops in the field and used to ferry guests to lavish parties for Marcos's relatives and friends. He empowered his cronies to get rich (to say nothing of the personal wealth he and Imelda amassed in New York real estate and Swiss bank accounts). A parliamentary regime controlled by elites favorable to the United States was far preferable to a pro-U.S. dictatorship as a means of countering the communists and benefiting U.S. business interests.

In the late 1990s, "color revolutions" (sometimes called "velvet revolutions")[38] broke out in a number of countries, including Slovakia (1998), Serbia (2000), Belarus (2001 and 2006), Georgia (2003), Ukraine (2004), Kyrgyzstan (2005) Uzbekistan (2005), Azerbaijan (2005), and Kazakhstan (2005). Coming as they did in strategic areas surrounding Russia, and involving remarkably similar tactics, much doubt about Western involvement has been raised. Are these Color Revolutions NATO's Fifth Column? Small groups' efficacy is revealed in many of the color revolutions—as is the hidden role of U.S. agencies.

In the 1986 Philippines uprising, the CIA maintained twenty-four hour direct contact with RAM mutineers and provided them real-time intelligence on Marcos's troops movements. CIA-sponsored coups d'états occurred in Iran in 1953, Guatemala in 1954, and Brazil in 1963. In 1973, the CIA engineered protests by housewives banging pots and pans in the streets of Santiago and encouraged a strike by truck drivers to destabilize Allende's socialist government. Unrecognized U.S. intervention sometimes obscures its bloody imposition of neoliberalism in Chile in 1973, in Thailand in 1976, and in Korea and Turkey in 1980. Today, direct CIA involvement in regime change is often unnecessary, since other government agencies have taken up the very same projects that used to be their province. A more recent form of U.S. intervention has been to foster dissent through NGOs and civil society and to bombard target countries with propaganda broadcast by the U.S. and UK media.

After the presidential election in 2009, opposition forces in Iran went into the streets to contest election results, but long before that occurred, they had a series of meetings with Western foundations. The Iranian Mehr News agency reported:

"Half a year before the Iranian presidential elections, the CIA was preparing an orange revolution scenario. CIA agents met Iranian oppositionists and gave them instructions in Turkey, Azerbaijan, Kuwait, and the UAE [United Arab Emirates]. The Woodrow Wilson Center and Soros Foundation are accused of setting up an Iranian revolution plan and providing $32 million funding to fulfill the strategy."[39]

CIA involvement in Eastern European struggles against communism has a long history. Since the end of the Cold War, American foundations like NED, Heritage House, AFL-CIO, and Freedom House, have stepped up their activities in countries near Russia. They helped create a web of "NGOs" that are increasingly dependent upon government funds for the bulk of their incomes. In Central and Eastern Europe from 1990 to 1999, "democracy assistance" grants, many from the U.S. Agency for International Development, totaled slightly less than $1.5 billion.[40] After the appearance of democratic movements throughout the world, global capital sought to use them for their own purposes. Massive protests complete with color-coded shirts and banners were orchestrated and financed from outside the country in question. Among the many forces arrayed against regimes unfriendly to U.S. corporate interests were leftovers from the war on communism like Voice of America, Radio Liberty, and Radio Free Europe. Newcomers like billionaire international speculator George Soros contributed mightily to overthrow governments unfriendly to his interests.

Another group involved is the National Endowment for Democracy (NED), the organization implicated in attempting to overthrow Chávez in April 2002.[41] Destabilization of Iran following the 2009 presidential election was remarkably similar to "color revolutions" in Georgia (Rose), Ukraine (Orange), Kyrgyzstan (Tulip), Lebanon (Cedar), Belarus (Denim), Iraq (Purple), Myanmar (Saffron), Venezuela (White), Armenia (Daffodil), and Moldova (Twitter).[42] Of all these, the most likely to have direct CIA involvement were the Rose (Georgia in 2003) and Orange (Ukraine in 2004) Revolutions.

Working behind the scenes, U.S. agencies are able to mobilize NGOs with great effect. In December 1997, at an event in Vienna under the sponsorship of the Foundation for a Civil Society, NGO workers and student activists gathered to explore the lessons of antiregime activists in Bulgaria, whose tent city in downtown Sofia had been attacked by police in January. The resultant outrage had helped spark an electoral defeat of incumbent president Zhelyu Zhelev. At the brainstorming session in Vienna, a key idea emerged—to use rock music to mobilize young people—a suggestion contributed by U.S. Peace Corps member Mike Hochleutner.[43] Getting internationally known sports and music figures— including American hip hop artist Coolio, they successfully used a "Rock the Vote" campaign organized by Marek Kapusta to enlarge a 20 percent youth voter turnout into 80 percent—costing Slovakian incumbent Vladimir Meciar the 1998 election.

Freedom House then helped assemble a conference in Slovakia of regional activists, many of whom had never traveled abroad, that "read like a 'who's who' of future revolutionaries."[44] A retired U.S. Army colonel, Robert Helvey, conducted extensive training in nonviolent tactics for participants. Helvey had already been active on the Burmese border in 1988 (where activists recounted that he had helped to sap their fighting strength). He undertook at least eight other missions between 1992 and 1998 with Gene Sharp, head of Boston's Albert Einstein Institution. Although Sharp and Helvey advocate nonviolence as a tactic, they consistently utilize it solely against regimes unfriendly to the United States, and they have ties to the Pentagon. In the opinion of F. William Engdahl, they are responsible for many incidents of protest: "The concert-master of the tactics of Saffron monk-led nonviolence regime change is Gene Sharp, founder of the deceptively-named Albert Einstein Institution in Cambridge, Massachusetts, a group funded by an arm of the NED to foster U.S.-friendly regime change in key spots around the world. Sharp's institute has been active in Burma since 1989, just after the regime massacred some 3,000 protestors to silence the opposition. CIA special operative and former U.S. military attaché in Rangoon, Colonel Robert Helvey [also retired U.S. army[45]], an expert in clandestine operations, introduced Sharp to Burma in 1989 to train the opposition there in nonviolent strategy. Interestingly, Sharp was also in China two weeks before the dramatic events at Tiananmen Square."[46]

Describing his Burmese mission, Helvey reported, "The only thing I have done is to expose them to the potential of nonviolent sanctions and showed them that nonviolent sanctions can be planned and executed like any other kind of warfare."[47] Yet an activist affiliated with the Burmese parliament in exile bitterly complained that Helvey and Sharp's contribution had been to "disarm and make the Burmese movement less powerful."[48]

For Helvey, "A military victory is achieved by destroying the opponent's capacity and/or willingness to fight. In this regard, nonviolent strategy is no different from armed conflict, except that very different weapons systems are employed."[49] Helvey was an active-duty U.S. officer in Vietnam, who "never thought what he did in Vietnam was wrong."[50] Faithful servant of U.S. interests, Helvey had never been interested in nonviolence since his perception was that it arose with "Vietnam-era 'flower-children, peaceniks and draft dodgers.'"[51] While at Harvard University as a U.S. Army Senior Fellow at the Center for International Affairs from 1987 to 1988, Helvey met Gene Sharp and helped integrate nonviolence into the Pentagon's arsenal of weapons. (Sharp was at Harvard after he had been assisted by Professor Thomas Schelling to receive Pentagon funding.) The two men then embarked on a worldwide campaign, often with U.S. funds, to use their weapon of nonviolence to further U.S. goals.

With funding from Freedom House in the United States, a private group in Belgrade printed five thousand copies of Gene Sharp's book, *From Dictatorship to Democracy*, and Robert Helvey arrived to conduct direct training sessions of Serb activists at the Budapest Hilton in March 2000. Helvey's main focus was "how to subvert the regime's 'pillars of support,' including the police and armed forces." He especially cautioned them that the international donors would be alienated if violence was used and would not contribute financial support.[52] Slovak activists also heavily influenced the Serbian student group *Otpor* (Resistance), and traveled often to Serbia to help adapt their get-out-the-vote campaign against Milošević, who had remained in power despite NATO bombings beginning in

March 1999. In 2000, *Otpor*, the Center for Civic Initiatives, and other groups were given at least $40 million by the U.S.-based International Republican Institute and National Democratic Institute to use in their campaigns against Milošević.[53] Not only did *Otpor* take U.S. government funds, it lied to its members about it, and when the truth was subsequently revealed, many of its most altruistic adherents resigned in protest.[54]

In October 2000, dozens of cars formed a caravan to Belgrade under the banner of *Otpor* that brought in anti-Milošević miners from Kolubara—the caravan that delivered the coup de grace against Milošević. On October 5, 2000, after an election won by the opposition candidate but which Milošević insisted required a runoff, crowds attacked the parliament building, setting it on fire. Heavy fighting resulted in the death of at least one woman and four other people being wounded. Radio Television Serbia was captured and set afire, as was a nearby police station.[55] While the parliament continued to burn that evening, about a hundred thousand people rallied to demand Milošević's departure from power. The next day, he resigned. What NATO bombings had failed to achieve was accomplished through other means.

These same activists, especially Kapusta, then traveled to Georgia to help oust Eduard Shevardnadze in November 2003. Georgia's "Rose Revolution" of 2003 was led by the student movement *Kmara* (Enough) and was funded by George Soros's Open Society Institute (OSI) with support from Belgrade's Center for Nonviolent Resistance. The same groups that were instrumental in overthrowing Shevardnadze then moved to Ukraine, where the Orange Revolution swept into power in 2004. Ukraine's student movement led by *Pora* (Time's Up) was assisted by veterans of *Otpor* and *Kmara* and funded by U.S.-based Freedom House and the National Democratic Institute. While protesters surrounded parliament for weeks, Ukrainian Security Service, the country's secret police, warned the opposition of a coming crackdown and, because they sided with the protesters, effectively undercut the regime's repressive powers.

Led by the student group *Kelkel* (Renaissance), Kyrgyzstan's Tulip Revolution was next. Inspired by *Otpor*, *Pora*, *Kmara* (Georgia), *Zubr* (High Time) Belarus, *Kahar* (Protest) Kazakhstan, and *Yok* (No) Azerbaijan, the Kyrgyz movement was also linked to many of the same U.S. foundations. Givi Targamadze, a former member of Liberty Institute and chair of the Georgian Parliamentary Committee on Defense and Security, had consulted Ukrainian opposition leaders on the technique of nonviolent struggle before he advised leaders of Kyrgyz opposition during the Tulip Revolution. After three people died in riots in capital, the government of President Askar Akiayev collapsed in March 2005.

According to cables released by WikiLeaks, key activists in Egypt and Yemen, were trained and funded by the International Republican Institute, the National Endowment for Democracy, and Freedom House.[56] At least one leader of the Egyptian protests received money to travel to Belgrade for a week of training by former *Otpor* activists who had helped overthrow Slobodan Milošević in 2000. These examples illustrate the power of small groups to help spark successful uprisings. What is of importance here is also the global perspective infused by outside support and the financial resources made available to carefully selected groups. Although useful to overthrow regimes, these same types of groups are by themselves often unable to break the existing system's stranglehold on the form of politics and structural imperatives of the economy. Global capitalism offered these young reformers a readymade alternative.

Of course, the wave of People Power sweeping the world helped animate people, so in many cases no outside help was necessary to motivate people to act. From the Cuban Revolution to the New Left of 1968, from Asia's uprisings to the Arab Spring, popular insurgencies erupted without the pull of doctrinaire parties and ossified theories. Rather those movements emanated from ordinary people's aspirations to be free. More often than not, popular movements' dreams are drowned in bloody repression by the forces of order. Sadly, governments around the world continue to perpetrate violence while speaking of the need for civil behavior. When indigenous insurgencies do succeed in accomplishing immediate objectives, grassroots energies often collapse in joyous celebrations or physical exhaustion. Mobilizations end as political parties and professional activists rush to steal the fruits of popularly won victories. Resulting power struggles bring political deadlock, movements are depoliticized, and global capital expands within political systems that are more efficient and streamlined.

To convince people of the need for qualitatively different organizing principles for management of the vast social wealth, cultural activists need to work in advance of revolutionary crises to prepare people's consciousness and stimulate their dreams. As history remains a phenomenon out of anyone's control, popular uprisings are one of the few vehicles available to citizens to change the course of their lives. Recent insurgencies point us toward understanding which constituencies we can expect to become activated in the future.

NOTES

1   See the 1973 edition of the now-defunct *Great Soviet Encyclopedia*. For a critique, see Herbert Marcuse, *The Aesthetic Dimension: A Critique of Marxist Aesthetics* (Boston: Beacon Press, 1978).

2   Paul Wood, *The Challenge of the Avant-Garde* (New Haven: Yale University Press, 1999), 270.

3   Reprinted in Charles Harrison and Paul Wood, eds., *Art in Theory 1815–1900: An Anthology of Changing Ideas* (Oxford: Blackwell, 1998), 40.

4   This painting was destroyed on February 14, 1945, when the British Royal Air Force used incendiary bombs to destroy the German city of Dresden, killing tens of thousands of people.

5   Reprinted in Harrison and Wood, *Art in Theory*, 797.

6   Quoted in Theda Shapiro, *Painters and Politics: The European Avant-Garde and Society 1900–1925* (New York: Elsevier, 1976), vii. Britain had long lagged behind France in both avant-garde aesthetic and political developments so much that the first English use of the term "avant-garde" was in 1910 in a newspaper review in the *Daily Telegraph* (at least according to the *Oxford English Dictionary*).

7   See Harrison and Wood, *Art in Theory*, 186.

8   See Tristan Tzara, *Dada Manifesto*.

9   Herbert Marcuse, *Counterrevolution and Revolt* (Boston: Beacon Press, 1972), 103–4.

10   Ibid., 107.

11   Marcuse, *Aesthetic Dimension*, 35.

12   Ibid., 72–73.

13   Interview, Stew Albert, Portland, Oregon, December 3, 1999.

14   See Zia Krohn and Joyce Lagerweij, *Concrete Messages: Street Art on the Israeli-Palestinian Separation Barrier* (Arsta, Sweden: Dokument Press, 2010).

15   Jacques Rancière, *The Politics of Aesthetics* (London: Continuum, 2004), 9.

16   Carlos Gabetta, "Argentina: IMF Show States Revolt," *Le Monde Diplomatique*, January 2002, as quoted in Starr, *Global Revolt*, 77.

17   John Jordan and Jennifer Whitney, *Que Se Vayan Todos: Argentina's Popular Rebellion* (Montreal: Kersplebedeb, 2003), 42.

18   See James Petras and Henry Veltmeyer, *What's Left in Latin America? Regime Change in New Times* (Surrey, UK: Ashgate, 2009) for further discussion.

19   See Roger Burbach, "Ecuador's Popular Revolt: Forging a New Nation," in *NACLA Report on the Americas* 40, no. 5 (September–October 2007): 5. For parallel European developments, see Carl Boggs, *Social Movements and Political Power: Emerging Forms of Radicalism in the West* (Philadelphia: Temple University Press, 1986).

20   Ellen Barry, "For Protesters in Moldova, the Revolution Will Be Tweeted," *International Herald Tribune*, April 9, 2009.

21   "Protests Against U.S. Beef Imports Transforms into a Huge Festival," http://english.hani.co.kr/arti/english_edition/e_national/292014.html.

22   See Ronda Hauben, http://www.columbia.edu/ percent7Erh120/other/netizens_draft.pdf.

23   Candlelight protests in Korea have a long history, dating at least to 1975 when Oh Choong-il and Kim Dae Jung used them to dramatize the darkness of military dictatorship. In 2002, after two Korean schoolgirls were tragically killed by a U.S. military vehicle, months of candlelight protests transpired, spreading to Moscow, Washington, D.C., and wherever Koreans found themselves. After a solitary online posting, some fifteen thousand people came to the first candlelight vigil on November 30; two weeks later, more than a hundred thousand protesters held candles in downtown Seoul.

24   So great was the power arrayed against movements in both Burma and Korea that when insurgent movements were being massacred by their own militaries, rumors spread that U.S. aircraft carriers had come the rescue. In the case of Korea, the carrier had been sent to support the military regime, not the insurgents in Gwangju. In Burma, no such American vessel entered Burmese waters. Even when false, rumors carry within them hopes and desires. U.S. power was clearly expected to intervene on the side of democracy. Disappointment was everywhere evident.

25   Yun Seong-Yi, "Political Participation in the New Internet Era," *Korea Herald*, January 18, 2008. For a prescient analysis of participatory democracy, see Michael Hauben, "Participatory Democracy From the 1960s and SDS Into the Future On-line," available at http://www.columbia.edu/~hauben/CS/netdemocracy-6os.txt.

26   Robinson, *Promoting Polyarchy*.

27   Quoted in James Davis, "This Is What Bureaucracy Looks Like: NGOs and Anti-Capitalism," *The Battle of Seattle: New Challenges to Capitalist Globalization* (New York: Soft Skull Books, 2002), 178.

28   Nerfin, "Neither Prince Nor Merchant," 172.

29   See James Petras, "NGOs: In the Service of Imperialism," *Journal of Contemporary Asia* 29, no. 4 (1999): 429–40.

30   *The Economist*, quoted in Heather Gautney, *Protest and Organization in the Alternative Globalization Era: NGOs, Social Movements, and Political Parties* (New York: Palgrave, Macmillan, 2010), 89.

31   Gautney, *Protest*, 88.

32   Quoted in James Davis, "Bureaucracy," 177.

33   John Keane, *Global Civil Society?* (Cambridge: Cambridge University Press, 2003), 83.

34   Jody Jensen and Ferenc Miszlivetz, "Global Civil Society: From Dissident Discourse to World Bank Parlance," in *The Languages of Civil Society*, ed. Peter Wagner (New York: Berghahn Books, 2006), 196–97.

35   See *New Left Review* 62: 141.

36   Petras, "NGOs: In the Service of Imperialism."

37   An important counterexample can be found in William Blum's "Anti-Empire Report," December 19, 2004, http://killinghope.org/bblum6/aer16.htm.

38   See Timothy Garton Ash, "Velvet Revolution: The Prospects," *New York Review of Books* 56, no. 19 (December 3, 2009): 20–23.

39   PanArmenian.net, June 29, 2009, as quoted by Rick Rozoff in "West's Afghan War and Drive into Caspian Sea Basin," http://groups.yahoo.com/group/stopnato/message/40624, July 10, 2009.

40   Sarah E. Mendelson and John Glenn, eds., *The Power and Limits of NGOs: A Critical Look at Building Democracy in Eastern Europe and Eurasia* (New York: Columbia University Press, 2002), 5, 191–92.

41   Eva Golinger, *The Chavez Code: Cracking U.S. Intervention in Venezuela* (New York: Monthly Review Press, 2007).

42   Rozoff, "Afghan War."

43   Arias-King, "Orange People," 44.

44   Ibid.

45   Ackerman and Duvall, *A Force More Powerful*, 475.

46   Engdahl, "Chokepoint!"

47   Ackerman and Duvall, *A Force More Powerful*, 475.

48   Interview with Burmese activist Aung Kyaw So in Maesot, Thailand, November 2008.

49   Robert L. Helvey, *On Strategic Nonviolent Conflict: Thinking About the Fundamentals* (Boston: The Albert Einstein Institution, 2004), xi.

50   Interview with Gene Sharp, Boston, March 3, 2011. For a recording, see http://eroseffect.com.

51   Helvey, *Nonviolent Conflict*, xii.

52   Ackerman and Duvall, *A Force More Powerful*, 485–86.

53   Johansen, "Waves of Nonviolence."

54   Tina Rosenberg, "Revolution U: What Egypt Learned from the Students Who Overthrew Milošević," *Foreign Policy*, February 16, 2011.

55   Sharp, *Waging Nonviolent Struggle*, 336. On March 3, 2011, I interviewed Gene Sharp at the Albert Einstein Institution in Boston and discussed with him concerns about U.S. support for nonviolent revolutions. The interview is available on my website, http://eroseffect.com.

56   Ron Nixon, "U.S. Groups Helped Nurture Arab Uprisings," *New York Times*, April 14, 2011.

CHAPTER 14

The Changing Face of the Proletariat

Modern conditions of production today offer the objective
possibilities for the development of generalized self-management of
production and of the economy by those who do the work.

—Serge Mallet

With labor emancipated, everyone becomes a worker, and
productive labor ceases to be a class attribute.

—Karl Marx

IN THE COURSE of the twentieth century, as revolutionary change became institutionalized in Russia and China, a fundamental revision in the theory of insurgencies transpired. From a weapon of the weak, Marxism became an instrument
for state dictatorships ruled by communist parties. In the advanced capitalist
countries, revolutionary change failed to materialize, and academic Marxism
was enshrined as a labor metaphysic, an opium for intellectuals that helped
to pacify them as the worldwide wave of change receded. Anarchism was savagely suppressed in Spain no less than in Russia, while its American varieties
(from Argentine to the United States) suffered a less violent but no less thorough
defeat. Once a vibrant theory resonating in the streets of Barcelona, the mines of
Colorado, and the pampas of Argentina, anarchism became a doctrine of marginalized self-righteousness isolated from popular movements.

The receding tide of revolution left behind a flotsam of parties and jetsam of
theories, whose contemporary utility is dubious. In 1968, the French Communist
Party stood against the wildcat strike of ten million workers and students. In 1977,
the Italian Communists aided the police to suppress student and youth protests.
Just as these outmoded organizations militantly opposed radical upsurges, so too
did their theories stand against the changing conditions for revolutionary change.

While Marx insisted upon distinguishing between the proletariat's objective economic conditions (class-in-itself) and subjective historical emergence (class-for-
itself), Marxists focused almost exclusively on comprehending class through the
single lens of objectivistic categories of production. Soviet and Chinese Marxism's
transformation from ideologies of revolution into tools of governance stigmatized
popular uprisings as "spontaneity." Amid a surfeit of attention to economic categories of production, scant attention was paid to the constituencies of movements for change as they emerged in concrete history.

For many Marxists and syndicalists, the category "working class" implies a
preference for manual workers' leadership capabilities and hegemony. One of the
reasons for the Left's irrelevance to nearly all recent uprisings is a metaphysical
definition of the proletariat. Tied to rigid ideological presuppositions, Left parties
have long lacked the flexibility to perceive the emergence of new social forces.[1]
While theorists like Harry Braverman have made significant explorations of the
working class, rigid categories of production continue to delineate the limits
of academic, or analytical, Marxism. Seldom do self-appointed theorists of the
working class mention women or minorities, and only in rare cases (as Herbert
Marcuse did in his final book) do they even consider the possibility of freedom
meaning to live without the compulsion to work.[2] At a time when it is possible
for human beings to work twenty hours per week for twenty years and to retire
with enough money to live decently, the state-capitalist system demands we
work longer hours and for more years in order for governments and corporations
to continue to function. The Soviet Union's variety of state socialism was little
better. Indeed, that variety of Marxism was rightly perceived as wanting to make
the entire world into a factory.

Much like medieval theologians who debated how many angels could dance
on the head of a pin, idealistic categorical imperatives define many leftists' means
of analyzing the strategic value of sectors of the population. For mainstream
democratization theorists, a bias exists in favor of the middle class as the vehicle
of democratization, while academic Marxists insist rigidly that the working class
is key, even to the point of excluding from conferences and journals those they
regard as outside the boundaries they neatly patrol.[3] For many Marxists, the
"proletariat" functions as a collective father figure, a thing-in-itself fixed once
and for all time in a frozen metaphysic universally "valid" yet nowhere relevant.

The history of recent uprisings provides a rich empirical resource from which
to evaluate the political positions of sectors of the population, to gauge the concrete historical meaning of "class-for-itself." Revolutionary subjects reveal themselves in concrete praxis, not in the obscure calculations and charts of "analytical
Marxians." Proletarian dogmatism of the Left leaves it playing in the academic
sandbox or searching the refuse bin of history for a nonexistent "master class."

In order for the Russian revolutionaries to seize power, Lenin had to convince many people of the development of capitalism in a very backward economy
and to threaten to leave his Bolshevik party on the eve of the insurrection; Mao
had to reorient his party to the reality of peasants as their main constituency and
was expelled from the Party for advocating rurally based struggles; Ho Chi Minh

had to overrule his Chinese and Russian advisors at Dien Bien Phu; Fidel had to pose the mountains as the revolutionary base, not the cities. What is needed today is for visionary activists similarly to risk being called heretics and revisionists, to risk ostracism and banishment from circles of those who self-righteously believe in their correctness.

Flexibility was the hallmark of all revolutions of the twentieth century, and in the twenty-first century, fluid conceptualization and adjustment to changing conditions is even more of a necessity. The character of "class-for-itself" (the subject of revolutionary change) may still be defined as the proletariat in philosophical categories: the determinate negation of capitalist society, the vast majority of the people, and those having "nothing to lose but their chains." Yet, if we are to be specific and evaluate concrete history, we need to analyze the changing constituencies of social movements as revealed in practice, not in the stale pages of arcane texts.

Enlarged Base of Revolution: Middle Strata and Lumpenproletariat

Beginning with formulations of the "new working class" in 1968, research gradually uncovered new groups central to political struggles within advanced capitalism, and not only in Europe and the United States.[4] At that time, students were in the leadership of insurgencies all over the world—from China to Mexico, and Paris to New York. Although factory workers in France and Poland became activated, the expectation that workers (as defined by objective categories of material production) would lead struggles was increasingly disappointed by empirical reality. When groups of employees did play leading roles in struggles, it was often people involved in immaterial production (white-collar workers, off-line office and health care workers, and proletarianized professionals), while factory workers' activation often followed in the wake of popular uprisings. In Asian uprisings as in the overthrow of Eastern European bureaucratic dictatorships and the Arab Spring, from the alter-globalization movement to the Arab Spring, similar dynamics were unveiled. Students and proletarianized professionals often led the movements, while workers erupted after the peaks of democratization uprisings had opened space for protest.

Uprisings in the Philippines, South Korea, Nepal, Bangladesh, Taiwan, and Thailand all drew extensive participation from constituencies defined in the media as "middle-class." So involved were urban employees of government and corporations that many mainstream theorists postulated the middle class as the main constituency of democratization. Thailand's uprising was widely characterized in Western media as the "cell phone mob," despite the fact that transport workers and students were key participants. China's Tiananmen Square protest was almost always described as a student movement, although workers became a key group that could be relied upon—and were flocking to the Square as the student movement waned. Gwangju's uprising is thought by many people to have been a student movement, although the city's urban poor and transportation workers were vital to the insurgency. Nearly all uprisings under scrutiny in this book involved technical and white-collar workers, teachers and students, writers, journalists, government employees, and proletarianized professionals, including doctors, professors, and lawyers. The significant roles played by these groups can be ignored only at the peril of remaining unconcerned with historical accuracy. Simultaneously, the mainstream media's characterization of the paramount importance of the middle class demeans subaltern groups and diminishes the contributions of manual laborers and the urban poor.

Insofar as material conditions of production play significant roles in the formation of historical actors, an explanation of the leading role of students and professionals can be found in changing economic conditions. Enormous technological breakthroughs of the twentieth century induced universities to abandon their classical position as ivory towers. Instead they moved to the center of research and development and became important resources for the maintenance of imperial control. In the United States, Harvard provided mangers of many countries' governments, while MIT developed advanced weapons systems for the Defense Department.[5] From within such institutions of war and political domination arose visionary student moments. Universities' involvement in the economy and politics was accompanied by a vast expansion of higher education. Today there are something like ninety million postsecondary students in the world, whose numbers have skyrocketed from fifty-one million in 1980 and eight-two million in 1995.[6]

The affinity of intellectuals for revolution predates the changed character of production in the twentieth century. A powerful force attacking Czarism, Russian students in the nineteenth century were called the "proletariat of thought."[7] Beginning in 1968, hundreds of thousands of students constituted progressive forces with enormous visions. They fought for their own freedom and simultaneously acted in solidarity with people around the world. As revealed in their praxis, students and the middle strata possess great capacities for self-organization. While students are adept at sparking struggles, they are commonly unable to sustain them. Concentrated on campuses for a limited number of years and comprised mainly of young people, student struggles are often dissipated after key initial moments. They have a tendency to engage in petty debates and arguments. Their toleration for hardship is limited when compared to other sectors of the population. During the Gwangju Uprising, for example, once the fighting had begun in earnest, many students melted away and returned to their homes, while others left the city to find safe refuge. At the same time, the urban poor and working people flocked to the front lines. The city's bus drivers and taxi drivers rallied the population on the night of May 20, just after the military had used deadly force and people's fighting spirits appeared to be diminishing. Factory workers at the city's largest employer, Asia Motors, provided the insurgents with dozens of vehicles, including freshly made armored cars, and they brought their heavy equipment downtown to help clear the streets of burnt-out chassis and other debris after the city was liberated. In Thailand in 1992, although students sparked the popular uprising, the participation of transport workers and union members was significant. In China, as the ranks of students thinned, the Beijing Autonomous Workers' Federation became a growing force. Working-class motorcyclists provided key intelligence functions in both Beijing and Bangkok. In Bangladesh, Nepal, and South Korea, working people became activated as a class immediately after the initial breakthroughs. Based upon recent historical praxis, students are the blasting caps of revolutionary upsurges, while workers and poor people are the dynamite. Even when the working class was clearly in the lead, as in Poland, leftist partisans recoiled from citizens' staunch religious conservatism and hierarchical organizations. As Daniel Singer recognized, emergent subjects of revolution often do not conform to expectations.

The more modern capitalism evolves, the number of workers directly involved in production constitute an ever-smaller fraction of the population. Traditional union organizations have declined precipitously in membership. Structural reasons related to the reorganization of production have directly contributed to these changes. As early as 1968, Brazilian activist Ladislas Dowbor noted that "the growth of the modernized sector generates the crisis of traditional industries. . . . As a result, the working class is progressively expelled from the process of production, swelling the class of marginals and leaving an ever smaller, better paid and relatively satisfied working class with no inclination at all towards the revolution." André Gorz elaborated these observations further in 1980: "The traditional working class is now no more than a privileged minority. The majority of the population now belongs to the post-industrial neo-proletariat which, with no job security or definite class identity, fills the area of probationary, contracted, casual, temporary and part-time employment."[8] The trends Gorz perceived decades ago have continued to intensify. In South Korea today, about half of all jobs are part-time and without benefits. In the United States today, unions represent fewer than 15 percent of workers, with government employees, teachers, and other white-collar workers constituting a huge proportion of their dues paying members. In 1988, estimates were that less than 10 percent of workforces were employed in manufacturing in Indonesia, the Philippines and Thailand, while the middle class was about 20 percent in Thailand and the Philippines (where 45 percent of the country lived in poverty).[9]

As the number of the marginalized and impoverished swell because of capital's incessant accumulation of wealth among the super rich, movements will increasingly involve poor people. Although the media and mainstream academics denigrate their participation in social movements, during many of the uprisings in Asia, the urban poor, or lumpenproletariat, acted when uprisings broke out. In Nepal, lumpen were important Maoist recruits and brought great strength as fighters. Prostitutes in Gwangju helped hide members of the Citizens' Army when many other people would not get involved. Many sex workers insisted on donating blood and worked with citizens groups on a number of teams. The city's gang leaders rose at one of the first general assemblies and pledged to work together with the mobilized citizenry. While the government characterized citizens as "rioters" and saw them all as "the lumpenproletariat classes, hooligans, scavengers, the jobless, laborers, shoeshine boys, and beggars. . . . The uprising was a struggle in which all citizens participated, not just these groups. The situation was an extreme emergency, where everyday life was suspended. . . . The

Gwangju citizens' system of voluntary division of work and impromptu organization worked to a surprising degree. The fact that the urban poor stood in the vanguard of street fights, and criminal gangs declared their cooperation with citizens' self-governing activities, was the manifestation of their civic spirit."[10] Within the Black Panther Party and the Algerian Revolution, the lumpenproletariat played significant roles, yet theories derived from their nineteenth-century actions in Paris have been frozen into metahistorical judgments.

In recent times, both the middle strata and urban poor also supported authoritarian rulers. In Thailand, the urban middle class vacillated in support of democracy. Experiences of uprisings and movements provide practical experiences from which we can extrapolate and project. In 1973, the engineering students in Thailand led assaults on police stations, but in 1976, some of the same individuals were part of the brutal mob that attacked Thammasat University and killed dozens of students. In the 1970s, middle-class homemakers were mobilized against Allende and his socialist government, while in the 1990s, they turned against the Pinochet dictatorship.

However one draws boundaries and creates divisions among the overwhelming majority of the population who are compelled to work in order to eat, the structural position of many off-line workers is precarious—particularly in the era of neoliberalism, when massive layoffs from privatization and corporate downsizing are all too common. Comprehended as a "new working class" by Serge Mallet, André Gorz, and Herbert Marcuse, others insist this is a new "middle" class. Educated enough to be managers, their jobs defy the traditional distinction between mental and manual work. The vast majority are order-takers, working in alienated hierarchies under order-givers. Within contemporary economies, the new working class is scandalously disenfranchised and often understand themselves as more intelligent than power holders. The very concepts "new working class" and "middle class" indicate contradictory conceptions of these groups. Managers and those who make decisions and give orders occupy a very different position than white-collar order-takers. As Val Burris cautions, "What is not consistent with the empirical evidence is any theory that treats all white collar employees as members of a single cohesive class—whether as part of the working class or a separate middle class."[11]

Empirical research in Asia analyze these groups' structural position and their involvement in social movements. In South Korea, Hang Sang-Jin analyzed the formation of what he named the "middling grassroots."[12] Different from the propertied middle class, who experienced great poverty after the Korean War, the middling grassroots were postpoverty employees (like baby-boomers in the United States) and emphasized postmaterialistic values such as participation and self-expression rather than the conservative, materialistic values of the propertied middle class. In Taiwan, Yun Fan's survey of activists' backgrounds found that they were twice as likely to come from upper and upper-middle-class backgrounds (including children of white-collar parents) while shopkeepers, farmers, and workers produced comparatively few activist progeny. (These latter groups comprised 67 percent of population but produced only 30 percent of 146 activists surveyed.)[13] After completing an eight-country study, Michael Hsiao concluded that the first generation of the salaried middle class supports democracy, while the second generation is more complacent and conservative. Hsiao counted more than 57 percent of Taiwan as members of the middle class.[14] If we regard stratification based upon income, salaried employees are a huge constituency, possibly even a majority of workers. In Nepal, one report stated that for the first time, the middle class—defined as those earning between U.S. $10 to $100 per day—rose from 33 percent of the developing world to 57 percent in 2006. [15]

The role of these strata in the movements for democratization at the end of the twentieth century was so striking that one ignores them at one's own peril. Mainstream democratization theorists emphasized the progressive character of off-line employees:

> Because of their access to communications and organizational resources, white-collar groups, particularly within the professions, play an important role in anti-government protests . . . arbitrary government authority can pose threats not only to their careers but also to professional norms, such as the integrity of the law or of universities. Except during periods of intense polarization, proletarianized professionals are inclined to press for constitutionalism. Their incorporation into popular democratic movements is often pivotal to the process of political transition, in part because it affects the government's calculus concerning the use of coercion.[16]

Marxist theory has an ideological predisposition against the favorable valuation of these groups. In 1950 (almost exactly the same time that C. Wright Mills explored their domination and alienation in *White Collar*), C.L.R. James, Raya Dunayevskaya, and Grace Lee Boggs analyzed these sectors with extraordinary criticisms: "The most obviously reactionary, the most easily recognizable is the counter-revolution of the middle classes. Because capitalism in its present stage, state-capitalism, faces them with complete liquidation and absorption into the proletariat, they propose the complete destruction of capitalism and return to a new medievalism, based on natural inequality."[17] Reacting to the rule of terror in the Soviet Union and McCarthyism in the United States, their analysis was bleak and uncompromising: "The rationalism of the bourgeoisie has ended in the Stalinist one-party bureaucratic-administrative state of the Plan. In their repulsion from this rationalism and from the proletarian revolution, the middle classes fall back upon the barbarism of Fascism. The anti-Stalinist, anti-capitalist petty-bourgeois intellectuals, themselves the victims of the absolute division between mental and physical labor, do not know where to go or what to do." Immanuel Wallerstein reached a similarly pejorative conclusion, when he referred to intermediate layers as "political allies for the ruling stratum and models of upward mobility for the unskilled majority."[18]

The emergence of student movements, the civil rights movement in the 1960s, and subsequent Asian uprisings, provide fresh historical data for analysis. Before New Left movements emerged, C.L.R. James wrote: "In 1950 the universal is as far beyond 1917 as 1917 was beyond the Paris Commune." With these words, he anchored his analysis in uprisings and in history's empirical progression, key means to comprehend the emergence of new social forces and the changing character of material conditions.

Gender and Uprisings

Advanced capitalism brought women out of the house and into the offices and factories of global corporations, and women are today widely integrated into the global workforce. At the same time as universities moved to the center of production and politics, households were rapidly transformed by the imperatives of advanced capitalism. Extended and nuclear family structures were decimated by imperatives of the economic system. Since most families require two breadwinners to make ends meet, most women are compelled to find employment outside their homes. Their unpaid labor in homes has been superseded by capitalist penetration of people's everyday lives through the fast food industry, medical institutions, and expansion of schooling. Previously autonomous arenas of the life-world have been colonized by the system's incessant drive to integrate fresh territories into the orbit of profitable activity. Neighborhoods have become sites of contested terrain with struggles against capital's incessant drive to profitably exploit everyday life. Once marginalized from the public sphere, women are increasing central to it. Their proletarianization is a structural reason for their increasing participation in social movements.

Since 1968, the critique of patriarchy has gradually widened to include millions of people. The potential for a world-historical transformation of capitalist patriarchy, a genuine contemporary revolution, poses a world without war and without wasteful production for the super rich, a world in which humanity's vast resources are turned toward meeting basic human needs, a world in which we preserve and restore the environment and provide opportunities for all to develop their creative capacities according to their own self-definition. No matter how much the system makes such dreams appear to be utopian and unrealistic, ordinary people intuitively grasp the simple fact that modern technology makes such a world possible. They know that work could be reduced to a minimum rather than being enforced as people's central life concern—let alone extended into seniors' golden years. If it is possible to overthrow the patriarchal performance principle that today dominates human lives, women will be central to such an endeavor. Already, in the course of Asian uprisings, one catches a glimpse of their potential for facilitating and leading social transformation, although all too often, existing patriarchal political structures seek to integrate emergent female leaders into positions of power (as global capital does with all subaltern groups posing the potential of fundamental opposition).

Europeans and Americans have a tendency to view Asia as particularly patriarchal in comparison to the West, yet in recent times, a new generation of Asian women leaders has emerged to lead democratic governments and political parties—from Cory Aquino in the Philippines (1986), Benazir Bhutto in Pakistan (1988), Khaleda Zia and Sheikh Hasina Wajed in Bangladesh (1990), and Aung San Suu Kyi in Burma (1988). For her courage and tenacity, Suu Kyi was awarded the

TABLE 14.1 **Contemporary Asian Antigones**

Country	Female Leader	Relationship	Male Leader	Fate of Male Leader
Philippines	Corazon Aquino	Widow	Benigno Aquino	Assassinated
Nepal	Sahana Pradhan	Widow	Pushpa Lal Shrestha	Deceased
Burma	Aung San Suu Kyi	Daughter	Aung San	Assassinated
Bangladesh	Sheikh Hasina Wazed	Daughter	Sheikh Mujibur Rahman	Assassinated
Bangladesh	Khaleda Zia	Widow	Ziaur Rahman	Assassinated
Pakistan	Benazir Bhutto	Daughter	Zulfikar Ali Bhutto	Executed
Malaysia	Wan Azizah Wan Ismail	Wife	Anwar Ibrahim	Imprisoned/ on trial
Indonesia	Megawati Sukarnoputri	Daughter	Sukarno	Died during house arrest

Nobel Peace Prize in 1991. Significantly, no major female leaders emerged in any European movements of the same period. Although these leaders' roles in Asian uprisings were demeaned as revolutionary "pin-up" girls, whose photos adorn the posters of the movement,[19] substantial criticisms can also be formulated.

In every one of the Asian cases, the female leader is either the daughter or widow of a martyred male leader, as indicated in TABLE 14.1. Family ties—women's traditional domain—remain central to women's roles, even within movements seeking to create a new social order. That may be one reason why none of these female leaders formulated particularly visionary aspirations for her country's future.

To be sure, female leaders are not confined to democratic insurgencies. One need only recall Megawati Sukarnoputri, Indira Gandhi, and Park Geun-hae to realize that women can be just as hierarchical—even dictatorial—as men. In mentioning the meaning of the above conservative women leaders in contemporary Asia, however, one cannot help but note that every single one of these women also came from a father who was head of the government—that is, a patriarchal legacy made their leadership possible.

The role of these prominent personalities in uprisings are little different than those of male leaders. The personalized bickering of Khaleda Zia and Hasina Wajed in Bangladesh often results in violence. Aung San Suu Kyi's personal hold over her followers is as rigidly hierarchical and mystified as in the case of many charismatic male leaders such as the Dalai Lama. If we focus attention instead on the situation of thousands of women activists rather than on "Great Woman" of history, a different picture emerges. Women constitute far and away the core of activist insurgencies. When uprisings fail and leaders are killed, women are often the ones called upon to pick up the pieces and prepare for the next stages of struggle. When prominent personalities are incorporated into reformed power structures, the majority of women remain among the poorest, least powerful, and most visionary members of society.

During the Gwangju Uprising, a feat often portrayed as consisting solely of heroic armed struggle, women were central to the life of the liberated city and what has been called the "absolute community." Beginning in 1978, an all female organization, Song Bak Hue (송백회—"Pure Pine Tree Society"), facilitated women's participation in the movement and provided a significant bridge among activists, including many imprisoned men. Once the uprising broke out, women from Song Bak Hue became one of the main forces organizing the daily rallies at Democracy Square. Women were essential to publishing big character posters and the daily newspaper, The Fighter's Bulletin (투사회보). While some women carried carbines, most of the fighters were men. Although they participated fully in street actions, women were often caught in "normal" female roles, like serving food in public kitchens, managing community drives for donations of blood and money, and caring for the wounded and dead. As discussed in more detail in Asia's Unknown Uprisings Volume 1, liberated Gwangju provided a taste of a genuinely free society, yet within that space, women's roles were not dramatically different than during normal episodes of everyday life. Within the Citizens' Army, not one woman was among the leaders. When the military was poised to reenter the city, women and youth were excused from the final battle and asked to leave Province Hall. Nonetheless, about a half dozen women remained and fought alongside several hundred men.

Inside the South Korean labor movement of the 1970s, female textile workers played key roles. During the 1987 June Uprising, women sponsored a national Day Against Tear Gas that helped to provide the uprising a continuing national focus. When thousands of women circulated among riot police and passed out roses, they effectively neutralized many hard-line regime supporters. Tired of being confined to subaltern status, Korean women increasingly organized themselves. After the June Uprising of 1987, the women's movement succeeded in changing antiquated family law, especially the Confucian registration system that had long marginalized women. As a remarkable testament to the cultural transformation of Korea, the "world's most Confucian society" saw teenage girls lead the entire country in candlelight protests that involved millions of people—including the country's trade unions.

In Tibet, as early as 1959, women's leadership and united capacity for action were vital to the uprising in Lhasa. Thailand's 1973 students included prominent contingents of middle and high school girls. The role of Catholic nuns in the Philippines in 1986 is legendary. Despite Chai Ling's destructive role in Tiananmen Square and her subsequent defection from the ranks of committed activists, she emerged as arguably the most significant leader of the 1989 insurgency. Women's courage in 1990 Nepal was central to the movement's capacity to withstand fierce repression. In all of these cases, the seldom-celebrated contributions of ordinary women to uprisings were vital.

Female Archetypes and Democratization

One of the reasons for lack of attention to female participation in social movements is that patriarchy permeates society, deforming even the most revolutionary of movements. Whether we live in America or Korea, in Europe, Asia, or Africa, women are systematically subordinated, discriminated against, compelled to work double shifts as mothers/housekeepers and employees, reduced to objects of sexual desire, and subjected to violence by men. Their contributions to overall accomplishments are often minimized or ignored. Although regarded as marginal, women are key members of the proletariat, whose labor generates profits in factories and offices, and their unpaid domestic labor is vital to reproduction and maintenance of the labor force.[20] These two structural positions place them firmly in the center of society.

By interjecting noneconomic concerns into the movement's aspirations and inner life, women play a vital role in transforming the movement from within, in leading men to live differently, and pointing us all in the direction of values like reciprocity (not hierarchy), cooperation (not competition), and love of life in all forms (rather than devaluing it).[21] Many women already have democratic patterns in their daily lives. Sociolinguist Deborah Tannen came to the conclusion that in their everyday conversation patterns, U.S. women tended to establish intimacy along horizontal lines while men tended to establish hierarchy.[22] Alain Touraine believes the women's movement is "most able to oppose the growing hold exercised by giant corporations over our daily lives."[23] If Marxists reify categories of production and seek to make the whole world into a factory, reducing humanity to the proletariat, feminism is a vital counterforce that organically constitutes human life in domains other than work. As Marcuse so eloquently reminds us: "In a free society . . . existence would no longer be determined by life-long alienated labor."[24]

The potential outcome of women's participation, especially when their aspirations are given free expression from the grassroots, is enormous. Patriarchy predates capitalism and is so embedded in our consciousness (and unconscious) that overthrowing it would result in the most radical of all conceivable revolutions. By radically transforming everyday life, a feminist revolution (one that also rejects other forms of oppression) would be the most far-reaching and democratic of all, ensuring that all people would be free in their daily lives to determine their own destinies. As is intuitively obvious, women would benefit from a feminist revolution, but as studies have increasingly shown, so would men. On average, women live many years longer than men. If men were granted the space to raise children and to care for the elderly, to spend more time in their families and circles of intimacy and less in the stressful environment of the workplace and public arenas of power and wealth, their life expectancies—to say nothing of the quality of their lives—would noticeably increase. Many leftists comprehend feminism, the "politics of identity," and "new social movements" as undermining working-class unity. Although often regarded as being lost with the emergence of fragmented "new social movements," universal interests may actually reside in the specificity of subaltern groups. The women's movement, for example, while at first glance appearing to be based upon the interests of only half of society, actually contains within it the promise of the liberation of all humans from oppressive patriarchal relationships.[25]

Part of the problem involved in discussing the relationship of women to uprisings is that although women are often heavily involved, patriarchal accounts of courage and media bias in selection of spokespersons often minimize women's roles. Within movements, women are often relegated to subordinate positions. In the early 1960s, women in the Student Nonviolent Coordinating Committee—one of the main organizations of the U.S. civil rights movement—typed the memos while men wrote them; women mimeographed the press releases while men spoke to the cameras. Not only were women made to work behind the scenes, they were also explicitly denigrated as activists. In both Germany and the United States, male leaders of the main student organizations of the New Left initially regarded demands for women's liberation with great hostility. (In all fairness, I should add that soon thereafter, feminism became an integral part of every major organization of the movement in the United States and subsequently in Germany as well.) Women are sometimes mistreated by male activists, even in such liberated moments as the Oaxaca Commune, where some women felt they were "fighting two different fronts—the system and the men inside our own movement."[26]

When Kathleen Cleaver, the first woman on the Central Committee of the Black Panther Party, was asked by a reporter about the role of women in the organization, she snapped back, "No one ever asks me what the role of men in the revolution is!" Her point is well taken. In the Black Panther Party in 1969, two-thirds of the members were women, and although it suffered murderous police attacks in which dozens of its members were killed, the organization led the way in openly supporting women's (and gay) liberation and sought to establish respectful relationships based upon equality and upon playing similar roles.[27]

Feminism's broad impact on democratization movements in the United States, Italy, and Germany was due in part to women's development of their own autonomous organizations as a power base for theory and practice. Independent women's organizations deepened the overall movement's commitment to revolutionary change. In Italy, the autonomous feminist movement set an example of a "politics of the first person" in which individuals did not take orders from higherups and where groups operated according to principles of self-managed consensus. Feminism's notion of autonomy was vital to the subsequent emergence of autonomous youth and workers' movements.[28] In South Africa, women within the African National Congress, committed to insuring women's participation in all decision-making bodies, made the democratization movement more effective and sensitive to women's concerns and leadership.

Although Europeans and Americans often espouse the belief that females there are more liberated than in Asia, where are the women leaders of insurgent movements in the West? In both Egypt and Asia, history is full of women political leaders. Some two thousand years ago, the Trung sisters were at the forefront of a successful Vietnamese independence movement against China. After their initial defeat, the Chinese Han regrouped and sent an even larger army to retake Vietnam. Mounted on elephants, the Trung sisters again led the resistance, but when it became clear the Chinese would win this battle, they took their own lives rather than be captured. These Vietnamese women emerged from a strong tradition of female leadership in Vietnam, including the passing of land from one generation of women to another.

Ancient Greek civilization's continuing universal appeal explains why during the Iraq War, antiwar actors began to perform Aristophanes's play *Lysistrata*, which was written in 411 BCE to protest the Peloponnesian War. Using a tactic also described in William Hinton's book about modern China, *Fanshen*, women in Aristophanes's play withhold sex from their husbands in order to wage peace.

Antigone and Chunhyang

Although not necessarily founded on real people, archetypes and ancient legends reveal something essential about cultures. Since they embody patterns of behavior familiar to particular cultures, they are transmitted from one generation to another for hundreds of years. In my view, dimensions of Korean culture have universal appeal similar to the Greek mythological character of Antigone. In Sophocles's play that bears her name, Antigone defied tyrannical King Creon of Thebes, who ordered that her brother's corpse be left in a field for vultures. Declaring that religious laws are more important than secular ones, Antigone retrieved Polyneices's body and gave him a proper burial. For her crime, she was sentenced to starve to death. Rather than await a slow and painful end, she hanged herself—just as her mother, Iocasta, had done after learning she had given birth to her son's (Oedipus) daughter—to Antigone.

Antigone has similarities to a mythological woman known to every Korean—Song Chunhyang. According to legend, Chunhyang refused to submit to the sexual demands of Byon Sa-to, the king's newly appointed governor-general of Cholla province (the region around Gwangju) who ruthlessly raised taxes and demanded that local women satisfy his sexual desires. Chunhyang's loyalty to Lee Mong-young, the son of the previous governor, and her desire to remain faithful to him alone (a version of patriarchal monogamy), led her to resist Byon Sa-to's demand that she be his lover. For her stubborn resistance, the governor ordered her severely beaten again and again, bringing her to the point of death. At the governor's birthday celebration, she was to be executed, but Lee Mong-young secretly returned to Cholla. Horrified to learn that Byon had tortured so innocent and beautiful a person as his lover Chunhyang, he organized a palace coup that expelled the evil governor and returned Cholla to harmony. The story of Chunhyang epitomizes the purity of Cholla and has come to be the most widely performed play using the region's unique *pansori* singing (a kind of Jeolla blues).

Koreans are so modest that they often deflate the significance of their own culture. Thus, the normal interpretation of Chunhyang is that she represents Korean women's subservience to men during the Chosun dynasty, a perspective from which there could be no more antifeminist story than Chunhyang's. At one point in the Chosun dynasty, patriarchal monogamy was modified for men to permit them to have a concubine in addition to a wife (although children born to concubines were considered inferior). The ideal wife guarded her chastity and continually sacrificed herself to her husband and her family. Women's intelligence was so undervalued (often regarded as impossible) that few were taught to read. Even as late as 1930, nine of ten Korean women were illiterate.

Not only was Chunhyang an "inferior" child of a concubine, but her lover was from the *yangban*, the aristocratic upper class—weaving a class dynamic into the plot. Chunhyang's unwed mother was a concubine, and because Lee Mong-young's father was a powerful *yangban*, he and Chunhyang were an impossible couple. Despite his love for Chunhyang, Mong-young took a wealthy noble's daughter for his wife while he was in the capital preparing for life as a high public official. This dimension of the story of Chunhyang is nothing but a recitation of the freedom of the rich (and men) to merrily cavort while the poor (and women) remain behind. Her lover freely leaves her behind and marries a rich woman, while she is expected to remain faithful to him. Despite conservative elements embedded in the plot, another interpretation is possible: Chunhyang's individual resistance to unjust central authority, no matter how conservative the cause, is an example of the affirmation of the individual's right to choose his or her own destiny. Antigone's act of resistance was to care for her brother's corpse (a traditional role for women—to care for her male relatives) while Chunhyang's was to control *her own live body*. Despite her refusal to accede to the governor's demands, Chunhyang's story has a happy ending, unlike the lives of Antigone, Cleopatra, and the Trung sisters, all of whom committed suicide.

In Im Kwon-tek's movie version, *Chunhyang*, her stubborn refusal and sacrifice helped to precipitate larger demands for self-determination. An indigenous uprising emerged alongside the palace revolt led by Mong-young, and after Chunhyang's liberation and recovery, the king announced a tax holiday for the region that lasted many years. Chunhyang thus becomes a democratic role model since her rebellious behavior led to a change in government officials and policy. Not only did she get her man, albeit as a concubine, but more importantly, she affirmed the chosen way of life of the community in the face of the attempted penetration of the indigenous life-world by outside authority.

Are archetypes and traditional cultural forms resources that can be mobilized for liberatory social movements? Or are they impediments to such freedom struggles? Perhaps they are both. Gwangju communalism, a daily facet of life, can provide both wonderfully rich everyday experiences, ones that are significant resources for collective actions, and a social superego that obstructs individual liberty. Confucian public space often diminishes the worth of younger people and women, and Asian feminists often correctly understand its excessive patriarchal dimensions. In the United States as in much of the West, collective action is inhibited by advanced social atomization and ingrained patterns of competition, individualism, and male egotism. In contrast, Korean communalism, while hierarchical and sometimes authoritarian, facilitates communal consciousness. Thanks to the communication channels it makes possible, Korean sociability may be one of the country's great natural resources. The gentleness of Confucian everyday life prefigures a free society and stands in stark contrast to daily American violence, whether observed in civil violence or police recklessness.

Modern Asian Antigones send out signals to millions of women, and not only in Asia, that the possibility of their political involvement is real. These "Great Women" were elevated to prominence by insurgent social movements, but they are not particularly radical. Future social movements will no doubt be more heavily constituted by and for women, in part because of the legacy left by their elder sisters.

NOTES

1   See the discussion of Michael Zweig in *Asia's Unknown Uprisings Volume 1*, chap. 10.
2   Marcuse, *Aesthetic Dimension*, 28–29.
3   A recent example is American Sociological Association President Erik Olin Wright's refusal in 2011 to approve a panel on autonomous social movements because he considered them not to be "working-class."
4   As a beginning point, see Serge Mallet's essays on the new working class in *The New Working Class* (Bristol, UK: Spokesman Books, 1975) and *Bureaucracy and Technocracy in the Socialist Countries* (Nottingham, UK: Spokesman Books, 1974).
5   See the award-winning film by Shin Eun-jung, *Verita$: Everybody Loves Harvard* (2011).
6   Keane, *Global Civil Society?*, 129.
7   Fishman, *Insurrectionists*, 119.
8   André Gorz, *Farewell to the Working Class: An Essay on Post-Industrial Socialism* (Boston: South End Press, 1982), 69.
9   John Girling, "Development and Democracy in Southeast Asia," *The Pacific Review* 1, no. 4 (1988): 333.
10   Choi, *Gwangju Uprising*, 37–39.
11   Val Burris, "The Discovery of the New Middle Class," *Theory and Society* 15 (1986): 344–45.
12   Han Sang-Jin, "The Public Sphere and Democracy in Korea," in *Korean Politics: Striving for Democracy and Unification*, ed. Korean National Commission for UNESCO (Elizabeth, NJ: Hollym, 2002), 266–67.
13   Yun Fan, "Taiwan: No Civil Society, No Democracy," in *Civil Society and Political Change in Asia: Expanding and Contracting Democratic Space*, ed. Muthiah Alagappa (Stanford: Stanford University Press, 2004), 168; Also see Richard Robison and David Goodman, *The New Rich in Asia: Mobile Phones, McDonald's and Middle-Class Revolution* (London: Routledge, 1996), 10.
14   Interview with Michael Hsiao, Taipei, February 3, 2009.
15   See Shrishti Rana, "Don't Forget Kathmandu," *Kathmandu Post*, April 11, 2009, 6.
16   Haggard and Kaufman, *Political Economy*, 31.
17   C.L.R. James, in collaboration with Raya Dunayevskaya and Grace Lee, "The Ideological Crisis of the Intermediate Classes," in *State Capitalism and World Revolution* (Chicago: Charles H. Kerr Publishing Company, 1986), 113–35.
18   "Structural Crises," in *New Left Review* 62 (March–April 2010): 139.
19   Callahan, *Cultural Governance*.
20   See Martin Oppenheimer's excellent book *White Collar Politics* (New York: Monthly Review Press, 1985) for an early appreciation of women's proletarianization.
21   Gorz, *Farewell*, 84–85, Herbert Marcuse, "Marxism and Feminism," in *The New Left and the 1960s*, ed. Douglas Kellner (New York: Routledge, 2005), 165–72.
22   See Tannen's insightful book, *You Just Don't Understand: Women and Men in Conversation* (New York: Ballantine Books, 1990).
23   In Gorz, *Farewell*, 85.
24   Marcuse, *Aesthetic Dimension*, 28–29.

25 For further discussion of the universal interests of the species, see the last chapter of my book *The Subversion of Politics: European Autonomous Social Movements and the Decolonization of Everyday Life* (Oakland: AK Press, 2006).

26 Barucha Calamity Peller, *Women in Uprising: The Oaxaca Commune, the State, and Reproductive Labor* (2011), http://readthenothing.files.wordpress.com/2011/07/oaxaca-commune3.pdf.

27 For more on the Panthers, see Cleaver's essay, "Women, Power and Revolution" in *Liberation, Imagination, and the Black Panther Party* (New York: Routledge, 2001).

28 See *The Subversion of Politics* (Korean translation published in 2000).

CHAPTER 15

Uprisings in Comparative Perspective

> The usual opinion that internal disturbances or wars occur mainly in the periods of impoverishment, or vice versa, is fallacious. This does not mean that the opposite statement, that wars and revolutions occur mainly in the period of prosperity, is a universal rule. It means . . . that war, internal disturbances, and economic fluctuations all move fairly independently of one another and that the causes of war and revolutions are not mainly economic.
>
> —Pitrim Sorokin

> The new movements have stirred intense debate over the relationship between economic crisis and political change, the viability of mass insurrection, the role of labor, the definition of democracy, and the significance of personal and cultural factors in creating a new society.
>
> —Carl Boggs

FOR DECADES, SOCIAL scientists have sought to locate specific variables and relationships that could predict the occurrence of social insurgencies, an elusive goal that continues to animate thousands of researchers in the social movement industry. Filling abstract hypotheses with empirical data, investigators produce administrative social research potentially useful to the control center. Yet because the hypothetical-deductive methodology subsumes the unique character of social reality beneath the rubric of a standardized formula, it often obscures rather than enlightens.

As early as 1937, Pitrim Sorokin analyzed thousands of cases of "social disturbances" in the quest for a universal formula. Much to his surprise, Sorokin found, "that war, internal disturbances, and economic fluctuations all move fairly independently of one another and that the causes of war and revolutions are not mainly economic."[1] This finding leaves unanswered a host of questions. Why do uprisings occur when they do? Why do some succeed while others fail? Why do some momentary successes—as in the 1986 overthrow of Philippine dictator Marcos—not lead to longer run system alterations? How should we understand why different results come from similar actions? Are there relationships between one uprising and another?

For uprisings under consideration in this book, none of the predictive variables generated by academic research seems robustly correlated to all occurrences—not economic factors, peaks of protests, number of deaths, role of regime insiders, or religion. While uprisings' popular participation and intensity do appear to indicate deeper subsequent democratization, not every case validates this relationship. Rootedness in civil society is also an important contributing factor, especially since such a resource enhances autonomous organization and collective leadership. Rather than locating the primary cause of uprisings in domestic economic and political variables, the relationship of one revolt to another seems most significant. Uprisings cluster in an eros effect of concatenation and mutual reinforcement. During the Arab Spring of 2011, this phenomenon was readily visible. Lubricated by Facebook, YouTube, and SMS texting, the intuitive popular capacity to join uprisings was robust.

Economic Factors

Following in the footsteps of Sorokin's empirical work, subsequent research correlated declining status and falling economic position with right-wing movements. The classic example is the rise of Nazism following the German economic crisis after World War I. In 1933, Arthur Raper uncovered an inverse correlation between hundreds of racial lynchings in the American South from 1901 to 1930 and the price of cotton.[2] The higher the price of cotton, the more peace reigned, but when the price of cotton fell and hardships set in, the number of lynchings dramatically increased. While social science can claim very few of its empirical findings as universal, the insight that periods of prolonged economic hardship and falling status produce right-wing, even dictatorial, social movements, although contradicting the common belief that the working class will rise up against hardship, seems valid in many different times and places.

While it is often thought that progressive movements will emerge as a result of economic crisis, left-wing revolutionary upheavals instead appear to be generated when ascendant prosperity and rising expectations are followed by a sharp drop-off in economic growth. James Davies formulated such a "J-curve" after investigating the Egyptian revolution of 1952 and Russian revolutions at the beginning of the twentieth century.[3] Taken as a whole, data related to Asian uprisings at the end of the twentieth century does not validate Davies's hypothesis. In Indonesia, the Philippines, and China, economic crises—especially

TABLE 15.1 **Inflation and GDP Growth Rate Before Uprisings**

Country (Uprising)	Years	Inflation	GDP Growth Rate	Years
Nepal (1990)	1980–1990	9.1%	7.2%, 4.2%	1988, 1989
Bangladesh (1990)	1980–1990	9.6%	2.9%, 2–5%	1988, 1989
Philippines (1986)	1980–1986	18.2%	-7.3%, -7.3%	1984, 1985
Indonesia (1998)	1998–1999	58.5%, 20.5%	4.7%, -13.1%	1997, 1998
Thailand (1992)	1980–1992	4.2%	11.6%, 7.9%	1990, 1991
South Korea (1987)	1980–1987	5%	6.9%, 12.4%	1985, 1986
Taiwan (1990)	1980–1987	1.3%	4.9%, 11.6%	1985, 1986
China (1989)	1988–1989	18.8%, 18.0%	11.3%, 4.1%	1988, 1989

Sources: Junhan Lee, "Primary Causes of Asian Development: Dispelling Conventional Myths," *Asian Survey* 42, no. 6: 825; China Statistical Yearbook, 2002 as cited in China Institute for Reform and Development, *Thirty Years of China's Reforms: Through Chinese and International Scholars' Eyes* (Beijing: Foreign Languages Press, 2008), 81.

inflation—caused great fears among people and contributed to the unrest. In the Philippines and Indonesia, negative GDP growth was experienced prior to the uprisings, reaching minus 13.1 percent during the IMF crisis in Indonesia. Prior to the overthrow of Suharto, more than twenty million citizens saw their standards of living plunge below the poverty line. In the Philippines under Marcos, the economy stagnated for years before people sent him into exile. Yet economic crises were not of great importance universally. South Korea's economy grew a healthy 12.4 percent in the year before the June 1987 uprising, and Thailand's economic output increased an average of 10 percent in the two years prior to 1992. Data in TABLE 15.1 indicate that no uniform economic conditions can be discerned prior to recent Asian uprisings.

If economic crises lead to uprisings, then we should have seen major mobilizations throughout the region during the IMF crisis of 1997. Korea's general strike against neoliberalism began in December 1996, well before the crisis first broke out (in Thailand in July 1997). Later in 1997, Korea's economy lay in ruins, a reason used to quiet the working class in the name of national salvation. In Thailand, after more than one million people fell through the poverty line by 1998, people's response was to save themselves rather than go into the streets to protest. In the Philippines leading up to 1986, a severe economic downturn preceded Marcos's ouster, yet so did years of patient preparation by RAM officers, Cardinal Sin, and the democratic opposition. The timing of the mutiny was more a function of political factors like the increasingly successful communist war of attrition and decreasing U.S. satisfaction with Marcos. Clearly in Indonesia in 1998, significant economic dislocation caused by the IMF crisis contributed greatly to the success of student mobilizations against Suharto. In China as well, the economy's problems were significant prior to 1989.

In 1959, Seymour Martin Lipset wrote a seminal article in which he hypothesized that a middle-class threshold for democracy existed before democratization could be long-lasting.[4] Although Lipset's hypothesis was subsequently accepted as truth, it does not appear to be absolutely valid—at least not for the occurrence of uprisings in the countries discussed here. Data in TABLE 15.2 reveal

TABLE 15.2 **GNP Per Capita at the Time of Uprising**

Country	Year	GNP/capita
Nepal	1990	$170
Bangladesh	1990	$210
Nepal	2006	$268
China	1987	$290
Philippines	1986	$560
Indonesia	1998	$636
Thailand	1992	$1,840
South Korea	1987	$2,690
Taiwan	1987	$5,325

Sources: Junhan Lee, "Primary Causes of Asian Development: Dispelling Conventional Myths," *Asian Survey* 42, no. 6: 823; Roger V. Des Forges, Ning Luo, Yen-bo Wu, eds., *Chinese Democracy and the Crisis of 1989: Chinese and American Reflections* (Albany: SUNY Press, 1992), 224, http://www.studentsoftheworld.info/country_information.php?Pays=NEP.

a wide variation in levels of economic prosperity, yet in all the countries, there was lasting democratization. Uprisings' success does not appear to be a function of the creation of a large middle class nor of GNP per capita.

Both of Nepal's successful uprisings occurred despite a low level of economic prosperity. The country's first act after the 2006 uprising was to abolish the monarchy altogether. While it may still be too early to determine if democracy will continue, the wide range of economic status indicates that, for these countries at least, the correlation between levels of economic development and uprisings is not significant. In Asia at the end of the twentieth century, uprisings were apparently not primarily moments in the movement of capital, as economic determinists maintain.

Neither does the identity of colonizing powers appear to be a significant factor, since former Dutch colonies (Indonesia, Taiwan) as well as places previously ruled by the United States (the Philippines), Japan (Taiwan, Korea) and Britain (Nepal, Bangladesh, Burma) all experienced strong democratization uprisings. The failure of former French colonies (Vietnam, Cambodia, and Laos) to be part of this wave of movements may be more a factor of intensive U.S. bombing during the Indochina War (which decimated their societies and economies) than of their colonization by France. Even here, a counterexample can be found in South Korea, where people rose up only seven years after their country had been devastated by U.S. air power during the Korean War (1950–1953) to overthrow the Syngman Rhee dictatorship.

Protest Peaks and Depth of Democratization

The relationship of confrontation politics to patient organizing efforts is often portrayed in either/or terms,[5] yet my research reveals that they often complement each other. In country after country, uprisings provided a surge in longer-term organizing and contributed to the outbreak of strike waves, the mushrooming of civil society organizations, and the proliferation of autonomous media. One reason for the portrayal of street actions as disparaging to (and even antagonistic to) organizing is that professional activists and academic "observers" are threatened by the sudden entry of popular movements into "their" space. As uprisings begin, new autonomous voices crowd out professionals' exalted positions as spokespersons for subaltern groups. When the oppressed speak for themselves, some of the first to drown out their voices are those who claim to represent them.

More often than not, uprisings create surges of movements in their wake, even when the movement (as in Burma and Tibet) is brutally suppressed. Immediately after democratic breakthroughs in Nepal, Korea, Thailand, and Bangladesh, workers' movements erupted that expanded unionization and insisted upon improved wages and working conditions. Women's movements in Nepal, Bangladesh, and South Korea won new government protections as well as changes in everyday lives. Unlike legislation or organization building, uprisings can stimulate social transformations of everyday life because they unlock ingrained patterns of behavior and challenge routinized structures of domination. Uprisings are significant vehicles for reclaiming state-dominated arenas, and their erotic and emotional energies are vital to resurgent civil societies.

Studying the character of democratization produced by the post–New Left surge in the 1980s and 1990s, we can observe that the more intense the uprising, the greater the depth of democratization, and conversely, in those countries without significant popular mobilizations, democratization was least robust. In Pakistan, for example, the death of President Zia al-Haq in a plane crash led to elections won by Benazir Bhutto in 1988. For many political scientists, these elections were proof of the presence of democracy, even though the country was soon engulfed once again by dictatorship. In South Korea, on the other hand, where mobilizations were widespread and lasted for many years, democratization was so vigorous that very few people ascribe any chance at all to the reimposition of a military regime. It appears to be the case that without significant protests in the streets, even limited, formal democracy has little hope to be respected by elites.

The wave of Asian uprisings predated transformative events in Eastern Europe, and unlike Europe's 1989 revolutions, they did not flow from decisions made by world leaders to end the Cold War. Uprisings in East Asia were generally not produced by elite decisions but by direct actions of an activated citizenry. Can this help explain why Asian people's lives generally improved after their popular breakthroughs (unlike the top-down revolts in the former Soviet Union and East European republics, where life expectancies have fallen)? Can we correlate peaks of movements with uprisings' lasting effects?[6] As displayed in TABLE 15.3, Gwangju's activated citizenry consisted of some 43 percent of the population, an astonishingly high percentage that might explain why they were able to overwhelm the military that night (although it does not explain their defeat on May 27, 1980, and the subsequent seven long years of Chun's U.S.-backed dictatorship). The high rate of participation in Gwangju, however, might be an indication why the city continued to propel insurgencies in Korea and why South Korean democracy ultimately prevailed. TABLE 15.3 delineates movement high points.

Like other abstract formulas, the political protest peak model does not seem to apply uniformly. In Rangoon, some 36 percent of the city mobilized for

TABLE 15.3 **Peaks of Urban Protests**

City	Date	Number of Protesters at High Point	Metropolitan Population	% Population
Bangkok	October 13, 1973	500,000	3,500,000	14%
Gwangju	May 21, 1980	300,000	700,000	43%
Manila	February 23, 1986	1,000,000	7,725,000	13%
Seoul	June 1987	1,000,000	10,000,000	10%
Rangoon	August 8, 1988	500,000	2,800,000	18%
Rangoon	September 8, 1988	1,000,000	2,800,000	36%
Beijing	May 20, 1989	1,000,000	12,000,000	8%
Kathmandu	April 6, 1990	400,000	1,100,000	36%
Bangkok	May 17, 1992	300,000	6,220,000	5%
Jakarta	May 20, 1998	1,000,000	9,000,000	11%
Kathmandu	April 22, 2006	1,000,000	1,900,000	53%

democracy on September 8, 1988, but severe repression led to decades of dictatorship. In Lhasa on March 19, 1959, practically the entire city answered the call to defend the Dalai Lama, yet the battle in which thousands of people were killed resulted in Chinese victory and the city's submission to colonization. In Seoul on June 26, 1987, the largest mobilization was about one million people—only 10 percent of the population—yet the movement's breakthrough was robust and long-term.

Counting the Deaths

To no one's surprise, military dictatorships' stupidity is matched only by their brutality, by the interests of "rational" elite actors whose self-interest is to maintain power by any means necessary. Is there a correlation between the number of people killed during uprisings and government stability? The numbers in TABLE 15.4 would seem to indicate that the more people killed by a regime, the better its chances of remaining in power. Although international public opinion and domestic constraints increasingly prevent governments from exercising the full brunt of their violence on their own citizens, the military in Burma has certainly shown little restraint, nor did Assad and Gaddafi in 2011. Even though the Romanian regime killed hundreds in 1989, it was overthrown. Like other abstract formulations, even heavy repression cannot always explain regime change—or lack of it.

When compared to other continents, the number of casualties during Asian uprisings is quite low. Samuel Huntington counted twenty thousand total deaths (heavily concentrated in South Africa and other parts of Asia) in thirty democratization efforts from 1974 to 1990.[8] Compared with millions slaughtered in U.S. wars in Asia or tens of thousands killed in Latin American conflicts, Asia's civility when dealing with its political problems seems evident. Some thirty-four people (mainly students) were killed in Athens in 1973 when the Greek dictatorship used tanks to seize control of the Polytechnic in 1973. In 1989, the uprising in Venezuela against the IMF-imposed austerity program cost 276 lives by official count, but

TABLE 15.4 **Deaths During Uprisings**

Place	Year	Number Killed
Lhasa	1959	5,000
Thailand	1973	77
Gwangju[7]	1980	240
Manila	1986	12
Korea	1987	1
Burma	1988	3,000
Tibet	1989	250
Beijing	1989	250
Taiwan	1990	0
Nepal	1990	62
Bangladesh	1982–1990	105
Thailand	1992	52
Indonesia	1998	1,188
Nepal	2006	21
Egypt	2011	840

Note: Numbers used are conservative and reflect official counts when available.

that figure is far too low. More reliable estimates are in the thousands. According to official reports, nearly eight hundred were killed in the overthrow of Romanian dictator Ceausescu in the same year.

Role of Military and Regime Insiders
In their typology of democratic transitions, political scientists pay a great deal of attention to elite dynamics. From the outside, analysts may be able to tell us that the transition in Hungary involved the transformation of a communist elite into a capitalist one, while in Czechoslovakia, a new elite emerged. Yet such a perspective cannot begin to comprehend the lived experience of the uprisings, to comprehend the ways in which people's lives were transformed, or which specific class actors were involved in creating and leading the movements.

Far more than is generally realized, significant defections to insurgencies occurred within the ranks of militaries. In the Philippines, dissident army officers led the mutiny against Marcos and called forth a million supporters with the help of the Catholic Church. Even soldiers sympathetic to Marcos refused to drive their tanks over citizens massed in the streets. In China, the army similarly refused to impose martial law for two weeks while the citizens of Beijing mobilized peacefully to stop them. As one commander proclaimed publicly, "We are the people's army. We will never fire on the people." General Xu Qinxian of the Thirty-Eighth Army refused to follow orders to use force, as did more than 100 officers and 1,400 enlisted men who deserted when violence became intense. In 1973, Thai General Kris Sivara refused to send additional troops or resupply ammunition to Bangkok, effectively limiting his rival's capacity to repress the demonstrations. The Royal Thai Navy openly supported the students, and Air Force personnel organized protests against the repression. During the Gwangju Uprising, General

Chung Oong refused to agree to orders to use troops against protesters. On three separate occasions, he insisted police would be sufficient.[9] His Jeolla-based unit successfully negotiated their peaceful retreat during heavy fighting at the train station. As residents of the Gwangju area, they had no wish to participate in the bloodletting—and people permitted them to evacuate in peace. Gwangju's police chief also refused to order his men to open fire, an act for which he was arrested. In Burma, border police, immigration officials, and Air Force personnel all joined protests on September 9, 1988. Eleven of the celebrated "Thirty Comrades" who led the independence movement supported democracy. In Indonesia, the army permitted students to occupy the parliament building (and once Suharto had left the presidential palace, gently expelled them).

In the case of Burma, Bertil Lintner surmised that if any general had marched on Rangoon to carry forward the banner of democracy in 1988, there was a good chance the movement could have succeeded. Looking at the country's prospects for democracy, a left-wing military coup may be its best chance, although Burmese officers are notorious for gang-raping minority women and accruing vast fortunes for themselves—not for altruistic actions. So brutal is the military that David Tharekabaw, vice president of the Karen National Union, told me that without an armed force protecting citizens, calling them into the streets for protests was little more than organizing a massacre.[10]

The coordination of military action—or at least the threat of it—with massive protests is certainly an effective means of enacting regime change. Autonomous military force was significant during Nepal's 2006 uprising, when the Maoist armed forces combined their attacks with urban mobilizations. In the Philippines, RAM's mutiny was key to the massive uprising. The church's outspoken support for mutineers sapped the morale of Marcos's troops, who were unable to mount an effective counterattack on the rebels' bases. At a minimum, the military must be neutralized, either through the government's decision not to employ its full force or by being so divided that it is unable to repress the popular mobilization.

Alongside defections within the armed forces, high-ranking government officials also dissented. At a critical moment in China, the Foreign Ministry insisted Zhao Zhiyang was still premier, even though Deng Xiaoping had replaced him with Li Peng. In Thailand in 1992, former Bangkok Mayor Chamlong took over leadership of protests, and many national ministries publicly decried the military's use of force. In Nepal, the country's foreign minister criticized the excessive violence employed by the Royal Army, and workers in many ministries staged "pen-down" strikes to support the movement. In the Philippines, governors and high officials defected to the opposition, and in Indonesia, parliamentary leaders annulled Suharto's reelection and called for his impeachment. Regime insiders who sympathized and sometimes participated in Asian uprisings is an understudied dimension. Many democratization theorists insist that for revolutions to succeed, uniting with such forces is a vital need. Insisting that some section of the existing elite must go over to the side of the insurgents for them to be successful, Alfred Stepan concludes, "One is tempted to argue that societal-led upheavals by themselves are virtually incapable of leading to redemocratization."[11]

Civil Society

In European history, the schism of the Roman Empire into East and West in 285 CE created two very different social systems. In the East, the Emperor became head of both the Christian church and the Byzantine state in Constantinople. After Rome was overrun and sacked twice by Germans, the Pope was reduced to an appendage of political power. Combined with the Protestant Revolution a millennium later, the net effect was to forge an autonomous secularism in Western Europe, helping to create a space in which citizens could assert their rights. This outcome of Western Europe's historical development has been hypostasized as the model that all societies must take in order for "civil society" to exist.

Jürgen Habermas in particular has posited a long list of requirements in order for "genuine" civil society to be said to exist: a free press and literacy, individual rights, civility, and sites for collective deliberation.[12] For Habermas, as for many other theorists, Western European privacy and atomization stand in sharp contrast to Asia and the East, where he believes the bourgeois individual did not develop. Privacy and individual rights in Germany (for example) are considered fundamentally different than in Asia's densely packed cities. In Habermas's view, coffee houses in eighteenth-century Europe contributed greatly to the public sphere and civil society. Following in his footsteps, many people have asked whether or not Asia's teahouses might be considered similar domains. For those who hold European society in high regard, the answer is "no."[13] From my experiences, many teahouses and even street corners in Asia might be more of a civil space than the interiors of Europe's finest cafés—and I have spent a great deal of time in both venues. Neighbors in Asia often have more long-lasting and cooperative roles in each other's lives than in the United States, where people often do not even know members of their community at all. Harvard professor Henry Louis Gates can attest to this observation. In 2009, he returned home from a trip to China and discovered he had misplaced his house key. After he broke into his own house, someone in the neighborhood phoned the police, who arrested him, an African–American, inside his own home in an affluent district of Cambridge.

Instead of locating Asia's heritage of values and relations as a resource, many Western observers point to the dearth of American-style voluntary groups and conclude that there is no civil society.[14] John Keane notes that "in early modern usages, 'civil society' was typically contrasted with the 'Asiatic' region, in which, or so it was said, civil societies had manifestly failed to appear."[15] To be sure, vibrant roots of civil society in Asia are known. No less than a hundred disparate women's newspapers were published in Beijing between 1905 and 1949, and Chinese chambers of commerce in market towns were said to number at least 2000 in 1912, with about two hundred thousand merchant members, and an additional 871 associations in larger cities.[16] While democracy is formulated as a European (Greek) invention, research has revealed republican forms of government in ancient Sumerian cities.[17] In India, republics arose in the Ganges plain with elected leaders and assemblies, which gave rise to egalitarian breakaways from the Hindu caste system such as Jainism and Buddhism.[18] Seeing its roots in Asian philosophers like Lao-tzu, Mencius and Confucius, Kim Dae Jung persuasively postulated Asia's cultural traditions as possibly providing a base from which new "global democracy" could be constructed.[19]

In Gwangju, activists reminded me that even under the harsh terms of the military dictatorship, they spread word of movements by taking food to neighbors' homes (사발통문)—a longstanding tradition in Korea, especially when fresh *kimchi* is made—in order to whisper news and organize events. Civil institutions were of tremendous importance during the Gwangju Uprising of 1980, including the YMCA, YWCA, Namdong Catholic Cathedral, Women's Pure Pine Tree Society, Nok Du Bookstore, Wildfire Night School, Clown Theater Group, and the Artists' Council. Nonetheless, leading American Koreanists insist that civil society did not reawaken until the elections of 1985.[20] In Taiwan, where forty years of the harshest repression (the "White Terror") resulted in untold thousands of state-sanctioned murders of political dissidents, civil society—the creation of a "subaltern counterpublic"—was the only place where activism could occur.

A similar pro-European bias can be located in the work of conservative commentator Lucian Pye, who posited Protestantism as an ideal basis for civic culture and suggested Asia's lack of it might mean it would be the last continent to democratize.[21] As Asia's economies grew rapidly in the 1970s and 1980s, Singapore's Lee Kwan Yew and Malaysia's Mahathir Mohamad embraced "Asian values" as a reason for their success. They believed that unlike the West, Asians prize family above individual, social order over individual freedom, and hard work over leisure. Yet for all the talk of "Asian" values, the continent is incredibly diverse, embracing lands from Iraq to Korea and Siberia to Sri Lanka. Even if we limit ourselves to East Asia, diversity is much greater than many people appreciate. Among the ten countries studied in this book, two are Islamic (Bangladesh and Indonesia), one is Hindu (Nepal), three are Confucian (China, Taiwan, and South Korea), one is Catholic (Philippines), and three are Buddhist (Thailand, Burma, and South Korea). South Korea also has many Protestants, possibly one-third of its population. Where once Confucian values were blamed for lack of business acumen and the ease with which Western businesspeople took advantage of polite Orientals, today Confucian culture is positively correlated with wealth.[22]

Conservative American anticommunism obscured the existence of civil society in East Europe by insisting the "totalitarian" state had swallowed all autonomous elements of society, yet there seems to be general agreement today that uprisings there at the end of the twentieth century emanated from civil society. As the cunning of history invalidated much Cold War propaganda on both sides, the political practice of *Solidarność* in Poland (a predominantly Catholic society) caused Polish dissidents to talk of "the rebellion of civil society against the state."[23]

Since many Western theorists believe civil society is a function of economic development, they therefore expect the trajectory of the West and its kind of civil society to be the future of "less developed" countries.[24] In actuality, changing dynamics at the end of the twentieth century might reverse the political truism that "the country which is more developed industrially only shows, to the less developed, the image of its own future."[25] The 1997 IMF crisis in Asia was followed a decade later by the global economic meltdown that began in the United States. As infrastructure deteriorates and the government assumes more powers, predictions that the United States is becoming a Third World country increasingly appear true. Rather than the West showing the East its future, the opposite may be occurring.

Throughout these two volumes, I have pointed to ways in which Asia's traditional civil society, so different from the West's, became great sources of strength for social movements. From the tree and the drum which Korean villagers could use to announce grievances and find consensual means of resolving them, to Chinese people's right to petition for redress of grievances, and Nepalese understanding of the dharma's meaning that kings should rule justly, cultural traditions—however dated and old-fashioned—became operative means of rallying opposition against ruling powers. As Larry Diamond and others point out, "civil society has played a crucial role in building pressure for democratic transition and pushing it through to completion."[26] If Asia only had weak civil societies, how could democratization movements have succeeded?

Autonomy and Centralization

High on the list of factors leading to short-term successful outcomes for uprisings are autonomous initiatives of many diverse grassroots groups within decentralized structures of authority. We can best comprehend these dynamics in a more precise analysis of the history of uprisings themselves. The centrally organized 1948 Jeju Uprising failed to preserve national unity as participants hoped, while the spontaneous and autonomous Gwangju Uprising led to a protracted and successful effort to imprison Chun Doo-hwan and Roh Tae-woo as part of the democratic transition. Arrests of movement leaders in Gwangju prior to the uprising helped make the movements more spontaneous and grassroots. The multitude became central, demands were visionary, and solidarity was unobstructed by ideological (and personal) disagreements among leaders. Can we generalize to say that the more autonomous the uprising, the greater its short-term success?

As discussed at length in *Asia's Unknown Uprisings Volume 1*, Korean uprisings in Jeju and Gwangju were essentially similar in their aspiration for autonomous self-determination in the face of increasingly heteronomously determined social relations dominated by the United States. They were both against the international megalith—the *Gesamtkapital* of corporate/government power that is today preponderant in local affairs around the world. These uprisings are normally understood in the context of national dynamics, yet cross-national comparisons between Jeju and the Taiwan uprising of February 28, 1947, reveal similarly tragic outcomes in the massacre of tens of thousands of innocent civilians in countries divided at the end of World War II by an Anglo-American decision to fight a Cold War against communism.[27] By coincidence, the first killings in Jeju came only one day after the killings began in Taiwan. In both cases, the forces of order resorted to massive violence in order to retain control. In Taiwan, tens of thousands were killed—their corpses thrown into the sea or left in the fields to rot.[28] In Jeju, at least 30,000 were killed on an island with a population of only 150,000.

Although both were moments when human freedom confronted slavery, Jeju and Gwangju comprised differing universes of discourse. While the Jeju Uprising was centrally organized down to some of its smallest details, the Gwangju Uprising was spontaneously enacted and spread beyond people's dreams (or nightmares). Their differences bear a striking resemblance to those between the Old Left and the New Left. The above remarks only begin to analyze the Jeju Uprising, but they also clarify the extent to which the uprising was centrally organized and controlled. The South Korean Labor Party had a centralized structure on the entire island down to the village level, and the organization also controlled the People's Committees, the de facto government from 1945 to 1948. Although they peacefully cooperated with the Americans after the Japanese defeat, people had little choice but to rise after police, obeying the orders of U.S. officers, opened fire at an elementary school on March 1, 1947, and killed three people. When a general strike was then suppressed and many of the island's young people tortured—some to death—the uprising resulted. Extraordinarily centralized, it began with simultaneous signal fires at eighty-nine volcano cones. Fighters were organized into centrally commanded regiments and battalions with self-defense forces at the village level.

Unlike on Jeju, Gwangju's uprising was entirely spontaneous, a reaction to the invasion of the city by brutal paratroopers who attacked its citizens. On Jeju, the SKLP was clearly the leadership, but in Gwangju, no organization was in control. When the uprising began, most movement activists were under arrest or had already fled the city. Horrific brutality inflicted by paratroopers on citizens led to a spontaneous citywide uprising in which people drove the military out of the city and held it for a week. People spontaneously created mobile strike forces and formalized the Citizens' Army, a Settlement Committee, and a Struggle Committee; they cared for corpses and grieving family members; healed the wounded; and cleaned up the liberated city. The Citizens' Army instructed all civil servants, including the disarmed police, to return to their posts; they took charge of gasoline distribution, traffic control, and information coordination. Tens of thousands of people gathered for daily rallies where a form of direct democracy was practiced that held ultimate decision-making power over negotiations with the military. A daily Fighters' Bulletin helped organize resistance to the impending counterattack—all without a centralized authority giving people orders from above—whether from a supreme commander or central committee. Crime rates were significantly attenuated and people cooperated with one another like seldom before.

On Jeju, numerous incidents of insurgents killing police were recorded. Sources indicate only approximately 5 percent of those killed in Jeju were victims of insurgents—some 1,764 people, including soldiers, election administrators, policemen, and members of right-wing organizations.[29] In Gwangju, by contrast, very few soldiers or police were killed, and there were no executions. My interviews with more than fifty members of the Citizens' Army (published in two volumes in Korean) revealed that many captured soldiers were released unharmed by the insurgents. One soldier was even given back his rifle (but not his ammunition) so his superiors would not punish him.

Years later, the incongruity between Jeju and Gwangju was still operative. From the very first trials in Gwangju, people threw garbage at the judges, and families of the dead and wounded organized resistance. On Jeju, where the horrific murders and brutality were far greater, it took decades for whispers about the carnage to be heard. In 1960, after students ended the Rhee dictatorship, the Chang Myon government opened an investigation of the massacre on Jeju, but the day after Park Chung-hee's 1961 coup, the investigators were arrested. The dictatorship clamped down on truthful investigation of the past, and any public hint of the massacre would have to wait until 1978, when Hong Ki-yong published a short story, "Aunt Sooni." In 1987, during the Great June Uprising, the Student Union at Jeju National University held the first commemorative service for those who had been massacred.[30]

Understanding this dialectic of autonomy and centralization within Korean political development lends insight into Burma, the Philippines, and Tibet. The Philippines was organized from the top down and led by segments of the military and Church. Although the 1986 People Power Uprising succeeded in displacing Marcos, the movement had comparatively little impact on the system of rule by the rich. The Dalai Lama's leadership of Tibet's movement and Aung San Suu Kyi's titular role in Burma also lend a top-down character to those movements, which constrains their impact. Along with a stringent adherence to nonviolence imposed by these two charismatic and courageous leaders, their authority disempowers creative grassroots action. The international moral high ground may be theirs, but domestic political efficacy is narrowed. The genius of Suu Kyi's father was to unite all minorities fighting for independence with the majority Burmese, but his daughter's rigid pacifism leaves minority groups isolated from the urban opposition and the opposition without a unified strategy. Although more than a dozen armed struggles were waged by ethnic minorities, the junta was able to pacify or defeat them one at a time, until it achieved control over the whole country. Suu Kyi's pacifism implicitly asserts the moral superiority of the majority over minorities—who have little choice but to fight in order to survive. In Tibet, many freedom fighters committed suicide in Mustang in 1971 when the Dalai Lama ordered them to lay down their weapons as a result of China-U.S. detente.

In Burma, years of oppressive dictatorship suddenly culminated in the uprising of 1988. At the beginning of the year, no one could have guessed that an altercation in a teashop in Rangoon would quickly develop into the government's apparent demise and the rise of neighborhood councils controlling the entire country. As the movement suffered terrible repression, an uprising was planned for precisely 8:08 a.m. on 8–8–88, when the city's dockworkers walked off their jobs. Within hours, the entire city was on strike, and within days, the whole country. The situation developed in ugly directions when activists killed suspected infiltrators. One of the first acts of students in their liberated university dormitories was to execute three fellow students they believed had informed to the authorities. As the struggle intensified and many people were killed, crowds cheered when captured police officers were publicly beheaded without trials.

Other significant variations can be located between the uprisings. While Gwangju people united as one into an "absolute community" and general assemblies of tens of thousands of people made important decisions at "Democracy Square," Burmese protests lacked both the graceful unity of all people and the capability to have daily meetings of tens of thousands in a liberated space. Whenever people gathered in the streets, the military bloodily dispersed them. In Gwangju, during days of brutal military attacks, citizens beat back the paratroopers and liberated the city. The example they set in their spontaneous capacity for self-government and the organic solidarity of the population surpassed that of the Burmese uprising.

During the height of the Burmese protests, the government suddenly released from jails around Rangoon thousands of criminals, compelling neighborhoods to cordon themselves off behind bamboo fences and to maintain around the clock patrols to guard against thieves, rapists, and assorted antisocial miscreants.[31] This phenomenon is the opposite of what occurred in the case of Gwangju. The discrepancy between the two cases is even greater when we recall that in Gwangju, dozens of people died assaulting the city's prison in attempts to liberate prisoners. In Burma, the government released prisoners since it knew they would terrorize the populace.

In Rangoon, Aung San Suu Kyi and a small group of notables quickly became the movement's leadership. Inside Gwangju, no one of the stature of Aung San Suu Kyi emerged as the single most important leader of the movement. Although the military singled out Kim Dae Jung as the leader, he was in prison during the entire uprising and did not even know it had happened until weeks afterward. Before the uprising began, dozens of other activists had been arrested, creating a vacuum on the streets within which the popular movement developed fresh organizations and collective leadership. Without a central command, the integration of small groups' initiatives was sufficiently powerful to drive the military out of the city on May 21. Rather than being vertically structured, the Citizens' Army was organized horizontally with no central authority or single leader having the final power to make decisions. The people themselves became their own government, and essential needs were met through cooperation. The decentralized and autonomous character of the Gwangju Uprising served to strengthen the movement. In contrast to the prevailing view of centralization meaning strength and efficiency, does the decentralization of the Gwangju Uprising indicate the power of autonomy and decentralization? These factors (unity, participatory democracy, and spontaneity) indicate greater chances for an uprising's short-term efficacy.

Of course, there are tremendous differences between South Korea and Burma. A Confucian society, South Korea is one of the world's largest economies, a member of OECD, and a "semiperipheral" country with modern infrastructure, advanced production facilities, and burgeoning high-tech sector. Korea's economic growth over the past thirty years has been spectacular. Per capita GNP, only $100 in 1963, exceeded $20,000 in 2007. With a democratic system since 1992, Korea's economy has expanded and moved into high-tech industries. While global statistics are only now becoming standardized, Korea is often considered the "world's most wired society." As in other indications of development, Burma is an IT basket case with only two Internet servers in 2007, when it had no mobile phone service in the country's new capital.

Measured in discrete units of time, direct insurgencies may fail. Their leaders may either be killed or imprisoned, many others may also suffer causalities, and groups that openly express themselves may again become dormant and silent. However, uprisings' open expression of grievances and visions, even when bounded in time, undermine the existing system's stranglehold on defining political reality. After popular insurgencies, existing parties begin to lose the type of approvals they had earlier. Huge political gaps develop which the parties have either to deal with by making genuine changes or risk becoming irrelevant. Sometimes the impact of particular uprisings, however brief their eruption, goes on for many decades. The ultimate destruction of previously legitimate political parties and outmoded norms of everyday life may take place slowly, but the impact of insurgencies persists.[32]

While a longer-term perspective indicates the need for strategic insurgent organizations, the past years of repression and brutality in Burma speak volumes to the disadvantages of centralized leadership. Aung San Suu Kyi was under house arrest for most of two decades, and the movement remained marginalized. Pacifists' critique of insurgents' "violence" does not seem to be an issue for many movement participants—although it certainly is for elite ones, including NGOs. Although armed, the Gwangju People's Uprising is remembered in Korea as a nonviolent movement since it stopped the brutality of the military. Despite the oft-repeated myth that the 1986 overthrow of Philippine President Marcos was strictly nonviolent, an armed rebel force that used its weapons with lethal precision led the movement.[33]

While Nepal and Burma's uprisings were planned in advance and organized from the top-down, the Gwangju Uprising was a spontaneous reaction to military attack. The violence among people in Nepal and Burma stands in sharp contrast to the Korean situation. In Nepal, political differences were often the source for altercation and even physical confrontation. As in Burma, many police were killed in the streets without trials. More than one account tells us that during the "voluntary" blackouts in 1990, houses that did not turn off their lights had their windows broken, after which the inhabitants were told that if they continued not to comply with the blackout, their houses would be burned down.[34]

Does humanitarian treatment of captured enemy combatants lead to greater success later? In China, unlike Gwangju, citizens disrespected the lives (and even some of the corpses) of young soldiers who followed orders to suppress the protests. In such a situation, while a few soldiers may have been killed, the net effect was to boomerang against the citizens' movement. If there was any hope for the movement to succeed, it lay in the capacity of ordinary people to reach out with love and solidarity—to effect an erotic bond—with the soldiers of the People's Army, as occurred on May 20 when hundreds of thousands of citizens blocked the army but also fed them. On June 3, a far different scenario unfolded, as brutality on both sides was meted out.

This review of possible explanations for the occurrence of uprisings reveals no single satisfactory dimension to which we can point—except perhaps the influence of one uprising on another. The eros effect, arising as it does from the unconscious, cannot be verified scientifically and was not even comprehended as having occurred in East Asia's string of uprisings since they were spread out over many years. Interviews of key activists in every country I visited indicated that great inspiration and energy crossed borders and taught lessons. If the Asian movements had erupted within months of each other rather than years apart, as during the 2011 Arab Spring, no doubt more recognition would have been given to their "meaningful coincidences."

NOTES

1   Pitrim Sorokin, *Social and Cultural Dynamics*, vol. 3: *Fluctuations of Social Relationships, War, and Revolution* (New York: American Book Company, 1937), 238.

2   Arthur Raper, *The Tragedy of Lynching* (Chapel Hill: University of North Carolina Press, 1933), 31.

3   James C. Davies, "Toward a Theory of Revolution," *American Sociological Review* 27, no. 1 (February 1962): 5–19.

4   Seymour Martin Lipset, "Some Social Requisites of Democracy: Economic Development and Political Legitimacy," *The American Political Science Review* 53, no. 1 (March 1959): 69–105.

5   See Alagappa, *Civil Society*.

6   See Junhan Lee, "Primary Causes of Asian Development: Dispelling Conventional Myths," *Asian Survey*, 42, no. 6, 823, 831. Lee sought to do so but lacked empirical data to understand the real peaks. I am indebted to his methodological suggestion.

7   Figures are from the May 18 Memorial Foundation. Government compensation programs reflect lower numbers, in part because some families refused to register.

8   Huntington, *Third Wave*, 194

9   Interview with Chung Oong, Seoul, December 4, 2009.

10 Interview in Maesot, Thailand, November 5, 2008.

11 Alfred Stepan, "Paths toward Redemocratization" in *Transitions from Authoritarian Rule: Comparative Perspectives*, vol. 3, eds. Guillermo A. O'Donnell, Philippe C. Schmitter, and Laurence Whitehead (Baltimore: Johns Hopkins University Press, 1991).

12 Callahan, "Comparing the Discourse," 281–82.

13 See Susanne H. Rudolf and Lloyd I. Rudolf, "The Coffee House and the Ashram: Gandhi, Civil Society and Public Spheres," in *Civil Society and Democracy*, ed. Carolyn M. Elliott (Oxford: Oxford University Press, 2003), 377–404. Even in regard to Asian teahouses, the argument is made elsewhere that the nature of discussions does not reach the lofty height of individual autonomy attained in European cafés.

14 The case of Korea is discussed at length in *Asia's Unknown Uprisings Volume 1*. Gregory Henderson found "amorphousness and isolation in social relations." See Henderson, *Korea: The Politics of the Vortex* (Cambridge: Harvard University Press, 1968), 4.

15 Keane, *Global Civil Society?*, 31. On the next page, Keane continues his commentary on Europeans' views: "Civil societies was impossible in Muslim society."

16 Gordon White, Jude Howell, and Shang Xiaoyuan, "Market Reforms and the Emergent Constellation of Civil Society in China," in *Civil Society and Democracy*, ed. Carolyn M. Elliott (Oxford: Oxford University Press, 2003), 266–67.

17 See Thorkild Jacobsen, "Primitive Democracy in Ancient Mesopotamia," *Journal of Near Eastern Studies* 2, no. 3 (1943): 159–72.

18 Romila Thapar, *A History of India* (Harmondsworth: Penguin Books, 1966), 53. See Goody, "Civil Society," 156.

19 Kim Dae Jung, "Is Culture Destiny? The Myth of Asia's Anti-democratic Values," *Foreign Affairs* 6, 189–94.

20 Bruce Cumings, "Civil Society in West and East," in *Korean Society: Civil Society, Democracy and the State*, ed. Charles Armstrong (London: Routledge, 2002), 24.

21 Lucian Pye, *Asian Power and Politics: The Cultural Dimensions of Authority* (Cambridge: Belknap Press, 1985).

22 See Larry Diamond, ed., *Political Culture and Democracy in Developing Countries* (Boulder: Lynne Rienner Publishers, 1993).

23 See John Ehrenberg, "Civil Society," *New Dictionary of the History of Ideas* (New York: Scribner's, 2004).

24 See for example, Girling, "Development and Democracy," 332.

25 Karl Marx, Preface to the first German edition of *Capital: A Critique of Political Economy* (New York, International Publishers, 1967), 8–9.

26 Diamond et al., *Consolidating*, xxx. Yet as Muthiah Alagappa notes, NGOs and civil society can also be impediments to democratization.

27 See Lai et al., *Tragic Beginning*.

28 While the exact number of killed will never be known, estimates range from ten thousand to over one hundred thousand. On April 1, 1947, seven Taiwanese associations estimated the number slaughtered at fifty thousand. Ibid., 158.

29 Rimwha Han and Soonhee Kim, "Jeju Women's Lives in the Context of the Jeju April 3rd Uprising," presented at the international conference, The Jeju Sasam Uprising and East Asian Peace: International Legal Issues and Human Rights in 21st Century Korea, Harvard University, April 25, 2003.

30 Chang-sung Hyun, Young-hee Cho, Chan-sik Park, Seok-ji Hahn, Chang-hoon Ko, "The Resistance of the People and the Government's Countermeasures: The Historical Flow and Significance of the Case Studies from 1000 Years in Jeju," *Journal of Island Studies* 3, no. 1 (Spring–Summer 2000): 27.

31 Confirmed to me in e-mails with Bertil Lintner, April 9, 2006.

32 Discussions with Basil Fernando contributed greatly to my analysis here.

33 See Mercado's excellent book, *People Power*, especially pages 226, 232, 258, 308.

34 Routledge, "Backstreets," 568.

CHAPTER 16

The System Is the Problem

> We have a system that might be called global governance without global government, one in which a few institutions—the World Bank, the IMF, the WTO—and a few players—the finance, commerce, and trade ministries, closely linked to certain financial and commercial interests—dominate the scene, but in which many of those affected by their decisions are left almost voiceless.
>
> —Joseph Stiglitz, Nobel Prize–winning economist

> Standing armies shall in time be totally abolished.
>
> —Immanuel Kant, 1795

"HUMANS ARE BORN free yet everywhere are in chains." This immortal phrase remains as true today as when it was written by Jean-Jacques Rousseau in 1762. Despite amazing technological breakthroughs and dizzying economic expansion, the human condition remains substantially unworthy of the word "freedom." Potential abundance for all is twisted into weapons used in unending wars that mercilessly slaughter uncounted thousands of people. The capitalist world economy excludes the voices of the vast majority of human beings, while its systemic imperatives compel a billion people to teeter on the edge of starvation—and compels all of us live to work in order to eat. Everyday tens of thousands of people die from hunger and easily preventable diseases. Environmental devastation proceeds at dizzying speeds.

Profit-hungry corporations and militarized nation-states scandalously squander humanity's vast wealth despite a collective consciousness among millions of ordinary people that all weapons of mass destruction should be outlawed, that billionaires' wealth belongs to humanity, and that much more democracy is needed. Encumbered by obsolete property relationships and outmoded political forms, humanity stands today at a crossroads. Either we will create new, more democratic forms of governance or witness the erosion of planetary freedoms (including the prosperity enjoyed by many people).

No matter who sits in the White House or runs global financial institutions and corporations, the problem is not with the individual men and women at the top: the system is the problem. Its basic rules breed crisis after crisis. It is responsible for hundreds of millions of impoverished human beings at its periphery. It demands wars. It destroys our natural environment. Modern versions of colonial predecessors, global institutions such as the World Trade Organization (WTO), International Monetary Fund (IMF), and World Bank (WB) enforce these rules. They promise more prosperity through "free" trade, future prosperity from IMF "bailouts," and an end to poverty through World Bank "assistance," but they deliver continuing suffering and misery while they undermine global stability. At a time when human beings could work twenty hours per week for twenty years and live well in the remainder of our time on this planet, these global institutions insist we all must work longer hours and more years for less money. The 2008 global economic crisis is but a small foretaste of tragedies this system will produce.

The Best and the Brightest

One means to portray the systematic nature of the problems humanity faces is to take the case of the "best" of modern U.S. presidents. In American popular culture, John Kennedy is often associated with the word "Camelot" and remembered for Jackie's beauty. Yet, tragically, it was he—one of the most liberal U.S. presidents in history—who ordered the largest chemical warfare program in history (when Vietnam was sprayed with massive quantities of "Agent Orange," a gentle sounding phrase hiding one of the most deadly chemicals known to humans). Alongside Saddam Hussein, Kennedy was head of a modern state that sanctioned chemical warfare on civilians. Indeed, Hussein's Hallabja massacre pales by comparison: it was one attack that killed about eight thousand people, while JFK ordered years of chemical warfare that killed untold thousands of people and caused horrific birth defects and cancer for decades.

Despite all his apparent differences with JFK, Republican President Richard Nixon continued the use of Agent Orange—another example of basic agreement between the two parties in the United States. Republican George Bush attacked Afghanistan, and Democrat Barack Obama widened the war. During his term in office, Obama's Secretary of Defense was Bush-appointee Robert Gates, ex-CIA director and ex-Chairman of Fidelity Funds, the nation's largest mutual fund company. The first director of Obama's National Economic Council was Lawrence Summers, disgraced former president of Harvard University who helped implement the international response that deepened and prolonged the Asian IMF Crisis of 1997. Alongside U.S. wars against Iraq and Afghanistan, "liberal" Obama and company wage wars in Libya, the Philippines, Somalia (through Ethiopian proxies), and Colombia; they arm Israel and permit it to overrun and besiege Palestinian towns and cities; they encourage the revival of German and Japanese militarism; they attempt to isolate the Chávez government in Venezuela; they remain outside the purview of the International Criminal Court, and refuse to sign a new international protocol to the 1972 biological warfare treaty. On his watch, the United States rejected a global treaty banning landmines, which 150 countries supported, despite clear evidence of thousands of innocent people being killed every year by "leftover" mines. They develop miniature nuclear "bunker-buster" bombs (in defiance of international treaties to which the United States is a signatory).[1] During the first two and a half years of Obama's presidency, Wall Street profits were six billion dollars higher than during *all eight years* of Bush II.

When I refer to any of these presidents, I do not wish simply to focus on one man and his administration; it is the *system* that I wish to place under scrutiny. "Democratic freedom" that allows citizens the choice between the lesser of two evils every four years is no freedom at all—unless of course, we mean the "freedom" to select Coke or Pepsi, McDonald's or Burger King, but not to choose between war and peace, elite greed or shared prosperity. The system today offers no alternative to massive military spending, to corporate control of the economy, or to environmental devastation. Within such structural imperatives, history provides a great deal of evidence of how even "progressive" leaders only exacerbate problems. Although Hollywood remakes continually celebrate the distance of current U.S. policies from those of Nazi Germany and Japan during World War II, a great deal of continuity exists. More than a century before President Obama bowed to Japanese Emperor Akihito in 2009, U.S. collaboration with Japan's emperor resulted in the secret 1905 Taft-Katsura memorandum, recognizing Japan's right to "establish suzerainty of Korea" in exchange for Japan's agreement not to interfere with U.S. domination of the Philippines. Although this bilateral agreement was kept secret for decades, Japan immediately sent its first Governor-General to Korea, formally annexed the country in 1910, and brutally ruled it until 1945.

Immediately after World War II, U.S. policymakers made Japan and Germany their new best friends—quickly isolating former allies Russia and, after 1949, China. In West Germany and Japan, U.S. administrators embraced former Fascist operatives and integrated them into U.S. structures of military and economic control. Rather than being put on trial for war crimes, German rocket scientists and Japanese biological war experts became favored guests. A few high officials were tried and executed, and while Germany underwent partial de-Nazification, Japan still refuses to recognize or apologize for its wartime crimes—including massacres in cities like Nanjing, testing of bioweapons on prisoners, and the kidnapping of more than two hundred thousand women (half of them from Korea) who were used as sex slaves ("the Emperor's gifts to his loyal troops"). During World War II, Japan's "Greater East Asian Co-Prosperity Sphere" ordered rice exported from Vietnam to Japan as fuel for its industry because of an oil shortage. When famine resulted from 1944 to 1945, at least a million and a half (possibly two million) Vietnamese starved to death in the North (where the population was under fourteen million). If not for the uprising of the whole people (*khởi nghĩa*) in 1945 that liberated rice stores from Japanese control, thousands more would have starved.

Behind wars in which millions of ordinary people perish, world elites collaborate with each other. President George W. Bush's grandfather (and President George H.W. Bush's father), Prescott Bush, owned several large corporations that worked for Hitler and the Nazi regime.[2] More recently both presidents Bush and coworkers like James Baker were involved with the Bin Laden family in the Carlyle Group, a well-connected Washington merchant bank specializing in buyouts of defense and aerospace companies.[3] The Carlyle Group was one manifestation of transnational policy implemented by U.S. ruling circles as the global economy's expansion shifted to the global South. In order to continue reaping the rewards of capital expansion, the transnational elite opened its doors to local leaders who emerged in the space opened by uprisings against authoritarian regimes— men such as Fidel Ramos in the Philippines and Thaksin in Thailand. Getting rid of "cronyism" may sound desirable, but the end result was greater profits for transnational banks and corporations. For millions of people, the net effect was deepening impoverishment and marginalization.

During the last centuries, liberals have continually led the capitalist system's expansion in the name of progress. We are all aware of the hideous crimes of Nazis, but "enlightened" forms of European capitalist civilization have intensified the slaughter of native peoples in the periphery and created a centralized world system that demands militarism as a key organizing principle. While Americans continually celebrate our superiority over Nazis and Japanese Fascists, since World War II, over ten million people have been killed in U.S. wars around the world. Johan Galtung estimates twelve to sixteen million lives were extinguished in seventy U.S. interventions—and that was before recent wars in Iraq and Afghanistan.[4]

In the last half of the twentieth century, the United States slaughtered over five million Asians during the "Cold" War. In just three years, somewhere between three and five million people were killed in Korea, the vast majority of them innocent civilians. Cities were routinely reduced to rubble and ash. Thousands of civilian refugees were massacred and the United States employed biological weapons, yet it still will neither admit nor apologize for these actions.[5] Instead, before it moved its killing fields to Iraq, it sent them to Indochina, where it used more firepower than had been used in all previous wars in history combined, killing at least two million people and leaving millions more wounded or made refugees. Chemical warfare was systematic: over twenty million gallons of Agent Orange were sprayed on Vietnam. For every man, woman, and child in South Vietnam, the United States sprayed a gallon of Agent Orange, dropped forty pounds of napalm, half a ton of CS gas, and more than a thousand pounds of bombs (the equivalent of seven hundred Hiroshima atomic bombs)—all on people whose only wrongdoing was to struggle for national independence.[6]

On a personal level, Americans are known as friendly and relaxed, breathing democracy and exhaling liberty. Many Americans today pride themselves on "liberating" Afghan and Iraqi women from crass patriarchal domination, yet the murderous method used to free Iraqis from Saddam Hussein can only be compared historically to the slaughter inflicted by the Mongols in 1258, when they massacred some eight hundred thousand people and ended the Abbasid Caliphate.

In 2005, media attention portrayed the plight of Iraqi prisoners in U.S. custody in Abu Ghraib as exceptional. Sadly, such abuse has a long and tragic history. During the Vietnam War, suspected Viet Cong were routinely tortured with electric shocks or thrown out of helicopters. Evidence from the Korean War also indicated U.S. violation of norms of decency—if not international law. In the prison camp on Koje Island, Australian journalist Wilfred Burchett documented dozens of cases of medical experimentation (including the use of disease-carrying lice) and torture.[7]

The continuing reason for these wars is not simply the misguided decisions of a few errant policymakers and sadistic youth but rather the structural imperatives of the current economic regime. The very success of the system itself is the problem, not merely the frail human beings holding weapons. Most to blame are politicians, presidents, CEOs, and billionaires who make decisions to produce millions of weapons and to deploy armed soldiers to every corner of the planet, yet even they are caught in capitalism's global web. The key recognition here is that structural imperatives of the existing world economic regime demand system change.

In the Name of Freedom and Democracy
Recent uprisings in Egypt and the Arab world, like their predecessors in East Asia decades earlier, are propelled forward by vague promises of democracy and freedom. In the name of deposing dictators and correcting "corrupt" capitalism, movements drew in tens of thousands of adherents—including global corporate managers desiring to penetrate previously closed markets, to access labor forces unavailable to international capital, and to shore up dictatorial regimes reborn as "democracies." Like a wolf in sheep's clothing, corporate capitalism's capacity to brand itself as benign, even progressive and enlightening, disguised its murderous reality.

Common sense holds that increasing core democracy and overthrowing dictators should produce more enlightened policies and improvement in the lives of all human beings. Yet in this concluding chapter, I hope to clarify a dialectic of enlightenment and enslavement in the inverse relationship between the expansion of formal democracy and increasing human misery. For two centuries, progressive thinkers and policy-makers guided by "enlightened" values of the American and French revolutions presided over the system's most successful expansion. The global penetration of the capitalist system resulted in rapid economic development and important forms of individual liberty—but it also produced genocidal imperial conquest and an unstable economic behemoth. Perfecting "the machine instead of smashing it," revolutionary change at the end of the eighteenth century helped propel the nascent world system centered in Europe into a framework of international domination, concentrated military power in nation-states, and accumulated the world's wealth in the hands of giant corporations and banks. For the United States, the dialectical irony of history means that it is both a multicultural beacon of freedom as well as a white European settler colony founded on genocide and slavery.

Beginning in the sixteenth century, as peripheral areas were rapidly assimilated into Northern European economic structures, increasing political democracy in the North coincided with intensified exploitation in the South. When European settlers incorporated previously autonomous regions in the Americas, Southern Africa, Asia, and most recently, Israel, they committed genocide to steal the land of indigenous peoples. Besides exterminating tens of millions of Native Americans, European colonialists enslaved tens of millions of Africans. Estimates of the number of Africans killed in the slave trade range from fifteen to fifty million human beings.

From their earliest days, Northern European settler-colonists practiced biological warfare. Lord Jeffrey Amherst, after whom towns in Massachusetts, New York, and New Hampshire are named to this day, was celebrated because he devised a scheme to rid the land of indigenous people without risking white lives. He gave Native Americans blankets carrying smallpox virus, wiping out entire villages under the guise of providing assistance. The extermination of indigenous peoples was accelerated after the American Revolution, and in the century after it, nearly all indigenous peoples were systematically butchered. Although these acts are widely regretted today, the United States has never renounced such violence. Indeed, several towns and one prestigious university are still named for Amherst. One of the fanciest restaurants near prestigious Amherst College in Massachusetts is called the "Lord Jeff."

In a similar vein, white European settler-colonists purposely wiped out the buffalo, seeking to deprive native peoples of their primary source of food. Between 1872 and 1874, it is estimated that 3,700,000 buffalo were slaughtered (only 150,000 of them by Native Americans). From 1874 to 1883, as settler colonialism in Western North America intensified, some eight million buffalo were massacred. Far from feeling guilty for this form of biological warfare, "Buffalo Bill" staged a "Wild West" circus-style show to celebrate it, touring not only the East Coast of the United States but also Europe.

In the name of freedom, the United States annexed nearly half of Mexico in 1848 with the aim of expanding "Anglo-Saxon democracy" and "Manifest Destiny." Dozens of U.S. soldiers, the St. Patrick's Brigade, were executed under orders of General Zachary Taylor for refusing to fight against Mexico. At the end of the nineteenth century, as manufacturers looked for international markets, the United States (led by men experienced in the Indian wars) conquered the Philippines. At least two hundred thousand Filipinos perished from the war and disease.[8] The director of all Presbyterian missions hailed the slaughter of Filipinos as "a great step in the civilization of the world."[9] President William McKinley explained, "I heartily approve of the employment of the sternest measures necessary." For Theodore Roosevelt, the murders in the Philippines were necessary for the triumph of "civilization over the black chaos of savagery and barbarism." In 1900, Senator Albert Beveridge of Indiana summarized the mentality of American power: "We are the ruling race of the world. . . . We will not renounce our part in the mission of our race, trustee, under God of the civilization of the world."

Mark Twain and the Anti-Imperialist League stood in opposition to U.S. global conquests, but imperial ambitions were far too strong. Between 1898 and 1934, American Marines invaded Honduras seven times, Cuba four times,

Nicaragua five, the Dominican Republic four, Haiti and Panama twice each, Guatemala once, Mexico three times, and Colombia four times. In 1915, over fifty thousand Haitians were killed when U.S. troops mercilessly put down a peasant rebellion.[10] Marines were sent to China, Russia, and North Africa—wherever American investors needed help.

France's Great Revolution unleashed Parisian enlightenment on the world. Its dialectic of enlightenment and enslavement in Vietnam was graphically illustrated when French colonial authorities placed a full-scale replica of the U.S. Statue of Liberty atop the Hanoi pagoda of Le Loi, a national hero who led the victory against the 1418 Mongol invasion. (Le Loi's mythology includes Hoan Kiem, or Returned Sword, Lake, where a golden turtle gave him the magical sword he used to drive the Mongols out. With peace restored, the turtle subsequently reappeared to reclaim the sword. Here is a real Camelot, a story not unlike that of King Arthur in British folklore.) "Enlightened" French colonialism was brutal and deadly: Indochinese recall that dead human beings fertilized every tree in the country's vast rubber plantations that gave life to Michelin tires.

The strongest French imperial expansionists were staunch anticlerical "progressives" who regarded themselves as ideological heirs of the French Revolution. They were "enlightened" liberals, much as John Kennedy and members of his administration were "enlightened" liberals who believed they were carrying forth in the tradition of the U.S. revolutionary heritage. As Minister of Education, Jules Ferry defied the Catholic Church in France by making education universal, secular, and obligatory, but he later became the first French prime minister to make intensification of colonialism his overriding platform. Ferry believed that it was France's duty to civilize inferior people, and on May 15, 1883, a full-scale expedition was launched to impose a protectorate on Vietnam.[11]

Conservatives in France objected to this colonial expansion. As Vietnam disappeared, subsumed under the names of Tonkin, Annam, and Cochin China, even the identity of Vietnamese people was attacked as the French referred to them as Annamites. Bringing with them "civilization," French troops burned the imperial library at Hue in 1885, whose ancient scrolls and manuscripts were a repository of centuries of wisdom. Here we see the spatial expansion of the liberal values of the Enlightenment and the French Revolution—values that became the basis for France's "civilizing mission" (*mission civilisatrice*), just as the American Revolution was later turned into "Manifest Destiny."[12]

Under the direct influence of its great revolution, France proclaimed a crusade against Algerian slavery and, in the name of instituting orderly and civilized conditions, was able to break up Arab communal fields of villages, including lands untouched by "barbarous" and "unenlightened" Ottoman rulers. As long as Islamic culture had prevailed, hereditary clan and family lands were inalienable, making it impossible for the land to be sold. After fifty years of "enlightened" French rule, large estates had again appeared, and famine made its ugly appearance in Algeria.

In the name of civilization and liberal democracy, the British destroyed the communal ownership of village land in India, structures that had sustained local culture for centuries, a communal tradition surviving invasions by Persians,

Greeks, Scythians, Afghans, Tartars, and Mongols but which could not resist the "perfection" of the liberal principles of the British state. Under British enlightenment, large estates developed, and peasants were turned into sharecroppers. In 1867 the first fruits of British liberalism appeared: in the Orissa district of India alone, more than one million people died in a famine. Such famines were hardly indigenous to India, with its "backward" traditions (according to European values), but were brought by the "enlightened" liberalism of European democracy, through the spatial extension of the principles of "democratic" capitalism.

In every period, people believe they have advanced beyond the follies and barbarism of the past, yet even today, "enlightenment" and enslavement continue to proceed hand in hand. "Enlightened" China devastates Tibet in the name of destroying feudalism and superstition. In the name of freedom, the United States brings misery to millions of ordinary Afghanis, Iraqis, and Pakistanis. Even after all American combatants leave Iraq, "rational" U.S. warfare will continue to kill and maim for decades because of the residual effects of hundreds of tons of expended depleted uranium.[13]

Despite—or more accurately, because of—the spatial extension of proclaimed liberal values, there were four times as many deaths from wars in the forty years after World War II than in the forty years prior to it. From 1992 to 2002, the world's total income increased by an average of 2.5 percent per year, while the number of poor people increased by one hundred million. The top 1 percent of the world has the same income as the bottom 57 percent and the disparity is growing.[14] While the world spends something like a trillion dollars a year on its militaries, one adult in three cannot read or write, one person in four is hungry, and the planet's ecological crisis intensifies.

Structural Imperatives of the World System

Clearly the capitalist world system has dramatically developed technology and created huge amounts of wealth. Yet, it has now reached its productive limits and is destroying its very accomplishments. Ironically, its very successes undermine its own continuation. The existing system's structural imperatives are enforced by seemingly banal patterns of investors moving money to reap profits in financial markets, by banks and corporations making investment decisions solely on the basis of profit, and by governments' needs to provide people with security and stability. The corporate system's rules capture all of us in a cycle of enlightenment and enslavement because of its structural requirements for:

- Wars and Weapons
- Bubbles and Busts
- Billionaires and Beggars
- Profits and Pollution

First Structural Imperative: Wars and Weapons

Since the Great Depression of 1929, militarism has become the primary solution to stagnation in the world economy—and not only for the United States. Two hundred years have passed since Kant told us that, in time, standing armies would be totally abolished, yet there are more soldiers under arms today than ever before in history. World governments spent a record $1.46 trillion on militaries in 2008, a year of huge economic crisis, despite which—or should I say, as a result of which—global military spending grew 4 percent to a level 45 percent higher than a decade earlier. U.S. military spending increased nearly 10 percent in 2008 to $607 billion (about 42 percent of the world's total). In the number-two position was China with expenditures one-seventh of the United States (estimated at $84.9 billion).[15] In 2001, global military spending (conservatively estimated) rose 2 percent to $839 billion, or 2.6 percent of world GNP—about $137 for every man, woman and child on the planet.[16] That number increased to $217 in 2008.[17] Since 1948, the United States has spent more than $15 trillion on its military—more than the cumulative monetary value of all airports, factories, highways, bridges, buildings, machinery, water and sewage systems, power plants, schools, hospitals, shopping centers, hotels, houses, and automobiles.[18]

No matter who sits in the White House, militarism has long been and will surely remain at the center of U.S. foreign policy and economic development. Whatever their party, U.S. presidents—like senators and congressional representatives—have vigorously underwritten a vast expansion in the nation's military power and continually endorsed wars as an instrument of foreign policy against nations that posed no direct military threat. When the Cold War ended as the Soviet Union imploded, the promised peace dividend never materialized. Instead, the United States demonized Islamic terrorism and North Korea as reasons to ramp up arms expenditures, to create wars in Iraq and Afghanistan, and to expand American military presence around the world. In 2008, the United States had over 250,000 troops on 700 foreign bases in 130 countries.[19]

With a quarter of world population, 20 percent of its productive capacity, and 13 percent of its trade, Northeast Asia has been the primary area of world economic growth in the past two decades, and is poised to become a central power in the twenty-first century. Rather than reaping a peace dividend with the end of the Cold War, East Asia became the site of a regional nuclear arms crisis and massive buildup of conventional military forces. Armament sales to East Asia, a means of recovering U.S. trade dollars, soared amid exaggerated threats of war. In Taiwan, the threat of China is continually used to sell more arms systems.[20] U.S. disinformation exaggerating the North Korean threat plays a vital role in selling advanced "missile defense" weapons systems to Japan and South Korea. We know from experience that the CIA greatly exaggerated the Soviet Union's capabilities during the Cold War, and the Bush administration infamously—and falsely—insisted Iraq had "weapons of mass destruction." Overstating Pyongyang's nuclear and missile capabilities is a successful U.S. marketing strategy to sell missile systems to Japan, South Korea, and Taiwan—all countries that hold billions of dollars in foreign reserves that can be recouped through the sales of expensive "defense" weapons.[21]

Today in Northeast Asia a regional war could be waged without directly involving the United States. In a worst-case scenario, U.S. policymakers could opt to initiate a "limited" war in which Koreans would fight other Koreans. Minimal U.S. casualties might make such a war palatable to the American public.[22] Massive military exercises in 2010 off the coasts of China and North Korea follow a pattern. From 1976 to 1993, "Operation Team Spirit" threatened invasion and nuclear war on the DPRK. Every day U.S. planes capable of dropping nuclear weapons approached the 38th parallel. Although they veered off at the last minute, for people in the DPRK, the possibility of a U.S. nuclear attack was a daily reality for decades. In the 1980s and 1990s, North Korea reported more than 7,900 provocative acts per year, and the United States admitted to many of the same incidents, including daily high-altitude surveillance flights over North Korea. Over the years since the 1953 armistice, at least ten U.S. planes, including an EC 121 spy plane, have been shot down by the DPRK. In March 2003, the United States deployed a dozen B-52 bombers and an equal number of B-1s to the U.S. Pacific territory of Guam, within range of the DPRK. Is it any wonder that Pyongyang developed its own nuclear weapons?

With continuing stagnation in the world economy since the 2008 economic crisis, the system's incapability to provide for steady state growth amid peace strongly indicates the need for system transformation. If the present structural imperatives continue to pattern the world economy, global political elites will continue to use unconstrained military spending in order to prevent global stagnation and aggrandize national power.

Second Structural Imperative: Crisis of Bubbles and Busts

A recurrent problem of the existing world system is its cyclical patterns of booms and busts. In 2008, the near meltdown of the world's financial infrastructure made the system's instability apparent, yet similar traumas have continually manifested themselves. Explosive financial crises plagued Mexico from 1994 to 1995, much of East Asia from 1997 to 1998, Russia and Brazil in 1998, and Argentina beginning in early 2002. During the high-tech bubble of the late 1990s, the price of Internet startup stocks skyrocketed and then collapsed. As much as $7 trillion worth of assets vanished, leading to the recession of 2001 to 2002.[23] New crises are continually regenerated precisely by business-as-usual, by the cardinal rule of maximizing individual gain rather than meeting more generalized human needs, a rule that is central to the capitalist economic regime.

A leading cause of recent crises is that banks and corporations sought to increase global profits as their domestic profits declined.[24] Stagflation in the late 1970s meant that interest rates hardly kept up with inflation, so wealthy U.S. bankers—led by the Rockefeller family—attacked domestic wages and the welfare state and "financialized" everything they could to squeeze greater profits. Willing suppliants in countries like Korea, where dictator Chun Doo-hwan bloodily came to power only with U.S. help, made easy pickings. By the late 1980s, more than seventy Third World countries had undergone structural adjustment programs, forms of "shock therapy" that drastically loosened state controls of economies. As the IMF took control of nations' economies, riots broke out in dozens of countries from 1976 to 1986.[25] Like a baby learning to speak, the movement opposed to corporate-led globalization was born in dozens of diffuse and militant actions.

With growth rates slowing, the world economy has entered what Immanuel Wallerstein considers its final crisis. The average annual growth rates in GNP per capita from 1965 to 1989 for low- and middle-income countries was:

1965–1973   4.0 percent
1973–1980   2.6 percent
1980–1989   1.8 percent[26]

Giant corporations need new markets and financial resources to continue growing. As international investors, led by New York and Tokyo bankers, rushed to solve the stagflation crisis of the late 1970s, neoliberalism was developed to cure the problems of the system. In 2008, the financial crisis revealed the short-term character of this "solution." The incessant drive to increase profits led to cries for "liberalization"—meaning foreign penetration of financial sectors. The push for market controls to replace governmental ones resulted in an epidemic of crises. In country after country, deregulation was followed by a banking crisis, as TABLE 16.1 indicates.

For investors, paper losses bring sadness, but the world's poor suffer tragedy. In 2008, when the entire world economy nearly collapsed, investors lost trillions of dollars in wealth, but more people at the periphery of the world system experienced starvation. The number of the world's starving people, which had declined to 848 million from 2003 to 2005 rose to about 963 million in 2008.[27] Global structural unemployment in the aftermath of the crisis left more than 30 million people unemployed in the world's wealthiest seven countries.

In the long run, these trillions of dollars in losses from crises will have to be repaid by the world's workers and farmers—not by its bankers and executives. U.S. taxpayers will pay for the gargantuan assistance floated to major financial institutions in 2008 whose mercurial return to prosperity indicates how much big banks and corporations benefit from crises. During the IMF-Asian financial crisis of 1997, Indonesia saw its exchange rate plummet 73.5 percent in less than eight months (from July 1, 1997 to February 18, 1998), while South Korea's currency fell 48.1 percent and Thailand's 43.2 percent.[28] Twenty-one million Indonesians and one million Thais were pushed below the poverty line. Thailand's taxpayers were

TABLE 16.1 **Banking Crises and Decontrol of Financial Sectors**

Country	Crisis	Decontrol of Interest Rates	Abolishing Direct Credit Controls	Increasing Competition	Allowing International Capital Flows	Privatization	Deregulation
Indonesia	1997–2002	1983	1983	1988		1996	1992
Korea	1997–2002	1991	1982	1981	1996	1983	1988
Malaysia	1997–2001	1991	1976	1985			1989
Philippines	1998	1983	1983	1993	1995	1995	
Thailand	1997–2002	1992	1980	1992	1992	1993	1993

Source: Ilan Noy, "Banking Crises in East Asia: The Price Tag of Liberalization?" *Asia Pacific Issues: Analysis from the East-West Center* 78 (November 2005): 6.

compelled to pay for losses totaling 35 percent of GDP—to say nothing of lost revenues from foregone output undercut by the crisis. Yet George Soros prospered spectacularly after he led an investors' stampede to take $100 billion out of the region in a few weeks. The IMF's bailout of foreign speculators only exacerbated the collapse of the real economy and deepened the recession throughout East Asia in 1998.[29] Taxpayers of Korea, Indonesia, and Thailand repaid the IMF loans made in 1997, because they had no alternative but to accept the "help" of the IMF—and its conditions for "assistance."

Neoliberalism means first and foremost privileges for Japanese and U.S. banks and corporations. Pressure by the United States for financial deregulation and trade liberalization were foremost among the objectives of U.S. policy and resulted in military dictatorships in Chile, Thailand, South Korea, and Turkey. As we saw in the case of the Gwangju Uprising, the United States rejected political liberalization and heavily pushed economic liberalization—even in the midst of the uprising when hundreds of people were massacred. Foreign demands for reform sought to strip the developmental state of its powers to control corporate growth and economic accumulation. As a result, the ties of corporate sectors in South Korea and Taiwan were loosened vis-à-vis their own national governments while strengthened in relation to the global economy. When local elites proved unable to control the corporate sector, they also lost their legitimacy in the eyes of the population. During the 1997 IMF crisis, Jeff Garten, President Clinton's undersecretary of commerce, bluntly stated, "Most of these countries are going through a dark and deep tunnel. . . . But on the other end there is going to be a significantly different Asia in which American firms have achieved a much deeper market penetration, much deeper access."[30]

From 1997 to 2008, the capitalist system's ever-larger spirals of booms and busts dragged into its orbit more people than ever. In the late 1990s, no less than $4.6 trillion in investor wealth vanished on Wall Street—about four times the size of losses in the 1987 crash.[31] Increasing flows of capital is one cause: in the 1970s, wealthy nations annually invested $34 billion outside their borders. By 1990, the annual flow of foreign investments was more than six times as much—some $214 billion.[32] The daily turnover in world foreign exchange and financial markets amounted to $1.5 trillion in 1998—up from $15 billion in 1973 and $820 billion in 1992.[33] By 2003, global financial markets daily trafficked $1.3 trillion—more than a hundred times the amount of global trade.[34]

In Asia, the IMF, WTO, and WB implement policies favorable to U.S. investors, to knock down the doors long closed to U.S. corporations and banks by state-aided economies. Once the "crony" regimes were overthrown and more "democratic" ones installed, U.S. goods and investments flowed into the region—leading to integration into the global web of corporate economic control. Within that web of systemic crisis tendencies, the IMF crisis of 1997 was used to purchase assets at fire sale prices. As Walden Bello recounted,

> All the talk about the Asian financial crisis being caused by crony capitalism could not obscure the fact that it was the liberation of speculative

capital from the constraints of regulation, largely in response to pressure from the IMF, that brought about East Asia's collapse. The IMF also came under severe public scrutiny for imposing draconian programs on the Asian economies in the wake of the crisis—programs that merely accelerated economic contraction—while putting together multi-billion-dollar rescue packages to save not the crisis economies, but foreign banks and speculative investors.[35]

In poor countries, the imposition of corporate control required parliamentary democracy to stifle indigenous elite opposition to penetration of their areas of control by U.S. and Japanese corporations. Political liberalization became a suitable vehicle for the expansion of global corporations' markets, financial infrastructure, and neoliberal agenda. The "Third Wave" of democratization—severed from its meaning as an expansion of substantive democracy—suited corporate expansion of the world economy. As before in history, "liberalization" went hand-in-hand with global capitalism's expansion. Emerging parliamentary systems were appropriate vehicles for the expansion of global corporations' control in the semiperiphery and periphery.

When global corporations shifted their focus to emerging markets, U.S. banks and corporations abandoned many inner cities. Much of the United States was hollowed out by American corporations moving to more profitable arenas of investment, and African American mayors were permitted to be elected to govern shells of former prosperity like Detroit (much as Obama inherited an economy broken by the Bush-Cheney years).

The IMF, WB, and WTO—the "real axis of evil"—play vital roles in short-circuiting liberatory impulses. Using popular insurgencies to broaden market control of economies, they help to supplant indigenous elites (read as "crony") who tried to keep U.S. and Japanese banks and corporations at arm's length. Usurping the erotic energy of popular movements, international institutions of capital turn demands for freedom into consumer goods, gadgets, and gimmicks. With IMF "assistance," laborers employed in local businesses are transformed into willing employees of transnational capital, while simultaneously local economic elites become subservient to global capital within reformed political structures. Giant corporations control an ever-growing share of people's wealth as global economic integration proceeds. When markets succeed in making much of the world subservient to global corporations, the need for raw American power, embodied in CIA coups and genocidal wars, has largely been superseded.

Through "free" trade and "free-market" financial transactions, new markets and arenas for investment were opened. Capital's declining rate of profit was offset temporarily by driving smaller producers out of business, enabling global corporations to increase market share and profits. The net effect of financial crisis after crisis has been to accelerate huge concentrations of capital. As long as the current world economic regime remains in place, similar crises will recur with the certainty of the common cold—and they will grow in magnitude as transnational banks and corporations hold more of the world's wealth.

In 2000, the world's top fifty financial institutions controlled $50 trillion in assets—roughly a third of global wealth. It is estimated that the world's three hundred largest corporations control half of the world's output of goods and services. These giant corporations dwarf nations. Exxon, for instance, has more ships than Great Britain. Considering the hundred biggest economies in the world, fifty-one are now global corporations and only forty-nine are countries.[36] The combined sales of the world's top two hundred corporations are far greater than the combined economies of 182 countries. Total employment of the top two hundred corporations is only 18.8 million, less than one one-hundredth of one percent of the planet population. World exports of goods and services totaled over $11 trillion in 2005—nearly a doubling in seven years, but fully one-third of world trade consists of transactions among various units of the same corporation.

Third Structural Imperative: Billionaires and Beggars

"Structural violence" and inequality are continually deepened by the world's economic regime.[37] In the last decade of the twentieth century, as the world's wealth was grabbed by the super rich, the number of billionaires tripled, and the world's 1,100 richest people had almost twice the assets of the poorest 2.5 billion. Alongside a thousand billionaires today stand a billion paupers who barely have enough to eat.[38] Uneven regional development means there are more telephones in Manhattan than in sub-Saharan Africa. The income disparity between the world's poorest 20 percent and richest 20 percent rose from one to thirty in 1960, to one to sixty in 1990, to one to seventy-four in 1994.[39] Even in the "advanced" economies, thirty years ago, multinational CEOs made 35 times the wages of an average employee; today the figure is more than 350 times.[40]

According to the United Nations, more than seventeen thousand children died every day from hunger in 2009—a total of more than six million that year. UNICEF estimates that up to thirty thousand children under the age of five die of easily preventable diseases every day in the Third World.[41] That means that every decade, more than a hundred million children under the age of five die of unnecessary causes, including diarrhea, whooping cough, tetanus, pneumonia, and measles—diseases easily preventable through cheap vaccines or simply clean water. Those lucky enough to survive starvation and disease face lifelong problems. In November 2009, the UN Children's Fund reported that nearly two hundred million children under the age of five were stunted by a lack of food. The Food and Agriculture Organization reported that one in six people on the planet—over a billion people—are affected by hunger.[42] As the 2008 financial crisis began, the UN's Millennium Development Goals Report 2008 concluded that an additional hundred million people would be pushed into "extreme poverty."

In such a world, there can be no lasting peace. As long as the wretched of the earth, those at the margins of the world system, are dehumanized, branded as terrorists, and kept on the verge of starvation, they have no alternative but to find justice by any means necessary. The structural violence of an economic system based upon short-term profitability constitutes an ongoing crisis of greatest urgency. The existing economy's unreasonability will become more visible as it squanders humanity's wealth, destroys traditional cultures wholesale, and plunders the planet's natural resources. Already, austerity measures imposed by the IMF have resulted in higher food prices, a drop in real wages in the Third World, and declining gross national products in many countries. Third World debt has increased by 34 percent to $2.5 trillion.[43] Despite promises of debt reduction for the world's poorest countries, since 1996 only about $1 billion has been erased, less than 5 percent of debt of the world's forty-one poorest countries. To pay off the entire debt of the Third World would cost less than the amount spent by wealthy countries to shore up their financial institutions in the crisis that began in 2008. If thirty thousand people were dying in Europe every day, would world leaders hesitate to save their lives immediately?

Fourth Structural Imperative: Profits and Pollution

Not only does the world economic regime devalue human life, it treats all of Nature as an "externality" of little importance. The system's self-expanding value requires increasing incorporation of resources into the pool of available materials for generating profits. Fish stocks decrease and ocean pollution reaches deadly proportions, while forests are clear-cut or burned off due to global warming. As climate change, hunting, and habitat loss proceed with economic growth and population increase, an "extinction crisis" endangers one in four mammals and one in three amphibians.[44]

Included in Nature degraded by capitalism is not only external Nature, that is, trees, rivers, mountains, and air, but also inner nature, that is our psyches, imaginations, and communities. The present system colonizes everyday life, dehumanizes work, and destroys communities. Since labor, the creative application of our life-forces to shaping the world, has become a commodity to be bought and sold, more and more of us are increasingly compelled to accept positions in life that are terribly alienating and hierarchical as opposed to life-affirming and cooperative. We live in order to work, rather than living with the freedom to choose how to live out our lives.

Families are under attack since atomization is consumer society's preferred form. Profitability demands that builders create multiple luxury spaces for the rich while millions of people are homeless. Nowhere in the monetary equations of the construction industry do we find communal homes for ordinary people who would like to live together, a solution that makes sense for child-rearing as well as for seniors and many others currently isolated by the capitalist cutting up of living space for profitability rather than community.

Humanity's precious resources are squandered in unneeded tunnels in the Alps and Pyrenees, massive bridges connecting Denmark and Sweden, highways from Prince Edward Island to the Canadian mainland, Boston's Big Dig, redundant World Cup stadiums—to say nothing of unending wars and wasteful military spending. What these projects have in common is that they provide massive profits to a handful of giant corporations. And here lies the crux of the problem. These corporations are not democratically controlled. They operate according to one law: profits must increase from one year to another. Democracy has nothing to do with the international institutions they've created; rather the dictates of the IMF, WB, and WTO compel nations to follow orders. The United States currently has the sole permanent seat on the World Bank's Board of Directors and has effective veto power over major decisions. It has stopped the World Bank from providing funds to Vietnam and Afghanistan (when it was under Soviet rule) and refused to allow the PLO to have observer status.[45] The WTO is so opaque that major decisions are made in secret caucuses in the "Green Room" to which only a handful of poor countries are selectively invited by the world's wealthy countries. Most countries are excluded. The key issue that saw talks break down was agricultural subsidies paid by OECD countries to their own farmers, who could then dump their products on poorer countries' markets at prices below those that local small-scale farmers could afford. Such subsidies in the rich countries rose from $182 billion in 1995 (the year the WTO was created), to $280 billion in 1997, and $362 billion in 1998.[46] Malian cotton farmers, Kenyan corn farmers, and Haitian rice growers cannot possibly compete against billions of dollars in subsidies paid to their counterparts in the global North.

In September 2009, the G-20 summit in Pittsburgh agreed to turn the G-20 into the world's top economic forum, thereby acknowledging that the advanced countries should not (and cannot) control the world economy. The G-20 accounts for some 85 percent of the global economy and over half of the total economy of developing nations. For some observers, this change signifies an important advance in global economic democracy. Even if the G-20 member states reorganize the capital structure of the International Monetary Fund (IMF) and World Bank, does cooperation of nations—each of which is ruled by an elite that owns a large share of all wealth and income—mean more democracy for everyone? Or does it mean strengthening the very structures that perpetuate humanity's central problems? "Hot money" was the problem of the 1997 IMF crisis, and "derivatives" and "secondary mortgage market" problems caused the 2008 crisis, but both are avatars for international capital's control by individual investors.

Created by generations of laborers, humanity's collective wealth is controlled by a few hundred transnational corporations through the most undemocratic of means—and for ends benefiting only a small minority. According to the logic of "enlightened" neoliberal economics, these corporations must either grow or die according to the market's dictates. Of course, when Wall Street banks were threatened with extinction in 2008, the U.S. government quickly abandoned its rhetoric and produced the biggest welfare program in history to rescue them.

Using the real axis of evil—the WTO, IMF, and WB—giant corporations continue to enrich themselves while impoverishing many people. The World Bank calculated that sub-Saharan Africa's income declined by more than 2 percent after WTO negotiations were implemented.[47] In Haiti, after the country agreed to a bailout that required them to accept "Miami rice" from the United States, rice growers went out of business. Today, Haitians eat mud pies. Kenya was self-sufficient in food production before an IMF "assistance" program. Today, the country imports food at high cost.

Without the IMF's "help," China, Hong Kong, Singapore, and Malaysia have prospered while countries that accepted the fund's assistance have stagnated and undergone crisis after crisis. During the 1960s and 1970s, Latin America's income grew by 75 percent, but in the 1980s and 1990s (after IMF structural adjustment programs), growth fell to 6 percent. Average incomes in former communist Eastern European countries and sub-Saharan African countries also fell with IMF help.[48] In fact, in all areas affected by IMF structural adjustment programs— Eastern Europe, South Asia, Latin America, Caribbean, sub-Saharan Africa—the absolute number of people living in poverty increased in the 1990s.[49]

Even if some of the above irrationalities of the present system are reduced, the structural contradictions of the system will inevitably result in the continual reappearance of war. Although Filipinos voted to expel the United States from its huge base at Subic Bay after the ouster of Marcos in 1986, U.S. troops are back in the Philippines as part of the "war on terror." To be strategically effective, popular movements need to develop a long-term vision of global structural transformation. The system's imperative for militarism requires new structural imperatives, one emphasizing human needs not corporate profits. With real democracy, unlike rule by professional politicians, all weapons of mass destruction would be outlawed and standing armies be made obsolete. As long as the wealth accumulated from centuries of labor remains dominated by the "enlightened" and "rational" principles of efficiency and profitability, the system's structural imperatives will breed war and insecurity.

How has this situation evolved? Has it been democratically decided that we, the human species, should live under these conditions? Rather than having been reasonably chosen, the current world system has been imposed by the power of the strongest, by the dead weight of the past, and decidedly not by the life forces of the present. From the French and American to the Russian and Chinese revolutions, the power of nation-states has been reinforced, as each country has sought to rise in the hierarchical architecture of the world system. Few people would disagree with the idea of totally abolishing weapons of mass destruction—not just nuclear, chemical, and biological weapons but also so-called conventional ones like fighter jets, bombers, landmines, artillery, and automatic weapons. Only through popular insistence upon nonmilitary forms of conflict resolution will humanity's future fate improve beyond our abysmal reality.

Toward a Reasonable System

Creating a new system may seem overwhelming, yet a growing international consensus agrees on the need for a fundamental restructuring of the world system to decentralize and bring under self-management the vast social wealth of humanity. Already the first steps have been taken in defining the outline of a new set of structural imperatives, including:

1. Markets alone are not sufficient for regulation of production and distribution.
2. Billionaires' wealth and power should be curtailed.

3. Democracy should be expanded to include direct popular decision-making.
4. The public sphere (human rights, labor rights, and Nature) should be protected.
5. All people's basic needs should be met.[50]

Global gatherings like the World Social Forum (WSF) have sparked people's imaginations. A whole series of other meetings around the world has produced detailed sketches of an alternative based upon self-sufficiency and steady state economic output, not production for profit of international investors but for human needs.[51] Cross-national meetings of farmers involved with Via Campesina have brought representatives from over fifty-six countries together and endorsed general notions such as that production techniques and consumer applications should seek to preserve natural ecosystems and encourage the use of appropriate technologies and non-resource-depleting energy sources.

The WSF is inhibited by its foundation sponsors from taking political positions or sponsoring global actions, and its many problems reveal the need for alternatives to it.[52] Nonetheless, sheer numbers of participants at WSF meetings reveal the growing global support for systematic change. Attendance has grown beyond anyone's expectations, as illustrated in TABLE 16.2 below.

In 2009, the Beijing Asia-Europe People's Forum and the Social Forum in Belem issued calls for democratic administration of the world economy and socialization of finance and industry—two of many voices calling for a reasonable solution to humanity's precarious existence and the planet's wanton destruction. Through regional meetings such as these, transparent and democratic institutions of global economic governance could replace the WTO, WB, and IMF.

As early as 1970, the Black Panther Party convened a Revolutionary People's Constitutional Convention that used principles of direct democracy to draft the outline of a new system. Meeting under extraordinarily repressive conditions in Philadelphia, the general assembly of ten thousand activists approved the

TABLE 16.2 **World Social Forum Attendance**

Year	Place	Attendance
2001	Porto Alegre, Brazil	20,000
2002	Porto Alegre, Brazil	50,000
2003	Porto Alegre, Brazil	100,000
2004	Mumbai, India	80,000
2005	Porto Alegre, Brazil	155,000
2006	Caracas, Venezuela	60,000
2006	Bamako, Mali	15,000
2006	Karachi, Pakistan	30,000
2007	Nairobi, Kenya	40,000
2009	Belém, Brazil	133,000

Sources: Heather Gautney, *Protest and Organization in the Alternative Globalization Era: NGOs, Social Movements, and Political Parties* (New York: Palgrave, Macmillan, 2010).

final documents—admittedly fragile first steps, but bold ones. They called for the abolition of the standing U.S. military, grassroots people power, and a world federation of free states, in which people could participate as citizens of paradise while insisting upon ethical standards for appropriate behavior in international politics and economy.[53]

Destruction of the world's militaries would undoubtedly send the global capitalist system into a calamitous depression—all the more reason for people to discuss this issue as part of the need to develop a completely different world system. If the wizards of high finance can afford trillions in government spending to keep the banks afloat, as they did in 2008, then we can certainly find ways to keep economies stable during a period of transition to a peace economy. In the present system, everyone is dependent upon major financial institutions and investors' profitable choices to continue daily economic operations. According to Walden Bello, "deconstruction" of corporate-driven globalization would mean that the IMF would be decreasingly asked for "assistance" and ultimately be converted into a research group. The World Bank's powers would be reduced through creation of regional—and more participatory—financial institutions funded by bonds.[54] A means to limit financial transfers might empower nation-states (or regions) to control investment decisions inside their borders. Since the UN is composed of representatives of nation-states, hundreds of the world's societies are not represented. Locally based, regional structures for decentralized governance would not only permit indigenous people to govern themselves, they would facilitate equitable redistribution of resources and encourage the articulation from below of autonomously conceived cultural and political needs.[55]

The Ongoing Global Uprising

A global revolution with pluralist and decentralized forms is already underway. Visible in Asia's uprisings, Latin American insurgencies, and the alter-globalization movement, ordinary citizens' aspirations for people power and more democracy have emerged everywhere. While now seemingly marginalized, the international movement today involves more activists than at any other point in the historical evolution of our species. While the airwaves broadcast a version of history that emphasizes the need for central authorities and social conformity, beneath the radar, people's understanding and self-guided actions constitute a powerful undercurrent. As we become increasingly aware of our own power and strategic capacities, our future impact can become more focused and synchronized. One tendency we can project into the future is the activation of a global eros effect, in which synchronous actions unify people across the world.

The real axis of evil—the IMF, WB, and WTO—will not willingly relinquish their grip on humanity's vast wealth. Globally synchronized struggles by hundreds of millions of people are needed to create lives worthy of being called "free." It is my hope that this history of recent Asian insurgencies will help inform future uprisings—which, however reluctantly undertaken, are necessitated by the systematic crisis tendencies of the existing world system. Sad and joyous, full of suffering while bringing forth tears of happiness, uprisings are moments of extreme desperation, during which human hearts act according to people's fondest dreams. By understanding these dreams and remaining true to them, we become capable of a future of freedom.

NOTES

1 Thom Hartmann, "The Genetically Modified Bomb," Common Dreams News Center, September 10, 2003, http://www.commondreams.org/views03/0910-15.htm; Ethirajan Anburasan, "Genetic Weapons: A 21st Century Nightmare?" United Nations Educational, Scientific and Cultural Organization, October 12, 2003, http://www.unesco.org/courier/1999_03/uk/ethique/txt1.htm.

2 On October 20, 1942, the U.S. government seized Prescott Bush's bank operations in New York City because they were linked to the Nazis. The Trading with the Enemy Act was invoked to seize Union Banking Corporation, directed by Bush. Along with E. Roland Harriman, three Nazis, and two others, Bush owned all UBC's stock. German interests in the Silesian-American Corporation, long managed by Prescott Bush and his father-in-law George Herbert Walker, were also seized on November 17, 1942. Prescott Bush was a key player in Hitler's build-up of arms and monies to finance his war. In 1942, a U.S. government inquiry determined that Bush's bank was heavily involved with *Vereinigte Stahlwerke* (United Steel Works Corporation), which was subsequently found to have produced approximately 50.8 percent of Nazi pig iron; 41.4 percent of Nazi universal plate; 45.5 percent of Nazi Germany's pipes and tubes; and 35.0 percent of Nazi Germany's explosives. See Webster G. Tarpley and Anton Chaitkin, *George Bush: The Unauthorized Biography*, *Executive Intelligence Review* (January 1991), http://www.tarpley.net/bush2.htm.

3 See Andrew Wheat "The Bush–bin Laden Connection," *Texas Observer*, November 9, 2001, http://www.texasobserver.org/showArticle.asp?ArticleID=480.

4 Johan Galtung, "The Korean Peninsula: Moving from the DMZ to a Zone of Peace." http://wagingpeacekorea.org/board/view.php?id=hero&page=5&sn1=&divpage=1&sn=off&ss=on&sc=on&select_arrange=headnum&desc=asc&no=15. He also considers there to be two thousand nations yearning for autonomy within two hundred states. Since World War II, there have been more than a hundred wars in which twenty-five million people have been killed and seventy-five million wounded. Kristin Dawkins, *Global Governance: The Battle over Planetary Power* (New York: Seven Stories Press, 2003), 96

5 International Scientific Commission on Biological Warfare in Korea and China, *Report*, 1952. Leading up to the U.S. war on Iraq, President George W. Bush often referred to the "Korean Model." Some one hundred thousand South Koreans opposed to division were killed under the U.S. military government and its progeny from 1945 to 1950 (*before* the Korean War). For Korea, to represent a "model" for U.S. international relations speaks volumes to the character of the U.S. government. In 2005, when discussing the idea of maintaining U.S. troops in Korea, Senator John McCain mentioned that, "We've been in South Korea . . . for sixty years." Secretary of Defense Robert Gates reminded us that Korea's example stands, "in contrast to Vietnam, where we just left lock, stock and barrel." Lest we think Democratic Party leaders are much different, Clinton administration defense secretary William Perry pledged to keep troops in Korea even if it were to reunify. Apparently, even after its disastrous wars in Korea and Vietnam, U.S. strategy for global domination still involves encircling China, and a land base on East Asia's mainland is a vital piece to Pentagon planners.

6 George Katsiaficas, ed., *Vietnam Documents* (New York: ME Sharpe, 1992), 146.

7   See Alan Winnington and Wilfred Burchett, *Plain Perfidy: The Plot to Wreck Korean Peace* (1954).

8   See Wolff, *Little Brown Brother*. John Tirman believes as many as four hundred thousand Filipinos may have been killed (*Deaths of Others*, 18).

9   Noam Chomsky, "The United States and Indochina: Far from an Aberration," in *Coming to Terms: Indochina, the United States and the War*, eds. Douglas Allen and Ngo Vinh Long (Boulder: Westview Press, 1991), 165.

10   Catherine A. Sunshine, *The Caribbean: Survival, Struggle, and Sovereignty* (Boston: South End Press, 1985), 32.

11   See Robert Aldrich, *Greater France, A History of French Overseas Expansion* (New York: St. Martin's, 1996), 98.

12   One cheering spectator is Francis Fukuyama, who argued that contemporary American-style representative democracy is the desired endpoint of human development, that we have reached the "end of history." Although he now recognizes the alternative offered by China, Fukuyama wrote that the battle of Jena in 1806 (when Napoleon defeated the Prussian monarchy) marks the consolidation of the liberal-democratic state, and that the principles and privileges of citizenship in a democratic state only have to be extended. For Fukuyama, there is "nothing left to be invented" in terms of humanity's social progress. See his article "The End of History," *The National Interest* 16 (Summer 1989), 3–18. For Fukuyama, the spatial extension of the principles of the French Revolution means that the rest of the world will likewise experience human progress.

13   Depleted uranium has been used in armor-piercing projectiles because of its extreme density. The Pentagon has admitted that 320 metric tons of DU was left on the battlefields of Iraq but Russian estimates placed the amount closer to 1,000 metric tons. DU has a half-life longer than the age of the solar system and has been linked to Gulf War syndrome and thousands of deaths and deformed fetuses in Iraq. A UK researcher estimated that half a million people would die from its radioactivity in Iraq before the end of the twentieth century. See Neil Mackay, "U.S. Forces' use of depleted uranium weapons is 'illegal'" *Sunday Herald*, March 30, 2003 (http://www.truthout.org/docs_03/printer_040103F.shmtl).

14   See Arundhati Roy, "Not Again," *Guardian*, September 27, 2002.

15   The Stockholm International Peace Research Institute 2009 report.

16   Other reports estimated a global average of 3.5 percent of GDP, with Taiwan's expenditures reaching 6.3 percent. Arirang, August, 10, 2003.

17   Compared with $12 billion in 2005, the U.S. DOD agreed to sell or transfer more than $32 billion in weapons and military equipment in fiscal year 2009. Direct commercial sales rose quickly as well with foreign governments acquiring export licenses for $96 billion in weapons, up from $58 billion in 2005.

18   Joel Andreas, *Addicted to War: Why the U.S. Can't Kick Militarism*, 3rd ed. (Oakland: AK Press, 2004), 44. If we add the current Pentagon budget to foreign military aid, veterans' pensions, the military portion of NASA, the nuclear weapons budget of the Energy Department, and the interest payments on debt from past military spending, the U.S. spends more than a million dollars a minute every minute of every day. Inside the U.S., the Pentagon owns more land than the size of South Korea; its holdings almost match the entire landmass of North Korea.

19   These statistics only begin to put the problem in proper perspective. See Bernd Debusmann, "Fading Superpower, Rising Rival Nations," *Korea Herald*, August 29, 2008.

20   Thom Shanker, "Arms Deal to Taiwan Riles China," *New York Times*, October 4, 2008.

21   In 2006, the United States approved the sale of nine interceptor missiles to Japan in a

deal worth $458 million. In October 2008, the United States announced it was selling Taiwan more than $6 billion in advanced weapons, including $3.1 billion in Patriot Advanced Capability-3 guided missile systems, a sophisticated array of missiles, radars and control systems designed to defend against missiles and aircraft. Also included in the proposed deal (which was finally approved in January 2010) were $2.5 billion worth of Apache attack helicopters and support systems. South Korea's Defense Reform 2020 initiative involves spending tens of billions of dollars on a low-altitude missile shield PAC-3 system as a step toward joining the U.S.-led global ballistic missile defense initiative. An air-and-missile-defense system, dubbed the Korea Air and Missile Defense (KAMD) network, intended to enter service by 2012, when Seoul takes over wartime operational control of its forces from the United States, will meld early warning radars, Aegis-based SM-2 ship-to-air missile systems, and modified PAC-2 interceptors. In addition to already deployed KDX-III destroyers, ROK plans to commission one more hull by 2012 (per-unit price is about $1 billion), build more indigenous three-thousand-ton KSS-III submarines, and more Aegis-class ships.

22 Here is one pragmatic reason why keeping U.S. troops in Korea may actually serve as a deterrent to war. The United States would be less likely to use weapons of mass destruction in Korea if it were to mean many American soldiers would also die in the ensuing conflict. Paik Nak-chung first brought this insight to my attention.

23 Walden Bello, "A Primer on the Wall Street Meltdown," http://links.org.au/node/657.

24 Gérard Duménil and Dominique Lévy, "The Economics of U.S. Imperialism at the Turn of the 21st Century," *Review of International Political Economy* 11, no. 4 (October 2004): 663.

25 See John Walton, "Urban Protest and the Global Political Economy: The IMF Riots," in *The Capitalist City: Global Restructuring and Community Politics*, ed. Michael Peter Smith and Joe R. Feagin (London: Basil Blackwell, 1997), 364; and John Bellamy Foster and Fred Magdoff, "Financial Implosion and Stagnation: Back To The Real Economy," in http://monthlyreview.org/2008/12/01/financial-implosion-and-stagnation.

26 Huntington, *Third Wave*, 311.

27 UN Food and Agriculture Organization statistics. See Javier Blas, "World's Hungry Close to One Billion," *Financial Times*, December 9, 2008.

28 Lowell Dittmer, "Globalization and the Asian Financial Crisis," in *East Asia and Globalization*, ed. Samuel S. Kim (Lanham: Rowman & Littlefield, 2000), 36.

29 See Stiglitz, *Globalization*.

30 "Worsening Financial Flu Lowers Immunity to U.S. Business," *New York Times*, February 1, 1998. One of Obama's chief economic advisors was Lawrence Summers, also Clinton's secretary of the treasury. Assessing the state of Argentina in 1999, a few years before the crisis hit, Summers wrote: "Today, fully 50 percent of the banking sector, 70 percent of private banks, in Argentina are foreign-controlled, up from 30 percent in 1994. The result is a deeper, more efficient market." Quoted in Walden Bello, *Deglobalization: Ideas for a New World Economy* (Manila: Ateneo de Manila University Press, 2006), 78.

31 With trillions of dollars changing hands in investment markets, casino capitalism produces severe downturns following record booms. Losses totaled 80 percent by June 1932, 60 percent by April 1942, 50 percent by October 1974, and nearly that much by October 2008. "How This Bear Market Compares," http://www.nytimes.com/interactive/2008/10/11/business/20081011_BEAR_MARKETS.html?hp, accessed October 12, 2008. Also see Bello, *Deglobalization*, 14.

32 Samuel S. Kim, *East Asia and Globalization* (Lanham: Rowman & Littlefield, 2000), 8.

33 Benjamin Cohen, "Phoenix Risen: The Resurrection of Global Finance," *World Politics* 48, no. 2 (1996): 268–96; UN Conference on Trade and Development, *World*

Investment Report 1999, 477–83; Beinart, "An Illusion for our Time: The False Promise of Globalization" *New Republic*, October 20, 1997, 20–24; David Goldblatt, David Held, Anthony McGrew, and Jonathan Perraton, "Economic Globalization and the Nation-State," *Alternatives* 22, no. 3 (1997): 269–85; David Goldblatt, David Held, Anthony McGrew, and Jonathan Perraton, "The Globalization of Economic Activity," *New Political Economy* 2, no. 2 (1997): 257–77, as cited in Kim, *East Asia*, 28.

34   Keane, *Global Civil Society?*, 174.
35   Bello, *Deglobalization*, 5.
36   Sarah Anderson and John Cavanagh, "How Important Is the Market to the Economy?" Corporate Watch, Summary of Findings, 2000, http://www.globalpolicy.org/component/content/article/221/47211.html.
37   Johan Galtung, "Violence, Peace and Peace Research, *Journal of Peace Research* 6, no. 3 (1969), 167–91.
38   In 2010, *Forbes* magazine counted 1,210 individuals worth $1 billion or more, with a combined wealth of $4.5 trillion—more than the holdings of the world's four billion poorest people. For analysis, see James Petras, "Billionaires Flourish, Inequalities Deepen as Economies 'Recover,'" http://theglobalrealm.com/2011/04/22/billionaires-flourish-inequalities-deepen-as-economies-"recover"/.
39   Keane, *Global Civil Society?*, 90.
40   David Rothkopf, "Change is in the Air for the Financial Superclass," *Financial Times*, May 16, 2008, 9.
41   Elizabeth Olson, "UN Says Millions of Children Die Needlessly," *New York Times*, March 14, 2002, 13. In late 2008, the Global Call to Action against Poverty estimated that fifty thousand people around the world die unnecessarily each day. More than half are children under the age of five who perish from hunger or poverty. In Africa alone, every day 7,000 people die of malaria, 6,000 of HIV/AIDS, and 1,500 of tuberculosis. All together, almost eleven million children die annually of preventable causes.
42   "U.N. Says Hunger Stunts 200 Million Children," *Korea Herald*, November 13, 2009, 15.
43   Dawkins *Global Governance*, 19, 31.
44   James Kanter, "1 in 4 Mammals Threatened, Study Says," *New York Times*, October 6, 2008.
45   Bello, *Deglobalization*, 60.
46   Ibid., 72.
47   Stiglitz, *Globalization and Its Discontents* (New York: Norton, 2002), 61.
48   "Global Capitalism: Can It Be Made to Work Better?" *Business Week*, November 6, 2000, 42–43.
49   Bello, *Deglobalization*, 68–69 (quoting a World Bank study by Mattias Lundberg and Lyn Squire).
50   Dawkins, *Global Governance*, 118–20.
51   See John Cavanagh and Jerry Mander, eds., *Alternatives to Economic Globalization: A Better World Is Possible* (San Francisco: Berrett-Kohler, 2004); William Fisher and Thomas Ponniah, eds., *Another World Is Possible: Popular Alternatives to Globalization at the World Social Forum* (London: Zed Books, 2003); Dada Maheshvarananda, *After Capitalism: Prout's Vision for a New World* (Washington, D.C.: Proutist Universal Publications, 2004).
52   Thanks to James Petras for his critical insights into the WSF. Also see Stellan Vinthagen, "Is the World Social Forum a Democratic Global Civil Society?" in *The World and U.S. Social Forums: A Better World Is Possible and Necessary*, eds. Judith Blau and Marina Karides (Leiden: Brill, 2008).
53   The documents are contained in Kathleen Cleaver and George Katsiaficas, eds., *Liberation, Imagination, and the Black Panther Party* (New York: Routledge, 2001).

54   Bello, *Deglobalization*, 108–12. If the WTO were to find few nations willing to meet in its infamous Green Room, back room decisions by the world's most powerful economies could not be imposed on others. Simultaneously, Bello urges construction of a "pluralist system of global economic governance" that respects cultural diversity and creates a steady state, ecologically harmonious economy and encourages appropriate technologies and non–resource-depleting energy sources. Many specific details need to be worked out by regional assemblies.

55   Samir Amin, "The Future of Global Polarization," in *Globalization and Social Change*, eds. Johannes Schmidt and Jacques Hersh (London: Routledge, 2000), 40.

INTERVIEWS

THAILAND
Prof. Vipar Daomanee, Thammasat University, Bangkok, October 28, 2008.
Prajak Kongkiriti, Bangkok, October 28, 2008.
Somchai Homlaor, Human Rights activist attorney Bangkok, October 28, 2008.
Prof. Naruemon Thabchumpon, Chulalongkorn University, Bangkok, October 29, 2008.
Prof. Ji Ungpakorn, Chulalongkorn University, Bangkok, October 30, 2008.
Parinya Thevanaruemidkul, Bangkok, October 30, 2008.
Somsak Kosaisook, Bangkok, October 31, 2008.

BURMA
Dura, Seoul, South Korea
Sann Aung (in Bangkok, Thailand) November 1, 2008.
Aung Kyaw So (in Maesot, Thailand) November 4, 2008.
Aung Moe Zaw (in Maesot, Thailand) November 5, 2008.
David Tharekabaw (in Maesot, Thailand) November 5, 2008.

TAIWAN
Prof. Michael Hsiao, Academia Sinica, Taipei, February 3, 2009.
Sue Huang, Taipei, February 3, 2009.
Tien Chiu-Chin, Taipei, February 4, 2009.
Yi-cheng Jou, Taipei, August 6, 2009.
Michael Lin, Taipei, August 11, 2009.
Frank Chen, Taipei, August 12, 2009.
Wu Jieh-min, Taipei, August 15, 2009.

NEPAL
Keshar Jung Rayamajhi, Kathmandu, April 10, 2009.
Deepak Kumar Bhattarai, Gopi Krishna Bhattarai, Pawan Roy, Punya Bhandari, Bhawana Bhatta, Kathmandu, April 11, 2009.
Prakash Man Singh, Kathmandu, April 12, 2009.
Shalik Ram Jamkattel, Kathmandu, April 12, 2009.
Madhav Kumar Nepal, Kathmandu, April 12, 2009.
Subodh Raj Pyakurel, Kathmandu, April 13, 2009.
Indra Mainals, Patan, April 14, 2009.
Professor Lok Raj Baral, Kathmandu, April 15, 2009.
Bimal Sharma, Kathmandu, April 16, 2009.
Sudip Pathak, Kathmandu, April 24, 2009.
Professor Jagadish Pokharel, Kathmandu, April 26, 2009.
Yog Prasad, Kathmandu, April 26, 2009.
President Ram Baran Yadav, Kathmandu, April 26, 2009.
Professor Kapil Shrestha, Kathmandu, April 26, 2009.
Professor Mukunda Pathik, Kathmandu, May 2, 2008.
Ram Chandra Pokharel, Kathmandu, May 2, 2009.

PHILIPPINES
Peter Rahon, Manila, May 29, 2009.
Mary Racelis, Manila, May 29, 2009.

Raul Socrates Banzuela, Manila, May 30, 2009.
F. Sionil José, Manila, June 1, 2009.
Corazon Juliano-Soliman, Manila, June 2, 2009.
Senator Gregorio Honasan, Manila, June 2, 2009.
John Carroll, Manila, June 4, 2009.
Edicio de la Torre, Manila, June 5, 2009.

CHINA
Dingli Shen, June 24, 2009.

BANGLADESH
Aini Elias, Dhaka, May 9, 2010.
Amirul Haque Amin, Dhaka, May 10, 2010.
Ashim Kumar Ukil, Dhaka, May 10, 2010.
Dr. Beena Shikdar, Dhaka, May 11, 2010.
Dr. Mushtuq Husain, Dhaka, May 10, 2010.
Fazlul Haque Milan, Dhaka, May 11, 2010.
Gopal Chandradas, Dhaka, May 11, 2010.
Adilur Rahman Khan, Dhaka, May 11, 2010.
Ataur Rahman, Dhaka, May 11, 2010.
Md. Shariful Islam, Dhaka, December 22, 2010.

OTHERS
Stew Albert, Portland, Oregon, December 3, 1999.
Basil Fernando, Dhaka and Hong Kong, December 22–23, 2010.
Gene Sharp, Boston, March 3, 2011.

The author interviewing Nepali President Ram Baran Yadav.

With Maoist leader Shalik Ram Jamkattel (center) and Manik Lama.

With Madhav Kumar Nepal.

With Burmese activists on the Thai border.

In Bangladesh with activists including Adilur Rahman Khan (center) and Basil Fernando (to his left).

With Philippines Senator Gregorio Honasan.

Receiving an award from the May Mothers' House in Gwangju. Photo by Choi Seong-uk.

With former South Korean Prime Minister Kim Geun Tae.

CREDITS

Previous portions of part of this book have appeared as:

"The Unfinished Struggle for Democracy in Bangladesh," *Democracy and Human Rights* 11, no. 2 (2011) 389–420.

George Katsiaficas interviewed by Kourosh Ziabari, "U.S. Human Rights Policy is Self-Serving and Duplicitous," *Teheran Times*, May 1, 2011, http://www.tehrantimes.com/index_View.asp?code=239724.

"The Eros Effect and Arab Uprisings: Interview with David Zlutnick," April 6, 2011, http://www.youtube.com/watch?v=DhjTw77W6-I, http://www.counterpunch.org/zlutnick04222011.html.

"The Real Egyptian Revolution Is Yet to Come," *Sri Lanka Guardian*, February 14, 2011, http://www.srilankaguardian.org/2011/02/real-egyptian-revolution-is-yet-to-come.html.

"The Eros Effect Comes to Cairo," *Egyptian Gazette*, February 16, 2011. http://213.158.162.45/~egyptian/index.php?action=news&id=14994&title=The%20Eros%20effect%20comes%20to%20Cairo.

"Nepal's 2006 People's Uprising," *Democracy and Human Rights* 10, no. 3 (2010).

"Reading Signs of Change," in *Signs of Change: Social Movement Cultures 1960s to Now*, eds. Dara Greenwald and Josh MacPhee (with Exit Art) (Oakland: AK Press, 2010).

"Uprisings and Civil Society: Nepal's 1990 *Jana Andolan*," *Democracy and Human Rights* 9, no. 2 (2009), 317–60.

"Comparing Uprisings in Korea and Burma," *Socialism and Democracy* 23, no. 1 (March 2009).

"Ideen der Studenten Bewegung von 1968: politische und philosophische Auswirkungen," *Korean Journal of German Studies* (December 2008).

"Asia and South Korean Social Movements," *Conference Book* (Pacific and Asia Conference on Korean Studies (PACKS), Hanoi, November 24–26, 2008).

"Korean Candlelights in History," *Jumeokbab*, September 2008, 10–15 (in Korean and English).

"1968 and Alterglobalization Movements," *Conference Book*, Ideas and Strategies in the Alterglobalization Movements, Gyeongsang National University, May 2008.

"Aesthetic and Political Avant-Gardes" in *Historical Memory and Cultural Representation: 4.3 and 5.18 Cultural Movements* (Gwangju: Chonnam National University, 2003).

"The Anonymous People" by Basil Fernando, used by permission of the author.

ABOUT THE AUTHOR

George Katsiaficas is author or editor of eleven books, including ones on the global uprising of 1968 and European and Asian social movements. Together with Kathleen Cleaver, he coedited *Liberation, Imagination, and the Black Panther Party*. A longtime activist for peace and justice, he is international coordinator of the May 18 Institute at Chonnam National University in Gwangju, South Korea, and teaches at Wentworth Institute of Technology in Boston.

Index

1968, xx, 9–23, 26, 27, 30, 33n12, 33n13, 34n33, 42, 58, 131, 132, 140, 292, 293, 350, 359, 361, 363, 364–68, 371, 380, 381, 394, 397, 401, 406, 413, 419, 422, 424, 425, 426, 429,

228 Incident/Massacre (Taiwan), 176–83, 189, 201

Abhisit Vejjajiva, 335

Agency for International Development (AID), 79n137, 416

Alam, S.M. Shamsul, 275, 276

Albright, Madeleine, 345, 353

Algeria, 12, 368, 461

All-Burma Students' Union, 86, 87, 101

All-Burma Students' Democratic Front, 94

All China Federation of Trade Unions (ACFTU), 146, 152

All Nepal Free Student Union, 243

All Nepal Women's Association, 235

All Party Students' Unity (APSU) (Bangladesh), 266, 273–75

All-Taiwan General Labor Union, 179

Alliance of Independent Journalists (Indonesia), 354

Alliance of Taiwan Aborigines, 194

Alliance of Youth for Self-Government (Taiwan), 174, 180,

Almonte, Jose, 48, 74n9

Alsa Masa (Philippines), 61

Amatya, Tulsi Lal, 241

American Revolution, xx, 1, 363, 460, 461

anti-Americanism, 26, 27, 63, 415

Antigone, 430, 434–36

April 3rd Faction (China), 132

Aquino, Benigno, 37, 42, 193, 430; assassination of, 43–46

Aquino, Corazon (Cory), 15, 37–39, 44–45, 48–49, 52–59, 64–74, 369, 429, 430; government, 59–63; snap election, 46–48

Arab Spring, 1, 10, 31, 58, 361, 364–71, 376–77, 400, 410, 419, 424, 439, 453

Aristophanes, 367, 434

Arroyo, Gloria (Macapagal-Arroyo), 39, 65–69, 70–73

Arroyo, Jose Miguel, 72

Artists' Council for a Free Gwangju, 447

Asia Human Rights Commission (AHRC), 70, 243, 383

Assembly of People's Deputies (Tibet), 112

Assembly of the Poor (AOP) (Thailand), 331–32

Autonomous Student Federation (China), 126, 152, 154

Autonomous Student Union (ASU) (China), 125, 139, 141–42, 144, 148, 153, 155, 157, 158

Awakening (Taiwan), 190, 193

Awami League (AL) (Bangladesh), 266, 267–72, 277–78, 282

Bamboo Union (Taiwan), 190

Bangladesh Nationalist Party (BNP), 266, 268–72, 273, 277–78, 282

Baral, Lok Raj, xxi, 253

BBC, 86, 99, 221, 248, 322

Beijing Autonomous Student Union (BASU), 151, 154

Beijing Autonomous Workers' Federation (BAWF), 128, 137, 145–46, 149, 152–59, 425

Bello, Walden, 344, 466, 473, 478n54

Belo, Carlos, xix, 355

Bhattarai, Barburam, 240

Bhattarai, Krishna Prasad, 218, 230, 232, 234, 256

Bhumibol, King Adulyadej (Thailand), 290, 297, 298, 300, 308, 327, 335

Birendra, King (Nepal), 212, 215, 217, 229, 230, 237, 242

Black Bloc (BB), 407–8

Black Panthers, 10, 372

Boggs, Carl, 23, 438

Bouazizi, Mohamed, 368, 377

British colonialism, 82, 267

Buck-Morss, Susan, 32

Buddhism, 90, 91, 96, 105–6, 117, 212, 235, 241, 304, 317, 321, 334, 446

Burmese Bar Association, 100

Bush, George H.W., 74, 131, 458, 474n2

Bush, George W., 74, 205, 242, 348, 456, 457, 458, 463, 467, 474n5

Bush, Prescott, 458, 474n2

Cambodia, 82, 98, 292, 374, 441

Camdessus, Michel, 349

Camp Crame (Philippines), 49, 50, 54, 55

Campaign for Popular Democracy (CPD) (Thailand), 288, 314–15, 319, 336

candlelight protests (South Korea), 2, 392, 409, 410, 411, 420n23, 431

Carlyle Group, 73, 458

Ceausescu, Nicolae, 13, 16, 20, 217, 218, 444

"cell phone mob" (Thailand), 14, 328–29, 424

Central Academy of Fine Arts (China), 147, 157

Central Intelligence Agency (CIA), 31, 456, 463, 467; in Burma, 101; in Indonesia, 345; in the Philippines, 39, 46, 49, 50, 61, 73; in Thailand, 305; in Tibet, 107–8, 113; involvement with NGOs, 414–17

Chai Ling, 127, 143, 148, 151, 155, 156, 158, 161, 170n117

Chalard Vorachad, 315–16, 319

Chalard Worachat, 288, 315, 319

Chamlong Srimaung, 155, 288, 316–21, 324–25, 334, 445

Chand, Lokendra, 229, 240

Chang Myon, 450

Chávez, Hugo, 12, 409, 416, 456

Chen Fang-ming, 173

Chen Shui-bian, 174, 190, 201, 203

Chen Xitong, 160, 170n123

Chen Yi, 175, 177

Chiang Ching-kuo, 182, 183, 186, 190, 192, 194, 195

Chiang Kai-shek, 41, 82, 106, 112, 129, 175, 181, 182, 183; Memorial Hall, 174, 198, 199; Square (Taiwan), 6, 14, 352, 380

Choi Jungwoon, 372

Chou En-lai, 104, 111, 122n7

Chuan Leekpai, 315, 327

Chuang Chui-sheng, 179

Chun Doo-hwan, 2, 5, 17, 34n21, 93, 140, 141, 147, 204, 448, 464

Chung Oong, 390, 391, 445

Chunhyang, 434–36

Citizens' Movement for Free Elections (NAMFREL) (Philippines), 46

civil society, 3, 13, 28, 31, 360, 363, 367, 376, 380, 391, 401, 407, 412, 413, 414, 415, 439, 441, 446–48; Bangladesh, 271, 277, 285n34; China, 130, 131, 138, 154, 170n103; Korea, 6; Nepal, 213–217, 234–37; Philippines, 64, 68, 69, 72; Taiwan, 191,194, 202, 203, 205; Thailand, 5, 306, 322

Cleaver, Kathleen, 433

Coalition of Thai Artists, 305

Cold War, 17, 22, 366, 372, 416, 442, 447, 448, 458, 463

Collective Campaign for Peace (COCAP) (Nepal), 253

"comfort women" (Taiwan), 175

Communist Party of Burma (CPB), 82

Communist Party of China (CCP), 106, 127, 129, 152, 159, 162, 163, 166

Communist Party of Nepal–Maoist (CPN-M), 211, 241, 255

Communist Party of Nepal–Marxist Leninist (CPN-ML), 255

Communist Party of Nepal–Unified Marxist Leninist (CPN-UML), 240, 255, 257

Communist Party of Thailand (CPT), 306, 310, 311

Communist Party of the Philippines (CPP), 42, 47, 59, 75n36

Confederation for Democracy (CFD) (Thailand), 288, 316, 319, 320, 325, 326, 330

Confederation of Nepalese Professionals, 212, 252

Confucianism, 3, 52, 129, 130, 138, 143, 431, 435, 447, 451

Congress of the Filipino People (KOMPIL), 45, 65, 66

Constituent Assembly (Nepal), 212, 215, 243, 251–55

Crown Property Bureau (CPB) (Thailand), 333

Cruz, Rene, 52

Cui Jian, 126

Cultural Revolution (China), 130, 131, 132, 162, 166n10; in Tibet, 113

Cunningham, Philip, 158

Czech, 16–17, 19–21. See also Velvet Revolution (Czechoslovakia)

Dada, 136, 401, 404, 405, 406

Dahal, Pushpa Kamal (Prachanda), 255, 257

Dalai Lama, 104, 106–12, 114, 117, 119–21, 122n7, 123n38, 123n61, 430, 443, 450

Dare-to-Die Squad (China), 154, 155

Davies, James, 439

Democratic Progressive Party (DPP) (Taiwan), 174, 193, 195–98, 201–5

Deng Nan-jung, 197

Deng Xiaoping, 114, 128, 130, 132, 139, 162, 445

Dhaka University (Bangladesh), 266, 269, 270, 273, 274, 282

Dhaka University's Central Students' Union (Bangladesh), 272

Dili Massacre (Indonesia), 344, 347

Dixit, Kanak, 254

dob-dob monks (Tibet), 108, 109

Drapchi Prison (Tibet), 119

EDSA (Epifanio de los Santos Avenue) (Philippines), 38, 39, 48, 50, 52, 54–57, 63–74

Egypt, 31, 361, 364, 368–70, 401, 418, 433, 444, 459

Encuentro (Zapatista), 376

Enrile, Juan Ponce, 41, 48–50, 52, 54–57, 60,

Eros Effect, xx, 10, 33n15, 52, 92, 128, 139, 140, 150, 169n73, 193, 217, 220, 227, 317, 318, 352, 360, 361, 364, 365, 368, 371, 381, 397, 401, 407, 439, 453, 473; activating the, 376–77; revisiting the, 371–76

Ershad, Muhammad, 2, 7, 8, 29, 266, 267, 269–79, 282, 284

Estonia, 19, 20

Estrada, Joseph, 8, 38, 39, 63–65, 65–69, 70–71, 73, 410

Export Processing Zones (EPZ) (Bangladesh), 45, 60, 280, 282, 284

Facebook. See social media

Fan Yun, 194

Fan Zhongya, 139

Farmers' Confederation of Thailand (FCT), 304, 307, 308

Farmers' War of 1894 (Tonghak Uprising) (Korea), 4, 383

fatwa (Bangladesh), 278

Federation of Independent Students of Thailand (FIST), 304

Federation of Labor Unions of Thailand (FLUT), 303, 308

feminism, 10, 360, 432, 433; Nepal, 236; Taiwan, 186, 187;

Feminist Dalit Organization (FDO), 235, 256

Feng Congde, 127, 141, 148, 155,

Fernando, Basil, xx, 359

Fighters' Bulletin (South Korea), 449

Fighting Peacock (Burma), 85, 87, 96, 100

First Quarter Storm (Philippines), 15, 42

"Flying Tigers" (China), 127, 152, 154, 156

Ford, Gerald, 346

Foreign Direct Investment (FDI), 43, 312, 329

Foreign Trade Bank, 92

Forum for the Protection of Human Rights, 221

Forum Kota (Indonesia), 7

France, 98, 129, 365, 384, 385, 386, 388, 390, 393–96, 401–3, 405, 419n6, 441, 461; activism, 9, 10, 293, 294, 374, 394, 401, 406, 424. See also 1968, French Revolution, Paris Commune

French Revolution, 14, 363, 395, 396, 461, 475n12

GABRIELA (General Assembly Binding Women for Reform, Integrity,

Leadership, and Action) (Philippines), 62, 77n96

Gaddafi, Muammar, 368, 443

"Gang of Four" (China), 130, 131, 132

Gangdruk, Chuzhi, 109, 122n33

Garrison Command (Taiwan), 177, 178, 180, 181, 189

General Federation of Nepalese Trade Unions, 228, 256

"Generation 88" (Burma), 81, 99, 100

Germany, 7, 10, 13, 14, 16, 19, 21, 22, 27–29, 140, 167n13, 183, 296, 366, 394, 405, 406, 407, 433, 446, 457

GLBT (Gay, Lesbian, Bisexual, and Transgender Movement) (Thailand), 331

Gorbachev, Mikhail, 17–21, 126, 140, 142, 144, 147, 151, 366

Government of the Union of Burma (GUB), 97, 303

Great Britain, 129, 468. *See also* British colonialism

Great Hall of the People (China), 126, 138, 147, 151, 158, 159

Great Leap Forward, 113, 130, 150, 314

Greece, 11, 23, 120, 221, 359

Green Movement, 19

Gregory, Dick, 147

Gwangju People's Uprising of 1980, xix, 1, 5–6, 10, 13–14, 23, 26, 29, 68, 93, 127, 140, 147, 164, 221, 258, 296, 318, 322, 352, 363, 370–72, 376–77, 406, 409, 411, 415, 425–27, 431, 434–35, 442, 444–52, 466; and the Paris Commune, 380, 382, 383–94, 397, 399n51

Gyanendra, King (Nepal), 212, 216, 242, 243, 249–51, 254, 256

Gyi, Aung, 90

Habermas, Jürgen, 446

Habibie, B.J., 353, 355

Han Chinese, 6, 106, 108, 114, 120, 165, 191, 433

Hau Po-tsun, 201, 204

Havel, Vaclav, 16, 20, 59

Headquarters for Defending the Square (HDS) (China), 148

Hegel, G.W.F., 359

Higgins, Andrew, 149

Ho Chi Minh, 33n13, 373, 423

Honasan, Gregorio, xx, 15, 38, 42, 48, 50, 60, 93

Hong Kong, 127, 137, 148, 153, 155–56, 159, 161–62, 166, 183, 197, 201, 330, 363, 383, 471

Hong Sung-dam, 384, 406

Hsieh Hsueh-hung, 178–80, 182, 183, 186

Hsu Hsin-liang, 193

Hsu Te-hui, 179

Hu Jintao, 119, 151, 166

Hu Yaobang, 125, 128, 133, 134, 136, 137, 138, 168n44

Huang, Peter, 185

Huang Chao-Chin, 177

Huang Hsun-hsin, 166

Hungary, 7, 15–19, 21, 139, 140, 382, 387, 444

hunger strike, 20; Burma, 93; China, 126, 127, 142–48, 149–51, 153, 155–56, 158; Nepal, 228, 235; Taiwan, 198, 200; Thailand, 7, 288, 296, 308, 315, 316, 319; Tibet, 119,

hunger strike command (China), 148

Huntington, Samuel, 1, 3, 22–29, 83, 130, 231, 313, 373–74, 443

Ibrahim, Anwar, 65, 356, 430

Imagination of the New Left: A Global Analysis of 1968, The (Katsiaficas), 33n12

IMF crisis of 1997, 30, 64, 65, 440, 447, 456, 466, 470; in China, 163; in Indonesia, 344, 345, 348–50, 353; in Thailand, 289, 332–34

"Independence Uprising Organization" (Tibet), 118

Independence War (Bangladesh), 265

Indonesian Democratic Party, 347

Informal Sector Service Center (INSEC) (Nepal), 253

Insein Jail (Burma), 85, 92

Internal Security Operation Command (ISOC) (Thailand), 304, 305

International Workingmen's Association (IWA) (France), 386, 388

Israel, 26, 98, 369, 407, 456, 460

James, C.L.R., 428

Jamkattel, Shalik Ram, 244

Jardiniano, Tagumpay, 55

Jatyo Samajtantrrik Dal (JSD) (Bangladesh), 268

Jiang Zemin, 134, 151, 166

jinglees (Burma), 85, 89, 92, 93

Jittravadee Worachat, 319

Johnson, Lyndon, 23
Joint Coordination Committee (Nepal), 223
Joint Trade Union Coordination Centre
 (Nepal), 256
Jose, F. Sionil, 40, 52
Jung, Carl, 371, 374–75, 378n27
Kant, Immanuel, 29, 455, 462–63
Kaohsiung Incident (Taiwan), 174, 179, 181,
 182, 183–89, 193, 195, 201
Kapunan, Eduardo, 48
Karki, Laxmi, 219
Kennan, George, 372
Kennedy, John F. (JFK), 23, 113, 456, 461
Kent State, 10, 140
Kilusang Mayo Uno, 53, 59
Kim Dae Jung, 42, 43, 75n21, 420n23, 446,
 451
Kim Young-sam, 147
King, Jr., Martin Luther, 10, 14, 140, 374
Kissinger, Henry, 23, 27, 113, 268, 346
Klima, Alan, 287, 318, 328
Ko Yuna-fen, 181
Koirala, Girija Prasad, 230, 232, 251, 252
Koirala, Krishna Prasad, 249, 251
KontraS (Indonesia), 354, 356
Korean War, 5, 27, 42, 184, 292, 377, 427,
 441, 459, 474n5
Kraprayoon, Suchinda, 2, 7, 141, 288, 315,
 316, 319, 320, 324–26, 334, 367
Kropotkin, Peter, 394–97
Kuomintang (KMT), 82, 106, 107, 129, 174,
 175–205
Lee Jae-eui, 393
Lee Myung-bak, 205, 410
Lee Teng-hui, 174, 190, 196, 198, 200–201,
 204
Li Honglin, 133
Li Peng, 118, 119, 126, 127, 139, 145, 150–52,
 155, 158, 162, 200, 445
Li Yizhe (Guangzhou democracy activists),
 132
Li Yuan-chen, 187
Libya, 364, 368, 456
Lilley, James, 192
Lintner, Bertil, 80, 92, 102n15, 445
Lipset, Seymour Martin, 3, 23, 440
Lissagaray, Olivier, 380, 389
Liu Guogeng, 159, 161
Long March (China), 106, 152
Lu, Annette, 187, 203
Lukang Rebellion, 191

Lysistrata (Aristophanes), 367, 434
MacArthur, Douglas, 40, 175
Mahendra, King (Nepal), 211, 215, 220
Man Singh, Ganesh, 217, 226, 237–39, 246
Marcos, Ferdinand, 15, 29, 31, 37–74, 86,
 140, 141, 192, 204, 347, 360, 361, 415,
 439, 444; ouster, 2, 5–6, 12, 39, 50, 193,
 217, 218, 313, 328, 345, 369, 370, 371,
 440, 450, 452, 471; regime, 41–43; snap
 election, 46–48
Marcuse, Herbert, 10, 11, 168n53, 360, 363,
 371, 375, 400, 405, 419, 423, 427, 432
Maung Maung, 80, 90, 93, 94
McKinley, William, 460
Mendiola Massacre (Philippines), 38, 60
Milošević, Slobodan, 31, 99, 417–18
Mimang (People's Party) (Tibet), 108
Molotov-Ribbentrop Pact (1939), 17, 19
Moro National Liberation Front (MNLF)
 (Philippines), 42, 52, 72
Movement for the Restoration of
 Democracy (MRD) (Nepal), 217, 219, 223,
 230–32
Mubarak, Hosni, 31, 361, 368–70, 381
Nasrin, Taslima, 266, 278
National Administration Reform Council
 (NARC) (Thailand), 310
National Coalition Against Dictatorship
 (Thailand), 306
National Council of the Union of Burma
 (NCUB), 101
National Democratic Front (NDF)
 (Philippines), 38, 47, 60
National Endowment for Democracy
 (NED), 31, 46, 101, 415–18
National League for Democracy (NLD)
 (Burma), 6, 81, 95–99, 101
National Student Center of Thailand
 (NSCT), 293–98, 301, 302, 304, 306
NATO, 21, 129, 418
Ne Win, 2, 6, 80–83, 85–86, 141
neoliberalism, 8, 22, 32, 61–64, 71, 72, 195,
 196, 239, 283, 288, 289, 330, 332, 336,
 360, 363, 376, 377, 397, 413–15, 427, 440,
 465–67, 470; in Thailand, 311–15. *See
 also* IMF crisis of 1997
Nepal, Madhav Kumar, xx, 249, 250, 257,
 263n131
Nepal University Teachers' Association
 (NUTA), 223

Nepali Congress Party (NC), 211, 214–18, 221–23, 230–32, 237–40, 252, 254, 256,
New Art Movement (Indonesia), 346
New Left, 9, 11, 13–17, 23, 295, 366, 371, 419, 428, 433, 442, 449
New People's Army (NPA) (Philippines), 42, 43, 47, 52, 59, 60, 72, 75n36, 415
NGOs, 30, 31, 412–19; in Bangladesh, 266, 276–79, 283; in China, 164; in Indonesia, 354; in Nepal, 236, 247, 253; in the Philippines, 40, 45, 52, 61–64, 66, 68–73; in Taiwan, 193, 201–3; in Thailand, 314–16, 319, 323, 329–32
Nixon, Richard, 22, 82, 113, 365, 373, 456
North Korea, 141, 165, 463, 464, 475n18
Nya-Tri-Tsenpo, 105
Obama, Barack, 27, 369, 456, 457, 467
OECD, 451, 470
Olalia, Rolando, 38, 59, 60
Old Left, 9, 16, 449
Organization for Student Struggle (Bangladesh), 266, 269
Padma Kanya University (Nepal), 222, 223
Palestine, 12, 270, 336, 368, 378n11, 407, 456; Intifada, 370
Pancha (Nepal),
Panchayat system (Nepal), 211–12, 215–17, 220, 223–26, 229–35, 237–39, 241, 246, 259n4
Panchen Lama, 104, 105, 111, 118, 119, 120, 123n61
Papadopoulos dictatorship (Greece), 11, 26, 303
Parinya Tevanarumitrakun (Thailand), 316, 319
Paris Commune, 14, 131, 153, 382, 395, 397, 402, 428; and Gwangju Uprising, 383–94, 399n51
Park Chung-hee, 41, 386, 450
Party Politburo, 7, 145, 151
Peng Meng-chi, General, 179, 181
People Power Party (PPP) (Thailand), 335
People's Alliance for Democracy (PAD) (Thailand), 334, 335
People's Congress (China), 133, 134, 151, 153, 166, 170n100, 123n61
People's Consultative Assembly (Indonesia), 346, 349, 355
People's Daily (China), 126, 139, 140, 152
People's Global Action (PGA), 376

People's Liberation Army (PLA) (China), 7, 158, 160; in Tibet, 107, 109, 111, 112, 123n61
People's Liberation Army (PLA) (Nepal), 256–57
Petras, James, xx, 31, 413, 414
Phatharathananunth, Somchai, 5, 342n156
Philippine Democratic Party (LABAN), 15, 44
Pol Pot (Nepal), 258, 311
Poland, 7, 9, 16, 17, 18, 21, 28, 34n19, 139, 168n48, 424, 426, 447
Poudel, Ram Chandra, 252, 254
Power of Virtue Party (*Palang Dharma Party*) (PDP) (Thailand), 316
Prachanda (Pushpa Kamal Dahal), 255, 257
Pradhan, Sahana, 230, 430
Prague Spring, 9, 17, 18, 20
Prapas Charusathiara, 292, 296, 298, 301, 302, 308
Qing Dynasty, 105, 173, 174
Radio Bandido (Philippines), 50
Radio Nepal, 215, 220, 229, 248
Rahman, Sheik Mujibur, 265, 267, 268, 269, 430
Ramos, Fidel, 48–50, 54, 56, 59, 62, 63–65, 71, 74, 93, 289, 458
Rangoon Institute of Technology (RIT) (Burma), 80, 83, 84, 101
Rangoon University (RU) (Burma), 82–85, 94
Rapid Action Battalion (RAB) (Bangladesh), 280, 281, 284
Raval, Vinay, 220
Reagan, Ronald, 5, 44, 47, 54–56, 347
Red Shirts (Thailand), 289, 290; and Yellow Shirts, 334–37, 370, 392
Reform the Armed Forces Movement (RAM) (Philippines), 15, 42, 46, 48–50, 61, 62, 415, 440
reformasi era (Indonesia), 13, 353–56
Reforms and social movements, 204
Reyes, Angelo, 67
Rhee, Syngman, 5, 293, 391, 392, 441, 450
Roh Tae-woo, 5, 29, 369, 448
Romania, 7, 13, 16–18, 21, 28, 29, 217, 226
Royal Nepalese Army (RNA), 242, 244, 248
Rudé, George, 28

Russia, 17, 18, 21, 22, 101, 113, 366, 394, 396, 397, 415, 416, 422, 457, 461, 464. *See also* Soviet Union

"Saffron Revolution" (Burma, 2007), 81, 99–102, 392, 416, 417

Saleh, Ali Abdullah, 368

Sangharsha Bulletin (Nepal), 221

Sant Hathirat, 316, 319

Sein Lwin, 2, 80, 85, 89

Serbia, 129, 415, 417–18

Settlement Committee (SC) (Taiwan), 173, 174, 177–82

Seven Party Alliance (SPA) (Nepal), 212, 243, 245, 247, 249–53, 263n111

sex workers, 426; Bangladesh, 266, 279; Nepal, 236; Taiwan, 187, 203; Thailand, 292, 330

Shekhar, Chandra, 218

Shih Ming-teh, 205

"silent generation" (Taiwan), 183–89

Sin, Jaime (Cardinal), 14, 38, 39, 41, 44, 46, 48–50, 64–66, 440

Sison, Jose Maria, 59, 61

Sivara, Kris, 301, 302, 308, 444

Sivaraksa, Sulak, 52, 292, 337n1

social media, 14, 99, 364, 365, 374, 382, 400–401, 410, 411, 439

Socialist National Organization (JSD) (Bangladesh), 268

Solarz, Stephen, 189, 260n54

Somsak Kosaisook (Thailand), 317, 319, 321, 322, 328, 334

Sorokin, Pitrim, 438, 439

Soros, George, 332, 344, 414, 415, 416, 418, 466

Sotelo, Antonio, 48, 54

Southern Alliance Association (Taiwan), 173, 178

Soviet Union (USSR), 7, 16, 17, 19, 20, 21, 22, 30, 42, 113, 129, 139, 168n53, 364, 366, 394, 428, 442, 463. *See also* Russia

"Stealth Coup" (Bangladesh), 266, 281

Stiglitz, Joseph, 332, 455

Street Poetry Revolution (Nepal), 215

Student Federation of Thailand (SFT), 314–16, 319–20

Subianto, Prabowo, 351

Subversion of Politics, The (Katsiaficas), 33n15

Suharto, Mohammed, 2, 8, 29, 58, 204, 332, 344–56, 440, 445

Sukarnoputri, Megawati, 347, 355, 430

Suu Kyi, Aung San, 6, 65, 80, 81, 90, 95–97, 100–102, 327, 429–30, 450–52

Syria, 364, 368

Taft-Katsura Agreement (1905), 63, 346, 457

Taher, Abu, 268

Tahrir Square, 58, 369, 381

Taiping Rebellion (China), 4, 130

Taiwan National University (TNU), 186, 190, 197

Tan Kuan-san, 109

tangwai (extraparliamentary opposition) (Taiwan), 8, 187, 188, 191–93, 201

Tenzin, Champa, 114

Tet Offensive (Vietnam), 9, 10, 33n13, 41

Thai Rak Thai Party (Thailand), 289

Thaksin Shinawatra, 289–90, 333–36, 458

Thammasat University (Thailand), 287–89, 292, 296–300, 306–9, 318, 331, 334, 352, 380, 427

Thanom Kittikachorn, 11, 287, 288, 292–94, 300–305, 308, 319

Thapa, Kamal, 240, 256

Thompson, E.P., 28

Tiananmen Square (China), 6, 15, 20, 23, 26, 118, 119, 125–28, 130, 134, 136–38, 140–61, 166, 198, 200, 205, 217, 220, 316, 380, 394, 407, 417, 424, 431

Trade Union Congress of the Philippines (TUPAS), 45, 46, 314

Truman, Harry S., 129, 184

Truth and Reconciliation Commission (Nepal), 238, 253

Tunisia, 364, 368, 370

Twitter. *See* social media

UN (United Nations), 19, 69, 70, 83, 100, 107, 186, 256, 257, 282, 334, 347, 412, 413, 468, 473

UNICEF, 217, 468

United Front for Democracy against Dictatorship (UDD) (Thailand), 335, 336

United Left Front (ULF) (Nepal), 211, 217–18, 222–23, 230–32, 238–39, 263n111

United Kingdom. *See* Great Britain

United National Democratic Organization (UNIDO) (Philippines), 44

United National People's Movement (UNPM) (Nepal), 217, 229, 232

United People's Front (UPF) (Nepal), 239, 240

United Revolutionary People's Council (Nepal), 242

United States of America, activism, xix, 9, 11, 142, 303, 365, 372, 377n4, 405–6; feminism, 10, 186–87, 433–36; IMF Crisis, 163–64; international violence, 3, 40, 345, 374, 460; intervention, 6, 26, 31, 39, 58, 82, 107, 175, 184, 186, 188, 195, 231, 238, 242, 305, 347, 368, 415–19; involvement with NGOs, 412–19; neoliberalism, 62–63, 195–96, 204–7, 289, 360, 376, 413–16, 466; support of dictatorships, xix, 5, 11, 22–27, 30–31, 40–45, 54, 56, 93, 175, 187, 250–52, 268, 282, 305, 345, 352, 360–61, 370, 384–85, 415, 442, 464, 466; war, 3, 5, 15, 22, 24–27, 40–42, 61, 129–30, 184–85, 242, 272, 292, 307, 345, 361, 365–67, 373, 377n4, 415–19, 434, 441, 448, 456–59, 462–64, 471, 474n5. See also anti-Americanism

University of Science and Technology (UST) (China), 133–34

USSR. See Soviet Union. See also Russia

Urban Industrial Mission (UIM) (Philippines), 69

Velvet Revolution (Czechoslovakia), 18, 19, 140, 168n48

Ver, Fabian, 46–50, 54–55

Vietnam, 7, 9–10, 33n13, 41, 42, 61, 63, 185, 288, 304, 346, 350, 363–65, 374, 377n4, 417, 433–34, 441, 457, 461, 470; War, 3, 11, 15, 22–23, 26–27, 129, 292, 373, 391, 456–59, 474n5. See also Ho Chi Minh, Tet Offensive

Wallerstein, Immanuel, 16, 185, 414, 428, 465

Wang Dan, 142, 143, 148, 154, 162

Wang Xizhe, 132

Weber, Max, 347

Wei Jingsheng, 132

Weng Tojirakan, 319

White Lotus Rebellion (China), 130

"White Terror" (Taiwan), 174, 183, 184, 189, 191, 194, 196, 361, 447

Wild Lily Student Movement (Taiwan), 198–200

Wolfowitz, Paul, 22, 47

Women's Action Network for Development (WAND) (Philippines), 62

Women's Rights Charter (Nepal), 235

Workers-Employees Unity Council (Bangladesh), 266, 270

World Bank (WB), 30, 32, 59, 63, 72, 158, 238, 242, 267, 282, 312, 344, 348, 352, 363, 365–67, 406–9, 413–14, 455–56, 466–67, 470–73

World Social Forum (WSF), 32, 472

World Trade Organization (WTO), 14, 30, 32, 64–65, 72, 163, 363, 365–67, 376, 414, 455–56, 466–67, 470–73, 478n54

World War II, 3, 25, 27, 33n13, 40, 92, 129, 167n13, 175, 267, 334, 363, 371, 376, 405, 448, 457, 458, 462, 474n4

Writers' Association (China), 133, 134

Wuer Kaixi, 128, 137, 139, 141–42, 148–51, 156, 200

Xu Qinxian, 160, 444

Yadav, Darsan Lal, 244

Yadav, Ram Baran, xx, 257

Yan Mingfu, 143

Yangtze River Commentary, 132

Yellow Shirts (Thailand), 8, 289–90, 334–37, 370, 392. See also Red Shirts

"Yellow Tiger" (Thailand), 287, 298

Yemen, 364, 418

Yin Chung-jung, 184

YMCA, 14, 387, 447

Yoon Sang-won, 363, 392

yushin system (Park Chung-hee), 386

YWCA, 14, 387, 392, 393, 447

Zapatistas, 15, 336, 366, 376, 377

Zedong, Mao, 42, 107, 113, 122n7, 129, 130, 131, 135, 145, 146, 150, 171n137, 175, 423

Zeitgeist, 7, 11, 191, 194

Zhao Ziyang, 119, 126, 127, 128, 137, 141, 145, 146,148, 151, 152, 155, 162, 445

Zhou Enlai, 130

Zhou Yongjun, 139, 141

ABOUT PM PRESS

PM Press was founded at the end of 2007 by a small collection of folks with decades of publishing, media, and organizing experience. PM Press co-conspirators have published and distributed hundreds of books, pamphlets, CDs, and DVDs. Members of PM have founded enduring book fairs, spearheaded victorious tenant organizing campaigns, and worked closely with bookstores, academic conferences, and even rock bands to deliver political and challenging ideas to all walks of life. We're old enough to know what we're doing and young enough to know what's at stake.

We seek to create radical and stimulating fiction and non-fiction books, pamphlets, T-shirts, visual and audio materials to entertain, educate and inspire you. We aim to distribute these through every available channel with every available technology — whether that means you are seeing anarchist classics at our bookfair stalls; reading our latest vegan cookbook at the café; downloading geeky fiction e-books; or digging new music and timely videos from our website.

PM Press is always on the lookout for talented and skilled volunteers, artists, activists and writers to work with. If you have a great idea for a project or can contribute in some way, please get in touch.

PM Press
PO Box 23912
Oakland, CA 94623
www.pmpress.org

FRIENDS OF PM PRESS

These are indisputably momentous times—the financial system is melting down globally and the Empire is stumbling. Now more than ever there is a vital need for radical ideas.

In the six years since its founding—and on a mere shoestring—PM Press has risen to the formidable challenge of publishing and distributing knowledge and entertainment for the struggles ahead. With over 250 releases to date, we have published an impressive and stimulating array of literature, art, music, politics, and culture. Using every available medium, we've succeeded in connecting those hungry for ideas and information to those putting them into practice.

Friends of PM allows you to directly help impact, amplify, and revitalize the discourse and actions of radical writers, filmmakers, and artists. It provides us with a stable foundation from which we can build upon our early successes and provides a much-needed subsidy for the materials that can't necessarily pay their own way. You can help make that happen—and receive every new title automatically delivered to your door once a month—by joining as a Friend of PM Press. And, we'll throw in a free T-shirt when you sign up.

Here are your options:

- **$25 a month** Get all books and pamphlets plus 50% discount on all webstore purchases

- **$40 a month** Get all PM Press releases (including CDs and DVDs) plus 50% discount on all webstore purchases

- **$100 a month** Superstar—Everything plus PM merchandise, free downloads, and 50% discount on all webstore purchases

For those who can't afford $25 or more a month, we're introducing **Sustainer Rates** at $15, $10 and $5. Sustainers get a free PM Press T-shirt and a 50% discount on all purchases from our website.

Your Visa or Mastercard will be billed once a month, until you tell us to stop. Or until our efforts succeed in bringing the revolution around. Or the financial meltdown of Capital makes plastic redundant. Whichever comes first.

Asia's Unknown Uprisings Volume 1: South Korean Social Movements in the 20th Century

George Katsiaficas

ISBN: 978-1-60486-457-1
$28.95   480 pages

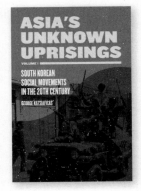

Using social movements as a prism to illuminate the oft-hidden history of 20th century Korea, this book provides detailed analysis of major uprisings that have patterned that country's politics and society. From the 1894 Tonghak Uprising through the March 1, 1919, independence movement and anti-Japanese resistance, a direct line is traced to the popular opposition to U.S. division of Korea after World War Two. The overthrow of Syngman Rhee in 1960, resistance to Park Chung-hee, the 1980 Gwangju Uprising, as well as student, labor, and feminist movements are all recounted with attention to their economic and political contexts. South Korean opposition to neoliberalism is portrayed in detail, as is an analysis of neoliberalism's rise and effects. With a central focus on the Gwangju Uprising (that ultimately proved decisive in South Korea's democratization), the author uses Korean experiences as a baseboard to extrapolate into the possibilities of global social movements in the 21st century.

Previous English language sources have emphasized leaders—whether Korean, Japanese, or American. This book emphasizes grassroots crystallization of counter-elite dynamics and notes how the intelligence of ordinary people surpasses that of political and economic leaders holding the reins of power. It is the first volume in a two-part study that concludes by analyzing in rich detail uprisings in nine other places: the Philippines, Burma, Tibet, China, Taiwan, Bangladesh, Nepal, Thailand, and Indonesia. Richly illustrated, with tables, charts, graphs, index, and footnotes.

"George Katsiaficas has written a majestic account of political uprisings and social movements in Asia—an important contribution to the literature on both Asian studies and social change that is highly-recommended reading for anyone concerned with these fields of interest. The work is well-researched, clearly-argued, and beautifully written, accessible to both academic and general readers."
— Prof. Carl Boggs, author of *The Crimes of Empire* and *Imperial Delusions*

"This book makes a unique contribution to Korean Studies because of its social movements' prism. It will resonate well in Korea and will also serve as a good introduction to Korea for outsiders. By providing details on 20th century uprisings, Katsiaficas provides insights into the trajectory of social movements in the future."
— Na Kahn-chae, Director, May 18 Institute, Gwangju, South Korea

Fire and Flames: A History of the German Autonomist Movement

Geronimo
with an Introduction by George Katsiaficas
and Afterword by Gabriel Kuhn

ISBN 978-1-60486-097-9
$19.95   256 pages

Fire and Flames was the first comprehensive study of the German autonomous movement ever published. Released in 1990, it reached its fifth edition by 1997, with the legendary German *Konkret* journal concluding that "the movement had produced its own classic." The author, writing under the pseudonym of Geronimo, has been an autonomous activist since the movement burst onto the scene in 1980–81. In this book, he traces its origins in the Italian *Autonomia* project and the German social movements of the 1970s, before describing the battles for squats, "free spaces," and alternative forms of living that defined the first decade of the autonomous movement. Tactics of the "Autonome" were militant, including the construction of barricades or throwing molotov cocktails at the police. Because of their outfit (heavy black clothing, ski masks, helmets), the Autonome were dubbed the "Black Bloc" by the German media, and their tactics have been successfully adopted and employed at anti-capitalist protests worldwide.

Fire and Flames is no detached academic study, but a passionate, hands-on, and engaging account of the beginnings of one of Europe's most intriguing protest movements of the last thirty years. An introduction by George Katsiaficas, author of *The Subversion of Politics*, and an afterword by Gabriel Kuhn, a long-time autonomous activist and author, add historical context and an update on the current state of the Autonomen.

"The target audience is not the academic middle-class with passive sympathies for rioting, nor the all-knowing critical critics, but the activists of a young generation."
— Edition I.D. Archiv

"Some years ago, an experienced autonomous activist from Berlin sat down, talked to friends and comrades about the development of the scene, and, with Fire and Flames, *wrote the best book about the movement that we have."*
— Düsseldorfer Stadtzeitung für Politik und Kultur

Portugal: The Impossible Revolution?

Phil Mailer
with an afterword by Maurice Brinton

ISBN: 978-1-60486-336-9
$24.95   288 pages

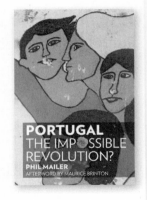

After the military coup in Portugal on April 25, 1974,
the overthrow of almost fifty years of Fascist rule, and
the end of three colonial wars, there followed eighteen
months of intense, democratic social transformation
which challenged every aspect of Portuguese society. What started as a military
coup turned into a profound attempt at social change from the bottom up and
became headlines on a daily basis in the world media. This was due to the intensity
of the struggle as well as the fact that in 1974–75 the moribund, right-wing
Francoist regime was still in power in neighboring Spain and there was huge
uncertainty as to how these struggles might affect Spain and Europe at large.

This is the story of what happened in Portugal between April 25, 1974, and
November 25, 1975, as seen and felt by a deeply committed participant. It
depicts the hopes, the tremendous enthusiasm, the boundless energy, the total
commitment, the released power, even the revolutionary innocence of thousands
of ordinary people taking a hand in the remolding of their lives. And it does so
against the background of an economic and social reality which placed limits on
what could be done.

*"An evocative, bitterly partisan diary of the Portuguese revolution, written from a
radical-utopian perspective. The enemy is any type of organization or presumption of
leadership. The book affords a good view of the mood of the time, of the multiplicity of
leftist factions, and of the social problems that bedeviled the revolution."*
— Fritz Stern, *Foreign Affairs*

*"Mailer portrays history with the enthusiasm of a cheerleader, the 'home team' in
this case being libertarian communism. Official documents, position papers and
the pronouncements of the protagonists of this drama are mostly relegated to the
appendices. The text itself recounts the activities of a host of worker, tenant, soldier
and student committees as well as the author's personal experiences."*
— Ian Wallace, *Library Journal*

*"A thorough delight as it moves from first person accounts of street demonstrations
through intricate analyses of political movements. Mailer has handled masterfully the
enormous cast of politicians, officers of the military peasant and workers councils, and
a myriad of splinter parties, movements and caucuses."*
— *Choice*

Organize!: Building from the Local for Global Justice

Edited by Aziz Choudry, Jill Hanley & Eric Shragge

ISBN: 978-1-60486-433-5
$24.95   352 pages

What are the ways forward for organizing for progressive social change in an era of unprecedented economic, social and ecological crises? How do political activists build power and critical analysis in their daily work for change?

Grounded in struggles in Canada, the USA, Aotearoa/New Zealand, as well as transnational activist networks, *Organize!: Building from the Local for Global Justice* links local organizing with global struggles to make a better world. In over twenty chapters written by a diverse range of organizers, activists, academics, lawyers, artists and researchers, this book weaves a rich and varied tapestry of dynamic strategies for struggle. From community-based labor organizing strategies among immigrant workers to mobilizing psychiatric survivors, from arts and activism for Palestine to organizing in support of Indigenous Peoples, the authors reflect critically on the tensions, problems, limits and gains inherent in a diverse range of organizing contexts and practices. The book also places these processes in historical perspective, encouraging us to use history to shed light on contemporary injustices and how they can be overcome. Written in accessible language, Organize! will appeal to college and university students, activists, organizers and the wider public.

Contributors include: Aziz Choudry, Jill Hanley, Eric Shragge, Devlin Kuyek, Kezia Speirs, Evelyn Calugay, Anne Petermann, Alex Law, Jared Will, Radha D'Souza, Edward Ou Jin Lee, Norman Nawrocki, Rafeef Ziadah, Maria Bargh, Dave Bleakney, Abdi Hagi Yusef, Mostafa Henaway, Emilie Breton, Sandra Jeppesen, Anna Kruzynski, Rachel Sarrasin, Dolores Chew, David Reville, Kathryn Church, Brian Aboud, Joey Calugay, Gada Mahrouse, Harsha Walia, Mary Foster, Martha Stiegman, Robert Fisher, Yuseph Katiya, and Christopher Reid.

"This superb collection needs to find its way into the hands of every activist and organizer for social justice. In a series of dazzling essays, an amazing group of radical organizers reflect on what it means to build movements in which people extend control over their lives. These analyses are jam-packed with insights about anti-racist, anti-colonial, working-class, and anti-capitalist organizing. Perhaps most crucially, the authors lay down a key challenge for all activists for social justice: to take seriously the need to build mass movements for social change. Don't just read this exceptionally timely and important work—use it too."
— David McNally, author of *Global Slump: The Economics and Politics of Crisis and Resistance*

Moments of Excess: Movements, Protest and Everyday Life

The Free Association

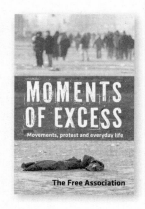

ISBN: 978-1-60486-113-6
$14.95   144 pages

The first decade of the twenty-first century was marked
by a series of global summits which seemed to assume
ever-greater importance—from the WTO ministerial
meeting in Seattle at the end of 1999, through the G8
summits at Genoa, Evian and Gleneagles, up to the
United Nations Climate Change Conference (COP15) at Copenhagen in 2009. But
these global summits did not pass uncontested. Alongside and against them, there
unfolded a different version of globalization. *Moments of Excess* is a collection of
texts which offer an insider analysis of this cycle of counter-summit mobilisations.
It weaves lucid descriptions of the intensity of collective action into a more sober
reflection on the developing problematics of the 'movement of movements'. The
collection examines essential questions concerning the character of anti-capitalist
movements, and the very meaning of movement; the relationship between
intensive collective experiences—'moments of excess'—and 'everyday life'; and the
tensions between open, all-inclusive, 'constitutive' practices, on the one hand, and
the necessity of closure, limits and antagonism, on the other. *Moments of Excess*
includes a new introduction explaining the origin of the texts and their relation to
event-based politics, and a postscript which explores new possibilities for anti-
capitalist movements in the midst of crisis.

"More than a book, Moments of Excess *is a tool for 'worlding' . . . it speaks to
questions that are crucial in creating a better world, all the while asking and opening
more questions . . . Reading this book, I felt like a part of a conversation, a conversation
that I didn't want to end."*
— Marina Sitrin, editor of *Horizontalism: Voices of Popular Power in Argentina* and
(with Clif Ross) *Insurgent Democracies: Latin America's New Powers*

*"Reading this collection you are reminded that there is so much life at the front-line, and
that there is no alternative to capitalism without living this life to the full. The message
is clear: enjoy the struggle, participate in it with your creative energies, be flexible and
self-critical of your approach, throw away static ideologies, and reach out to the other."*
— Massimo De Angelis, author of *The Beginning of History: Value Struggles and
Global Capital* and editor of *The Commoner*

*"Wonderful. Fabulous. The Free Association's work have been writing some of the most
stimulating reflections on the constantly shifting movement against capitalism—always
fresh, always engaging, always pushing us beyond where we were . . . exciting stuff."*
— John Holloway, author of *Change the World Without Taking Power* and
Crack Capitalism